# The WPA Guide
# to 1930s New Mexico

# The WPA Guide to 1930s New Mexico

*Compiled by the Workers of the Writers' Program
of the Work Projects Administration
in the State of New Mexico*

*Foreword by Marc Simmons*

## THE UNIVERSITY OF ARIZONA PRESS
TUCSON

Originally published as *New Mexico: A Guide to the Colorful State*
Copyright 1940 by the Coronado Cuarto Centennial Commission

THE UNIVERSITY OF ARIZONA PRESS

Copyright © 1989
The Arizona Board of Regents
All Rights Reserved

Manufactured in the United States of America
♾ This book is printed on acid-free, archival-quality paper.
93  92  91  90  89    5  4  3  2  1

Library of Congress Cataloging-in-Publication Data

[New Mexico, a guide to the colorful state]
The WPA guide to 1930s New Mexico / compiled by the workers of the
  Writers' Program of the Work Projects Administration in the State of
  New Mexico ; foreword by Marc Simmons
      p.    cm.
  Reprint. Originally published: New Mexico, a guide to the colorful
  state. New York : Hastings House, 1940. (American guide series)
  Bibliography: p.
  Includes index.
  ISBN 0-8165-1102-0 (alk. paper)
    1. New Mexico — Description and travel — Guide-books.   2. New
  Mexico.    I. Writers' Program of the Work Projects Administration in
  the State of New Mexico.
  F794.3.N49 1989
  917.89'0452 — dc19                                             88-27891
                                                                      CIP

British Library Cataloguing in Publication data are available.

# Foreword

In my large personal library of Southwestern books, the volume entitled *New Mexico: A Guide to the Colorful State* has long occupied a prominent place. First published in August 1940, this splendid work formed part of the American Guide Series, embracing books on the then forty-eight states plus a subsidiary line of regional and municipal guides. All were written by federal writers of President Franklin D. Roosevelt's Work Projects Administration (WPA). I am pleased to contribute this Foreword to the New Mexico volume, now being reissued by the University of Arizona Press under a new title. It serves as an appropriate companion to the Press's *WPA Guide to 1930s Arizona*.

At first glance, these guides might easily be dismissed as dated and inaccurate. After all, they were compiled nearly a half century ago, when the Southwest was a very different place and information on its land, people, and history was small in quantity compared to that available today. It is perhaps a measure of the quality of the Federal Writers' Project that the guides still have considerable value as reference and research tools. I've lost count of the times over the last twenty-five years that I have pulled the New Mexico book off the shelf to search for background information on one of the dozens of subjects treated succinctly and forthrightly in its pages. It is the sort of volume that people seriously interested in the state always want to have close at hand.

A word about how the New Mexico guide came to be written and about the people involved in the effort can serve as a useful introduction to this new printing. Indeed, the long struggle to get the book written and into the hands of readers itself casts an interesting light on a troubled segment of New Mexico history, the decade of the 1930s.

That was the period when drought and depression were delivering twin punches to the economy of the Southwest. In a bid to ease the labor crises that had enveloped the nation and to provide long-needed public improvements, President Roosevelt signed an executive order in May 1935 establishing the Works Progress Administration (later renamed the Work Projects Administration). Through it the president intended to replace many of the simple relief programs, which he thought were undermining individuals' self-respect, with work relief projects that encouraged self-reliance and a sense of independence. To that end, the WPA was instructed to develop small, useful projects that could be carried into the remotest corners of America and that would assure maximum employment among all sectors of society.

Among the beneficiaries were to be the nation's writers and artists, a large number of whom were then on relief. New Mexico, especially, stood to gain because of its old and flourishing colonies in Taos and Santa Fe. Much of the art produced under this program, including murals in public buildings, has come to be regarded as a significant part of the cultural heritage of the state. The entire government project, offering federal support and subsidies to those involved in creative arts, was of a size and character unprecedented in the history of the country.

At the head of the WPA in Washington was Harry Hopkins, an idealistic and energetic man who was eager to help people but who, because of his impatience with the stubborn ways of bureaucracy, sometimes failed to get his progessive ideas across. One smart move he made was to select a bright, up-and-coming New Mexico politician, Clinton P. Anderson, to head the state's work relief program.

As Anderson tells it, Hopkins came to Albuquerque one day to help dedicate the new Little Theater, built with WPA funds and labor. After the morning ceremonies, the pair climbed into a car to motor north to Santa Fe and a lunch meeting with Governor Clyde Tingley, an ardent supporter of Roosevelt and the New Deal.

As they reached the turnoff to Santo Domingo Pueblo, Hopkins insisted that they stop to observe a ceremonial dance that they'd learned was in progress. At the village entrance, however, Indian guards barred their way. The guards explained that the dance was a sacred fertility rite and that outsiders were forbidden to watch.

Anderson forcefully remonstrated with them, explaining that his guest was a dignitary from Washington who had control over some of the Pueblo's federal funds. That brought a grudging opening of the door. The ceremony thus revealed proved to be no disappointment. Hopkins was mesmerized by the lines of dancers and the music of chanters and drummers. After Anderson had reminded him for the third time of the appointment with Tingley in Santa Fe, he replied that lunches with governors were a dime a dozen, but Indian dances like this were important and unique. That little episode convinced young Anderson that while Hopkins was well intentioned, he was also impractical.

Afterward, Anderson was promoted to WPA field coordinator for the western states, but owing to a brisk efficiency that brought him into conflict with Hopkins, he was fired in 1936. Nevertheless, he continued to maintain an interest in a particular WPA project, the American Guide Series, and when the New Mexico volume appeared in 1940, he was the author of the foreword. Of course, his greatest fame was to come later when he played a prominent role in national politics as a U.S. senator.

The American Guide Series was an outgrowth of the Federal Writers' Project of the WPA, established in each state to furnish gainful employment to qualified authors. Initially there was some confusion over what the guides ought to contain and what audience they should attempt to reach. In time, however, the project's director, Henry G. Alsberg, decided that the books should include both comprehensive road tours and substantive essays on history, geography, archaeology, and folklore. In this way they would benefit tourists as well as armchair travelers and other readers. The format also seemed to guarantee that the guides would preserve their usefulness in the long term.

Like his boss, Harry Hopkins, Alsberg was of a romantic frame of mind, and this shaped his vision of what the guides should be. He was primarily interested in scenic and human-interest subjects presented in such a way as to stir the emotions of readers and lead them to new and unexpected discoveries in each state. But his vision also encompassed practical considerations, as he never lost sight of the fact that the chief purpose of the guides was to serve economic ends. In the first stage, their writing would give work to contributors, and in the second, the published books could be expected to lure visitors to out-of-the-way places, which would thereby profit through a boost in tourism. As he put it, the intent was to encourage people to "see America first."

That phrase was not original with Alsberg; he borrowed it from the writings of Charles F. Lummis, who had made his own discovery of the Southwest in the mid-1880s and had spent the remainder of his life vigorously promoting its cultural and natural wonders. Seeing America first, for Alsberg, meant keeping Americans on this side of the Atlantic during vacation time and attracting visitors from abroad, which translated into more millions spent on tourism, further reducing unemployment. It was this heady prospect that fueled enthusiasm for the nascent American Guide Series.

In 1936 Ina Sizer Cassidy, the wife of Santa Fe artist Gerald Cassidy, was named state director of the project in New Mexico. She considered herself an amateur historian and a doyenne in the society of the local arts colony. Moreover, her appointment had been obtained largely through the influence of her friend Commissioner of Indian Affairs John Collier. None of this augured well for the smooth running of the program, and in truth, problems soon appeared.

It became evident that Mrs. Cassidy did not have a firm grasp of what Washington expected or desired with regard to the content of the New Mexico guide. As a federal handbook made plain, all areas of the state were to be covered, but Mrs. Cassidy's attention was focused on the area she knew best — Santa Fe and vicinity. In addition, she viewed the guide as an opportunity to promote "fine writing" and her own opinions. Those aims increasingly got in the way of the series goal: to give accurate information to travelers and general readers.

Another problem arose among the project writers scattered around the state, who eventually numbered sixty in all. Those in out-of-the-way places were able to acquire some of the history of their localities from old-timers, but lacking access to libraries and archives, they could do little in the way of serious historical investigation. Furthermore, many of the authors were only marginally qualified. This placed a heavy burden on the small editorial staff in Santa Fe.

Nonetheless, the writing of New Mexico's guide moved ahead by fits and starts, with periodic demands by Washington officials for thorough revisions. Mrs. Cassidy was removed as head early in 1939 and was succeeded by

Aileen Nusbaum, the author of *Zuni Indian Tales*. In the few months she served as acting state director, Nusbaum whipped the guide into shape for publication. She was followed by Charles Ethrige Minton, who wrapped up some of the final details.

Although the WPA had funded the preparation of the guide, its formal sponsors at the local level were the University of New Mexico, whose faculty had provided some editorial assistance, and the Coronado Cuarto Centennial Commission, under the directorship of Clinton P. Anderson. The commission's function was to conduct a major celebration commemorating the four-hundredth anniversary of the launching of the Coronado expedition in 1540, and it considered its cosponsorship of the guide to be a logical and suitable tie-in. Unhappily, the book — brought out by the New York publisher Hastings House — was late, and first copies did not reach New Mexico until September 1940, after most of the Coronado activities were finished. Many contributors were displeased by the garish orange binding and by the lettering in clashing blue, and New Mexicans generally reacted unfavorably to the insipid subtitle, *A Guide to the Colorful State*. Still and all, they found more to praise than to condemn, and the book was soon accepted as a standard reference work. In 1945 the University of New Mexico Press assumed the copyright and brought out a second edition, which included a list of errata.

In addition to a lengthy section of essays, the guide presented twenty-five tours, ready-made for visitors wishing to see both the state's celebrated points of interest and its scenic and historical treasures hidden away in remote corners. The work was visually enhanced by a series of photographic sections that included reproductions of paintings by some of New Mexico's outstanding artists. A series of maps, a calendar of annual events, and a historical chronology rounded out the guide's useful features.

Marta Weigle, in her splendid book *New Mexicans in Cameo and Camera* (Albuquerque: University of New Mexico Press, 1985), a compendium of New Deal documentation, notes that in New Mexico the pronunciation of WPA sounded, to Spanish ears, very much like *El Diablo a pie*, meaning "the Devil on foot" (p. xiv). So that's what the federal program came to be popularly called, "The Devil on Foot." While it may have been a devilish task to produce *New Mexico: A Guide to the Colorful State*, the original goal of creating a work of lasting significance was admirably achieved.

The new title bestowed here, *The WPA Guide to 1930s New Mexico*, reflects the value that has emerged most recently from its pages because of the picture it gives of the state as it existed just before World War II. Still, the general reader today, like his predecessor a half century ago, will most appreciate the rich store of informative nuggets that in many cases are recorded in these pages and nowhere else. Whether or not the Devil actually had a hand in the finished work, New Mexicans and the legions of travelers who continue to visit New Mexico can take pleasure in having this incomparable guide accessible once more.

Marc Simmons

# Contents

## Part I.  Before and After Coronado

## Part II.  A City, a Capital, and an Art Center

## Part III. The Most Accessible Places

*Part IV. Appendices*

# *Illustrations*

## AGRICULTURE: INDUSTRY—*continued*

Spanish-American Farm Village along the Rio Hondo
*Courtesy Farm Security Administration*
Threshing Wheat with Horses, Tres Ritos
*Courtesy New Mexico State Tourist Bureau*
Tres Ritos, a Typical Farming Community
*Courtesy New Mexico State Tourist Bureau*
Drying Washed Wheat, Jacona
*Courtesy New Mexico State Tourist Bureau*
Washing Wheat, Jacona (Note Strings of Chili in Background)
*Courtesy New Mexico State Tourist Bureau*

Oil Wells near Hobbs
*Courtesy New Mexico State Tourist Bureau*
Panning Gold, near Santa Rita
*Courtesy New Mexico State Tourist Bureau*
Open Pit Copper Mines, Santa Rita
*Courtesy New Mexico State Tourist Bureau*
Irrigated Farms, Carlsbad Reclamation Project
*Courtesy Bureau of Reclamation*
Conchas Dam
*Courtesy U. S. Engineer's Office*

## THE LAND                                    *Between 24 and 25*

Rio Grande Canyon
*Ernest Knee*
Sandstone Formations Near Santa Fe
*Ernest Knee*
Cimarrón Canyon
*Ernest Knee*
Organ Mountains (Northeast of Las Cruces)
Field of Evening Primroses near Cimarrón
*Ernest Knee*
San Juan Valley, near Farmington
*Courtesy New Mexico State Tourist Bureau*
The Enchanted Mesa, as seen from Ácoma
*Courtesy New Mexico State Tourist Bureau*

"White Sands" (Gypsum), a National Monument
*Courtesy New Mexico State Tourist Bureau*
Eroded Sandstone Formations near Cuyamungué
*Ernest Knee*
Aspens, Sangre de Cristo Mountains
*Ernest Knee*
In the Sangre de Cristo Foothills
*Ernest Knee*
Dome and Onyx Drapes, Carlsbad Caverns
*Courtesy National Park Service*

## ALONG THE HIGHWAY                          *Between 268 and 269*

In Northern New Mexico
*Ernest Knee*
US 66, East of Grants
*Courtesy New Mexico State Tourist Bureau*

Lumberjacks in Lincoln National Forest
*Courtesy New Mexico State Tourist Bureau*

MISSIONS—*continued*

CITIES AND TOWNS                    *Between* 176 *and* 177

## *Maps*

# General Information

*Railroads:* Atchison, Topeka & Santa Fe Ry. (AT&SF), Southern Pacific Lines (SP), Denver and Rio Grande Western R.R. (D&RGW). Santa Fe and Southern Pacific are transcontinental lines with branches covering important points in State.

*Airlines:* Transcontinental and Western Airlines (New York to Los Angeles), stops at Albuquerque; Varney Airlines (Pueblo, Colo. to El Paso, Texas), stops at Ratón, Santa Fe, and Albuquerque.

*Busses:* The main interstate bus lines are: Greyhound Lines, New Mexico Transportation Co., White Star Coaches, Page Way Stage Lines, Lee-Way Stages, Cannon Ball Stage Line, Parrish Stage Lines, Rio Grande Motor Way, Rio Grande Stages, Santa Fe Trailways, T.-N.M. & O. Coaches, All-American Bus Lines. Local and freight lines in addition.

*Highways:* Main traveled routes are patrolled by State Police. No inspection at ports of entry except for commercial vehicles. Water and gasoline scarce on some rural routes. Never attempt to cross "dry" arroyos when water is running; watch out for livestock on unfenced highways. Do not disturb flowers or trees or shrubs bordering highways. Put out fires.

*Motor Vehicle Laws:* Passenger automobiles must be operated at such speeds as shall be consistent at all times with safety and the proper use of roads. Maximum speed for trucks and busses, 45 m. No licenses required of non-residents for three months. Maximum speed in residence districts, 25 m; in business districts, 20 m.; in school zones, road intersections, on blind curves, and blind grade crossings, on grades where driver's view is obstructed, 15 m. Minimum age for drivers, 16. Drivers are required to stop at scenes of accidents resulting in property damage or personal injury, and to report same to State Police or local authorities. Brakes and lights must be in good order. Rear lamps must exhibit a yellow or red light capable of being seen for 500 feet, with a white light to illuminate the number plate. A red reflector at least three inches in diameter required on the rear of every vehicle. Keep to the right, especially on mountain roads.

*Prohibited:* Parking on highways, passing on blind curves or on the crest of a grade, at grade crossings or intersections. Projecting luggage in front, or more than four feet in rear, or beyond fender line on left side. Driving without an unobstructed rear-view mirror.

*Accommodations:* Hotels numerous in cities and towns; guest ranches and lodges in mountain areas and environs of larger towns offer facilities for riding, pack trips, swimming, hiking, and sometimes golf. Motor camps numerous in and near towns, but scarce between, as distances between settlements are great. As yet relatively few tourist camps are equipped for trailer accommodation; three in Albuquerque.

*Liquor Laws:* No liquor sold on Sundays from 2 a.m. to 7 a.m. Monday.

*Climate and Equipment:* Winters are cold in the plateau and mountain sections. Travelers in summer should be prepared for hot dry weather but should have warm clothing for sudden changes of temperature due to abrupt changes in elevation. Nights are generally cool; cold in high altitudes. Cars should be equipped with chains, shovel, and towrope if venturing off main roads. Country subject to sudden torrential rains in summer months. Skiing equipment useful in winter months in mountains in various sections. Avoid drinking water outside towns; advisable to carry a supply of drinking water at all times and water for car in isolated districts.

*Recreational Areas:* New Mexico is one of the most attractive recreation areas. Game can be found in abundance and in great variety, due to the presence in this State of six of the seven life zones of North America. There are thousands of square miles of unspoiled mountain forests, and near primitive, remote villages are many recreational resources readily available to hunters and fishermen; also, there are numerous others easily accessible near less remote centers. For the latter, a motor car goes right to the spot; for the former, competent guides furnish pack equipment, horses, and dogs for hunting bear, bobcat, and mountain lion, as well as other game not predatory. Good roads lead directly to or very near many hunting and fishing places, many of them with adequate hotel accommodations, camp grounds, or other facilities.

*National Forests:* Regional headquarters, Albuquerque: Apache, west central section of State, US 60 and US 260; Carson, north central section, US 64 and US 285; Cíbola, central and west central sections, US 85 and US 60; Coronado, southwestern section, US 70-80; Gila, southwestern section, US 260; Lincoln, central and south central sections, US 54 and US 70-380; Santa Fe, north central section, US 84-85, US 64, and US 285.

Information about camping facilities available in national forest can be obtained from the forester in charge of each forest district.

*National Park:* Carlsbad Caverns, southeast section, US 62.

*National Monuments:* Aztec Ruins, northeast section, US 550; Bandelier, near Santa Fe, US 64, NM 4; Capulín Mountain, northeast, US 84; Chaco Canyon, northwest, US 66 and US 84; El Morro, west central, US 66; Gila Cliff Dwellings, southwestern (pack trips only) US 260; Gran Quivira, central, US 60 and US 54; White Sands, south central, US 70.

*State Parks:* Bluewater, west central, US 66; Bottomless Lakes, southeast, US 285 and US 380; Conchas Dam, east central, US 66-54; Eastern New Mexico, east central, US 70; Hyde, near Santa Fe, US 85 and US 64; Santa Fe, in Santa Fe, US 85 and US 64.

*State Monuments:* Abo, central, US 60; Coronado, north central, US 85; Gran Quivira, central, US 60 and US 54; Jémez, north central, US 84, NM 4; Lincoln, south central, US 380; Paako, north central, US 85, NM 10; Pecos, north central, US 84-85; Quarai, central, US 66, NM 10.

*Pack Trips:* Pack trips are necessary to get to New Mexico's trails through the national forests and mountain regions. These trips should not be attempted without experienced guides, as few of the trails are marked and it is dangerous to attempt such trips alone. There are numerous pack trails, but the best known ones go to the various national forests, where 78 areas have been developed especially to take care of tourists. In these areas can be found facilities such as tables, benches, overnight shelter, running water, and fire places. These camping areas are distributed over the following national forests: Carson, Cíbola, Gila, and Lincoln. Further information regarding pack trips and expert guides can be obtained from the Chambers of Commerce in the following cities: Las Vegas, Santa Fe, Española, Carrizozo, Lincoln, Tularosa, Corona, Alamogordo, Mountainair, Socorro, Albuquerque, Deming, Silver City, Taos, Reserve, Carlsbad, and Gallup. They also furnish information about trips not included in national forests.

*Fishing:* Lakes in New Mexico's southern portion afford warm-water game fishing. Elephant Butte Lake (*see Tour 1c*), near Hot Springs, is noted principally for large-mouth bass, weighing three to nine pounds. There are also perch, crappie, bream, and catfish. Every accommodation, including motorboat service, is available.

Southeastern New Mexico likewise has excellent bass, crappie, and catfish waters, the principal ones being McMillan and Avalon Lakes between Artesia and Carlsbad. Smaller lakes in the Pecos Valley near Roswell, Artesia, and Carlsbad, the Pecos River, and numerous smaller waters near Santa Rosa also offer good fishing.

*Trout Fishing:* Many of the best trout streams, including the Gila's west and middle forks, White Water, White Creek, and Big Dry Willow Creek, are in the Gila River drainage area, where pack trips are more satisfactory and ample facilities are available. The Sacramento and White Mountains have only limited fishing resources.

The Jémez Mountains, 50 miles west of Santa Fe, contain numerous fishing streams, the Jémez' east fork, the Guadalupe, Cebolla, and Las Vacas Rivers being the best. A State fish hatchery in the vicinity keeps the waters well stocked.

The Pecos River, its tributaries, and other streams heading in the Sangre de Cristo Range between Santa Fe and Las Vegas and northward, yield rainbow, native, and Loch Leven trout. Most of these streams are accessible by automobile, but some of the best can be reached only on horseback.

Fishing is excellent in streams and lakes near Taos Mountain, especially in regions where pack trips are necessary. Eagle Nest Lake, 30 miles northeast of Taos, near the highway, is unsurpassed for rainbow trout, as are the Cimarrón and Red Rivers.

One hundred miles northwest of Santa Fe, the Chama River and its tributaries, especially the Brazos, provide fishing and pleasant vacation spots.

The State's largest fish, rainbow and Loch Leven trout—often weighing 15 pounds—are caught in the Rio Grande, which provides 100 miles of fishing from Embudo to the Colorado State Line.

*Fish and Game Laws:* Game fish are defined as trout and salmon, bass, crappie, perch, catfish, bream, sunfish, and bluegill.
*Open Season for Fishing* (dates inclusive): General: Trout and salmon, May 15-Nov. 15; bass, crappie, perch, catfish, bream, sunfish, and bluegill, Apr. 1-Apr. 15, and June 1-Nov. 30. Open seasons for special waters differ; make local inquiry.
*Licenses:* Nonresident, $3. General hunting and fishing, $35.25. Licenses must be carried on person and exhibited to authorized officer upon request. Nonresident 15-day fishing license for Elephant Butte Lake and Lake McMillan, $1.25. Children under 14 years may fish without a license.
*Limits:* Trout and salmon, 25 fish or 15 pounds and 1 fish, minimum size 6 inches. Bass, 15 pounds and 1 fish, minimum size 9 inches. Crappie, 20 fish, minimum size 5 inches;—Chaves and Eddy counties bag limit 10, minimum size 6 inches. Catfish, 25 pounds and 1 fish,

minimum size 8 inches. Perch, 20 fish. Special regulations in regard to catfish in some counties.

*Prohibited:* To use any means of taking fish other than with hook and line, attached to rod or held in the hand; to use more than one line with or without rod, having more than two hooks, allowed to each person, except that more than two hooks may be used on artificial lures.

*Big Game Hunting:* Big game hunting includes bear, wild turkey, Abert squirrel, elk, antelope, and deer, including mule deer, Arizona and Virginia whitetail.

Deer inhabit practically every mountainous section of the State from the desert hills in the extreme south to the northern timber-line regions. Turkey and bear, not so widely distributed, inhabit most mountain areas.

The Gila Forest in Grant, Catron, and Sierra Counties is the largest and best known big game country, but as game has been forced back by roads in some sections, pack trips are recommended.

Big game abounds in the Magdalena and San Mateo Mountains, in the White, Sacramento, and Guadalupe Mountains, the Capitán Mountains, the Jémez Mountains, the Pecos Mountains on the Pecos watershed, the Rio Grande, the Rio Pueblo country between Mora and Taos, and the Canjilón-El Rito-Vallecitos country between the Rio Grande and the Chama River. These also have wild turkey.

The State's northeast section is characterized by large ranches having abundant game, but hunting is permitted only by consent of landowners. The region contains some open areas, however.

Hunters are urged to kill at least one predatory animal. Mountain lions, although not classed as game animals, provide good sport when hunted with dogs.

*Open Season for Hunting* (dates inclusive): Bear, Oct. 1-Dec. 10; deer, mule deer, Virginia and Arizona whitetail, horns 6 inches or more, Oct. 25-Nov. 15; elk (special permit required), Oct. 25-Nov. 15; squirrel, Oct. 25-Nov. 15; antelope, season to be set if conditions warrant; beaver, protected at all times.

*Birds:* Prairie chicken, season closed (1940) on account of drought conditions. May be opened later if number of birds justify. Quail (except bobwhite), Nov. 10-Dec. 10; doves, Sept. 1-Nov. 30; dusky or blue grouse, Oct. 1-Oct. 10; pheasants, date of season and bag limit to be determined later if conditions warrant; band-tailed pigeons, Oct. 1-Oct. 15; ducks, geese, brant, coot, jacksnipe, Wilson's snipe, rails and gallinules will conform to Federal regulations. Turkey, Oct. 25-Nov. 15.

*Waterfowl:* During seasons when waterfowl are plentiful, hunting is especially good along the Rio Grande, in the Pecos Valley, and on northern and eastern lakes. Depletion of ducks has occurred in New Mexico as elsewhere, but wild geese hunting is still above average. They are present in late fall and most of the winter on the larger streams and adjacent sloughs, and also on small lakes and ponds of northeastern New Mexico, where they congregate in great numbers to feed in grain fields.

*Licenses:* General hunting, nonresident, $30.25; big game, $25.25; bird, $10.25. Duplicate licenses, $1.

*Limits:* Bear, 1 per season; deer, 1 buck per season; elk, 1 bull elk with three or more points on each horn; squirrel, 5 per season; antelope, season undetermined. Birds: Quail, 12 per day or in possession; doves, 15 per day or in possession; dusky or blue grouse, 5 per season; band-tailed pigeons, 10 per season; turkey, 2 per season.

*No Open Season:* On mountain sheep, mountain goat, beaver, ptarmigan, sage hens, whitetailed deer, bobwhite, pintail grouse, cranes, swan, plover, yellow-legs, or insectivorous birds. No general open season on elk, antelope, pheasant, or prairie chicken.

*Prohibited:* To hunt between sunset and one-half hour before sunrise; to use steel or hard pointed bullets; to take game by any means other than ordinary shoulder gun or pistol or bow; to take birds with a gun larger than 12 gauge or .22 calibre rim fire rifle or pistol; to use highpowered rifle in shooting waterfowl; to hunt or carry firearms in any game refuge; to shoot at game from auto, from or across a highway.

## TAG YOUR BUCK AS SOON AS KILLED.

*General Service for Tourists:* N. M. State Tourist Bureau, State Capitol, Santa Fe; local chambers of commerce; National Forest Service; State Game and Fish Dept., Santa Fe.

*Boating:* At Elephant Butte Lake, formed by Elephant Butte Dam, a Regatta is held annually on the first Sunday and Monday of June. Cottages and power- and rowboats can be rented by the day, week, or month (*see Tour 1c*). At El Vado Lake, on the Chama River, formed by the El Vado Dam, cottages and boats are also for rent (*see Tour 7a*).

*Winter Sports:* A ski course constructed by the United States Forest Service, sponsored by the Santa Fe Winter Sports Club, affiliated with the United States Western Amateur Ski Association and the International Ski Association, is maintained at Hyde Park, Santa Fe, with a practice hill course and tow at 8,300 feet, and a three mile ski trail to 12,000 feet to reach numerous open natural ski courses in the Santa Fe National Forest. National ski courses are also in the Valle Grande in the Jémez Mountains. Los Alamos Boys School maintains a private ski course and skating pond at the school, situated on Los Alamos Mesa, 35 miles northwest of Santa Fe. The Santa Fe Winter Sport Club maintains two skating ponds in the city.

# Calendar of Annual Events

### JANUARY

| | | |
|---|---|---|
| First | at Indian pueblos | Dances. |
| Sixth | in Spanish-American villages | "Old Christmas," feast of the Three Kings. Performances of *Los Tres Magos.* |
| Sixth | at Indian pueblos | Installation of newly elected governors, usually followed by dances. |
| Sixth | at Taos Pueblo | Buffalo dance. |
| Sixth | at San Ildefonso Pueblo | Eagle dance. |
| Twenty-third | at San Ildefonso Pueblo | Feast Day of San Ildefonso (St. Ildephonseus). Annual fiesta and Buffalo dance. |

### FEBRUARY

| | | |
|---|---|---|
| Second | at San Felipe Pueblo | Candlemas Day—Dance. |
| Ash Wednesday | in Spanish-American villages | Beginning of Lenten Rituals of *Los Hermanos Penitentes* (The Penitent Brotherhood). |

### MARCH

| | | |
|---|---|---|
| No fixed date | at Indian pueblos | Opening irrigation ditches with ceremonies. |
| Holy Week | State-wide | Observance by usual religious customs, with processions in Spanish-American villages and in Catholic communities. |

## APRIL

| | | |
|---|---|---|
| Easter Sunday and three following days | at Indian pueblos | Spring Corn dances at Cochití, Santo Domingo, San Felipe, and other Indian pueblos. |
| No fixed date | at Indian pueblos | *Chongo* races. Ceremonial planting dances. |

## MAY

| | | |
|---|---|---|
| First | San Felipe Pueblo | Feast Day of San Felipe (St. Philip). Annual fiesta and spring Corn dance. |
| Third | Santa Cruz | Feast Day of Santa Cruz (finding of the Holy Cross). Annual fiesta and performance of *Los Moros y los Cristianos* (The Moors and the Christians). |
| Third | Taos Pueblo | Ceremonial races (dawn to sunset). |
| Fifth | Alamogordo | Mexican Independence Day celebration (*Cinco de Mayo*). |
| Fifteenth | San Ysidro | Feast Day of San Ysidro, patron saint of farmers. Observed in many Spanish-American villages. |
| Twenty-sixth | Albuquerque | Feast Day of San Felipe de Nerí (St. Philip of Nerí). Annual fiesta celebrated on Saturday and Sunday following May 26th, in Old Albuquerque plaza. |

## JUNE

| | | |
|---|---|---|
| First week | Ratón | Northern New Mexico musical fiesta. |
| First Sunday and Monday | Hot Springs | Elephant Butte Regatta. |
| Middle Two Weeks | Las Vegas | 120th New Mexico National Guard Engineers encampment. |
| Thirteenth | Córdova | Feast Day of San Antonio de Padua (St. Anthony of Padua). Observed in Córdova, San Antonio de Senecú, and other villages of which San Antonio is the patron saint. |

### JUNE—*continued*

| | | |
|---|---|---|
| Twenty-fourth | San Juan Pueblo | Feast Day of San Juan Bautista (St. John the Baptist). Annual fiesta and dance. |
| Twenty-fourth | Taos Village | San Juan Day. Corn dance. *Corrida del gallo* (chicken pull). |
| No fixed date | Santa Fe | Corpus Christi (first Thursday after Trinity Sunday). Celebrated on the Sunday following, by outdoor religious procession, 10 A.M., from the Cathedral of St. Francis; 7:30 P.M., from Cristo Rey Church. |
| First Sunday after Corpus Christi Procession | Santa Fe | De Vargas Memorial Procession of Our Lady of Victory, from the Cathedral of St. Francis to Rosario Chapel where services are held each morning the following week, commemorating De Vargas' reconquest 1692. |
| Second Sunday after Corpus Christi Procession | Santa Fe | Return of De Vargas Memorial Procession, with Our Lady of Victory, from Rosario Chapel to Cathedral of St. Francis. |
| Late in June | Roswell | Annual Good Will tour. |
| Late in June | Las Vegas | Water carnival at Storrie Lake. |

### JULY

| | | |
|---|---|---|
| First to third | Santa Fe | Elks' Celebration of Pioneer Days. |
| Second to fourth | Silver City | Annual rodeo. |
| Third to fifth | Carlsbad | Cavern City Cavalcade. |
| Fourth to sixth | Las Vegas | Annual Cowboys' Reunion. |
| Fourth | Cimarrón | Annual rodeo, the Maverick Club. |
| Fourth | Albuquerque | Pioneer Days, sponsored by Veterans of Foreign Wars (3 days). |
| Fourth | Madrid | Annual rodeo and 4th of July celebration. |
| Fourth | Mescalero | Annual fiesta, rodeo, and Indian dances at Mescalero, U. S. Indian Agency. |
| Fourteenth | Cochití Pueblo | Feast Day of San Buenaventura (St. Bonaventure). Annual fiesta and Corn dance. |

## JULY—*continued*

| | | |
|---|---|---|
| Twenty-fifth | Taos Pueblo | San Antonio Day. Corn dance. |
| Twenty-sixth | Taos Pueblo | Santiago Day (St. James). Corn dance. |
| Twenty-sixth | Santa Ana Pueblo | Feast Day of Santa Ana (St. Anne). Annual fiesta and dance. |
| Mid July | Cimarrón | Annual Horse Show. |
| Last Sunday July or first Sunday August | Santa Fe | Annual Horse Show. |

## AUGUST

| | | |
|---|---|---|
| Second | Jémez Pueblo | Feast Day of Nuestra Señora de los Ángeles (Our Lady of the Angels). Old Pecos dance. |
| Fourth | Santo Domingo Pueblo | Feast Day of Santo Domingo (St. Dominic). Annual fiesta and summer Corn dance. |
| Tenth | Picurís Pueblo | Feast Day of San Lorenzo (St. Lawrence). Annual fiesta and dance. |
| Mid August | Santa Fe | Annual "Poets' Roundup." |
| Middle Two Weeks | Las Vegas | 111th National Guard Cavalry Encampment. |
| Fifteenth | Zía Pueblo | Feast Day of Nuestra Señora de la Asunción (Our Lady of the Assumption). Annual fiesta and dance. |
| Twenty-second | Las Vegas | Annual Horse Show of 111th Cavalry (2 days) at Norman L. King Stadium, Camp Luna. |
| Twenty-second | Isleta Pueblo | Feast Day of San Agustín (St. Augustine). Annual fiesta and dance. |
| Third Wednesday to Saturday | Gallup | Annual Inter-tribal Indian Ceremonial. |
| No fixed date | Ratón | Elks' Celebration and Pioneer Days (3 days). |
| Labor Day Weekend | Santa Fe | Annual fiesta inaugurated by Governor Peñuela in 1712 (3 days). |

## SEPTEMBER

| | | |
|---|---|---|
| Second | Ácoma Pueblo | Feast Day of San Esteban (St. Stephen). Annual fiesta and dance. |
| First week | Deming | Annual rodeo (3 days). |
| First week | Magdalena | Annual rodeo. |
| Sixth | San Ildefonso Pueblo | Harvest dance. |
| Early September | Wagon Mound | Annual Bean Day and rodeo. |
| Early September | Taos | Taos County Fair and folklore contests. |
| Early September | Portales | Annual fair and rodeo. |
| Fifteenth | Jicarilla Apache Reservation | Ceremonial races and dance (3 days) at Horse Lake or Stone Lake. |
| Fifteenth to seventeenth | Carlsbad | Mexican colony rodeo and barbecue. Street dancing and singing. Celebrating Mexican Independence from Spain. |
| Sixteenth | Alamogordo | Mexican Independence Day celebration. |
| Sixteenth | Roswell | Mexican Independence Day celebration. |
| Eighteenth to twentieth | Lovington | Lea County Fair and rodeo. |
| Nineteenth | Laguna Pueblo | Annual fiesta and dance. |
| Twenty-ninth | Socorro | Feast Day of San Miguel (St. Michael). Annual fiesta and rodeo (2 days). |
| Twenty-ninth | Taos Pueblo | Sunset dance, eve of San Gerónimo Day. |
| Thirtieth | Taos Pueblo | Feast Day of San Gerónimo (St. Jerome). Annual fiesta and dance. |
| Late September | Farmington | Farmington Fair. |
| Late September | Clayton | Union County Fair. |

## OCTOBER

| First week | Roswell | Eastern New Mexico State Fair, rodeo and Old Timers' celebration. |
| First week | Shiprock Navaho Indian Agency | Annual Navaho Indian Fair. |
| Fourth | Santa Fe | Feast Day of St. Francis of Assisi (Patron Saint of Santa Fe). Celebrated on evening of October 3d, by procession from the Cathedral of St. Francis. |
| Fourth | Nambé Pueblo | Annual fiesta and dance. |
| Fourth | Ranchos de Taos | Annual fiesta. |

## NOVEMBER

| First | | Eve of All Souls Day. Celebrated as the Spanish "Halloween" with interesting old customs in Santa Fe, Spanish - American villages, and in many of the Indian pueblos. |
| Second | | All Souls Day (The Day of Dead. Spanish - American Memorial Day). |
| Eleventh | Alamogordo | Armistice Day rodeo and barbecue. |
| Twelfth | Tesuque Pueblo | Feast Day of San Diego (St. James). Annual fiesta and harvest Corn dance. |
| Twelfth | Jémez Pueblo | Annual fiesta and harvest Corn dance. |
| Late November or early December | Zuñi Pueblo | "Shalako" ceremonies and house dances. |
| After first frost | Navaho Indian Reservation | Navaho "Yei-be-chai" and Fire dance. |

## DECEMBER

| | | |
|---|---|---|
| Twelfth | Santa Fe | Feast day of Nuestra Señora de Guadalupe (Our Lady of Guadalupe) celebrated on Eve (December 11) of this day, with procession from the church of Our Lady of Guadalupe. Celebrated also in many Spanish-American villages. |
| December eighteenth to January fourth | Madrid | Annual Christmas festivities and electrical illumination. |
| Twenty-fourth | Santa Fe | Christmas Eve, little bonfires for El Santo Niño (The Christ Child) lighted before house doors and in the streets; also before candle-lit *Nacimientos* (Nativity scenes). |
| Twenty-fourth | Taos Pueblo | Night procession with torches. |
| Twenty-fourth | Indian Pueblos | Dances after Midnight Mass in the Pueblo Mission churches of Santo Domingo, San Felipe, Cochití, Tesuque, Santa Clara, Jémez, etc. |
| Twenty-fifth to twenty-eighth | Indian Pueblos | Dances at above and other Indian Pueblos on Christmas Day and 3 days following. |
| During fortnight before and after Christmas | Santa Fe | Performances of *Los Pastores* (The Shepherds) and *La Aparición de Nuestra Señora de Guadalupe* (The Apparition of Our Lady of Guadalupe) in many Spanish-American villages. |

## CORONADO CUARTO CENTENNIAL FOLK FESTIVAL CALENDAR

(Giving Principal Events from May 15 to November 1940)

| Date | City | County | Event |
|------|------|--------|-------|
| May 15 | Tucumcari | Quay | Final Folk Festival for Quay County combining best representatives from the community in the county. |
| May 23 | Clovis | Curry | Folk Festival, using Spanish customs, including folk dances, songs, and traditions. |
| May 23-25 | | Bernalillo County Schools | School and community festivals featuring Anglo and Spanish folk songs, dances, legends and traditional Spanish religious dramas to be played in many of the communities. |
| May 30, 31 | Hot Springs | Sierra | Community and School Festival with Anglo and Spanish folk songs, dances, and a fiddlers' contest. |
| June 2 | Santa Fe | Santa Fe | By Sociedad Folklórica. "Los Comanches." |
| June 15 | Ruidoso | Lincoln | "End of the Trail for the Caravan's Roundup." |
| June 16 | Capitán | Curry | Musical festivities including religious songs, traditional Anglo songs, old fiddlers, etc. |
| June 17 | Lincoln | Lincoln | "A Day in Old Lincoln"— one of the traditional highlights of the Lincoln celebration. Entire community participating in depicting customs and traditions of early Anglo and Spanish settlers in Lincoln |

CORONADO CUARTO CENTENNIAL FOLK
FESTIVAL CALENDAR—*continued*

| Date | City | County | Event |
|---|---|---|---|
| July 4, 5 | Mosquero | Harding | Annual Rodeo with Folk Festival as part of celebration. School children to participate in parade depicting pioneer days, folk dances, and songs with Old Timers taking part. |
| July 4, 5 | Las Vegas | San Miguel | Folk Festival in connection with annual 4th of July celebration. |
| July 18 | Clovis | Curry | Cowboys' Roundup, including cowboy ballads and legends. |
| July 27 | Glencoe | Lincoln | Fiesta de Los Rancheros—the traditional highlights of the Lincoln Folk Festival celebration. Entire community participating in depicting customs and traditions of early Anglo and Spanish settlers in Lincoln. |
| July 28 | Santa Fe | Santa Fe | By Sociedad Folklórica: "Adán y Eva," traditional Spanish religious drama. |
| July | Portales | Roosevelt | Old Fiddlers' Contest. |
| July | Socorro | Socorro | Community Folk Festival held in connection with the opening of new airport. Street dancing, featuring New Mexican folk dances, community sing, many county groups participating. |

CORONADO CUARTO CENTENNIAL FOLK
FESTIVAL CALENDAR—*continued*

| Date | City | County | Event |
|------|------|--------|-------|
| August 1 | Clovis | Curry | "Curry County Echoes of Long Ago" will feature Spanish and Anglo folk songs, dances, singing games, religious songs, fiddlers, and music festivals. |
| August 5, 6 | Dalhart, Texas | | Folk Festival sponsored by XIT Ranch Association. Anglo and Spanish folk songs, s q u a r e dances, cowboy songs, tall tales. All the surrounding ranch groups to participate. Held in connection with the Coronado Entrada. |
| August 20, 21 | Fort Sumner | De Baca | De Baca County Festival, in form of dramas, "Coronado's March to Quivira" and "Saga of Billy the Kid." |
| August 25 | Santa Fe | Santa Fe | Folk-dance pageant. |
| August | Portales | Roosevelt | Community Folk Festival. |
| Sept. 3-5 | Santa Fe | Santa Fe | Fiestas de Santa Fe. |
| October 6 | Santa Fe | Santa Fe | By Sociedad Folklórica: "Los Matachines." |
| October | Portales | Roosevelt | Folk Drama Contest. |
| November 24 | Santa Fe | Santa Fe | By Sociedad Folklórica: "La Aparición." |
| November | Socorro | Socorro | "49rs" Celebration, sponsored by Socorro School of Mines. Old Timers' parade, amusements of "49rs" days. |

## CORONADO ENTRADA

(Full length historical play by Thomas Wood Stevens depicting incidents in
Coronado's Expedition of 1540)

| | |
|---|---|
| May 29, 30, 31, June 1 | Albuquerque, New Mexico |
| June 5, 6 | Clovis, New Mexico |
| June 13, 14, 15 | Pampa, Texas |
| June 22, 23 | Ratón, New Mexico |
| June 28, 29, 30 | Santa Fe, New Mexico |
| July 12, 13 | Las Vegas, New Mexico |
| July 17, 18, 19 | Roswell, New Mexico |
| August 1, 2, 3 | Tucumcari, New Mexico |
| August 5, 6 | Dalhart, Texas |
| August 16, 17, 18 | Prescott, Arizona |
| August 24, 25, 26 | Hot Springs, New Mexico |
| August 30, 31 | Clifton, Arizona |
| September 6, 7, 8 | Farmington, New Mexico |
| September 16 to 21 | Amarillo, Texas |
| September 26, 27 | Socorro, New Mexico |
| September 30, | |
|    October 1, 2, 3, 4, 5 | Lubbock, Texas |
| October 11, 12, 13 | Las Cruces, New Mexico |

# PART I
## Before and After Coronado

# The State Today

NEW MEXICO today represents a blend of three cultures—Indian, Spanish, and American—each of which has had its time upon the stage and dominated the scene. The composite of culture which now, in the union of statehood, presents a harmonious picture upon casual inspection, is deceptive, for the veneer of Americanization in places runs thin indeed. It is difficult to think of a modern America in a village of the Pueblo Indians, while the inhabitants dance for rain. To be sure, a transcontinental train may thunder by, or an airplane soar overhead; but the prayers never stop, the dance goes on, and the fantastic juxtaposition seems to widen the gap between. Who could dream of the American Way in a mountain hamlet where the sound of the Penitente flute is heard above the thud of the scourges, and Spanish-American villagers perform medieval rites of redemption in Holy Week?

These are extremes of incongruity, but they are true. They diminish in the vicinity of the larger towns and cities and vanish altogether in some places; but their existence, strong or weak, colors the contemporary scene. New Mexico is a favorite camping-ground of the anthropologists because here they can study the living Indians in connection with their ancient, unbroken past and possible future. They can learn much about how people lived in medieval Spain by studying the ways of life in the remote Spanish-American villages of modern New Mexico; it has been said that if a Spaniard of those times should come to earth today, he could understand the Spanish spoken in New Mexico more readily than the modern language of his native land.

The interaction of the diverse elements of the population is slowly working towards homogeneity, dominated more and more by the irresistible middle current of Anglo-American civilization and the modern American tempo.

The mingling of the three racial elements early gave rise to the need of terms to differentiate them. Before the United States occupation the non-Indians of the region, as persons of Spanish descent and subjects of Mexico, were known as Mexicans, and proudly so. When the great influx of non-Spanish people occurred after 1848, the New Mexicans referred to them generally as "gringos." In origin, this term was not

3

one of opprobrium but simply meant any foreigner (not Spanish or Indian) who spoke the Spanish language without a good accent—unintelligibly. A Spanish dictionary published in 1787 shows that *gringo* (perversion of *griego,* Greek) was used in Spain long before Mexicans of the Southwest applied the term.

At the time of the annexation of the territory by the United States, the people of Spanish descent became United States citizens and were known thereafter as Spanish-speaking Americans to distinguish them from the Indians and the later immigrants from old Mexico. To distinguish the settlers from other parts of the United States, the prefix "Anglo" was added. Thus today the residents of the State are spoken of as Spanish-speaking Americans or Spanish-Americans, Anglo-Americans, and Indians. It is well to keep these distinctions in mind when thinking of New Mexico.

It must be remembered also that New Mexico's position as a border State, with an international port of entry and a considerable mileage on the boundary line between the United States and Mexico, has always been a factor in the State's life and character. Ties with Mexico are strong—one quite recent governor of the State was a Mexican gentleman born in Chihuahua. New Mexico—particularly the southern part—feels the effects of whatever diplomatic policies are current between the two nations at a given time, and always the State is faced with the familiar border problems of smuggling, illicit immigration, and the like. The exchange of spiritual and other influences is always in process—a condition which adds an interesting international flavor to the scene.

In the migratory annals of the United States, the direction of movement has been from east to west; in New Mexico (meaning in this instance all the southwestern states originally embraced in the old Spanish province of Nuevo Méjico) that direction did not hold. For three centuries preceding the United States occupation, the trend of settlement here was all from the south. Contact with the outside world was not from the east or from the Atlantic seaboard, but from Mexico City, and through Mexico from Spain. This difference in influences must be realized in order to appreciate the abrupt turn-about that came when the Spanish New Mexican frontier, with its face turned anxiously east, became a part of the last American frontier, with its face turned eagerly west, but it still has much of its habitual brooding introspection, induced by vast expanses of mountains and semiarid plateaus, by its shut-in valleys, and by the primitive mode of life that prevails everywhere outside of the towns—on ranches, in tiny settlements, in the Indians' villages and nomadic solitudes.

Homogeneous, New Mexico is not. Its cultural, regional variations follow perhaps inevitably its topographical divisions. Spanish settlement, with its roots in Chihuahua, spread like a tree up the central Rio

Grande Valley, branching east and west. In north central New Mexico today the Spanish element is still most prevalent, the only integral remnant of the northernmost fringe of Spanish empire in America.

Northeastern New Mexico, first penetrated from the east by trappers and traders and later developed by way of the Santa Fe Trail, is preponderantly Anglo-American. With the coming of the United States Army in 1846, the introduction of wagon and stagecoach roads over the Gila Trail to southern California, and the later advent of railroads and mining developments turned the Anglo-American trek down the Rio Grande Valley and into the southwestern part of the State and the mines of the Silver City area. East central and southeastern New Mexico, the western extension of the Great Plains and the Llano Estacado, was first developed as a cattle country soon after the Civil War; it is peopled largely by ranchers from Texas, and is still markedly Texan in character. South central New Mexico likewise received a large influx of Anglo-American immigration soon after the Civil War, when, as Eugene Manlove Rhodes has said, "the Mississippi valley moved in." The saints' names of many small Spanish villages were changed to the Scotch, Irish, or English cognomens of the later settlers. Across the middle of the State, too, the trek followed the railroad from Santa Fe and Albuquerque to the western border. In the far northwest the fertile San Juan Valley attracted Mormon homesteaders who, migrating southward from Utah, established themselves in the region bordering the great Rocky Mountain plateau country which was then and is today inhabited by the Navaho Indians, and which was in ancient times the cradle of the highest development of Pueblo Indian culture.

These general regional variations, following cultural development, are complicated by the many variations within any one region. Suddenly and without forewarning, from almost any point in the State, one may step from modern America into Old Spain, or into aboriginal Indian territory, within the space of a few miles, just as one passes from an almost tropic climate into an arctic one, due to the many abrupt transitions from plain to plateau, up mountains and down again.

With an average of only about four persons to the square mile, New Mexico is a sparsely settled State. The commerce required for the needs of such a population is conducted largely by Anglo-Americans or people of foreign descent, the native Spanish-Americans remaining the farmers and not infrequently the politicians. Due to the bilingual character of the population, a section was placed in the constitution of the State, when it was drawn up in 1910, to the effect that all laws passed by the legislature should be published in both English and Spanish for the following twenty years, and after that such publication should be made as the legislature provided. It is interesting to note that state court and legislative procedure is still to some extent bilingual, and interpreters stand ready in the legislature to translate from English into Spanish and vice versa. Some interpreters deliver a better and more eloquent speech in translation than the original. The fate of many a bill has rested in the hands of the interpreter.

New Mexico as a whole has been subjected to every boom that has swept the western land, but has emerged singularly unaffected by them. From the days of Coronado, who sought fantastic wealth, to the boom times of the Comstock Lode and Cripple Creek, search for treasure in the earth has been a fever in New Mexicans. The finds, though not permanent, have been spectacular in many instances; but the gold boom died just as the land boom and the cattle boom died. Today mining remains a lesser industry, confined to a few proved areas of coal and mineral deposits. Mining operations are scattered throughout the State, but the early promise of the industry has never been fulfilled. Oil, natural gas, and "dry ice" are the latest developments in the field, and they have prospered, especially in the southeastern part of the State, where Hobbs has mushroomed from a shanty oil town to the fifth largest city in New Mexico.

The patriarchal feudal system of Old Spain has left its stamp upon the land. It was the custom in Spanish times to portion out the land in vast grants for colonization to favored individuals, who had the right to collect tribute from the Indians living upon them; for more than two centuries this was the economic picture of the region. As these old grants contained the best farming and grazing lands in the territory, their withdrawal from the arable and productive domain greatly retarded the normal development of the region. Many of the original grants remain intact today, having changed hands after the United States annexation opened the country to speculators of the land grabbing era. Most of those robust and adventurous men anticipated the coming of the railroads and the boom in the cattle industry, and for some years they fared well indeed; but, as the land had done so often before, it overwhelmed the land grabbers and left them staggering with too much acreage and in some cases an insupportable load of taxes. Some of the old grants have been purchased by the Federal government and returned to the Indians, their original claimants; others have been broken up and sold in parcels; still others stand as they did in the beginning, idle, waiting for development by people with money enough to finance the task.

Huge areas also have been set apart as national forests and parks under Federal control. The timbered mountains, in addition to holding lumber reserves for the future, offer unlimited recreational facilities, camping, hunting, and fishing to the nation-at-large. These great primitive areas coupled with many national and state parks and monuments are among today's major attractions in New Mexico.

The fate of the vast cattle empire of the late nineteenth century, which spread from the southeast along the eastern slope of the Rocky Mountains, has been similar to that of the old Spanish grants. The empire has receded, leaving the great ranches of the early days broken up and sold, or languishing under burdens of delinquent taxes. The livestock industry is still of great importance in all parts of the State, although dry farming and irrigation projects have broken up the public range in many sections.

New Mexico remains, then, an agricultural State primarily. The country people of Spanish descent in the central sections are all small farmers, fighting fatalistically the reluctant earth with ancient irrigation systems and inadequate tools. Rich farming lands there are, but they form a minor part of the whole. Wherever a stream ventures out of the mountains, there, for as far as it remains above the surface, will be found little farms using the precious water. Often they are hidden in the folds of the hills, where the people, forming tiny hamlets, live now much as their forebears have lived for the past two or three centuries.

To a great extent, these are the people, too, who have guided the political destiny of New Mexico, for they still hold the balance of power between the two major parties. The political complexion of the State is not, however, so predictable as it used to be. Up to 1916, the Spanish-American population could be expected with fair reliability to vote Republican, but the old party lines are beginning to break down. Reasons for this early preference were an ingrained conservatism, a long-standing dislike of Democratic Texas and Texans, at whose hands the Spanish-speaking people felt they had suffered persecutions and indignities in the past, and the desire, if not the need, of a high protective tariff for New Mexico's products.

With the great land grants resting in the hands of the Spanish grandees, it was the *haciendado* who was the leader and the lawmaker. His *peons* tilled the fields and tended the herds. It was inevitable that the politics of the territory should follow the same feudal path. The grandee, or *patrón,* needed only to say the word, and such votes as were needed by him or his friends were forthcoming. As the *patrón* commanded, so it was done—as in the old days the *peons* had fought for him, so now they would vote for him. The result was that the territory was governed by *ricos,* the landowners, for the *ricos.* This was the situation at the beginning of the United States occupation. The rule of the eastern Tweed type of politician here found fertile soil, and the territory came under the control of professional Anglo-American politicians, who led the ambitious Spanish-Americans into a maze of political practices which resulted in the legend that the *haciendado* voted all of his sheep as well as his *peons,* when the need arose. With statehood for New Mexico, however, these old practices began to disappear and, except in the more remote sections, are gone from the scene.

As to the northern and southern political divisions of the United States, New Mexico appears sometimes to belong with the former and sometimes with the latter. During the Civil War, New Mexico as a territory sided in the main with the North, even stopping a Confederate army which had been sent to capture the territory and the California gold fields. Whatever the partisanship of the people today, politics remains one of the favorite preoccupations, for the Latin temperament delights in the special kind of intrigue and excitement which politics affords. It pervades their whole life, causing divisions within families and even within religious groups where such schisms seem irrelevant to the Anglo-American.

In those sections of the State which have been shown to be predominantly Anglo-American, the social life is that of the middle western small town which has been so widely and exhaustively described in the literature of the present century. In the central and northern sections of the State, this life is deeply colored by Spanish and Indian influences. It centers primarily around the home and the church, which have combined with the tyrannical land to perpetuate a fatalistic outlook as well as the old and proved ways of living.

For all its tyranny, however, it is a land of surpassing beauty and attraction. Its climate is almost universally benevolent, with clear air, brilliant sunshine, and in the plateau regions, brisk winters of dry and stimulating cold. Space is the keynote of the land—vast, limitless stretches of plain, desert, and lofty mountains, with buttes and mesas and purple distances to rest the eye. To all of this is added the interest of human life, lived here for countless ages.

The future of New Mexico, from a commercial and industrial point of view, is promising. The needs of the Nation have not yet pressed the resources of the State to development, but the time will come. Enough coal lies buried within its borders to supply the nation for thousands of years, after other more accessible supplies have been exhausted; and the same is true, in a lesser degree, or other minerals. The very factors—aridity, remoteness, and immense distances—that have retarded the exploitation of natural resources contribute immeasurably to the State's attractiveness as a national vacation-land.

# The Land

NEW MEXICO is the southeastern State of the Mountain group, bounded on the north by Colorado, on the east by Oklahoma and Texas, on the south by Texas and Mexico, and on the west by Arizona. The northwestern corner of the state, joining Arizona, Utah, and Colorado in a common corner, is the only place in the United States where four States so meet. In size, New Mexico is the fourth largest of the forty-eight States, its area embracing 122,634 square miles of land ranging in elevation from lofty mountain peaks to low arid plains and deserts.

Of the eight major physiographic divisions of the United States three are present in New Mexico. The major divisions are composed of provinces, and the provinces in turn of sections. Parts of four provinces and eight sections are in New Mexico. Seven of the eight sections lie within 50 miles of Santa Fe. Few other cities can claim such a strategic position.

The Southern Rocky Mountains Province lies in the north-central part of the State; the Great Plains Province, with its three sections —the Ratón, Pecos Valley, and High Plains—occupies the eastern third; the Colorado Plateaus Province, embracing the Navaho and Dátil Sections, is in the northwest quarter; the Basin and Range Province with its two sections, the Mexican Highland and Sacramento, occupies the southwest quarter and central portion.

The Rocky Mountain System of the Southern Rocky Mountains Province is made up of complex mountains of various types. This is the highest and most rugged part of the State, and contains Pleistocene glaciation and striking scenery, outstanding features of which are the Sangre de Cristo, Jémez, and Nacimiento Mountains, and the Rio Grande Canyon.

The Interior Plains of the Great Plains in the Ratón Section show dissected lava-capped plateaus, mesas, and buttes; deep picturesque canyons, volcanic cones; Park Plateau, Ratón Mesa group, Ocaté and Las Vegas Plateaus, and Canadian Escarpment.

Pecos Valley Section, of late mature to old plain, is a long trough occupied by the Pecos River, and includes the Roswell Artesian Basin. The High Plains Section shows the broad intervalley remnants of smooth river-formed plains; the Llano Estacado, or Staked Plains, is as flat as any land surface in nature.

9

The Intermontane Plateaus of the Colorado Plateaus Province, in the Navaho Section, show young plateaus, stripped structural-platform or rock terraces, retreating escarpments, mesas, cuestas, shallow canyons, and dry washes, to San Juan Basin, San Juan Valley, and Chuska Mountains. In the Dátil Section are found extensive lava flows, and volcanoes and volcanic necks, such as the Zuñi Mountains, Mount Taylor, and Cabezón Peak.

The Mexican Highland of the Basin and Range Province shows narrow isolated ranges of largely dissected block mountains separated by broad silt-deposited desert plains; rock pediments, alluvial fans, bolsons, playas (dry lake beds), salinas, and dunes. Sandía, Manzano, San Andrés, Caballos, Magdalena, San Mateo, Black, Mogollón, and many other ranges are here; also basins such as the Tularosa, Jornada del Muerto, and Plains of San Agustín; and the Rio Grande, a through-flowing stream of complex geologic history.

The Sacramento Section includes mature block mountains of gently tilted strata, block plateaus, and bolsons, such as the Sierra Blanca, Sacramento, and Guadalupe Mountains, and the Estancia Valley.

The great topographic relief of the State, 10,430 feet (from 2,876 to 13,306), is conditioned by great uplifts and displacements of the earth's crust. This relief is to a large degree responsible for the great range of rainfall in the State as well as for the temperatures above and below zero. There is also a definite connection between the contrasting physiographic relief and the presence in the State of six of the seven life zones present in North America; the Lower Sonoran, Upper Sonoran, Transition, Canadian, Hudsonian, and Arctic-Alpine, each with its distinctive assemblage of plants and animals.

The annual rainfall for the whole State ranges from 12 to 16 inches and, although 100 degrees of heat are not infrequent in the summer, the mean temperature for the year is about 50 degrees.

## GEOLOGY

Few other States possess a more remarkable array of diverse geologic features or a more complete record of geologic history than New Mexico. There are many breaks in the record; in some instances no strata were deposited; at other times strata were deposited only to be removed by subsequent erosion. But it is noteworthy that every period of the geologic time-table is represented in this State. The most ancient rocks in New Mexico are possibly 1,000 to 2,000 million years old and are so exposed in mountain ranges that to see them it is necessary to ascend rather than to descend, as required in the Grand Canyon of the Colorado in Arizona.

Throughout much of the Paleozoic era southern New Mexico was submerged beneath the seas from time to time, thus accounting for the presence today of marine sediments such as sandstones, limestones, and shales of Cambrian, Ordovician, Silurian, Devonian, and Mississippian ages in the southern half of the State.    In the following epoch, the Pennsylvanian, practically the whole State sank beneath marine waters, and thick sediments accumulated over extensive areas.    In the closing period of the era, the Permian, oscillations of level occurred with consequent marine and terrestrial deposits.    In the Permian Basin of southeastern New Mexico vast deposits of rock salt, gypsum, and potash salts accumulated.    These recently discovered potash deposits, vying in magnitude with Germany's, constitute a national resource of great value.

During Triassic and Jurassic times terrestrial conditions prevailed in the Southwest, continental deposits by wind, rivers, and lakes being made.    In the Cretaceous period most of the State was submerged for the last time, and marine strata of considerable thickness were deposited. In this period's closing stages the land rose again, and vegetation accumulated to form important coal beds.    The Laramide revolution, which ended the Mesozoic era, brought about uplift and displacements of the earth's crust.

Throughout the next era, the Cenozoic, continental deposits accumulated, as higher portions of the State were subjected to erosion, and great igneous activity began.    Both intrusion and extrusion of magmas (molten matter) occurred intermittently and from place to place.    It is believed that this activity began in the late Cretaceous and continued until recent times.    Further deformation of the earth's crust occurred, apparently, during the Cenozoic.    The deformations of the Laramide revolution and of the Cenozoic era and the igneous activity, particularly the intrusions, accompanied the emplacement of most of the State's ore deposits.    During the Pleistocene period mountain valley glaciers occupied some higher portions of the State.

Many of the Paleozoic rocks are at certain horizons abundantly fossiliferous.    From the Cambrian through the Permian era fossils are dominantly marine invertebrates such as corals, crinoids, brachiopods, clams, and snails; marine invertebrates occur again in Cretaceous beds. Plant fossils appear in Pennsylvanian and Permian strata, and most abundantly in the Upper Cretaceous, where great numbers contributed to the vast deposits of coal.    Vertebrates, such as fishes, amphibians, and reptiles, are found in the Pennsylvanian, Permian, and Triassic formations; in the Upper Cretaceous, fishes, turtles, and dinosaurs are not uncommon.    Cenozoic beds have yielded large numbers of mammalian remains.    In the San Juan Basin are the type localities of the well-known Paleocene formations, the Puerco and the Torrejón, with their unique fossil mammals.    Many new species and genera, particularly of fossil plants and vertebrates, have been described from New Mexico.

When studied further, the invertebrates will also doubtless yield many forms new to science.

Sedimentary, igneous, and metamorphic rocks are all present in the State in great variety.    Marine sediments, such as sandstones, limestones, and shales, and the terrestrial or continental deposits of rivers, lakes, glaciers, and the wind, have already been mentioned.    Intrusive igneous rocks occur as batholiths, stocks, dikes, sills, and laccoliths; extrusive igneous rocks in the form of volcanic cones, lava flows, and ash deposits cover large portions of the State.    Volcanism continued until fairly recent times, and some basaltic lavas are possibly less than 1,000 years old.    Metamorphic rocks are abundant in the pre-Cambrian basement complex and occur also in the aureoles surrounding the younger intrusive bodies.    What is generally conceded to be the finest display of volcanic necks in the world exists in the Mount Taylor-Rio Puerco region.

An investigation, still in progress, reveals that more than 275 species of minerals have been recorded in the State.    Many fine specimens can still be found, especially on the dumps of hundreds of abandoned mines. A number of minerals, for example some of the potash salts, either do not occur elsewhere in North America or are very rare.    Both metallic and non-metallic minerals have yielded richly.

Much of the State's striking scenery is in large part the result of deformations of the earth's crust.    Folds and faults of many varied types abound.    A standard classification of mountains recognizes: (1) residual mountains, or mountains of erosion; (2) volcanic mountains; (3) tectonic mountains, a group of mountains formed by displacements of the earth's crust, including fault rock (broken and displaced blocks), dome, and fold (folded rock strata); and (4) complex mountains, or those in which combinations of several of the above types occur.    Good examples of all except the pure fold type are found in New Mexico. The fault block type is particularly well developed and marvelously displayed.    Practically all of the deformation and its accompanying igneous activity have occurred within the past 60 million years, since the end of the Mesozoic era.

## SCENIC GEOLOGIC FEATURES

*Underground Waters:*    Carlsbad Cavern National Park; Bottomless Lakes State Park; several groups of hot springs and their deposits, notably the Soda Dam near Jémez Springs; Rosewell Artesian Basin; sinkholes of the Pecos Valley.

*Volcanic Features:*    Capulín Mountain National Monument, Bandelier National Monument, the great Valle Grande Caldera, the volcanic necks of the Mount Taylor-Rio Puerco field, Shiprock and associated peaks, Zuñi Salt Crater near Quemado, the very fresh lava of the Carrizozo and San José flows, the ice caves near Grants.

*Erosion and Weathering:* Chaco Canyon National Monument, El Morro (Inscription Rock) National Monument, Enchanted Mesa, Tucumcari Mountain, the volcanic necks already mentioned, Rio Grande Canyon near Taos, Cimarrón Canyon, the great Red Wall between Thoreau and Gallup, glacial phenomena of north central New Mexico, work of the wind at White Sands National Monument (one of the largest areas of gypsum sand dunes in the world).

*Miscellaneous Features:* Estancia Salt Lake, Zuñi Salt Crater, the great fault escarpments of such ranges as the Sandía, Manzano, Caballos, San Andrés, Sacramento, and others, Sweet's Ranch Petrified Forest, the Turquoise Hills, and the Santa Rita open copper pits.

## FLORA

In all, more than 6,000 species of flora have been recognized and recorded in New Mexico. Many of the trees and shrubs are entirely different from those of the rest of the country. The desert cacti, in season, turn into vast fields of flowers, most of which are not to be found in flower keys of the eastern and northern parts of the country. Many extraordinary forms of flora are peculiar to the southwestern deserts.

In the Lower and Upper Sonoran zones, which are sometimes grouped together under the term Sonoran Desert, the predominant vegetation in New Mexico is desert grass, creosote bush, mesquite, piñon pine, and soapweed; and valuable grasses: the gramas, the galleta, and buffalo give range value to the lands of Upper Sonoran elevation. Woody plants, like desert willow, screw-bean, valley cottonwood, and cacti, are found in variety. Higher elevation areas known as the Upper Sonoran zone contain most of the valuable grazing and dry-farming lands, where the principal crops are wheat, corn, milo maize, kaffir, and broom corn on the eastern plains and pinto (Mexican) beans in the Estancia Valley and near-by foothills.

The rough lands north of the plains are generally characterized by scrubby forests of juniper, piñon (nut pine), and oak. The parts of the Upper Sonoran zone which are not under irrigation are covered with such vegetation as sagebrush, snakeweed, and short grasses, with saltgrass and valley cottonwood along the rivers. The higher edges of the valleys are less arid and are generally covered with piñon, juniper, and a better stand of grass.

Certain steep broken areas of the Sonoran Desert, like the Gila River Basin in the southwest, have scattered growths of oak, juniper, and piñon and an abundance of food-yielding plants. In the canyons are a profusion of wild grape, currant, hackberry, walnut, and oak. Fruit-bearing cacti (*Opuntias*) and yucca (*Yucca baccata*) occur on the slopes.

Three varieties of yucca, commonly called soapweed (*palmita* or *amole*) grow in New Mexico. The roots, when crushed, make excellent suds used by the Indians and native Spanish-Americans in place of soap. The broad-leafed *Yucca baccata* (Dátil-date), found in foothills, bears large succulent seed-pods which the Indians used as food. *Yucca macrocarpa,* with thick wide stiff leaves, bears a smaller flower than the *Yucca aloifolia,* commonly called Spanish Dagger, or *Yucca elata,* which has narrow flexible leaves and tall branched flower stocks, commonly called God's Candles. Because of its widespread habitat, its ability to withstand drought, and its beauty, the yucca was chosen for the State flower.

Some sections are open country of scattered grass and desert shrubs, such as saltbrush, white and purple sage, and varied species of rabbit brush. In the San Juan River Valley in the northwest, all of which lies within the Sonoran Desert, the land is extremely fertile and, where irrigated, supports good yields of fruits, chiefly apples, pears, and peaches. The dominant plants in this section are the Utah juniper, buffalo berry, Rocky Mountain birch, and cliff rose.

Piñon and juniper are abundant in the broken country and over the foothills of the mountains. Oak becomes more conspicuous toward the upper borders of the zone. The Rio Grande cottonwood is large and shady along the valley streams, and other trees of the Upper Sonoran are the lance-leaved cottonwood, several willows, and the mountain mahogany. Scattered over the grassy plains and mesas are sages, yuccas, and cacti, and in some of the more arid regions, the bushy snakeweed, sometimes mistaken for sagebrush, and greasewood. Locoweed (*Astragalus*), with its purple or white flowers, is beautiful in full bloom, but it is the curse of some range lands, for it is poisonous to cattle.

The Transition zone is the important timber section of the State, the zone of the western yellow or ponderosa pine; the lance-leaved cottonwood, many varieties of oak, willow, and pine are also found in the forests of this zone, together with the New Mexico birch, maple, locust, the wild red plum, and the cherry. Some of the brushes are buckthorn, currant, gooseberry, thorn apple, barberry, wild rose, and snowberry. Wild hop, columbine, lupine, milk vetch, and rush are some of the herbaceous plants; dropseed, meadow grass, bluegrass, bromegrass, foxtail, and wheat grass are common.

The trees of the Canadian zone (which lies above 8,000 feet and is important for the water supply it stores for regions of lower elevations) are the bristlecone pine, western white pine, aspen, and Douglas spruce.

Engelmann fir, corkbark fir, and Siberian juniper grow in the Hudsonian zone, which lies around timberline. Currants and sedges of several species are found in this zone.

The flora of the Alpine zone, the smallest of all, is characterized by dwarf alpine flowers, mountain forget-me-nots, saxifrages, sedges, rushes, dwarf closed gentian, and alpine larkspur. No trees grow here, as the area is confined to the mountain peaks above timberline.

Plants enter largely into native Indian ceremonial rites, many species having definite uses, medicinal virtues, and healing qualities. The jimsonweed (*Datura stramonium*) is used to induce hallucinations, delirium, and convulsions, in which state the subject is supposed to be benefited by intercourse with the powers of the unseen world. The amole (*yucca*) root figures in many cleansing rites, and the wild herbs used by the Indians and Spanish-Americans would make a large catalogue. Mormon tea, *chimajá* (wild celery)—the latter a plant whose leaves and root both cooked and raw are edible—*yerbas buenas* (mints), *oshá* (mountain celery) and *yerba de mansa* (lizard's tail) are among those still gathered in New Mexico mountains as valuable foods and remedies.

## FAUNA

The first survey of New Mexico animals and birds was made in 1540 by Castañeda, the chronicler of the Coronado expedition. In making his reports, as required by the Spanish government, Castañeda mentioned chiefly the animals whose skins were found in the pueblos along the line of march, and he noted especially the buffalo, or "cows covered with frizzled hair which resembles wool." The few birds mentioned are of special interest, since they were the first recorded in what is now the United States. The Spanish chronicler noted that "a very large number of cranes and wild geese and starlings (purple grackles) live on what is sown. There are a great many native fowl in these provinces, and cocks (wild turkeys) with great hanging chins." Long robes and dresses made of the "feathers of the fowls" were seen, and "tame eagles which the chiefs estimate to be something fine."

Many expeditions, private and governmental, have augmented this first fragmentary report. William Gambel visited the State in 1841, mainly for the study of birds, and four years later James William Abert did considerable collecting. Dr. A. Wislizenus conducted a study of the flora in 1846, and subsequent students have furnished a wealth of information on the flora and fauna of New Mexico. A systematic survey of the State's bird life was undertaken in 1903 by Dr. C. Hart Merriam and Mr. Vernon Bailey, and continued after 1913 by the Biological Survey of the United States Department of Agriculture. Field work was carried on in every important valley and mountain range in New Mexico, and material gathered for a fairly detailed map of the six life zones.

More than three hundred species of birds have been recognized in New Mexico.   Fifteen species of fur-bearing animals and thirty species of game are listed by the State Game and Fish Department.

Rodents are the most abundant mammals in the Lower Sonoran zone and also occur in numbers in the Upper Sonoran.   Larger mammals in this zone include the beaver, civet cat, whitetail and mule deer, wildcat, fox, antelope, a few mountain sheep, and the Mexican cougar. This wide-ranging predator, commonly known as the mountain lion, though rare, is immensely destructive.   The timber wolf—*lobo* to Spanish-Americans—is also scarce but may sometimes be found ranging alone or leading a pack of mountain coyotes.   Prairie-dog towns are still seen in many places along the highways despite a vigorous program of the Department of Agriculture to bring them under control; they are considered harmful to both grass and farm crops.   Jack rabbits (hares) are still numerous, and occasionally a coyote, badger, or skunk is visible from the highway.

Terrapins often crawl around on the grasslands of the southeast far from streams or lakes, and the ornate box turtle is also found in this zone.   Snakes are non-venomous, except the rattlesnake and the rare coral snake.

The Abert squirrel and the porcupine thrive in the Transition zone, which is also the habitat of the Rocky Mountain lion, the mule deer, black bear, bobcat, and mountain coyote.   Otter, mink, and badger occur in this zone, as well as many of the smaller animals and rodents from the lower elevations.   The wild turkey, the ruddy duck, cinnamon teal, shoveler, dusky grouse, and many song birds breed here.

Mountain sheep, the Rocky Mountain woodchuck, the gray rock cony, and several birds, including the dusky shrew, nutcracker, and grosbeak are found in the narrow Hudsonian zone around timberline. There are mountain sheep also in the highest areas of the Alpine zone.

New Mexico has excellent possibilities for the propagation of game birds. Reclamation and other agricultural activities have helped to create conditions favorable to certain kinds, and recent extensions of game sanctuaries have given promising increases.   There are now 183 State, and one or two Federal, game reserve areas set aside as sanctuaries where game animals and birds may reproduce unmolested, all of them extremely important in the conservation of wildlife.   Areas in the lowlands are for prairie chicken, quail, and other game birds and in the mountains for big game.   No hunting of any kind is allowed within a game refuge.

Predatory animals are still a serious menace to wild game of all kinds in the State.   Due to State Game Department activities, wolves and mountain lions are no longer the serious menace that they were in past years. Wildcats and coyotes are still dangerous enemies, their prey ranging from barnyard fowl to adult deer and antelope.

Distribution of birds, as of all wildlife in the State, is influenced largely by altitude. The mountain bluebirds nest at various levels between 5,800 and 10,300 feet, while the white-tailed ptarmigan occupies the tops of the mountain ranges. Thrashers are found throughout the year in the extreme southwestern part of New Mexico; the chestnut colored longspur breeds far north of New Mexico, but enters the State in the fall to remain until April; the painted bunting nests in the extreme southern part of the State in the valleys of the Rio Grande and Pecos Rivers but deserts the State during the winter. The white-rumped sandpiper, the Baird sandpiper, and several other shore birds pass across New Mexico when traveling from their summer homes far north on the Arctic coast to their winter homes in lower South America.

About three hundred different species of birds can be found in New Mexico at almost any time of the year. Among them is the fiercest of all hawks, the duck hawk, which nests in overhanging cliffs. Bright-colored orioles, eight or ten varieties of wrens, four kinds of humming-birds—among them the calliope, the smallest in North America; forty-four different kinds of sparrows, the yellow warblers, finches, and many other small birds are found here. White pelicans are plentiful near Elephant Butte Dam; and common also is the crested roadrunner (the chapparal cock, or *paisano,* of Mexico), a grotesque bird that tries to outrun horses and automobiles on the roads. Magpies and jays, ravens, hawks, and eagles (whose feathers are prized by Indians) are found in the higher zones. Characteristic of the Lower Sonoran zone is the mourning dove, whose sweet, mournful note breaks the stillness of the semiarid plains. On the high timbered mesas and in mountain canyons, the Rocky Mountain magpie (*Pica pica hudsonia*) is the bane of campers. He does not hesitate to filch bright objects and for that reason is called the camp robber, a title bestowed elsewhere on the Canada jay.

It is now widely recognized that birds, by destroying farm and orchard insects, are directly instrumental in the conservation of agricultural output; consequently they receive increased protection every year.

The piñon supplies one of the more important of the natural game foods, and its nuts impart a fine flavor to the flesh of the game that fattens on them. Oak mast ranks second to piñon and is a more dependable source. Juniper berries, manzanita mast, desert sumac, and skunk-brush furnish food and cover for birds. Elderberry and chokeberry supply seasonal food to birds and animals, especially wild pigeons and songbirds; bears wreck the branches of the chokeberry to get its fruit.

Cacti produce succulent fruit even during the driest seasons, and yucca and sotol provide food for cattle and deer.

Streams of the higher elevations support only trout. New Mexico is aware of the value of its trout streams and the State Fish and Game Department is carrying on an efficient restocking system. The native blackspotted, or cutthroat, are unexcelled, and they are better adapted to New Mexican waters than most of the introduced specimens, such as the Loch Leven, rainbow, and eastern brook trout.

Millions of black bass, crappie, perch, channel catfish, and bream are planted annually in the warm waters of New Mexico to replace the less desirable native carp, suckers, and garfish. A peculiar type of gizzard shad, with a gizzard very similar to that of a hen, is found in Pecos Valley. Another interesting fish is the gambusia, which has been introduced in the river valleys to aid in mosquito control. It is the only fish in these waters which bears its young alive.

Cold-blooded vertebrates are most plentiful both in species and numbers in warm climates, and it is natural that the Upper and Lower Sonoran zones in New Mexico should be rich in reptilian life. The rattlesnake is the most widely distributed venomous reptile in the State. The black-tailed or green rattlesnake is occasionally encountered in the Guadalupe Mountains; prairie rattlesnakes are found over the high plains country north and east, and the large western diamond-back is found in the warmer valleys.

The venomous coral snake is met occasionally. Non-poisonous snakes include the western bullsnake, which grows to a large size but is harmless; the Mexican blacksnake; the coachwhip; the ring-necked snake; the puff adder, and several species of gartersnakes.

One of the odd reptiles of New Mexico is the glass snake, which is really not a snake at all but a legless lizard. Its peculiarity is its ability to shake off a part of its tail when attacked. While the aggressor watches the wiggling tail, the creature makes for cover.

The only poisonous lizard in the whole Southwest is the Gila monster, which inhabits the Lower Sonoran zone of Arizona. Many species of harmless lizards abound in New Mexico. Widely different groups are represented, such as the scaly rock lizards, bar-tailed Texas lizards, leopard lizards, Bailey's collared lizard, and western earless lizards. Three kinds of horned toads are found in the State. These interesting little creatures with tiny horns on their backs are sometimes captured and kept as pets.

Five species of toads are found in New Mexico but the leopard frog and the bull frog are the only true frogs in the State. Salamanders (*guajolote*), the many-ribbed triton, theuta, striped swift, the Sonoran skink, the prairie skink, and the southern brown-shouldered uta are found. Six species of turtle occur; the Sonoran mud turtle, yellow-necked mud turtle; the western painted turtle; tortoise terrapin, and the soft-shelled turtle; Cumberland terrapin are common on the prairies of the eastern sections. Besides the dry-land terrapin of these sections, there is the tortoise of the Lower Sonoran zone. The terrapin is carnivorous and lives on earthworms and insects; the tortoise is herbivorous.

One is likely to encounter many legends, exaggerations, and misconceptions concerning plants and animals in the State. Many insects are widely believed to be dangerous. Three of these are the tarantula, the centipede, and the vinegarroon.

The tarantula is a large, ugly, hairy spider, dark or light brown in color, which burrows into the ground or utilizes small holes from one to two inches in diameter. For all its ferocious appearance, the tarantula is unable to inflict more than temporary pain and injury. The centipede is another horrid-appearing insect more beneficial than harmful, for it devours other insects and small animals; its bite, while painful, is not serious. Wild stories are sometimes heard of the deadly vinegarroon, which is a sun spider (*solpugida*). They are known to the Arabs as wind scorpions and to the Spanish as spiders of the sun (*arañas del sol*). They are very swift and agile insects of nocturnal habits, living in warm desert regions. The vinegarroon is densely covered with hairs, has no spinning organs, and is entirely harmless.

Besides these three much slandered species, many other kinds of scorpions, harvesters, spiders, ticks, and mites are found in various sections. The majority prey upon other insects and so are beneficial, but some are serious plant and animal insect pests.

A few species of spider are exceedingly venomous, and a bite from one of these may result in great pain and even death. The most poisonous species in New Mexico is the Black Widow, a medium-sized black spider, the female of which has a red mark in the shape of an hourglass upon the abdomen. It lives under boards, logs, stones, and in outbuildings.

There are a number of species of ticks in various parts of the State: the most common in the southern and warmer parts of the Lower Sonoran zone is the *Argasine,* or chicken tick. Ear ticks, or the spinose ear ticks, give some trouble by getting into the ears of stock and pets, but there are no fever ticks in the State.

The sheep-scab mite, once one of the greatest pests sheepmen have had to deal with, by quarantine and dipping has been almost eradicated. Many other plant and animal mites offer less serious problems.

Grasshoppers, katydids, and crickets are widespread though not in exceptional numbers. Locusts are a minor menace in some seasons and require poisoning campaigns. Aphis, scale insects, leafhoppers, and other

*Homoptera* present the usual problems to orchardists and gardeners but are controlled by a variety of sprays.

Wild bees are plentiful, and there are a great variety of ants, beetles, and butterflies. The Rocky Mountain tent caterpillar is a dangerous pest in the forests, where it attacks and defoliates at least twenty-four varieties of trees and shrubs; one species even attacks the evergreens. A project of the Work Projects Administration has spent considerable time in Santa Fe searching for insect enemies of these pests (which have become alarmingly destructive in the mountainous sections) in order to utilize nature's means of combating them.

## NATURAL RESOURCES

Although its land area ranks fourth in extent among the forty-eight States, New Mexico has a water area of only 131 square miles, the smallest of any State in the Union. The conservation of the State's water resources is therefore a matter of the utmost urgency, particularly since the land is largely composed of vast arid and semiarid districts which require irrigation for abundant productivity. Water is thus more important to the State's present and future welfare than all the coal or gold or minerals within its borders.

About 350 square miles of New Mexico's area may be regarded as a vast plateau region, averaging 5,000 in elevation, intersected by numerous streams forming narrow valleys and deep gorges. The southern portion of the State is characterized by great stretches of plains, cut by muddy rivers, split by occasional north-south mountain ranges, and embracing fertile agricultural sections, all of which require irrigation.

Crops adapted to unirrigated districts are comparatively few in number; hence the great emphasis placed upon irrigation. In the irrigated valleys, where the moisture factor is largely under control, practically all crops of the Temperate Zones can be raised successfully. Some dry farming, or farming dependent entirely upon rainfall, is carried on in the higher altitudes in the Estancia Valley and above the northeast tier of counties, with periodic loss of crops due to drought. Plant adaptation has probably received the least attention among conservation measures.

Irrigation in New Mexico, practiced by aboriginal Indian tribes in prehistoric times, is the oldest in America, yet the problems attendant upon modern irrigation are far more complex than the simple diversion of water from streams into the fields. Any extensive reclamation scheme requires intelligent and farseeing planning, involving the expenditure of millions of dollars for dams, canals, and subsidiary works for the control of flood waters, erosion, silt, and drainage. In New Mexico, especially, the menace of silt carried by the rivers and streams is very great. It results in the reduction of the storage capacity of reservoirs, which unless controlled, can nullify, in a relatively short time, the most elaborate and expensive reclamation projects; and it dangerously raises the level and banks of rivers above the surrounding countryside. This often renders the land adjacent to the stream unsuitable for agriculture, and adds the menace of floods as well. The natural processes of disintegration, erosion from wind, rain, and torrential cloudbursts, will continue, but much can be done to control them.

New Mexico is divided into water basins, each with its special characteristics and problems. The river basins are the most important, and the greatest is the San Juan, in the northwestern part of the State. Next in importance are the Canadian, Rio Grande, Pecos, and Gila, with the Zuñi, San Francisco, and Sacramento Rivers as the lesser streams in New Mexico. Although the San Juan, a part of the great Colorado River drainage, belongs in one of the great water systems of the continent, it serves a smaller area in New Mexico than the Rio Grande and Pecos Rivers; the Rio Grande, with its source in Colorado, flows in a general southerly direction through the center of the State; the Pecos, originating in northern New Mexico, flows southeast across the State and into Texas.

During the Spanish and Mexican eras in New Mexico, irrigation was confined to the valley of the Rio Grande and its tributaries, owing to the proximity of hostile Indians, lack of engineering knowledge, and lack of capital for the purpose of creating extensive dams. Irrigation of large areas by modern methods was initiated in the last quarter of the nineteenth century, under the United States regime. The northernmost project on the Rio Grande proper is the Middle Rio Grande Conservancy District, an irrigation and flood-control development begun in 1930. This $10,000,000 project has for its purpose the drainage of about 120,000 acres of land, the checking of flood damage from the Rio Grande and its tributaries, and the installation of a modern and efficient irrigation system in the upper valley, a system that contains 363 miles of canals maintained by a small annual tax assessed against the irrigated acreage.

Lower on the river, near the town of Hot Springs, is the Elephant Butte Dam of the Rio Grande Federal Reclamation Project. Elephant Butte Reservoir, sometimes called Hall Lake, is 40 miles long and approximately three miles across at its widest point. The shore line is nearly 200 miles in extent, the lake covering an area of 40,000 acres to an average depth of 66 feet. The original storage capacity, somewhat decreased by silt deposition, was sufficient to cover 2,638,860 acres under a foot of water. The site of the old United States Army Post, Fort McRae, now lies beneath its surface. An engineering wonder, Elephant

Butte is of international significance, as it was built under a treaty agreement with Mexico, because the waters of the Rio Grande also irrigate Mexican lands.

Waters impounded in this reservoir irrigate 145 miles of valleys stretching through southern New Mexico, a section of southwest Texas, and south into Mexico. The principal valleys are those of the lower Rio Grande and the Mesilla. The reservoir not only regulates seasonal discharge of the river to meet irrigation requirements and the control of major floods, but also its enormous excess capacity makes possible the carrying of stored water from year to year. The dual service capacity has been demonstrated on several occasions since its completion. The reservoir abounds with warm-water fishes, bass, crappie, and catfish. A summer regatta with motor and sailboat racing and water sports is held annually.

Caballo Dam is a secondary structure on the Rio Grande below Elephant Butte, 11 miles south of Hot Springs. It is a conversion dam and was built to provide additional irrigation and power development for the valley areas. Its impounding capacity is approximately 300,000 acre feet. Additional supplementary diversion dams are provided at Percha, Leasburg, and Mesilla. An elaborate system of flumes, siphons, and several hundred miles of main canals supplement the dams; the whole provides irrigation and reclamation for an area of approximately 180,000 acres, divided into three main valleys by canyons through which the Rio Grande flows. The first division below the dam is the Rincón Valley, extending about 50 miles; next is the Mesilla Valley, extending south 55 miles; and then the El Paso Valley, extending 40 miles farther south.

As an additional step in the control and storage of flood waters in the Rio Grande Basin, El Vado Dam was built in 1935 on the Chama River, a tributary of the Rio Grande, at a point about 17 miles west of Tierra Amarilla. This dam impounds 200,000 acre-feet of water, and with other supplementary projects on Rio Grande tributaries, such as Carson Dam near Taos Junction, and Santa Cruz Dam north of Santa Fe, insures a better utilization and control of Rio Grande waters.

Near Carlsbad in Eddy County in the Pecos Basin is the Carlsbad Reclamation Project, the next largest system of storage dams associated with irrigation in the State. Started in 1888 as a private enterprise, the project met with repeated discouragement and failure. Eventually in 1904, after a series of disastrous breaks and floods which washed out the dams on three occasions, the owners of the system, the Pecos Irrigation & Investment Company, petitioned the Federal government to take over the project. President Theodore Roosevelt, under authority of the Reclamation Act of 1902, took over the assets of the company, and the Carlsbad system of dams is being completed successfully under government ownership. More than 30,000 acres of reclaimed land are watered by the project.

Comprised of two dams and their lakes, the McMillan and the Avalon, across the Pecos River north of Carlsbad, the project includes miles of main canals and intersecting ditches, the largest flume in existence, and an underground siphon. The system waters an area which extends hamshaped about the environs of the city of Carlsbad. The gates which regulate the water flow are of a type interesting to engineers and used nowhere else in the world.

Erosion in the Pecos River Valley, as elsewhere, is a major problem, for the river carries so much silt that Lake McMillan is already almost filled, necessitating a new project, the Alamogordo Dam, about 16 miles above Fort Sumner in the Sacramento Basin. Extensive experimentation in methods of erosion control are being conducted in the Pecos Valley in an effort to decrease the silt menace.

In the Canadian River Basin, where the Conchas Dam has been under construction in eastern San Miguel County, the river has a drainage area in New Mexico of 16,066 square miles.

Conchas Dam was started in 1935, under supervision of United States Army Engineers. The first concrete was poured April 13, 1937, and it was completed in October, 1939. Both concrete and earthen dikes are being built the total length, approximately four miles. Conduits are to be placed in the concrete sections to allow release of water during the dry seasons, and a 300-foot spillway will be used under normal conditions. The reservoir when completed will have a storage capacity of 600,000 acre-feet; 100,000 dead, or permanent, storage; 300,000 for irrigation; and 200,000 for flood control. The lake will cover about 25 square miles, extending 14 miles up the south Canadian River Valley and nine miles up the Conchas River Valley. Irrigation for about 60,000 acres in the vicinity of Tucumcari is expected, in addition to water for domestic uses and an adequate system of flood control.

Eagle Nest Dam, storing the headwaters of the Cimarrón River in Colfax County about 30 miles northeast of Taos, and built in 1918 to provide electric power and to irrigate approximately 70,000 acres in Colfax County, is within the Canadian Basin. The dam is 140 feet high and impounds 100,000 acre-feet of the flood waters of the Cimarrón River. This private project is in a setting of great natural beauty, the lake seeming to be a natural rather than artificial body of water. Its waters are stocked with trout by the State Game and Fish Department.

The flow of water in the Canadian River drainage is so erratic that reservoirs must occupy a commanding place in any scheme of water conservation and use in the region, and several projects have been planned.

The New Mexico portion of the Dry Cimarrón Basin lies in a mountainous plateau region of the northeastern corner of the State, with altitudes ranging from 8,000 feet at the source of the river to 4,600 feet at the New Mexico-Oklahoma State Line. The river flows mostly in a relatively narrow canyon eroded in the sandstones, but the valley opens out in places and offers some cultivatable areas. About 9,900 acres are now under irrigation, and about 8,600 additional acres are susceptible of irrigation. The basin in New Mexico has a population of only about 1,800, and there are no urban centers. Although the New Mexico lands encompassed in this basin are better suited to grazing, a large part of them are at present used for dry farming, for which they are not suited. As these lands are returned to grazing, a wide-spread system of small reservoirs will be required to store the local run-off. Irrigation is, however, the important problem, and the need in this section is for reservoirs to retain the winter run-off and the excess flow from torrential rains for application to the land at proper times. Several sites for such works have been tentatively chosen.

The San Juan River is the largest stream flowing into or through New Mexico; its annual discharge, two and one-half million acre-feet, is more than twice that of the Rio Grande. The San Juan rises in Colorado and flows through the northwest section of New Mexico for a distance of 100 miles. Its broad and fertile valley, when irrigated, produces abundant crops of fruit, vegetables, grains, and hay. Within the State of New Mexico, the waters of the San Juan River are capable, if fully utilized, of irrigating 600,000 acres, of which amount, about 50,000 are now so used. In connection with this basin, which is a part of the Colorado River drainage system, the terms of the Colorado River Compact are of present and future importance. Any proposed development of the irrigable area will take into consideration the allotment of these waters to the signatory States, in accordance with the compact. As the Navaho Indian Reservation now occupies about one-half of the total area of this basin, and the Southern Ute Reservation another portion of it, the co-operation of these agencies is essential to any development.

A serious condition of water erosion exists within the area, which could be greatly improved by halting overgrazing on Indian and other lands. It has been proposed to divert a portion of New Mexico's water in the San Juan to the Rio Grande by means of a transmontane diversion system. Future development of the San Juan Basin will determine the feasibility of such a plan.

The Gila River has a drainage area of about 13,500 square miles, 6,100 of which are in New Mexico. The river rises in the high Mogollón and Black Range Mountains of southwestern New Mexico and flows in a general southwesterly direction across Grant and Hidalgo Counties, in New Mexico, and finally joins the Colorado River at Yuma, Arizona. Above Cliff, New Mexico, northwest of Silver City,

# The Land

*Ernest Knee*

RIO GRANDE CANYON

SANDSTONE FORMATIONS NEAR SANTA FE *Ernest Knee*

*Ernest Knee* CIMARRÓN CANYON

ORGAN MOUNTAINS (NORTHEAST OF LAS CRUCES)

FIELD OF EVENING PRIMROSES NEAR CIMARRÓN

*Ernest Knee*

SAN JUAN VALLEY, NEAR FARMINGTON

THE ENCHANTED MESA, AS SEEN FROM ÁCOMA

"WHITE SANDS" (GYPSUM), A NATIONAL MONUMENT

ERODED SANDSTONE FORMATIONS NEAR CUYAMUNGUÉ     *Ernest Knee*

ASPENS, SANGRE DE CRISTO MOUNTAINS                    *Ernest Knee*

*Ernest Knee*                    IN THE SANGRE DE CRISTO FOOTHILLS

DOME AND ONYX DRAPES, CARLSBAD CAVERNS

the main stream and its tributaries are small mountain streams of normally clear water, occasionally flushed by sharp floods. Irrigation possibilities are meager and have been largely exhausted. Below Cliff to the San Carlos Reservoir in Arizona, a distance of 175 miles, the river passes through a series of canyons and valleys, where erosion is extremely active and cheaply constructed canals have served the valley lands. In New Mexico the water supply is generally adequate for areas now under ditches. The waters of the Gila irrigate a total of 7,700 acres in the State. With minor costs there could be added approximately 10,000 acres more on the New Mexico section of the basin. Ten dam sites have been investigated in the last few years, for storage, irrigation, flood control, and power, of which nine have been rejected for various reasons in favor of the projected site at the mouth of Redrock Cañon.

The San Francisco River, principal tributary of the Gila, joins the latter stream near Clifton, Arizona. It has a total run-off almost as large as that of the main stream, but more poorly distributed and supporting only minor irrigation developments.

Notable areas of fertile land exist in various parts of the State where irrigation by pumping underground water is feasible, provided sufficient power can be obtained for the pumping. It is estimated that 26,000 acres in Hidalgo County could be utilized in this way, with other closed basins in Luna County, the Tularosa Valley, the closed basin of San Augustine and the Estancia Valley, also of similar value. The latter lies near the geographic center of New Mexico, south of Santa Fe and east of Albuquerque. In this valley large areas are already devoted to dry farming, the principal crop being the famous New Mexico pinto bean. About 30,000 acres of land yield nearly 250,000 bushels of beans. With ground water irrigation this production could be doubled. In the entire Estancia Basin there are no permanent streams. The area was used for the grazing of sheep until homesteaders began its settlement for farming purposes in the present century.

Out of a possible irrigable area, exclusive of extensive new enterprises of 741,245 acres, the total irrigated land in New Mexico is about 600,000 acres. Underground water surveys are now in progress, and projected dams and systems will greatly increase the figures. A natural resources committee has made recommendations to the Federal government listing twenty-three projects for New Mexico river basins, for water conservation and development. The plans call for long-term development of the projects and are part of a nation-wide conservation scheme. The New Mexico allotment is $14,000,000.

*Forests:* The evergreen-carpeted mountain ranges, splashing brooks, wildlife, and scenic grandeur of which New Mexico is rightly proud are found to a great extent in the seven national forests which lie either entirely or partly within this State. They are the Carson, Cíbola, Gila, Lincoln, and Santa Fe National Forests, entirely inside the State; and the Apache and Coronado, which are in both New Mexico and Arizona. The national forests in New Mexico cover a total net area of 8,558,286 acres (1938).

These forests hold some of the most important natural resources of the State, and have played a vital part in its development. Protection of watersheds makes possible a gradual run-off of rain and melting snows, thereby insuring a steady, regulated flow of water for domestic use, irrigation and power, and preventing floods, erosion, and the resultant silting up of costly reservoirs.

A perpetual supply of timber and forage is assured by allowing use of timber-lands and ranges on a sustained-yield basis, worked out scientifically and proved by years of forestry experience. Fish and game abound, picnic nooks and camp-grounds are numerous, and forests are kept green by constant vigilance against that blackening scourge, the forest fire. All these things are made possible because the national forests are not restricted to any one use. Their administration provides for use by the public of timber, water, forage, wildlife, and other natural resources, on the principle of "the greatest good for the greatest number in the long run."

Stewardship of these, the public's forests, is entrusted to the Forest Service of the United States Department of Agriculture. In charge of local districts on each forest are the rangers, always ready to supply visitors with information or help. Each national forest is in charge of a supervisor, with headquarters at a town on or close to his forest. Forests of New Mexico and Arizona, comprising the Southwestern Region of the Forest Service, are under general supervision of the Regional Forester at Albuquerque.

These forests are made up of the woodland zone and saw-timber zone. The woodland zone may be subdivided into the evergreen oak type, which in the southern part of the State occurs at elevations of 4,500 to 6,000 feet, and the piñon-juniper type, occurring at elevations of 5,000 to 7,000 feet.

The woodland zone of the national forests in the State covers 3,000,000 acres at relatively low elevation, and is readily accessible and available for use for fuel, building materials, fence posts, etc. It provides shelter and food for game and wild fowl. Tree species of this zone are found in areas receiving fourteen or more inches of annual precipitation.

The saw-timber zone, embracing approximately 4,200,000 acres, may be subdivided into three broad types: ponderosa pine, Douglas fir, and spruce, each named for the species providing the major volume of timber. Aspen, valued mostly for the watershed protection and aesthetic reasons, occurs high in this belt. All require an excess of nineteen inches of annual precipitation.

Ponderosa pine occurs generally at elevations between 7,000 and 8,000 feet. It is estimated that 90 per cent of the saw-timber now being manufactured into forest products comes from this species. Douglas fir is found above the ponderosa pine area, usually at 8,500 to 9,500 feet. Spruce occurs above Douglas fir at 9,500 to 11,500 feet.

These types supply raw material for a considerable number of mills, of which there were 86 active in the State during 1935. The total cut of these mills from timberland depends directly upon general economic conditions. The annual average for the past few years has been 120,000,000 board feet. The total volume of saw-timber is, in round numbers, 11,266,000,000 board feet.

Success of Forest Service timber management policies is attested by the fact that some owners of private timberland adjoining national forests have arranged for management of their lands by the Forest Service, under co-operative agreement.

Water conservation is fundamentally linked with forest conservation in New Mexico. These enormous forest areas form a most effective means of controlling and equalizing the flow of streams and maintaining favorable water-flow conditions in the Rio Grande, Upper Gila, Pecos, San Juan and Canadian River drainages. Adequate watershed protection is, therefore, carefully worked out by the Forest Service.

Thousands of head of livestock depend upon these forests. In 1935, they carried 111,500 cattle and horses and 203,000 sheep and goats. Under scientific range management, destructive overgrazing is prevented. Sustained yield of forage year after year is assured by allowing on a range area only the number of livestock which grazing experts know it can support. Local stockmen receive first consideration in grazing permits. Range improvements installed by the Forest Service, including 3,200 miles of control fences, 77 corrals, and 282 water sources, have a cost value of nearly one and one-half million dollars.

Primitive areas, keeping virgin wilderness intact so this and future generations can see it in the natural state in which the pioneers found it, have been set aside. They are accessible only by pack trip. Foremost in New Mexico is the Gila primitive area embracing 600,000 acres of the Gila National Forest in the southwestern part of the State.

Deer and other big game, and wildfowl such as turkey and quail, are increasing in numbers due to maintenance of wild life refuges and to scientific wild life management of the national forests, in co-operation with the New Mexico Department of Game and Fish. Research on fish life and conditions in forest streams contributes materially to the success of stocking them. In recent years, 250 miles of fishing streams were developed to provide more shade, food, and other necessities of

fish life.   Improvements included 18,000 dams, shelters, and other structures, creating pools, shady spots, and other protection.

Conservation of the forests has taken the form of improving woods
practices among lumbermen; maintaining timber areas on a basis of
sustained yield; protecting forests against fire hazards; controlling destructive rodents, insects and tree blights; improving timber stands;
reforesting burned areas or newly acquired lands; checking soil erosion
on the national forests; improving ranges by re-vegetation, by construction of stock fences, reservoirs and watering places, and by eradication
of harmful plants; improvement of public picnic and camping areas and
construction of many miles of forest highways, roads, and trails.   These
arteries, primarily for administrative use and fire control, also give the
public access to areas attractive for recreation.

In such areas, public picnic and camping grounds have been developed, with hundreds of facilities such as tables and benches, overnight
shelters, running water, fireplaces, comfort stations, and refuse pits.
Care is taken to make these areas blend into the forests as much as
possible, and to do this natural materials are used in constructing the
facilities.

There are many principal areas like this, distributed over the following National Forests: Carson, 24; Cíbola, 17; Gila, 14; Lincoln, 10;
and Santa Fe, 24.   Hundreds of other locations, undeveloped, are a lure
to those who choose to leave the beaten path.

These forests belong to the people by rightful heritage, and are
theirs to use free.   They are waiting, ready with green depths, murmur-
ing streams, bracing air, and thrilling vistas.   Whether they will always
be waiting and ready, with the same natural beauty, depends on whether
the public leaves them as they found them, and is careful with matches
and campfires.

*Soil Conservation:*   With the settlement of New Mexico, as with
other southwestern States, vast areas have been deforested and planted
to crops, while more recently grassland areas have been opened either to
cultivation or to grazing. These changes have vitally affected the movement of water, a prime factor in preserving nature's balance.   Water
formerly absorbed into the ground for subterranean stores now runs off
directly into streams, with the consequently lowered subterranean water
level reducing the moisture and productivity of large areas.   Deep
arroyos have developed within less than a generation, and rainfall has
become a destructive agent.

The foliage, leafy floor, and roots of forests formerly retarded this
run-off but as a result of overgrazing, incalculable quantities of precious
top soils have already been washed away with resultant poorer forage in
many places.   Dust storms since 1934 and floods reaching the proportions of national catastrophes have impelled the Federal and State

governments, and increasing numbers of citizens, toward the proper control of these elemental factors.

Studies in soil erosion and measures for the preservation of soil fertility were commenced in 1934 by both the United States Government and the New Mexico Extension Service.   Conservation and control of unappropriated public range lands by the Government in the interest of stockmen and homemakers is one of its features.   Soils for use in making adobe (mud and straw) bricks for building purposes are also being investigated.   For centuries the Indians have made use of various clays in the manufacture of pottery, and the many kinds of clay available are now being considered for use in modern ceramics.   This may lead to an industry of national importance.   The most intensive studies of soils in the State have been made in the Rio Grande Valley, where 13 varieties have been distinguished.   While these soils will grow most of the Temperate Zone crops, much of the more fertile land has been submerged for long periods and is therefore deficient in bacterial life essential to the liberation of plant food.   Only proper tillage can overcome the deficiency, and this is one of the conservation problems now confronting the State.

Recent results of the application and expansion of soil conservation in New Mexico are phenomenal.   In this State, where more than 50 per cent of the land is publicly owned or controlled, the Soil Conservation Service (United States Department of Agriculture) works on problems of land use with such agencies as the Forest Service, Division of Grazing, Bureau of Reclamation, Resettlement Administration, State Extension Service, and the State Planning Board.   The Indian Service co-operates on Indian lands such as the Navaho Reservation and the pueblos.

The Soil Conservation Service has an office in Albuquerque for the management of the Southwest Region, which consists of Utah, Arizona, western Colorado, and all of New Mexico except the eastern tier of counties.   The region is divided into districts determined by drainage areas.   The Rio Grande District covering that river's drainage from its headwaters in Colorado, southward to Fabens, Texas, has its headquarters also in Albuquerque.   That portion of the State drained by the San Juan and Little Colorado Rivers is included in the Navaho District, with headquarters at Gallup.   The Gila River's watershed in southwestern New Mexico is included in the Gila District, whose headquarters are at Safford, Arizona.

Rainfall is light, and water scarce in all these districts.   Water for the few rivers along which the population and irrigated farming areas are concentrated comes from the upper watersheds.   As grass and trees are destroyed in those regions, the rivers become muddy with soil of the upper ranges, farmlands, and forests, and silt replaces space for water storage in reservoirs.

New Mexico's area is more than 90 per cent range land, but the people dependent on irrigated land and benefited by conservation work on the upper ranges are more numerous than those directly using range and forest. Consequently, only well-forested and well-grassed land will insure the future of stock raising and irrigation farming.

As all types of land are closely interrelated in soil conservation, the actual operation program may be divided into three categories: work on the range, dry farming lands, and direct protection of towns and irrigated lands.

Plant cover is maintained on range lands by proper use. As erosion control and adequate vegetative cover are directly dependent upon this proper usage a co-operative agreement between land users and the Soil Conservation Service is made before operations on range and farm areas are undertaken. The success of this plan is shown in the Laguna area, for example, where numerical adjustment of stock to the range's carrying capacity, with proper grazing practices, notably increased the forage and consequently the revenue in one year.

The diversion of water from arroyos and retardation of rain run-off by simple diversion dikes, contour furrows, spreaders, and stock tanks, also aids in securing an adequate plant cover.

A program for control of wind erosion in the plains area includes such measures as management of crop residues, strip cropping with erosion resisting crops, diversification of crops, or a variable cropping plan designed to maintain a vegetative cover, moisture conservation and uniform distribution through terracing and contour tillage, wind break trees, listing, and other tillage operations for emergency purposes to lessen further wind erosion in badly eroded areas until the vegetative cover is properly restored.

Examples of work on range lands are at the Navaho experiment station, Mexican Springs, Laguna Indian Reservation, Montaño Grant, Mariano Lake demonstration area, Sandía, San Juan, Fort Stanton, United States Marine Hospital Reservation, and Hatch-Rincón.

Disturbance of range and woodlands along short side drainages that run through towns and irrigated lands to empty into the Rio Grande and other rivers has led to flooding, silting, and destruction of municipal and other property. In many such instances the Soil Conservation Service co-operates with land users and municipalities to prevent continued destruction. As protection is needed immediately in these cases, types of engineering structures are employed which ordinarily would not be justified on range land.

The erection of detention dams in vicinities above certain towns prevents the torrential down rush of water, regulating its flow to a period of from 12 to 24 hours, thus preventing damage to the towns below. These structures, however, are designed for immediate protection, and agreements for correct usage of lands above the towns are made with occupants to provide for the gradual return of vegetative cover. Soil Conservation Service nurseries provide trees, shrubs, and grasses for erosion control planting.

Erosion in dry farming areas (farming where there is sufficient rainfall to support crops without irrigation) is due to cultivation on steep slopes; terracing for water detention; institution of strip cropping on steeper hillsides where clean-tilled crops have led to erosion; and to the removal from cultivation of certain areas where land is too steep to till without soil loss. Results of erosion work in dry farming areas are evident at San Antonio and Barranca-Abo.

*Minerals:* Rich in present and potential mineral wealth, New Mexico ranks twentieth (1935) among the States in total value of mineral production. Its mineral resources may be classified as metals, non-metallic minerals, and hydrocarbons, the value of metals being greater than that of non-metallic minerals and hydrocarbons combined. Chief among the metals are gold, silver, iron, lead, manganese, molybdenum, copper, and zinc.

Gold production is mainly from base-metal ores, the principal source in 1936 being the Pecos Mine in San Miguel County. The Hillsboro and Pittsburg Districts in Sierra County furnished the bulk of placer gold.

The output of silver practically parallels that of gold, a large portion of recoverable silver coming also from the Pecos Mine. Other silver-producing districts are the Central, Steeple Rock, and Pinos Altos Districts in Grant County, and the Mogollón District in Catron County.

Copper, which formerly led the State's total mineral output in value, is found in the Central District, the Santa Rita, Tyrone, Ground Hog, and San José Mines, Grant County, and the Pecos Mine in San Miguel County. Like copper, lead is produced chiefly from complex ores such as are worked at the Pecos and Ground Hog Mines.

For zinc, the ranking metal since 1933, the Pecos Mine, now closed, was also the largest producer, other mines being in the Central District, Grant County, and the Magdalena District of Socorro County.

High-grade iron ores occur in the vicinity of Fierro, Grant County. Manganese comes from the Little Florida Mountains in Luna County, and Boston Hill near Silver City; and molybdenum from the Red River District near Questa, Taos County, the second largest molybdenum mine in the United States. Other metals present in the State but mined only in a small way, if at all, are antimony, arsenic, bismuth, radium, tin, tungsten, and vanadium.

Among the non-metallic minerals are asbestos, barite, bentonite, building and ornamental stone, cement materials, chalk, clay and clay products, and feldspar. Fluorspar deposits are found near Deming in Luna, Dona Ana, Sierra, and in other counties. Deposits of Fuller's earth, graphite, guano, and gypsum covering a large area and occurring in thick beds of unusual purity, are worked in Chaves, Eddy, and Lincoln Counties. Limestone, lime, and lithium minerals are found in unusual deposits near Dixon, Taos County. Magnesite, meerschaum, and mica are mined near Las Tablas and Petaca in Rio Arriba County, and near Ojo Caliente, Taos County; and ocher, nitrates, petrified wood, and rich deposits of potash are found in Eddy County. Salt is recovered in Torrance County and Salt Lake, Catron County, by the process of solar evaporation, and at Carlsbad, Eddy County. Sand and gravel, sodium sulphate, sulphur, and turquoise are also found.

Important hydrocarbons are coal, petroleum, and natural gas. The Ratón District, Colfax County, is the most important coal producing district, followed by that of Gallup, McKinley County. Coal in the Ratón District is of bituminous grade, and that of the Gallup area sub-bituminous. Anthracite coal is mined in the Cerrillos District. Coal reserves in New Mexico are estimated at 192 billion tons, or sufficient for 70,000 years at the present rate of utilization.

The known oil reserves amount to at least 225 million barrels, the Hobbs fields, Lea County, being the chief center of petroleum production. Other fields are Jal, Copper, Eunice, and Monument in Lea County; the Artesia-Jackson-Maljamar field, Eddy and Lea Counties; and the Hogback and Rattlesnake fields, San Juan County.

Natural gas abounds in the southeastern part of the State in Lea and Eddy Counties, and San Juan County in the northwestern section. The search for oil in New Mexico has also led to the discovery of carbon dioxide gas in commercial quantities (used in the manufacture of dry ice) in Torrance, Harding, Union, and Mora Counties. The carbon dioxide gas well in the Estancia field in Torrance County about five miles west of Estancia, and approximately 40 miles east of Albuquerque, provides the dry ice manufacturing plant with what is said to be the purest natural supply of carbon dioxide gas in the United States.

*Game and Fish:* An adequate refuge system for all classes of game, in close co-operation with land owners, forms the basis of the plan for game conservation in New Mexico. Protection of wildlife on privately owned lands is mainly dependent upon the owner's co-operation, willingly given especially by proprietors of large ranches. In national forests it is dependent upon users of land allotments for grazing purposes.

All game on land owned by the Federal Government legally belong to the State. Conservation operations are, therefore, supported entirely by fishing and game receipts derived by the State game and fish department. However, under the Migratory Bird Treaty with Great Britain, migratory birds are wards of the Federal government, and subject to its control. Nevertheless, the State shares the responsibility, the Federal government restricting these limits.

The policy of the State department of game and fish is to maintain a large number of moderate-sized refuges, sanctuaries where game animals, and birds may reproduce unmolested and return to adjacent hunting grounds. These refuges—well distributed over national forests, public domain, privately owned, and State-leased land—are as permanent as possible. The total number has been increased to 201, embracing an area of 2,884,654 acres. With few exceptions these refuges are well posted and well respected and they demonstrated their value in greatly restoring and stabilizing game supplies.

Elk, completely exterminated about 1900, have been restored by importation. Wild turkeys are now replaced in a dozen sections where they were all killed out. Scaled and Gambel quail have been re-established in many areas, and propagated in new places. Pheasants have been introduced successfully into the larger irrigated valleys, and adult prairie chickens have been trapped and moved to new lands. Sage hens, procured from the Wyoming Game Department in exchange for native New Mexican species, have been reintroduced to several units of their former range. Canadian mountain sheep have been imported into the State's high regions, and numerous and successful beaver plantings are made in streams suitable to this animal.

Special rules for New Mexico, adopted to care for wild life interests on public domain grazing districts administered under the Taylor Grazing Act, are based on the principle that wildlife is entitled to a reasonable share in use of all public domain lands, and that in the allotment of domestic stock on grazing districts, allowance shall be made also for them. The Division of Wildlife Management of the United States Forest Service, with a regional office in Albuquerque, gives the State valuable aid in protection of game, provision of suitable habitats, and work on watersheds to maintain clear mountain streams.

Perhaps the most serious problem facing the State department of game and fish is the control of predatory animals, mountain lions and mountain-dwelling coyotes being the most vicious killers of game. For their extermination, the department employs hunters, encourages private individuals and stockmen to hunt these animals, and issues a coyote trapping bulletin giving detailed information and instructions in the latest, most practical, and scientific methods of extermination.

In restocking birds, the department has not depended upon fowl reared in captivity, but upon trapping birds from refuges where they are plentiful, and transferring them to other areas.

During the past five years the department has concentrated upon fish cultural operations, building up extensive State hatcheries. The State maintains six, and the Federal government two, hatcheries for scale and warm water fish including bass, crappie, blue gill, and bream. As a result, increasingly better trout fishing is evident in practically all of New Mexico's lakes and streams. Because El Vado Lake was stocked in the spring of 1935 with 420,000 rainbow trout from four to six inches long, the Chama River below El Vado Dam now affords excellent trout fishing.

In co-operation with the Work Projects Administration, projects have been initiated which have made possible valuable improvements at the Lisboa Springs, Park View, and Taos hatcheries. The Jenks Cabin hatchery is to be replaced by the Glenwood hatchery, which is more accessible and affords a better water supply.

Drainage canals in the Middle Rio Grande Valley have developed into unusually good fishing water, especially for trout. Hundreds of miles of new fishing water have been built up during the past three or four years in the midst of the State's most heavily populated area.

Adequate State game and fish laws, providing a safe and flexible system for the protection, development and use of wildlife for recreational purposes, are now in effect in New Mexico. Statutes provide for the recovery of specific amounts as civil damages for the illegal killing of game. A recent measure authorizes the seizure, confiscation, and sale of cars, aeroplanes, trucks, or other conveyances used in illegal transportation of game.

# Archeology

THE southwestern United States, New Mexico in particular, has been the scene of intensive anthropologic study. The reports of early explorers contain many references to the permanent villages of the sedentary Pueblo Indians and the countless ruins in all western and central parts of the State. The literary accounts, the concentration of the indigenous population, and the spectacular cave and surface ruins interested such students as Bandelier, Cushing, Fewkes, and Hewett in the archeology and ethnology of New Mexico soon after the science of anthropology was popularized. Successive studies throughout the past sixty years have improved the techniques of the science and developed the knowledge of the prehistory of the area until today New Mexico may be listed with such centers of acknowledged archeological interest as the Nile Valley and the "Fertile Crescent" in the Old World.

In New Mexico and adjacent southwestern States archeologists have traced the sequence of human occupation from the nomadic hunter contemporaries of extinct post-Pleistocene animals through localized horizons of hunters and seed-gatherers and phases of sedentary agriculturists to the organized inhabitants of village communities that survived the Spanish conquest. Ethnologists have described the different forms of culture possessed by the present day settled Pueblo Indians and the formerly hunting, now pastoral, nomadic Navaho and Apache. Over 20,000 Indians in New Mexico continue to live in much the same fashion as their pre-Columbian ancestors. Physical anthropologists have studied many groups of the indigenous population as well as the wealth of skeletal material collected in the course of ruin excavations. They have established several physical types and the chronological order of the appearance of the types in New Mexico. Philologists have recognized at least four linguistic stocks in the area, each of which may be subdivided into a number of dialects. Anthropo-geographers have appreciated the Southwest as one of the largest and most varied regions in the United States in which to study the inter-relationship of man and nature; the influence of environment on human physique and culture may be noted in three ecological zones.

The prehistory of New Mexico is divided into three general culture periods: the Folsom, the Basket Maker, and the Pueblo. The nature and age of the first complex explains the elusiveness of the remains; the culture period was the last to be established and is the least known.

Man was undoubtedly native to the Old World; evidence is accumulating which indicates that the Americas were invaded via the Bering Strait at least 15,000 or 20,000 years ago. Just what the first New Mexican looked like is unknown, as no authentic human remains have been found of sufficient antiquity to furnish information of the physical characteristics. However, following the last glacial period some types of modern man lived in New Mexico and left his chipped stone dart points embedded in fluvial deposits in conjunction with the bones of animals now extinct.

The Folsom culture derives its name from the site of discovery in northeastern New Mexico. A number of chipped stone dart points of unique shape were found associated with the skeletal remains of a post-glacial sub-species of bison. The artifacts are from one to three inches in length; they are thin and leaf-shaped, with a longitudinal fluting on each face, a concave base with ear-like projections, and carefully retouched edges. The knapping technique developed by the Folsom hunters compares favorably with the percussion and retouching method employed by the inhabitants of the Scandinavian countries during the late Neolithic and Early Bronze periods, and the "ripple flaking" of craftsmen belonging to the pre- and early-Dynastic Egyptian horizons.

During the past ten years many surface finds of Folsom points have been made throughout the plains from Canada to Mexico; and two camp sites of the early "Bison Nomads" have been discovered. The encampment about fifteen miles south of Clovis, New Mexico, in one of the series of shallow basins known as Black Water Draw, yielded an assortment of stone artifact types and contained the remains of a char-coal-filled hearth. The Folsom people hunted such animals as the giant ground sloth, musk-ox, three-toed horse, camel, four-pronged antelope, mammoth, etc., which existed in the early post-glacial period. The early nomads probably frequented the country that is now New Mexico approximately 10,000 to 15,000 years ago.

The length of the first period of time that elapsed between the bison hunters of the Folsom complex and the first Basket Makers is not known. The short, slender, long-headed Basket Makers may have been the physical descendants of the early hunters; culturally they were the intrusive carriers of maize agriculture in the Southwest, coming from a center located in Mexico.

The Basket Makers, so named because of the abundance of basketry found in their cave storage cists, burial places, and habitation sites, developed a succession of three culture levels that flourished from the beginning of the Christian era to the eighth century. Little is known of the Basket Maker I people. Archeologists believe that they were a partly nomadic group of hunters who possessed semi-permanent dwell-ings seasonally occupied while maize was being cultivated. The phase at first was hypothetical, assumed in order to explain the transition from the purely hunting and collecting to the agricultural forms of culture. The horizon was established by cave finds in southern Nevada and southwestern New Mexico.

The distribution of the Basket Maker, throughout the course of their second culture phase, included the greater part of what is now New Mexico. The rock-shelter and cave habitations of the people are particularly numerous in the San Juan drainage in northwestern New Mexico and adjacent areas. Debris accumulated and was preserved in a state of extreme dryness. The Basket Maker II people were true agriculturists, cultivating beans, squash, and a soft variety of maize.

There was a continuous improvement in the style of dwelling. The first Basket Makers probably lived in temporary shelters constructed of poles, brush, and skins; in inclement seasons they took refuge in caves. In time they excavated slab-lined storage cists and granaries in the floors of the rock-shelters; the dead were buried in a flexed position in some of the pits. The people of the Basket Maker III phase enlarged the constructions and evolved permanent dwellings.

The Basket Maker II people excelled in weaving. They made excellent twined and woven bags decorated with geometrical designs, coiled baskets, and twined and woven sandals with square, and later with scalloped and rounded, toes from such materials as apocynum, yucca, and juniper bark fiber, and from human and animal hair. In addition to sandals the men wore a g-string and the women a short, apron-like skirt. They had warm robes made of cordage wrapped with rabbit fur, and leggings and sandal padding of shredded bark and corn husks. Their weapons included the *atlatl* (throwing board and darts), clubs of wood and elk antler, and hafted stone knives. They had wooden planting-sticks and such grinding stones as troughed *metates* and *manos*. Crude unfired clay vessels, tempered with vegetable matter, were utilized; but fired ceramics were unknown to the forerunners of the Basket Maker III phase.

The third culture phase of the Basket period was a time of considerable change. Permanent villages were established, both in large caves and on suitable exposed locations; fired pottery, the bow and arrow, and soft varieties of maize were introduced. In the Chaco region of northwestern New Mexico the material culture shows a gradual development leading to the trait complexes of the subsequent Pueblo horizons; a definite demarcation between the Basket Maker III people and the following Pueblo I inhabitants seems to be lacking. Probably increased numbers of intrusive stocky roundheads absorbed the earlier population and, at the same time, adopted and elaborated much of the Basket Maker III culture to suit their own needs.

The third culture period, called Pueblo (Spanish; village) because the Spaniards found large numbers of Indians living in compact communities when they entered the Southwest in the sixteenth century, is divided into five phases.   Pueblo I and Pueblo II are termed Developmental; they are transitional stages from the Basket Maker period to the great or Classic Pueblo III phase.   The largest surface villages and cliff dwellings were built in Pueblo III times.   Pueblo IV is called Regressive; this phase was flourishing when the Spaniards entered what is now New Mexico.   Pueblo V, the Historic phase, pertains to the present-day Pueblo Indians.

The immediate origin of the roundheaded Pueblo people, with skull posteriors artificially flattened, is not known.   Some archeologists believe that consecutive waves pushed south along both sides of the Rocky Mountains eventually to settle in the northern reaches of drainages in the southwestern plateau.   The majority favor the more tenable theory that the roundheads were cognizant of agricultural methods before they reached the Southwest, coming north from Mexico with such possessions as soft varieties of corn, the domesticated turkey, and techniques including cranial deformation, coiled pottery, and horizontal masonry.

Professor A. E. Douglass, of the University of Arizona, developed a method whereby the age of the different phases of the Pueblo period could be determined.   He discovered that the date of construction of the prehistoric ruins in the Southwest could be established accurately by the study of the growth of tree rings in beams taken from ruins and old buildings.   Tree rings form a distinctive pattern; the width of the rings is slight in dry years and larger in years of greater precipitation.   On this basis master charts, or tree ring keys, have been made for several of the southwestern areas.   The Rio Grande chart has been carried back to 930 A.D.

A change of house type, as well as the round skull, marks the arrival of the Pueblo people.   The pit dwellings used by the Basket Makers were abandoned and rectangular rooms of horizontal masonry were built above the ground.   During the Pueblo I period these houses were crude, unit-type, one-storied buildings, usually in the form of an elongated rectangle, E-shaped, or in intermittent patterns.   Generally a square or circular subterranean or semi-subterranean ceremonial chamber (perhaps evolved from the pit house of the Basket Maker period), known by the Hopi Indian name *kiva,* was associated with the earlier dwelling-units; and as the size of the structures expanded, the *kivas* were enlarged and their numbers increased.

The ruins of the early Pueblo cultures are distributed over the entire plateau region from the Colorado River to eastern New Mexico, including southern Colorado and Utah.   This fairly large population occupied the area from about 800 to 900 A.D.

Cotton was added to the list of cultivated plants and was woven into cloth garments. Turkeys were domesticated, and a type of feather robe was made. Pottery came to be slipped, polished, corrugated, and incised—all of which were treatments unknown to the Basket Maker potter. Finer tempering material was used. The black-on-white pottery of northern New Mexico became distinct from that of northern Arizona; even local developments and fashions became recognizable.

The Mogollón complex flourished in southern New Mexico contemporaneous with the Developmental Pueblo phases in the north. It is differentiated from the true Pueblo development by the continued use of pit dwellings; by the possession of such accessories as the three-quarter grooved ax and shell gorgets (which may show affiliations with peoples to the East); and slate palettes and pottery vessels bearing the imprint of the paddle-and-anvil method of thinning the walls, which are characteristics of the Hohokam culture period of southern Arizona. Skeletal remains display a mixture of physical types. Possibly the Mogollón people represented a mixture of intrusive elements that mingled in southern New Mexico after the area was vacated by the northward-travelling initial waves of Pueblo Indian ancestors. At the end of the Developmental or the beginning of the Classic Pueblo phases, southern New Mexico received direct influence from the Pueblo culture; this contact or conquest resulted in the highly evolved, localized Pueblo III development in the Mimbres Valley.

Pueblo III, known as the Classic or great Pueblo period, is characterized by the building of the large surface pueblos and cliff dwellings of the San Juan area. There was, between 950-1200 A.D., a concentration of population in the more fertile and better watered valleys of New Mexico. Many of the scattered small villages of the earlier periods were abandoned. Large, terraced communal dwellings, some of three and four stories and containing over five hundred rooms, were built. Huge circular *kivas* were constructed, some reaching the amazing diameter of more than sixty feet. This tendency toward higher and more massive buildings, stronger walls and fewer exterior openings indicated the appearance of enemies, possibly the nomadic Shoshoni from the north and northwest, and, a little later, nomadic Athapascans from the east and northeast.

The concentration of Pueblo population and wealth in a few areas, accompanied as it must have been by an interchange of ideas and goods, produced a marked acceleration of cultural activity. Not only were larger communal dwellings and ceremonial structures erected, but the style of masonry was improved. The finest examples are found in the Chaco area. Here worked, sandstone slabs and spalls of selected size and shape were used to face a rubble core, with an excellent effect. Nowhere else, nor at any other time, did the pre-Columbian inhabitants of the Southwest surpass or even equal the masonry of the Classic period in northwestern New Mexico. For this reason such great ruins as Aztec, Chetro-Ketl, Pueblo Bonito, Peñasco Blanco, and others have been constituted parts of National Monuments and have been the subjects of extensive excavations.

There were changes and improvements in ceramics. A greater variety of colors was introduced, and the execution of form and detailed design reached a perfection hitherto unknown in Pueblo culture. The Pueblo III people counted their wealth in turquoise, shell, quartz, wood and stone beads, gorgets, bracelets, pendants, mosaics, and other forms of jewelry as well as in pottery.

During the period between 1275-1300 there occurred a marked drought which brought about the abandonment of many of the Pueblo areas in New Mexico and elsewhere in the Southwest. Apparently due to the lowering of the water table, reduction of vegetal cover and the consequent increase of desiccation, surface denudation, and erosion, such areas as the western Puerco, Chaco, and San Juan drainages became temporarily less suitable to the Pueblos than other regions to the south, west, and east. Large movements of population evidently took place which, in New Mexico, resulted in the complete abandonment of the northwestern portion of the State, as well as parts of the upper Gila, Mimbres, Tularosa Basins and other recognized Pueblo III areas.

Thus the scene was laid for Pueblo IV, or the Regressive period.

The Pueblo IV people were gradually drawn into the great river valleys of the Rio Grande and the Little Colorado. The Santa Fe region abounds in Pueblo ruins of this period; and the site at Pecos, those in the Galisteo Basin and on the Pajarito Plateau may be taken as examples.

There was a constant restriction of area during this Regressive period due to the onslaughts of the alien nomads, and later, the Spanish occupation. However, in various portions of New Mexico it was actually the period of highest cultural achievement. Large communal dwellings with their *kivas,* scattered small houses, and cavate lodges continued to be built. Among the most notable pueblos of this period are those of Hawikúh, Hálona (old Zuñi), and the villages on El Morro in the Zuñi country; Ácoma and Humming Bird in the Puerco —San Juan drainage; Giusewa, Amoxiumqua, and Astialakwa in the Jémez region; Tsankawi, Tchirege, Tyuonyi, Ótowi, and Puyé in the Pajarito Plateau; Paseoninge, Poshuouinge and Sapawe in the Chama drainage; Tsiquna and Kuapoge near Santa Fe; San Cristóbal, Pueblo Largo, Shé, Galisteo, San Lázaro, Tunque, Paako, and San Marcos in the Galisteo region; Pecos, Chilili, Quarai, Abó, Pueblo Colorado, Pueblo Blanco, and Tabirá (Gran Quivira) in the Manzano-Chupadero Mesa country; Pilabo, Kuaua, Puaray, Alameda, Perage, etc., along the main Rio Grande. Furthermore, most of the Indian Pueblos now existing were at or near their present sites during, not only the later part of the Regressive period (1540-1700 A.D.), but also before the coming of the Spaniards.

In general the material culture of early Pueblo IV was not greatly different from that of Pueblo III. The chief change is in the introduction of glaze paints in the decoration of pottery. Both polychrome and glazed paint wares were made in great quantities, while corrugated cooking pots and black-on-white decoration tended to die out.

Turkeys, maize, beans, and squashes continued to constitute the bulk of the Pueblo people's food, augmented by such game as bison, deer, antelope, and rabbit; and wild grass seeds, piñon nuts, and berries. Probably there was little change during the sixteenth century, but with Oñate's colonization came wheat, barley, oats, rye, turnips, cabbage, carrots, onions, melons, peaches, pears, apples, grapes, coffee, tea, etc., from the Old World; and "Irish" potatoes, sweet potatoes, chili peppers, tomatoes, chocolate, from the countries to the south. Prehistoric Indians of New Mexico smoked wild tobacco, sumac, and other herbs, as their stone and clay tubular and elbow pipes indicate; the cultivation of tobacco in the Southwest was introduced by the Spaniards.

A varied pattern of culture was created during the latter part of the Pueblo IV period with the introduction of the horse, donkey, cattle, sheep, goat, pig, and poultry; and there occurred important changes in textiles, ornaments, tools, kitchen wares, weapons, and clothing. The Plains Indians also modified Pueblo culture, when they introduced their articles of dress and certain dances new to the area now known as New Mexico.

Pecos Pueblo ruin, because of the intensive investigations carried on by Dr. A. V. Kidder of the Andover Academy, affords an excellent example of the Pueblo IV period. It is known to have been occupied from the thirteenth century to 1838; the few surviving Pecos Indians then joined the Jémez people. The Seven Cities of Cíbola in the Zuñi country have been identified, and Hawikúh, the largest, was excavated by Dr. F. W. Hodge of the Museum of The American Indian, New York. Zuñi is a concentration of the villages that prompted the penetration of the northern country by the Spaniards.

Archeology, or the study of ancient peoples through their remains, dwellings, and artifacts requires various techniques of research. The excavation of rooms, uncovering of skeletal and other materials, and describing the finds through text, photographs, maps, sketches, and museum displays does not constitute all of scientific archeology. Much valuable information has been lost by misinterpreted interest on the part of enthusiastic amateurs. During the last twenty-four years there have been developed or applied for the first time in New Mexico and the

Southwest techniques that require trained scientists. The result of their work has made the picture of the past cultures possible for those interested in New Mexico anthropology.

The Modern Pueblo period (1700 A.D.-present) also referred to as Pueblo V, falls within the field of history and must be considered under the division of Ethnology.

Today, in the pueblos of Taos, Picurís, San Juan, Santa Clara, San Ildefonso, Nambé, Tesuque, Cochití, Jémez, Santo Domingo, Zía, Santa Ana, San Felipe, Sandía, Laguna, Ácoma, Zuñi of New Mexico, as well as in the Hopi villages in northern Arizona, the visitor will be able to visualize the life of the ancient people as a rounded whole and to gain some conception of their social and religious life.

The National and State Monuments of archeological significance are Aztec Ruins N. M. (see Tour 9); Bandelier N. M. (see Tour 2A); Chaco Canyon N. M. (see Tour 6B); Coronado S. M. (see Tour 1b); El Morro N. M. (see Tour 6b); Gila Cliff Dwellings N. M. (see Tour 18); Gran Quivira S. & N. M. (see Tour 15); Jémez S. M. (see Tour 9); Pecos S. M. (see Tour 1a); Quarai S. M. (see Tour 15).

Archeological museums are maintained at several of the above mentioned Monuments, and also at the Museum of New Mexico, at Santa Fe; at the Laboratory of Anthropology, Santa Fe; and at the Museum of Anthropology of the University of New Mexico, Albuquerque. There are branch State Museums at Las Vegas, Carlsbad, Silver City, Ratón, Clovis, Portales, Lincoln, Mountainair, Farmington, and Las Cruces.

# *Indians*

THE peaceful aspect of the Pueblo Indians of New Mexico at the present time tells little of their strenuous past. Green fields and orchards surround their villages, strings of red chili festoon their adobe houses in autumn, and the sweet odor of burning piñon and juniper drifts across winter dance courts. The people, courteous and reserved, sell their pottery to visitors, allow them to attend certain dance-ceremonials, and watch them depart knowing that they belong to different races, and, in their own words, "think different thoughts."

Physically the Pueblo Indians belong to the roundheaded Mongoloid people who followed the long-headed Basket Makers into the Southwest. They are generally shorter and stockier than the nomadic tribes, and their facial expression is more placid; but as a whole the modern Pueblo Indians are not a homogeneous group. Actually they represent an aggregation of peoples brought together by intermarriage and cross strains of acculturation which has developed under environmental influences.

The first contact of the Spanish Conquistadores (1540) with the inhabitants of the area which is now New Mexico was with the Pueblo Indians. The land was claimed for the Spanish Crown and the Indians considered converts of the Catholic faith. Because of Spanish oppression in 1680 the Pueblos united and revolted, overthrowing the Spanish government and killing and driving out the alien settlers. In 1692-93 De Vargas reconquered the country and made peace with the Pueblos. During the first years of the seventeenth century, there came a certain expansion. The Pueblo villages with their outlying farms and flocks, secured from the Spaniards, proved tempting prey for the marauding Navaho, Comanche, Ute, and Apache. These nomadic or scattered Indians found it convenient, when hunting was poor, to raid the Pueblo villages whose frugal people kept stores of corn against drought and times of need. But after the advent of the military garrisons, first Spanish, then Mexican, and finally those of the United States, the Pueblo Indians began to enjoy increasing security. Old citadel dwellings on mesa tops were gradually abandoned, and villages in the more fertile valleys were built; however, many of these still retained, to a certain degree, the compact, defensive type of structure of ancient times.

The eighteen pueblos in New Mexico today, from Taos to below

Albuquerque and along the old Coronado trail westward from Isleta to Zuñi, occupy approximately the same lands that they held during the early Spanish occupation. Their land titles originated with grants from the Spanish Crown, ratified by the sovereignty of Mexico and subsequently confirmed by the Congress of the United States under the treaty of Guadalupe Hidalgo (1848). The Pueblo Indians thus own their lands by virtue of titles antedating American supremacy, differing in this respect from all other Indians in the United States. The one group of Spanish land grants provided for a tract measuring three leagues in each direction from the mission church. These grants averaged about 17,000 acres for each pueblo. Additions from time to time have been made to the lands of various villages in the form of Executive Order reservations from the public domain and by purchase.

Within the village, farming and grazing lands are assigned for use to individuals, and the tenure is allowed only as long as the land is worked or employed for productive purposes. Because of the complete security of the pueblos in modern times the tendency has been to build smaller and more isolated dwellings closer to their fields. The old Pueblo IV village of Ácoma is an excellent illustration; the pueblo is almost deserted for the farming areas.

The similarity of their problems and needs during recent years and the necessity of concerted action in dealing with the Indian Bureau have brought the Pueblos together. Their ancient all-Pueblo councils meet at intervals to discuss their general welfare and their contact with the Federal government. The latter supplies such facilities as schools and hospitals, instruction in modern farming methods, appropriations for soil erosion control and irrigation projects, seed selection, forestry, animal husbandry, care of grazing lands, and other matters.

Oñate (1598) is known to have given the Pueblo chiefs canes or "rods of office" in recognition of their authority. In 1620, a "law of the Indies" issued from the Crown at Madrid provided that the Pueblo Indians were to select their own temporal officers without interference from the Spaniards, but that these elections had to be approved by the local Spanish authorities, to whom the new "governors" of the villages displayed their canes. This custom was continued after the American occupation when Abraham Lincoln, in 1863, gave ebony canes with silver handles to the Pueblo governors, designated by them as the Lincoln canes.

This democratic form of government is still in force. A governor and his lieutenants are elected in each pueblo just before the New Year, and their induction into office occurs with great ceremony on Twelfth Night, or "old Christmas," the gift-giving day of the Spaniards, called by some Indians the "Day of the Three Kings." The Pueblo governor is the civic head of the village, dealing with the United States officials as well as presiding over the municipal affairs of the people.    However, the *cacique,* or high priest of their old religion, who keeps in the background, is still the real power.

Under their own system the people in some pueblos are divided into moities or halves, called the Summer and Winter, or the Calabazas (squash) and Turquoise People, each of which holds some executive power in religious participation for six months.    At times, each of these moities has its own *cacique,* and each is composed of different phratries or clan-groups.

The religious predicament of the Pueblos is a good example of what ethnologists call acculturation.    Having their own pagan beliefs, inherited from dim antiquity, they were converted to Christianity by the Franciscan missionaries of the seventeenth and eighteenth centuries. The result of this conversion was to drive the indigenous religion beneath the surface and to superimpose upon the belief in the old gods of nature a whole new pantheon of saints.    Most Pueblo Indians are baptized, confirmed, and married by Catholic priests, yet they continue to observe the old ceremonies and take part in certain rites.    The Protestant missions in, or near, several pueblos are working towards complete conversion; with what success only time will tell.

There is a marked similarity in ceremonial form, dress, and organization among all Pueblo Indians.    Efficacy in the different rites is believed to be achieved by accurate repetition.    Even the minute details of the ceremonies and the preparation of the artifacts used in them are of the utmost importance; and each prayer and act is directed in accordance with the ancient law of exactness.    Because of this remarkable adherence to old rules visitors today are privileged to witness certain ceremonies that had their origin in an early primitive culture.

All pueblos hold dance-ceremonials at appointed periods in the year. Each village celebrates the feast day of its Catholic patron saint with tribal dances, and the dates of these ceremonies are fixed by the Church calendar; however, the seasonal or impromptu dances occur at the instigation of the *cacique.*    Many pueblos have their own calendar, and their major ceremonies fall on dates controlled by their own method of count.    Actually their year terminates with the harvest, October being the beginning of the new season and the new year when the Winter People assume control of all ceremonial activities; the major rites are held at the time of the "turning-back-of-the-sun," or winter solstice. At the spring equinox the Winter People turn over the conduct of ceremonial affairs to the Summer moiety, and from that time on until the harvest, the ceremonies are prayer-forms for growth, fructification, and rain.

The most colorful of the autumn dances is given at Jémez in November.    This fiesta of their patron saint, San Diego, is attended by Navaho in great numbers, and often by a few Apache as well as Indians from the Rio Grande pueblos, all of whom come to trade as well as to see the elaborate Harvest Dance held on this occasion. But the most remarkable of all Pueblo dances is that of the Shalako at Zuñi.

Zuñi, probably by virtue of its remoteness and the fact that it has resisted both the Spanish influence and that of the Catholic church, has retained more of its ancient ceremonialism than any other pueblo. Although all pueblos have masked dances, Zuñi is the only one in New Mexico in which the general public, with the exception of Spanish-Americans, is admitted. Hatred of the Spaniards, inherited from Coronado's time, is manifested in this exclusion today. The Shalako ceremony, held in late November or early December, ceremonially closes the year as well as dedicates new houses. The Shalako, or giant messengers of the rain gods, are received into the pueblo at sundown and conducted to the new houses where they are entertained throughout the night with feasting and ceremonial dancing. They depart the following evening. The preparation for this ceremony lasts forty-nine days. The complexities of the rites attending the Shalakos' presence among mortals are staggering but the beauty and reverence of the ritual does not escape even the most cynical observers. From the time of the departure of the Shalako until after the winter solstice visitors are not admitted to the series of ceremonies that take place in Zuñi.

Many of the winter dances are prayer-forms for abundant game and the success of hunters, with offerings to the guardian spirits of the game for the necessary sacrifice. The Deer Dance at Taos and the Buffalo and Deer Dance at San Felipe, performed with symbolic costumes and pantomime, are beautiful.

In the spring the Pueblo Indians pray for rain and for the renewal of life everywhere. Prayer-sticks are planted in the fields, and dances are held in the *kivas,* or ceremonial chambers, as well as in the open. At many of the dances of this period the attendance of white people is by special invitation only.

The Corn Dance at Santo Domingo on August 4th is the greatest of the summer ceremonies in New Mexico. Both the Summer and Winter People, or, as they are called in Santo Domingo, the Calabazas and Turquoise, take part. Hundreds of Pueblo people dance in this ritual; and the visiting Indians, Spanish-Americans, and Anglo-Americans number into the thousands.

All pueblos have their religious societies, priests, warriors, medicine men and women, and delight makers, or holy clowns. The latter are believed to have brought laughter into the world and are, therefore, beings receiving reverence and affection. Their costumes are varied; the mud-heads of Zuñi are totally different in appearance from the black and white painted and corn-husk crowned delight makers of the Rio

Grande pueblos. There is, however, a great similarity in the general dance dress. The men usually wear a hand-woven white cotton kilt embroidered in the earth colors of red, green, and black wool and an embroidered sash of heavy white cotton material, or a so-called Hopi rain belt of braided white cotton finished with a long, symbolically knotted fringe. A kit-fox skin dangles from the belt at the back. Their hair, when long, hangs loose. Body-painting as well as headdress and ornaments varies with the dances. A quantity of silver, shell, turquoise, and coral jewelry is worn; and in most dances men have turtle-shell rattles tied below the left knee. In Santo Domingo the men wear a shell-trimmed band called a *bolso* (Sp., purse strap) over one shoulder which crosses the chest and back diagonally and is fastened at the belt. The Pueblo women's ceremonial costume comprises the traditional hand-woven black woolen square fastened over the right shoulder; leaving the left shoulder bare, it hangs to the knees and is confined at the waist with a long woven belt, usually red in color. Their hair hangs loose, the bangs covering the eyes. The *tablita,* or headdress, of thin wood, painted and decorated with feathers, and the details of mantle and accessories, change with the ceremonies. Much jewelry is worn. Women dance barefooted for the most part in the belief that strength (fertility) is drawn from the earth.

The linguistic division of the Pueblos presents an interesting picture. The eighteen pueblos in New Mexico are divided into three linguistic stocks: Tanoan, Keresan, and Zuñian. The languages are so different that they cannot be understood except by those familiar with the tongues. The Pueblos do not appear to have been greatly handicapped by this disparity of languages, for trading between the villages has always been extensive.

In spite of the persistence of the old ceremonies among the Pueblo Indians their social life is gradually undergoing a marked change. Modern education and the contact with the Spanish and English speaking people who have settled on or near Pueblo lands have influenced the majority of the Indians. The Tewa pueblos of San Juan and Nambé are becoming Spanish-American villages; Santa Clara is adopting Anglo-American customs; and the people of Isleta market in Albuquerque.

The little Tortugas settlement, not included in the total of eighteen pueblos, three miles south of Las Cruces, is said to have been founded by the survivors of the aged and disabled Indians who were left there by Otermín on his way to El Paso following the Pueblo Revolt in 1680. These Mexicanized Pueblo Indians offer a splendid example of cultural change within historic times; they no longer speak their ancestral language, nor do they hold to their old customs, but they do tell legends of their Tigua origin that are unmistakably Pueblo in character.

Some of the Pueblos will not tolerate a doctor in their village. Their medicine men and women have an extraordinary knowledge of the properties and usage of herbs, and they treat certain illnesses with their remedies as well as by mental suggestion. They practice magic, believe in witchcraft, and resist interference either from church or state.

Primarily agriculturists, the Pueblo Indians were pioneers in the use of irrigation which, in view of the comparative aridity of their lands, was a necessity. Before the coming of the Spaniards their crops were confined to maize, beans, squash, and cotton; after their contact with Europeans, wheat and other cereals, fruit, and vegetables were added. The Pueblos had no domesticated mammal save the dog; and the turkey was their only domesticated fowl. With the introduction of horses, cattle, sheep and goats, and poultry, the pattern of their culture changed and enlarged.

The history of ceramics in New Mexico is the story of its early inhabitants. The Pueblos have always excelled in this art. The methods and materials used today are those that were employed at the time of the coming of the Spaniards. They have never known the potter's wheel, but build their jars and bowls from a small molded base by means of clay coils, obliterated after the desired form is determined. The pottery is decorated, polished, and fired in open kilns.

After the Spaniards brought sheep to the Southwest, the Pueblos to some extent substituted wool for cotton. But unlike the Navaho, who still make sheep raising and wool weaving their major industry, the Pueblos of New Mexico, except Zuñi, and to a lesser degree Ácoma and Laguna, no longer make woolen blankets or rugs.

The schools are precipitating changes. Boys who attend government or mission schools are obliged to submit to the cutting of their hair. European-type clothes are issued, and the young Indian is in outward appearance just another American school boy. His own tribal games are replaced by baseball and football, and his interest is awakened in automobiles and machinery. For girls the change is less abrupt. They adopt the required form of dress while in school and discard it upon their return home; they attend classes and are taught the usual domestic sciences. The grade schools are well attended, although few young Indians apply for the higher forms of education.

Pueblo Indians are monogamous, but divorce is sometimes easily procured, for family ties are not as strong as those of clan. Marriages are not permitted between members of the same clan. The line of descent is matriarchal, the children belonging to the same clan as that of the mother. The father's affiliations are with his own clan and phratry.

After the Revolt of 1680, the Pueblo Indians continued their previous decline more rapidly, not only from wars but from pestilence until recent times when security and enlightened assistance checked their decrease and brought about a slow advance.

Upon acquaintance the Pueblo Indians are not unlike any other dwellers in small places. They fear gossip and ridicule and resist change. But they offer some characteristics that are theirs by right of heritage—the clan wisdom of an old race is, perhaps, the underlying principle. They are aware that they are a part, not spectators, of nature's phenomena; and they patiently accept the domination of the newer and stronger influence in material culture that must take over and mold their destinies along with its own.

The pueblos of New Mexico are Taos (*see Taos*); Picurís (*Tour 3a*); San Juan (*Tour 7a*); Nambé (*Tour 3a*); Santa Clara (*Tour 7A*); San Ildefonso (*Tour 2A*); Tesuque (*Tour 3a*) Santo Domingo (*Tour 1b*); San Felipe (*Tour 1b*); Cochití (*Tour 1b*); Santa Ana (*Tour 9*); Zía (*Tour 9*); Jémez (*Tour 9*); Sandía (*Tour 1b*); Isleta (*Tour 1b*); Laguna (*Tour 6b*); Ácoma (*Tour 6A*); Zuñi (*Tour 6b*).

## THE NOMADS

The present pattern of nomadic Indian culture was definitely changed after the Spaniards brought horses and sheep into the Southwest, and their story is the development from a war-like to a pastoral people.

In remote geological times the three-toed horse disappeared from the western hemisphere. Early Indians, hunting with spear and bow and arrow, were unaware of the existence of an animal that would carry man. The dog was their only beast of burden; their equipment was, of necessity, simple, and their progress slow. But in the early years of the seventeenth century the Spanish colonizers established ranchos around Santa Fe, and cultivated maize and exotic cereals, and bred horses and cattle and sheep. The nomads were quick to recognize the value of horses, and there followed years of effort in procuring the foreign animals, mainly through theft, that intensified the aggressiveness of their already belligerent character.

The main stocks from which the nomads of New Mexico came were two; the Southern Athapascan and the Shoshonean of northwestern America. The Ute and Comanche (whose history in New Mexico deals with their power in the past) represent important southern divisions of the great Plateau Shoshonean family.

Early Spanish writers have given different names to the Apache; and many divisions and subdivisions of the tribe make certain errors comprehensible. Coronado met bands of nomadic Indians whom he named Querechos. In 1598, the great colonizer, Oñate, mentions Apache; and Benavides (1630) in his famous "Relation" tells of the

Vaqueros, who have been identified as Coronado's Querechos. The earliest reference to the Navaho in Spanish chronicles is the citation by Benavides of the *Apaches de Narahú.*

In order more fully to understand the division of the Apache tribe during Spanish rule in New Mexico it is necessary to see the divisions and sub-divisions of the Athapascan or Apache people:

| | |
|---|---|
| Querecho or Vaquero | Mescalero |
| Navaho | Faraón |
| Chirícahua | Llanero |
| Piñaleno | Lipán |
| Coyotero | White Mountain |
| Arivaipa | Pinal |
| Gila | Gileño |
| Tonto | Mimbreño |
| Jicarilla | Mogollón |

The sub-tribes are divided again into bands, and the bands into groups formed by families.

The fort-like character of the large Pueblo Indian communal dwelling testified that the nomadic tribes preyed upon these people in pre-Columbian times; and it is thought that it was through Spanish defense that the Pueblo people were saved from extinction.

For example, the Navaho Indians comprise the largest tribe in the United States. They call the country of the San Juan drainage the ancient land of the Dine. Among their ancestors, and represented in their clans, are Pueblo IV people of the little Colorado and San Juan regions.

In 1776, Fr. Escalante, who attempted to blaze a trail from Santa Fe to the Pacific coast, describes the *Province de Nabajoo* as the land lying west of the Jémez range in north central New Mexico. On Escalante's map of that date he shows the northern boundary to be the San Juan River, then called the Rio de Nabajoo; the eastern line followed the Jémez range west of Abiquiu, and the western drainage of the Rio Puerco as far south as the Zuñi Mountains, and west as far as the Hopi pueblos. In the latter part of the eighteenth century, a Spanish document describes the Navaho country as bounded on the west by the Hopi, on the north by the Ute, on the east by the Pueblos, and on the south by the Gileño and Chirícahua Apache. It was stated that the Navaho did not change their dwelling places as did the rest of the Apache nation, but lived in fixed settlements where they raised maize. The name Navaho probably came from the Tewa word meaning small green fields.

In the year 1788 the Spaniards found themselves on excellent terms with the Navaho tribe. They hoped to achieve a lasting peace and conversion of the Navaho to Christianity, as well as to change their semi-nomadic mode of living to that of sedentary Indians.

According to tradition, at this time Antonio el Pinto, head chief of the Navaho people, built ten stone towers in his encampment to safeguard the women and families from the continuous invasions of the Gila Apache. This chief was obeyed and respected by his people, and in recognition of his relations with the Spaniards was given the title of general. The lesser chiefs were designated as *capitancillos*.

But peace was not to last. The Navaho, fearing the quiet of pueblo life and Christianity, joined the Apache of the east. During the years that followed the depredations of these tribes upon the pueblos of the Rio Grande and Zuñi, as also upon the Spanish settlements, created for the Spaniards the Indian problem inherited and aggravated by the impotent Mexican regime in 1822, and encountered by the United States in 1846. Treaties were made which the Navaho broke, open warfare existed, and it was not until Kit Carson with a regiment of New Mexican soldiers captured a number of the tribe in the Canyon de Chelly (1864) that they began to surrender. By the end of the year over 7,000 Navaho were captured and moved to the Bosque Redondo in east central New Mexico. There the Government tried to make farmers of them. The experiment proved a dismal failure; many died from disease and malnutrition, and for a time their spirit as well as their health was broken.

Again in their own land the Navaho resumed their nomadic and pastoral life. They appointed "head-men" whose duty it was to supervise a systematic form of trade. "Always take mares and ewes," was their motto. Those Navaho of sixty-odd years ago underwent every hardship that their tribe might grow and regain its former prestige.

At the present time over 22,000 Navaho live in New Mexico, principally in the 2,500,000 acres of reservation land in the northwestern part of the State. But their phenomenal growth since the time of their captivity has brought new problems. The total land allotment for the Navaho was expanded to over 15,000,000 acres; the Navaho, however, increased from 7,000 to over 45,000. What seems to be an immense amount of land for the tribe becomes understandingly inadequate when one realizes that their country is barren and almost treeless. Stock reduction and the control of grazing lands by the Government have become necessary.

Recently oil and gas resources were found in the San Juan region of the Navaho reservation. The head-men of that part of the tribe, in council, wisely decided to appropriate the income for tribal funds. Roads have been improved and excellent water wells have been located in various parts of the entire reservation.

The present democratic government of the Navaho by a tribal council under the supervision of the United States Commissioner on Indian Affairs and the superintendent of the Navaho deals with tribal problems. The Navaho capital has been established at Window Rock, Arizona. Chapter-houses have been built over the reservation where head-men meet and pass on local affairs; from these men are chosen the members of the tribal council. The ancient Navaho form of government, handed down from the first Dine, was a system of rule by four chiefs, the head, or first chief, having the power of a modern dictator.

The Navaho religion presents an excellent example of acculturation. These nomadic Indians have superimposed Pueblo creed and ritual upon the more primitive Athapascan beliefs. The result is an amazingly rich and varied ceremonialism that is completely their own.

*Shamans* or medicine men control all ceremonies. These elders of the tribe—priests, doctors, and temporal mediators—believe that the earliest cultures in the Southwest occupied the area of the San Juan drainage and northern New Mexico. They guard jealously all information regarding locations of sacred shrines and places identified with Pueblo Indian origin which are, in part, their own.

Certain rites of a minor character accompany every happening in Navaho life, but the great ceremonies, or chants, are solemn religious liturgies held for curative purposes and to further prestige. These ceremonies last from five to nine days, and are attended by thousands of Navaho. They are social gatherings as well as rituals, where trading, horse-racing, and display of finery are important factors.

The sand, or dry, paintings, an extraordinary art in itself, are made in the ceremonial *hogans* (houses) by *shamans* and their assistants during the last days of the ceremonies. These sacred paintings, representing elaborate symbolic figures and designs, are made with sands and minerals of different colors. The work is begun not long after sunrise and is destroyed and carried from the *hogan* before sunset.

The two greatest ceremonies of the Navaho are the Mountain Chant and the Night Chant, and on the last night of their presentation occurs one of the most spectacular performances of modern times. An enormous clearing is surrounded by a wall of evergreens against which an audience of probably two thousand or more Navaho stand and sit. From sun-down to dawn they watch a succession of ceremonial dances, jugglery, and legerdemain which takes place around a huge fire in the center. The great chants are usually held in the autumn and early winter "after the thunder sleeps."

The ceremonial dress of the Navaho is varied as they have freely borrowed from Pueblo and Plains Indians. There is always a certain barbaric splendor about them, for even in their usual dress their love of .rich colors and wealth of silver and turquoise jewelry add to their picturesqueness. The Navaho are the handsomest of the Southwest Indians. The men are usually tall and slender, with excellent carriage; the women, though much shorter, have a natural grace. Their wide, flounced skirts and tightly buttoned velvet blouses were introduced after their contact with white women in the past century.

Although the Navaho Indians derive their principal income from sheep, goats and horses, and a little from agriculture and the making of silver and turquoise jewelry, they are known as the weavers of the famed Navaho blankets. The wool used in the weaving is usually from their own sheep. It is carded, spun, and woven into blankets on vertical looms by the women of the tribe. The art of weaving came from the Pueblos. The probability is that the first Pueblo refugees during the Revolt of 1680, and the captives from raids on the Rio Grande and Zuñi villages, happened to be weavers; and thus the present pastoral pattern of Navaho life had its beginning.

They are content to drive their herds of sheep to the high mountain pastures in summer, living in crude shelters of brush and pole. The winter *hogans* are, however, distinctive of the Navaho landscape. Built of log and stone and covered with earth, these stout, hive-like structures are scattered singly or in groups of two and three among the piñon and juniper of the mesa tops, or along the floors of canyons near springs or arable patches of land. There are three types of *hogan*—the dwelling, the ceremonial lodge, and the sweat house; but with modern education rectangular stone houses are rapidly coming into favor.

From the eighteenth century to the present day the Navaho's principal means of transport has been the horse; but the automobile, or "chuggie," is fast replacing the herds that they once counted as part of their wealth.

Polygamy was practised after the Navaho returned from the Bosque Redondo. It exists today in certain areas, but, as divorce is easily obtained, the custom is dying out.

The Navaho, as a people, are extremely kind to all children and considerate of the aged. They are the most aggressive, hard-working and imposing of the various Athapascan tribes in New Mexico. The majority are in favor of education. They believe that the future of their people lies in the possibility of chosen members of the tribe meeting citizens of the United States on their own plane of civilization.

The picture of the beginning of eighteenth century New Mexico shows the Faraones (called the Apache hordes of Pharaoh), who were closely related to the Jicarilla and Mescalero Apache, located in the Sierra de Sandía and the Sierra de los Ladrones. De Vargas died (1704) while pursuing these hostile Indians near what is now the town of Bernalillo. Governor Mogollón declared war against them

(1712-1714), and a punitive expedition was sent against them in 1715. In the latter part of the century records show that the land occupied by this belligerent people lay between the Rio Grande and the Rio Puerco. The country of the Mescalero bordered it on the east, and to the south extended the frontier of Nueva Vizcaya.

The Jicarilla Apache, so named by the Spaniards because of their proficiency in making little baskets suitable for drinking cups, lived on or near the mountains of the same name in the northern part of the province of New Mexico, now southeastern Colorado, in the seventeenth century. The Comanche drove them from their country in 1716, and into the mountains and canyons between Taos and Picurís. For a short time they seemed to accept Spanish rule and the Christian faith, but they later joined the Mescalero and harried both Pueblo and Spanish settlements. The Jicarilla learned from the Pueblo Indians the manner of clearing fields and raising corn. In the eighteenth century their *rancherías* were on the banks of the Cimarrón, and they were considered a semi-agricultural people.

The Mescalero Apache ("mescal people" from their custom of eating mescal) inhabited the mountains near the Pecos River in the eighteenth century. To the east and south of them stretched the desert of Bolson Mapimi; the Plains Indian territory lay to the east, and to the north extended the "Comanchería." The land of the Comanche also bordered the Lipán on the north. At that time the Lipán were considered the most formidable of all the "savage" nations. Their territory was vast, extending east to the province of Coahuila, and south to the left bank of the Rio Grande.

During Spanish rule the Gileño, or Gila Apache, inhabited the mountains near the Gila River. To the west lay the land of the warlike Chiricahua Apache (Arizona), and to the east the country of the Mimbreño. The Mimbreño were a large tribe in the eighteenth century. They took their name from the Mimbres drainage where they lived. They were closely related to the Gileño of the west and the Mogollón Apache north of their own territory.

After the American occupation of the territory of New Mexico (1846), the United States Government soon learned that they had inherited serious problems. Among the Apache tribes cattle and horse stealing had become the accepted means of support. Formerly a hunting people, they simply took livestock instead of game.

In 1855, Governor Merriwether made a treaty with the Mimbreño and Mescalero, and encouraged them in developing farm lands. A reservation on the Upper Gila for southern Apache was recommended and authorized in 1860. However, a general outbreak accompanied the general Navaho uprising in 1863. After the successful suppression

*Indians*

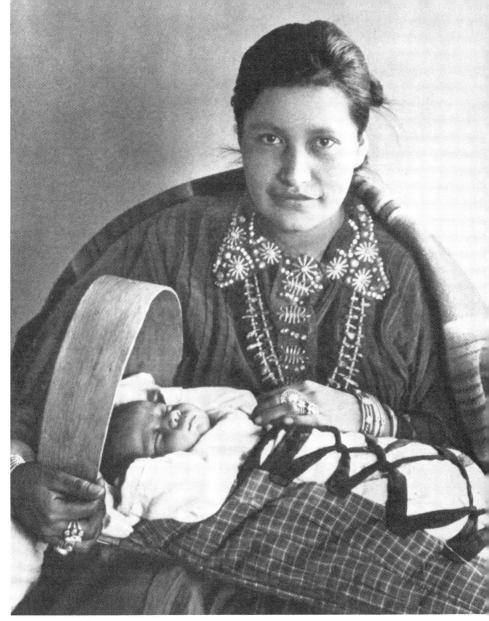

*Laura Gilpin*

NAVAHO MADONNA

NAVAHO WOMAN SPINNING

*Laura Gilpin*

*Laura Gilpin*

NAVAHO FAMILY

NAVAHO GIRL

*Laura Gilpin*

*Laura Gilpin*

SHEPHERDS OF THE DESERT

ÁCOMA, THE SKY CITY

*Laura Gilpin*

ZUNI PUEBLO AND GARDENS, ZUNI RIVER

*Mullarky*

CLOSEUP, PUEBLO BONITO RUINS, CHACO CANYON

TAOS PUEBLO

PETROGLYPHS, CHAMA CANYON

of the nomadic Indian revolt General Carleton brought 400 Mescalero to the Bosque Redondo where 7,000 Navaho were incarcerated.

Through the mismanagement of a party of soldiers, Cochise, the great Chirícahua chief, who had been friendly towards Americans, became the leader of a large band of southern Apache whose fanatical intent was to drive all white men from their lands. Believing that the withdrawal of troops from military posts in their territory was an acknowledgment of defeat, Cochise, and later Victorio, with a large number of Mimbreño, Mogollón, and Mescalero, terrorized the inhabitants of New Mexico, Arizona, and Chihuahua until 1880. Nana, Victorio's successor, was joined by Gerónimo and the warfare continued. It was evident that the future prosperity of the Territory of New Mexico would depend on the control of the Apache Indians. The United States Government made clear that it would not tolerate the continued plundering and murdering of its citizens, and took steps to establish order through military force. General Crook's experiment in training the southern Apache in the ways of civilization had failed. In spite of the fact that their farms yielded large crops the first year, Gerónimo incited them to revolt. General N. A. Miles compelled Gerónimo's surrender (1886) and the Apache tribes were finally conquered.

After years of administrative juggling two Apache reservations were established in New Mexico, the Jicarilla reservation of 750,000 acres in Rio Arriba and Sandoval counties, north of Santa Fe; and the Mescalero reservation of 427,320 acres in northern Otero County.

The Jicarilla Apache reservation is rich in forest lands, and tribal funds have been greatly augmented by the sale of timber. In the last eight years $330,000 worth of pure-bred sheep and goats have been issued to them, and an income from the sale of their surplus stock, owned communally, makes possible a small monthly payment to the very old tribal members. As a tribe the Jicarilla derive most of their income from sheep, supplemented with earnings from labor and a small amount from arts and crafts. For generations the Jicarilla have supplied a special type of water-carrying basket, as well as other baskets of beautiful workmanship.

The Mescalero reservation contains some of the best grazing country in New Mexico. The allotment of sections of land to individuals, as they demonstrate their ability, has done much to quiet this turbulent people.

The physical appearance of the Apache varies greatly. They are, with the Navaho, the tallest Indians in New Mexico. They are a shrewd people, honest in protecting property placed in their care; but their aggressive heritage and former habit of support through plunder have made a social readjustment within three generations difficult.

Polygamy is less general than formerly when warriors took wives as well as bartered for them.    There existed an ancient cross-cousin taboo that, among the Jicarilla, still persists.

The tepee is the most typical Apache dwelling, though the southern tribes used dome-shaped shelters consisting of a frame made of boughs covered with a thatching of leaves and bark.    The tepee, travois, and parfloche are elements in the Plains Indian material culture and are more often associated with those Apache whose lands adjoin the plains. Small houses are slowly being introduced by those Indians who have been educated in United States Government schools now living in settlements.

In times past Apache foodstuffs consisted of the products of the chase, principally buffalo, and roots (mainly maguey), and berries. Both bear and fish were taboo, although among some bands fish was caught and eaten.    The modern foodstuffs consist of mutton and corn supplemented by fruits, and such staples as coffee, etc.

The ritual life of the Jicarilla Apache may be divided into two parts; the shamanistic or personal, and the traditional or "long life" ceremonies.    The power of the *shaman* is continually stressed; they practice magic, perform cures, and direct the ceremonials or "sings." The most important of the "long life" ceremonies is the Bear Dance. This four-day rite, with sand paintings, is based on the legend of the Bear and the Snake which belongs to the Navaho as well as the Apache. The ceremonial relay race is run in mid-September.    This harvest festival, largely a time of trading and horse racing, is the principal gathering of the Jicarilla.    The fine pageantry of the Navaho ceremonies is lacking, for the Jicarilla regard for costuming, as shown in their habitual apparel, is scant.

Very little is known of the Mescalero ceremonials.    On the fourth of July they hold a fiesta followed by a four-day ceremony.    Medicine men chant in a huge tepee that is analogous to the Navaho ceremonial *hogan*.    Visitors are not welcome, and students are discouraged.

Later years have wrought a deplorable change among the Apache. Lacking the stamina of their Navaho relatives, they have been unable to resist both tuberculosis and whisky which have brought about a defeat more deadly than weapons of warfare.    With hospitalization and education, progress has been and is being made.    The Apache's land is more productive than that of the Navaho.    If they successfully adopt the ways of modern civilization they may regain the self-respect so necessary in establishing the proper morale of any people.

The Ute Indians formerly occupied the land which is now central and western Colorado, eastern Utah, and the upper San Juan drainage in New Mexico.    After De Vargas reconquered the country in 1692 there was a time of comparative peace, but beginning with the early

years of the eighteenth century the Ute joined the Comanche in per-
petrating their depredations.    In 1724, the Ute were at war with the
Jicarilla Apache, and captured one-half of their women and children.
Twenty-four years later war broke out between the Ute and Navaho.

It is certain that contact with the French influenced the Ute during the first half of the eighteenth century.    The Spaniards were fully
aware of the threatened French intrusion into New Mexico, and the
Ute, with other nomadic tribes, were quite willing to have their friendship bought with horses, cattle, and food; and this old "gift" custom
was later carried on by the Americans.

During the first part of the nineteenth century, the southern Ute
regarded the Jicarilla Apache country as their own.    The first agency
for both tribes was placed at Taos; later it was moved to Cimarrón.
The agency for the bands called Capote and Tabeguache was established
at Abiquiu.

After the American occupation of the Territory of New Mexico
the first treaty with the Ute Indians was made in 1849.    Peace and
amity were promised.    Four years later Governor Lande induced 250
Ute to farm on the Rio Pecos; but the Ute had little liking for soil
cultivation and were easily persuaded to join the Apache in an outbreak,
which was swiftly and effectively dealt with.

The Ute and the Jicarilla with the Pueblo were "Union" Indians.
A provision was made in 1861 for the Uintan band of Utes; and in
1863 the Tabeguache were assigned a reservation.    The final treaty,
however, made in 1868, set forth the boundaries of the reservation in
Colorado.    Seven years later this reservation was enlarged, and in 1879
the United States established the Ute reservation on the San Juan
River in northwestern New Mexico.

The Ute tribe is divided into three main groups: Tabeguache or
Uncompahgre, Kaivwach or White River, and Yoovte or Uintah.
Each group has, through contact and intermarriage, assumed certain
characteristics of its neighbors.    The relationship of the Ute and Jicarilla Apache, in spite of periods of warfare, has been of long duration.

Although the Ute people are not as tall as the Navaho and Apache
their height is greater than that of the Pueblo Indians.    Like their
Comanche relatives they are well built, but apt to become corpulent.
Their lack of friendliness characterizes their facial expression.

Originally brave and war-like, the Ute have become content to
live on Government allotments consisting of food and funds.    Up to
a short time ago the funds were largely spent for horse racing and
whisky.    With the introduction of a good school system the past years
have seen a great improvement.

Religious beliefs of the Ute Indians, like those of the other Plains tribes of Shoshonean stock, is governed by the Great Spirit. Their ceremonials or chants are of secondary importance.

The Ute are now considered Colorado Indians, but they still own grazing land north of the San Juan River in northern New Mexico.

About the beginning of the eighteenth century the Comanche left their country in southern Wyoming and migrated to the southern plains where, for over a hundred and fifty years, they fought other nomadic tribes, Pueblo Indians, Spaniards, and Americans. They were first seen in what is now New Mexico with the Ute in 1705; and with the Ute they attacked Taos pueblo; they raided Jicarilla Apache settlement, pueblos and Spanish ranches, and always they took horses.

The hostilities of the Comanche more than those of any other nomadic tribe prevented the Spaniards from establishing settlements in the Arkansas Valley. However, the Spaniards recognized the importance of the "Comanchería" as a barrier between New Mexico and the threatened French intrusion in the northeast and promoted friendly relations with the tribe. They were asked to attend the Taos fair in 1748-49 where they traded skins and captives for horses and foodstuffs. But the French supplied arms through the Comanche camps in Kansas and depredations continued. Treaties with the Spaniards were made and broken, and it was not until Anza became governor of New Mexico in 1778 that the Comanche problem was properly understood.

There existed at the time twelve bands of Comanche, each led by one or two chiefs who believed themselves to be the head of the whole tribe. No sooner would one chief make a treaty than it was repudiated by the others. Governor Anza adopted the aggressive method; he attacked the principal settlement of Cuerno Verde, their most noted chief, and later killed him. Peace between Spaniards and Comanche followed the year 1784. In 1786, Anza was instructed by General Ugarte to keep this peace with the Comanche, making gifts of horses and stores, and even paying salaries to certain chiefs who would make war on the Apache.

It was not until 1850 that the Americans discovered, through trial and error, the Comanche division into bands with little or no coalescence. From the beginning the Comanche were the terror of the Santa Fe Trail. Military protection by the United States assured the furtherance of the commerce of the prairies; and the establishing of this protected road through the Comanche country to Santa Fe was one of the steps towards the American occupation of the territory of New Mexico.

The Comanche like all nomadic tribes gave trouble during the first twenty years of the new government. The treaty of 1867 provided for a Comanche reservation in Oklahoma. In 1874-75 the Comanche joined their old enemies the Apache in an attack which was quickly quelled, thus establishing the supremacy of the United States Govern-

ment for all time.   The few Comanche left in New Mexico were attached to the Kiowa agency in Oklahoma.

The Comanche are a copper-colored people with a pronounced aqui-
line nose and thin lips, black hair and eyes, and little beard.   They are
of low or medium stature, well built, but with a tendency to corpulence.
The women usually age prematurely.   They were originally nomads,
and lived in tepees that were easily carried from place to place as they
followed the game.   Their continued travels curtailed the development
of culture and religion.

The Comanche religion is largely an individual matter; they believe
in the Great Spirit who is associated with the sun.   Polygamy was
formerly common.   Women were often stolen or bartered for, and
there existed little ceremony with courtship or marriage.   *Peyote,* an
alkaloid intoxicant from a cactus native to Mexico, was introduced
in comparatively recent times.

Horses were their medium of exchange, and in horses the Comanche
counted their wealth.   Their first horses were used as pack animals;
later they used them for pursuing game and in war.   They soon
acquired extraordinary skill in horsemanship, and this supremacy more
than anything else made them the greatest and most feared of the Plains
Indians.

# History

THE story of the discovery of New Mexico by the Spaniards, as recounted by Castañeda, starts with Nuño de Guzmán, Governor of New Spain in 1528, who had in his possession an Indian called Tejo (Te-ho) who told of going northward with his father to trade feathers for ornaments. They brought back large quantities of gold and silver, and saw "seven towns so large that they could be compared in size to Mexico and its suburbs, and that in them were whole streets occupied by silversmiths." These settlements were to be reached by "traveling northward between the two seas," and "across a grassy desert for forty days."

Guzmán organized an army of 400 Spaniards and 20,000 friendly Indians of New Spain, and set out in December, 1529, to find the fabled Seven Cities. He did not, however, find this promised land of riches, as he lost his way and followed up the Pacific Coast. Before the expedition's return to Mexico in 1531, Guzmán established Culiacán in the province of Sinaloa, which became an important outpost for later exploring expeditions.

Interest in those unknown regions flared up again when in April, 1536, a group of four almost naked men walked into the village of Culiacán. Their leader, Álvar Núñez Cabeza de Vaca, had started out from Spain for Florida in 1527, as royal treasurer of the Narváez expedition which met with misfortune, all of its members except De Vaca and a few companions being lost at sea or killed by Indians. The four final survivors, De Vaca, Andrés Dorantes, Alonso de Castillo Maldonado, and Estevan, the negro slave of Dorantes, wandered from the coast of Texas to the Spanish settlements on the Gulf of California.

The story of De Vaca's experiences was the first definite word to reach Mexico City about the northern region later to become New Mexico. Antonio de Mendoza, first viceroy of New Spain, determined upon an expedition into those northern lands. But first he planned to send out a small exploring party, and selected as its leader Marcos de Niza, a Franciscan friar who was with Pizarro in the conquest of Peru, and later a frontier missionary in the northern part of New Spain. Estevan accompanied Marcos as guide; they took six Indian interpreters and others as servants.

Marcos set out from Culiacán on March 7, 1539, following the west coast to the Sonora Valley where he stopped to rest and sent Estevan on ahead to explore and report back to him. If the country was unusually good Estevan was to send a cross two hands long; if it was as rich and populous as New Spain, a still larger cross. Four days later an Indian messenger returned with "a very large cross, *as tall as a man!*" The Indian told of seven great cities in the first province with houses two, three, and four stories high, ornamented with turquoise which he said was abundant. Farther on, he added, there were other provinces greater even than the Seven Cities.

Marcos immediately pressed forward over the deserts of Northern Mexico and southeastern Arizona. He did not overtake Estevan, however, who reached the Zuñi pueblo of Hawikúh, the first of the Seven Cities, and was killed there. Fray Marcos, upon learning of the Negro's death, did not turn back until May, 1539, when, according to his account, he beheld Hawikúh from the top of a nearby mesa, the Zuñi not permitting the friar to approach nearer. Fray Marcos erected a cross and took formal possession of the country for Spain, then returned to Mexico City and reported to the viceroy. He had claimed a whole new region for Spain; had seen the many-storied houses of the Zuñi; and Indians who wore turquoise suspended from their noses and ears. From these Indians on the way he had heard of great cities, populous nations, and lands abounding in wealth. These accounts lost nothing in the retelling as they passed from one adventurer to another.

Mendoza, the viceroy, immediately began preparations to conquer this country. He selected Compostela as the assembling place, appointed Francisco Vásquez Coronado as Captain-general of the expedition, and Marcos as guide. The army started its northward march, February 23, 1540.

Coronado followed the route of Marcos and Estevan. Going ahead of the main body, Coronado reached Cíbola July 7, and captured Hawikúh, which he named Granada. The pueblo contained no wealth but an abundance of provisions. The soldiers, disappointed at finding no treasures, complained so bitterly against Marcos that he returned to New Spain.

During the summer and fall exploratory parties penetrated to the Hopi pueblos and the Grand Canyon of the Colorado River in Arizona, the Rio Grande Pueblo country as far north as Taos, and east to the buffalo plains of the Llano Estacado.

In September, Coronado's main army reached Tiguex, near the present town of Bernalillo, where Coronado established winter headquarters. The Tiguex Pueblos revolted and were subjugated with such severity as to incur Indian hostility to the Spaniards for generations.

An eastern plains Indian called the Turk, a captive of the pueblo of Cicuyé (Pecos), told the Spaniards of a fabulously rich country far to the east named Quivira. Coronado listened eagerly and as soon as spring came started eastward with his entire force. Leaving Tiguex for the Eastern Plains April 23, 1541, the army stopped at Cicuyé (Pecos), and continued the march for two or three days, when in order to cross the Pecos River a bridge was built supposedly near Puerto de Luna, in present Guadalupe County. This was the first bridge known to be built in the present Southwest. Coronado's route led towards the northeast for a short distance, then turned in a general southeasterly direction to a point presumably near the headwaters of the Brazos River on the plains of Texas.

After thirty-seven days of marching, the food supply was almost exhausted and only buffalo meat was available. It became apparent that the Turk's directions were misleading—the Spaniards thought deliberately so. Coronado selected other Indian guides, sent the main army back to Tiguex, and with a picked body of thirty men marched towards the north, which the new guides said was Quivira's true location. Coronado pushed on as far as the Quiviras (Wichita Indians) in eastern Kansas, where populous cities and treasures of gold failed to materialize. From there he returned by a more direct route to Tiguex.

Early in April, 1542, after a winter of discouragement and dissension, Coronado and his army started back to New Spain. His report to Viceroy Mendoza in 1543 was a disappointment; the expedition was considered a failure, having added no gold to Spain, although Spanish possessions were increased by a vast territory, and the explorations formed the basis of the first definite geographic knowledge of the Southwest.

Three Franciscan friars, Juan de Padilla, Juan de la Cruz, and Luis de Escalona, who had accompanied Coronado, remained among the Pueblo Indians as the first missionaries and martyrs of New Mexico. Juan de la Cruz was killed by Indians at Tiguex, Luis de Escalona at Cicuyé (Pecos), and Juan de Padilla traveled northwestward to Quivira (now the state of Kansas) where he met martyrdom in 1544.

The next expedition, forty years after Coronado's, was initiated and led by Agustín Rodríguez for missionary purposes. Agustín was accompanied by Francisco López, Juan de Santa María, and twelve soldiers under Captain Francisco Sánchez Chamuscado. Proceeding from Santa Barbara in southern Chihuahua, they blazed a new trail into the Pueblo country up the Rio Grande to Puaray, one of the pueblos in the Provinces of Tiguex where Coronado had made his headquarters.

Eager to announce their discoveries, Juan de Santa María started back to New Spain but was killed by Indians on the way. After extensive explorations, the soldiers returned to Mexico, but Francisco and

Agustín refused to leave, and remained at Puaray where shortly afterwards they were put to death.

To ascertain the unknown fate of these Franciscans, the expedition of Antonio de Espejo and Bernardino Beltrán, 1582-83, was undertaken. After obtaining definite information of the friars' deaths, the expedition explored a large part of the Pueblo country, and returned down the Pecos River, thus opening a third line of approach to the Pueblo region of central and northern New Mexico. Another outstanding feature of the expedition is that Casilda de Anaya, the third white woman to enter New Mexico, made the trip with her soldier husband. Espejo reported the region as abounding in great mineral wealth, good grazing country, and "lands suitable for fields and gardens, with or without irrigation." His report was influential in the settlement of the new province.

The name "New Mexico," the oldest State name in the Union except Florida, is thought to have been first applied by Francisco de Ibarra in 1565, who called the country north of the settled Mexican provinces *un otro* or Nuevo Méjico. Following the Rodríguez expedition 1581-82, the name was used permanently, appearing in the Gallegos account of that expedition written and presented to the viceroy in 1582. Nuevo Méjico was also used on the title page of Luxán's journal dated 1583, of the Espejo expedition.

The first attempt to colonize New Mexico was made by Gaspar Castaño de Sosa, 1590-91, who with 170 persons, including women and children, and a wagon train of supplies entered by way of the Pecos River. After about a year among the Rio Grande pueblos, Castaño was arrested by Juan Morlete for having made an unauthorized entry, and was returned to Mexico City in chains.

Humaña and Bonilla also made an unauthorized entry, 1593-94, visiting the pueblos and traversing the northeastern plains probably to the Platte River. Humaña murdered Bonilla, and Indians killed the rest of the party except one New Mexican Indian called Jusepe who escaped and returned to Picurís. His story is the only account of what happened.

Don Juan de Oñate, a wealthy mine owner of Zacatecas, and son of a pioneer, made the next attempt to colonize the new region. The government, unable and unwilling to finance his proposal, granted him a contract September 21, 1595, when Oñate offered to equip an expedition at his own expense.

After numerous delays, the army of soldiers and settlers, numbering about 400, a baggage and supply train of 83 wagons and carts, and 7,000 head of stock, left Santa Barbara, February 7, 1598, for the north. On April 30, Oñate took formal possession of New Mexico at a point on the Rio Grande below El Paso del Norte.

Near Mount Robledo Oñate started ahead with a small escort to examine the country. On July 11 he established the first Spanish capital in New Mexico at the Tewa Village of Yugeuingge (called *Yunqueyunque* by Coronado), on the west bank of the Rio Grande, and christened it San Juan, adding *de los Caballeros* (St. John of the Gentlemen) "in memory of those noble sons who first raised in these barbarous regions the bloody tree upon which Christ perished for the redemption of mankind." (Villagrá, *Historia del Nuevo Méjico.*)

The main body of colonists following more slowly crossed the dread *Jornada del Muerto* (Journey of Death), and arrived five weeks later at San Juan, thus establishing the first permanent colony in New Mexico, and the second in the United States (the first being St. Augustine, Florida, 1565).

Work on the first Spanish irrigation ditch was begun August 11, 1598, and on the first church in New Mexico, August 23, it being dedicated September 8, to San Juan Bautista. The next day Pueblo chiefs of the region submitted and agreed to receive Christian missionaries. The Province was divided into seven mission districts with eight Franciscan friars.

From 1598 until 1601 the settlement was referred to as San Juan Bautista, but later was called San Gabriel del Yunque. San Juan de los Caballeros generally was used to denote the Tewa Pueblo on the east bank of the Rio Grande to which the Indians had moved. The Spanish capital remained at San Gabriel del Yunque until its removal to Santa Fe in the winter of 1609-10.

The first winter in New Mexico was fraught with hardships. Friendly Indians could not provide sufficient food for the colonists and mutiny developed among the soldiers. The colony stood firm, however, due to the courage of its sturdy pioneers.

On December 4, the Ácoma Indians revolted, trapping Oñate's nephew, Juan de Zaldivar, and eighteen of his men in their famous sky city on a mesa. Zaldivar, ten other soldiers, and a few servants were killed.

To punish the Ácoma, Oñate sent Vicente de Zaldivar, brother of the murdered Juan, with a picked force to recapture the pueblo. The battle began January 22, 1599, and raged until January 24, when the Spaniards gained the mesa top and were victorious. Setting fire to the pueblo, they sent the inhabitants to settle on the plains below. This ended organized Indian resistance to Oñate, and on December 24, 1600, relief forces from New Spain reached San Gabriel.

Oñate left San Gabriel for Quivira, June 23, 1601, to visit that section, going probably as far west as the present Wichita, Kansas, and traversing sections covered by Coronado sixty years before.

During Oñate's absence discontented settlers, soldiers, and all of the missionaries except one friar abandoned San Gabriel for the Santa Barbara mines or elsewhere. When Oñate returned November 24, the settlement was all but deserted. Vicente de Zaldivar followed the colonists, secured new missionaries and settlers, brought back some of the deserters, and San Gabriel flourished again.

Oñate set out for the South Sea (the Pacific Ocean), October 7, 1604, with thirty horsemen and two priests. He reached the Gulf of California, January 25, 1605, and took possession for Spain. The party started back to San Gabriel, saving themselves from starvation on the way by killing and eating their horses. On the return trip, Oñate left his name on Inscription Rock, now El Morro National Monument, April 16, 1605, instituting a practice followed by subsequent governors, soldiers, and priests.

Extensive expeditions, campaigns, and the exacting duties of governor had worn Oñate out, while huge expenditures from his own private fortune reduced him to poverty. The colony needed reinforcements which Oñate could not supply and which were not forthcoming from Mexico City. March 31, 1605, a secret report was made on New Mexico and Oñate's conduct, which doubtless inspired Philip III's order of June 7, 1606, that no more explorations be made in New Mexico, that Oñate go to Mexico City, and another governor be appointed. In despair Oñate resigned, August 24, 1607. The viceroy accepted his resignation but cautioned Oñate not to leave New Mexico without further orders, which should arrive in December, 1609, at the latest.

The viceroy chose Juan Martínez de Montoya, one of Oñate's captains, as governor, but the colonists, for reasons which they considered sufficient, did not permit him to serve. They elected Oñate as governor, but he declined; then they chose his son, Don Cristóbal. Sometime before March 5, 1609, the viceroy appointed Don Pedro de Peralta governor with instructions to found a new capital.

To Oñate was due the permanent settlement of New Mexico. He organized the first mission system among New Mexican Indians, explored the Southwest as extensively as Coronado, Espejo, and all of his predecessors combined, and blazed the trail to the Gulf of California. Villagrá's *Historia del Nuevo Méjico,* an epic poem in thirty-four cantos describing Oñate's conquest and settlement of New Mexico, the first poem written about any section of the United States, was published at Alcalá, Spain, in 1610.

Oñate and his son, Don Cristóbal, were permitted to leave New Mexico after the arrival of Peralta, which they did in the spring of 1610, but Don Cristóbal died on the way to Mexico. Oñate was charged with crimes committed in New Mexico, including refusal to obey royal decrees, lack of respect for the friars, mistreating the Indians, murdering some, and punishing the Ácoma and Jumano Indians with especial cruelty. He was sentenced with De Zaldivar and several others in Mexico City, May 13, 1614. Oñate was perpetually banished from New Mexico and fined 6,000 Castilian ducats. Some reason exists for believing that he was pardoned before 1624, as at that time he still bore the title of *adelantado,* and was entrusted with visitation of mines in Spain.

During the winter of 1609 and 1610, Peralta founded Santa Fe and moved the settlers from San Gabriel to the new capital. The mission supply service between Mexico City and Santa Fe was organized for sending supplies to missionaries and Spanish settlements via pack train every three years.

Colonization during the seventeenth century was slow. Spanish authorities were interested in New Mexico principally as a northern outpost. The region was considered a failure as a source of easily obtainable gold, and became, therefore, primarily a venture in missionary work, colonization, and frontier protection.

Eleven mission churches had been established by 1617. The Franciscan Mission Province was formed into the *custodia* of the conversion of San Pablo in 1621, with Alonzo de Benavides as *custodio.* Benavides, also agent of the Inquisition, arrived in Santa Fe, December 1625. The progress of mission work was remarkable. By 1626 there were 43 churches and 34,000 Christian Indians.

The seventeenth century was, therefore, the great mission-building period. San Esteban at Ácoma is an outstanding example. The missions covered a wide area, east as far as Pecos, west to Zuñi and the Hopi pueblos; along the Rio Grande as far north as Taos, and south to the mission of Nuestra Señora de Guadalupe, founded by Franciscans from New Mexico in 1659, at El Paso del Norte on the west bank of the Rio Grande (now Juárez, Mexico).

Spanish settlements, even though the population was relatively small, were spread far apart. Until 1680, Santa Fe was the only Spanish villa, or incorporated town. Santa Cruz de la Cañada, north of Santa Fe, was the second important village at that time, although Spanish settlements or *haciendas* extended from Taos to below Isleta on the Rio Grande.

The province was seriously handicapped by continuous friction between civil and religious authorities. Beginning with the administration of Governor Peralta in 1610, these caused grave disturbances culminating in the preparation by Santa Fe's *Cabildo* (town council) of a signed statement complaining against the Franciscans, and a letter sent February 21, 1639, to Mexico City appealing to the viceroy. The friars in turn made serious accusations against Governor Rosas, during whose administration this occurred, and declared that he persecuted them. These incidents assumed proportions of a major and often damaging conflict. As a result, several of New Mexico's governors felt the heavy hand of the Inquisition or ecclesiastical discipline either during or immediately following their terms of office.

By 1660 the conflict had become so grave that the Franciscans threatened to abandon the entire province. Governor Mendizabel consequently fell afoul of the Inquisition, and he, his wife, and three or four lesser officials were arrested and their property confiscated by the Holy Office.

Don Diego de Peñalosa, who succeeded Mendizabel as governor from 1661-64, forbade exploitation of Indians by the friars in "spinning and weaving cotton *mantas*." At the conclusion of his term Peñalosa was charged before the Inquisition in Mexico City with offenses against the clergy. A ruinous fine was imposed upon him and he was forced to march barefoot through the streets carrying a green candle. Unable to obtain redress from the viceroy, the ex-governor went to London and later to Paris where his schemes for conquest of the Quivira country east of New Mexico stimulated La Salle's expedition (1682), by which France set a limit to the expansion of Spanish possessions.

Exploitation of the Indians by imposed labor or tribute continued alternately by friars and governors, and the Indians' resentment of the suppression of their religion led to a series of sporadic uprisings beginning in 1640, the immediate cause being the whipping, imprisoning, and hanging of forty Indians who would not give up their own religion. In 1643 the Jémez Indians were discovered plotting with the Navaho to drive the Spaniards from New Mexico; and in 1650, the Pueblos of Jémez, Isleta, Alameda, San Felipe, and Cochití conspired with the Apache for the same purpose. These and the Apache outbreak of 1676, with the leaders and participants in each instance hanged, imprisoned or sold into slavery, culminated finally in the Pueblo Revolt of August 10, 1680, led by Po-pé.

The Pueblo Indians planned with Apache aid to murder or expel all Spaniards and to destroy Santa Fe. On August 9, two days before the time set for the uprising, the plot was discovered by Governor Antonio de Otermín. Apprised of this discovery, the Indians began their slaughter in the early morning hours of the 10th, leading eventually to the deaths of over four hundred Spaniards, including twenty-one priests. North of Santa Fe but few Spaniards escaped alive. Settlers near Santa Fe gathered in the capital, preparing for a last stand. Indian hordes gathered around the village and sent the governor two crosses, one white and one red. If he returned the white and promised to abandon the country, the Spaniards might go in peace. If he returned the red, meaning that the Spaniards would fight, the Indians threatened to massacre them all.

The Spaniards refused to surrender and sent back the red cross. The Indians then cut off Santa Fes water supply and began the siege. Starvation soon threatened the white men who sallied forth early on August 20, and attacked the sleeping Indians, killing three hundred and taking forty-seven captive. About one thousand five hundred others fled to the hills.

On August 21, which date marks the end of Spanish rule in New Mexico for thirteen years, the besieged Spaniards, numbering about one thousand men, women, and children, abandoned Santa Fe and started towards El Paso del Norte. Their settlement on the east bank of the Rio Grande was the beginning of modern El Paso, Texas.

When the Spaniards were gone, the Pueblos celebrated their victory. They destroyed official records, tore down and burned churches, washed baptized Indians with *amole* (soapweed) in the Santa Fe River to cleanse them of the stain, and annulled Christian marriages.

Several unsuccessful attempts to reconquer the province were made during the next ten years. In 1690, the Viceroy at Mexico City appointed Don Diego de Vargas Zapata Luján Ponce de León as Governor of New Mexico. August 21, 1692, De Vargas set out from El Paso with three hundred men for the reconquest. The army reached Santa Fe on September 13. The Indians blustered and threatened, but surrendered peacefully before night. De Vargas raised the royal banner, and on September 14, 1692, repossessed the country in the name of the King of Spain. He subdued the remainder of the province without losing a man or fighting a battle except for an encounter with the Apache, and then returned to El Paso.

De Vargas left again for New Mexico October 13, 1693, with seventy families, one hundred soldiers, and seventeen Franciscans, and re-entered Santa Fe December 16. In 1695 the Franciscan missions were re-established and the Villa of Santa Cruz de la Cañada refounded. The Pueblos rebelled again in June 1696, but were subdued. De Vargas ordered several Pueblo governors shot and subsequently the Pueblos gave little trouble.

Colonization increased and Albuquerque was founded in 1706, by Governor Don Francisco Cuervo y Valdés and named in honor of the Duke of Alburquerque, viceroy in Mexico City.

As war existed between France and Spain in 1719, New Mexico was threatened with French intrusion from the east. On June 14, 1720, Captain Pedro Villasur left Santa Fe with an expedition for the Pawnee Country to investigate French activity there. Near the Platte River in central Nebraska, Pawnee Indians, armed by French traders, attacked the party, killing Villasur and forty-four others. Only thirteen survived.

In 1723 the Spanish government forbade trade with the French, and limited trade with Plains Indians to those coming to Pecos and Taos, thus giving rise to the latter's annual fairs.

The Mallet brothers and seven or eight other French Canadian fur traders came to Santa Fe in 1739, by way of the Missouri and Platte Rivers through Nebraska, Kansas, and southeastern Colorado. Some of the men returned across the Plains to Illinois; others down the Canadian and Arkansas Rivers to New Orleans. This marked a new epoch, as the traders had penetrated to New Mexico through dangerous Indian country and had returned in safety. They also carried back the first definite information about the fur trade and internal conditions of the province.

Results were immediate and far-reaching. French officials in Louisiana became actively interested. More traders entered, although they were opposed. Toward the close of the French and Indian War, the ceding by France to Spain of all Louisiana west of the Mississippi River solved this particular frontier problem. The French peril ceased to exist, but there remained an even more dangerous one to guard against —the English.

Meanwhile, New Spain extended its missions and outposts on the California coast. In July, 1776, Escalante and Domínguez with eight companions left Santa Fe to find a trail to the new missions at Monterey, California. They traveled northwest up the Chama Valley to Abiquiu, across the upper San Juan Basin, through southwestern Colorado, across the Green and Grand Rivers, to Utah Lake in north central Utah, then southwest to Sevier Lake. The friars mentioned the existence of the Great Salt Lake farther north. With the trail to California uncertain and the rapid approach of winter, they turned back through the Grand Canyon and Zuñi, reaching Santa Fe January 22, 1777. Their trail from Santa Fe into central Utah became the first stage of the Spanish Trail from Santa Fe to Los Angeles.

Lieutenant Colonel Juan Bautista de Anza, who after founding San Francisco in 1776 became governor of New Mexico, instituted a vigorous campaign (1779) against the Comanche, former Spanish allies, because of their raids led by Chief Cuerno Verde upon Spanish settlers in the Rio Grande Valley. De Anza's command consisted of 645 men, including 85 soldiers and 259 Indians. In a battle ninety-five leagues northeast of Santa Fe in the present state of Kansas, the celebrated Comanche chief was defeated and killed. De Anza's route led in full view of the peak named later for Zebulon Pike.

In 1780 a smallpox epidemic following a three-year drought broke out among the Pueblos, Moquis, and Spaniards. Drought, famine, and pestilence carried off 5,025 Pueblo Indians.

Ever since the founding of San Antonio (1718) in the province of Texas (now the State), the Spaniards needed direct communication with Santa Fe. In 1787 a trail from San Antonio north to the region of Wichita Falls, then up the Red and Canadian Rivers, and on to Santa Fe was traced by Pedro (Pierre) Vial, a French frontiersman officially sent out from San Antonio.

Other routes to the East were opened shortly afterwards, but still there was none to St. Louis in Spanish Louisiana. Vial and two companions left Santa Fe May 21, 1792, with orders from the governor to find a direct route. Vial reached St. Louis and returned, thus making the first complete journey across what became the famed Santa Fe Trail.

During the latter part of the eighteenth century mineral prospects received new attention, although little actual mining was done during the Spanish era. The first big development was the Santa Rita copper mine discovered about 1800, but not extensively worked until 1804.

Spanish officials, thoroughly aroused by the westward expansion of the United States, due to the Louisiana Purchase in 1803, and by explorations into Spanish-American territory, were fearful lest restless Anglo-American pioneers overrun Texas and New Mexico. When news reached Governor Joaquín Alencastre of Lieutenant Zebulon M. Pike's exploration into Spanish territory, and of his erection of a cottonwood stockade—over which Pike raised the American flag—about five miles up the Rio Conejos in Colorado on the west side of the Rio Grande, Alencastre sent out a party of horsemen to arrest and bring the Americans to Santa Fe, where they arrived March 3, 1807. Pike was sent to Chihuahua under guard, and later escorted to the Louisiana frontier. Pike's report supplied the United States with the first authentic information about the Spanish Southwest.

Alencastre instituted measures to prevent additional American influences from entering New Mexico. Until Mexico gained independence from Spain, attempts to open trade with St. Louis were unsuccessful and the traders who at times did enter the province were expelled or imprisoned.

In 1810 Spain was overrun by Napoleon's armies and turned to its American colonies for support. A decree was issued providing for election of deputies from Spanish-America to the Cortes in Spain. On August 11 Pedro Bautista Pino was chosen to represent New Mexico. He was the province's first and only representative to Spain.

## UNDER THE REPUBLIC OF MEXICO
### 1821-1846

As soon as Mexico achieved independence from Spain, September 27, 1821, the new republic was ready to establish relations with the outside world, a policy that affected New Mexico.

William Becknell, of Missouri, a trader among the Comanche, was the first American to take advantage of the change.    In 1822 he brought the first wagons loaded with goods from Missouri across the Plains to Santa Fe, and earned the title, "Father of the Santa Fe Trail."  He was also the first trader to follow the Cimarrón route to San Miguel and Santa Fe.    Two years later the spring caravan brought $30,000 worth of goods to New Mexico; the traders returned with $180,000 in gold and silver, $10,000 worth of furs, and the Santa Fe trade was established.

The $10,000 of furs is significant as it relates to an almost forgotten phase of early American enterprise in New Mexico.    James O. Pattie, a Kentuckian, with a party of western frontiersmen trapped all over New Mexico and Arizona from 1824 to 1828.    In 1826 Ceran St. Vrain, veteran trapper, and a large party including the youthful Kit Carson, trapped beaver on the Rio Grande, the Gila, and Colorado Rivers.    A route for the Santa Fe Trail from Missouri to Taos was surveyed by the United States Government in 1825, but traders refused to follow its roundabout course, preferring the routes already in use.

The treaty of 1819, regarding boundaries between Spanish possessions and the United States, signed by both governments, was ratified by the Republic of Mexico in 1828.

In 1833 the first gold lode or vein west of the Mississippi River was discovered and worked on, the *Sierra de Oro* (mountain of gold), now known as the Ortiz mine.    Actually, however, gold was known and had been worked in the *Cerrillos* (little hills) of Santa Fe, and the arroyos to the south in the time of Governor Don Tomás Velez, 1749-54.    As early as the middle of the seventeenth century, lead and some silver had been mined in the region.

The first newspaper in New Mexico, *El Crepúsculo de la Libertad* (The Dawn of Liberty), was published in the summer of 1834 at Santa Fe by Antonio Barreiro on the first press in New Mexico—that owned by Don Ramón Abreu.    The printer was Jesús Baca.    This press was subsequently purchased by Padre Antonio José Martínez and moved to Taos where he published various pamphlets and school manuals for his students.

An uprising caused by dissatisfaction with the revised Mexican constitution, centralization of power, and imposition of taxes to which New Mexicans had not been subject before, took place August 3, 1837, and Lieutenant Colonel Albino Pérez, unpopular since his arrival in Santa Fe as governor, was assassinated.

The rebels entered Santa Fe August 10, and elected José Gonzales, a native of Taos, as governor, but General Manuel Armijo overthrew Gonzales and re-established the Mexican government's authority with himself as governor, January 28, 1838.    Armijo continued in office, except from April 28, 1844 to November, 1845, until the end of the Mexican period in New Mexico.

The year 1841 was marked by the attempt of Texas to get some of the profitable overland commerce going into New Mexico, and possibly as a concealed purpose, to induce the New Mexicans to throw off the yoke of Mexico and thus establish the Texas boundary claim to the east bank of the Rio Grande.

On entering New Mexico the members of this Texas-Santa Fe expedition were arrested, several were shot, and the others sent by Armijo to prisons in Mexico City. They were soon released due to pressure by the United States, Texas, and British Governments. Accounts of the prisoners' mistreatment aroused resentment adding to the strain already existing between the United States and Mexico.

President Polk announced war with Mexico, May 13, 1846, and the United States immediately began planning to invade New Mexico, Chihuahua, and California.

## AMERICAN OCCUPATION—NEW MEXICO A TERRITORY OF THE UNITED STATES
### 1846-1912

General Stephen W. Kearny, commanding the Army of the West, entered New Mexico at Ratón, reaching Las Vegas August 15, 1846, where he absolved the people from allegiance to Mexico and proclaimed himself governor. On August 18 General Kearny, having failed to meet the expected resistance from General Armijo in Apache Cañón, occupied Santa Fe without a shot being fired in his bloodless conquest, and again declared the end of the Mexican period and the beginning of the American. The construction of Fort Marcy, the first American military fort in New Mexico, was begun on August 23, on the high hill northeast of Santa Fe.

On September 22 General Kearny, hastening to organize a new government for New Mexico as a Territory of the United States, appointed officials including Charles Bent as civil governor, and Donaciano Vigil as secretary. Bent was a pioneer with influential business and social connections, having come to Santa Fe in 1826. He was a partner in the firm of Bent and St. Vrain, the largest fur trading company in the Southwest.

On September 25 General Kearny set out for California, leaving Colonel Alexander W. Doniphan in charge of New Mexico with orders to march southward to assist in the conquest of Chihuahua as soon as Colonel Sterling Price arrived to take command in New Mexico. Meantime, however, Navaho raids were growing so bold that Colonel Doniphan swept across the Continental Divide into the very heart of the Navaho country in the northwest, and forced them to make a treaty at Bear Spring November 22, the first United States treaty with the Navaho.

Scarcely more than a month later Colonel Doniphan's forces were victorious at Brazito, where the only battle of the Mexican War fought on New Mexican soil occurred on the afternoon of Christmas Day. The same American troops occupied El Paso del Norte which surrendered without a struggle December 28, and on February 8, 1847 began their advance on the city of Chihuahua.

With General Kearny and Colonel Doniphan both out of the territory, malcontents planned a sudden blow against American control before it became too firmly rooted, and called a general uprising for midnight of December 19. The plot was discovered and the leaders fled or were imprisoned. The revolutionary spirit was not subdued, however, and flared up anew in the Taos Revolt a month later when Governor Bent was murdered in his home at Taos, January 19, 1847, by local revolutionists and Indians from Taos Pueblo. Several other officials were also murdered and the homes of Anglo-American residents sacked.

The revolt spread, and preparations were under way to march upon the capital itself. Colonel Price, who had succeeded Colonel Doniphan in command, immediately left Santa Fe with 350 men for Taos, which he reached on February 3. The following morning the troops surrounded Taos Pueblo and fired on insurgents gathered in the church. The next morning the Indians begged for peace. The revolt failed, ending all doubt of American control, and placed the whole Territorial government in the army's hands, leaving scarcely more than the name of civil government for the next four years. Coincidental with American rule was the starting of the first newspaper in New Mexico, printed in English, the *Santa Fe Republican,* September 4, 1847.

The close of the Mexican War resulted in the treaty of Guadalupe Hidalgo signed February 2, 1848, providing (1) that Mexico give up all claim to territory east of the Rio Grande and cede New Mexico and upper California to the United States; (2) that the United States pay Mexico $15,000,000 besides settling American citizens' claims of $3,250,000 against Mexico; (3) that inhabitants of the ceded territory become American citizens unless moving out or formally declaring within a year their intention to retain Mexican citizenship; and (4) that they be "admitted at the proper time (to be judged by the Congress of the United States) to the enjoyment of all rights of citizens of the United States."

On October 10, 1848 a convention of delegates met at Santa Fe, and, protesting against the Texas claims to the east side of the Rio Grande and the introduction of slavery, petitioned Congress for a speedy organization of a civil territorial government. When the petition reached Congress it obtained no results.

Another convention meeting September 24, 1849 adopted a regular plan of territorial civil government and sent a delegate to Congress to urge its acceptance, but he was denied a seat.

During the same year a regular stage line was established between Independence and Santa Fe, making the round trip twice monthly and carrying the mail by yearly contract. Though irregular in the early years, this service was later increased to once a week and finally to three times a week.

A constitutional convention met in Santa Fe in May, 1850, and framed a constitution for the "State" of New Mexico; this was ratified June 20 by a decisive vote of the people, and submitted to Congress. A legislature, meeting on July 1 elected United States senators, and drew up a memorial to Congress denouncing the military officials' high-handed methods of controlling the government, and asking admission as a State.

This effort to secure statehood failed as Congress, on September 9, passed the compromise measures of 1850, one feature of which was the Organic Act of the Territory of New Mexico by which New Mexico became a territory with full civil government. The Organic Act also settled the long standing controversy with Texas over the region east of the Rio Grande. The claim of Texas had always been shadowy and uncertain, while that of New Mexicans who had occupied the territory for two centuries and a half was definite and beyond reasonable doubt. Congress organized the lands east of the Rio Grande as part of the Territory of New Mexico and paid Texas $10,000,000 to relinquish all claims. Congress also, September 27, 1850, authorized monthly mail routes east and the establishment of post offices.

March 3, 1851, James C. Calhoun (appointed March 29, 1849, first Indian agent west of the Mississippi River) was inaugurated as first Governor under the Organic Act.

The first legislative assembly meeting under the Organic Act in 1851, fixed Santa Fe as the capital, and divided the territory into three judicial districts; and at its second session the territory was divided into nine counties. Neither session passed a tax law.

In the summer of 1851 the Right Reverend John B. Lamy, bishop of the newly established Roman Catholic Vicarate Apostolic of Santa Fe, reached the capital and took charge of the diocese. Bishop Lamy instituted a series of extensive reforms and launched a program of education that made him famous in the Southwest.

Congress in the spring of 1853 authorized Jefferson Davis, Secretary of War, to send out exploring expeditions to determine the most feasible route for a railroad to the Pacific coast.    Two of the routes were surveyed through New Mexico.

Later, James Gadsden was sent by the President to Mexico City as a special commissioner with instructions to settle the boundary dispute with the Mexican government by buying the region west of the Rio Grande and south of the Gila River, including the proposed railway route and all of the disputed territory.    On December 30, 1853, he signed a treaty, the Gadsden Purchase, by which the United States paid Mexico $10,000,000 for all of the territory along the present southern boundary of the United States from the Rio Grande to the Colorado River.

United States land laws were extended to New Mexico by act of Congress, July 22, 1854, and the office of United States surveyor-general for the territory was created.    Two years later the surveyor-general investigated Pueblo Indian land claims and recommended confirmation of titles to eighteen Pueblos.    Fort Wingate was established in 1857, near San Rafael, and moved in 1860 to Shashbitgo (Bear), now known as Fort Wingate.

Mesilla Valley and Arizona applied to Congress in 1859 for establishment of a new territory out of the southern half of New Mexico to be known as Arizona.    Although the people of New Mexico favored the measure, it was not adopted.    Formation of the Territory of Colorado, February 28, 1861, reduced New Mexico in size, its northeastern section being included in the new territory.

The controversy between North and South leading to the Civil War was not of vital interest in New Mexico, nor was the question of Negro slavery an outstanding issue.    New Mexicans were accustomed to native peonage and to captive Indian slavery, but in 1861 there were only twenty-two Negro slaves in the territory.    As a conquered province New Mexico had formed no strong attachment to the Union. But as many of the early pioneers and traders over the Santa Fe Trail, and many American officers in the territory were Southerners, the inclination was toward the South.

When the conflict began, numerous resignations and desertions from the Union Army in New Mexico took place, the men joining the Southern forces.    However, when the first Southern advance came from Texas into New Mexico popular feeling went to the Union as the long standing controversy with Texas had bred much ill feeling and Texans were intensely unpopular with the average New Mexican.

Confederate territory reached to El Paso and the Confederate government was anxious to extend it westward to the Pacific coast.    As a transcontinental nation the Confederacy's prestige would be doubled and its credit and resources increased due to the California gold mines. Accordingly, Lieutenant Colonel John R. Baylor of the Confederate

Army came up by Fort Bliss, July 1, 1861, with 600 Texans, occupied Mesilla and captured Major Isaac Lynde's entire command which had abandoned Fort Fillmore.

One month later, August 1, Lieutenant Colonel Baylor organized by proclamation all of New Mexico south of the 34th parallel as the Territory of Arizona, which was recognized by the Confederate Congress. Governor Connelly issued a proclamation September 9 calling for volunteers to resist invasion "by an armed force from the State of Texas," the Confederacy not being mentioned.

Confederate General H. H. Sibley with an army of 2,300 entered New Mexico from Texas and marched northward for the major operation in the Territory. At Valverde, February 21, 1862, he met U. S. General E. R. S. Canby with a force of about 3,800. In a desperate all-day battle the Confederates were victorious. The Confederate forces captured Albuquerque and marched on to Santa Fe, which they occupied March 10 without opposition, the territorial officials having fled.

The Union Army, strengthened by Colorado Volunteers sent into New Mexico, surprised the Confederates on their way to Fort Union in Apache Cañon, near Glorieta, 15 miles southeast of the capital, and a fierce engagement took place. The Confederates retreated, many being captured by the Union forces. Another battle occurred on March 28 at Pigeon's Ranch, during which the Confederate supply train encamped at Cañoncito was completely destroyed. On discovering their loss, the Confederates fell back to Santa Fe, and the Federals returned to Fort Union.

Failure of the advance on Fort Union ruined Confederate plans. General Sibley evacuated Santa Fe, April 8, retreating down the Rio Grande, and Federal forces reoccupied the capital three days later. On April 15 the Union and Confederate forces met at Peralta, where a skirmish ensued, and the Southerners continued their retreat. When the "California Column" came in from the west, July and August, 1862, the Civil War in New Mexico was over.

Due to abandonment of military posts in 1861 for concentration of U. S. Army forces at strategic points during the Civil War period, the major portion of New Mexico was exposed to attacks by Indians, who, taking advantage of the situation, plundered settlements, murdered inhabitants, and drove off livestock.

Consequently an Indian policy was developed for the Southwest. It included rounding up the wild tribes, Apache and Navaho, from all parts of the territory, moving them to the *Bosque Redondo* (circular grove of woods) on the Pecos River near Fort Sumner. There, disarmed and subjugated, they were to be taught farming and made partially self-supporting.

Colonel Kit Carson, the great pathfinder and scout, was sent to subdue and bring in the Mescalero Apache and Navaho. Early in 1863 he had 400 at the Bosque Redondo, and 200 more by the end of the year. In 1864 Colonel Carson marched directly into Canyon de Chelly, the Navaho stronghold, defeated the Indians and transferred 7,000 to the Bosque Redondo.

The depredations of these nomadic tribes were temporarily checked, but the Bosque Redondo colonizing scheme did not work. The Indian nations were hostile among themselves, disease spread, and they faced starvation unless fed by the Government. The Mescalero fled from the reservation in 1866 and went on the warpath, resulting in a change of Indian policy. A peace commission, sent from Washington in 1868, signed a treaty with the Navaho allowing them to return to a reservation in their own country, northwestern New Mexico and northeastern Arizona, the latter territory having been formed February 24, 1863, out of the western half of New Mexico. Fort Sumner was consequently abandoned.

Peonage, or debt servitude, not covered by the Emancipation Proclamation and the Thirteenth Amendent (which applied only to Negroes), was formally abolished in New Mexico by Congress March 2, 1867. During the same year the Moreno gold district, Colfax County, was discovered, and the general incorporation act for mining and other industrial pursuits became a law. Rapidity of communication was effected by the arrival of daily mail from the east (1868), and the completion of the military telegraph line from Fort Leavenworth to Santa Fe July 8, 1869, an epoch-making event.

The alleged sale by Governor William A. Pile, 1869-71, of the Spanish Santa Fe Archives as waste paper was the outstanding feature of his administration. Only about one-fourth of the records were subsequently recovered.

With the erection of the diocese of Santa Fe into a metropolitan see by papal bull, February 12, 1875, the Right Reverend John B. Lamy became Archbishop of the Province.

The Lincoln County War, beginning in 1876, was a bloody feud involving rival cattlemen and political factions with Billy the Kid (William H. Bonney) taking a prominent part. As Territorial officials instituted no effective measures to stop this outbreak, President Hayes on October 1, 1878, appointed General Lew Wallace Territorial Governor for the specific purpose of ending the Lincoln County War. On October 7, the President ordered Federal troops to reinforce the civil authorities, but the war ended before they were called into action.

The first railroad track was laid inside the Territory November 30, 1878; the first locomotive crossed the summit of Ratón Pass on December 7. No other event was more important in transforming New Mexican life. A new era of progress and development was begun, the great cattle boom of the eighties resulting directly from the opening of eastern markets by rail.

With transportation facilities available for bringing in modern mining machinery and exporting mineral products, prospectors and capitalists came into New Mexico creating the first great mining boom, which began in 1879. Mining camps at Los Cerrillos were established in March, the White Oaks camp in September, and the Rio Arriba placer mines were located.

During April of the same year Chief Victorio and his band of Apache left the Mescalero Reservation and went on the warpath, spreading terror throughout southern New Mexico and Arizona until Victorio was attacked and killed in 1883 by Mexican troops in Chihuahua, where he had been driven by American forces. His death was followed by General George Crook's campaign against the Apache.

An echo of the Lincoln County War and an effective check to lawlessness in northeastern New Mexico was the shooting of Billy the Kid, July 14, 1881, by Sheriff Pat. F. Garrett.

In 1885, Gerónimo, one of the last outstanding chiefs of the Apache, fled from the San Carlos Reservation in Arizona and took up the bloody work of Victorio, terrorizing an even wider range than his predecessor. President Cleveland ordered General Nelson A. Miles to capture Gerónimo and place all Apache on reservations. Gerónimo surrendered on September 3, 1886.

When the cattle boom ended, an influx of eastern farmers began, followed by rapid agricultural development. The Pecos Valley became a thriving agricultural center through the discovery in 1888 and 1890 of quantities of artesian water. The Pecos Valley Irrigation and Investment Company's extensive system was begun in 1889, followed by other extensive irrigation and reclamation projects.

Education in New Mexico was advanced when Governor Edmund G. Ross signed, on February 28, 1889, a bill creating a university at Albuquerque, an agricultural college at Las Cruces, and a school of mines at Socorro.

To eliminate confusion and uncertainty relating to title of land grants in New Mexico and other States within territory acquired from Mexico in 1848 and 1853, Congress approved an act, March 3, 1891, for establishing a Court of Private Land Claims, which confirmed titles to almost 2,000,000 acres by June 30, 1904. The Pecos Forest Reserve was created by order of the President January 11, 1892. Seven national forests are now located in New Mexico.

When the capitol building burned May 12, 1892, many public documents were completely destroyed. This disaster, coupled with Governor Pile's alleged sale of the Santa Fe Spanish Archives as wastepaper in 1869-70, and the destruction of the early public documents by Indians during the Pueblo Revolt of 1680, has made the task of New Mexico's historians extremely difficult and given rise to numerous controversies.

With the declaration of war against Spain, President McKinley called on New Mexico, April 23, 1898, for its quota of 340 volunteer cavalrymen for service in Cuba as Rough Riders under Colonel Leonard Wood and Lieutenant Colonel Theodore Roosevelt. In eight days the entire quota was mustered into service. The Rough Riders landed near Santiago on June 22, in time for action two days later at Las Guasimas, the first engagement in Cuba. At El Caney and San Juan they won brilliant victories. Leaving Cuba August 7, they were discharged from service September 15.

New Mexico's capitol building now in use was completed and dedicated June 4, 1900, at Santa Fe.

Floods occurring on the Mimbres River, Grant County, August 29, 1902, rendered hundreds homeless, causing the Governor to ask public aid. During September and October two years later, the most disastrous floods in New Mexico's history took a toll of many lives and demoralized railroad traffic for two months.

A milestone in educational development was reached in 1909 when the United States War Department classed the New Mexico Military Institute as "distinguished," this being the first national recognition accorded one of the territory's educational institutions. Oil was discovered during the same year in encouraging amounts in a well near Dayton, Eddy County.

New Mexico's attempt to attain statehood was blocked again in 1906, when proposed joint statehood with Arizona was submitted to Congress and rejected by the people of Arizona. The Territory's long struggle culminated successfully, however, when Congress passed the Enabling Act and it was signed June 20, 1910, by President Taft. The Enabling Act provided for the admission of New Mexico and Arizona into the Union as separate States after each had adopted State constitutions. New Mexico lost no time in calling a convention of 100 members to draw up a State constitution. It was completed November 21, and adopted by the people January 21, 1911, but fell short of Federal requirements for admittance to statehood.

## STATEHOOD
### 1912

Certain constitutional changes asked for by Congress and President Taft, in August, 1911, were duly made; and, on January 6, 1912, New Mexico was admitted as a State into the Union—the 47th State. On January 15, William C. McDonald was inaugurated first State Governor.

The border town of Columbus, New Mexico, was raided March 9, 1916, by Francisco (Pancho) Villa and 800 or 1,000 of his followers, who set fire to houses and killed several citizens. A punitive expedition of 6,000 under Brigadier General John J. Pershing crossed the border at Columbus less than a week later, March 15, with orders to capture Villa dead or alive. A clash between Mexican and American troops followed April 12, at Parral, Mexico, resulting in diplomatic entanglements, and the United States Government relinquished the chase. Villa's raids recurred in Texas during May, and the President called out the National Guard along the entire Mexican border. The National Guard was mustered out of service April 5, 1917, after Villa's band ceased its raids across the international border.

Following the entrance of the United States into the World War, the New Mexico State legislature in a special session, opening May 1, provided for defense of the State and assistance of the Federal government by creating the State Council of Defense to mobilize and organize New Mexico's total resources, made provision for food conservation, and appropriated $75,000 for war purposes.

In June, 1,300 guardsmen were mobilized for Federal service at Camp Funston, Albuquerque. In September, the first detachment of New Mexicans, popularly known as "Battery A" (of the 146th Artillery), left for Camp Greene, North Carolina, and before the close of the year was in France—the first New Mexican unit to enter the trenches in Europe. The State's contribution to all branches of the service numbered 17,157 men, larger in proportion to population than the average for the whole country.

Food conservation as a war measure played an important part in influencing a majority of more than 16,000 to vote for the prohibition amendment to the State constitution, November 6, 1917.

The development of Hogback and Rattlesnake oil fields on Indian lands in San Juan County during 1922-24, provided definite assurance of New Mexico's position as an important oil State. Artesia oil field, Eddy County, was also discovered during this period.

Three miles of Carlsbad Caverns were surveyed in 1923 by Robert Holly, of the Federal Land Office, and Dr. Willis T. Lee, of the Geological Survey, and later in the same year were proclaimed a National Monument by President Coolidge. Carlsbad Caverns National Park was created by President Hoover, May, 1930. In 1936, the State of New Mexico counted among its assets seven National Forests containing approximately 9,000,000 acres.

The Pueblo Indian Lands Board was created by act of Congress, June, 1934, to settle non-Indian claims to land within, or in conflict with, Pueblo Land Grants.

In 1933, the United States and Mexican Governments ratified a treaty for regulating the course of the Rio Grande from El Paso to Fort Quitman, and for building the dam at Caballo, just below Elephant Butte Reservoir, to assist in the control of floodwaters of the lower Rio Grande.

The New Mexico Relief and Security Authority was established in 1935 by the State legislature to assist unemployed men and women unable to secure work on Federal projects.

# Agriculture and Stock Raising

THE process by which industry has driven agriculture into the background in other States has been to some extent reversed in New Mexico.

Farming has been carried on for centuries, first by the Pueblo Indians who are still farmers primarily; after 1598 by their conquerors, the Spanish colonists; and later by the descendants of the colonists, among whom farming and stock raising have always been of major economic importance. Although the farms were small, the herds of sheep and cattle were large, owing to the once unlimited free grazing area.

With the development of agricultural areas through reclamation and irrigation projects, farming in recent years has supplemented the already important industry of stock raising until their combined product exceeds in value the output of the State's other industries. The growth of dry farming (agriculture wholly dependent upon rainfall) has occurred chiefly in the northeastern and eastern portions of the State, where the average rainfall is 15.5 inches. Irrigation methods are used in the Rio Grande, Pecos, Mimbres, Gila, and San Juan River valleys and wherever water can be obtained from small streams. Artesian and pumping wells are used as additional sources, and such large storage reservoirs as those impounded by Elephant Butte, Santa Cruz, and El Vado dams.

There are in the State 41,369 farms, containing 34,397,205 acres of land, valued in 1937 at $170,150,410. Corn and wheat are the principal crops, the former (dating from pre-Columbian times) being the main crop of the Pueblo Indians. Chili (peppers) and frijoles (beans) are raised extensively by the small farmers of the central and northern plateaus. Cotton growing, first practiced by the Indians along the lower Rio Grande and then abandoned, is being revived in the southern part of the State; cotton production has already brought about a slight population shift, the native Spanish-American people having been displaced by imported Negro cotton pickers. Grains, sorghums, potatoes, legumes, and fruits are also grown in quantity.

An interesting agricultural development is the raising of sugar-beet seed in commercial quantities in the southern part of the State. Experiments carried on by the New Mexico College of Agriculture and Mechanic Arts have demonstrated that beet seed can be produced here in one year's time, whereas it takes two years in Germany, the former source of supply. Field beans in the central and northern sections are an important crop. A peculiarly New Mexican product, shipped to most countries in the western world, is the piñon nut, native to the foot-hills of the rough lands. The crop in good years—the trees bear heavily only once every four or five years—has a monetary value running into hundreds of thousands of dollars.

In 1936 a wheat crop of 1,023,000 bushels and a corn crop of 2,-185,000 bushels were harvested. A yield of 100,000 bales (500-pound) of cotton and a harvest of 288,000 bags (100-pound) of beans augmented the crop total for the year. Further increase in acreage, espe-cially in fruit, wheat, cotton, peanuts, and sweet potatoes, is assured by the recent irrigation project which has been initiated to put 5,000 acres of land under irrigation in the Fruitland area; and agriculture has an assured future in the Pecos Valley area, where conservation measures have progressed far enough to indicate that the valley has sufficient water supply to warrant increasing the acreage under cultivation.

Characteristic of the central and northern portions of the State are the small irrigated farms of the Spanish-American people in small moun-tain valleys and mesas. Individual holdings, divided as families in-creased in size, have become so small that now often half of the adult male population of the rural farming communities are obliged to leave their homes for as much as half the year to seek work and wages in the industrial area. This native Spanish-speaking population, com-prising approximately 52 per cent of the State's total, is naturally pas-toral and agricultural but it is gradually losing its land as more of the public domain, forest lands, and ancient grants, formerly freely avail-able for grazing purposes, is being withdrawn from its use. Of the three population groups using these lands, the Anglo-American minority has access to and controls the largest proportion.

Extensive experimentation and development of methods for insect pest control are carried out at the Agricultural Experiment Station of the New Mexico College of Agriculture and Mechanic Arts in co-operation with county, State, and Federal agencies.

The major insect menace in New Mexico comes from Mexican bean weevils, the wooly aphis (both aerial and subterranean forms), the giant apple-root borer, beetles, cotton bollworms, grasshoppers, cockroaches, onion thrips, peach twig borers, codling moths, and tent and pine tree caterpillars.

For the purpose of combating these, as well as garden insects and other pests, the experiment station publishes numerous bulletins giving methods of preventing infestations and for the treatment of trees, vegetables, shrubs, and other plant life with sprays and chemical dust compounds for which formulas are furnished.

The State extension service, with an agricultural agent in each county, co-operates with the United States Department of Agriculture in times of insect infestation. During 1934 and part of 1935, for instance, the extension service distributed necessary material for grasshopper control furnished by the United States Bureau of Entomology. The materials were prepared by Federal Emergency Relief labor under supervision of county extension agents, and were delivered to the farmers. An epidemic of leaf rollers during the same years was controlled by the agent's advice as to spraying. The extension service agent in Santa Fe County is continuously working on codling moth and aphis control.

Extensive research preparatory to the control of tent caterpillars by use of parasites was undertaken early in 1936 by the WPA Tent Caterpillar Laboratory in Santa Fe. Control operations were launched in the summer of 1937, with the liberation of parasitic flies in the Santa Fe District, and in the Red River, Arroyo Hondo, and Cabestro Canyons in the eastern division of the Carson National Forest. This was followed by liberation of other types of parasites during the summer in the same areas, and also in the Rio Pueblo country near Peñasco where new epidemics had sprung up, and on the Rio de Las Vacas in the Jémez Mountains.

Experimentation and methods instituted and practiced by the WPA Tent Caterpillar Laboratory differ from those of other agencies in that control of a major insect pest is being accomplished exclusively by the use of other parasites.

The livestock industry has undergone many changes in New Mexico since the first horses and sheep were brought into the province by Coronado in 1540. Although some sheep and cattle were introduced into the region by subsequent expeditions, they had disappeared before Juan de Oñate came with his four hundred colonists in 1598. With this permanent settlement the livestock industry in what is now the United States may be said to have begun. Until the rush of cattlemen into the region after the Civil War, sheep dominated the agricultural economy. They fed, clothed, and supported the people and were every man's stock in trade. Vast herds were owned by a relatively few *ricos* to whom the land grants had been made by Spain. They employed herders in great numbers, sometimes on a wage basis, but more often on a so-called *partidario* basis, a form of share cropping in the raising of sheep which is as old as Spanish colonization in New Mexico. Although the system varies, and has been modified in recent times, it remains esssentially share cropping with certain feudal implications. The conditions that favored the system were a land monopoly by the few and the existence of a large, underprivileged group.

It is estimated that a very few large operators own 75 per cent of

*Agriculture: Industry*

*Ernest Knee*

THE RANGE NEAR CIMARRÓN

WEIGHING COTTON, CHAVES COUNTY

TRUCK FARMING, NEAR BLUEWATER

*Lorin W. Brown*  REMUDA, NEAR SPRINGER

SPANISH-AMERICAN VILLAGE ALONG THE RIO HONDO

THRESHING WHEAT WITH HORSES, TRES RITOS

TRES RITOS, A TYPICAL FARMING COMMUNITY

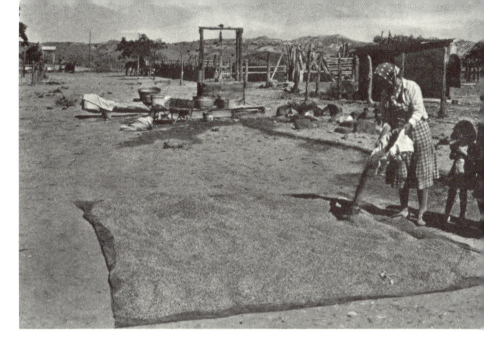

DRYING WASHED WHEAT, JACONA

WASHING WHEAT, JACONA    Note Strings of Chili in Background

OIL WELLS NEAR HOBBS

PANNING GOLD, NEAR SANTA RITA

OPEN PIT COPPER MINES, SANTA RITA

IRRIGATED FARMS, CARLSBAD RECLAMATION PROJECT

CONCHAS DAM

all the sheep in New Mexico. They also control most of the sheep-grazing land. To gain access to these lands the small operator is usually obliged to enter into a share cropping or *partidario* agreement with a large one. Under the terms of this agreement, which is seldom a written contract, the renter "borrows" a certain number of lambs, usually about twenty for each one hundred ewes rented, in addition to grazing fees for use of the land. The renter is responsible for all costs and risks of his venture and must, at the option of the owner, return the same number of ewes of the same age as those originally let. Theoretically, the remainder of the lambs and all of the wool belong to the renter; as the system operates, however, this is rarely true. The large owner extends credit to the renter for his outfit and for supplies for himself and family; and these must be settled for at rates that always apply in such systems of credit. Not all the large sheep operators use this share cropping system.

New policies in the extension of grazing privileges on Government-owned lands, such as the national forests and Indian lands, and new legislation governing the use of the public domain promise a more equable distribution of grazing privileges.

After the close of the Civil War, and before the coming of the railroads into New Mexico, cowmen who were engaged in the raising of livestock in other parts of the West and Southwest were attracted to the immense unoccupied grazing lands of the New Mexican Territory. The only serious threat to the business in those days, as it had been to the Spaniards and Mexicans, was from hostile Indians. The long drives first to army posts in New Mexico, and later to shipping points on the railroads in Kansas, were made at the risk of sudden and massed attacks by the Apache and Comanche. The principal railroad shipping points in the seventies were Dodge City, Abilene, and Newton, Kansas, and cattle were driven to these points from the great ranges and ranches in western Texas and New Mexico. The subjugation of the roving Indians and their confinement on the reservations removed the threat to these cattle movements, and almost simultaneously the railroads pushed deeper into the territory. The great days of the Chisholm and other famed cattle trails were not many but they gave rise to a wealth of romance, lore, and legend.

The end of the colorful cowmen, the somewhat lawless cowboys, and the vast herds was discernible at an early day, but prophets to see it were few. Stock raising as an industry in New Mexico climbed to lofty figures before and during the World War, but the factors that were to tumble it from such heights were already operating in the land. The public range was being opened to homesteaders; sheep were feeding on ranges where cattle could no longer find enough to eat; squatters and farmers were taking up the water rights and planting wheat on the great ranges of the *Llano Estacado* (Staked Plains) ; the cattlemen themselves found that it was more profitable to fatten cattle at the new rail-heads and shipping points, using the hay and grain that the farmers raised on the former grazing lands. Fences barred vast stretches of what had been anybody's range, and the cattlemen fell to quarreling and fighting among themselves. After the World War the bottom fell out of the cattle market, and many of the large operators were ruined.

A general view of the stock industry today presents a very different picture. The modern cattleman is a businessman. By scientific methods he has developed the haphazard practices of the old-time cowmen (who turned their stock loose on the public range and trusted to fortune and nature to return them a profit on it) into an efficient system in which the stock raiser knows the value and number of his herds, is familiar with their productiveness, and can figure with a fair degree of certainty his yearly profits. In the old days the "big" cattleman was one who owned from fifteen to thirty thousand head of cattle; the "big" sheepman owned as many as half a million head. Today a few cattlemen own more than three thousand; and ten or twenty thousand sheep is a big flock for one man or firm.

The large Bell ranch in Harding County and those in the neighborhood of Magdalena are the last outposts of the great ranches and the open range; elsewhere cattle are generally raised in small herds and fattened at shipping points on the railroads. In the San Juan area in the northwest, the huge crops of alfalfa are used to feed cattle in small herds. Oil and gas developments in the east and southwest have made that industry more profitable than stock raising; and in some areas sheep have driven out cattle altogether. Sheep are still raised in great flocks in some areas of the State, notably those in the north and the southwest, and by the pastoral Indian tribes—formerly nomadic huntsmen—the Apache and Navaho.

It is said that there are as many head of livestock in New Mexico today as there were twenty or thirty years ago, but they are confined to half the former area. In 1936 there were 2,337,000 sheep and lambs and 991,000 cattle on the farms; horses, mules, and hogs totaled 222,000.

In 1916, an excellent year for the industry, the value of livestock in the State totaled $22,000,000. In 1938, the total valuation, inclusive of cattle, calves, sheep, and lambs, was more than $56,000,000; and horses, mules, and swine increased this total by another $7,000,000. This was the best year in a decade.

# Industry, Commerce, and Labor

ALTHOUGH New Mexico's largest enterprise is the entertainment of the thousands of visitors who enjoy its vast recreational resources every year, the State embraces a number of industries native to the soil.

With the discovery of gold in the Fray Cristóbal Mountains in 1683, the mining industry began. Pedro de Abalos recorded the *Nuestra Señora del Pilar de Zaragoza* mine, which he discovered while on the northern campaign of Governor Cruzate for the reconquest of the province, following the Pueblo Indian Rebellion of 1680. Turquoise was mined by Aztec and Pueblo Indians before the coming of the Spaniards; an old mine, the *Chalchilhuith,* in the Cerrillos hills near Santa Fe shows the workings of prehistoric Pueblo Indians who mined with stone hammers and axes. Many early mines are mentioned in the Spanish archives in Santa Fe, as it was the search for precious metals that led the Spaniards to the conquest of the land. Miners from Mexico found and opened the great copper deposits at Santa Rita, near Silver City in 1800. Twenty years before the great gold excitement at Coloma, California, and thirty years before the finds on Cherry Creek in Colorado, gold was mined near Santa Fe in the Ortiz Mountains. In 1833 the first gold lode or vein discovered and worked west of the Mississippi was on the famous *Sierra del Oro,* now known as the Ortiz Mine; but actually gold was known and had been worked in the Cerrillos (Sp. little hills) south of Santa Fe, in the time of Governor Don Tomás Velez, 1749-54. As early as the seventeenth century lead and some silver had been worked in this region.

Mining regulations in the form of royal decrees, issued by various viceroys in Mexico, date back to the seventeenth century. The establishment and organization of mining boards and tribunals, relating to silver mines in operation, was a matter of grave importance to officials and settlers in this area, as well as to those farther south in Mexico.

At present nearly all of the gold found in New Mexico comes from base-metal ores. Practically all placer districts in the State yield small quantities of gold, but the amount from this source during recent years has been insignificant as compared with the total gold production. In 1915 gold from New Mexico was valued at $1,461,000, a figure which has never again been equalled. Beginning with 1918 it dropped considerably, due to impoverishment of resources and decreased activity in the Elizabethtown, Mogollón, San Pedro, and Oro Grande districts. During the five year period from 1925 to 1929 the value of gold production varied between a low of $405,803 in 1926 and a high of $727,-162 in 1929. During the depression the value fell as low as $479,753 in 1932. By 1934 it had increased to $954,380, in 1935 it had reached $1,170,225, and in 1936 production dropped to $1,156,295. About 35 per cent of the gold represented in the last figure was produced at the Pecos Mine in San Miguel County. The bulk of placer gold came from the Hillsboro and Pittsburg districts in Sierra County.

Silver production has about equalled that of gold. It reached a peak of $1,162,208 in 1916. In 1918 it declined considerably. From 1926 to 1929 the output varied between $281,383 in 1926 and $597,784 in 1929. The lowest figure for silver production during the depression was reached in 1932 when the output was $322,143. By 1934 it had increased to $686,400 and in 1935 to $763,242. In 1936 production was valued at $900,941. Over 50 per cent of the recoverable silver output in 1935 was from the Pecos Mine in San Miguel County. Other silver-producing districts are the Central, Steeple Rock, and Pinos Altos districts in Grant County and the Mogollón district in Catron County.

Copper reached its maximum output in 1917 with 105,568,000 pounds valued at $28,820,064. A drop occurred in the post-war period, with partial recovery during the following years. In 1929 and 1930 copper accounted for about 70 per cent of the value of New Mexico's total mineral output. An enormous decrease in copper production resulted from the closing in 1934 of the Chino Mines in Grant County, which formerly produced over 82 per cent of the State's total output. In 1935 the total value of the copper mined in New Mexico was only $373,915 compared with $1,890,400 in 1934. In 1936 this rose to $582,544. Most of the copper at present comes from the Ground Hog and San José Mines in Grant County. The Chino Mines reopened in January, 1937. With this resumption copper may again lead New Mexico's metals.

Zinc reached its high point in 1929 with $4,548,060. Though it had fallen to $3,145,392 in 1930, in that year it represented nearly 22 per cent of the value of all metals produced in New Mexico, ranking next to copper. Since 1933 it ranks first among the State's metals. In 1935 the mine production of zinc was $1,947,088 and in 1936, $2,-066,800. The Pecos Mine in San Miguel County was the largest producer of zinc. There are valuable mines also in the Central district of Grant County, and in the Magdalena district in Socorro County.

Lead has always held a somewhat subordinate position among New Mexico metals, reaching its height in 1929 with $1,402,431. In 1930 the value of lead was only 7 per cent of the total of all metal. In 1935 its value was $583,120; in 1936, $609,592.   Like copper it is produced chiefly from complex ores, such as are being worked at the Ground Hog Mine.

High grade iron ores are found near Fierro in Grant County. Manganese used in the manufacture of steels and dry batteries comes from the Little Florida Mountains in Luna County and Boston Hill near Silver City.   Molybdenum, used in making molybdenum steel, is mined in the Red River district near Questa, Taos County.

The richest concentration of metal-bearing minerals now appears to be the Silver City area, but the potential mineral wealth of the State is much too vast to estimate.   The value of total mineral production in New Mexico shows a sharp increase from approximately $5,000,000 in 1905, the year after the United States Geological Survey began to keep detailed records of mine production, to a peak of over $43,000,000 in 1917.   A drop occurred after the World War with a brief recovery in 1920.   In 1921 all minerals responded to a world-wide slump, but from 1921 to 1929 there was a steady increase in production, reaching a total of over $37,000,000 in 1929, followed by another sharp decline for 1930 due to the depression which began in that year.   In 1933 New Mexico ranked fourteenth in mineral production with an output valued at $23,355,000.

A rapidly growing and suddenly developed industry in New Mexico is that of petroleum, more than half of which comes from the Hobbs fields in Lea County in the southeastern part of the State.   In 1936 New Mexico's output of petroleum products was 26,804,000 barrels; the fields, in addition to the above, being the Jal, Copper, Eunice, and Monument in Lea County; the Hogback and Rattlesnake fields in San Juan County and the Artesia-Jackson-Maljamar fields in Lea and Eddy counties.   This output was valued at $22,033,000.   Natural gas from these fields is piped to various New Mexico cities, El Paso, Texas, and as far south as Cananca, Mexico.

An interesting development in the search for oil has been the discovery of carbon-dioxide gas (used in the manufacture of dry ice) in commercial quantities in Torrance, Harding, Union, and Mora counties.   An experimental plant recently erected in Torrance County is so successful that market demands are greater than its daily output of thirty tons.

Oil tests have also resulted in developing artesian water wells in areas where abundant water for irrigation may eventually prove more valuable than if tests for oil had been successful.

Coal has played an important part in the mining activities but has suffered as an industry from competition with oil and natural gas.   It is mostly of a bituminous or sub-bituminous grade.   A small anthracite deposit occurs in the Cerrillos district south of Santa Fe.   The industry in 1935 gave employment to an average of 2,457 persons, paid over $2,000,000 in wages and produced 1,300,00 tons valued at $3,750,000.

Nonmetallic mining in New Mexico is an industry of growing importance. Newly discovered potash deposits are the leaders in this field, with fluorspar and others gaining in importance. The known supplies of gypsum are practically inexhaustible.

After the annexation of the territory by the United States, according to the historian Ralph E. Twitchell, the only currency of any volume here was that distributed by the Federal government to army contractors and troops. Coin of all kinds commanded a big premium, and large quantities were transported across the Plains by merchants and traders, with little loss through robbery or otherwise. Long credits were given by these merchants, and immense quantities of merchandise were handled by large firms whose headquarters were in Santa Fe. Today the commercial picture, with few large enterprises and countless small ones, with banking facilities in every city, county seat, and town, is very different from that of the early days.

After an unsuccessful attempt to organize the Bank of New Mexico in 1863, when the legislative assembly granted a provisional charter to a number of prominent citizens of New Mexico, no attempt to institute a bank was made until 1870. In that year Lucien B. Maxwell, having sold the famous Beaubien and Miranda land grant, applied for a charter for a national bank which was organized at Santa Fe as the First National Bank of Santa Fe. The original stock certificates of this bank bore a vignette of Maxwell with a cigar in his mouth; and "the trusting nature of the promoter of this institution," says Mr. Twitchell, "is well illustrated by the fact that he signed in blank more than a hundred of the stock certificates, so that his absence at his home in Cimarrón might not interfere with the expected activity in stock dealings."

The organization of banks in other parts of the State progressed slowly at first. Las Vegas had one in 1876 and another in 1879. Albuquerque followed with a new bank in 1881, and Silver City, at this time a roaring mining town, had a series of banks of uncertain stability. The Silver City National Bank, however, has weathered all the financial storms that have assailed the town. After the turn of the century, banking organization proceeded rapidly, and prospered up to and through the World War period, when large livestock loans were made on a basis of prevailing prices which ran as high as $60 and $70 per head. After the war, when the extraordinary demand ceased abruptly and deflation started, prices dropped, many stockmen were impoverished, and as a result, many banks failed. Commerce was long in recovering from this blow, and the cattle industry has not yet regained its former eminence in the State's economic structure.

The growth of industry and commerce has not been extensive enough to affect greatly the essential economic and social aspects of the native people, who are naturally agricultural and pastoral. Relatively few have become miners and wage earners permanently, though the inadequacy of land has forced about half of the rural population in the north central counties to seek supplementary work for a part of the year. What labor is employed in industry is largely Spanish-American. Most of the unskilled railroad labor is also Spanish-American, although Pueblo and Navaho Indians are being drawn into this work, and in those cities where the railroads maintain shops a definite industrial aspect is added.

Native arts and crafts, in addition to the older weaving and silversmithing of the Navaho Indians, have in the last decade been revived among the Pueblo Indians and lately among the Spanish-American people. These activities represent a growing industrial nucleus that may, if it can be maintained in the face of machine competition, become significant (see *Arts and Crafts*). In establishing vocational schools in many of the towns and villages, Federal and State authorities have taken cognizance of this possibility. It remains questionable, however, whether a handicraft industry can thrive in this machine age.

The commerce that has accompanied the ebb and flow of industrial activity in New Mexico has changed in character as the interests it served have changed. Today few commercial enterprises, with the exception of the railroads, exist that are comparable to the great trading concerns of Santa Fe Trail days, concentrated in Taos and Santa Fe. The trading firm of Seligman Brothers, for example, engaged in the "Santa Fe Trade," loaded in Kansas City in one day, 83 wagons carrying approximately 3 tons each for transportation over the Plains. No banks or banking institutions existed here in Spanish or Mexican times. The large mercantile houses served the country's banking needs. It was many years after the old trail was closed to commerce before the small merchants and ranchers discontinued the practice of carrying their "bank accounts" with the big merchants of Santa Fe, Las Vegas, and Taos.

Industrial labor has fared better than agricultural, although unionization has been slow, due to the individualistic nature of the Spanish-American. For the same reason radical political movements have gained meager foothold among the working men of the State, finding adherents mostly in the mining areas, where the State's major labor troubles have arisen, and among the unemployed. Labor legislation in the form of mine-safety laws, workmen's compensation and security laws, a prevailing wage law and a wage collection law has substantially strengthened the position of the laboring man. Meanwhile a small but determined unemployed Spanish-American group has attempted to conquer the ancient heritage of fear, reluctance, and inertia—the residue of peonage—and to organize for their collective protection.

New Mexico's labor troubles have had complex backgrounds, but certain factors are prominent as causes.  As a point of contact with the Mexican nation below the Rio Grande, the State has been faced with some labor problems evoked by its geographical position.  Cheap labor has been easily available from Mexico, and mine operators, especially coal operators pressed to keep production costs at the minimum, have taken advantage of this.  A large floating or migratory element of workers has resulted, most of whom are willing to work at subsistence wages or less.

Exploitation of these workers has been easy and unionization difficult.  Sporadic efforts to organize the labor in coal camps have been made, chiefly in Gallup, Dawson, Ratón, and Madrid.  In 1922 a Nationwide strike of coal miners resulted in breaking the union at Gallup, ending union efforts in that place for almost a decade.  In 1933 another strike was more successful, the workers gaining union recognition and collective bargaining.  From the point of view of labor gains, this was probably New Mexico's most important strike.

The railroad brotherhoods represent the oldest union organizations in the State.  In 1922 a national strike of railroad shopmen was broken in New Mexico, but certain concessions were gained.

In the recent resurgence of labor organization, New Mexico has shared in the activity; but progress is slow because the native workers need knowledge, articulate leadership, and bolder assertions of labor's right to organize.  Attempts are being made to organize the agricultural workers in the southern part of the State and to bring the laborers in the lumber industry into some kind of organization.  It is felt that success in these two fields would materially strengthen the position of labor in New Mexico and give impetus to the much needed desire of working men to better their wages, working conditions, and living standards.

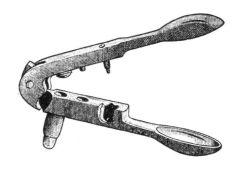

# Transportation

NEW MEXICO, next youngest and fourth largest of the States, is now served reasonably well by its transportation systems. The Santa Fe and the Southern Pacific railways cross it; and branches of major lines weave in and out of canyons to mines, oil and potash fields, and recreation centers. The caravans of one hundred and eighty-two freight bus lines, ninety-seven of which are interstate, ply the highways on regular schedules. Sixty-one passenger bus lines, twenty-eight of which are interstate, carry the traveler over the vast and colorful expanse of the State to almost every village and hamlet. For those who prefer to journey by air, transcontinental planes stop regularly at well-equipped fields.

The history of transportation in New Mexico extends back, of course, into antiquity when goods were carried on human backs. Still later the dog became the beast of burden, but both of these methods still prevailed among the Indians when the Spaniards came. After Coronado's conquest (1540), the horse, mule, burro, and ox were introduced; and following Oñate's permanent settlement of New Mexico (1598) the pack train came into general use. These trains, which slowly made their way from Chihuahua in Mexico to Santa Fe over El Camino Real (The Royal Road), consisted of from five to as many as five hundred burros and mules, with loads securely strapped on their backs. Later came the carreta, with solid wooden wheels, and ox-timbrils, huge two-wheeled carts.

El Camino Real was a very important road in New Mexico's early development. At least as early as 1581 it was traveled by three missionary friars and their escort. From Vera Cruz on the eastern coast of Mexico, this famous highway ran to El Paso, and thence along the right bank of the Rio Grande to Socorro and Albuquerque. From Albuquerque it climbed northward along the flank of the Sandías, ascended La Bajada to the mesa, and crossed the plateau to the foothills of the Sangre de Cristo at the village of Santa Fe.

As early as 1609, committees representing the Church and State met in Mexico City to decide upon a definite method of transporting goods to the new province. This new service became known as the Mission Supply. Every three years thereafter a train was organized and sent to New Mexico, returning to Chihuahua with salt, copper, turquoise, blankets, as well as Indian slaves to be sold in the mining areas of northern Mexico. Until the development of Santa Fe trade with the East, this service, serving the settlements as well as the missions, was the chief means of bringing merchandise to New Mexico; and the trade, which grew to enormous proportions, was carried on until the middle of the nineteenth century over the oldest highway in the United States.

From Coronado's time until the dawn of the Santa Fe trade with the East, no important advancement was made in the type of transportation facilities used. It remained for the indomitable will of the eastern trader, his insatiable curiosity to learn what lay beyond, and his love of an adventurous life to make the Santa Fe Trail, with its eastern terminus in Independence, Missouri, a great and living artery of commerce. Constant improvements in ways of transportation, initiated by these traders, encouraged and hastened the development of modern railroads and bus lines. It was in 1821 that Captain William Becknell, Father of the Santa Fe Trail, assisted by four companions, freighted goods by pack-horses from Missouri to New Mexico. In the following year, he left Franklin, Missouri, with twenty-one men and three wagons, and turned the first wagon wheels over the thick buffalo grass of what was to become a famous road. Becknell was also the first trader to follow the Cimarrón route to San Miguel and Santa Fé. His trail-blazing marked the third epoch in the history of transportation in New Mexico.

Before 1821, fur traders had followed up the Arkansas River, after striking it at Great Bend, to Las Animas River. They then had crossed the divide separating the Arkansas from the Canadian, and had gone down the Canadian Valley east of the Sangre de Cristo Mountains. When the route was changed in 1822, half of it was placed within Mexican territory. Traders then crossed the Arkansas at the upper end of the Great Bend, entered Cimarrón Valley, and crossed the divide to the Canadian in New Mexico. The way to Santa Fe was well known, but the annual caravan established the principal route.

Despite danger from Indians and trouble with the Spanish and Mexican governments, the value of goods carried over the Trail rose from $15,000 in 1822 to $450,000 in 1843, and to more than $5,000,000 by 1855. The long and dangerous trek over deserts and mountains was rewarded by the high prices for which eastern goods were sold, as well as by furs acquired for a song and carried homeward. When the Trail was first opened, calico sold at two or three dollars a yard in Santa Fe. The new route was less dangerous and twelve hundred miles shorter than the old trail to Mexico, and tapped a rich market no longer available to El Camino Real. In consequence of this, New Mexico began to face east instead of south.

Santa Fe was a hospitable place, and when the whips of the drivers were heard, everyone in the town turned out in welcome. After the goods were discharged at La Fonda, the old inn, liquor flowed freely and women were kind. Gaming tables were busy. At Santa Fe, goods from the East were reloaded on organized wagon trains, which thereupon proceeded south to Chihuahua, thereby connecting the new Trail with the old one to Mexico and California. The covered wagons of Becknell's time were replaced by the improved Conestoga and Murphy wagons, accompanied later by carriages and "Democrats," light one- or two-seated spring wagons. Until the coming of the railroads in the eighties, the Santa Fe Trail was one of the main highways of transcontinental travel. Its importance can be inferred from the fact that in 1860 trade movements over the Trail involved in personnel and equipment the following: nine thousand and eighty-four men, three thousand and thirty-three wagons, twenty-seven thousand nine hundred and twenty oxen, and six thousand one hundred and forty-seven mules.

Mules, indeed, were an important factor in the establishment of the route. California had a great number of mules, noted for their size and quality. Some of the New Mexicans took woolen blankets to California to exchange for Indian goods, but decided instead to trade them for mules. The appearance of these huge beasts in New Mexico "caused quite a sensation" (Warner, *Reminiscences of Early California*) because in form and size they were so superior to those used in freighting over the Trail. Thereupon there sprang up a trade in mules "which flourished for some 10 or 12 years."

An experiment in transportation, shared by New Mexico, was the introduction of camel trains by the American Army in 1855. At first they were a great success, making faster time than wagon or mule pack trains. But, before long they became of little use as the fine sharp gravels of the deserts cut and lacerated their tender hoofs, and turned them into limping cripples. In addition, they were a nuisance in the fact that they frightened other beasts, especially mules, which often brayed incessantly in astonishment and terror.

There were other important roads, some of which were especially used in driving great herds of cattle to the markets. Charles Goodnight and Oliver Loving blazed a trail to Cheyenne. This, the Goodnight and Loving Trail, used in the sixties, lay up the Pecos from Fort Sumner to Las Vegas, up the Santa Fe Trail to Ratón Pass, and by Trinidad and Pueblo to Denver. Cooke's Route, which opened the first wagon road across the continent to California, was the path of the Mormon Battalion in 1847. Beale's Wagon Road was one of the first in northern New Mexico and Arizona. Blazed in the fall of 1857, it followed the route near the 35th parallel surveyed by Whipple in 1853, running from Fort Defiance in New Mexico to the Colorado. Another famous thoroughfare of early New Mexico was the Butterfield

Trail which connected St. Louis and San Francisco. After entering New Mexico through El Paso, it ran northward along the east bank of the Rio Grande to Mesilla, crossing the river there and running toward Cook's Peak near Deming, and thence to Shakespeare, just below Lordsburg, and across the present boundaries of the State. "On its better stretches fast stage coaches could travel 165 miles in 24 hours."

Wagon and pack trains carried freight and a few passengers, but credit for development of travel and mail services in New Mexico during the wagon era really belongs to the pony express and stagecoach. In 1849, the year of the California gold rush, the first monthly mail stage began to operate between Santa Fe and Independence, Missouri. Another monthly mail line, connecting Santa Fe and San Antonio, Texas, was of considerable importance to the area served because it made better time than the stage from Missouri. In October 1857, service on both the western mail lines was placed on a weekly schedule, and six-mule instead of four-mule coaches were used. During the same year was established the Butterfield mail stage to towns in southern New Mexico. This line connected with that from San Antonio. The original Overland Pony Express did not cross New Mexico, but an independent pony express from Denver to Santa Fe was established in 1861. This service over the old Taos Trail lasted only one year.

The Butterfield system was discontinued in March 1861, when provision was made by Congress for the transfer of the assets of the Butterfield line to the Central Route; but stages on the Santa Fe, Texas, and several small intrastate lines continued to carry passengers and mail. During the next three decades improved physical equipment made it possible for wagon trains to cover the route in shorter time, and with pack trains they carried the freight until the Atchison, Topeka and Santa Fe Railroad descended the south slope of Ratón Mountain in January 1879. The era of wagon transportation in New Mexico ended in the early eighties.

Meanwhile, surveys had been made to find a southern rail route to the coast. Two of these surveys, those on the 32nd and 35th parallels, passed through New Mexico, and both were reported as feasible. But it was not until December 7, 1878, that the first locomotive came over Ratón Pass, and it was not until after the completion of the Ratón tunnel (2,011 feet through Ratón Mountain) in the fall of 1879 that New Mexico was opened to railway service. Las Vegas celebrated the arrival of the "iron horse" July 4, 1879; and on February 9, 1880, Santa Fe was reached with an eighteen-mile spur from Lamy. The triumphant entry into Santa Fe, 853 miles from the Missouri River, was marked by a huge celebration. Eventually the Santa Fe Railroad was extended to Albuquerque and then south and west to Deming, where it linked with the Southern Pacific Railroad which had come in from California in 1881. A branch of the Santa Fe was also constructed to El Paso; and another from Albuquerque crossed the State Line through Gallup into Arizona. In later years the Belén cut-off from Texico to Dalies created a cross-state route linking the New Mexico trackage in a transcontinental system.

Almost simultaneously with the building of the Santa Fe, the Denver and Rio Grande Western Railroad was extended into New Mexico, entering from Antonito, Colorado, just north of the State Line. A branch was also built from Antonito to Chama in Rio Arriba County, thence to Durango, Colorado, and again southward to Farmington, New Mexico. In 1880 the main line was extended directly south to Española, and in 1885 to Santa Fe. During the period 1880-1910 much trackage was laid in New Mexico to mines, lumbering areas, and resorts, but by 1920 the smaller lines were absorbed by the three main systems now existing in the State.

The coming of the Atchison, Topeka and Santa Fe, the Denver and Rio Grande, and the Southern Pacific completely transformed New Mexican life. New towns were built. Large ranches were created, mines were opened, land values boomed, and New Mexico began to come into its own.

On March 14, 1903, the legislature passed an act making all post roads public highways, though the only highway taken over during the territorial period was El Camino Real. It extended from Ratón to Anthony, fifteen miles north of El Paso. With the coming of the automobile the need of good roads was realized, and in 1913, a year after New Mexico became a state, the legislature authorized a $500,000 bond issue, the proceeds of which were allotted pro rata among the counties for highway building and improvement. Other funds were raised, but not until 1919, when the State was empowered to deal with the Federal government, did highway building begin in dead earnest. Today there are approximately 62,277 miles of road, of which 12,737 miles are Federal and State highways.

Two interstate airlines cross New Mexico. Eastbound and westbound planes of Transcontinental Western Airways, Inc., traveling between Los Angeles and New York, made daily landings at Albuquerque. The Varney Line, from Pueblo, Colorado, to El Paso, Texas, lands at Ratón, Santa Fe, and Albuquerque.

# Folklore

THE Indians of New Mexico have no written language. Their myths have passed orally from generation to generation, and one of the principal tasks of modern ethnologists has been to record and preserve them. In detail these mythic beliefs vary from tribe to tribe, and yet throughout the land occupied by the Pueblo and Navaho Indians there are fundamental similarities and uniformities that afford a basis of thought for a lore of a grandeur and beauty comparable to the great myths of the world.

The mythic core of the Indians of the Southwest can be divided into three parts: the creation myths, the legends which are largely epic narrations, and the folktales and fables.

The Age of the Beginning, or the concept of the origin of the universe held by the Pueblo and Navaho, explains everything in their lives—the heavens, the earth with its plants and animals, and finally man. It explains their relation to one another and their tribal origins. The Pueblo and Navaho alike believe that they emerged from a series of worlds below the surface of the earth. The Pueblo Indians place the point somewhere near their present respective domains, while the Navaho relate that they came to the earth's surface through a sacred lake located in the La Plata Mountains of southwestern Colorado. The general story tells of world levels that are symbolic of the stages of development in the evolution of life. From living matter in water the Mist People, who filled the primal dark world, evolved through insect, reptile, bird, and mammal forms. Finally man, followed by his brothers—the lower examples of animal life—climbed to the world of sunlight and understanding where they were given the shapes they now possess. Man brought with him a tree, maize, and magic.

Closely allied to the creation myths are the legends of the migrations and the parts played by gods and heroes in the early history of the various tribes. This period is called the Age of the Gods or the Great Age. All things were gigantic. Colossal birds dwelt on peaks and huge serpents lived in caves and canyons. The Twin Gods of War slew the enemy giants and beasts who preyed upon the people. Sober-faced Indians today will point to the lava flows, volcanic necks, and dark buttes found throughout the mountain regions of the Southwest, and say that they are the blood and bones of the monsters of this period.

Practically every strange formation in New Mexico is associated in one way or another with the holy people.

The greatest single factor, however, to influence the whole trend of thought of the Pueblo Indians was the cultivation of corn, and the stories and rituals that sprang from the development of this cereal formed the major portion of the second group's legends.

## THE CORN MAIDENS OF ZUÑI

Paiyatuma, the God of Dew, Dawn, and Music, brought the seven Corn Maidens, with their magic wands, to the land of Cíbola. When the morning mists had cleared away and the Dawn God's piping faded, the people of Zuñi found seven plants of corn growing in their dance court, and near the plants stood seven maidens lovelier than the morning stars. The people chanted prayers of thanksgiving to Paiyatuma, and they promised him that they would cherish the maidens and the substance of their flesh. They built a bower of cedar branches for the Corn Maidens and they lighted a fire in the bower. All night the maidens danced to the music of the chants and the drum and the rattle. They danced by the growing corn and motioned upward with their magic wands, that the people of Cíbola would have corn and plenty.

But as time went on the people were not satisfied. There were those among the young man who looked upon the maidens amorously. There were those who plucked at their garments as they danced. The God of Dew called his daughters to his house of the rainbow. "Athirst are men ever for that which they have not," he said. "The people of Cíbola must experience want."

There followed years of trial and famine. Many were the men who went in search of the lost maidens. Finally four holy youths were sent to the Land of Summer. There they found Paiyatuma playing upon his flute and butterflies and birds flying around him. There also were the Maidens of Corn. After the proper offerings and promises were made the God of Dawn gave the four youths the growing plants with the substance of the maidens' flesh, but the maidens went forth as shadows and were seen no more of men. (Adapted from "Zuñi Folk Tales," by Aileen Nusbaum.)

Today corn that is for seed is held by the Pueblo Indians as sacred; it is put into the earth reverently and watched over daily, and for those who remember the story the Corn Maidens come at dawn and motion the plants upward toward the sun.

The Indian folk tales and fables of the third group are built around culture heroes and animals. There are countless stories of this nature told in every Indian village and campsite. The Tewa Tale (E. C. Parsons), "Coyote Steals Fire," is typical of this series.

## COYOTE STEALS FIRE

Long time ago (hao) they always took care of the fire; they did not let them blow it out, they always kept it up. At Yungeowinge, some people were living, and their fire went out. Down at Tekeowinge they were having a big dance, pokwashare. They said, "Where can we get fire? Ours is all gone. Let's go and tell Coyote to go with us. Maybe he can get fire." They made up a bundle of chips and rags, to burn well, to tie on his tail. They said, "Let's not let him know it, so he will bring the fire." They went down to Tekeowinge and the dance began, man and woman, man and woman, man and woman all around. One of those people was watching his fire, sitting near the fireplace. So Coyote old man began to dance with them. The man keeping the fire was watching the dancing. Coyote was turning round, turning round, he put his tail into the fire, it caught fire. He began to run and they ran after him. He was coming to Kosowe. They were pretty nearly catching him. There was Sawe. Coyote said, "Tiupare, help me! They are nearly catching me." So Sawe put the fire on the back of its neck, and flew up the tree. Just then they overtook Coyote. Then they went back home, and when they went back, Sawe brought down the fire to Coyote. So Coyote brought the fire. He wanted to cross the river to Yungeowinge. He could not cross. He said, "If I cross, the fire will go out." He did not know what to do with the fire. He saw some Poteyi. He said, "Won't you help me?" They said, "All right." They took the fire. They began to burn their hands and they said, "r-r rehro." Just the same they still say in just the same way, "r-r rehro." Thus Coyote took the fire to Yungeowinge. They said, "Thank you," and they paid him well. And after that they did not let the fire go out. Thus it passed at Chamita.

Among the Pueblos sometimes the original purity of the Indian folk tale has been confused by Hispanic influences and accretions, but for the most part the bulk of folk material is amazingly free from European dominance.

*Spanish:* The Spanish Colonists in the Southwest have cultivated their traditions as faithfully as any other linguistic group in the United States. From the San Luis Valley in southern Colorado, down the Rio Grande valley of New Mexico into Texas, may be found vigorous remains of sixteenth and seventeenth century folklore. Their musical repertoire includes traditional ballads brought from Spain by the early conquerors, religious songs with a strong flavor of the Gregorian Chant, and lyric *canciones* or songs of the past century. The philosophy of the common people is still contained in the old *proverbios* or proverbs, similar to those Cervantes put in the mouth of Sancho Panza. In isolated communities where modern forms of entertainment are scarce, the folk tale thrives as the literary entertainment of the common people.

The remote source of Spanish-American folk tales is undoubtedly Spain, but the more immediate source is Mexico. There seems to be surprisingly little Indian influence, although there were certain modifications brought about by the geographical conditions and the flora and fauna of the new country.

The following is a brief summary of a New Mexican folk tale gathered from oral traditions entirely. It gives a fair idea of the Spanish-American folk tale in New Mexico as it survives today:

### LOS TRES HIJOS
(The Three Sons)

"Once upon a time there lived an old couple who had three sons. The father gave them their inheritance. The oldest son invested his money wisely and became rich. The second son was not as capable, but he managed to live quite happily on what his father had given him. But Juan, the youngest son, was a spendthrift. He soon became penniless, and then started to seek his fortune.

"On his way Juan met an old man who promised him that if he, Juan, would live with him for seven years, during which time he would be content with his desert home, and not cut his hair, or trim his nails, or shave, he would be allowed to wear a magic coat with pockets always filled with gold. He could spend the money or bury it, yet the pockets would never be empty. For nearly seven years Juan remained in the desert and every day he buried a quantity of gold pieces near a large cactus. He grew so ugly and dirty because of the conditions of the promise that he frightened people, and therefore he was arrested and put into prison. In jail he met the father of three beautiful daughters. They formulated plans to escape, Juan furnishing the money to pay the jailer for their release. The man promised Juan that he would give him one of his daughters in marriage when he had completed his term of seven years in the desert.

"Soon after the expiration of the term, Juan, cleansed and groomed, and appearing as a very handsome youth presented himself at the house of the man and his three daughters. They invited him to dine. The youngest daughter's ring fitted him perfectly, and it was understood that this was the girl he was to marry. Juan went back to the desert, uncovered the treasure he had buried, and returning, married the beautiful girl. I believe," the narrator concludes, "that they are still living happily, unless they are dead."

Although there are elements in this story that can be traced to better known tales, it is a characteristic Spanish-American folk tale because of the blend of old world origin and new world setting.

There is the story of *Juan Catorce*—John Fourteenth, a local variant of the Paul Bunyan legend. There are tales of princes and peasants, of witches, of tricksters and saints, that enrich the store of New Mexican folklore.

The Spanish folk song is an intrinsic part of the Southwest. No other group in the United States is more given to singing, with the possible exception of the southern Negro, than the Spanish-American people of New Mexico. They have today a three-fold repertoire, consisting of [1] the traditional ballads brought from Spain by the Conquerors, [2] the lyrical *canciones* or songs and the racy *corridos* or popular ballads that in the last fifty years have found their way up from Mexico, and [3] the religious ballads and songs called *alabados*.

New Mexican folk songs have changed with social and economic changes. Songs of neighboring areas have been adapted to the Spanish-American people's own tempo and rhythm. Even the words may be changed—a proof that the song is truly popular and capable of rebirth in a different soil.

Pageants and plays are important features of the folkways of the country. These productions are intimately associated with the life of the people; and because of their oral transmission and the many local variations they are colored with genuine folk influences.

The early Spaniards came with a dual mission to the new world—to conquer and to convert. To hasten conversions the first missionaries utilized adaptable features of both the Christian and the pagan religions. In the absence of a common tongue, pantomime and mimicry were resorted to, and the *auto sacramental* or religious plays, served to bridge the deficiency of speech. Some of the first *autos* to be given in New Mexico bore such titles as *Adán y Eva* and *Caín y Abel*. The second cycle of religious plays was based on the New Testament. This cycle began with *San José*, Saint Joseph, and was usually followed by *Las Posadas*, The Inns. *Las Posadas* dealt with the Nativity, beginning with the effort of Mary and Joseph to find lodging in Bethlehem. These were usually followed by one of the two most popular of the Spanish-American plays, *Los Pastores*, The Shepherds. *Los Reyes Magos*, The Magi Kings, and *El Niño Perdido*, The Lost Child (Jesus) preceded *La Pasión*, The Passion, which completed the New Testament cycle with the death of Christ.

In addition to these primarily instructive *autos*, and among the other old plays brought from Spain, is *Los Moros y Los Cristianos*, The Moors and The Christians, enacted on horseback. This *auto* was first presented in New Mexico by Oñate's soldiers in 1598. It represents the defeat of the Moors by the Christians.

Indigenous to the New World is *La Aparición de Nuestra Señora de Guadalupe,* The Apparition of Our Lady of Guadalupe. This play presents the miraculous appearance of the Virgin to the Indian, Juan Diego, in Mexico. A purely native New Mexican play, *Los Comanches,* The Comanches, also performed on horseback, is not of a religious nature, but is based on the capture by the Comanche Indians of two daughters of a prominent Spanish family. Although the story is generally given annually in Taos and Tomé, a small village near Albuquerque, it is also performed in other Spanish-American villages.

Today religious dramas may be found in any Spanish-American settlement in New Mexico where, during the Christmas season, they are presented by a local cast. In some instances the comic element in the play is the source of the greatest entertainment, for sometimes the best actors are cast in these roles. In the transmission of the popular plays from generation to generation no attempt is made to keep them intact; in fact, entire scenes may be omitted or added; and if the music usually associated with a similar play is particularly pleasing to a director, he may unhesitantly incorporate it in his own production. Thus are these folk plays preserved, if not in their purest form, yet as a living part of the folk life in New Mexico.

*Anglo-Americans.* Tales of buried treasure have contributed their share to the stock of New Mexican legends. In the early days of the Spanish occupation it was believed that the padres, on being warned of an Indian attack, hurriedly buried their church vessels and relics in caves or pits near their missions, leaving crude signs or maps to mark the place. Another source of hidden treasure was buried loot of bandits. This gold and other coin was supposed to have been hidden in ruins and caves throughout the State. Some old-timers say that a blue light or flame appears at night above the location of such treasures. Be that as it may, the numerous excavations in church ruins and caves testify to the still existing credulity of treasure seekers.

The story of the Lost Padre Mine of Isleta is one of the most persistent tales in New Mexico. It is told that a padre at the Indian pueblo of Isleta once possessed an exceedingly rich gold mine in which a considerable number of workers were employed. During an attack by Apache Indians the Isleta miners refused to work, and abandoned the mine. The padre, needing more gold, made a last trip to the mine. He was captured by the Apache and died in captivity. The mine has never been located.

The coming of Americans from the East introduced new elements into the already rich folk legendry. They brought a more vivid point of view and traditions that had their origins in other frontier regions. There were the buffalo hunters, the desert rats, and the cowboys. Folk tales concerning the adventures of early explorers and mountain men

and Indian scouts who charted the wilderness sprang up almost over-
night; the stories of Frémont, Kit Carson, Doniphan, and old Bill
Williams have added color to the Anglo-American conquest of New
Mexico.

Among the tales of the early plainsmen and buffalo hunters is the
story of the hunter on the Staked Plains, who, with a party killing
buffalo, was overtaken by a "norther" (a plains blizzard) while far
from camp. Having scant clothing, no shelter, and no matches, and
being bewildered by the storm, he bethought himself to crawl inside a
green buffalo hide, wrapping it tightly about him. When morning
came he found that the hide had frozen stiff and that he was unable to
move or extricate himself. Several days afterward he was found and
released by his companions. Upon being questioned as to how he
managed to survive the experience he explained that, had it not been for
the possession of a quart of whisky and a good set of teeth, he "surely
would of froze to death."

In more recent times an interesting source of folk stories has been
New Mexico's bad men—Billy the Kid, Black Jack Ketchum, "Buck-
shot" Roberts, Tom O'Foliard, and other gun-fighters of the territorial
days, when many men acted on the theory that "the law didn't come
west of the Pecos." All through the Ruidoso country stretch the trails
of "Beely the Keed" or "El Cabrito," as he was called by the Spanish-
speaking people, who loved him too well to betray him. The wild
escapades of this outlaw culminated in his "capture by shooting" by
Sheriff Garrett of Lincoln County. He died at the age of twenty-one
after gaining the reputation of having killed a man for each year of his
life, leaving behind him a lasting legend of a western Robin Hood. A
number of people in remote parts of the State believe that the Kid is
still alive in Mexico, despite the fact that the circumstances of his death
are well authenticated.

Typical of the stories told of those reckless days is an incident in the
career of Clay Allison, the notorious "Corpse-maker" of Colfax County.
One day a desperado named "Chunk" disagreed with Allison over a bet.
Chunk, seeking to trick Allison, invited him to dinner at the hotel.
Taking their places at the table, each laid his pistol beside his plate, and
when coffee was served in large mugs, they facetiously used their guns
for spoons, each keeping a sharp eye on the other. Chunk, after stirring
his coffee, pretended to lay his weapon aside, but instead rammed it
under the table and fired at Allison. His bullet went wide. One shot
from Allison, and Chunk fell forward on his plate, dead.

The stories of these early outlaws are often charged with dry humor.
One of the numerous yarns told about rustlers deals with one Joe
Asque. Narrowly escaping a sheriff's posse at Lake Valley, he hid on
Carrizo flats. At this point there was much good water, and watching

the stock come to drink, Joe's itching rope longed for action, and so, choosing a string of five fat saddle horses, he headed them east. Fifteen miles farther he came to a wooded canyon, where he saw a wagon approaching with two men in it. He prepared to greet them but as the team came abreast it stopped, and Joe found himself gazing into the black hole of a Winchester. "Put them up and get down," the men told him. Joe, armed only with a six-shooter, obeyed. His captors tied his hands behind him and slipped his own rope over his head. Then the wagon was driven to the nearest tree, where the rope was tied to a branch, and Joe forced to step off the wagon, where he was left hanging with his toes just clear of the ground. Joe was small and light, which saved his life. The knot in the rope happened to be under his chin, and although it was hard for him to breathe, he did not actually choke. After some time he freed his hands, and with his pocket knife cut the rope. Later, in commenting on his experience, Joe said the hanging was not so bad, but riding his old horse bareback for a hundred miles to his home range certainly made him mad.

The cowboys have left many ballads which reflect the hardy life of the outdoors and the camaraderie of trail and camp. Many of the tales of cowboy and sheepmen were composed around the campfire, where men talked and sang under the stars. The popular ballad, "Little Joe the Wrangler," first published in 1908 and claimed for various writers in the Southwest, was composed by N. Howard (Jack) Thorpe, a cowboy, around such a campfire. Others originated in small settlement supply stores, which also served as "hang-outs" for punchers, cowmen, and prospectors. There on winter nights the men sat around a big stove and "swapped yarns." Such a group of weather-beaten men were gathered one night when one of them said: "I was at the Seven Springs Canyon last week and things shore look bad. That old dog, Soldier, took over an hour to travel ten feet from the corral to the house."

"How come?" asked several of the boys.

"W–e–l–l, it was this-a-way. You know old Uncle Johnnie Root who lives there? Though he has a bunch of cattle, he is still an old prospector, always out to find the richest gold mine ever, and he had a shaft in the hill by his house. Well, a couple of weeks ago he thought he would drive his shaft a little deeper. So he dug up his fuse, caps and giant, but found the giant had bin froze. So he poked six sticks into the oven to thaw out, and leaving old Soldier in charge, started for the corral. He just closed the gate when there was a terrible noise and he see his roof blow straight up. Johnnie ambled over to the hole in the ground where his house had bin but outside of a box of crackers and a necktie, he couldn't find nothing.

"Then he began to whistle for his dog, Soldier. All day he hunted and late in the evening he heard a whimper and spied old Soldier on the topmost branch of a big pine, where he had been tossed by the explosion. That dog was so tickled to see him that he jumped. He landed on his four feet all right, but that two hundred foot drop drove all four legs up into his body, leavin' only his paws sticking out. He seems to have recovered and his legs are firmly knit, but you can see if you go to Seven Springs, he can't step over an inch at a time and it takes him a hour of hard work to crawl ten feet."

Tales of the cattle trails in the Staked Plains country, of early ranchmen and railroaders, help to swell the volume of New Mexico folklore. Though many collections of cowboy and ranch, of Spanish and Indian folklore have been published, there is still a vast fund of material yet to be recorded.

# Contributions to the Language

N EW MEXICO has contributed generously to the idiomatic speech of the United States. The vernacular of the State took form and color from English, Spanish, French, and the American Indian tongues. It has not only broadened the everyday speech of New Mexico but has enriched the American language with many words of universal appeal. These various language influences were effective during the colonization by Spanish Conquistadores and the influxes of French and Anglo-American trappers, traders, trail blazers, and pioneers who absorbed the Spanish idiom and added their own to the region. Later, the cattle empire made its special contributions.

Since New Mexico was a province of Spain and Mexico for more than 200 years, Spanish words such as cañón, lariat, stampede, and barbecue naturally found their way, with but slight changes, into the English vernacular. Many of the Spanish or Anglicized words of Spanish origin which are listed as belonging to the New Mexico idiom may be in general use elsewhere. But the first contact between Anglo-Americans and Spanish-speaking population occurred in New Mexico and also at a date earlier than in the surrounding States. Some words now in common usage in the Southwest date back to the era when New Mexico was the home of various Indian tribes. Among these words, still preserved in something like their original form, are *chimajá, punche* or *puncho, tegua* or *tewas* and *tombé.*

Many other Indian words found in the regional idiom have come into English through a form of Mexican-Spanish that derives mainly from the original Aztec or Nahuatl. Examples of these are *chicle, chili, chocolate, coyote, jacal* (hacal), *mescal, metate, mesquite, sotol, tamale, tapadero, tequila, tomate* and *zacatón.*

French fur trappers, as early as 1733, and continuing through Santa Fe Trail days, left their mark in such words as "cache," "fawche," "sashay," "travee," furnishing another artery of lingual exchange between east and west.

The Anglo-American trappers, traders, and pioneers liberally seasoned New Mexico's speech, dating this period with "all set," "big talk," and "blaze away." Many of the words in this linguistic heritage are now intrenched in our national vernacular. They recall the trail and its life and frequently stem from Anglicized variants of the Spanish.

Mining activity with its "high grader," "hill nutty," and "pay dirt," brought a small but richly expressive contribution. The era of early transportation used Spanish terminology. The whole pack-train outfit, in charge of a *mozo* or *arriero* was known as the *atajo* (*hatajo*). The animals, burros, mules, or horses, made up the *remuda*. The pack-saddle and equipment (*the aparejo*) was secured to the animals by *cinchas* and *látigos,* while the halter became a *hackamore* (*jáquima*).

The cattle-raising era, following frontier trail days, was responsible for the Anglicization of numerous Spanish terms as they appear in that part of the present national vocabulary which deals with this industry. Practically all the cowboy equipment was obtained from Spanish-American sources. The *bronco* of today and the mustang of yesterday came from the same source, and the names of the animals and articles used were also of a common origin. Fresh mounts were secured from the *remuda* or *caballada,* and the horse-wrangler who was generally a descendant of Mexican-Spanish *caballerango.*

One outstanding example of a cowboy term of Spanish derivation is "dogie," a motherless calf. The usual explanation of the term is that it came from "doughie," "dough-guts," or "dough-bellies," used by cowboys in referring to motherless calves with abnormally extended bellies, the result of being forced to subsist on a grass instead of milk diet. According to N. Howard (Jack) Thorpe, an old time cowboy, it was derived from the Spanish word *dogal,* "to tie by the neck." Spanish-American vaqueros, when milking a cow, tied the calf with a rope that allowed it to nurse only one teat, leaving the rest for the milker; the name which the milker used for the calf was "dogal," corrupted by Anglo-American cowboys to "dogie."

Changes in Spanish words adopted into the English vernacular were not confined solely to spelling and pronunciation: sometimes the original words also acquired different meanings; for example, *rodeo* to the Spaniard and early border ranchman meant a roundup of livestock on the range. The present day application of *rodeo* (Anglicized to rōdeo) means an exhibition of professional cowboy contestants before paying spectators.

The general adoption of common Spanish words from the written language may be said to have begun with General Pike's Journal in 1807, and to have continued by other chroniclers of the New Mexican scene, who introduced or gave *baile, fandango, frijoles, hacienda, rancho, rebozo, señoritas, siesta,* and *tortillas* to the eastern readers.

The significance of the Mexican War and the American occupation of New Mexico (1846) included the absorption of more than a few Spanish words into the vocabularies of United States soldiers, as a result of their daily contacts with the Mexicans.

Two outstanding contributions, *gringo* and *"greaser,"* terms respectively designating American and Mexican, came from this period. Contrary to common fallacy, the origin of *gringo* was not from the popular army song of the day *Green Grow the Rushes O,* but was a corruption of the Spanish word *griego*—Greek. It was first used as such in Spain where Greeks employed in the Spanish Army were called *gringos.* Ultimately the word came to mean all foreigners and is commonly used in this sense today in Mexico and South America. In New Mexico, where *gringo* was first used to designate all non-Spanish speaking peoples, it is today applied particularly to Anglo-Americans.

While they were originally used to designate nationalities alone, *gringo* and *greaser* were later used as terms of contempt. Whipple in his "Explorations" (1856) records his attendance at a ball where the natives were "heard talking . . . of gringos . . . ," and he adds in a footnote: "*gringos* . . . Mexican term of contempt." Today in Santa Fe, Spanish-American school children often call each other, if frecklefaced, *gringo salado;* and in games of robbers and police the robbers are always called *gringos.*

No etymology for the term *greaser* is known. It appears to have been coined by *gringos* or other foreigners of the early American occupation period to designate the Mexican workman. Stories of its origin vary, one contending the name was given because of their love of greasing their hair to intensify the dark color; another is that it came from the excessive use of oils and fats in Mexican cookery. Another story also relates that in the days of oxcarts and freight wagons, there was always a Mexican *peón* assigned to grease the axles and he was called the *greaser.* The present use of either *gringo* or *greaser* is considered a taunt or term of contempt.

The Santa Fe Trail freighters of the early sixties recognized two classes among Spanish inhabitants, the *ricos* (rich) and *peones* (poor) To the latter class they applied *greaser* contemptuously.

The revolution in Mexico, in 1910, with Villa's raids into New Mexico and General Pershing's pursuit across the Rio Grande, gave Spanish terms a new interest, especially in the press reports, and also served to revive the term *gringo.*

Contemporary literature relating to the Southwest, including the prose or poetry of Charles F. Lummis, Mary Austin, Willa Cather, J. Frank Dobie, Alice Corbin, Nina Otero, Harvey and Erna Fergusson, and N. Howard Thorpe, demonstrates how spontaneously the native-born or naturalized people of that region employ the language handed down from the Conquistadores. Many who now employ these words are not aware of their Spanish origin. Spanish continues to be the sole language of some of the State's native-born Spanish-Americans, while others of Spanish extraction use English and Spanish with equal facility.

# GLOSSARY

| | | |
|---|---|---|
| ABARROTE | (ah-bar-o'tä) | Retail grocery (local usage). |
| ABAJO | (ah-bah'ho) | Lower. *Rio abajo,* lower river. |
| ACEQUIA | ('ah-sä'kē-ah) | Canal, thence irrigation ditch. |
| ADIÓS | (ah-dē-os') | Goodby. |
| ADOBE | (ah-dō'bä) | Unburnt, sun dried bricks of earth mixed with straw. |
| AGUA | (ah'wah) | Water. |
| AGUARDIENTE | (ah-gwar-dē-än'tä) | A term for whiskey or brandy. |
| ALAMOGORDO | (al-ah-mo-gor'do) | Round (or fat) cottonwood tree. |
| ALBONDIGAS | (al-bon-dē'gahs) | Meat balls. |
| ALFORJA | (ahl-for'hah) | Saddle bag. |
| ALGODONES | (ahl-go-do'nes) | Cotton fields. |
| ALTO | (ahl'to) | High. *Pino alto,* tall pine. |
| AMIGO | (ah-me'go) | A friend, *Amigo mío,* my friend. |
| AMOLE | (ah-mo'lä) | Palmillo plant called soap-weed; soap is made from its roots. |
| ANCHO | (ahn'chō) | Broad. *Rincón ancho,* broad corner. |
| APACHE | (ah-pah'chä) | Apache. Indian word for enemy. |
| APAREJO | (ah-pah-rä'ho) | Pack-saddle and equipment. |
| ARENA | (ah-rä'nah) | Sand. *Llano arenoso,* sandy plain. |
| ARRIBA | (ah-rē'bah) | Upper. *Rio arriba,* upper river. |
| ARRIERO | (ah-rē-är'o) | Mule driver. Especially for pack-trains. |
| ARROYO | (ah-rō'yō) | Wash from flood waters. |
| ATAJO | (ah-tah'ho) | A short-cut. |
| BAILE | (by'lä) | A ball, dance. |
| BAJADA | (bah-hah'dah) | A sharp descent. |
| BELIN'KA | | Navaho for American. |
| BIENVENIDO | (bē-än-vä-nē'dō) | Welcome. |
| BIG LOOP | | The lasso of a cattle-thief. |
| BONITO | (bo-nē'tō) | Pretty. *Pueblo bonito,* pretty pueblo. |
| BOOTHILL | | A kind of burial ground. |
| BOOTZIES | | Indian term for Mexican sweet-cakes. |
| BOSQUE | (bōs'kä) | Thickly wooded area. |
| BOTAS | (bō'tahs) | Boots. |
| BOX CANYON | | A canyon with one entrance |
| BULTO | (bōōl'tō) | Bulk, bust (Scul.) and locally: image of saint carved in wood. |
| BRAND-BLOTTER | | A person who illegally alters a brand. |
| BREAKS | | Many small rough canyons. |

| | | |
|---|---|---|
| BRONC-PEELER | | A cowboy who tames horses for riding and range work. |
| BROOMIES | | Wild horses. |
| BRUJA | (broo'hah) | A witch. |
| BUENOS DIAS | (bwāy'nōs-dē'as) | A greeting, Good day. |
| BUENAS TARDES | (bwāy'nahs-tar'dās) | Good afternoon. |
| BULLDOGGING | | To throw (a steer) by seizing its horns and twisting its neck. |
| | | |
| CABALLADA | (cah-bah-yah'da) | A herd of horses. |
| CABALLERANGO | (cah-bah-yār-an'gō) | A herdsman; a wrangler of horses (local usage). |
| CABALLERO | (cah-bah-yā'rō) | A gentleman; a horseman. |
| CACHE | (kash) | To hide away. A place of concealment. |
| CACIQUE | (kah-sē'kā) | A wiseman or councilman of an Indian tribe. |
| CALABOZO | (kah-lah-bo'so) | Jail. |
| CALIENTE | (kah-lē-ān'te) | Hot. |
| CAMINO | (kah-mē'nō) | Road or highway. |
| CAMPIÑAS | (kahm-peen'yas) | Fields. |
| CAÑADA | (kahn-yah'dah) | Land between. |
| CANCIÓN | (kahn-sē-ōn') | A song. |
| CAÑÓN | (kahn-yon') | A ravine. |
| CANTINA | (kahn-teen'ah) | A saloon. |
| CANTO | (kahn'tō) | A chant. |
| CANTORES | (kahn-tor'ās) | Official chanters. |
| CAPULÍN | (kah-poo-leen') | Choke-berry or choke-cherry. |
| CARNE | (kar'nā) | Meat. |
| CARRETA | (kah-rā'tah) | Two wheel cart. |
| CASA | (kah'sah) | House. |
| CENA | (sā'na) | Supper. |
| CERRO | (sā'rō) | Hill or peak. |
| CHAMIZO | (chah-mē'sō) | Brush used as kindling wood. |
| CHAPAREJOS | (chap-ah-rā'hōs) | Chaps. |
| CHAPARRAL | (chah-par-rahl') | A low growing brush. |
| CHAPARRAL COCK | | State bird of New Mexico. The road-runner. |
| CHAPS | (chaps) | Leather protectors used by cowboys (abbrev.). |
| CHARRO | (chah'ro) | Gaudy clothes of embroidered fabrics. Also an ill-bred person. |
| CHICO | (chē'kō) | Small. *Rio chico,* little river. |
| CHIHUAHUA | (chē-wha'wha) | A city in Mexico. |
| CHIMAJÁ | (chē-ma-ha') | A medicinal herb; locally wild celery. |
| CHONGO | (chōn'gō) | The queue style in which hair is worn by the men of the Isleta Indian tribe. |
| CHOUSING | | Hurrying cattle or horses. |
| CHUCK WAGON | | Wagon used during a roundup for cooking and carrying foodstuffs. |

| | | |
|---|---|---|
| CHUPADERO | (choo-pah-dā'ro) | Cattle tick. |
| CÍBOLA | (sē'bō-lah) | Buffalo. |
| CIENEGA | (sē-ā'nā-gah) | A marshy place. |
| CIGARRITO | (sē-gar-ree'tō) | Cigarette, particularly of cornhusk paper. |
| CINCHAS | (sēēn'chas) | The saddle girth. |
| CLAN | | An Indian group usually named for animals, seasons or vegetables. Each pueblo may have several clans. |
| COCINERO | (kō-sēē-nā'rō) | Cook. |
| COLCHÓN | (kōl-chōn') | A mattress. In early days it was placed on floor and used as bed. |
| COMIDA | (kō-mē'dah) | Dinner, food. |
| COMO LE VA? | (kō-mō-lā-vah') | How are you? |
| COMPAÑERO | (kom-pahn-yer'o) | Friend or companion. |
| CONCHAS | (kōn'chahs) | Shell or flat silver discs. |
| CONQUISTADORES | (kōn-kees-tah-dō'rās) | The early Spanish explorers of New Mexico. |
| COUNT COUP | | Trailsmen's term for counting victims of a battle. |
| COWPOKE | | A cowboy. |
| COW-WOOD | | Dried manure chips used for fuel. |
| COYOTE | (Sp. kō-yō'tā) | A small species of wolf. Common to plains of North America. The prairie wolf. |
| CREASED | | To be slightly injured by a knife or bullet. |
| CRISTO | (krē'stō) | Christ. |
| CRITTER | | An animal. |
| CRUCES | (crū'sēs) | Crosses. |
| CUMBRES | (kōōm'brās) | A mountain ridge. |
| CUNA | (kōō'nah) | Cradle; also a kind of dance. |
| CUTTING CATTLE | | Separating cattle from a herd. |
| DÍA | (dē'ah) | Day. |
| DIABLO | (dē-ah'blō) | Devil. |
| DINE | (din-nā) | The people. Navaho name for themselves. |
| 'DOBE DOLLARS | | Mexican dollars (*pesos*). |
| DOGAL | (dō-gahl') | To tie by the neck. |
| DOGIE | (dō'gē) | Motherless calf. |
| DOS REALES | (dōs-rā-ah'lās) | Twenty-five cents; two bits. |
| DRIFT | | To travel aimlessly. A drifter is such a traveler. |
| DRIFT FENCE | | A fence erected to stop cattle from drifting. |
| DUEÑA | (dōō-ān'yah) | Chaperone. |
| DULCE | (dōōl'sā) | Sweet, also candy. |
| DUST THE TRAIL | | To travel a trail. To start or leave. |
| DUSTING PAN | | Pan used in placer mining. |

| | | |
|---|---|---|
| EAR-MARK | | To cut ears of cattle for identification. |
| ESCONDIDO | (es-cōn-dē'dō) | Hidden. *Rincón escondido,* hidden corner. |
| ESTUFA | (es-tōō'fa) | Indian council chamber, like a kiva. (Derived from Spanish stove because of the heat in the ill-ventilated structures.) |
| FAJAS | (fah'has) | Bright girdles woven and worn by Indians. |
| FANDANGO | | Dance. |
| FARO | (fä'ro) | A gambling game. |
| FEEL LIKE CHAWIN' | | Trailsmen's term for hunger. |
| FIESTA | (fē-es'ta) | A feast and celebration of carnival spirit. |
| FILIGREE | | Mexican ornaments of intricate, lacy designs, woven of gold or silver wire. |
| FLAME THROWER | | Cowboy term for gun. |
| FLOUR GOLD | | Fine gold dust. |
| FOFARRAW | | Trailsmen's term for fancy dress. |
| FONDA | (fōn'dah) | Inn. |
| FREEZE ON TO IT | | Trailsmen's term to hold fast. |
| FRIJOLES | (frē-ho'lās) | Beans. |
| FUZZIES | | Poor quality horses. |
| GERÓNIMO | (Her-on'ē-mo) | Jerome. |
| GILA MONSTER | (hē'lah) | A poisonous lizard. |
| GLORIETA | (glō-rē-ā'tah) | Bower, arbor. |
| GOLONDRINA | (gō-lōn-drē'na) | The swallow. |
| GRACIAS | (grah'se-ahs) | Thanks. |
| GRACIAS A DIOS | (gra'se-as ah-dē'ōs) | Thanks to God. |
| GRAMA | | A wild grass. |
| GRAN QUIVIRA | (grahn-kē-vē'rah) | New Mexico National Monument. |
| GREASER | | Term of contempt for Mexican. |
| GRIEGO | (grē-ā'gō) | Greek. |
| GRINGO | (grēn'go) | A term of contempt for Anglo-Americans or any, except Indians, not speaking Spanish. |
| GROUNDING | | Cowboy term for letting bridle reins touch ground; horse then stands without tying. |
| GRUB-LINE RIDER | | Usually a lazy cowboy who rides from one ranch to another without offering to work or pay for his food or shelter. |
| GRUBSTAKE | | Food and supplies furnished a prospector for interest in located mines. |

| | | |
|---|---|---|
| GUACO | (gwah'-kō) | Bee balm, a plant, the roots of which are used to obtain a dye for decorating pottery. |
| GUITARRA | (gē-tar'rah) | Guitar. |
| HACIENDA | (ah-sē-ān'dah) | A ranch house. |
| HACKAMORE | (hack'a-more) | Halter or headstall. |
| HAIR BRANDING | | Brand made by burning only hair. A temporary brand used on trail herds. |
| HATAJO | (ah-tah'hō) | Herd or flock. |
| HEELING | | Roping a calf by hind legs. |
| HERMANO MAYOR | (ār-mah'no mah-yor') | Chief brother, headman. |
| HERMOSO | | Beautiful. *Ojo hermoso,* beautiful spring. |
| HIGH-GRADER | | One who steals rich ore from mines. |
| HILL-NUTTY | | An eccentric miner or prospector. |
| HOGAN | (hō'gan) | The Navaho house, a crude octagonal structure of adobe-covered logs. |
| HOMBRE | (ōm'brā) | Man. |
| HONDA | (ōn'dah) | Sling, locally; a loop or ring on lariat end to slip a rope through and make a large slipknot. |
| HONDO | (ōn'dō) | Deep. *Arroyo hondo,* deep arroyo. |
| HOORAW | | Derision. |
| HUECO | (wā'kō) | Hollow. *Cerro hueco,* hollow peak. |
| HUMP YOURSELF | | Trailsmen's term for haste or diligent work. |
| HUNG UP | | An accident in which a cowboy is unseated from his horse and his foot caught in a stirrup. |
| INDITA | (ēn-dē'tah) | Little Indian; a kind of song. |
| INJUN-BROKE HORSE | | A horse broken for mounting from either side. |
| ISLETA | (ēs-lā'tah) | Islet or little isle. |
| JACAL | (ha-kahl') | A crude hut. |
| JÁQUIMA | (ha'kē-mah) | Headstall or halter (same as hackamore). |
| JERKY | | Sun-dried meat. |
| JORNADA DEL MUERTO | (hor-nah'-dah moo-ār'to) | Journey of death. |
| JUMP UP A LOT OF DUST | | A big roundup, or great haste. |
| KAYAKS | (ki'aks) | Pack-saddle bags. |
| KIVA | (kē'vah) | Indian ceremonial chamber with entrance by ladder through roof. |

| | | |
|---|---|---|
| KO-KO | | Zuñi Indian gods. |
| KOSHARE | (kō-shar'ā) | Keres Indian for ancestral spirits; delight makers. |
| LADRÓN | (la-drōn') | Thief. |
| LAGUNA | (la-gōō'nah) | Lake. |
| LAMY | (lah-mē) | John B. Lamy, 1814-1888. Archbishop of New Mexico. Town pron. Lā'mē. |
| LÁRIAT | (lah'ri-at) | A lasso. |
| LASSO | (lah'sō) | A rope used to catch stock; made of buffalo hide or rawhide in early days. Now commonly of hemp, forty to seventy feet in length. (Sp. lazo.) |
| LAS VEGAS | (vā'gahs) | The meadows. |
| LÁTIGOS | (lah'tē go) | Cinch-strap. |
| LINE CAMP | | A camp established on the far boundaries of a ranch. |
| LINE-RIDER | | A cowboy who guards ranch boundaries, turning back stray stock and repairing fences. |
| LLANO | (yah'no) | A plain. |
| LOCO | (lō'cō) | Crazy. |
| LOMA | (lo'mah) | A low hill. *Loma prieta,* dark hill. |
| LONGHORN | | Spanish cattle brought into Texas from Mexico; so designated because of their long horns. |
| LUMINARIAS | (lōō-mē-nah'rē-ahs) | Small bonfires. |
| MADRE | (mah'drā) | Mother. |
| MAGUEY | (mah-gā') | Century plant. Lasso ropes, sisal, and an intoxicating drink are made from it. |
| MALPAIS | (mahl-pah-ēs') | Volcanic rock (lava). |
| MAÑANA | (mahn-yah'nah) | Tomorrow. |
| MANTA | (mahn'tah) | Mantle or small shawl. |
| MANZANA | (mahn-zahn'ah) | Apple. |
| MARIJUANA | (mar-e-whah'na) | An herb of the hemp family intoxicating in its effect when smoked. |
| MATACHINES | (ma-tah-chē'nās) | Aztec drama dance. |
| MAVERICKS | | Unbranded range stock. Name derived from Sam Maverick, a Texan, who left most of his cattle unbranded. |
| MAYORDOMO | (ma-yōr-do'mō) | Foreman. |
| MESA | (mā'sah) | Table. High table or table land. |

| | | |
|---|---|---|
| MESQUITE | (mes-kēt') | A desert shrub. |
| MESILLA | (mā-sē'ah) | Little table land. |
| MESTIZO | (mes-tē'-so) | Indian half-breed. |
| METATE | (mā-tah'tā) | Stone upon which corn is ground by hand. |
| MILPAS | (mēl'pahs) | Fields; maize lands. |
| MIMBRES | (mēm'brās) | Place of willows. |
| MOIETIES | (moi'ē-tēs) | A social division among the pueblos. |
| MONTE | (mŏn'tā) | A gambling game. (Sp. forest or hills.) |
| MORADA | (mō-rah'dah) | A meeting or chapter house of Penitentes. |
| MORO | (mō'rō) | Moor. |
| MORRO | (mō'rrō) | Headland, bluff. *El morro,* the headland. |
| MOUNTAIN CANARY | | Nickname for a burro. |
| MOZO | (mō'sō) | Young man, youth, man servant. |
| MUERTE | (moŏ-ār'tā) | Death. |
| MUSTANG | | Horses directly decended from Spanish mestaños brought by the conquistadores. An unbroken horse. |
| NESTERS | | Homesteaders. |
| NIGHT-HAWK | | Man who guards the saddle horses at night during a roundup. |
| NORTE | (nŏr'tā) | North. |
| NUEVO | (noŏ-ā'vo) | New. |
| OCOTILLO | (o-ko-tē'yo) | A wild thorny desert shrub. |
| OJO | (ō'hō) | Eye, spring (of water). |
| ON THE PROD | | Angry—cowboy ready to fight. |
| ORO | (ō'rō) | Gold. *Cerro oro,* gold hill. |
| PADRE | (pah'dray) | Father, priest. |
| PÁJARO | (pa'ha-ro) | Bird. |
| PALAVER | (pal-ă'ver) | To discuss. |
| PASTORES | (pahs-tō'rās) | Shepherds. |
| PATIO | (pah'tē-o) | Inner court yard. |
| PATRÓN | (pah-tron') | Boss. |
| PAY DIRT | | Gold bearing sand. |
| PEÑA | (pān'yah) | Rock. |
| PEÑASCO | (pān-yas'cō) | Large rock. |
| PENITENTE | (pān-ē-tān'tā) | A secret religious order, practicing flagellation and crucifixion. |
| PEÓN | (pāón) | A poor person or servant. |
| PESO | (pā'sō) | Mexican and other Spanish-American unit of currency. |

| | | |
|---|---|---|
| PEYOTE | (pā-yō′tā) | A species of cactus; the ripened seed is used by Indians in ceremonials. |
| PENOLE | (pā-no′lā) | Parched Indian corn mixed with cold water. |
| PIKI | (pē′kē) | Indian paper-thin bread of ground corn; baked on a hot stone. |
| PIÑÓN | (pēn-yōn′) | An edible pine nut. |
| PINTO | (pēn′tō) | Spotted. |
| PLACITA | (plah-sē′ta) | A little plaza. |
| PLAZA | (plah′zah) | A square park around which native towns are often built. |
| PALOVERDE | (pah′lo-vār′dā) | A green bush. |
| POCO TIEMPO | (pō′kō tē′āmpō) | Pretty soon, short while. |
| POLVADERA | (pol-vah-dā′rah) | Dusty. |
| PORTERO | (pōr-tā′rō) | Porter. Also a gap between cliffs or fingers of lava rocks. |
| PRONTO | (prōn′tō) | Right away, quick. |
| PUERCO | (poō-ār′ko) | Dirty. *Rio Puerco*, dirty or muddy river. |
| RAMRODDING THE OUTFIT | | Bossing the range. |
| RANCHEROS | (rahn-chā′rōs) | Ranchers. |
| RANCHO | (rahn′cho) | Ranch. |
| RATÓN | (rah-ton′) | Mouse. |
| REAL | (rā-ahl) | Royal. |
| REBOZO | (rā-bo′so) | Woman's shawl. |
| REMUDA | (rā-moo′dah) | The herd of horses used in a roundup. |
| RIATA | (rē-ah′tah) | Rope, lasso. |
| RICO | (rē′kō) | Rich; "rich people." |
| RIDE THE RIVER WITH | | Cowboy term for trustworthiness. |
| RÍO | | River. |
| ROAD RUNNER | | The chaparral bird. |
| RODEO | (ro′dā-o) | Public performance presenting the chief features of a roundup. |
| RUN MEAT | | A buffalo hunt. |
| RUNNING IRON | | A straight iron rod used for branding. |
| SALA | (sah′lah) | Reception room or dance hall. |
| SALADO | (sah-lah′do) | Salty. *Rio salado*, salty river. |
| SAN | (sahn) | Saint or holy. |
| SANDÍA | (sahn-dē′ah) | Watermelon. |
| SAN FELIPE | (sahn-fā-lē′pā) | Saint Philip. |
| SANGRE DE CRISTO | (sahn′grā dā crēs′to) | Blood of Christ. |
| SAN JUAN | (sahn whan′) | Saint John. |
| SANTA ANA | (sahn-tah′nah) | Saint Anne. |
| SANTA CLARA | (sahn′ta klah′-ra) | Saint Clara. |
| SANTA FE | (sahn-tah fā′) | Holy Faith. |
| SANTOS | (sahn′tos) | Images of Saints painted on wood, cloth, or skins. |

| | | |
|---|---|---|
| SARAPE | (sah-rah′pā) | A blanket, sometimes used by men as a large shawl or covering. |
| SASHAY | | Exuberant pantomime; also to travel. |
| SCRATCHING | | Cowboy term for using spurs. |
| SEÑOR | (sān-yōr′) | Mr. |
| SEÑORA | (sān-yo′ra) | Mrs. |
| SEÑORITA | (sān-yor-e′ta) | Miss. |
| SHALAKO | (shah′lah-ko) | Zuñi rain messenger. Zuñi dance of the new house ceremonies. |
| SHAMAN | (shah′man) | Indian medicine man. |
| SIERRA | (sē-ārr′ah) | Mountain. |
| SIMPLE AS A KIT BEAVER | | Trailsmen's term of stupidity. |
| SIPAPU | (sē-pah′pŏŏ) | Sipaphe, the land of; the underworld in certain creation myths. |
| SOD-BUSTER | | A homesteader or one who plows. |
| SOLEDAD | (so-lā-dahd′) | Solitary. *Peña soledad,* lone rock. |
| SOMBRERO | (sōm-brā′rō) | Hat. |
| SOPAPILLAS | (so-pah-pē′yahs) | Squares of short biscuit dough fried in deep fat until puffed up; also called *buñuelos* (būn-yā′lōs) |
| SPANISH SUPPER | | Trailsmen's term for a meager meal. |
| SQUASH BLOSSOM | | A manner of wearing the hair in large loops over each ear, formerly affected by Hopi Indian maidens. Also Indian handmade silver ornaments in the form of squash blossoms. |
| TABLITA | (tah-blē′tah) | Colored plaques, symbolically decorated with designs and feathers, worn by Pueblo Indian women during dance. |
| TRAIL HERD | | Cattle driven for long distance from range to market. |
| TRAILSMEN | | Term applied to frontier trappers, mountaineers, and sometimes to people of the overland wagon trains. |
| TRAVEE | (tră′vē) | Travois; two long poles strapped to a horse, one end of the poles dragging the ground; used by Indians to transport supplies and household goods. |

| | | |
|---|---|---|
| TRUCHAS | (troo'chahs) | Trout. |
| TUMBLEWEEDS | | Ripened Russian thistle bunches. |
| | | |
| VADO | (vah'do) | A ford over a river. |
| VALSE DESPACIO | (vahl'sä däs-pah'sē-o) | A slow waltz. |
| VAMOS | (vah'mos) | Let's go. Am. slang: get out. |
| VAQUERO | (vah-kā'ro) | A cowboy. |
| VERDOSO | (vĕr-dō'sō) | Verdant. *Ojo verdoso*, verdant spring. |
| VIGILANTE | (vĕ-hē-lahn'tā) | Frontier citizens organized to control lawlessness. |
| VILLA | (vĕ'ah) | Town. |
| VINEGARROON | (vēnä-gah-rŏŏn') | The whip-scorpion. So called because it emits a vinegar-like scent. |
| VIVA VIVA | (vē-vah, vē-vah) | Hurrah, Hurrah. |
| | | |
| WHITE-FACES | | Hereford cattle. |
| WRANGLER | | Cowboy who tends the horses at a ranch or on roundups. |
| | | |
| YE-BET-CHAI | (yā'bä-tchī) | A Navaho dance. |
| YESO | (yā'sō) | Gypsum. *Cerro yeso*, gypsum hill. |
| YUCCA | (yŭc'ah) | Spanish bayonet plant; state flower of New Mexico. Used for making brushes and weaving baskets. Root used for soap. |
| | | |
| ZACATÓN | (sah-kah-tōn') | Tall wild grass. |

# Religion

WHEN Fray Marcos de Niza planted the cross on the hill near Háwikuh in 1539 and claimed the country for the Spanish Crown a new chapter in the annals of the promulgation of the Christian faith was written.

For nearly three centuries Franciscan missionaries had journeyed to the far corners of the earth for the purpose of harvesting souls. Martyrdom was courted; fear for personal safety was non-existent. A spirit of service in the Glory of God fired these zealots; and following Coronado's conquest in 1540 and his return to Mexico two years later, three Franciscans, Frays Juan de Padilla, Juan de la Cruz, and Luis de Escalona, remained as the first missionaries, and they became the first martyrs in the new land. When the Conquistadores failed to find cities or mines of fabled wealth in the region that was to become New Mexico, the country was saved from possible abandonment by the courageous Franciscan friars. In June 1581, Fray Augustín Rodríguez and two companion Franciscans with twelve soldiers under Captain Francisco Sánchez Chamuscado, traveled north from Mexico to explore the region, learn the languages, and convert the Indians. When the soldiers withdrew, the friars refused to leave, and all were killed. Concern for their unknown fate inspired the relief expedition of Antonio de Espejo and Fray Bernardino Beltrán in November 1582.

The first church was built in New Mexico in the new capital at the old pueblo of Yunque-Yunque across the Rio Grande from the present village of San Juan in 1598 by Oñate, assisted by eight priests and two lay brothers, religious of Saint Francis. This church was dedicated to San Juan Bautista. The Spaniards called their first capital San Juan, but moved to San Gabriel about a year later and in 1610 to the Royal City of Santa Fe.

By 1617 the friars had built eleven churches and had converted 1,400 Indians. New Mexico became primarily a mission area and its history was intimately linked with the Roman Catholic Church. Under the direction of the Superior of the College of Saint Francis, established in the City of Mexico, the missions of New Mexico were elevated to a *custodia* of the Franciscan Order in 1617 and were given the name of Saint Paul. Fray Alonzo de Benavides was appointed custodian, and the territory was placed under the bishopric of Durango. In Benavides' famous "Memorial" to the King of Spain, Philip IV, in 1630, he states that there were 250 persons living in Santa Fe, but only fifty of these were armed.

Finding but a poor chapel in connection with the governor's head-quarters in Santa Fe, Benavides built a church and convent—the church he called the Parroquia—and re-established numerous missions in the Indian Pueblos.  It was some years later that the church of San Miguel was built in the Indian quarters in Santa Fe called the Analco (*see Architecture*).

Fray Benavides was the first authorized agent of the Inquisition in New Mexico.  But Bandelier says that "the Inquisition had no manner of sway or jurisdiction over the American Indians . . . It never inter-fered nor was permitted to interfere in matters of faith or belief of the aborigines."  However, serious difficulties arose between the governors and the Franciscans, the latter being accused of assuming extraordinary powers as ecclesiastical judges and officials of the Inquisition.

Conflicts arose due to other causes.  The resettlement of Indian villages in larger units with proper churches to facilitate religious train-ing resulted in temporary reduction of tribute for the royal treasury and for private owners of large land grants holding Indians in *encomienda* (the right to levy tribute).  Employment of Indians at missions caused dissension.  Colonists' claims to Indian labor often conflicted with those of missionaries, "conflict between Church and State characterized the administration of every province of the Spanish empire in America.  In New Mexico it was the most important phase of political history dur-ing the seventeenth century," says France V. Scholes in *Church and State in New Mexico in 1610-1650.*

The Pueblo Rebellion of 1680 was led by Po-pé, a Tewa Indian medicine-man and a native of San Juan pueblo.  Po-pé and his followers impressed upon the Pueblo Indians that their gods had ordered the revolt and that all Spaniards must be expelled or killed.  The religion of the Pueblo Indians (*see Folklore and the Indians*) was based upon age-old myths and rituals that dictated almost every act of their lives; and for those natives who had been converted to the Christian faith the throw-ing aside of the new teaching was not difficult.  With the expulsion of the Spaniards, the pagan beliefs prevailed, and churches were desecrated and destroyed.  It was not until De Vargas reconquered New Mexico in 1692 that the Roman Catholic Church was re-established.

De Vargas was given 100 soldiers to help keep the peace.  Fray Salvador de San Antonio was appointed Custodian; in 1695 the new villa and church of Santa Cruz de la Cañada was built on the site of the old village; and in 1706 Albuquerque was settled and the church of San Felipe de Nerí was established.

It was during the latter part of the seventeenth century that the

Jesuits accomplished the conversion of the Pima Indians and Father Kino and Father de Campos built their chain of missions in that part of the province of New Mexico that was later to become Arizona.

The Franciscans, however, controlled the missions around Santa Fe after the resettlement of New Mexico. In the early years of the eighteenth century, the missions did not thrive; this was due both to the temporary success of the rebellion, when the Indians' belief in their old gods held sway, and to the controversies that raged between Franciscans and episcopal authorities, which weakened the Church's power. During Spanish rule, no bishop visited the province after 1760; and subsequent to Mexico's independence, the Church suffered considerable loss.

A movement to extend religious instruction reached New Mexico in 1828 when a college for young men was opened in Santa Fe. During the same year several missions were converted into parishes and provided with secular priests following a law passed by the Mexican Congress expelling all native-born Spaniards. This forced many Franciscans to leave the country.

The Church's second period of growth in New Mexico dates from the occupation of the Territory by the United States in 1846. The Vatican elevated the Territory into a vicariate apostolic July 19, 1850. The Reverend John B. Lamy, a priest of the Diocese of Cincinnati, was consecrated bishop. Upon his arrival in Santa Fe in 1851, because he had not been previously announced, Juan Felipe Ortiz, the *vicario* in charge, refused to recognize his credentials, and it was necessary for him to make the long journey to Durango in Mexico where Bishop Zubiria resigned all claim to the American portion of his diocese. Bishop Lamy had left the Reverend Joseph P. Machbeuf, the able lieutenant who had accompanied him from the East and was later to become Bishop of Colorado, in Santa Fe. Upon his return Bishop Lamy found that severe disciplinary measures had to be taken: Father Gallegos was removed from his parish in Albuquerque and Father Martínez of Taos, because of his activity in political quarters as well as opposition to Church authority, had to be excommunicated.

Bishop Lamy instituted extensive reforms and carried forward heroic work in education. Religious conditions improved rapidly; sixteen years after his arrival Bishop Lamy had repaired the majority of the old churches and built 85 new ones. The cornerstone of the impressive Cathedral of Saint Francis of Assisi was laid, July 14, 1869, in Santa Fe. This large stone church was built over the old Parroquia.

The Jesuit Order was introduced in the Territory in 1867, the priests founding a school at Albuquerque and a college at Las Vegas in 1877. The Jesuits launched the publication of a religious newspaper *Revista Católica* (Catholic Review) in 1875. An act to incorporate the Society of Jesuit Fathers of New Mexico was passed January 18, 1878, by the Territorial Assembly over the Governor's veto, but it was later annulled by Congress as unconstitutional.

The Diocese of Santa Fe was elevated into a metropolitan see in February 1875 by Pope Pius IX, and Lamy became Archbishop. Ralph Emerson Twitchell wrote of Archbishop Lamy, who died February 14, 1888, that he was ". . . equally at home in the hut of the Indian, the cabin of the miner, or in the Vatican at the feet of the Pontiff." Willa Cather commemorated him as Father Latour in *Death Comes for the Archbishop.*

The Penitentes (Penitent Brotherhood) adhering to the belief of atonement through physical suffering, were introduced into New Mexico in 1598 by Oñate and the Franciscans accompanying him. This cult stems directly from the Third Order of St. Francis, of which Oñate himself was a member. As the Third Order was a Franciscan institution of lay members and, according to its constitution, could only be governed by priests of the order, it ceased to have canonical existence following the exodus of Franciscans from New Mexico in 1828. The centuries-old custom of religious penance was, however, too deeply ingrained to be given up by the native people. What was left of the Third Order in New Mexico carried on as local brotherhoods in isolated communities; and during the Mexican regime, when secular priests were all too few to administer to the widespread parishes, the members of the brotherhood themselves performed many priestly rites, as well as acts of mercy and charity enjoined in the precepts of the original Third Order, of which religious penance was only one phase.

Following the American occupation and the elevation of New Mexico into a bishopric under Bishop Lamy, the ecclesiastical authorities of the Roman Catholic Church made various attempts to suppress the Penitentes, public penance having been banned by several papal bulls, some of them even antedating the introduction into America of such Old World customs. But in spite of opposition, the Penitente Brotherhood continued to exist, and still exists in the more remote communities of New Mexico, although the severity of their self-imposed penance has been considerably modified. The Brotherhood is divided into two classes: the Brothers of Light consisting of the *Hermano Mayor,* head of the organization, the Reader, the Healer, etc., and the penitents, called the Brothers of Darkness. These men, during the times of public penance, cover their heads with a black cap and their only clothing consists of short white cotton drawers. They are the flagellants and cross bearers and pull the Cart of Death.

The Penitentes are most active during Lent. Their processions to and from local shrines and a neighboring cross-topped hill, symbolizing Calvary, constitute a form of primitive Passion Play. The chanting of the psalm "Miserere," and the plaintive notes of the *pitero* (small flute) can be heard near the mountain villages north of Santa Fe almost every evening during Holy Week. The Penitentes resent the intrusion of curious onlookers, although certain outdoor ceremonies and processions may be witnessed by outsiders, providing they gain permission and remain at a respectful distance; but the ceremonies of initiation and those carried on in the *morada* are guarded as secret. Guaranty of religious freedom in the State protects the Penitentes in their religious rites; and the Church's former unbending opposition has been modified to a more tolerant attitude toward what is a genuine and deeply sincere religious folk-survival.

Not until after the American occupation did Protestant missionaries come to New Mexico. Labor as they would, however, the early missionaries made but little progress until the 1860's when the first substantial results were obtained. Difficulties encountered were due partly to natural barriers of language and customs, and partly to the relatively small Anglo-American population. The building of railroads into New Mexico, causing an influx of eastern immigrants, was of great assistance to all Protestant denominations.

Baptist missionaries were first in the new field with the arrival of the Reverend Henry W. Read at Santa Fe in July 1849, and the first Protestant church in the Territory was also Baptist, being dedicated at Santa Fe on January 15, 1854. Following these came the Methodists with the Reverend E. G. Nicholson, who reached Santa Fe in 1850. The successful establishment of a school at Watrous in 1871 by the Reverend Thomas Harwood led to the opening of other Methodist mission schools. Then came the Reverend W. T. Kephardt, sent by the Presbyterian Missionary Union in 1851, but little was accomplished by this denomination until the Civil War period.

During the summer of 1863, the Right Reverend J. C. Talbot, Missionary Bishop, held the first service of the Protestant Episcopal Church at Santa Fe, but a regular organization was not established until 1880. The same year a congregational organization was effected, the first church being erected in Albuquerque, which led to other churches in various parts of the Territory.

Other Protestant denominations in New Mexico include: Seventh-day Adventists, Brethren (Plymouth), Christadelphians, Disciples of Christian Lutherans, Christian Reformed Church, Christian Scientists, and Salvationists.

As a result of the steady increase of the Protestant population in New Mexico, nearly every town or village of consequence now has its Protestant as well as Roman Catholic church, and Indian Protestant mission schools are being successfully maintained in or near Indian pueblos and reservations.

An influx of Mormon families into New Mexico for the purpose of colonization began during the last quarter of the nineteenth century. Among these was a group of families setting out from Utah in the winter of 1877-78, under the leadership of Luther C. Burnham. Traveling in covered wagons, some drawn by oxen, these religious pioneers were three months in making the hazardous journey, which ended with their settlement at Ramah.   Later Burnham moved to the Fruitland mesa on the San Juan River, where he and nearly all the other settlers lived in a long fort-like adobe building for protection against hostile Indians.   Burnham became first Mormon Bishop in the territory, which was known as "Burnham's Ward."

Another Mormon settlement at Luna, six miles east of the Arizona State Line, was established by the families of John and George Earl and John and William Swapp in March 1883, and the Mormon community of Carson was founded by W. K. Shupe in 1909.   These and other Mormon communities maintain their religion and traditions to the present day.

In Las Vegas, in 1885, was built the first Jewish temple, preceding by several years the one in Albuquerque.

In that part of the State sometimes called "Little Texas," because the remote communities were settled by people from central Texas, there exists the sect of Penticostals, or Holy Rollers.   These pioneers brought with them their equivalent of the Penitentes' emotional release —the one through penance in physical suffering, the other in emotional excitation in religious fervor—which gave drama and color to an ordinary drab and emotionally starved existence.   It is highly problematical whether or not the Holy Rollers would have gained a foothold during the days of Indian attacks; but after the people from Texas and Oklahoma gained physical security and life became a grim battle with the land and boredom, it is easy to understand their urge for emotional expression.   Today their three-day singing festivals are well known throughout southeastern New Mexico.

# Education

PRIOR to the coming of the Franciscans, who brought with them the Old World concepts of education, the Indians of the Southwest already had evolved a traditional system of instruction which was suited to their needs. Indian youths were taught the meaning of tribal dances and legends, the making of pottery, the construction of dwelling places, the preparation of food and herbs, and the conversion of pelts and hides into clothing.

After the missionaries converted the Indians to the Christian faith, the neophytes attending early mission schools were taught the Mass in Latin. In March 1609, the viceroy instructed Governor Peralta "to teach all the Indians, especially the children," the Spanish language. They were also instructed in the handicrafts and agriculture of the white man. No provision was made, however, for the formal education of descendants of the Spanish conquistadores until August 1721, when public schools were established in New Mexico by royal decree. Little came of this, as the schools were closed shortly afterward for lack of funds. Not until Mexico won its independence from Spain was a practical movement launched toward general education for the common people. Meanwhile instruction of both Indians and Spaniards was left to the church. This led to the founding of at least one mission school in each Spanish settlement and similar schools in most of the Indian pueblos.

On April 27, 1822, the provincial deputation passed a law to establish public schools in New Mexico; yet in 1832 there were only six. Governor Albino Pérez' proclamation, July 16, 1836, relating to the institution of a public school system, was the first of its kind issued by a governor of New Mexico. The proclamation was without practical results.

When the United States annexed the territory, the native peoples were found to be generally illiterate. The extreme isolation of communities was largely responsible for this condition, and from 1800 until General Kearny's occupation of the region in 1846 education had been a private endeavor. Within a few years this condition began to change, and the promotion of parochial education was accelerated by Archbishop Lamy, who established at Santa Fe in 1851 the first English school in the territory. The following year a boarding school for girls, the

Loretto Academy, was opened in Santa Fe, and in 1859 a similar institution for boys, St. Michael's College, was established there. In 1854 the United States Congress granted the territory 46,080 acres of land for aid in establishing universities. Yet until 1889 there was not a public college or high school in the entire territory.

The territorial legislature in 1850 provided for a school in each settlement to be supported by a tax of fifty cents per child. This was not popular, however, as peonage still prevailed and the upper class resented being taxed for the education of the peons. In 1889 a bill was passed by the territorial legislature providing for the location of a university at Albuquerque, a school of mines at Socorro, and an agricultural college at Las Cruces.

The University of New Mexico opened its doors June 15, 1892. Congress granted 111,080 acres of land to the university on June 21, 1898, and later granted 200,000 acres from the total provided by the enabling act for the territory approved June 20, 1910. Revenue derived from timber sales, and from oil, gas, and other mineral leases, goes to the support of the university, which has been approved by the Association of American Universities and is a member of the North Central Association of Colleges and Secondary Schools. Its extension division is a member of the National University Extension Association. The 1938-39 resident enrollment was 1,556. The total enrollment was 2,745. The university now consists of five colleges and a graduate school, with a total of twenty-one departments.

Land grants for revenue for the New Mexico College of Agriculture and Mechanic Arts near Las Cruces total 250,000 acres. The college has charge of all agricultural activities—regulatory, research, extension, and teaching.

The curricula offered at the New Mexico School of Mines, opened in 1892, include mining, metallurgical and geological engineering (mining and petroleum options), and general courses. Revenue is derived from 200,000 acres apportioned to the school from Federal land grants. Its situation is especially fortunate, as field geology and mine surveying can be studied to advantage in the immediate vicinity.

In 1891 the first public school law of consequence was enacted, with Amado Chávez as superintendent of public instruction; and under his supervision definite progress was made. A successor, Hiram Hadley, 1905-07, is credited with having inaugurated the present system of education.

Common schools were allotted 8,464,000 acres of public lands for revenue from the two Federal land grants. During the present century advancement in education in the State has been rapid. In 1934 there were 1,229 public schools with an average daily attendance of approximately 100,000. Teaching standards have risen steadily, and college work is now required of all applicants for teaching positions. Ninety-seven per cent of the revenue collected by the State sales tax is apportioned to the counties for educational purposes.

Because of the existing bilingual problem—more than 50 per cent of the school children are Spanish-speaking—an educational program for New Mexico could hardly be patterned after that of any other State. In 1930 the San José Training and Experimental School was created for the purpose of giving a period of intensive training to cadet teachers in methods and techniques particularly adapted to the teaching of the non-English-speaking child. This project has done much, not only toward solving the problem of teaching the bilingual child, but also toward centering State and national attention on the problem.

In the late summer of 1936 the State Department of Education, in co-operation with the New Mexico Educational Association, the State University, and the General Education Board, launched a three-year program for the improvement of instruction. Through the use of laboratory schools it was planned to develop a special curriculum and technique in teaching to eliminate the high rate of retardation in the elementary grades, due in large measure to the bilingual problem.

Vocational training has been introduced in some public schools, so that, with a less formal system of education, larger numbers of students will remain longer in school and be encouraged to go on to high school work. The program covers vocational education in home economics, agriculture, trade, and industrial and vocational rehabilitation. In the trade and industrial division most classes are held in conjunction with high schools. Funds made available by Congress through the Smith-Hughes Act of 1917 for vocational education are used in connection with this work and are administered through the Federal Board of Vocational Education of the Department of the Interior. They are matched dollar for dollar by the State for the local schools. A development known as the community type of vocational school has also been made a part of the county school system, and practical education is given to boys and men lacking educational advantages. Handicraft trades have been featured, so that the economic level of the community can be raised. As a result, exportation of handicraft products has increased, providing a livelihood for many in villages where employment formerly had been limited.

State institutions in addition to those already referred to include the New Mexico Normal University, Las Vegas; the New Mexico State Teachers College, Silver City; and the Spanish-American Normal School, El Rito, for training teachers in rural Spanish-speaking communities. Total grants of public lands by Congress to normal schools aggregate 300,000 acres.

New Mexico is one of twenty-seven States now providing junior colleges.   The objectives of the Eastern New Mexico Junior College (officially Eastern New Mexico Normal School), established at Portales in 1934, include a general educational background for two years of college, music, art, and literature, vocational skill for those not going into the professions, and preliminary work for those who will go on to college to prepare for specific professions.

The New Mexico Military Institute, Roswell, opened September 1898, was established as a junior college in 1914.   It provides thorough academic and military training for young men of high school and junior college age.   One hundred and fifty thousand acres of public lands were allotted to the military institute by Congress.

Other State institutions are the New Mexico School for the Deaf, Santa Fe; the New Mexico School for the Blind, Alamogordo; the Home and Training School for Mental Defectives, Los Lunas; the New Mexico Industrial School for Boys, Springer; and the Girl's Welfare Home, Albuquerque.   Public land allotments to the deaf, industrial, and blind schools total 150,000 acres.

The forty-four Indian schools in the State are supervised by the Federal government.   These are of four types: non-reservation boarding, reservation boarding, day, and mission.   The majority are situated in or near pueblos and Indian settlements.   Attendance in 1935 was 9,271.   The present policy of the Indian Office is to prepare Indian youths practically and fully to make the most of their tribal resources and crafts, and to train them so that when they leave school they will find native ties strengthened rather than broken or weakened.

Among the private institutions are three college preparatory schools: the Los Alamos Ranch School for Boys, Ótowi; the Brownmoor School for Girls, near Santa Fe; and the Sandía School for Girls, at Albuquerque.   These draw pupils from the East and Middle West, mostly.

Continuing in the traditions of the Franciscan friars who first brought education to New Mexico, the Catholic Church maintains sixty-five grade schools, high schools, and colleges throughout the State which provide religious instruction courses as well as secular studies.

# Literature

NEW MEXICO'S literary tradition begins with the orally transmitted myths, legends, and rituals of the Indians who were native to the soil when the Spaniards came and who still inhabit it. This primitive literature, unrecorded until the nineteenth century, extends far back in time and is still an integral feature of contemporary literature.

In the sense of the written or printed word, New Mexican literature began with the old Spanish chronicles of exploration and conquest. These basic sources of history rank among the great original adventure books of the world. In human interest and genuine literary flavor, these straight-forward tales of priests, conquerors, and soldiers seem today as fresh and modern as when they were written—especially so in New Mexico, where so much of the landscape and terrain through which adventurers journeyed remains unchanged. Because of the barrier of language, less has been known of these Spanish narratives than of similar early chronicles of the eastern colonies, but fine English translations of the most important New Mexican narratives have been made and are now available in book form.

One more purely creative work of this early Spanish period is the first known poem conceived on the soil of what is now the United States. This is the famous *Historia de la Neuva Mexico* by Captain Don Gaspar Pérez de Villagrá—an epic in thirty-four rhymed cantos, celebrating the conquest and permanent settlement of New Mexico in 1598 by Don Juan de Oñate.

Villagrá, himself a member of Oñate's expedition, shared in its hardships and glories, as recounted in his poem, culminating in the battle of Ácoma, 1599, in which he took an important part. His book, addressed to King Phillip III of Spain, was published in Alcalá, Spain, in 1610. An English prose translation by Gilberto Espinosa has recently been published by the Quivira Society.

Another phase of early Spanish literature in New Mexico is represented in the religious plays, traditional songs, ballads, and folk tales, brought from Old Spain and still surviving among the descendants of the early colonists.

Little distinction exists between the Spanish and Mexican regimes, as far as literary influences are concerned, since the old traditions, rooted in Spain, continued to flourish on the new soil.

English literature in New Mexico may be said to have begun in the early nineteenth century with the travel books of Anglo-American and European visitors, whose recording of the New Mexican scene is variously sympathetic or biased, due to the vast difference in background and according to the diverse temperaments of the observers. These books, with a few exceptions, overlap, or are subsequent to, the Mexican regime, 1821-46.

An early, unwilling visitor to New Mexico (who withal seems to have enjoyed certain features of his stay) was Lieutenant Zebulon Pike. His *Journal of a Tour Through the Interior Parts of New Spain* covers his arrest and enforced march from the upper Rio Grande in southern Colorado through Santa Fe and on to Chihuahua in 1807. Throughout the journey, Pike gives intimate and vivid pictures of the manners and customs of the New Mexican people, their villages and settlements, from the point of view of an outsider.

Written during the Mexican era and almost unknown today, is a small book by an author also named Pike, but not to be confused with Zebulon Pike. Albert Pike, of Confederate War fame, was the author of what is widely regarded as the best version of the words to "Dixie," and, in later life, was one of the founders of modern Masonry. His *Prose Sketches and Poems, Written in the Western Country,* published in Boston in 1834, was the result of a visit to New Mexico in 1831-33. His poems, a quaint mixture of Byronic and Shelleyan influences in conjunction with such subjects as "The Bold Navaho" or "The Vale of Picurís," represent much of the same quality that is found in early romanticized American landscape painting. Albert Pike was, so far as known, the first Anglo-American poet of New Mexico. His prose stories and sketches convey to the reader today the same strangeness of scene which then impressed itself upon the sensitive young poet from the East.

With the advent of the Santa Fe Trail days, the era of American pioneer narratives may be said to have begun. But the journals of the early beaver-trappers and traders preceded the later regularly organized trail traffic. Jacob Fowler, the Patties, and others recorded their adventures in manuscript—to be printed then or later. Some, like Kit Carson, told their stories—grudgingly, under pressure—long after the event. The great book of the Santa Fe Trail is Josiah Gregg's *The Commerce of the Prairies* (1844), which is not only a saga of the trail —from Leavenworth to Santa Fe, and from Santa Fe to Chihuahua— but an illuminating portrayal of everything connected with it, and particularly valuable for its description of life in New Mexico in the 1830's. Another book of pertinent interest is *Wah-to Yah,* or *The Taos Trail* (1850), by Lewis H. Garrard, who, as a young man bent upon adventure, joined a Santa Fe caravan and recorded his life on the prairies with zest and exhilaration. Garrard's overland trek to New Mexico is an interesting companion piece to Richard Henry Dana's sea voyage around Cape Horn to Mexican California in *Two Years Before the Mast* (1840).

Meantime, during this period, many travel books on Mexico by European visitors, Wislizenus, Brantz Mayer, and others, devoted considerable space to the northern province, New Mexico. One of these travelers was the young Englishman, George Frederick Ruxton, who journeyed up the Rio Grande Valley in the fall of 1846 and visited Taos just a short time before the uprising of 1847. His *Life in the Far West* (1847) and *Adventures in New Mexico and the Rocky Mountains* (1848) give firsthand pictures of his experiences in New Mexico at that time.

Immediately after the American occupation, 1846, another class of travel books is found in the reports of the U. S. Army officers and topographical engineers assigned to New Mexico and the Southwest. The reports of Emory, Abert, Marcy, Cooke, Johnston, Sitgreaves, and others, published as U. S. Senate Executive Documents, are anything but dull. Reading them, one is impressed by the high calibre and general cultural background of the young officers who wrote these reports. A book of more popular character and enduring literary interest is *El Gringo, or New Mexico and Her People* (1854), written by W. W. H. Davis while United States Attorney in the early territorial days. This book, with its detailed and intimate accounts of New Mexican life in the 1850's, so far as many aspects of native life are concerned, has never been superseded. It was largely drawn upon by later writers of the native scene. Particularly interesting also is James F. Meline's *Two Thousand Miles on Horseback* (1867). Numerous other books of the territorial era have furnished source material for the many books on New Mexico's frontier life in all its varying phases.

In any account of New Mexican writers, the name usually first mentioned is that of General Lew Wallace, who is said to have completed his novel *Ben Hur* in 1880 in the Palace at Santa Fe, where as territorial governor he divided his attention between Christian gladiators in Rome and the affairs of Billy the Kid in New Mexico. *Ben Hur* of course owed nothing to New Mexico, but Wallace is usually mentioned as the first New Mexican "author." Mrs. Lew Wallace (Susan E.) meantime was recording her interesting and lively impressions of the contemporary scene in letters to an eastern newspaper, later published in a small book called *The Land of the Pueblos* (1888).

Hardly, however, was *Ben Hur* off the press, when the first of the Billy the Kid books began to appear; notably Sheriff Pat F. Garrett's *Authentic Life of Billy the Kid* (1882), who, as the subtitle naively remarks, was "captured by killing." Since then the Lincoln County

War has been continuously waged in print. Other famous gunmen of New Mexico have been celebrated in subsequent New Mexican frontier narratives, but none so much fought over or provocative of immediate argument as Billy.

The last quarter of the nineteenth century was characterized by the advent of historians, archeologists, and ethnologists, for whom New Mexico presented a rich field. The first Anglo-American histories of New Mexico were naturally devoted to its conquest by the United States and were, for the most part, written by men who had shared in the campaigns of Generals Kearny and Doniphan and James Madison Cutts, Philip St. George Cooke, F. S. Edwards, J. T. Hughes, and others. Apparently the first American historian to turn his attention to the early Spanish history of the newly acquired territory was W. W. H. Davis, mentioned above, whose *Spanish Conquest of New Mexico* was published in 1867. Hubert Howe Bancroft's comprehensive *Arizona and New Mexico* (1889) was followed by the work of resident historians: L. Bradford Prince, Benjamin Read, a native New Mexican, William G. Ritch, Ralph Emerson Twitchell, and Charles F. Coan. Since then much important work in special fields has been published by later historians, among whom, in New Mexico, Lansing B. Bloom and George P. Hammond of the University of New Mexico are leading authorities.

In uncovering New Mexico's past, historians and archeologists naturally had to work hand in hand, because New Mexico's history is closely connected with its archeological sources and with its still contemporary aboriginal life. In this respect the work of Adolphe F. Bandelier, who was both historian and archeologist, is outstanding. From a literary point of view the works of such men as Bandelier, Frank Hamilton Cushing, and Dr. Washington Matthews are particularly valuable. Cushing's *Zuñi Creation Myths* and *Zuñi's Folk-Tales,* Dr. Washington Matthews' *Navaho Legends* and his transcripts of the great Navaho Mountain and Night Chant ceremonials, and Bandelier's *The Delight Makers* (1890), a vivid re-creation in fiction of prehistoric America, gave a new and larger conception of the aboriginal scene and stimulated the imagination of later writers.

One of the first to feel this influence was Charles F. Lummis, much of whose inspiration was gained from his association with Bandelier, and whose series of popular books on New Mexico, *The Land of Poco Tiempo, Strange Corners of Our Country, The Spanish Pioneers,* and many others are still favorite introductions to New Mexico. Until the turn of the century, indeed, Lummis seems to have been almost the only author *per se* in New Mexico—except the cowboys. After the Indians and Spaniards, the Anglo-Americans who first became intimately related to the soil were the cowboys.

They were poets first in their own right, with their improvised night-herding or cattle-trail songs; and then books began to be written about them.  In 1881 Emerson Hough, as a member of the staff of the weekly newspaper *Golden Era,* at the boom mining town of White Oaks, gathered the material for his novel *Heart's Desire* (1905), incorporating the well-known cowboy, prospector, and eastern magnate pattern—less familiar then than now.  Hough's novels were followed by his substantial books on the western frontier.  In the first decade of the twentieth century, a real cowboy, Eugene Manlove Rhodes, who had been wrangling horses and punching cattle for the Bar Cross on the Jornada del Muerto, had his first stories published in Lummis' magazine *Out West.*  In 1904 he left New Mexico for the East, with his banjo and a suitcase full of stories, and landed in the fold of the *Saturday Evening Post.*  When he died in 1934, Rhodes had ten books to his credit, as well as many stories not yet collected in book form—all authentic tales of the veritable soil and soul of the New Mexican cattle range.  Swift-moving and keen with philosophic wit, his books will out-live the rank and file of mere "westerns."  Rhodes is buried on the top of Rhodes Pass—named for him before his death—of which a vivid description is given in one of his novels, *Stepsons of Light* (1921).  The scenes and characters of his other novels, thinly veiled by fictitious titles, are readily discerned by old-timers.

Cowboy songs are classed as "folk," but individual authors some-times become folk-poets before they know it.  In 1908 N. Howard (Jack) Thorpe, cow-puncher and rancher, published a small collection of *Songs of the Cowboys,* including several of his own.  Among these was "Little Joe the Wrangler," widely sung wherever cowboys con-gregate, as well as over the radio and on the phonograph.  A second enlarged edition of *Songs of the Cowboys* was published in 1921, includ-ing more of his own songs.  Thorpe's *Tales of the Chuck Wagon* (1926) and other stories published in magazines reflect more than forty years' intimate knowledge of New Mexican life and practically every square inch of its terrain.

An early novel, with the scene laid in southern New Mexico, is Florence Finch Kelly's *With Hoops of Steel* (1900).  The stories by Thomas A. Janvier in *Santa Fe's Partner* (1907) furnished a lively record of the time when mail and passengers were transported by stage-coach from the railroad terminus at Española to Santa Fe, with one stop for lunch at the Bouquet Ranch at Pojoaque.

In the second decade of the twentieth century, books on or about New Mexico began to appear, first slowly and then with an accelerated pace, until their number now is almost bewildering.  These are about equally divided between native-born or resident New Mexican authors and other writers for whom the New Mexican scene presents some special interest. The visitor, first impressed by the composite scene, usually asks eagerly: "What book shall I read *to tell me all about it?*" There isn't any one book that can do this—the field is too varied. The only answer is to refer the reader to the bibliography and let him choose for himself.

Under general literature many nationally known names are included, indicating that New Mexico's literature, although regional in character, is not merely regional in interest or quality. Some of these authors were of established reputation before coming to New Mexico or writing about it; as for instance the late Mary Austin, who came to live in Santa Fe in 1918 and was subsequently identified with New Mexico as she had previously been with California; or Willa Cather, whose *Death Comes for the Archbishop* was the result of a literary sojourn.

One interesting feature of the growth of New Mexican literature is the number of writers who have, so to speak, developed on the soil. It may be that the advent of eastern writers, during and after the World War, had something to do with awakening native-born New Mexicans to a tardy appreciation of their own soil, just as the soil itself had power of re-creating the imaginative vision of the newcomers. In either case, or both cases, modern literature in New Mexico indicates a deepening sense of reality and individual vision.

The poets were among the first to feel and express the spirit of the country. Books of verse that reflect this spirit are: *Red Earth* (1920), by Alice Corbin; *Breakers and Granite* (1921), by John Gould Fletcher; *Caravan* (1922), by Witter Bynner; *The American Rhythm* (1923) and *The Children Sing in the Far West* (1928), by Mary Austin; *Birds, Beasts and Flowers* (1923), by D. H. Lawrence; *Fandango* (1927), by Stanley Vestal; *Mountain against Mountain* (1928), by Arthur Davison Ficke; *Along Old Trails* (1928), by William Haskell Simpson; *Foretaste* (1933), by Peggy Pond Church; *Altantides* (1933), by Haniel Long; and *Horizontal Yellow* (1935), by Spud Johnson. The work of these and other poets of New Mexico is represented in national and southwestern anthologies.

The field of creative fiction is comparatively small but distinguished. Harvey Fergusson, of Albuquerque, grandson of Santa Fe Trail pioneers, had two eastern novels to his credit when in 1921 he turned to his native scene in *Blood of the Conquerors*—probably the first realistic novel of contemporary New Mexico. He followed this with four other regional novels, including *Wolf Song* (1927), a story of Spanish and Anglo-American life in Taos of the Kit Carson era, in interesting contrast to Willa Cather's *Death Comes for the Archbishop,* published the same year. Miss Cather's book is based on the life of Archbishop Lamy and the French priests, whose advent in the 1850's did so much to change the scene in Taos and elsewhere in New Mexico.

Mary Austin, who had written much on the Southwest before her death in 1934, gave her usual individual touch to *Starry Adventure* (1931), a novel in which the landscape itself is a spiritual force, almost more important than the human beings motivated by it. Her *One Smoke Stories* (1934) are brief pungent tales of native life—Indian and Spanish. In these, as in her other work, as well as in her autobiography, *Earth Horizon* (1933), is revealed her feeling of man's close identification with the spiritual life of the soil.

Paul Horgan's novels, notably *No Quarter Given* (1935), envisage the contemporary scene through the medium of characters whose psychological problems are variously solved or complicated by the effect of a new environment. *The Royal City of the Holy Faith* (1936), in a different vein, presents in fictional form three separate periods in the history of New Mexico, centered in the Palace of the Governors in Santa Fe.

Also imaginatively projected around life in the Palace is Eugene Manlove Rhodes' *Penalosa* (1936), a reprint of a chapter from his out-of-print book, *West is West* (1927). This is a dramatic picture of the Inquisition, of which Penalosa, during his term as Governor (1661-64) became a victim.

Not precisely fictional, but in the realm of creative prose—almost poetry—is Haniel Long's *Interlinear to Cabeza de Vaca* (1936), which also recasts an old story through modern interpretive vision.

Raymond Otis, whose *Fire in the Night* (1934) is a novel of Santa Fe's younger generation, entered a new field in his *Miguel of the Bright Mountain* (1936), the story of a young novitiate's mystical absorption in the rites of the Penitentes, followed by *The Little Valley* (1937), both highly sensitized portrayals of life in small Spanish communities.

Bandelier's *Delight Makers* had a prehistoric background, but modern novelists have attempted a perhaps even more difficult literary feat in dealing with present-day Indian life. *Under the Sun* (1927), by Dane Coolidge, and *Wind-Singer* (1930), by Frances Gillmor, are semihistoric stories of Navaho life, leading up to the present. Oliver La Farge's *Laughing Boy; a Navaho Romance* (1929), awarded the Pulitzer prize for that year, is a mixture of poetry and realism—the stark aridity and commercial cheapness of "white man" civilization set against the age-old religious ceremonialism of Navaho life, with the modern Indians' struggle to bridge the two. His short stories in *All the Young Men* (1935) and his more recent novel, *The Enemy Gods* (1937), carry on various aspects of the same theme.

A new note is added to New Mexican fiction in Conrad Richter's *Early Americana and Other Stories* (1936) and *The Sea of Grass* (1937). The latter novel is a skillfully woven piece of romantic-realism, involving the lives of a single family, against the primitive background of the high upland range of desert grass, cut and ploughed and destroyed by homesteaders.

While no one novel or story of the late D. H. Lawrence can be singled out as definitely New Mexican, the spirit of the country is a part of the texture in several. More direct impressions are recorded in his verse, mentioned above, and in several articles on New Mexico. The vivid personality of this strange genius has left its impress on the mountain slope above Taos, where he spent some of the later years of his life and where he is buried. Biographically, also, his impress remains in three books written about him, centering largely on his life in Taos; *Lorenzo in Taos* (1932), by Mabel Dodge Luhan; *Lawrence and Brett* (1938), by Honorable Dorothy Brett; and *Not I but the Wind* (1934), by his wife, Frieda Lawrence.

New Mexico has probably more native drama than any state in the Union, with its yearly calendar of indigenous Navaho and Pueblo Indian dances and ceremonies, as well as Spanish folk plays—the latter first introduced in 1598 and still performed annually. These are recorded in folklore and anthropological publications.

Modern plays on New Mexico that have been published as well as produced include: *El Cristo* (1926), a one-act folk play by Margaret Larkin; *Night over Taos* (1932), a poetic drama based on the Taos revolt, by Maxwell Anderson; and *Russet Mantle* (1936), a play of modern life in Santa Fe, by Lynn Riggs.

The ever-increasing number of books on frontier life and adventure prove that the "vanishing frontier" is anything but vanishing, so far as literary popularity is concerned. New Mexico's share in this field includes many books of a general character, as well as several first-hand accounts of territorial days which pick up the thread of frontier life where the earlier original pioneer narratives left off. Of especial interest are three books on the Socorro-Dátil-Mogollón section of New Mexico—a region rich in history, romance, and beauty but apparently the least-known part of the State.

*Fifty Years on the Old Frontier* (1923), by James W. Cook; *Some Recollections of a Western Ranchman* (1928), by Honorable William French; and *Law and Order Ltd.* (1928), the story of Elfego Baca, by Kyle S. Crichton, cover approximately the same scene and period, from different angles and racial backgrounds. The Honorable William French, of French Park, Ireland, was one of a number of "younger son" Britishers who became ranch owners in New Mexico in the 1880's. Captain James W. Cook, an American, who started out as a guide for English sportsmen in Wyoming, became manager for one of them on the W. S. ranch at Alma, subsequently acquired by French. Elfego Baca, an enterprising scion of an old Spanish family of Socorro, figured as deputy sheriff in the celebrated "Frisco War," in which all three participated. The first two books also give firsthand accounts of the Apache campaign in New Mexico; and French's book, which goes on where Cook's New Mexican chapters leave off, includes his experiences with members of the famous "Wild Bunch" of Montana, all of whom, at one time or another, while hiding out from the law, found employment on French's ranch and, as French naively remarks, proved exceedingly able and efficient in restoring law and order on the ranch while there. After the departure of the "Wild Bunch," French became discouraged by the general lawlessness in that part of the country and removed to Colfax County in northeastern New Mexico, where the town of French was named for him.

In another book of the same period, *Riata and Spurs* (1927), Charles A. Siringo, the cowboy-detective, tells of tracing the "Wild Bunch" all the way from Montana to Alma, only to find that they had left Alma before he arrived. Siringo, after years of adventure, settled on a ranch near Santa Fe in the later part of his life, and was a familiar figure in the Plaza, riding his white horse, Sailor Gray, accompanied by his favorite Russian wolf-hound.

The Lincoln County War of 1877-81, resuscitated by Walter Noble Burns' *Saga of Billy the Kid* (1925), came actively to the fore again with reprints of earlier books on the subject and with new books such as George W. Coe's *Frontier Fighter* (1934) and the *Real Story of Billy the Kid* (1936), by Ex-Governor Miguel A. Otero. George Coe, who fought and rode with Billy the Kid, is still living near Lincoln, and Governor Otero lives in Santa Fe. These two books give valuable firsthand accounts of the generally misunderstood background of the Lincoln County War and the part that politics as well as the U. S. Army played in it. Much evidence supporting the true background is also supplied in Major Maurice Garland Fulton's annotated 1927 edition of Pat Garrett's book on Billy the Kid, mentioned above. Governor Otero's book includes a rare photograph of the idealistic young Englishman, John G. Tunstall, whose death precipitated the later stages of the war.

Recent studies of frontiersmen include Stanley Vestal's *Kit Carson* (1928) and *Mountain Men* (1937); and *Old Bill Williams* (1936), by Alpheus A. Favour. Bill Williams was one of the early group of trappers and traders who worked in and out of Taos, but his early life in Missouri, the circumstances of his coming to New Mexico as guide for the United States survey of the Santa Fe Trail in 1825, and his tragic death as a result of Frémont's disastrous fourth expedition are less generally known. Other pioneer characters—trappers, traders, prospectors, cowboys, outlaws, and "lady-wildcats"—are vividly portrayed in books by Duncan Aikman, Frederick R. Bechdolt, Dane Coolidge, Eugene Cunningham, T. M. Pearce, and N. Howard Thorpe.

Historical accounts of the frontier, the Santa Fe Trail and cattle range, are given by Will C. Barnes, R. L. Duffus, J. Evetts Haley, Emerson Hough, William McLeod Raine, and others.

Edwin L. Sabin's *Kit Carson Days, 1809-1867,* published in 1914, is probably the most authoritatively complete account of Carson's life and his period, with abundant indication of Carson's extraordinary military services to the Government through two wars and as Indian Agent. Incidents of his earlier life are simply and directly told in *Kit Carson's Own Story of his Life,* as dictated to Colonel and Mrs. D. C. Peters about 1856-57. The original manuscript, a straight-forward narration of facts published by Blanche Grant in 1926, lacks the heroics supplied by Peters in his book, which so greatly annoyed Carson.

Books of general descriptive interest by New Mexican writers include *The Land of Journey's Ending* (1924) by Mary Austin; *Caballeros* (1931) by Ruth Laughlin Barker; *Rio Grande* (1933) by Harvey Fergusson; *The Sky Determines* (1934) by Ross Calvin; and *When Old Trails Were New* (1934) by Blanche Grant. Two books with special emphasis on the Spanish background are *Old Spain in Our Southwest* (1936) by Nina Otero; and *Brothers of Light, The Penitentes of the Southwest* (1937) by Alice Corbin Henderson.

Among popular books on contemporary Indian life may be mentioned: *Ácoma, the Sky City* (1926) by Mrs. W. T. Sedgwick; *Desert Drums* (1928) by Leo Crane; *The Rain Makers* (1929) and *The Navaho Indians* (1930) by Mary Roberts and Dane Coolidge; and Erna Fergusson's *Dancing Gods* (1931), an account of Indian ceremonials in New Mexico and Arizona. D. H. Lawrence's *Mornings in Mexico* (1927) also includes two vividly impressionistic chapters on Pueblo Indian dances.

For a general introduction to Indians and archeology, *Indians of the Southwest* (1913) by Earle Pliny Goddard is an authentic and convenient handbook. Dr. A. V. Kidder's *Introduction to the Study of Southwestern Archaeology* (1924), Edgar L. Hewett's *Ancient Life in the American Southwest* (1930), and *Indians of the Rio Grande Valley* (1937) by Edgar L. Hewett and Adolph Bandelier present the results of modern research in readable form for the layman and whet the serious student's appetite for the many monographs and books of a more scientific nature on these subjects.

Folklore, appealing alike to adult or juvenile reader, is well represented in New Mexico literature. Indigenous Indian, Spanish, and Anglo-American myths, legends, and folk tales are significantly intermingled in many popular books. Among these may be mentioned: *Indian Stories from the Pueblos* (1929) and *Native Tales of New Mexico* (1932) by Frank G. Applegate; *Zuñi Indian Tales* (1926) by Aileen Nusbaum; *Coronado's Children* (1930) by J. Frank Dobie; *Navaho Tales* (1927) by William Whitman; *Tewa Firelight Tales* (1927) by Ahlee James; *Waterless Mountain* (1931) and *Dark Circle of Branches* (1933) by Laura Adams Armer; *Tay-Tay's Tales* (1922) and *Tay-Tay's Memories* (1924) by Elizabeth Willis DeHuff; and *The Burro of Angelitos* (1937) by Peggy Pond Church. Charles F. Lummis and Frank Cushing were earlier contributors to this field. For the erudite student, a wealth of material is furnished in the publications of the Bureau of American Ethnology, the *Journal of American Folklore,* and the *American Anthropologist.*

In the publishing field, New Mexico has several book-publishing firms and monthly or quarterly publications. The former class includes: The University of New Mexico Press, Albuquerque; the Quivira Society (publishers of translations of original Spanish narratives, edited by Dr. G. P. Hammond of the University of New Mexico); The Rydal Press, Santa Fe (publishers of limited editions); and Writers' Editions, Santa Fe. The last named, sponsored by a group of Southwestern writers, is incorporated as a nonprofit co-operative publishing enterprise—said to have been unique in the United States when founded in 1933.

Magazines include the *New Mexico Historical Review* (quarterly); *El Palacio* (monthly), a news bulletin and commentary on archeological activities; the *New Mexico Quarterly,* of general literary interest, published by the University of New Mexico; the State-published magazine *New Mexico* (monthly), featuring illustrated articles of contemporary and historic interest.

Taken as a whole, perhaps the outstanding feature of contemporary literature in New Mexico is its largely regional character. This seems due less to intention than to an instinctive reaction on the part of the writers to the influence of the native soil and scene. Incidentally, the difference between sectionalism and true regionalism may be recognized by reference to the regional character of much great literature. The claim for New Mexican literature is, not that it is great, but that it is largely genuine and a direct product of the soil.

# Music

THE music of the early Indian nowhere appears to be better preserved than in New Mexico, where, among the Pueblo, Navaho, and Apache Indians, it has been handed down by rote from one generation to another from prehistoric times. Since Indian music is not characterized by Western concepts of harmony, no comparison with European music is possible. To ordinary white ears, says D. H. Lawrence, the Indian's song sometimes sounds like a rather disagreeable howling around the drum.

Singing, to the Indian, like dancing, is part of ceremony, part of ritual. Against the backdrop of the mesas and the mountains, in the center of the plaza of his pueblo, the Indian sings as he dances for rain, for favor in the hunt, to make the corn grow.

Lawrence, who lived for many years in Taos, describes a Taos Indian dance as follows:

"The Indian singing, sings without words or vision. Face lifted and sightless, eyes half closed and visionless, mouth open and speechless, the sounds arise in the chest. He will tell you it is a song of a man coming home from the bear-hunt: or a song to make rain: or a song to make the corn grow: or even, quite modern, the song of the church bell on Sunday morning. . . .

"The dark faces stoop forward, in a strange race-darkness. The eyelashes droop a little with insistent thuds. And the spirits of the men go out in the ether, vibrating in waves from the hot, dark, intentional blood, seeking the creative presence that hovers forever in the ether, seeking identification, following on down the mysterious rhythms of the creative pulse, on and on into the germinating quick of the maize that lies under the ground, there, with the throbbing, pulsing, clapping rhythm that comes from the dark, creative blood in man, to stimulate the tremulous, pulsating protoplasm in the seed-germ, till it throws forth its rhythms of creative energy into the rising blades of leaf and stem."

For every occasion there is a song and a dance; the Indian repertoire is as extensive as that of the white man. In some ceremonies lasting several days, definite groups of songs are sung, with only rare instances of repetition. Among these are the Shalako of the Zuñi, the Yebechai of the Navaho, and the corn dance of the Santo Domingo Pueblo, where as many as six hundred performers faultlessly synchronize their movements into a superb pageant.

Songs of one tribe differ from those of another in various ways, as the native folk music of Europe differs among the nations. Not only does the melodic style and rhythmic composition vary, but its manner of execution may also be vastly different. The Pueblo songs are pitched in medium and low voice, while those of the Navaho are often high.

Types of songs may also bear a tribal identity. The Eagle, Buffalo, Deer, Corn, Basket, and Turtle dances belong to the Pueblos. The Navaho, besides their healing songs in the Night and Mountain chants, sing round or circle dance songs. Plains Indian songs adopted by the Pueblo Indian differ greatly from their own in tempo and melody. The Apache, in addition to their distinctive Devil and Bear dance songs, enjoy back and forth and circle dance songs.

Hunting, traveling, work songs, and lullabies are found varying greatly in composition and interpretation in all of the New Mexico tribes.

With the tribal ceremonies, the percussion accompaniment varies, rattles being used for the Navaho Night and Mountain chants and some of the Pueblo ceremonies, while the drum is used by the Pueblos in the Corn and other dances. Apache use the drum also, preferring soft toned ones similar to the water drum of the Indians of the Atlantic seaboard. Of late years the Apache use drums made of lard buckets, in preference to the Pueblo wooden drum, for they carry a louder, more resonant tone.

With the advent of the United States Government Schools, the missionary activities of various religious organizations, passing of the patriarchs of the tribes, and with the consequent loss of ancient melodies, musicians fear the disappearance of much of this invaluable tribal music unless it is scientifically recorded before it is too late.

Some such recordings have been made: notable is a collection of Zuñi songs by Dr. J. Walter Fewkes, of the Hemenway Archeological Expedition (1890). These were made on phonograph cylinders, from which, with the aid of a harmonium (small organ with metal reeds) Mr. Benjamin Ives Gilman recorded some of the melodies, including the "Song of the Rabbit Hunt," and the sacred dance of the Ko-Ko, and published in *A Journal of American Ethnology and Archaeology, Vol. 1.*

A collection of Santo Domingo Pueblo songs, by Frances Densmore, U. S. Bureau of Ethnology, has been published (1938) by the Southwest Museum, Los Angeles.

More than two thousand Navaho sacred ceremonial songs have been made on phonograph records under the sponsorship of Miss Mary C.

Wheelright. These are deposited in the Museum of Navajo Ceremonial Art, at Santa Fe.

Natalie Curtis, in her *The Indian's Book,* has recorded many of the
songs of New Mexico's Pueblo Indians, while composers like Thurlow
Lieurance, Charles Wakefield Cadman, Jean Jeancon, and others have
recorded some melodies, transposing them to fit our musical scale, but
in the process losing much of the Indian characteristics.

There remains much still to be done to preserve for future generations this valuable music, not alone for the Indian, but also as a point
of departure for aesthetic achievements in the field of true American
music.

## SPANISH MUSIC

Spanish music was first introduced when Cortés came to the American continent in 1519, bringing with him the folk songs of the mother
country, where for centuries *trovadores* and *juglares* had been composing and singing romances or ballads built around the lives of their
heroes, or dealing with subjects of love, religion, or war.

The Spanish ballad of the sixteenth century used sixteen syllables
to a verse and was usually assonated instead of rhymed. The sixteen-
syllable verses were unpliable, so they eventually were broken down
into octosyllabic meter which, with greater variety of themes, was
employed in a subsequent composition known as the décima. This
décima consisted of forty-four lines, a four-line introduction followed
by four stanzas of ten lines each, with the first line of the introduction
becoming the last line of the first stanza, the second line of the introduction becoming the last line of the second stanza, and so on. This
stanzaic form was first used by Lope de Vega in Spain and is still
recited as poetry in New Mexico, though not so frequently sung.

As the spirit of conquest moved the Spaniards on to new lands,
their songs went with them, Coronado and his men bringing them into
New Mexico. But it was not until the first colonizing expedition of
Juan de Oñate, in 1598, that they became a part of New Mexican
culture. Since the Spanish expeditions were made for the glory of
God, as well as the acquisition of land and wealth for the Crown, the
Franciscan missionaries were a vital part and, in some instances, the
dominating force of each expedition. Among these missionaries, who
had been well trained in letters and in the arts, were found some musi-
cians of ability, and it is to them that credit for the introduction of
European music in the New World must be given.

From Spanish historical documents we find that the first music
teacher was Fray Cristóbal de Quinones. He is credited with having
brought the first organ into what is now the United States; he installed
an organ in the chapel of the monastery at San Felipe Pueblo and

trained the Indians to sing the church services. He died in 1609. Thus,

> At the time that Jamestown was founded and thirteen years before the Pilgrims set foot on the Massachusetts coast, New Mexico could not only boast of a music teacher who had enjoyed the benefits of a musical education such as the church schools of the day afforded, but was in possession of an organ. . . . Before 1630 many schools were in operation which included music in their curriculum. The first boys' choirs within the present United States were those which supplied the music for the mission churches of New Mexico. Churches and monasteries were supplied with organs which were transported overland from Mexico City, a six months' trip in those days. A century before Boston claims to have had an organ (1713) there were many organs in the "Great Unknown North," as the Spaniards termed the land of the Pueblos. As far as Spanish dominion extended, there was music.

The second teacher was Bernardo de Marta, a Spaniard who came into New Mexico about 1600.

One form of Spanish-American folk song prevalent at that time, and still heard today, is the *alabado,* a religious ballad, an outgrowth of Gregorian Chant. This form has little melodic interest, is primitive and monotonous, but very moving when sung by a large number of voices. The Penitentes still use this form of song in their services, often to the accompaniment of a crude flute. It is used also at wakes.

Other song forms which have developed within New Mexico are the *indita, cuando, corrido,* and lastly the *canción popular.* The *indita* dates approximately from the time of Maximilian and is a combination of song and dance. The words tell a story, the refrain is lyric and amorous. It is composed of eight syllable rhymed verses. The *corrido,* always heroic in its subject matter, is a modern development of the ballad. Its music pattern is a definite one in four-quarter rhythm, usually with guitar accompaniment, and is never danced. It is often a melodramatic narrative almost always naming the day and date of the episode with which the poem deals. The *cuando* has no definite pattern and is practically obsolete now; formerly it told of adventures and always ended each stanza with the word *cuando* (when). Out of these earlier forms, since the first quarter of the nineteenth century, has developed the *canciones populares,* literally, popular songs, very singable in melody and rhythm. These date from the first quarter of the nineteenth century and are common to every locality. In all of this Spanish-American folk music very little Indian influence is felt, with the exception of the *indita.*

Nowhere else in the United States has the study of Spanish-American music been more seriously followed than at the University of New Mexico. Dr. Arthur L. Campa, Director of Research in Folklore and Professor in Modern Languages, with financial help from the Rockefeller Foundation and the late Senator Bronson Cutting, has made recordings and subsequent transcriptions of a large number of folk songs which illustrate the different types found within New Mexico. Aurelio Espinosa's great contribution to research in this field has been widely recognized.

With co-operation from some Latin-American organizations and through the public schools both children and adults are now given an opportunity to learn these songs and sing them under musical direction. Frequently a small amount of folk dancing accompanies the singing. Also, to those who want it, instruction is given in playing stringed instruments which comprise the native *típica* orchestra.

## ANGLO-AMERICAN MUSIC

"All lonely people sing," says Margaret Larkin in *Singing Cowboy,* "and much of the cowboy's work is done in solitude. Singing relieves the monotony of the night watch, or the day's ride on the range." To the new frontier of the West, after the Civil War, came men and boys from Kentucky, Illinois, Louisiana, and Ohio; with them they brought their folk-tunes—English and Scottish ballads, Irish reels, Negro spirituals, and sentimental songs of the day—and to these they added words that told of their experiences in cow camp and cattle range.

Miss Larkin says,

There always were one or two fellows in an outfit who were said to have a voice, and they sang the solo stanzas while the rest of the group joined in with Whoopee ti yi yo, or the yell that took the place of the chorus. If there was any accompaniment, it was the guitar, supplemented by fiddle and an accordion at dances. Fiddling and singing were highly regarded accomplishments, and the cowboy who could do either was in demand in frontier celebrations.

Some of the most popular cowboy songs sung on the New Mexican ranges were "The Strawberry Roan," "Little Joe the Wrangler," "When the Work's All Done This Fall," "Jack O' Diamonds," "The Santa Fe Trail," "By the Silvery Rio Grande," and "Ridin' Down That Old Texas Trail." The songs are usually sentimental, dealing with loneliness and death. Typical is the last stanza of "When the Work's All Done This Fall":

Poor Charlie was buried at sunrise, no tombstone at his head,
Just a little slab-board, and this is what it read,
Charlie died at daybreak, he died from a fall,
And the boy won't see his mother when the work's all done this fall.

To the tune of "The Little Old Log Cabin in the Lane," Jack Thorpe, one of the venerable old-timers on New Mexico ranges, wrote "Little Joe, the Wrangler."

> It was little Joe, the wrangler, he will wrangle never more,
> For his days with the roundup they are o'er;
> 'Twas a year ago last April when he rode up to our camp,
> Just a little Texas stray and nothing more.

The song tells how they taught little Joe to wrangle horses, and then one day while camping on the Pecos, a storm came up, the herd stampeded, and in a flash of lightning they saw Little Joe out in front of the herd bravely trying to head them off; the next morning he was found in a washout mangled to a pulp.

Many of the songs are based on actual experiences; there probably was a "Little Joe" whose death inspired Jack Thorpe. The song was the way the cowboy told of an important event, and even relayed news. One of the most famous New Mexican songs is "Billy the Kid."

> I'll sing you the song of Billy the Kid,
> I'll sing of the desperate deed that he did;
> Way out in New Mexico long, long ago,
> When a man's only chance was his old forty-four.

In some sections of the State, particularly in the east, old-time singing conventions are popular. These are well organized into local, county, and district groupings, and furnished by their all-day Sunday-singings, a recreational activity which is thoroughly enjoyed. It is an interesting observation that most of these groups still prefer to use shaped notes for sight singing, a carry-over from southern United States.

Despite the basic wealth of folk music in New Mexico, the development of music as a fine art has been exceedingly slow. Within the last ten years, however, great strides have been made in music education through higher State institutions of public instruction and city school systems. In the latter there has been an especially noticeable impetus in instrumental instruction. Most of the schools in incorporated towns and cities now have orchestras or bands. In Albuquerque an annual program is given by the public schools in which five hundred children participate in band and orchestral ensemble. School credit is allowed in many of these places for instrumental study as well as glee club and chorus participation. Music departments of State institutions have steadily grown stronger and within the last year the University of New Mexico has developed its music department until it now awards a Bachelor of Music degree.

A State Federation of Music Clubs exists with chapters in various towns of the State. Some civic orchestras exist, notably the one in Albuquerque, with a membership of approximately seventy pieces, and one in Ratón with fifty pieces. In Albuquerque, a Junior Orchestra with twenty-five members is also maintained. In some places there are community choral organizations directed by competent leaders in which

# Missions

*Laura Gilpin*

MISSION, RANCHOS DE TAOS

TAOS PUEBLO MISSION IN THE MOONLIGHT

*Ernest Knee*

*Ernest Knee*

PENITENTE CHAPEL, NEAR ESPAÑOLA

CHURCH OF SAN MIGUEL (1621), SANTA FE

REREDOS, CHURCH AT SAN JOSÉ

*Ernest Knee*

*Ernest Knee*

CHURCH AT SAN JOSÉ

SANTUARIO, CHIMAYÓ

*Laura Gilpin*

OUR LADY OF GUADALUPE–
WOODCARVING BY NEW MEXICO SANTO MAKER

*Laura Gilpin*

NEW MEXICAN SANTO DE BULTO

REREDOS, CRISTO REY CHURCH, SANTA FE

*Ernest Knee*

music lovers may participate. Organizations of this character are doing distinguished work in Santa Fe, Albuquerque, and Clovis. At least four cities in the State now have thriving community organizations which sponsor concerts of high artistic merit by nationally known artists.

With the advent of the Federal Music Project of the Work Projects Administration instruction in various branches of music has been made available to thousands who would otherwise be unable to have it. This program includes instruction-direction for community projects in which the performers are paid by Federal funds. With the co-operation of school authorities, rural schools that never received music instruction have been provided with teachers or supervisors. Teachers have also been provided for State institutions whose budgets have been too small to extend music opportunities. Among these are the Girls' Welfare Home, The Penitentiary, and the Crippled Children's Hospital. Communities have been supplied with instructors of orchestral and band instruments and these in turn have become organized playing groups that contribute to community entertainment. Another of the most interesting undertakings of the Federal Music Project has been the promoting of an awakened interest in our Spanish-American folk music. During the two years the Federal Music Project has functioned in New Mexico, it has offered musical instruction to nearly 10,000 people, and given 736 free public concerts.

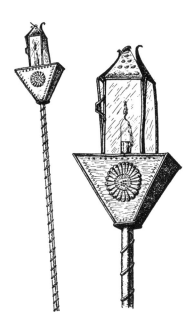

# *Architecture*

ARCHITECTURE more than almost any other art reflects the history and culture of the people and region to which it is related. The architecture of New Mexico based on forms and materials indigenous to the State is particularly representative, modifications having occurred with successive invasions and subsequent changes in social conditions.

Broadly speaking, the history of New Mexico divides itself into three great periods, accompanied by major cultural changes. The first of these is the prehistoric, or pre-Columbian, era extending from the dim horizons of antiquity to the invasion by Coronado in 1540. This was followed by the Spanish era which began with the conquest and extended through three centuries of Latin influence, including the period under Mexican administration, until the American occupation in 1846. The last period, beginning with this date and extending to the present, may be subdivided into two parts: the Territorial, which lasted more or less until the advent of the railroads, and the modern, reflecting the vast cultural changes due to improved technology.

The buildings discovered by the first Spanish explorers were evolved by inhabitants who had lived in this country for unknown centuries. Built of materials found in the desert and adjoining mountain regions, the plans and shapes of those structures resulted from adaptation of materials to the needs of the builders. Since there was no influence present extraneous to the American continent, these edifices may be said to be truly American, and as their influence can still be felt in contemporary New Mexican architecture, the latter possesses a unique heritage in the United States.

As the Indians of the Southwest were a sedentary agricultural people instead of nomadic, they were, more or less, permanently attached to definite sites near their fields. Archeologists find that probably the earliest habitations were caves, and that later, although sometimes concurrently, houses large enough to care for the whole community were erected. These would correspond to modern apartment houses and were occupied by groups rather than by individuals due to the necessity for defense against enemies tempted by the corn stored in them. The necessity for defense was one of the principal factors in the planning and form of the buildings.

The basic unit of these structures was a rectangular cell-like room, a shape which permitted the greatest number of units in a given area. The units were arranged in terraces four or five stories high, each tier receding the depth of one room. Lower and inner rooms were used for storage, the upper and outer ones as living quarters. In certain instances, especially where the apartments were built around a central court, the outer walls were kept flush, only rooms facing the court being set back in receding tiers.

By eliminating large openings in walls of the ground floor, the structure was easily converted into a stronghold by the simple process of withdrawing the ladders which provided access to the upper terraces.

Walls were built either of stone or adobe, depending upon which was more easily available. When the walls were of stone, they were often made of tabular slabs readily obtainable from near-by ledges. The slabs were laid in adobe mortar, sometimes being fitted with such care, as at Pueblo Bonito, that little mortar was required, especially when the joints were filled with a mosaic of spalls which left hardly a chink between the main stones.

Adobe, apparently used from time immemorial, was cast or puddled into place in the walls in stratified layers in a most ingenious fashion. The walls were then finished with a smooth coating of adobe inside and out. The interior of the rooms was also coated with white gypsum or a light colored clay and often, especially in ceremonial rooms, decorated with a contrasting color.

Roofs were formed by placing round logs, or *vigas* as they are referred to locally, six or eight inches in diameter, at regularly spaced intervals across two opposite wall tops. Over these were placed smaller poles crossed at right angles on which long grasses, rushes, small branches, or split sticks were laid closely, and over all a thick layer of mud was spread. These roof surfaces also served as floors for the rooms above.

To provide drainage the entire roof sloped gradually to openings in the side wall in which *canales* (water spouts) were placed extending out over the wall to carry off rain water.

The main supporting *vigas* were cut and trimmed laboriously with primitive stone axes. Because of the work involved, old timber was re-used wherever possible. When a *viga* so used did not fit its new position, it was permitted to protrude beyond the exterior wall, thus producing a characteristic feature of Pueblo Indian architecture: the projecting *viga*.

Wooden doors were not used, openings probably being covered with blankets or hides. Access to rooms on the ground floor was possible only through trap doors in the roof. The upper floors were reached by ladders or masonry steps on the exterior. Windows were simply small holes with no sash of any kind and were used principally to let the smoke out and the air in; they also were probably used to shoot arrows through.

Apparently no chimneys were employed during the prehistoric era, fires usually being built in a sunken or raised pit in the floor, the smoke escaping through a hole in the roof. Rudimentary fireplaces existed, but they had no chimneys.

It should be noted that the multiple-house as described is typical, but there were many variations of the main type. The principal features of this main type, however, have survived to the present day as buildings of stone masonry or adobe in this style are still being erected. The adobe's characteristic softness of outline, due to erosion and battered exterior walls, is an important feature of the New Mexico landscape. The rectangular terraced masses, flat roofs, protruding *vigas,* wood ceilings, and white exterior walls are a heritage, from time immemorial, of the early inhabitants of New Mexico.

The *kivas* (ceremonial chambers), usually subterranean and circular, had, contrary to the general rule of no chimneys, highly complicated ventilating flues connected with fireplaces. The great *kiva* of prehistoric times stood apart from other buildings and projected above ground only far enough to insure drainage. The roof in which a hatchway provided the only entrance to the interior was either flat or cribbed, and rested on pillars which rose at intervals from a continuous bench around the circular wall within.

*Kivas* as found today do not greatly vary from this traditional plan. Excellent examples of the old circular type built partly above ground are to be found in the south plaza of San Ildefonso Pueblo, at Nambé, Santo Domingo, and Cochití; San Juan, Santa Clara, and Tesuque have the rectangular type attached to other buildings. The *kivas* at Taos are below ground with tops and entrances slightly above ground. Fine examples of the prehistoric type of underground *kiva* are present in the cave in Bandelier National Monument, at Aztec National Monument, and Chetro Ketl in the Chaco Canyon National Monument.

The *kivas* which have been brought completely above ground are still circular within although enclosed in rectangular walls and joined to other unrelated buildings. *Kivas* are of the greatest interest architecturally, but have not influenced subsequent architecture in the State as have the great pueblos, or multiple-houses.

When the Spanish soldiers and priests came to New Mexico important architectural changes occurred, but these changes were due only to new plan requirements, improved tools, and methods of construction; the materials remained the same until the advent of the Anglo Americans. Retention of the same materials accounts for the harmonious blending of the old and new.

Unquestionably the greatest architectural influence was at first exerted by the priests who must have been persons of extraordinary ability and fortitude, judging by the many great churches they built under adverse conditions throughout New Mexico. These structures are still used as precedents for monumental buildings in the Pueblo-Spanish style. The priests brought a knowledge of European building methods and an enthusiasm kindled by memories of the Renaissance in Spain. The basis for comparisons in this category is the great church and adjacent monastery at Ácoma. Missions at Laguna Pueblo, San Felipe Pueblo, and others are also noteworthy.

As the priests started their churches, they were brought, however, face to face with the fact that the Indians who were to build them were conservative, had their own building traditions, and that the ancient materials imposed limitations beyond which they could not go. The priests may have wanted to introduce vaulted ceilings and arches, but it was simpler to stay within the construction methods known to the people and safer to avoid arches when using material so easily weathered as adobe. In general they even avoided the arch where stone was used. This practice constitutes one of the principal differences between New Mexico and the later California missions.

Certain changes were made, nevertheless. The plan of Christian churches, usually coffin shaped, narrowing at the sanctuary or else cruciform, was adopted. Where adobe was used (as in the majority of cases) the priests introduced a novel method to the Indians, the making of adobes in the form of pre-cast bricks mixed with straw and sun dried. This became the standard method of adobe construction, the old method of puddling being gradually abandoned. The walls of the churches were greatly thickened in contrast with the rather thin walls formerly constructed. The spans were increased to accommodate large congregations, and heavier timbers were necessarily brought into use even though the roof construction remained essentially the same.

One of the greatest innovations was the introduction of the iron axe and adze. With these tools *vigas* were no longer confined to the round form previously used but were rectangular in section; they also made possible the shaping of decorative capitals to crown pillars or columns and corbels, often in the form of pilaster caps, for support of the roof-beams. Finally and most important, doors, windows, and frames of wood could be made; these, however, were probably not used generally by the Indians in their community houses until they began to feel safe from enemies; but at an early date the Indians began the use of selenite in window openings—an innovation possibly suggested by the priests.

A typical mission church is characterized by massive dignity and simplicity, often relieved by detail of grace and charm (*see Tour 6A,*

*Ácoma*). The nave was lighted by rectangular windows placed high in the walls, frequently on one side only. The walls of the sanctuary were usually carried higher than that of the nave, thus permitting a one-story opening above and in front of the altar which illuminated it from an invisible source of light. This effect produced a feeling of mystery and reverence in the beholder. The interior walls were invariably plastered smooth with adobe and whitened with gypsum. Designs were painted on them with colored earths in the form of dadoes, or bands at the base of walls, and embellishments usually in traditional Indian patterns. The *vigas* were richly carved in many cases, the designs being more reminiscent of Moorish Spain than of the Indian world. This was also true of the corbels supporting the ceiling beams, the capitals over the columns supporting the choir loft, and the beams of the exterior *portales* or porches of the mission facade or the cloister of an adjacent monastery. These *portales,* so characteristic of New Mexican architecture, were probably introduced by the priests but may have come in with secular buildings.

Native materials and methods of construction, with the modifications outlined above, were also adopted for secular buildings. The Spanish house plan was suitable for use in New Mexico due to the similarity in climates. The typical house of the better type was built around a patio with *portales* facing the enclosure—an arrangement providing shelter from wind and sun and also a measure of defense in case of attack, an important consideration in past centuries.

The houses were rarely built more than one or two rooms wide, communication being from room to room. Windows, not glazed in the early days, were usually small, barred with wooden grilles, and provided with wooden shutters on the inside. Few doors opened to the outside, usually one at the front and one at the back, leading to the corral.

Shutters and doors were sometimes paneled and beautifully carved, but more often were simple hand-hewn planks held together with cross bars. They were not hinged, as iron was scarce, but secured to the frame by pivots made by extending the stile into pockets in the frame. Floors were of earth or covered with thin stone slabs. Fireplaces with chimneys came into general use, commonly being built into corners with the walls used as supports for chimneys. High-walled corrals for safe-keeping of livestock in time of trouble were usually attached to the houses.

Many variations of the above plan occurred, including houses with no *portales,* others with *portales* across the front with flanking wings. Some houses were two-storied, as evidenced by the so-called oldest house in Santa Fe, but certain features were common to all: the uneven contours of earthen walls, rectangular masses, flat roofs, wood ceilings, and white interior walls, characteristic of buildings in pre-Columbian times.

Few architectural changes other than those already referred to took place during the three centuries of Latin domination. Homes of the wealthy *haciendados* or *ricos* up and down the Rio Grande Valley were finer than those of the poorer people, but the difference was doubtless mainly only in size and detail. As communication with Mexico became more regular and established, iron, tin, glass, and other refinements of living were imported which led to slight modification of the buildings, but in essentials they remained the same.

A variant in the prevailing rectangular mass was the occasional *torreón* (round tower) used for watchtowers or defense. An example exists at Manzano, but like the round *kivas* of the Indians and their pre-Columbian watchtowers, these structures did not influence the main current of architectural development.

The raising of the American flag in 1846 signaled the beginning of profound changes in the architecture of New Mexico. These changes were slow at first and keyed to the tempo of caravans crossing from the United States into the new Territory. As the Santa Fe Trail became safer for travel, increasing numbers of Anglo-Americans began to arrive with new materials and architectural ideas based on those of the communities from which they came.

Millwork and brick were imported from St. Louis and Kansas City. The small grilled and glassless windows began to give way to double-hung glazed sashes often provided with slatted shutters on the outside. Slender, squared columns replaced the heavy hewn ones; *portal* parapets were ornamented with wood trim. Door and window openings were also trimmed. Painted woodwork further helped to recall eastern precedents. Finally, with the introduction of brick kilns and lime plaster, the old adobes were capped with a protecting cornice of brick in ornamental patterns, and walls were coated with lime stucco.

Nevertheless, since these changes occurred relatively slowly and were made with the original structures as a base, the fundamental rectangular mass and the old plan remained with many of the characteristic details.

The changes described above produced a type similar in detail to the architecture of Monterey, California, but still fundamentally New Mexican as to essentials of construction. The style is extensively used and is known as Territorial to distinguish it from Pueblo-Spanish. Examples of the former are present in Santa Fe, notably Sena Plaza and two homes near the intersection of Canyon Road and Camino del Monte Sol. The new Public Welfare Building, the State Supreme Court Building, and the Municipal Building in Santa Fe are in this same style found also throughout the State.

Some changes, even though not always extensive, occurred in most houses, especially the introduction of glazed sash. Even the ancient communal houses of Indians felt the new influence. The Indians gradually began to feel comparatively safe from enemies, and the resultant tendency was no longer to build terraces and fortress-like houses but to break up into individual smaller units where they could be nearer their fields. Thus the difference between an Indian pueblo and a Spanish-American village tended to decrease.

In towns, especially Santa Fe, where land was relatively expensive, two-story buildings were common and often had a two-story porch in front. The Plaza at one time was almost completely surrounded by such buildings. In some sections, notably Las Vegas and the east slope of the Rockies, many houses of this type are present, further modified by a wood shingle roof in place of the traditional flat dirt one.

With the advent of the railroad in 1878, two outstanding factors which had influenced the architecture of the State were changed. Builders were no longer dependent on local or native materials, and buildings were no longer subject almost exclusively to the native tradition. As a result, buildings of every type and description were erected and the newer towns began to resemble the Middle West and the East —reflecting Anglo-American culture rather than that of New Mexico.

During this period many important public buildings were erected, including the first State capitol in Victorian Gothic style, replaced later by the present domed capitol in neo-English Renaissance style.

The tendency to build outside of the local tradition had actually begun, however, even before the railroad was introduced, one of the most notable examples being the great Cathedral of St. Francis in Santa Fe, a stone Romanesque structure, which replaced the original old, adobe *Parroquia*.

Not even the venerable Palacio Real, or Governor's Palace, in Santa Fe escaped unscathed. This building is so old that some of its walls are constructed of puddled adobe, a technique typical of the pre-Columbian era, although the walls were probably built or rebuilt by Indians after the Pueblo Revolt of 1680. Nevertheless, even this building was trimmed and modernized to the extent of including a delicate Victorian balustrade across the length of the parapet.

During the first decade of the twentieth century a reaction set in and certain individuals began to realize that the ancient traditional forms not only had aesthetic values, but were admirably adapted to the climatic conditions of the country. Appropriately, among the first buildings to reflect this reaction was the Governor's Palace. Under the competent direction of archeologists this structure was brought back to a state approximating the original based upon a plan found on an old map in the British Museum. So successful was this venture that from then on the State's native architecture has been adopted increasingly by Anglo-Americans. Notable examples are the New Mexico State Art Museum, the Laboratory of Anthropology, the Headquarters Building, 3rd Region, National Park Service, Santa Fe, and the new buildings at the University of New Mexico at Albuquerque.

Certain problems have arisen in adapting such rigid modern materials as brick to forms characterized by softness of contour due to use of the hands instead of trowels in plastering and to the erosion of adobe.

One solution is to lay the brick by eye instead of plumb or level as adobes are laid, and to clip corners where rigid lines are too harsh. Another solution is the adoption to a large extent of the modified Territorial style which permits far more rigid lines. Another legitimate solution is frank expression of the structural materials used. This tends to produce a "modern" structure but the characteristic features of the ancient forms can be retained in the adoption of rectangular masses, flat roofs, set-backs, and much of the detail. Where adobe is still used —as it is to a large extent because of its economy and unique insulating qualities—no such problems exist.

That the renascence of indigenous building has proved eminently practical as well as fitting is borne out by the large number of public and private structures in Pueblo-Spanish style erected since the first decade of the present century. In Santa Fe and Taos, where the movement has been most persistent, any number of modern houses reveal the successful use of the old traditions. The Carlos Vierra house in Santa Fe is often cited as an excellent example of domestic architecture in the Pueblo-Spanish style.

It may be the objection of some that in this article too much stress has been laid upon local traditional types when, as a matter of fact, probably the majority of buildings in New Mexico are not in the tradition. This extensive architecture not based on the old forms does not harmonize with indigenous types and a detailed description of such buildings would not be specifically characteristic of New Mexico. No extraneous architecture of significant interest has appeared in the State. Furthermore, as nowhere else in the United States, can a style of architecture be found which traces its descent in an unbroken line from aboriginal American sources; this unique and valuable heritage is worth stressing.

# New Mexican Art

ALMOST anywhere in New Mexico one's boot might turn up from the earth potsherds with fragments of the design still visible. These are the ancient remains of the art of the Pueblo Indians, a sedentary and grain-growing people, living in adobe villages along the water courses of New Mexico who developed the art of decorating and firing clay pottery. Even today every village has its own distinctive designs, despite friendly intercourse among the Pueblo tribes.

From the day she is able to walk, the Indian girl is taught to make a spherical bowl by coiling layers of clay one above the other and polishing the whole to smoothness with an inherited polishing stone. Often to her brother falls the task of applying the designs and firing. Taking a slender brush of yucca fibre between his fingers, and dipping it into vegetable or mineral color, he applies it to the smooth surface of the unfired pot. So much are these strong geometric designs and sure whorls part of the mental configurations of the Pueblo Indian that they were not affected by the transplanted designs of Renaissance Spain or the later Machine Age. For a kiln, a circle of sturdy tin cans is formed, and a few strips of iron act as modern supports, replacing the green branches and stones of ancient use. Into this the pottery is placed, covered by sheep-dung to maintain a hot, even fire.

Attempts to introduce the potter's wheel and a modern kiln have failed, and museum workers and private groups interested in encouraging the art have emphasized the quality of the pottery and the revival of authentic designs, made in the old way. Today the pottery of such people as Marie and Julián Martínez of San Ildefonso pueble sets such a high standard of skill and beauty that appreciation of the genuine art is increasing and the souvenir "rain god" and clay "Mexican sombrero" are falling into disfavor.

At the outdoor Indian market, such as the one held during the summer months before the Palace of Governors in Santa Fe, a comparison of the designs of the various pueblos is possible. From the northern pueblos of Picurís and Taos come bean pots of micaceous gold clay. From San Ildefonso and Santa Clara come bowls, jugs, and plates of luminous black and earthy red, some of them so highly polished as to shine like metal. On the Rio Grande the old villages of Santo Domingo and Cochití produce bold black geometric designs on a creamy buff background. Zía draws upon its pottery conventionalized deer, birds, flowers, and seeds, naively and yet harmoniously arranged. From the western pueblo of Zuñi comes pottery of cold red, with brown and white designs that unite complex triangular figures with rotund whorls. The close-knit geometrics of the hardfired Ácoma pottery, and the accurate cross hatching of fine-line work of the neighboring Laguna, make the pottery of the part of New Mexico lying between Albuquerque and Gallup one of the most interesting ceramic sections in the world.

Pueblo pottery is comparatively soft and porous, for too much heat is apt to warp it and destroy its color and finish. A well-fired pot rings clearly when tapped. In good pottery, the decorations, in black, white, the ochreous clays, and the Ácoma types of orange, red, and yellow, are painted on before the pot is fired. Colors like blues, greens, and purples, painted on after firing, denote pottery made solely for the tourist trade.

*Navaho Weaving.* It is believed that the Navaho women actually learned to weave from the Pueblos, even as the men learned silversmithing from the Spanish colonists; but long ago they outgrew their teachers and forgot them, and today the arts of weaving and silversmithing are Navaho arts. Although the Spaniards brought the sheep as well as the horse to the new country, a Spanish official recorded in 1795 the fact that already Navaho weaving was "of more delicacy and taste than that of the Spaniards."

During the nineteenth century, Navaho blankets evolved from the narrow horizontal striped designs of the Pueblos and became the fine patterns of rhythmic stripes and terraces. To her own subtle gamut of vegetable dyes, the Navaho woman added tropical indigo which she obtained by trade from the Spaniards, and sometimes combined with it the brilliant cochineal red of Bayeta, an imported English red flannel; blankets made with this flannel came to be called "Bayeta." In the 1850's a Navaho sarape was one of the most desired garments on the frontier; it brought $60 on the open market, and was so tightly woven it could hold a bucket of water. It was sought by *haciendados* far below the Mexican border, and the so-called "chief blanket" of broad bold red, white, and blue stripes was traded and treasured by Indians as far north as Canada.

The Navaho loom of that Golden Age of weaving is the same as the loom of today: two sturdy upright poles with the necessary cross poles. The women commence weaving from the bottom, working upward, placing the weft threads through the suspended net of strong warp threads and "battening" down with a flat stick each thread as it is placed. If the battening is done thoroughly and the warp is of a strong, tightly-spun wool, a firmly woven blanket is the result. During the pre-Civil War period the Navaho loom produced unbordered blankets in horizontal stripes and terraces. At this period the rhythmic spacing of stripes, never monotonous, was the highest achievement of the Navaho weaver. It has never since been equaled. For a good example of such a striped blanket a collector today will gladly pay $2,500.

In 1863 the free-roaming Navaho tribe was brought into its first sustained contact with civilization. Kit Carson was commissioned by the United States Government to round up the tribe, destroy its sheep, and conduct the remaining Indians to a forty-mile tract of farm land in the eastern section of the State at Bosque Redondo. For four years, while Indians attempted to become farmers, the army officers provided the women with brightly dyed machine yarns and requested rugs made in their own souvenir designs. That was the beginning of the modern bordered rug.

In 1867 the 7,000 remaining Navahos were given 4,000 head of inferior sheep and sent back to their old country. Aniline dyes and Germantown yarns were introduced. From the 1860's to the 1890's, serrated diamond patterns appeared in the blankets woven by the Indians for their own use. By the end of the century traders introduced among them cotton string for warps and gaudy package dyes. No longer did the old harmonious rhythm of stripes dominate the loom. Instead, a central heterogeneous pattern enclosed by a rectangular border prevailed. The clumsy thick weaving on a cotton string warp, poorly dyed, had one major result: the Navaho ceased wearing the product of his own loom. The introduction of lightweight, factory woven blankets for sale on the reservation relegated the Navaho loom to the further production of rugs for the tourist market. Symbolic stories and designs were conceived by the traders, colors were dictated, and Navaho weaving was wholly directed into the tourist channel. Present day blankets show the result of this forced evolution. Although the intricate designs a Navaho woman weaves today are far more complex than those woven by her grandmother, she has not yet learned to arrive at beauty and harmonious proportion through her often bizarre patterns.

Some efforts have been made to encourage the Navaho weaver to return to the more simple designs and colors of the past. "Revival" blankets of vegetal dyes have generally not proved successful. Their wan colors have never duplicated the warmth and brilliance of the past. Better aniline dyes have been introduced; the degenerating quality of the wool on the reservation has called forth some effort to save the old Navaho sheep from extinction. The kinky wool of modern sheep is best suited to factory spinning.

In the Two Grey Hills district, traders have sent wool to Boston for factory scouring and carding. Rugs from this section are note-worthy for their enduring quality. Their designs, unfortunately, are not comparable with their quality. Just so long as the hurrying public believes that a Navaho rug must be gaudy to be Indian—just so long must both weaver and purchaser suffer.

Present day Navaho blankets that best uphold the old tradition of tight weaving and dignified design are the saddle blankets still widely in use among all Indians and westerners. About the size of the aver-age bathroom rug they are purchasable for about five dollars, and one seldom sees among them a poor design, poor weaving, or fantastic color-ing. The diamond twill, the herringbone, the simple small stripe, characterize most of these blankets, with large yarns of tassel at the four corners. It is hoped that in time the grotesque designs of large modern Navaho rugs will be modified by the weavers themselves into a more unified and harmonious whole.

*Navaho Silversmithing.* Itinerant Spanish silversmiths taught the Navaho the art of working in metal about a century ago. In 1864 while the tribe was confined by the United States Army at Bosque Redondo, coils of brass and copper wire were issued to the Indians who lost no time in hammering the metal into bracelets. After the tribe's release, when silver coins began to find their way to the reserva-tion, the Navaho converted the white man's money into silver buttons, harnesses, squash blossom necklaces, and into the large flat silver shells (called *conchas*) which they strung on a leather strap and wore about the waist. With such ornament they could fare far and wide, cutting off a button when it became necessary to purchase a bag of tobacco. Silver jewelry became the medium of exchange. And at that time—when the Navaho hammered his silver into artistic forms for himself and his family to wear—the most beautiful silver was made. Today it may be seen in museum collections, and occasionally bought from traders who universally refer to the old silver as "pawn." The Indians' perpetual indebtedness to the trader leads to the trader's acceptance of Indian jewelry in pawn. The silverwork of this period is character-ized by its substantial weight and its boldness and simplicity of design.

About 1900 the Navaho learned of the better silver content in Mexican pesos, and for thirty or more years, most Navaho jewelry was made of this malleable money. The early years of the twentieth century evolved the use of turquoise (the ancient precious stone of Southwestern Indians) massively combined with the white metal.

Traders took a growing interest in the silver work, and it was intro-duced to early railroad tourists as souvenirs of the Indian country. To conform to tourist demands the jewelry was steadily reduced in cost (and thus in weight of silver) so that an essential quality of the old jewelry—its substantial weight—was lost. In conforming to popular imagination about "symbolic" Indian designs, the trader introduced among the Indians new dyes, swastikas, thunderbirds, etc.—which had never been a part of the old silversmith's kit, but which are still widely publicized and purchased as symbolic Indian jewelry.

Today there are three main groups of Indians working in silver: [1] the scattered group, of about 500 smiths, living mostly in the southern part of the Navaho reservation adjacent to Highway 66, who are strongly influenced by the traders who supply them with silver and designs; [2] the equally large and shifting population of young men (of all tribes) who work, on a weekly salary, in the benchwork system of city souvenir shops; [3] the young Indians who are being trained in the best tradition of their grandfathers at the United States Indian schools.

Reservation silversmiths still work with a hammer bought from the trader, and a piece of railroad iron picked up along the tracks for an anvil. Mexican pesos, no longer available, have been replaced by the little one-ounce slugs of silver supplied by the trader. Sandpaper, pliers, tongs, punches, nippers, vices, hammers, shears—all are obtained from the trader. Where once the Indian soldered his silver work with silver dust mixed with his own saliva and native alum got from the ground, he now asks for borax at the store. To decorate the surface of his hammered silver, the reservation Navaho employ dies which they themselves have filed from bits of scrap iron. These dies are little design "elements" which they press into the warm silver. These small elements-of-the-design possess no description: in their very namelessness lies their authenticity. Although reservation traders have demanded mass-production of low-priced souvenirs in "symbolic" designs, there are still Navaho making traditional silver jewelry for their own and their family's use. Such silver is generally heavy in weight, simple in design, with a soft surface polish obtained by patient rubbing with buckskin. There are still old smiths who pour liquid silver into a sandstone mold to form those buckles and bowguards which they themselves wear. And "file" work—the beautiful bracelets of pure silver, in a series of painstakingly filed ridges—can be found in the more remote trading posts. Gradually the gasoline blow torch (instead of charcoal) is being introduced on the reservation, and it is in itself a factor to be considered in the changing of design, for it makes possible the quick soldering of commercial silver wire, and other small surface ornaments, which the trader has introduced.

Since the tremendous increase in travel, souvenir shops and souvenir-producing factories have sprung up in most Southwestern cities. Young Indian silversmiths can find employment at their trade, but it necessitates working in an assembly line. Here they are paid weekly salary to monotonously stamp out hundreds of catalogue bracelets and rings from large sheets of silver. They have little, if any, control over the design, and the amount of hand-hammering and hand-polishing that is required of commercial silver wire, and commercial "boxes" that hold the machine-polished turquoise, is at a minimum.

With the loss of originality and the beautiful proportion that characterized old Navaho design has come a perfection of technique both on the reservation and in the city shop. Technically, the modern Indian silversmith, though less of an artist, is a more finished workman.

The Government, in its effort to encourage traditional Indian silversmithing, maintains three very good schools for Indian craftsmen in New Mexico. Silver working shops may be visited in United States Indian schools at Santa Fe, Albuquerque, and Fort Wingate. Here young Navaho and Pueblo boys become expert craftsmen in all the old skills and designs of their people working under master Navaho silversmiths, and producing the finest present-day Indian silverwork. Unfortunately, a large percentage of the boys on leaving school enter bench-work shops in the city where they have little opportuntiy to develop their hand training.

The United States Indian Arts and Crafts Board has established standards for judging Indian jewelry, and sometimes the Board's stamp of authenticity may be found on the underside of the jewelry. To meet its approval a piece of Indian jewelry must [1] be hand-hammered of silver slugs not less than 900 fine; [2] be fashioned by hand-made dies which contain only one single element of design which is applied with hand tools; [3] contain appliquéd ornaments made by hand; [4] contain genuine turquoise, handcut and polished; [5] be of hand-polished silver.

*Indian Painting.* The most recent art to attain high development among the Indians of New Mexico is painting in water color. This ancient technique had its origins in the paintings on cliff dwellings, in the decorating of ceremonial rooms or *kivas,* and in the painting of leather shields and cotton dance kilts.

The old-age precision with which the Pueblo Indians decorate pottery and the Navaho make their intricate sand paintings, has influenced the fine draughtsmanship and sense of decoration that characterizes Indian pictures. The art of painting a portable picture or filling a rectangle of paper with color and movement dates almost wholly from the beginning of the present century and illustrates how quickly and keenly this naturally artistic race can adapt itself to a new medium of expression.

Dr. Edgar L. Hewett and other present-day archeologists in the Southwest were the first to place paints and paper in the hands of Indians. Indifferent to European laws of perspective, placing simply that which was in the distance above that which was in the foreground, the early painters gradually evolved in draughtsmanship and complexity, until today a very strong and individual American Indian school of painting has taken root.

In 1922 Doctor Hewett wrote: "The Indian race may attain to a place equal to that of the Orientals, whose art in many respects, such as its flat, decorative character, absence of backgrounds and foregrounds, freedom from our system of perspective, unerring color sense and strangely impersonal character, it strongly resembles."

Three full-blooded Indian youths, painting in their own style, were given special encouragement. The boys were Awa Tsireh, of San Ildefonso, Fred Kaboti, a Hopi, and Ma-Pe-Wi, from Zía pueblo. In 1925 the Newberry Library in Chicago showed a score of Awa Tsireh's water colors. In 1927 Ma-Pe-Wi, Awa Tsireh, Tonita Peña, and Crescencio of San Ildefonso had paintings at the International Art Center in New York City.

In the United States Indian Schools as late as 1928, Indian children were prohibited from painting Indian subjects, until a United States Congressman expressed the changing sentiment, slow but sure in coming to the surface: "Who wants to go West to buy a picture painted by an Indian of three apples on a plate?"

In 1929 a Sunday edition of a newspaper in Madrid, Spain, acclaimed a water color of a "Zuñi Basket Dance" shown among the paintings of the Pueblo Indians in the Congress of Folk Arts held at Prague. By 1931 Oqwa Pi of San Ildefonso was exhibiting in the Museum of Modern Art in New York City.

But it was September of 1933 before the Indian Bureau in Washington decided upon the need of a department of painting in the Santa Fe Indian School. The paintings of the students have been exhibited at the Royal College of Art in London, at the Trocadero in Paris, in shows all over the European and American continents. Large murals have been executed by the Indian youths in their laboratories and dining rooms; and in Government and private buildings, depicting ceremonial dances, scenes of the hunt, of wild life, and of typically Indian industries. A permanent exhibit is usually to be found at the Santa Fe Indian School, while adult Indians will show you their paintings in their own homes. The nominally priced pictures may be obtained from artists living in the pueblos, from the Indian Schools, the Santa Fe Art Museum, the better shops, and the professional galleries.

## SPANISH COLONIAL ART

During the period of Spanish colonization of New Mexico, Spain was at the height of her artistic glory. It was the period of Velásquez and El Greco, and among the lesser artists Ribera (who visited Italy and had been converted to the style of Corrégio) ; Zubarán, a painter of religious pictures, who leaned toward ecstatic, saintly heroes; and Montañez, an eloquent sensualist and head of the school of Spanish sculpture. In 1680 the gentle Murillo was born in Seville, which became the center of Spanish art, and where the Italian Rennaisance took root. His pictures of the Virgin were tempered with tenderness such as the colonists of New Mexico found sadly lacking in the new province. Despite difficult transportation over the trail from Mexico, the first Spanish settlers imported many religious paintings and carvings. Thus the local art derived from sources in the mother country, and for a long time pictures like those of Murillo were models for the early creative efforts of New Mexican artists.

To supply the great love the colonists felt for religious art, paintings were executed under the direction of missionary priests. These pictures were not rendered in the accomplished style of the Continental artists. They were painted on hand-hewn wood or on skins, with earth colors and vegetable dyes used by the Indians. There was a deliberate effort to cling closely to the traditions and refinement of the European models; but the artists were untutored. The result was a primitive adaptation of Spanish painting.

In the Pueblo Rebellion of 1680, the churches were razed, the paintings brought from Europe were arrow-holed, and many possessions damaged. The reconstruction period moved the local artists toward a more native expression, since they could no longer rely on imported models. As generations passed, the minds of the artists strayed from tradition, and they relied more on their own conceptions, drawn from environment.

The saintly images called *santos* became primitive in feeling and technique. A local school of art developed, with its own style and in the native mediums. It was an art of passionate extremes, sensual, yet morbidly ascetic and stoical. It was a folk art, adapted to its environment with simplicity of design.

The New Mexican carvings were of several types. The *bultos* were carved of soft wood, generally the roots of cottonwood, coated with gesso and colored. Other *bultos* were made by impregnating a cloth or a skin with gesso and stretching it over a framework of reeds. The cloth was molded to the framework and decorated. The crucifixes were classed with *bultos*. Often a crucifix has several carved objects at the base of the pedestal.

The *retablos* were paintings on wood, generally hand-hewn pines. The wood was shaped, then the surface treated, covered with gesso and painted. The *retablos* varied in size from miniatures to the large *reredos,* the back screen of an altar consisting of several *retablos*. Still other *santos* were painted on tin and canvas.

The altars, when carved, followed a simplified baroque of the Spanish schools. The side altars often contained locally painted saints. Sometimes, instead of carving, the pieces were painted to represent carving. The altar in the church at Laguna, rich in color, with twisted columns dividing the panels of Saints, is considered by many the finest in New Mexico. In the church at Ranchos de Taos is a large *retablo* which suggests the New Mexican school in many carvings—the San Miguel, the San Ysidro, and the agonizing Cristo on the Cross.

New Mexicans were so strongly devoted to their old images that they regarded them as holy relics. Later the French priests brought pasty-looking French pieces. Then began an influx of Currier and Ives prints and European lithographs, ridiculously embellished to tease the Latin fancy. But the Penitentes never accepted the importation and their *moradas* contain many of the original *retablos* and *bultos,* safe from collectors.

There were many carved and panelled chests (*cajas*). The carvings were simple geometric designs, yet often a border was used with birds and animals cut in repeated half-circles. There were great unadorned chests for food and smaller ones for clothing, often painted in popular flower motifs. Often the household had only one large chair, reserved for the priest. Since his visits were infrequent, the chairs were little used and many of them passed on from father to son.

Furniture had two styles: the formal uprightness of the Spanish and the grace of the Empire. There seems to be no native example of the rococo, such as was used in table supports in Spain. In fact there are no examples of tables except small ones, with supports hand carved in imitation of turnings. The cupboard (*trastero*) often possessed an imposing height, with paneled and grilled doors swung to a center fastening. A fancy carving in relief often graced the top. Hinges were embracing hooks of iron.

Little dating of furniture can be done except by American occupation. The early craftsman used the full mortise and tenon for strength in the soft wood. Later the hard pieces of eastern manufacture were brought in by wagon trains, and the craftsman discontinued this type of joinery, seeing it was not used in the importations.

One of the most fascinating means of decorative embellishment was the use of straw laid on a coat of pitch. Used on chests and crosses, its golden scheme made a splendid contrast with the blackness of the pitch. Little of the craft has been revived, except recently at the Spanish-American Normal School at El Rito and on the New Mexico Art Project.

The Conquistadores depended upon the Indians for spinning and weaving. In 1804 the viceroy wrote to Mexico asking for master-weavers to instruct the local craftsmen. His request was granted and the Bazan brothers, Don Ricardo and Don Juan, came to New Mexico. After a short stay in Santa Fe they settled in Chimayó which became the center of the weaving industry. The best blankets, of handspun wool, colored with vegetable dyes, were done about 1850. Indigo, brazil wood, and cochineal were imported from Mexico; others were made from local plants.

The pattern sources varied. A popular one was the zig-zag which Mary Austin attributes to the influence of Indian pottery. Older pieces use repetitive design with variations, and a color harmony resulting from limitations of the hues. Some patterns are derived from Mexico; others, from local sources, are quite primitive.

After the American occupation the old craft gradually fell into discard. It has been somewhat preserved in Chimayó due to the demand for the blankets by curio companies. Commercial dyes were used in the 1880's as they were easier to use than the old vegetable dyes. The machine-spun wool was used a great deal after the turn of the century, when Chimayó blankets were made for the tourist trade.

The revival of weaving came after the contemporary artists became interested in native crafts. The revival was slow because little information was available on the older practises. Vegetable dyes were occasionally used but with results far inferior in color and durability to those used by early workmen. Later, private enterprises bought and sold blankets with the result that the demand far exceeds supply. Weaving again became a highly perfected art; at no time have the standards of workmanship been lowered to meet the demand, and the craftsmen in the villages of New Mexico are again producing their woven materials of handspun, vegetable dyed yarn which is equal to the best of the former period.

The women practised embroidery in a beautiful, decorative manner. Animal and plant forms were used as motifs. The art was probably practised less professionally than weaving, being part of the education of the leisure class women. *Colchas* (bedspreads) and altar cloths were thus embroidered. The long coarse stitchery, caught down with a short cross stitch, was executed upon handspun cloth called *jerga,* and composed an all-over pattern. The *sabanilla* or altar cloth was an all-over embroidery.

The paper flower is a very popular art in New Mexico today. Girls master it early in life. New flowers are made to adorn altars at fiesta time, and they are also used in weddings. Before the manufacture of crepe paper, colored tissues were used. A hundred years ago chicken feathers were put to decorative uses of this kind, a practise that probably came from Mexico. These flowers were often arranged on *bultos* and the whole protected by cases made of tin and glass.

The blacksmith made iron locks and hasps, spear heads, axes, knives, copper or brass kettles, and an occasional article of tin such as a lantern or a candle holder. Tin craft flourished with the importation of European lithographs and Currier and Ives prints. The prints were fragile and to protect them tin frames were worked into forms of stars, birds, and leaves, combined with spiral ropings made from thinly cut, twisted strips.

From tin are made decorative mirrors, candelabra, flower pots, pitchers, crosses, and boxes with painted glass sides. The painting of the glass had a delicate charm of which few examples are left. Designs were usually in simple colors combed into waves while the paint was wet. These undulations often formed a background for more formal patterns. It is thought that tin came into use largely because of the use of silver by the rich.

Iron and tinsmithing have been corrupted least of all the crafts by the machine age, and it is difficult to distinguish new pieces from old examples as to quality, design, and workmanship.

The jewelry in gold and silver, known as filigree, emphasized delicacy of ornamentation. Much of the silver filigree doubtless came from Mexico, where that metal is plentiful and cheap. Although brooches, rings, combs, and earrings were made both in Europe and Mexico, they did not have such fine tracery as was turned in New Mexico. It remained in vogue until the early part of the twentieth century when the silver made by the Indians replaced it in popularity.

Frank Applegate was one of the first artists to take a major interest in local crafts. The Spanish-Colonial Art Society, organized by him and Mary Austin, has been active in preserving the older objects, and the State Department of Vocational Education has done much to promote the revival of local folk art. In 1932 the University of New Mexico became interested in the program and formed a department to study old pieces and their practicability for modern use. Photographs and drawings were made of private collections and furnished to the vocational schools teaching various folk crafts. These schools supply the State and elsewhere with an array of fascinating articles, useful and decorative, in the traditional Spanish-Colonial design.

Through the arts of the native people, the contemporary artists who visited New Mexico found a deeper fulfillment than is afforded by mere "picturesqueness." During a time when it was proper to go to Europe for traditional background, they stumbled upon sources which made them feel at home in North America, the sources existing in the Spanish-Americans. It gave to those modern explorers a sense of art heritage which they could not find in any other place in their homeland.

## THE MODERN ART MOVEMENT

In the fall of 1898 two young artists, Bert Phillips and Ernest L. Blumenschein, driving a camp wagon on a sketching trip from Denver to Mexico City, stopped at the Taos pueblo, and, fascinated by the paintable landscape and the colorful Indians, they sold their team and remained to begin the Taos Art Colony. True, a number of painters had been through the area before—the Kern brothers who came with the U. S. Army in 1846; Sauerwine, painter of Indians; Remington, famous for his Montana cowboys and scenes from army life; but Blumenschein and Phillips, by their exhibitions throughout the country, popularized the region. Blumenschein spent the winters in New York, but Phillips became a ranger in the Carson National Forest, and his paintings mirror his intimate knowledge of the country.

Other painters followed—Joseph Henry Sharp, Irving Couse from New York, Oscar Berninghouse from St. Louis, Walter Ufer from Chicago. In 1914 the Taos group organized the Taos Society of Artists which held regular spring and autumn exhibits in art centers like New York, Boston, and Philadelphia. Fame of the Taos colony spread to the Old World, and from Russia came Nicolai Feschin and Leon Gaspar, from Austria Joseph Fleck, and from England came John Young-Hunter, the portrait painter, and Dorothy Brett.

In 1923 a group called the New Mexico Painters was formed which combined both the Taos and the Santa Fe colonies, with Mr. Blumenschein as secretary. It included Victor Higgins and Walter Ufer of Taos, and Frank Applegate, William P. Henderson, Jozef Bakos and B. J. O. Nordfelt of Santa Fe. This organization sent paintings on circuits of the entire country.

In 1925 Burt Harwood settled in Taos and erected an art gallery which housed the paintings and art objects he had collected in years of travel in Europe. At his death the gallery was left to the town as an art and community center, and named the Harwood Foundation. Around this central building smaller studios were erected for use by visiting artists. In 1930 the Harwood Foundation was taken over by the University of New Mexico for its summer art school, and in 1932 it was named the Taos School of Art under the direction of Emil Bisttram who came from the Roerich Museum in New York.

Santa Fe followed Taos as an art center, through the efforts of George Bellows, Robert Henri, and Albert Growl, who lived there in the second decade of the century. They were followed by Warren E. Rollins, Sheldon Parsons, William P. Henderson, Gustave Baumann, Gerald Cassidy, Louise Crow, Kenneth Chapman, Carlos Vierra, Frank Applegate, and Olive Rush. In 1917, Henri and Bellows, with the assistance of Edgar L. Hewett, established the Santa Fe Art Museum with a policy, unique in the history of American art, of free exhibition space to all artists. The museum itself was built largely through the financial assistance of Frank Springer, famous paleontologist, who had befriended Donald Beauregard. Beauregard's paintings now line the walls of the second floor of the museum, and he made the sketches for the murals in St. Francis Auditorium adjoining the museum, but his untimely death prevented his execution of them, and Kenneth Chapman and Carlos Vierra collaborated on the final work.

In the 1920's a number of artists came to Santa Fe to settle, among them John Sloan, Randall Davey, Julius Rolshoven, Allan True, Raymond Jonson, Alfred E. Hayward, Albert H. Schmidt, Howard Ashmun Patterson, Datus Myers, Henry Balink, Bruce Saville, Allan Clark, Eugenie Shonnard, and D. Paul Jones. In 1920 the Santa Fe Arts Club was organized; it sponsored exhibits in various parts of the country. Also in 1920 came five young painters who called themselves *Los Cinco Pintores:* Jozef Bakos, Walter Mruk, Fremont Ellis, Willard Nash, and Will Shuster. They bought land on the Camino del Monte Sol, and built adobe homes and studios, beginning the colony of artists and writers who now live in that section of Santa Fe. They exhibited together in various parts of the country for about five years when in 1926 they joined with the Taos artists in the New Mexico Painters Society.

A new group of painters came around 1930, consisting of Gina Knee, Charles Barrows, E. Boyd, Cady Wells, and Jim Morris. They formed the Rio Grande Painters, who exhibited together for a few years, despite the diversity of their talents and interests.

Considerable activity developed in Albuquerque around the Art Department of the University of New Mexico and the New Mexico Art League. The Art League was formed in 1929 by a group of faculty members and students who have since then held yearly exhibits on the campus of the university. The University Art Department, founded in 1928, is headed by Ralph W. Douglass, painter and former cartoonist for the Chicago Daily News. The faculty consists of Raymond Jonson of Santa Fe, Loren Mozley of Taos (who directed the summer sessions in Taos), Mela Sedillo Brewster, in Spanish Colonial Arts and Crafts, and F. E. Del Dosso, teacher of design.

A number of individual artists work in Albuquerque. These include Brooks Willis, Howard Schleeter, Gisella Loeffler Lacher, and Edma Pierce. Known particularly for his Indian dance designs in tempera, Paul Flying Eagle Goodbear, a Cheyenne Indian, has attained considerable fame. Of the artists who have come to draw upon the history and landscape, there are Carl von Hassler, Carl Redin, Winifred D. Thompson, Inez B. Westlake, and Jim McMurdo.

Scattered across the State are various artists who have attained national recognition. In San Patricio is Peter Hurd; Fritz Broeske is in Las Vegas; in Texico is Pedro Cervantez, a strong primitive, former student of Vernon Hunter, who spent his formative years in Texico and has painted some of the most significant pictures of the Southwest.

Most recent organization of artists in New Mexico is the Transcedental Painting Group, founded at Taos in the summer of 1938. The purpose of the movement is to carry painting beyond the appearance of the physical world, through new concepts of space, color, light, and design, to imaginative realms that are idealistic and spiritual. The members of the group are Raymond Jonson, one of the world's leading non-objective painters, Bill Lumpkins, well-known modernist, Emil Bisttram, one of America's leading experimenters and teachers, Robert Gribbroek, Lawren Harris, the famous Canadian artist, Florence Miller, and H. Towner Pierce.

Despite the number of artists, the various colonies, and the groups that formed and reformed during the last three decades, there is no characteristic school of art in New Mexico. The forces of Europe and the East are strong in the State because most of the artists came from other places, and brought their training and temperaments with them. The painted record of New Mexico scenes has already become stereotype: an adobe house making a pattern of light and shade, the terraced lines of a pueblo, village scenes and country landscapes at various seasons of the year, and in different lights, deep-lined Indian faces and scenes from the lives of Cabeza de Vaca, Oñate, and Coronado. Today the artists of the State are trying to catch the life of New Mexico in free rhythms and modern moods.

In recent years, the strongest single factor in encouraging art in the State has been the New Mexico Art Project, which was opened in October 1935. Both the depression and ill-health—the latter of which brought many artists to New Mexico—made the employment problem of Southwestern artists a particularly urgent one. Many artists had been forced to give up painting entirely. During the first four years of its operation, 206 individuals were employed at various times. Well-known artists were given a chance to paint without restraint, and often, under these circumstances, produced some of their finest works. The project also developed a number of young artists. This encouragement stimulated creative activity and produced fresh and vigorous works. Easel paintings were distributed to the tax-supported public institutions, and many of them were chosen for national circulation and exhibition. Objects of arts and crafts were in great demand at exhibitions and educational institutions. Permanent and important works were the murals made in public buildings and educational institutions. In the work of the Index of American Design, part of the WPA art program, Spanish and Colonial arts and crafts were documented for permanent record. For the general public, Art Centers were established in Gallup, Melrose, and Roswell, where traveling national exhibits were shown free. These small communities became art-conscious, and fostered such activities as art-workshops, lectures, and classes in art education at the Art Centers.

# PART II

## A City, a Capital, and an Art Center

# Albuquerque

*Railroad Station:* Santa Fe Station, Silver Ave. and 1st St., for Atchison, Topeka and Santa Fe Ry.

*Bus Stations:* Union Bus Station, W. Copper Ave. and 6th St., for Interstate Busses, Southwestern Greyhound, Pacific Greyhound, New Mexico Transportation Co., San Juan Basin Stages and Inter-City Transit lines. Santa Fe Trailways Station, W. Copper and 5th St., for Santa Fe Trailways (transcontinental) System.

*City Busses:* Fare 10¢, regular service.

*Taxis:* Fare 15¢ upward, according to number of passengers and distance.

*Airports:* Municipal Airport, 3 *m.* SE. of city off US 66, S. on Yale Ave., for all lines; Taxi fare 50¢, time 10 minutes. Private airport 5 *m.* E. of city, reasonable fees.

*Traffic Regulations:* Speed limit 25 miles per hour; reduce speed at school zones. Regulation traffic lights, with signs regulating L., R., and U turns. Signs designate parking time-limits: One-hour limit in downtown section, 8 a.m. to 6 p.m.; ten-minute limit on the east side of post office. No L or U turns on W. Central Ave. from 1st to 7th St.

*Street Numbering:* Central Ave. N. and S. dividing line; 1st St. E. and W. dividing line.

*Accommodations:* Nine hotels, tourist courts, camps, and trailer parks; boarding houses; convalescent homes.

*Information Service:* Chamber of Commerce and American Automobile Association (A.A.A.), 319 N. 4th St.; Albuquerque Civic Council (Health-seeker information), Sunshine Bldg.

*Radio Stations:* KOB (1180 kc.); KGGM (1230 kc.).

*Theatres and Motion Picture Houses:* Albuquerque Little Theatre, San Pasquale Ave., local productions; Carlisle Gymnasium, Villagrá Ave., concerts and conventions; Hodgin Hall, University Campus, 2000 E. Central Ave., public lectures; Albuquerque High School Auditorium, E. Central Ave. and Broadway Ave. Eight motion picture houses.

*Athletic Fields:* University of New Mexico Stadium, Villagrá Ave.; Lincoln Stadium, W. Coal Ave.; Tingley Field, Rio Grande Park, S. 14th St.

*Swimming:* Municipal Beach, Laguna and Kit Carson Blvds., nominal fees, swimming suits rented, open summer season; Y. M. C. A., Central Ave. and 1st St., nominal fees, memberships, open all year; Highland Park, 900 E. Silver Ave., pool for children, free, open summer season.

*Tennis:* Twelve municipal (free) courts in various city parks.

*Golf:* Albuquerque Country Club, Laguna and Kit Carson Blvds., 18 holes, greens fee $1.20 for all day, monthly dues $6.60 with greens fee of 10¢ for 9 holes, limit 20¢ per day, caddies available; Sandía Golf Club, N. 4th St., 9 holes, greens fee 35¢ weekdays, 60¢ Sun.

*Riding:* Riding stables maintained by several concerns, horses rented, reasonable fees. (Consult Chamber of Commerce.)

*Hunting, Fishing, and Outdoor Sports:* Pheasant, quail, goose, duck, and rabbit hunting in season within short driving radius of city; fresh water angling in adjacent irrigation canals in season; skiing and winter sports in near-by Sandía Mountains.

*Baseball:* Tingley Field, Rio Grande Park, S. 14th St.

*Annual Events:* Easter Sunrise Service, Albuquerque Choral Club, University Stadium, Villagrá Ave.; Easter Egg Hunt, Easter morning, Rio Grande Park, S. 14th St.; Pioneer Days' Celebration; Satiric Art Ball, Albuquerque Society of Artists, Carlyle Gymnasium, Villagrá Ave.; Fiesta de San Felipe de Nerí, Old Albuquerque Plaza; Fall Festival and State Fair; Indian dances and ceremonials in nearby pueblos.

ALBUQUERQUE (pronounced Al-boo-kur-keh, 4,943 alt., 35,378 pop.), New Mexico's largest city and principal banking, industrial, railroad, and air lines center, owes much of its commercial development to an equable climate and to the rich timber, mineral, and agricultural resources in its vicinity. The population figures are taken from the 1940 census returns.

In the fertile valley of the Rio Grande, where the river sweeps in a broad curve from the north, the city is flanked east and west by tawny mesas and blue mountains. Fifteen miles to the east the Sandía Mountains rise 6,000 feet above the surrounding mesas to form the eastern ramparts of the valley. To the west, beyond the Rio Grande, snow-capped Cebolleta (Mt. Taylor) reaches an altitude of 11,389 feet. Nearer the city, to the northwest, five extinct volcanic cones accent the horizon. Other ranges northward and to the south are distantly visible above the reaches of the valley.

There are two Albuquerques, the old and the new. Old Albuquerque, locally called Old Town, the third villa established by the Spanish after their conquest of the province of Nuevo Méjico in the sixteenth century and their reconquest in the seventeenth, was the center of the trade, religion, and culture of the Spanish Province for almost two hundred years, and it still retains much of the color of this earlier leisurely period. The new Albuquerque, today's modern business section, is less than sixty years old, but already it serves a wide trade area and is brisk with transcontinental traffic. The two places, so different in tempo and appearance, are joined by Central Avenue (US 66), where the architecture from Old Town eastward to the business district records the periods through which the towns have passed, from the low squat adobe Provincial days, through the Victorian era, to the modern downtown skyscraper.

Cottonwoods, tamarisks, and poplars line miles of streets and parkways squarely laid out; parks are numerous and neat. There are many beautiful houses with patios and broad landscaped lawns and gardens. In various sections an effort has been made to harmonize modern structures with a semblance of territorial or Spanish-Pueblo design. The newer suburban districts and part of the business section follow this trend, though sometimes at the expense of unity of style. The older districts often have row after row of adobe, stucco, and brick homes. Frame dwellings are comparatively rare, and buildings are usually one or two stories in height, although in the business sections higher structures break the skyline.

The streets of Old Town and the outlying districts are lined with ancient flat-roofed houses typical of an earlier day. The plan of Old

Albuquerque with its central Plaza was that of all early Spanish towns in the Province of New Mexico. The thick-walled adobe church, *convento,* and other houses facing the enclosure formed a fortlike protection against marauding Indians. In the eighteenth century the livestock was corralled there at night; at a later period the Plaza was used as the market place for overland freight wagons. Spanish folkways are still evident in the *fiestas* and *bailes* (native dances), and especially on religious holidays, when participants in elaborate raiment carry the image of their patron saint in solemn procession and chant softly to violin or guitar accompaniment. Today the Old Plaza is content with memories, while the vigorous young town to the east marches on.

Youth seems to predominate on the crowded streets downtown, for the city is an educational center. The business man, the health seeker, and the retired executive jostle tourists en route east or west; and, mingling with them, Indians in gaudy blankets offer for sale the turquoise and silver jewelry and the pottery they make. Occasional cowboys in boots and ten-gallon hats mingle with a sprinkling of Spanish-Americans, the men wearing sombreros and the women fringed *tápalos* (shawls). In the evenings the streets are ablaze with the kaleidoscopic lights of modern signs, some of them pictorial representations of Indians at work or mountains in changing colors.

Although inhabited for generations by the Indians, the Rio Grande Valley at the site of present-day Albuquerque was first seen by white men when a detachment of Coronado's troops under Hernando Alvarado explored it in 1540. Other explorers followed, and after Oñate's time (1598), ranches developed in this vicinity, but no towns were founded. The ranches and haciendas were destroyed during the Pueblo Rebellion (1680) when the Spanish were driven from the province and sought refuge in El Paso.

Albuquerque was founded in 1706 by Don Francisco Cuervo y Valdés, twenty-eighth Governor and Captain-General of New Mexico, who removed thirty families from near-by Bernalillo and located them on the Rio Bravo del Norte (fierce river of the north), as the Rio Grande was then known, "in a goodly place of pasturage." He honored his patron saint, Francisco Xavier, and the Duke of Alburquerque, viceroy of New Spain, by naming the villa San Francisco de Alburquerque, from which came the common appellation of the "Duke City." Because the villa was founded without consulting King Philip V, however, the viceroy diplomatically renamed it San Felipe de Alburquerque, Felipe being Spanish for Philip. Eventually the first "r" was dropped, and it became Albuquerque. One of the first structures was the Church of San Felipe de Nerí, now a landmark, erected on the north side of the plaza in 1706.

Governor Cuervo y Valdés had progressive ideas regarding sanitation and protection which he put into practise in the new villa, with the result that it rapidly surpassed neighboring settlements both in size and in population, and soon became a place of considerable importance in trade routes. With a population periodically augmented by settlers seeking protection from possible attacks by marauding Indians, the town grew slowly but steadily. In 1790, the population was 5,959.

The villa was an important military post during the Spanish and Mexican regimes, second in importance only to Santa Fe and El Paso del Norte. After the American occupation in 1846 it was one of the important outposts of the US Military Department until 1870, when it was the headquarters for General Phil Sheridan. Many famous American army men were stationed here during this time, among them Generals Rucker, Miles, Sherman, and Sibley, and the peaceful plaza of the old Spanish town, usually scene of the gay communal life, a market place by day and a fiesta scene by night, became a drill ground for American troops.

Albuquerque was still an isolated frontier town during the Civil War, and the sympathies of the residents fluctuated. Although several skirmishes occurred in the vicinity, the post was alternately occupied by Union and Confederate forces with only a few shots fired. In 1862 Captain Enos, with a small Union command, was informed of the approach of Confederate General Hopkins Sibley with a large force. Realizing that defense was impossible, Enos loaded all available wagons and started them for Santa Fe, then fired the army storage houses to destroy remaining supplies. After his departure, Southern sympathizers extinguished the blaze and saved much of the provisions, which they turned over to General Sibley. He occupied the post without opposition for two months, but on learning that strong Union forces were advancing under Colonel R. S. Canby to take the town, Sibley hastily evacuated, burying eight heavy howitzers, or Napoleon guns, which he had previously captured from Union forces. Two of these cannon, later unearthed, are now in Robinson Park.

Sibley's sudden departure left the town in confusion. Suspicion and jealousies were rampant, and public officials abused their power by "legally confiscating" property of "accused" persons who had no recourse when, at public auctions, their effects were purchased by their accusers at far below actual value.

The decade following the Civil War brought an influx of eastern and mid-western farmers and livestock raisers who were looking for cheap land, and many who were attracted by the fertile valley and high grassy mesas settled in Bernalillo County.

Outside connection by telegraph first came in 1875. Completion of the Atchison, Topeka, and Santa Fe Railroad (1881) gave impetus to the town's growth, and under direction of the New Mexico Town Company, a railroad subsidiary, New Albuquerque was surveyed and platted in November 1880. The obstinacy of a landowner near Old Albuquerque in the matter of a right-of-way and the desire for a roadbed along the higher levels near the foothills away from the river made it necessary for the railroad to route two miles east, and the location of new Albuquerque, like that of many other western towns, was conditioned by the route of the railroad. In the usual procedure of the frontier, the first city lots were sold from a railroad flatcar.

# Cities and Towns

*Ernest Knee*　　　　OLD PALACE OF THE GOVERNORS (1610), SANTA FE

STATE SUPREME COURT BUILDING, SANTA FE

ENTRANCE, LITTLE THEATER, ALBUQUERQUE
Fresco, *Los Moros y Cristianos,* by Dorothy N. Stewart

LIBRARY, UNIVERSITY OF NEW MEXICO, ALBUQUERQUE

TERRITORIAL MEETING HOUSE, SANTA FE

PATIO, CASSIDY HOUSE, SANTA FE
Portal Incorporates Carved Choir-Loft Beam

STATE CAPITOL, SANTA FE

ADMINISTRATION BUILDING, UNIVERSITY OF NEW MEXICO, ALBUQUERQUE

CADETS ON PARADE, NEW MEXICO MILITARY INSTITUTE, ROSWELL

*Charles Vierheller*
AIRVIEW, BUSINESS DISTRICT, ALBUQUERQUE

STREET SCENE, CLOVIS—SOUTHERN NEW MEXICO

STREET SCENE, HILLSBORO—NORTHERN NEW MEXICO

Because of the considerable number of Union and Confederate veterans who remained after the Civil War, there was for many years ill feeling between Northern and Southern sympathizers. Further distinctions were sharply drawn between Americans and Spanish-American settlers, when the latter were forced into a minor role in civic affairs. The new town began at once to be important commercially to a larger territory through connections with the East by rail and wire. A mass meeting to discuss incorporation was held July 28, 1884, and the first mayor, Henry Jaffa, was elected in 1885. In 1890 the town was incorporated as a city.

From the time when the Conquistadores introduced a few hundred sheep, wool growing had been a principal industry of the region. The wool was brought from surrounding ranches to Albuquerque by ox-drawn wagons, horses, and even burros; buyers came from Boston, St. Louis, and Philadelphia. The earliest banking was done by merchants, who accepted the wool growers' cash for safe keeping and advanced them trade credit. As wool growing assumed increasing importance in the vicinity, Albuquerque became a commercial banking center. Today the gross annual sale of sheep and lambs is over $10,000,000.

These early days, typical of western towns, saw colorful and sometimes fatal events, but by degrees the unruly element was subdued, chiefly through the efforts of Governor Stover's Vigilante Committee. Albuquerque's amusement facilities ran the gamut from the noisy, flamboyant honky-tonk to the imposing opera house of the period. Among the stars appearing at the latter were Nordica, Pavlova, and Paderewski. Most of the saloons had faro layouts, roulette wheels, and poker. Faro was the most popular with miners fresh from the diggin's, cowboys, cattle buyers, and drummers from the East. These places, gleaming with glassware and polished bars, bore such picturesque names as *The Bucket of Blood, The White Elephant,* and *The Free and Easy.* The hamlet of the 1880's, ultimately lost its boisterousness as it grew from village to town and from town to thriving city.

By 1870 parochial schools had been founded, but the most significant educational advance came in 1889, when the territorial legislature created the University of New Mexico. The census of 1890 showed a population of 3,785, but twenty years later the city had grown to 11,020. In 1917 the commission manager form of government was adopted.

The expansion of irrigation projects in the valley region added to the wealth of the Albuquerque area and led to the establishment of packing plants and canning factories for agricultural products, especially fruit. Grazing lands on both sides of the valley support thriving wool and livestock industries, bringing an annual income of millions of dollars, two-thirds of which is locally controlled. Many vineyards and orchards dot the valley, and from the near-by mountains come several million pounds of piñon nuts annually shipped all over the United States.

The city's industries also include sawmills, sash and door factories, sheet metal, brick, and tile works, the Santa Fe Railway shops, an oil refinery, and oil distributing plants. At the junction of three Santa Fe lines—one from Chicago, one from El Paso, and one from the Pacific Coast—the Santa Fe shops and division point, with a yard trackage totalling 50 miles, employ several thousand men. In addition there are many smaller industries, and the city is noted for its ornamental metal and woodwork plants; also Indian and Mexican handicrafts. These, with Federal and State government agencies augmenting its income, give the city an annual pay roll of more than thirty million dollars. Average bank clearings of $170,000,000 indicate its financial importance, and a municipal airport ranking in area with the largest ports in the country gives the city facilities for transcontinental air traffic.

Long ago physicians realized the benefits that Albuquerque's year-around climate offered sufferers from pulmonary ailments, particularly tuberculosis. Many millions have been invested in sanatoria and convalescent homes, and the Federal Government has established hospitals here for Indians and for war veterans. The city's reputation as a health resort is significant as a factor in the business and social structure.

There are many city schools, seven parochial schools, several denominational and preparatory schools, and a U. S. Indian training school. There are fifty-two churches of various denominations, six civic clubs, numerous fraternal and church societies, and various women's organizations. Civic co-operation has established a mile-long fresh-water bathing beach, a municipal zoo, a dozen parks, a Little Theatre building, and a city beautification plan that includes the planting of vacant areas. There are also choral clubs, a city band, and a civic symphony orchestra. Playground and recreational facilities have been developed in 185 acres of parks and in three Community Centers. One of these comprises 18 acres with a community house and adjacent amphitheatre for 3,000 persons, developed entirely by NYA labor.

## THE STATE UNIVERSITY

Situated on E. Central Ave., extending from University Ave., east to Girard Ave., and from E. Central Ave., north to E. Roma Ave., is the University, the State's foremost institution of learning. On the high east mesa, overlooking the city, about a mile from the business section, the university campus consists of 315 acres, with large shade trees, shrubs, and spreading lawns, against the background of foothills and the Sandía Mountains. The buildings are all Pueblo Indian style, dominated by the new massive University Library building.

The university was created as a territorial institution by act of the legislature on January 28, 1889, due largely to the efforts of Bernard S. Rodey, who has been called the father of the university and in whose honor Rodey Hall was named. The new institution was opened June 15, 1892, in rented rooms as a summer school; it began regular year-round instruction when the first building was erected on the campus in September of that year. The early buildings were in general of Victorian-Gothic style, but in 1905, under President Tight's administration, the modified type of Pueblo architecture was adopted and the university buildings as a group became unique among those of American educational institutions. When New Mexico was admitted to statehood the university became a State institution. A land grant of 312,709.42 acres, including the timber, oil, mineral, and other rights, was made by the United States Government to be held in trust by the State for the benefit of the university.

Growth of the university has been very rapid. In 1928 the College of Education was organized; in 1935, the General College; and in 1936, the College of Fine Arts, which includes a department of native Spanish-American handicraft, spinning, weaving, and furniture making, together with folk dances, and a summer branch school of art at the artists' colony at Taos.

Fortunately the university is situated in a region unsurpassed in archeological remains, and many of these important ruins are owned by or under the jurisdiction of the institution. The Department of Archeology has therefore gained international importance; classes have the advantage of practical excavating experience in the field, with a full lecture program and field laboratory. Extensive excavating has been done in Chaco Canyon and other Southwestern sites.

## CAMPUS TOUR

*(Unless otherwise stated, all buildings are open during school hours.)*

1. The ADMINISTRATION BUILDING, Coronado and Quivira Aves., built in 1936 of reinforced concrete and finished in modified Pueblo style architecture, houses the administrative offices in the west wing of the first floor; in the east wing is the Department of Anthropology and the MUSEUM OF ANTHROPOLOGY (*open class days 9-5—adm. free*) which contains exhibits of Southwestern archeological material and artifacts. On the second floor, the west wing is occupied by the Geology and the Philosophy Departments. The GEOLOGY MUSEUM (*open class days 9-5—adm. free*) is designed to serve the general public and to supplement the usual instructional program. In the east wing, second floor, is the Physics Department. The entire third floor is occupied by the Psychology Department.

2. The STUDENT UNION BUILDING, Coronado Ave., west of the Administration Building, contains club rooms, lunchroom, and cafeteria, a co-operative book store, offices for student publications, and a large ballroom.

3. The UNIVERSITY LIBRARY, Coronado and Villagrá Aves., east of the Administration Building (*open daily except Sundays and Holidays during school term, 8 a.m. to 10 p.m.*), erected in 1938, was made possible through a PWA grant. The building, housing the Department of Library Science, is a massive pueblo-style structure of reinforced concrete, two stories with a main central tower four stories in height to accommodate the book racks and book elevator. The first

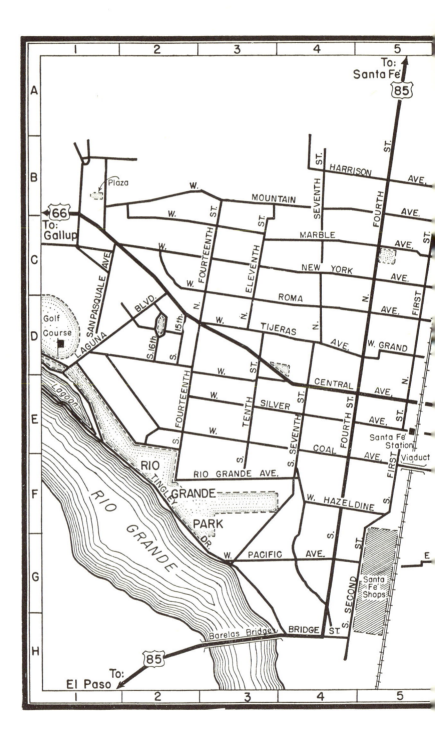

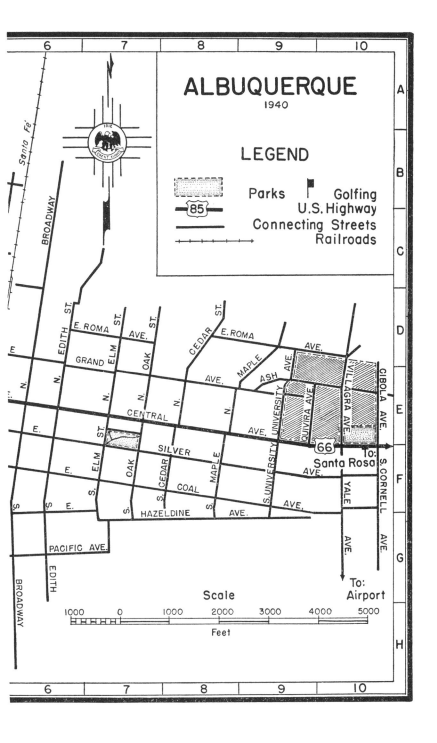

# ALBUQUERQUE
1940

## LEGEND

Parks

85

Connecting Streets

Golfing

U.S. Highway

Railroads

Scale

1000  0  1000  2000  3000  4000  5000

Feet

floor contains the loan desk in the main lobby, the general offices, and several reading rooms. The main reading room extends along the north side of the building. It is 35 feet wide and 192 feet in length. It is designed to resemble the interior of a pueblo church. There are fifty carved ceiling beams, *corbels,* and diagonal *latillas.* The lighting fixtures of wrought iron and pierced tin with mirrors are beautiful examples of native craftsmanship; the huge chandelier in the main reading room measures more than five feet in diameter and seven feet in height. All the furniture, the desks, and catalogue cases are hand-carved to give an interior effect that is Indian in design and entirely authentic for the Southwest.

On the second floor are study rooms for seminars, research cubicles, and the large Coronado Room which contains a valuable collection of regional literature. The general library, established in 1892, contains approximately 75,000 volumes, ultimate capacity being 300,000 volumes. The Coronado Room contains more than 1,500 volumes, and is a repository of Southwestern and early Latin-American history, and miscellaneous New Mexicana. The furniture in this room was designed and made by the NYA project of Las Cruces. On the second floor are several other loaned book collections, also a map room and staff room with kitchenette.

While the University Library was established primarily for the use of the University faculty and students, it maintains a loan and extension service for residents of the State. A branch camp-school library supplies books to field students when classes are being held at various archeological sites in the Southwest region.

4. The PRESIDENT'S HOME, Villagrá Ave., north of Library (*private*), is a good example of the Pueblo Indian type of architecture.

5. The DINING HALL, Quivira Ave., houses branches of the Department of Home Economics; the hall is used for banquets on occasion and at other times for current art exhibits.

6. The CARLISLE GYMNASIUM, Villagrá Ave., was named for a university student who gave his life in the World War. The building is well equipped for basketball and other indoor sports, and houses the Department of Physical Education. The huge court floor is also used at times for assembly gatherings and as an auditorium. Adjoining the gymnasium on the west is a modern outdoor swimming pool.

7. The STADIUM BUILDING AND ATHLETIC FIELD, Villagrá Ave., is opposite the gymnasium. The east side of the building on the west side of the playing field forms the Stadium with grandstand and bleacher seats for approximately 8,000. The Athletic Field is the scene of varsity gridiron battles, track meets, and other field events. Within the building are classrooms, offices, and locker rooms, with the Department of Music on the second floor.

8. HOKONA HALL, the women's dormitory, is another example of Pueblo style architecture. The name Hokona means "Butterfly Maiden," a Pueblo Indian deity. Exterior wall designs include representations of the Pueblo symbols of butterfly, mountain, and lightning.

One of the first buildings erected in the Pueblo style, Hokona Hall has the added charm of age in its setting among trees of the campus.

9. KWATAKA HALL is the men's residential hall. The name is a Hopi Indian term for "Man-Eagle." In characteristic architectural design, the building constitutes another attractive unit of the campus ensemble. The exterior walls are decorated with symbolical drawings representing strength, alertness, and swiftness.

10. The PUBLIC HEALTH LABORATORY, Quivira Ave., a PWA project, houses the State Health Laboratories.

11. HADLEY HALL, University Ave., houses the Department of Engineering.

12. The SCIENCE HALL contains the Department of Mathematics, a large Science lecture hall, and the State Oil and Road-materials Testing Laboratories.

13. RODEY HALL, a reproduction of the old church of Taos, was originally the Assembly Hall. It is now the Campus Theatre, with offices of the Drama Club and the Department of Dramatic Art in connection.

14. HODGIN HALL, the Educational Building, is the oldest structure on the campus. Originally a square brick building, it was remodeled (1908) in Pueblo design, and is now occupied by the College of Education, Modern Languages, the Extension Division, and other departmental offices.

15. The COLLEGE OF FINE ARTS, Quivira and Central Aves., formerly the Library Building, is another of the older buildings that has been adapted to the Pueblo style, with the exception that it has many windows. Here are housed several branches of the Art Department, including that of Spanish-American handicrafts, and Folk-dancing. The larger classroom walls show a series of murals by Raymond Jonson; these are abstract compositions depicting the various sciences. In the sculpture studio is another mural series by Willard Nash, impressionist representations of the different sports.

16. SORORITY AND FRATERNITY HOUSES, Roma and University Aves., are grouped generally together with ten chapter houses in the vicinity. Most of the fraternities have chapters at the university; the houses being equally attractive in architectural and decorative effect. Pi Kappa Alpha has its home in a unique Indian *kiva,* a building which has all the appearance of a Pueblo ceremonial chamber.

## OTHER POINTS OF INTEREST

17. OLD TOWN PLAZA, W. Central Ave. (US 66), N. 2 blocks on San Felipe Road, is the central portion of the original land grant made by the King of Spain, when Governor Cuervo y Valdés founded the villa in 1706. Here it was, according to old archives, that the Governor, his secretary, and witnesses plucked up stones and grass, flung them to the four points of the compass, at the same time shouting: "Long live the King!" The plaza was originally surrounded by an

adobe wall; in 1881, it was enclosed by a picket fence, and in 1937 the present stone wall was erected as a WPA project. The plaza has always been the center of communal life in Old Town and the scene of many historical events. Four flags have flown from its tall flagpole as Spain, Mexico, the Confederacy, and the United States claimed the territory.

18. CHURCH OF SAN FELIPE DE NERÍ, NW. corner of Plaza, except for a remodelled facade and other minor changes, stands exactly as it was built by Father Manuel Moreño and thirty families, who came with Governor Cuervo y Valdés when he founded Albuquerque in 1706. It was built originally to withstand firebrands and battering rams, such as were used during Indian uprisings. Thus the windows are twenty feet from the ground and the adobe walls are more than four feet thick. The original ceiling support is still used. Around a spruce tree trunk is built a spiral stairway leading to the choir loft. Hand-carved confessionals, altars, and various images and statues of unknown age produce an Old World medieval mood. In some of the side rooms are the original floors, worn thin and splintered. In the parish registers, dating from its founding, an almost complete record of the church in old Spanish script is found. According to these records, consecutive Sunday services have been held in the ancient edifice without missing a single Sunday since the church was opened by Father Moreño (1706).

19. ORIGINAL CONVENTO OF SAN FELIPE DE NERÍ CHURCH, NE. corner of Plaza, built shortly after the church, was used for more than a century as the abode of the Franciscan missionaries in this region. At times, while Albuquerque was a military post, soldiers were quartered in the building. It has been brick-faced and a second story added in recent years. At present it serves as the parish house.

20. The CASA DE ARMIJO, E. side of Plaza, once belonged to the wealthy Armijo family. A greater portion of the building is approximately two centuries old, the front section having been remodeled from time to time. During the Civil War the old Casa became the headquarters for both Union and Confederate officers. At present it is occupied by artists, writers, and crafts shops; still retaining its Spanish dignity, for the carved wooden doorways, deep-sunk windows, and an ancient patio lend charm to thick adobe walls.

21. HUNING CASTLE, 1424 W. Central Ave., now a private day school, was for many years an impressive landmark. It was inspired by castles in Hanover, Germany, the native land of the builder, Franz Huning. Mr. Huning, grandfather of Erna and Harvey Fergusson, New Mexico authors, was a prominent figure in the progress of Albuquerque. Emigrating from Germany he reached St. Louis in the gold rush days of '49 at the age of eighteen, joined a freighting caravan and traveled overland to Santa Fe, later coming to Albuquerque. His home, the "Castle," was a show place in territorial days. The main walls of the building are five feet thick. The finished lumber

was freighted from Illinois, some materials were brought from England, and the castle was five years in the building, due mainly to slow
travel over the old Santa Fe Trail.

22. The VINCENT WALLACE HOUSE, 1429 W. Central,
across the street from Huning Castle (*private*), is one of the two first
residences built in new Albuquerque (1882). Vincent Wallace was a
relative of General Lew Wallace, author of *Ben Hur* and governor of
the Territory of New Mexico. It is believed that Lew Wallace wrote
portions of his historical novel in this house, and here also, the famous
composer Puccini wrote sections of the scores of *La Bohème* and *The
Girl of the Golden West*.

23. ROBINSON PARK, W. Central Ave. and 8th St., (1880) is
a triangular area of greenery and huge shade trees providing a restful
spot near the business district. It was reserved as a park when the
townsite of new Albuquerque was laid out. Two brass howitzers
(cast in Boston, 1853), captured and later buried by Confederate General Sibley in Old Albuquerque during the Civil War, stand in the
park, and there is also a fountain built in tribute to John Braden who
gave his life, in Territorial days, to save the lives of a group of children
caught in a fire on a Fourth of July float. Braden managed to stop the
runaway horses, but died from severe burns.

24. The RIO GRANDE PARK AND ZOO, S. on Laguna Blvd.,
facing Tingley Drive along the Rio Grande (*admission free*), is an
80-acre landscaped area containing many beautiful trees. There are
playgrounds for children, tennis courts, several wild fowl ponds, and
a representative collection of animals and birds native to the Southwest
region.

25. The MUNICIPAL BATHING BEACH, Laguna and Kit
Carson Blvds., just west of Rio Grande Park, is an artificial lake of
constantly changing, pure water, diverted underground from the Rio
Grande, with depths from two to fifteen feet. There are modern housing facilities, with lifeguards in attendance along the three miles of
white sand beach.

26. THE HARVEY INDIAN MUSEUM, adjoining the Al-
varado Hotel, Gold Ave. and 1st St. (*8:30-6—adm. free*), may be entered through the hotel, or from the corridor facing the railroad at the
Santa Fe Railroad station. Housed in a California Mission type of
building, the museum occupies several large rooms and contains fine
examples of authentic early Indian arts and crafts from Mexico and
New Mexico. Indian craftsmen demonstrate silversmithing and Navaho weaving.

27. The U. S. VETERANS' HOSPITAL, end of Parkland Drive,
almost a small village in itself, is built so that the ensemble is a fair
reproduction of the Taos Indian pueblo. The massive buildings, with
recessed story-levels, constitute a striking landmark on the high mesa
several miles east of the city. The capacity is 250 beds.

28. The U. S. INDIAN HOSPITAL, 1 *m.* NE on Dartmouth
Ave., an imposing modern structure surrounded by trees, shrubs, and

velvety lawns, is devoted to the Government's medical aid for Indians. The capacity is 150 beds.

## SANDÍA LOOP AND RIM DRIVE

Albuquerque—Tijeras Canyon—Sandía Crest—Bernalillo—Albuquerque.

US 66; Rim Drive; US 85. 65.5 *m.*

This drive, which can be made in five hours or less, passes into the rugged Sandía Mountains to an observation point (two miles above sea level) where a vast panorama of the State can be seen. Several public camping and picnicking grounds along the route. Crest Road open from May to November.

ALBUQUERQUE. From Central Ave. and 1st St., 0 *m.,* proceed eastwardly on Central Ave. (US 66), entering TIJERAS CANYON (5,800 alt.), at 10.1 *m.,* and continuing through TIJERAS VILLAGE (467 pop.), 15.1 *m.*

At 17.1 *m.* (R) beyond the roadside filling station is an almost perfect sandstone dome with an incline from the surrounding cliffs which form a natural corner. On the walls of the formation are numerous pictographs of prehistoric origin.

FOREST PARK 18.5 *m.* (R) is a mountain resort, privately owned, where meals, cabins, and saddle horses are available.

At 22.1 *m.* is the junction with NM 10 (L). Proceed over NM 10 and Loop Drive through Tejano Canyon past TREE SPRINGS, 27.6 *m.,* above which point is the winter sports region where ski and toboggan tournaments are held.

At 29.6 *m.* is junction with Sandía Crest Road (8,652 alt.). Upward over this road through forests of aspen to SANDÍA CREST OBSERVATION POINT, 34.2 *m.* (10,678 alt.). Leave car at parking level and walk 20 yards to top. Most of the mountain ranges in the State visible from this point.

Returning, retrace to junction (L) with Loop Drive 42.5 *m.,* descend into Las Huertas Canyon and proceed to BERNALILLO 51.2 *m.* (*see Tour 1b*) and junction with US 85 (L). Proceed southwestwardly to Albuquerque and junction with US 66 at 4th St. and Central Ave., then (L) over Central Ave. to point of beginning, 65.5 *m.*

OPTIONAL RETURN: Retrace route from Observation Point to Albuquerque.

## OTHER POINTS OF INTEREST IN ENVIRONS

Isleta Indian Pueblo, 12 *m.* (*see Tour 1b*); Sandía Pueblo, 13.4 *m.;* Cíbola National Forest, 16 *m.;* Coronado State Monument, 18.6 *m.;* Santa Ana Pueblo, 29 *m.;* San Felipe Pueblo, 29 *m.;* Zía Pueblo, 37 *m.;* Jémez Pueblo, 51 *m.;* Santo Domingo Pueblo, 40 *m.;* Laguna Pueblo, 51 *m.* (*see Tour 6b*); Ácoma Pueblo, 67 *m.* (*see Tour 6A*).

# Santa Fe

*Railroad Stations:* Cor. E. San Francisco and Shelby Sts. for busses to Lamy for all trains of Atchison, Topeka and Santa Fe Ry.; 432 Guadalupe St. for Denver and Rio Grande Western R. R.
*Bus Stations:* Union Bus Depot, 126 Water St., for Southwest Greyhound Lines, New Mexico Transportation Co., Intercity Transit Lines, Chama Valley Lines; Cor. E. San Francisco and Shelby Sts. for Hunter Clarkson, Inc.; Union Bus Depot for Santa Fe Trailways.
*Airport:* Municipal Airport, 5.7 m. SW. city on Albuquerque Road (US 85); taxi fare $1.00.
*Taxis:* 25¢ upward, according to distance and number of passengers.
*Traffic Regulations:* Turns permitted either direction at intersections except one-way sts.; vehicle on the right has the right-of-way; parking limits designated on st. signs and orange curbs; one-way to R. around the plaza except on N. side; make way for police and fire cars.

*Accommodations:* Hotels, tourist camps, boarding houses; dude ranches in environs.

*Information Service:* Chamber of Commerce, 114 Shelby St.; New Mexico Tourist Bureau, State Capitol Building.

*Radio Station:* KVSF (1310 kc.).
*Theatres:* Three motion picture houses on San Francisco St.; occasional plays by Santa Fe Players.

*Annual Events:* Santa Fe Fiesta, three days, Labor Day week-end; Corpus Christi, 1st Thurs. after Trinity Sun.; De Vargas Memorial Procession, following week; Annual Horse Show, Annual Poet's Roundup, Elk's Celebration of Pioneer Days; New Mexico Kennel Club Dog Show, spring; Feast Day of Nuestra Señora de Guadalupe, Dec. 12; Feast Day of St. Francis of Assisi, Oct. 4.

SANTA FE (6,996 alt., 20,227 pop.), capital of New Mexico, started life in 1609 with the florid title of the Royal City of the Holy Faith of Saint Francis—*La Villa Real de la Santa Fé de San Francisco*. It has been a capital continuously for more than 300 years, and the flags of four nations—Spain, Mexico, the Confederacy, and the United States— have flown over its ancient Palace of the Governors, a building which still stands along the north side of the plaza and whose history is the history of Santa Fe and New Mexico. It is the oldest capital within the boundaries of the United States.

Never an industrial city, and even now sixteen miles from the main line of the railroad, Santa Fe nestles in the little valley of the Rito de Santa Fe where it emerges from the foothills of the Sangre de Cristo Mountains on the east. To the south are the Sandía Mountains; in the west is the Jémez Range. Surrounded by those snow-covered mountain peaks, in a land of vast distances and deep colors, this spot, from ancient times, has been a magnet for travelers. Today its major industry is the tourist and vacation trade. The summer nights are cool, and in winter the noon hours are warm. Snow lies on the high mountain peaks of the Sangre de Cristo until late in June. In July the summer rains bring mountain freshness to the valley. The average annual rainfall is 14.34 inches. The year-round average mean temperature is 48.9 degrees F. (winter average low 29.3 degrees, summer average high 68.7 degrees.)

The charm of the Royal City is quickly felt. The ancient narrow streets and the brown adobe houses are thick with deeds and memories. In the evening the fragrance of piñon smoke fills the air, for Santa Fe is a city of fireplaces. It is a town of patios where hollyhocks nod, where towering cottonwoods spatter with shade, here a crumbling gateway, there an ancient wall whose adobe bricks show through the broken earthen plaster. From the eminence of a near-by hill is visible, sunwashed in the daylight, thick on the floor of the valley and scattering to the foothills, clusters of flat, rectangular adobe houses along winding roads; and in the center of town, above the roof tops and the occasional smokestacks and the arms of the cottonwoods, the glistening dome of the State capital. From the same hill at night the town's glimmering lights are a handful of stars flung across the valley.

Santa Fe has seen much history in its crooked streets and venerable plaza; it has seen wars and rebellions, Catholic feasts and devout processions; Spanish men-at-arms, soldiers of Mexico, the Confederacy, and the Union; the bull-whackers and caravans of the Santa Fe Trail; Spanish women in black shawls, and the Indians from the near-by pueblos wrapped in blankets; for here are blended, as nowhere else in the United States, the full rich patterns of three distinct cultures—Indian, Spanish, and American.

The settlement was founded in the winter of 1609-10 by Don Pedro de Peralta, third governor of the Province of Nuevo Méjico, at a spot known to the Pueblo Indians as Kuapoga, or "the place of the shell beads near the water." Ruins, almost obliterated when the Spaniards came, showed that it was once the site of a Tano Indian village. Today's dwellers, in digging foundations for their homes, frequently unearth remnants of the prehistoric past in the form of pottery fragments, implements, and human bones.

When Peralta came to Santa Fe, he built the *palacio* for a fortress, laid out the plaza, and planned a walled city. At various places today the ruins of the ancient wall may still be seen. In the Palace, built the year the town was founded, sixty Spanish governors ruled the vast territory over a period of 212 years, and maintained the Spanish borderlands against invasion from the north. From the time of its founding to the present day, the town has been a continuous seat of government.

By 1617, with only forty-eight Spanish soldiers and settlers in the province—a province which extended from the Mississippi to the Pacific, from Mexico as far north as people roamed—the Franciscan friars had built eleven churches, had converted 14,000 Indians to the

Roman Catholic faith, and had prepared as many more for conversion. Throughout the Spanish times Santa Fe was the center of both the explorations and the missions to the Indians. From Chihuahua through El Paso del Norte came caravans and settlers on a route which came to be known as *El Camino Real,* The Royal Highway. But trouble with the Indians continued throughout the seventeenth century, for though they nominally accepted conversion, they persisted in their old forms of worship. Bancroft says that in 1645 there was a rising of the Indians near Santa Fe because forty of their number had been flogged and hanged by the Spaniards for refusing to give up their faith. From year to year conditions grew more serious until, in 1680, under the San Juan Indian, Po-pé, the northern Pueblos revolted. The Spanish colonists who were not killed by the Indians sought refuge in the Palace of the Governors where they were besieged; and though they succeeded in beating off the Indians, they saw that it was impossible to continue to hold the town. They abandoned it and fled to El Paso del Norte.

For twelve years the Indians held Santa Fe; they occupied the Palace of the Governors, had their own Indian governor, and turned the chapel into a *kiva* where they worshipped their gods in their old way. Then, in 1692, De Vargas, the newly appointed governor of the province, marched on Santa Fe and made a peaceful entry. He spent the rest of the year subduing the Indians of the northern province, and returned to Mexico. The next year when he returned to Santa Fe, he brought with him a little statue of the Virgin, called *La Conquistadora.* Pausing before his entry on the spot where Rosario Chapel now stands, he made a vow that yearly homage would be paid to "Our Lady of Victory" in remembrance of her aid. This vow, fulfilled without omission in the streets of the Royal City today, is known as the De Vargas Procession.

Since then, in many ways, the Catholic faith of the Spaniards has colored the life of the town. In June, on Corpus Christi Sunday, the Blessed Sacrament is carried beneath a golden canopy for public veneration, an event decreed by Pope Urban IV. The De Vargas Procession follows on the next Sunday, in which the statue of *La Conquistadora* is carried to Rosario Chapel. A novena of Masses is said between this procession and the returning of the statue to the Cathedral of St. Francis, her permanent abode. Since 1875 Santa Fe has been the seat of a Holy See. Archbishop Lamy, the "Bishop Latour" in Willa Cather's *Death Comes for the Archbishop,* built the Cathedral of St. Francis in 1869 on the site of the old adobe Parroquia. Today Santa Fe, the City of the Holy Faith, remains one of the great centers of Catholicism in North America.

When Mexico gained independence from Spain in 1821, and the flag of the new republic was raised over the Palace of the Governors, the plaza was named *La Plaza de la Constitución.* Always the social and commercial center of life in the town in Spanish Mexican times, the plaza was "an open space of mud dirt," the marketplace for Indian wares and garden produce. Here the captains and the *ricos* had their homes, while their servants lived across the river in a little settlement called *Analco,* an Aztec word meaning "on the other side of the water," clustered about the old chapel of San Miguel. After the entry of General Kearny, the Americans planted trees and alfalfa in the plaza, and so it remained for many years; in recent times flagstones have been laid among the old trees. During the Mexican regime, the governors continued to live in the Palace.

On the 18th of August, 1846, General Kearny marched his United States troops into Santa Fe, and after taking supper with the Mexican Lieutenant-Governor, hoisted the American flag over the Palace of the Governors, and, in a bloodless victory, New Mexico became a province of the United States. From that time down to the present the Stars and Stripes have flown above the ancient Palace, except for two weeks during the Civil War when Santa Fe fell into the hands of the Confederates. On February 18, 1862, after the Confederate victory at the battle of Valverde, the Southern forces under General Sibley marched to Albuquerque and then to Santa Fe, where valuable Federal supplies had been concentrated. The Union forces retreated to Fort Union, and in the ensuing battle at Apache Canyon, the Federal army chased the Confederates down the Rio Grande, and re-entered Santa Fe.

Mexican Independence in 1821 opened Santa Fe trade with the States. Before this time all the trade had been with Chihuahua in Mexico by way of the Camino Real, and the Spanish governors guarded this trade route jealously against encroachment from the North. But the Mexican governors were lenient and American traders, following William Becknell, "the father of the Santa Fe Trail," were unmolested. On November 6, 1822, Becknell brought a wagonload of goods from Missouri for which he had paid $150 and sold for $700, thereby discovering rich profit in the overland trade. Despite the hardships of the journey, the danger from Indians along the way, and the exorbitant imposts—as well as bribes—the trade flourished.

Gregg, in his *Commerce of the Prairies,* describes the entrance of a caravan into the Royal City:

> The arrival of the caravan always was productive of great excitement among the natives. "Los Americanos! Los Carros! La entrada de la caravana!" were to be heard in every direction. Crowds of women and boys flocked around to see the newcomers. . . . Each wagonner must tie a brand new "cracker" to the end of his whip, for on driving through the streets and the *plaza pública* everyone strives to outvie his comrades in the dexterity with which he flourishes this favorite badge of authority.

The caravans were unloaded at La Fonda, the inn at the end of the Trail, under the eyes of dark girls who hid their faces in lace mantillas, lounging soldiers from the barracks, and expressionless Indians wrapped in blankets. After the travelers were refreshed there were *bailes,* gambling halls, and bar rooms, where men laughed, danced, gambled, and sought friendly black eyes smiling behind shawls.

In 1849 a stage line was established over the Santa Fe Trail between Independence, Missouri, and Santa Fe. In the sixties the Santa

Fe Trail was mostly a military road connecting Missouri and New Mexico. In the seventies, with the coming of the railroads, the freighters and stagecoaches began to disappear, and by the eighties the old Santa Fe Trail was dead.

In 1879 the Santa Fe Railroad crossed Ratón Pass and came down toward Santa Fe. But it was found that a main line through the town would necessitate an expensive stretch of road uphill from Glorieta Pass to Santa Fe, so the Santa Fe junction was placed at Lamy, then eighteen miles south of the town; today the only connection with Santa Fe that the road maintains is a freight track. Passengers travel by motorbus.

The coming of the railroad in the eighties brought a period of prosperity to the town. It was during the next thirty years that the conglomerate of architectures which face the plaza was built up. Today the ancient Palace of the Governors still stands guard over the north side of the plaza. On the other three sides are store fronts on the street level of one- and two-story brick buildings of the style of the nineties, which rub elbows with Spanish-Pueblo buildings and even with the pseudo-Greek temple of the town's only bank. It was only in the last decade that the town became conscious of the unique type of architecture which is its heritage and returned to the authentic Pueblo style. Variations upon the Pueblo style are the Art Museum built in 1917 and the new La Fonda built in 1929 at opposite corners of the plaza.

With statehood in 1912 New Mexico's capital began a new chapter in its history. Federal as well as new State buildings were erected, schools were built, and a permanent population of government employees came to live in the town. Between 1880 and the admission of New Mexico to the Union, the population had been static, hovering between five and six thousand. But by 1920 it had jumped to 7,236, by 1930 it was 11,176, and today it is said to be over 20,000. In recent years the town has experienced a minor building boom.

The native Spanish-speaking population, which composes sixty per cent of the townspeople, separates the colorful from the drab; expensive mansions stand shoulder to shoulder with primitive adobe houses on the same sunny hillsides, following the same simple lines. Spain is stamped upon the town, for to Spain the Royal City was tied through two centuries by the Chihuahua Trail. The cowboys who clicks along the sidewalk in his high-heeled boots inherited his trade, his horses, his outfit, his vocabulary, and his methods from the Spaniards; the old man who takes his siesta on a bench in the plaza may count among his ancestors a Spanish don who owned a *rancho* as big as Delaware. The low, flat-roofed houses, the masses of rectangular walls, and the small windows are Spanish architecture modified by the aboriginal Indian culture which found expression in adobe building. And in the rooms of the Palace stalk the ghosts of conqueror, peon, and slave. Today children on the street still chatter in Spanish, and families still bear old Conquistador names like Delgado, Otero, Ortiz, and Sena.

In winter especially, when the Anglos are at work at home, Santa Fe becomes an old Spanish town again. Then the accents of Spain are not drowned out by English voices; the Spanish-Americans predominate in the streets; and when spring comes and the nights grow warm, they flock to the plaza to hear the band play and walk for an hour or two while the children romp under the trees. They follow the old custom of the promenade—it is their plaza again.

Although painters, musicians, and novelists have come since 1900 to absorb the beauty of the town and its surroundings, archeologists are credited with having discovered the ancient city for the nation as a whole, for it is located in the center of one of the most interesting culture areas on the continent. These scholars came and dug in the ruins and lived with the Indians, and at least one of them, Adolph Bandelier, left writings which are minor classics in the field. His *The Delight Makers* is a fictionalized story of the life in the prehistoric cliff dwellings of the near-by *Rito de los Frijoles*.

Santa Fe has many celebrations during the year, due in part to the love of song and dance of the Spanish population, and in part to the fondness of local artists and writers for a good time. Christmas Eve bonfires are lighted in front of the Cathedral, around the plaza, and before many of the houses; lights are placed around the roof tops. But the town's gayest scenes come in September when the community fiesta, ordained by the Marqués de la Peñuela in 1712 to commemorate the reconquest of New Mexico by De Vargas, turns the ancient square into a carnival ground. For three days the place is given over to street dancing, native and Indian markets, tribal dances by Pueblo Indians, and parades. The original purpose of the celebration is recalled by a solemn march to the Cross of the Martyrs and in the historical pageant in which De Vargas rides again, entering the city and planting the cross and the royal banner once more in the plaza before the Palace of the Governors while the Alcalde, in brocaded satin coat, reads the ancient edict.

In season and out, on the streets and in the stores and homes, one meets people from everywhere in the world, drawn here by a rich historic past, a wealth of archeological material, the blended cultures of three races, and the flood of sunshine on mountain, valley, and desert.

## POINTS OF INTEREST

1. THE PLAZA, bounded by Palace Ave. on the N., San Francisco St. on the S., Washington Ave. on the E., and Lincoln Ave. on the W., is the center of town, and from it most of the streets radiate. It is a peaceful old square, with trim flagstones, walks, and benches, and pleasant arching trees. In Spanish times it was much larger and included the whole block now occupied by the post office and the buildings along the east side; it was then unpaved, a lake of dust in dry times, a sea of mud in wet; it was the market place for the produce of the Rio Grande Valley, sold by Indians and Spaniards. When the

Americans came, they enclosed it in a white picket fence, planted it to alfalfa, reduced it to its present size, and built two-story adobe buildings with portals supported by spindly columns on the three sides confronting the Palace. It was at the Plaza that the wagon trains ended their strenuous journeys over the Santa Fe Trail, and here the ox-drivers, cowboys, and gamblers caroused in and out of the eight saloons that at one time graced the square; here criminals were locked in stocks or flogged in public view; here Billy the Kid once sat in chains. Today, except for the Palace, the Plaza is surrounded by an odd assortment of buildings; some ugly remnants of the early railroad days which now house business establishments; others, more recent, built in the more indigenous Pueblo and Spanish styles. In the center of the square is the SOLDIERS' MONUMENT, erected after the Civil War by the citizenry, which reads on the south side, "To the heroes of the Federal Army, who fell at the battle of Valverde, fought with the rebels, Febuary (sic) 21, 1862." On the west side the word "rebels" occurs again, a designation of the enemies of the Republic which probably does not occur on such an inscription elsewhere in the country. A granite slab marker denoting the end of the Santa Fe Trail, erected by the D. A. R. of the Territory in 1910, is a few paces east of the monument. In the northeast sector of the square rests a pair of old cannon, dating from the American occupation. Along the north sidewalk near by stands the marble marker designating the spot where General Kearny, on August 19, 1846, read his proclamation of the "peaceful Annexation of New Mexico." The bandstand which stands directly opposite the entrance to the Palace is the eminence from which, on summer Sunday evenings, the Conquistadores band holds forth to the delight of as many Spanish-speaking people as can crowd into the plaza.

2. THE PALACE OF THE GOVERNORS, N. side of the Plaza (*Open week days, 9-12 and 1-5, Sundays, 2-4, adm. free*), is an adobe structure that has reputedly stood since the winter of 1609-10. After a number of renovations, it was finally restored to its present state in 1909, from some old plans found in the British Museum. Originally the Palace was the most imposing and important part of the royal *presidio,* an all-purpose fortress built by the followers of Don Pedro de Peralta. It extended east and west along the north side of the plaza for a distance of 400 feet, and north and south more than double that distance. The whole area was surrounded by an adobe wall, and all the buildings within this enclosure were known in ancient Spanish times as *Casas Reales,* or Royal Houses. These included the palace proper, quarters for the soldiery, and several buildings used for governmental purposes. A pair of low towers stood at either end on the plaza side; the west tower was used for the storage of powder and military equipment and the east tower housed a chapel for the use of the garrison. Adjoining and connecting with the tower at the west end were the dungeons. A portal, or covered porch, under which many an Indian and Spanish prisoner of war was hanged, extended the whole length of the building along the south facade in much the same manner

as the present. The two ends of the building were shortened and the towers removed during the later Spanish occupation.

In the great Pueblo Revolt of 1680, the *presidio* was besieged for five days by a force of 3,000 northern Pueblo Indians. The Spanish governor of the time, Don Antonio Otermín, heard of the rebellion in time to strip the churches of sacred images and to summon all loyal persons to the shelter of the *presidio;* but his precautions availed little. With a force of barely 150 armed men he led the colonists in a surprise attack upon their besiegers, cut his way out of the city and left all to the Indians, who burned much property of the hated oppressors. Church buildings were razed and their contents burned; the Palace was cleared of archives and furnishings, which were also burned in the Plaza, and the building itself was made over into a pueblo, the chapel desecrated and turned into a kiva. So great was this blow to Spanish prestige and power that twelve years passed before a successful attempt to reconquer the province was made. With the arrival of Captain-General De Vargas and his successful assault on the walled pueblo that the Indians made of the *Casas Reales,* the next 130 years of Spanish rule from the Palace began. The building was restored, but the friars refused to use the profaned chapel for Christian purposes until De Vargas reminded them that the Moors in Spain had similarly desecrated the churches. Unrest among the Pueblo tribes persisted for some years, and *el palacio* was the scene of endless councils seeking a plan for the subjugation of the Indians. Intrigue among his own officials caused the imprisonment of De Vargas, but he was later exonerated by his king and reappointed governor of the province in 1701. He died in Bernalillo and was buried in Santa Fe in 1704.

The story of the Palace during the eighteenth century is a narrative of military activities and a monotonous succession of Spanish governors, 28 in number. The Mexican regime, which lasted for 25 years, quartered its governors in the Palace, as Spain had. Until 1907, when the present executive mansion was built, the Palace was occupied by American Territorial governors from the time of General Stephen Watts Kearny's peaceful conquest of the region from Mexico in 1846. By act of the New Mexico Legislature in 1909, THE MUSEUM OF NEW MEXICO was established and located in the Palace. Since that date it has also been the headquarters for the SCHOOL OF AMERICAN RESEARCH of the Archeological Institute of America and the HISTORICAL SOCIETY OF NEW MEXICO.

The architecture of this building represents the earliest application of Spanish methods and ideas to indigenous materials and limitations. Arches are notably absent, for the adobe bricks of which the walls are made were believed incapable of supporting the arch construction. The use of flat roofs and *vigas,* or roof beams, was borrowed directly from the Indians. Indeed, the whole structure, with the exception of doors and windows and the covered portal along the front, which were Spanish innovations, is constructed in the aboriginal style of Pueblo building. The existence of "puddled" adobe walls, a method similar to the modern practice of pouring concrete between forms, an example of which is shown under glass in the Territorial Room, has given rise to the conjecture that parts of the building were pre-Spanish. This work might have been done, however, during the Indian occupation of the premises after the Pueblo Revolt of 1680. The molding of adobe into bricks was a process unknown to the Indians until after the coming of the Spaniards.

The building is a hollow rectangle with a grassy patio in the center. In the east rooms, on the right of the entrance hall, where murals by Carl Lotave are shown, are exhibits by the Historical Society of New Mexico of every era in New Mexican history. The TERRITORIAL ROOM (1846-1912), is the first one encountered east of the entrance. Here are displayed among many objects of the American occupation, a painting by the late Gerald Cassidy of the Santa Fe Plaza as it was thought to have looked about 1850, a portrait bust of Lew Wallace, Territorial Governor in 1878, and the chair he used while working on the novel, *Ben Hur*. Paintings and photographs on the walls show the appearance of the early plaza and *palacio*. Also displayed is a piano brought across the plains over the Santa Fe Trail by oxcart in 1871.

In the MEXICAN ROOM (1822-1846), adjoining on the east, are cases displaying textiles of the period, hooked rugs, Mexican blankets of wool, and *colchas,* or counterpanes, distinctly a New Mexican achievement. On a sheet of hand-woven cloth was worked an all-over pattern in wool with tapestry stitch, in free designs usually taken from native pottery. Other objects manufactured or in use during this period are also shown here.

A narrow hallway east of this room contains the portraits of all the territorial and state governors who have held office since Kearny's entry in 1846.

The ECCLESIASTICAL ROOM, occupying the southeast corner of the building, contains the collections of the Spanish Colonial Arts Society, consisting of religious objects from the entire historical period of Santa Fe. A display of early Spanish ecclesiastical paintings on skins, canvas, and thin slabs of wood, *santos* or *retablos,* are shown, together with a carved stone *retablo,* and many *bultos,* or images carved in the round. A beautiful old reredos, from a former church at Llano Quemado, a village near Ranchos de Taos, stands against the south wall.

The LIBRARY extends from this corner north to the northeast corner of the building. It contains the collections of the Genealogical Library of the Stephen Watts Kearny Chapter of the D. A. R. and the combined libraries of the Museum of New Mexico, Historical Society of New Mexico, and the School of American Research. Noteworthy are the books of the Benjamin Read Historical Collection. The most valuable items in this collection, a group of forty-one Spanish *documentos inéditos,* are now stored in the vault. A fine portrait of New Mexico's first poet, Don Gaspar de Villagrá, by the late Gerald Cassidy, hangs on the north wall. Rooms along the north wing are occupied by offices and are not open to the public.

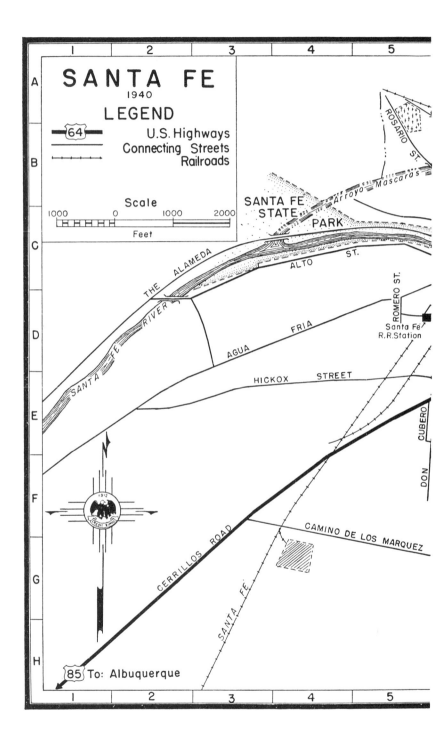

# SANTA FE
### 1940
## LEGEND

━━64━━    U.S. Highways
_____    Connecting Streets
+++++++    Railroads

**Scale**

1000    0    1000    2000

Feet

ROSARIO ST.

SANTA FE
STATE
PARK

Arroyo Mascaras

THE ALAMEDA

ALTO ST.

SANTA FE RIVER

FRIA

AGUA

ROMERO ST.

Santa Fe
R.R.Station

HICKOX STREET

CUBERO

DON

CERRILLOS ROAD

CAMINO DE LOS MARQUEZ

SANTA FE

85 To: Albuquerque

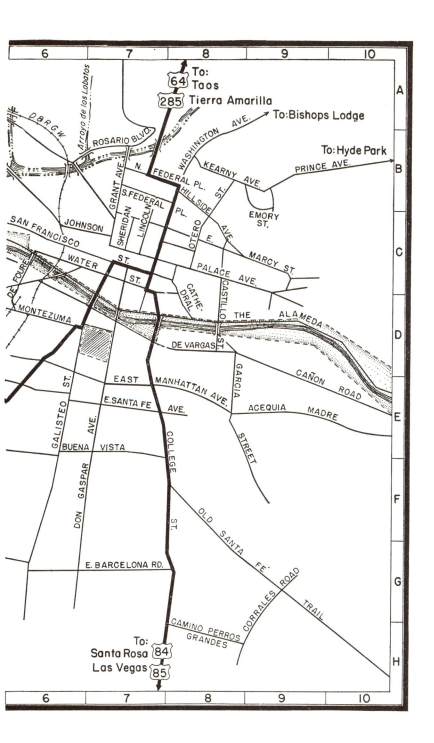

West from the Ecclesiastical Room is the LATE SPANISH COLONIAL ROOM (1693-1821) where objects of local manufacture used during that period are exhibited. This adjoins the EARLY SPANISH COLONIAL ROOM (1539-1680), where the earliest historical objects are displayed. The crude articles shown indicate the early Spaniards' poverty in tools. In this room are also some archives bearing the signatures of De Vargas and the Duke of Alburquerque. Portraits, by Gerald Cassidy, of the Duke of Alburquerque and Juan Bautista de Anza, Spanish governor from 1778 to 1789, hang on the east wall of this room.

The remaining exhibition rooms are given over to Indian displays. In the PECOS ROOM adjoining are found pottery and artifacts from the ruins of Pecos pueblo, until 1838 an occupied Indian village. In the PUYÉ ROOM to the west are more specimens of pottery and artifacts from the great cliff dwellings at Puyé, excavated by the Museum of New Mexico from 1907 to 1911. On the walls above the cases are mural paintings by Carl Lotave, depicting the ruins and their environment. Paintings by this artist also adorn the walls of the RITO DE LOS FRIJOLES ROOM adjoining. Here are displayed remains recovered from the ruins in the Bandelier National Monument. In this room, formerly divided by a partition, Governor Lew Wallace is said to have worked on the last three chapters of *Ben Hur*.

In the southwest corner of the Palace is the HALL OF ARCHEOLOGY. General archeological exhibits here reveal examples of the Classic period of Pueblo culture, which varies in different localities from 1000 to 1600 A.D.

The first room in the west wing is the CHACO CANYON ROOM containing specimens gathered by the Museum excavators in the area in 1920, 1921, and 1922, and by the University of New Mexico since 1929. Three plaster reproductions of typical *kivas* of the region stand against the east wall. Many photographs of the ruins hang on the walls, and cases filled with objects of archeological interest repay inspection.

The last room on this side is the MIMBRES AND CHIHUAHUA ROOM, exhibiting pottery and artifacts from the Mimbres area in southwest New Mexico and the Chihuahua section lying south of it, largely in the Mexican State of that name.

The rooms on the left of the main entrance, originally the public and private offices of the governors, are the executive offices of the Museum and Historical Society. The fireproof vault recently completed to house the priceless collection of archives dating from the De Vargas occupation in 1693 adjoins the private office of the director. These archives have had a checkered history, some of them reputedly having been sold at one time by a Territorial governor for wrapping paper and only a part of them recovered.

3. The MUSEUM OF NEW MEXICO ART GALLERY is on the NW. corner of the Plaza, at Palace and Lincoln Aves. (*Open week days, 9-5, Sun., 2-4, adm. free.*) Dominating the northwest corner of the Plaza, the museum building was erected in 1917 on the

site of the old Ft. Marcy military headquarters building, which had been used for military purposes since early Spanish times. Like the Palace across the street, it is administered jointly by the State of New Mexico and the School of American Research of the Archeological Institute of America. Funds for its construction, in the amount of $120,-000, were raised by public subscription and individual donations, matched by the State Legislature. Since the people own the building, the Museum offers any artist the use of its exhibition space, making it free to the exhibitor and the visitor.

The New Museum, as it has come to be called, is an architectural composite of six of the ancient Spanish missions built by Franciscan friars. Designed by the firm of Rapp & Rapp, of Santa Fe, with a number of local artists as consultants, the towers and balcony were inspired by the church at Ácoma; the missions in the pueblos of San Felipe, Cochití, Laguna, Santa Ana, and Pecos contributed details of the exterior.

Built around a grassy patio with cloistered walls, the museum has gallery space for more than 200 pictures. The entrance hall displays examples of Indian art in all its forms, including the latest development, water-color paintings by such outstanding Indian artists as Awa-Tsireh, Fred Kabotie, Ma-Pa-Wi, Tonita Peña, and Otis Polelonema. The galleries forming the east wing are given over to monthly exhibits by resident and visiting artists. The long room on the north houses the museum's permanent collection, with works by such nationally known artists as Gerald Cassidy, Birger Sandzen, Donald Beauregard, J. H. Sharp, John Sloan, W. Herbert Dunton, Julius Rolshoven, George Bellows, Frank Sauerwine, W. H. Holmes, Carl Lotave, Cartaino Scapitta, and Bush-Brown. The annual Fiesta exhibition in September fills all the available gallery space.

4. ST. FRANCIS AUDITORIUM, like an old chapel turned to different uses, occupies the entire west end of the building. Here are found the mural paintings depicting scenes from the life of St. Francis of Assisi, sketched and planned by the artist Donald Beauregard and finished, after that artist's untimely death, by Kenneth M. Chapman and Carlos Vierra.

Upstairs over the east wing is another gallery which contains the first gift to the permanent collection, a group of paintings by Donald Beauregard, given to the museum by Frank Springer, its principal benefactor. The room over the north side is used by the Women's Museum Board.

5. The NEW CITY HALL, on the corner of Washington Ave. and Marcy St., one block N. of the plaza, was erected in 1937 with Federal aid. Designed by John Gaw Meem, of Santa Fe, it is a Spanish-Colonial two-story structure, built of hollow tile and plaster. The north wing houses the mayor's office, the council chambers, and other city government offices; the south wing is used by the police department, and on the second floor of this wing is the city jail.

6. The FEDERAL BUILDING, at the N. end of Lincoln Ave., two blocks from the Plaza, was started before the Civil War. The first appropriation of $20,000 was made by the Congress in 1850, and four years later $50,000 additional funds were appropriated for its completion. The money was sufficient, however, to raise the building only one story and a half. The Civil War interrupted both the work and the funds to carry it on, and it was not until the late eighties that enough money to finish the structure was appropriated. The building now houses the U. S. District Court rooms and other federal offices. Recently a new wing was added; also an underground sprinkling system was installed.

7. The KIT CARSON MONUMENT stands in front of the Federal Building at the S. entrance. Although Kit Carson's grave is in Taos, this memorial was erected by the members of the local post of the Grand Army of the Republic.

8. The SCOTTISH RITE CATHEDRAL, at the corner of Washington Ave. and N. Federal Place, is a large red stucco building of Moorish design. The structure contains a lobby, classrooms, banquet hall and kitchens, an auditorium, and a completely equipped stage. Occupying the entire space above the proscenium arch is a mural painting representing Boabdil delivering the keys of the Alhambra to Ferdinand and Isabella.

9. OLD FORT MARCY AND THE GARITA, dominating the city from this hilltop, are now only a group of mounds. Here, however, was erected in 1846 by the Volunteer American soldiers of the American Army of Occupation an elaborate system of earthworks for the protection of the town. The fort was named for Captain Marcy of the U. S. Army, the discoverer of the headwaters of the Canadian River. The site affords a splendid panorama of the city and surrounding country. The Garita, somewhat lower on the slope, was a diamond-shaped prison with towers at the corners. It was a Spanish stronghold for prisoners condemned to hang, later used by the Americans for a guardhouse.

10. ALLISON-JAMES SCHOOL, NE. corner Federal Place and US 64, under the direction of the Board of Domestic Missions of the Presbyterian church, was established here in 1866. It is a coeducational institution for Spanish-American children of junior and senior high school age. The six buildings on 18 acres of land, valued at $195,000, are California Mission style.

11. The CROSS OF THE MARTYRS, crowning a low northern summit of the city, W. of US 64, was erected by community effort in recent years to commemorate the slaying of twenty-one Franciscan missionaries in the Pueblo Revolt of 1680.

12. The CHURCH OF SANTO ROSARIO, or Rosario Chapel, stands in a sandy plain to the S. of Griffin St., about two miles from the plaza. It is said to be a part of the chapel which De Vargas raised in his camp after the reconquest of Santa Fe in 1692. The image of the Virgin, *La Conquistadora,* which De Vargas reputedly brought

with him at the time and which he credited with his victory, is carried annually to this chapel in the early summer and left for a week.

13. ST. CATHERINE'S INDIAN SCHOOL, on Griffin St. W. of Rosario Chapel, stands on historic ground. This Catholic school is an order established by Mother Catherine Drexel of Philadelphia for the education of Indian children in the West and Negro children in the South.

14. The NATIONAL CEMETERY, across the road from St. Catherine's Indian School, is the burial place of New Mexico veterans of every American war.

15. The PUBLIC LIBRARY, 121 Washington Ave. (*Hours, noon to 9, Sat. from 10 to 9*) was started in 1907 by the Santa Fe Women's Board of Trade. The collection of belletristic and Southwestern literature comprises more than 25,000 volumes, kept up to date by regular purchases. Reading rooms with tables are provided. The building was remodelled in the Territorial style in 1932. Decorations of the entrance hallway are in true fresco by the Santa Fe artist, Olive Rush.

16. SENA PLAZA, one block E. of the Palace, on Palace Ave., is a successful restoration of the old Sena home (*circa* 1840) in the original spirit of a typical and old building, constructed around a patio. The architectural style is Territorial, distinguished by the slender posts supporting the portal, and the coping of brick surmounting the walls. It is now an office building. W. P. Henderson was the architect.

17. The U. S. POST OFFICE, on the W. side of Cathedral Place, was built in 1921 under the supervision of James A. Wetmore, architect, with local consultants. It is a good example of the Spanish-Pueblo style of architecture applied to a modern building, and is significant as one of the few Federal buildings done in local architectural style. The structure houses the U. S. Land Office, the Weather Bureau, the U. S. Public Roads Bureau and other offices in addition to the postal department.

18. ST. VINCENT'S HOSPITAL AND ORPHANAGE, 210 E. Palace Ave., half a block E. from Sena Plaza, is the only hospital in Santa Fe. This Catholic institution was founded by Archbishop Lamy, who enlisted the Sisters of Charity in Cincinnati in the work of establishing a hospital, sanitarium, and orphanage in Santa Fe.

19. The CATHEDRAL OF SAINT FRANCIS, opposite the Post Office, stands as an enduring monument to Archbishop Lamy, his priests, and the Catholic people of New Mexico. The cornerstone was laid in 1869, eighteen years after Archbishop Lamy arrived in Santa Fe. The site chosen by him was occupied first by the church and monastery erected in 1622 by Friar Alonso Benavides and destroyed by the Indians in 1680, and a second church, or *Parroquia,* was built there in 1713. In constructing his cathedral, Archbishop Lamy, whose statue stands at the entrance to the cathedral, built the new walls around this old second edifice and used it during the construction operations so that not a Mass was missed while the cathedral was rising. The sacristy in the rear of the cathedral is an actual part of the old *Parroquia.* The

native sandstone used in the walls has a richness of color which adds to the beauty of the cathedral's Romanesque lines. The height of the middle nave is fifty-five feet, the ceiling is arched in the Roman style and made of a very light volcanic stone obtained from the summit of a hill about twelve miles from Santa Fe. The interior of the cathedral is dominated by the high altar, under which Archbishops Lamy, Salpointe, and Esquillon lie buried. Tradition has long placed the remains of the great re-conqueror, De Vargas, under the cathedral altar, but late researches indicate that he lies elsewhere.

To the left of the altar in the Sacred Heart Chapel is the STATUE OF LA CONQUISTADORA, over two hundred years old, which is carried through the streets of Santa Fe to Rosario Chapel in the annual De Vargas Procession in June. The chapel to the right is dedicated to San Antonio, where a painting done by Pascualo de Veri in 1710 depicts *Christ at Gethsemane.*

Back of the high altar, through the sacristy and behind a locked door which will be opened upon request, is the MUSEUM where one of the finest pieces of ecclesiastical art in America was formerly kept. This is the stone *reredos,* removed from the old Military Chapel, La Castrense, which stood in the middle of the block on the south side of the Plaza until about 1850. It was given by Don Antonio Marín del Valle and his wife in 1760. The rare beauty and grace of the old stone carving can now be appreciated for it has been removed from its former cramped surroundings to the Cristo Rey (Christ the King) Church completed early in 1940. The museum contains also a collection of primitive paintings and carvings in wood from old churches, and a carved stone panel of Our Lady of Light, to whom the military chapel was dedicated. Two friars who came to New Mexico more than three hundred years ago lie buried beneath board markers set into the east wall of this room. These are the only known graves of the fifty-three Franciscans who came with the Conquistadores.

20. LA FONDA, San Francisco and Shelby Sts., at the SE. corner of the Plaza, stands on the site of the old Fonda, or Inn, the adobe building which served for hotel purposes from the beginning of the American occupation in 1846 and marked the end of the Santa Fe Trail. The old structure was the most notable landmark of the Trail days, and was the rendezvous of Spanish grandees, trappers, traders, pioneers, merchants, soldiers, and politicians. Like most of the buildings of the time it was one-story high and built around a central patio, with a large corral and stables on the south. During the American military occupation, Santa Fe, centered at this inn, was noted for the brilliance of its society. The patronage of the old place dwindled as more modern accommodations were provided, and the building fell into disrepair. A large part of the old building stood until 1925, when a modern hotel, financed by a group of Santa Fe citizens, was raised on the site. Three years later the structure was purchased by a private company, enlarged, redecorated, and remodelled, but the old name was retained.

21. LORETTO ACADEMY, S. of La Fonda on College St., is one of the oldest educational institutions in the West. The first building of the academy was erected in 1853; today there are five buildings, one of which, the chapel, is severely Gothic. Above the altar in the chapel is a golden statue of the Virgin, and a spiral staircase, winding apparently without support—which has given rise to mystic legends about its construction—leads to the gallery above. Today the academy is devoted to the education of Catholic girls of grammar and high school age.

22. SAN MIGUEL CHURCH, SE. corner College and De Vargas Sts. (*adm. 25¢*), is one of the oldest churches standing in the United States. Built about 1636 for the use of the Indian slaves of the Spanish officials, the church was all but destroyed by the Indians in the Pueblo Revolt of 1680. De Vargas partially restored it when he recaptured the province in 1693; and later, in 1710, it was completely restored by the Marqués de la Peñuela, the Spanish governor at the time. The exterior of the building has changed its appearance many times since, but the walls are the same, and the back of the church retains its original massive lines. After ringing thrice at the door, one is admitted by a Brother who will point out the ancient beam carved with this legend: *El Señor Marqués de la Peñuela hizo esta fabrica, el Alfres Real Don Augustín Flores Vergara, su criado, Año de 1710* (The Marqués de la Peñuela erected this building, the Royal Ensign Don Augustín Flores Vergara, his servant. The year 1710.)

The church contains among others, large rectangular paintings of the Annunciation by Giovanni Cimabue on the altar. The color of these ancient pictures remains rich and beautiful in spite of their age, and in one of them are two narrow holes said to have been made by the arrows of hostile Indians when the painting was being carried in an outdoor procession.

San Miguel church is now used only by the Christian Brothers and the students of St. Michael's College, which adjoins it on the south, for their chapel. It is opened for public worship only on St. Michael's Day and on Holy Thursday.

23. ST. MICHAEL'S COLLEGE, facing College St. between De Vargas and Manhattan Sts., was founded in 1859 by the Christian Brothers as a Catholic school for boys. It was incorporated by the Territorial Legislature in 1874, and in 1887 the present dormitory was built, a quaint building, with long narrow windows, grey shutters, balcony, and pegged railings. The later additions are modern brick buildings. The gymnasium is one of the largest and best equipped in the State, and the auditorium has a seating capacity of 2,000.

24. The SUPREME COURT BUILDING, on the NE. corner of De Vargas and Don Gaspar Sts., houses the Supreme Court, the State Law Library, the offices of the Attorney General, and the State Treasurer. It is a Spanish-Colonial building, with well-kept gardens in the rear, and was built in 1937 at a cost of $320,000. All of the windows are trimmed with bronze and adorned with the Zía sun

symbol. This is one of the many completely air-conditioned buildings in the State. The architect was Gordon F. Street.

25. The STATE CAPITOL BUILDING, on Galisteo St., at Montezuma, stands on the site of the first State capitol, which was built by the authorization of the Territorial Legislature in 1884, after a long struggle to keep the capital at Santa Fe. It was a towering Victorian structure of stone, surrounded by a low stone wall and open, treeless fields. This building burned to the ground in 1892 and the present structure, composed of two wings and a large central dome, was built in 1900. It contains most of the offices of the State government, including the two houses of the legislature. Its architecture has been described as neo-English Renaissance. The Santa Fe firm of Rapp & Rapp were the architects.

26. The NEW MEXICO PUBLIC WELFARE BUILDING, across from the capitol on the W. side of Galisteo St., was built with FERA funds and dedicated in 1935. John Gaw Meem was the architect. This building houses the offices of the Work Projects Administration and certain offices of the U. S. Treasury Department. Paintings by WPA artists hang on the walls of the corridors. The architecture of the building is interesting as a successful adaptation of the New Mexico Territorial style to modern usages.

27. The SANTA FE COUNTY COURTHOUSE, located on the SW. corner of Grant and Johnson Sts., two blocks west of the Palace, was built at a cost of $202,000, including equipment and architect's fee, and dedicated on January 7, 1940. Forty-five per cent of the cost was a grant from PWA, the remainder being owners' fund (bond issue). Designed by John Gaw Meem, it is a large two-story structure in modified Spanish-Pueblo style.

28. The MUSEUM OF NAVAHO CEREMONIAL ART (*Open 9 to 12 and 1 to 4:30 weekdays, and 1:30 to 4:30 Sun., adm. 25¢*), 2 m. SE. of the Plaza on Camino Lejo, off the old Pecos Road, is "an interpretation in modern form of a Navaho Ceremonial Hogan." Its purpose is stated as follows: "It is planned as an integral background for the exhibition of sand paintings and as a repository for the myths, music, poetry, sacred lore, and objects connected with the Navaho religion; the intention being to perpetuate for the general public, for research students, and for the Indians themselves, this great example of a primitive people's culture." The house is the gift of Miss Mary Cabot Wheelwright, and was designed by William P. Henderson as a synthesis of the types of Navaho ceremonial hogans. It contains the most important and complete collection of reproductions of Navaho sand paintings in the world.

29. The LABORATORY OF ANTHROPOLOGY, E. of the Museum of Navaho Ceremonial Art on a 50-acre site (*Adm. is free at all times. Hours 9-12 and 1-5 daily except Sun. and holidays. Personal attention without charge is given to all visitors by museum attendants.*) was organized in 1923 when a small group of enthusiastic citizens of Santa Fe, fearful that in another decade the opportunity might be

gone forever, started to assemble by gift and purchase a collection of Indian pottery of the Southwest which would demonstrate scientifically and chronologically the development of the art from earliest Spanish times to the present. Under the name of the Indian Arts Fund, they incorporated their organization, maintained and even increased the collection through many financial vicissitudes. This remarkable accumulation of pottery, and the idea which brought it into being, became the nucleus of the Laboratory of Anthropology when the latter institution was incorporated in 1927 as a privately conducted scientific and educational institution, dedicated broadly to the purpose of research in every phase of man's activities in the Southwest, from earliest prehistoric times to the present. Built in 1931, in the early Spanish-Pueblo style of architecture, the buildings include a museum, lecture hall and laboratory unit, a garage-storage unit, and the director's residence. Designed by John Gaw Meem, the architect's plans include numerous other units, to be added as occasion requires.

Four halls, equipped with the latest type of cases, are devoted to exhibits resulting from the research of staff members and to displays of choice specimens illustrating the archeology and ethnology of the Southwest. These rooms are on the left of the entrance hall and from them the lecture room opens. On the right of the entrance is the LIBRARY planned to hold 10,000 volumes, with a reading room open to the public. The 4,000 items already catalogued are devoted almost exclusively to the general subject of Anthropology, with particular reference to the history of man in the Southwest. Offices of the staff occupy the remaining space on the main floor.

Important as a museum feature of the laboratory are the great collections of Pueblo pottery, Navaho and Pueblo textiles, silver, basketry, and the arts and crafts of other tribes. Each specimen has been carefully selected to show some particular phase in the development of Indian art in the Southwest. These, owned and used co-operatively by the Laboratory and the Indian Arts Fund, Incorporated, are shown to visitors under the guidance of museum attendants who also supervise their use by pupils of Indian schools, adult Indian crafts workers, and by artists, writers, students, and all who can in any way promote an interest in the revival and improvement of native arts.

The bulk of these collections is kept on the lower floor, where storage space and vaults are provided for safekeeping. Also on the lower floor are the workrooms of the research staff where studies in progress include an archeological survey of the Southwest, studies of Southwestern Indian Art, Technology of Southwestern Ceramics and the Dendrochronology of the Rio Grande area. This latter work consists of tree-ring dating of ruins by analysis of wood remains.

The laboratory offers to the fullest extent possible its facilities and co-operation of Federal, State, and private institutions and agencies conducting studies in the Southwest.

30. The NATIONAL PARK SERVICE REGIONAL HEADQUARTERS, located near the Laboratory of Anthropology on the

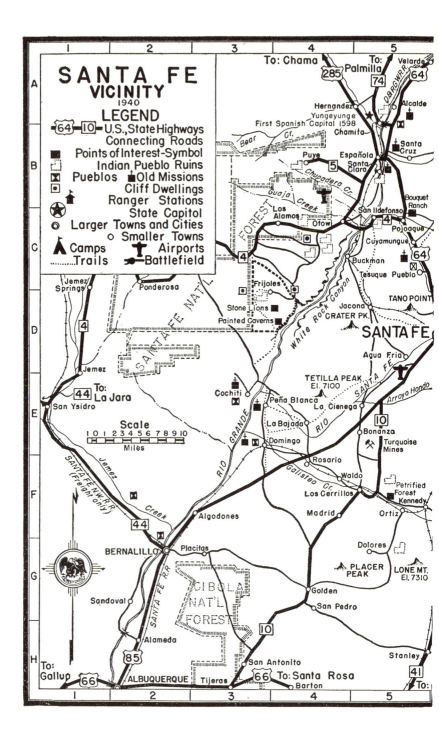

SANTA FE
VICINITY
1940
LEGEND
64─10 U.S., State Highways
Connecting Roads
Points of Interest-Symbol
Indian Pueblo Ruins
Pueblos ● Old Missions
Cliff Dwellings
Ranger Stations
State Capitol
Larger Towns and Cities
○ Smaller Towns
Camps        Airports
Trails       Battlefield

To: Chama
285  Palmilla   To: 74   Velarde
64
Hernandez   Alcalde
Yungeyunge
First Spanish Capital 1598
Chamita   Santa Cruz
Bear   Cr.
Puye   Española
Chupadera Cr.
Santa Clara
5
Guaja Creek
Los Alamos   San Ildefonso   Bouquet Ranch
Otowi   4   Pojoaque
Cuyamungue
Buckman   64
Tesuque Pueblo
Frijoles   TANO POINT
Stone Lions   Jacona
Painted Caverns   White Rock Canyon   CRATER PK.
SANTA FE

Jemez Springs   Ponderosa
SANTA FE NAT'L FOREST

4   Agua Fria
Jemez
TETILLA PEAK   SANTA FE
44  To: La Jara   El. 7100
San Ysidro   Cochiti   Peña Blanca   La Cienega   Arroyo Hondo
Scale   La Bajada   RIO
10 1 2 3 4 5 6 7 8 9 10   Domingo   10
Miles   Bonanza   Turquoise Mines
Rosario
Waldo
Petrified Forest
Los Cerrillos   Kennedy
Algodones   Madrid   Ortiz
44
BERNALILLO   Placitas   Dolores
PLACER PEAK   LONE MT.
Sandoval   CIBOLA NAT'L FOREST   Golden   El. 7310
San Pedro
Alameda   10
85   Stanley
To: Gallup   San Antonito   41
66   ALBUQUERQUE   Tijeras   66 To: Santa Rosa   To:
Barton

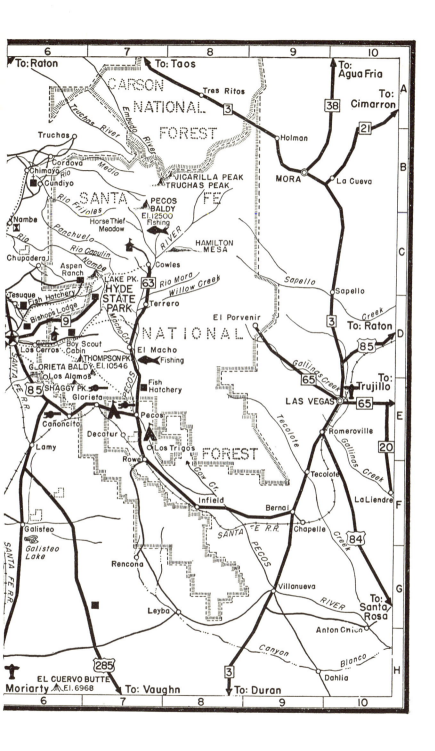

old Pecos Road, is one of the largest all-adobe structures in the United States. With its patio, it covers an acre of ground, and more than 200,000 adobe bricks were used in its construction. It houses the offices of Region III of the National Park Service, which includes New Mexico, Arizona, Texas, Oklahoma, Arkansas, and the southern parts of Colorado, Utah, and Nevada.

31. The SANTA FE INN, E. from the National Park Service Building, to sign of turnoff, is a Spanish-Pueblo building. Formerly the Sunmount Sanatorium, it was remodelled in 1938, and is today one of the more fashionable hotels in the Santa Fe area. The building, erected in 1915 at a cost of $90,000, was the first building in Santa Fe that returned to the old traditions for modern purposes.

32. CAMINO DEL MONTE SOL takes its name from a conical hill near-by, called *Monte Sol,* so named because of its prominence and position, where it catches the first and last rays of the sun. The street was once known as the center of the artist colony. Houses of artists lined the street on both sides and were, for the most part, built by the late Frank Applegate, beloved artist and writer. At 439 Camino del Monte Sol is the MARY AUSTIN HOUSE, which is now the property of Arsuna, an art center.

33. EL CAMINO DEL CAÑÓN is an ancient thoroughfare extending R. from the Alameda, following the Santa Fe River into the mountains for 10 or 12 miles. In pre-Spanish days it is said to have been the Indian trail from the lower Rio Grande Valley to Taos. The road has been closed to traffic, however, beyond the eastern city limits in the interests of public health, for the area contains a reservoir for the city water supply and the drainage which flows into it. Turning left at the point where the Camino del Monte Sol joins it, on the return to the Plaza, one passes many fine native adobe houses which often enclose garden patios.

34. GUADALUPE CHURCH, on the corner of Agua Fría and Guadalupe Sts., is the spiritual and social center of a very old section of Santa Fe, a region which has been little affected by the change of modern times. Deeply shaded by trees, the doorway is decorated by a panel of Mexican tiles depicting the Virgin of Guadalupe, the patron saint of Mexico. Although the present church is relatively new, having been restored in 1880 and again remodeled in 1918 after a fire, its history goes back to the early 1800's, when the original Guadalupe Church was built. Its present style suggests that of the California missions, particularly because of the stone walls which surround it and the many trees within its enclosures. Over the high altar is a copy of the original painting of Our Lady of Guadalupe, and beside it are paintings so old that their subjects are no longer discernible; fine old carved *vigas* and *corbels* adorn the high ceiling.

35. The GOVERNOR PÉREZ MONUMENT, about 2 m. W. of the Plaza on Agua Fría St., is a limestone marker erected by the D.A.R., on the spot where Governor Albino Pérez was assassinated in 1837. Enclosed by an iron rail, the stone commemorates a rebellion

evoked by a vicious system of taxation under Mexican rule. Taxes were levied on each vehicle bringing foreign merchandise into the city, on each animal employed by foreign merchants to carry such goods, and a tax of 25¢ per head on all sheep and cattle sold in the city. Encouraged by General Manuel Armijo of Albuquerque, a rich man of great power, the citizens rose in revolt against the tyranny of the system. The Governor, resisting, met defeat north of Santa Fe and fled to the Palace, to make good his escape from the city on the following day. His enemies overtook him in flight near Santa Fe, however, and he fell before the lances of the Indians. He was decapitated, and his head, impaled on a spear, carried triumphantly to the plaza.

36. AGUA FRÍA RANCHES, an area W. of Santa Fe on Agua Fría St., was formerly a prosperous ranch community with farms plentifully watered by the Santa Fe River. With the growth of the city, however, the water needed for irrigation was diverted for city uses, and the Agua Fría District passed as farming land except for the few who were able to dig wells and pump water. It will be noticed while driving west on the old road that the ranches become scattered and the buildings are for the most part in need of repair. Names on the mail boxes that dot the roadside are mostly Spanish, and some recall the great names of the Conquistadores.

37. The OLD SCHOOLHOUSE RUIN, on the S. side of Agua Fría 4.4 m. from the Plaza, is the site of a prehistoric Indian settlement. Although a number of late adobe houses have been built on the site, the mounds can be seen extending a considerable distance eastward. Here is ample evidence that Indians had settled the little valley long before the coming of the Spaniards, for slightly beyond, on the other side of the Rito de Santa Fe, partly excavated and plainly visible from the road, is Pueblo Pindi.

38. PUEBLO PINDI, a ruin, was named Pindi (Tewa Indian turkey) because of the profusion of turkey bones, eggshells, and turkey-pens found on the site. A tree-ring analysis shows the pueblo to have been occupied for about seventy-five years, at the end of which time the inhabitants are thought to have moved across the river to the above-mentioned schoolhouse site. Part of the pueblo has been washed away by the river, which often runs in flood during the summer rains, but enough remains to indicate that the pueblo once stood three or four stories high in places, with massive blocks of rooms terraced like the present pueblo of Taos. Two hundred rooms were excavated, five *kivas* were uncovered, and several plazas located. It is estimated that there may have been as many as 250 rooms in the pueblo originally.

39. AGUA FRÍA CHURCH, 5 m. from the Plaza of Santa Fe on the Agua Fría Road, was the center of the old village of Agua Fría. The church is still used by the people of the district, who celebrate their fiesta on June 24th. The Feast of San Isidro, their patron saint, is celebrated on May 15, and San Pedros Day on June 29. The place is gay, too, at Christmas time, when the church is garlanded with paper flowers and festooned with red Christmas bells. Small bonfires burn all

about on Christmas Eve, just as they do in the city only five miles away—but it seems far more remote than that. The old wood carver, Celso Gallegos, has his house here. He has earned a small portion of fame for his saints and figures fashioned from knots of pine and juniper. Spreading cottonwoods line the ditches, now too often dry.

40. The UNITED STATES INDIAN SCHOOL, 2 m. SW. from the Plaza on the R. of Cerrillos Road (Albuquerque highway), was started in 1899 with a Congressional appropriation of $31,000. Its 106 acres were donated by citizens of Santa Fe. Since the school is supported by the Federal government, no tuition is charged, and the enrollment is limited to 400 Indian boys and girls. The students do institutional work to pay for their room and board. Indian children from the Southwest, principally the Pueblo, Navaho, and Apache, are here given the opportunity to appreciate and understand the best of their own inheritance, and to borrow from the white man's civilization those things which prove advantageous and useful to them after leaving school.

The school emphasizes arts and crafts, including painting, designing, weaving, beadwork, basketmaking, potterymaking, silversmithing, and woodcarving. On the grounds is the Charles F. Lummis Indian Hospital, where Indians from the pueblos and reservations in northern New Mexico receive free medical treatment; it is also headquarters for the public health work of the U. S. Indian Service in this area.

41. The NEW MEXICO STATE POLICE BUILDING is on the S. side of Cerrillos Road, about 1.5 m. from the Plaza. The building, erected with WPA funds, and designed by W. C. Kruger, was finished in 1936. The structure contains cells, a fingerprint room, dormitories for officers, offices, and a target practice pistol range.

42. The NEW MEXICO SCHOOL FOR THE DEAF, on the N. side of Cerrillos Road, about 1 m. from the Plaza, is a State institution, founded in 1887. With the aid of WPA funds the school has been enlarged since 1935 with three new buildings, one devoted to agricultural training, another to administration, and a third for a dining hall and library.

43. The NEW MEXICO STATE PENITENTIARY (*visitors permitted; adm. 25¢*), off Cerrillos Road a quarter mile to the SW., dates from 1884, when a bill authorizing its location in Santa Fe was passed by the territorial legislature. The institution has been thoroughly modernized, with new quarters for women prisoners, a prison farm and orchard under irrigation, and institutional facilities within the walls. Most of the bricks and hollow tiles used in the city have been manufactured in the penitentiary, and New Mexico's motor license plates are made here.

## POINTS OF INTEREST IN ENVIRONS

Bishop's Lodge, 3 *m.;* Circle Drive, views of Rio Grande Valley, 2 *m.;* Tesuque Indian Pueblo, 10 *m.;* Nambé Indian Pueblo, 23 *m.;* San Ildefonso Indian Pueblo,

25 *m.;* Bandelier National Monument, cliff ruins in Rito de los Frijoles Canyon, 45 *m.;* Los Alamos Ranch School, ranch school for boys, 35 *m.;* Santa Cruz, 26 *m.;* Chimayó, 32 *m.;* Truchas, 38 *m.;* San Juan Indian Pueblo, 30 *m.;* Santa Clara Indian Pueblo, 28 *m.;* Puyé Cliff Dwellings, 40 *m.;* Taos and Taos Indian Pueblo, 75 *m.;* Turquoise Mines, 15 *m.;* Cochití Indian Pueblo, 30 *m.;* Santo Domingo Indian Pueblo, 30 *m.;* San Felipe Indian Pueblo, 40 *m.;* Apache Canyon, 20 *m.;* Pecos Pueblo Ruin, 30 *m.;* Pecos River Valley, for fishing, mountain scenery, 35 *m.;* Hyde Park, for skiing, 7 *m.;* horseback trails to Hyde Park, Little Tesuque Canyon, over the divide to Cowles, Lake Peak, Windsor Trail, and other trails mostly unmarked; services of guides desirable.

# *Taos*

*Railroad Station:* At Taos Junction, 20 *m*. W. via US 64 and NM 96 for Denver & Rio Grande Western R.R.
*Bus Station:* Columbia Hotel, S. side of Plaza, for Santa Fe Trailways and Valley Transit Lines.
*Taxis:* Cars for hire at local garages; sight-seeing service during summer months.
*Traffic Regulations:* Slow traffic in narrow, winding streets at intersections; one-way traffic around central plaza; one-way streets indicated.

*Accommodations:* Six hotels, cabin camps, private rooms.

*Information Service:* Hotels and taverns.

*Motion Picture Houses:* One.
*Swimming:* Ponce de León Hot Springs, 7 *m*. SE. of city, outdoor pool bathhouses.
*Riding:* Inquire locally about horses.
*Tennis:* Two dirt courts, 0.5 *m*. from city, open to Tennis Club members, small fee.
*Fishing:* Canyon of Rio Grande River, 15 *m*. S.; Hondo Canyon, 14 *m*. N.W.; Taos Canyon, 3 *m*. E.; other small streams in vicinity.
*Pack Trips:* Guides and equipment available for two-day to two-week trips through mountains; inquire locally.

*Annual Events:* San Gerónimo Fiesta, Sept. 30; Taos Pueblo Corn Dance (Indian Sun Down Dance), evening Sept. 29; Spanish-American carnival, Sept. 29; Deer Dance, Buffalo Dance, Matachines at Indian Pueblo, Christmas-New Year's holidays; Turtle Dance, early spring; Spanish-American pageants and Saint's Day processions, throughout year.

TAOS (pronounced to rhyme with house) is in reality three towns—the Spanish town (Don Fernando de Taos), the Indian Pueblo (San Gerónimo de Taos), and the old Indian farming center (Ranchos de Taos (*see Tour 8a*)—all separate entities, yet from the beginning closely knit together in interest.

In the vicinity of these three villages are other smaller settlements, from one to five miles apart, all properly members of the Taos community, representing extensions of Spanish colonization in the middle of the eighteenth century; the melodious Spanish names, such as Talpa, Cañón, Placita, Córdoba, Prado, and Cordillera, suggest their Old-World character. The two principal villages, the Indian pueblo of San Gerónimo and the Spanish Don Fernando de Taos, the latter generally called simply Taos, lie close against the base of a section of the Sangre de Cristo Mountains rising abruptly east. Because of the difficulty of approach no railroads have been built to them. Visitors enter Taos over highways through beautiful canyons by bus or motorcar ninety-nine miles southwest from Ratón, or seventy-five north from Santa Fe. But whether they enter the plateau through the Cimarrón Cañon with its pine trees, its eastern approach, or through the Rio Grande Canyon with its huge igneous rock cliffs, its southern portal, the ascent is almost as thrilling as Promotheus' cerulean adventure must have been to him when he climbed up into the land of the gods.

The first impression upon emerging on to the plateau is that of the freshness and purity of the rarefied atmosphere, the clearness of the light, making all colors pure and luminous, and the quietness, with the little villages lying peacefully, seemingly asleep, the tall, blue mountains, screen-like, behind them.

Many towns are situated near great mountains; but most of them are right in the mountains, or so close under them that they do not have the wide panorama that Taos commands, which prompted D. H. Lawrence, on his first visit, to write: "I think the skyline of Taos the most beautiful of all I have ever seen in my travels around the world."

In appearance like scattered stones carelessly thrown at the foot of the mountain backstop, the light-colored houses—square and hard as stones, but not made of stone—are fashioned of mud (adobe). The thick layer of creamish, tannish, or reddish mud filling all the cracks makes the houses as snug as birds' nests. Every year or two they must be replastered with mud mixed with sand and straw. More straw is used in Taos than in other places in the State, giving the houses a golden glint in the sunshine. Nevertheless, they have a gloomy look. They seem to be crouching close to the ground for protection from some unknown thing, and seem little taller than the hollyhocks screening their tawny walls.

Don Fernando de Taos (7,050 alt., 1,847 pop.), of which 80 per cent is Spanish-American and 20 per cent Anglo-American, is the seat of Taos County, where three languages and three races, Indian, Spanish, and Anglo-American, intermingle; it is also the home of the Taos art colony.

The village is a small trading center for the surrounding ranches. Its flat-roofed, one-story stores cluster around and front upon three sides of the small plaza, or town square, where the life and much of the history of the village centers. Parked in solid flanks facing the shops (parking against the plaza enclosure is prohibited) are seen the automobiles of residents, of ranchmen and tourists, trucks from near-by ranches and from distant cities, freight-laden, sometimes interspersed by horse-drawn, covered wagons from the pueblo or the ranches close by.

The plaza sleeps undisturbed in the sun, the old well in the center and the bandstand ordinarily giving no sign of life. Life and interest in the town's activities are evident along the uneven sidewalks, fronting the stores where white-robed Indians lean against a sunny corner to watch the Anglos pass or to visit among themselves, Spanish-speaking residents from near-by ranches here to barter produce for manufactured necessities, and sightseeing tourists peering in curio windows. Artists laden with sketch-easel and paint box, or new canvases to hang in the gallery, thread their way among the others, or stop to arrange a posing date with one of the Indians.

In the plaza, the heart of Fernando de Taos, as of every Spanish town, the light skin of the English-speaking residents, the dusk of the soft-spoken Spanish, and the blanketed bronze of the Indian prove exciting contrasts in the brilliance of the New Mexico sun. Occupying today the spot around which the first small group of settlers built their homes, the plaza is still the center of communal life, and the oldest walls of the earliest houses are now hidden behind modern buildings. Some of the rooms in La Fonda (hotel) on the south side were in use in 1832 as the Bent and St. Vrain Store, but the long *portales* which were built over the sidewalks after the fire of 1932, when many buildings had to be restored, give to the plaza a quaint, old-time look. Two roads have recently been paved to the village limits—and despite many protests the plaza, too, was oiled.

Relatively bare of trees in Spanish times, except in the vicinity of water courses and ditches, the town now has many beautiful ones. Those in the plaza are of recent planting, their predecessors having been destroyed by the fires that razed the buildings at various times in recent years. The rows of cottonwood trees over-arching Pueblo Road were planted by an Anglo-American citizen in the 1890's—for in almost every instance in New Mexico it has been the Anglo-American who has been the planter of trees for their own sake.

The citizens have had the wisdom to preserve the architectural traditions of the village, to keep the walls of their houses low and the roofs flat, to use the native materials, adobe and crude pine beams. Consequently, Fernando de Taos is distinctive, its buildings and dwellings almost uniformly appropriate to the land, the beauty which nature has bestowed only occasionally marred or spoiled by extraneous architectural intrusions. Some of the modern interpretations of the Spanish-Pueblo style are wild in detail, but the whole effect is preserved by adherence to the fundamental structural principles.

Fernando de Taos has surrendered less to the powerful current of Americanization than any town of its importance in New Mexico. Nowhere in the State do the three cultural elements, Indian, Spanish-American, and Anglo-American live in such close proximity and, in the main, with such tolerant disdain for one another. The Indians work for wages in the town, tinker with the white man's automobile in some garage, but they go home to the pueblo at night to immerse themselves in the timeless, Pueblo traditions.

Fernando de Taos is thought to have been named for Don Fernando de Chaves, one of its leading citizens in the seventeenth century, but also it has been called Fernández de Taos and San Fernández de Taos. Since 1884, however, when a young postmaster, finding too many different addresses going through his hands, despairingly suggested to Washington that the town be listed as "Taos," the shorter term has been used, though Don Fernando de Taos is the legal name.

Don Fernando de Taos was incorporated as a village in 1932, and since then has acquired a water system, electricity, a sewage disposal plant and a fire truck. In later years fire has been the scourge of Taos; a series of disastrous conflagrations levelled two sides of the plaza on successive occasions; and on December 15, 1933, the Don Fernando Hotel, which occupied the southwest corner, burned. Without adequate fire protection it was impossible to stop these blazes which at the time threatened the very existence of the town.

Fernando de Taos has no factories. A large percentage of the population is occupied in local trade or in the creative arts, the native crafts including carding and spinning, weaving, tin work, wood-carving and the making of Spanish-Colonial pine furniture.

The Loma (Spanish hillock) west of the plaza, once the village pasture, overlooks the village and a great expanse of Taos valley south. Here many of the artists live, in low-built adobe houses crowding in with the one- and two-room Spanish-American homes. In appearance a black gash of studio window is often all that distinguishes them.

Above a history full of revolutionary bloodshed and sturdy insistent pioneering, Fernando de Taos has held its head. For security against enemies, the Spaniards who first settled the valley early in the seventeenth century built their houses close to the Indian pueblo which had been discovered in 1540 by their compatriot, Hernando de Alvarado, whose followers had been so attracted to the valley that within a few years some of them returned. Later, colonists from Oñate's little community at San Gabriel on the Rio Grande, forty miles south, sought the fertile lands and plentiful waters of the region around the pueblo. The Indians were friendly and the settlers, most of whom had been soldiers in Oñate's command, set up their homes and farms unmolested.

In succeeding years the Indians, becoming alarmed at the growth of the Spanish community in their midst and displeased at the frequency of intermarriages between the girls and boys of the two races, decided in council to ask the Spaniards to move "a league away" from the confines of the pueblo—which the newcomers did with good grace. Thus the two villages separated.

For long, however, the interests of the Spanish town and the Indian pueblo lay close together: they needed the mutual protection of arms on the one hand and of numbers on the other, for the roving tribes of Apache, Ute, Comanche and Navaho Indians made frequent attacks upon both, seeking food and captives for slaves and uniting the destinies of the two for about three hundred years. As settlement increased and the need for farm lands became greater, small groups settled near their farm centers, bringing into being small villages clustering about the first villages.

Although Fray Pedro de Miranda built a church on the edge of the pueblo before 1617 for the combined settlements, bad blood appeared between the Indians and the Spaniards, and in 1631 this priest and two Spanish soldiers forfeited their lives. This ill-feeling increased until in 1650 a great revolt against Spanish rule was planned from the Taos

Pueblo only to come to naught because the Hopi, far away in Arizona, refused to join in the plot. However, thirty years later (1680), led by Po-pé of San Juan, who made his headquarters at Taos Pueblo, the Indians successfully rebelled and cast the Spanish from the land (*see History*). It was not until Captain-General De Vargas, after his re-conquest in 1692, marched up the Rio Grande to Taos, visiting all pueblos on the way, that the settlement was re-established on the old site.

Fernando de Taos was endangered by the hostility and attacks of the Apache, Ute, Navaho and Comanche, the latter particularly causing trouble. In 1760 a band of them attacked the town and carried away fifty women and children who were never recovered. Soldiers were sent after them and four hundred of the Indians were massacred. From that time on the Comanche left the town alone and there was never another Comanche raid in Taos Valley. However, the rear walls of the houses in Don Fernando were joined together to form a rectangular fortress, with only two gates through which cattle and sheep were driven at evening.

An agricultural settlement, Don Fernando became early in its history a trading center. During the eighteenth century its annual trade fair was the meeting-place of the Plains and Pueblo Indians, traders from Mexico and Old Spain, and *haciendados* and villagers from all over the Southwest. The fairs rapidly outgrew the new policy of seek-ing the friendship and trade of the Plains Indians, for whom Taos Pueblo had always been the nearest source of supplies of blankets, corn, and later of Mexican goods. A motley array gathered there each sum-mer, and Taos became the busiest village in the province. Gradually French trappers came, and after 1802, when Thomas Jefferson con-cluded the Louisiana Purchase and all the center of the continent fell into the possession of the United States, the American trappers swarmed into New Mexico. From 1815 to 1837 the "Mountain Men" (as they wer called) trapped fur-bearing animals, fought Indians, and opened new lands. These trappers, a race of men apart, who did so much for the development of Fernando de Taos, were solitary, courageous, and hardy, preferring the life of hardship on mountain trails to the soft amenities of civilization. They were men of action, whose speech was as picturesque as their dress. Many nationalities were represented among them: French, French-Canadian, English, and American. Their names are clues to the complex of natures and nationalities found in Don Fernando de Taos in the middle of the nineteenth century: the Robidoux Brothers, Bill Williams, Christopher (Kit) Carson, Milton Sublette, Bautiste LaLande, the Bent brothers, Ceran St. Vrain, Richens Wootton, Jedediah Strong, and others.

Contemporaneous with these mountain men and traders was a Spanish priest, Padre Antonio José Martínez, born in Abiquiu, who came to Fernando de Taos in 1826 and for forty years championed the cause of his people and strove to bring enlightenment and education to their lives. Single-handed, he fought ignorance and superstition, started a school for boys and girls, the first co-educational venture in the South-west. He operated a printing press, said to be the first brought to New Mexico, and published a paper called *El Crepúsculo* (the dawn), and further advanced his people's interest by serving in the first general territorial assembly at Santa Fe. Although unfrocked by Archbishop Lamy in 1854, after a quarrel, Padre Martínez never forsook his own people, fighting to the last to improve them. It has never been settled whether in the violent times after American annexation he favored or resisted the new regime. He was accused of helping to foment the uprising of 1847, which resulted in the death of Charles Bent, but evidence tends to exonerate him of this charge.

More trouble was ahead for the settlement. In 1837 the *alcalde* (mayor) was arrested on some trivial pretext and imprisoned by the Mexican government. All the town rose to arms and marched upon Santa Fe. The government, caught off its guard, was ready to agree to anything. At the instigation of Manuel Armijo, a leading politician, the insurgents elected as governor an Indian from the Taos pueblo! But Armijo quickly shot him and stepped into his office.

Another rebellion followed when the Spanish residents planned to overthrow the new government (*see History*). Arousing the Taos Indians, who had no grievance against the United States, by giving them plenty of *aguardiente* (liquor—Taos lightning) an attack was made on the new Governor, Charles Bent, who was scalped alive and then mur-dered in his home (*see below*).

Still another flurry of excitement promised a different kind of reputation for Fernando de Taos before the village settled down to its present character of peaceful refuge. As early as 1866 gold was found in quantity in the mountains, north, known as the Red River Country, but the incessant dangers from Indian attacks prevented its exploitation until the end of the nineteenth century. Prospectors roamed the hills for fifty years, getting grubstakes in Taos village and vanishing into the wilderness; but eastern capital was not attracted until the 1890's.

To the basic and underlying character of Fernando de Taos these alarms and excursions added little. It remained a small Spanish town in the United States, a fact which made few demands upon it save in such emergencies as the Civil and Spanish Wars. In the former in-stance, Kit Carson and some other citizens nailed the Union flag to a cottonwood pole in the plaza and stood by for a while to see that it stayed there—and that seemed to settle the matter. In the Spanish unpleasantness in 1898 there developed some antagonism toward Amer-icans, and racial hatred flared dangerously. Two artists, new arrivals, were jailed; the sheriff, a Spanish-American, was shot, and for a few days threats to "make sausage of the Americans" were heard on the plaza. The trouble blew over, however, and Fernando de Taos began to feel the power of law and order. The bad men of both sides decided to leave, and the village settled down to a well-behaved existence.

The fame of Fernando de Taos today, apart from the beauty of its setting, bears little relation to that of its past.   As the place of residence of some thirty nationally-known writers and artists, it is known throughout the land as an art colony.   The first known writer to come was Lewis H. Garrard, then eighteen years old, who arrived in 1845, two years before the massacre of Governor Bent.   He wrote about his experiences in a book called *Wah-to-yah, or the Taos Trail,* a volume that remains the most authentic record of the time.   The first artists to arrive were two brothers, E. M. and R. H. Kern, who accompanied Colonel J. C. Frémont in 1848.   Fernando de Taos is a place to which artists and writers have been attracted ever since, for it is remote from those elements of American civilization that tend to make cities so inhospitable to creative work.

Fernando de Taos as an art colony grew out of one man's enthusiasm for a village he had never seen, and a broken wagon wheel.   Joseph Henry Sharp, a young painter sketching in New Mexico in 1880, so enthusiastically reported what he had heard about the charm of remote Taos village that his two friends, Bert Phillips and Ernest L. Blumenschein, determined to seek western adventure and follow the sun to Mexico, stopping on the way to visit the little New Mexican village of Sharp's glowing enthusiasms.   Accordingly, going by train to Denver, they bought a camping outfit and headed south, painting as they journeyed.   Thirty miles from Fernando de Taos a wheel was broken and, on the flip of a coin, Blumenschein was elected to ride horseback and carry the wheel into town for repairs.   Phillips remained to guard the camp outfit.   Three days were required to make the round trip and have the wheel repaired.   Blumenschein, thrilled with the place, decided that here their journey ended and here they remained.   Later, Sharp joined them, followed by Irving Couse.   For many years they were the only painters working here.   For exhibition purposes they organized the Taos Society of Artists, sending exhibitions to eastern art centers carrying the charm of New Mexico and attracting the interest and attention of other artists.   Thus began a regular pilgrimage to this out-of-the-way spot where is found in the Indian culture a definite American esthetic source, and in Spanish an established religious art tradition which has had its effect upon the art of the United States, as Barbizon, Fontainebleau and other continental art movements had on contemporary European art.

SAN GERÓNIMO DE TAOS, familiarly called simply Taos Pueblo, the oldest of the three towns bearing the name Taos, is situated two and a half miles north of Don Fernando de Taos.   It is reached by the Pueblo Road, leading from the plaza.   Permission to use a camera must be obtained from the Governor but the privilege does not carry permission to photograph individuals.   (*Parking fee 25¢.*)

The ruins of the old mission, erected 1704, can be seen on the east edge of the pueblo.   The standing walls are four feet thick, with remains of twin towers in the ruined pile of adobe.   The present small adobe mission built about 1848, at the pueblo entrance, faces the plaza, and stands on the traditional site of the original church, built by Fray Pedro Miranda in 1617, but destroyed in 1680.

Two large adobe communal houses, four and five stories in height, today appear much as they did at the coming of the Spaniards in 1540. They face each other, separated by Taos Creek which flows through the larger central plaza. Immense pine logs, hand hewn, provide foot bridges across the stream at each end of the plaza. Here on moonlight nights young men come and sing.

Until about 1890, the only entrance to the terraced rooms was by means of ladders leading to hatchways in the roofs. As the danger of attack decreased and finally disappeared, doors and windows were cut in the adobe walls, but ladders remain on the outside since the great dwellings contain no inside stairways. The large main groups are surrounded by smaller houses and by pole-supported *tapestes* (Spanish, platforms), used for the storage of alfalfa, corn and other produce. Firewood is sometimes stored in the space beneath the platform. *Hornos* (Spanish, ovens) for baking are near the houses, and tall ladder-ends protruding indicate the presence of underground *kivas,* where the men of the tribe hold their meetings and teach the boys the ancient ceremonies and traditions. Women enter the *kivas* only on certain ceremonial occasions. Visitors are not allowed.

They teach their children early in the ways of the Indian, shield them from too close contact with strangers, and preserve the ancient ways and modes of thought with vigor seldom found in a primitive people amidst modernism and change. They are a handsome, distinguished, and independent people, always courteous, but never currying favor with the white man.

They are chiefly farmers and stockmen, though a few keep small stores generally designated by a blanket hung up outside the door. Several are painters, others are workers in beads and drum-makers. As among all Pueblos, the women are the heads of the families and keep the homes. Very little pottery is made here, the traditional kind being cooking pots and large storage jars in brown with scant decorations in applied designs of the clay in the same color. Both sexes are employed as servants in Fernando de Taos, the men also serve as gardeners, garagemen, and models for artists. But they take great pains to guard themselves against the influences and changes to which they are exposed by their proximity to white people.

The pueblo abounds in ancient ceremonialism. The dances of Taos are noted for their beauty and precision. The Deer and Buffalo Dances, alternately performed on Christmas Day and Twelfth Night, are always beautiful and elaborate, combining dramatic symbolism with ritualistic movements of great beauty. The Corn Dance is also given as in other pueblos, and there are many dances for rain.

The Sun-Down Dance is always performed on the eve of the Fiesta of San Gerónimo, their patron Saint, September 30, the most important event of the year. With green aspen branches held upright in their hands, the Indians dance in thanksgiving for harvests, dance to the sun, giving an effect of a small green branch rhythmically dancing.

Next morning after Mass in the church, the traditional race between the north and south pueblos is run, always on the courses leading into the upper end of the north pueblo. The winning side, it is popularly said, gains the right to name the governor for the following year. The Indians themselves say that the race is for the purpose of assuring the Sun Father of their ability and willingness to lend him their strength to augment his waning vigor. However, this may be not the real significance but only a reason given to satisfy inquirers. The secrets of the ceremonies are carefully guarded.

## POINTS OF INTEREST
### (*DON FERNANDO DE TAOS*)

1. The PLAZA around which the first Spanish settlers built their homes is still the center of life in the village. The buildings around it today are nondescript pseudo-territorial and pseudo-Spanish-Colonial. Where the flagpole now stands the first residents drew water from a community well. Here, after the massacre of 1680, when the rear walls of the houses were joined to make a rectangular fortress, sheep and cattle were driven at night for safety. Here the covered wagons of trail days rumbled warily in, to be greeted by the cheers of the villagers, noted for their hospitality, their *fandangos,* and their brew of raw whiskey, called "Taos lightnin' " by the mountain men. The roads branching out from the plaza are still in use, as winding and narrow as the original cow-paths. Most of them follow the old trails. The Navaho Trail, which led west across the Rio Grande at Wamsley Crossing to the great plateau on the west bank of the river where wild horses once roamed, is now a well traveled road to *La Otra Banda,* as the county west of the river is called. The Picurís Trail led to the pueblo of that name and probably followed much the same course as the present highway to the south. The Kiowa Trail ran along the base of the mountains, and the old Taos Trail followed the route of the present NM 3, north of the Colorado line, and east to Bent's Fort on the Arkansas River. The Santa Fe Trail followed the route of US 64, and the Cimarrón Route was the same until it turned east to pass through the present town of Springer. Thus the plaza is the hub of the wheel of activity in Taos County; the spokes are the trails which converge in it. Over these, past and present-day travelers have passed to Taos where the Old West is entrenched, and out again into the world.

2. The COURTHOUSE, a two-story building near the center of the N. side of the plaza, is the third building on the same site to be used as a hall of justice and seat of government for Taos County, the first dating from the Mexican era and the second from 1880. The present building, built in the fall of 1933 (the former razed by fire in 1932), is notable for the fresco paintings by the Taos artists Lockwood, Bisttram,

To: State Highway 3

ARMORY PLACE

MARTYRS PLACE

GOV. BENT ST.

N. PUEBLO AVE.

ROAD

PLACITA

DIBBLE LANE

TERESINA ST.

DON FERNANDO AVE.

PADRE MARTINEZ

DOÑA LUZ

PLAZA DE TAOS

SANTA

LA FONDA LANE

DE GEORGE'S ST.

BENIGNA LEE ST.

KIT

CARSON AVE.

DRAGOON LANE

MORADA RD.

DEDOUX ST.

FE RD.

PUEBLO AVE.

OJITOS

LANE

SANTA FE TRAIL

64

To: Santa Fé

64

To: Raton

# DON FERNANDO DE TAOS

1940

## LEGEND

—64— U.S. Highways
— Connecting Streets

Cemetery

Scale

300 200 100 0        300        600

Feet

Phillips, and Higgins, which were done on a WPA Project. The compositions are allegorical because the historical events of Taos are yet subjects of bitter controversy. The largest, by Victor Higgins, depicts *Moses, the Law Giver; Aspiration* is by Emil Bisttram; *Avarice Breeds Crime,* and *Justice Begets Content* by Ward Lockwood; and *Obedience Casts Out Fear* by Bert Phillips. Five other panels, *Transgression* and *Reconciliation* by Emil Bisttram, *Superfluous Laws Oppress* and *Sufficient Law Protects* by Ward Lockwood, and *The Shadow of Crime* by Bert Phillips, complement the first.

3. The HEPTAGON GALLERY (*open daily 10-9, adm. 10¢*), a few doors away on the same side of the plaza, is an exhibition gallery maintained by a group of artists including Bisttram, Dasburg, Kissel, Higgins, Adams, and Lockwood. The work of these and other Taos artists may also be seen in various shops around town and by appointment at the artists' studios.

4. LA FONDA HOTEL, occupying most of the S. side of the plaza, was in former times the old Bent and St. Vrain store, established in 1832.

5. The KIT CARSON HOUSE, on the N. side of Kit Carson Ave., is part of a group of buildings built around a patio. The house at the front, labelled The Kit Carson House, now belongs to the Bent Lodge, No. 42, of the Masonic Order. From 1858 to 1866 this was Kit Carson's headquarters, office, and home. Carson lived in rooms at the back of the patio and used the front for offices and commissary. In recent years an old-style portal has been added to the house, otherwise very plain in design.

6. KIT CARSON CEMETERY lies at the end of Dragoon Lane, extending N. from Kit Carson Ave. Here, Kit Carson and Padre José Martínez are buried. The tombstone on the Carson grave was put up by the Masons in the 1880's.

7. HARWOOD FOUNDATION (*open daily in summer 10-12 and 2-5, free*), S. side of Ledoux St., consists of a group of studio apartments in Pueblo type architecture, a library, and a large exhibition room. The Foundation was established in 1923 by Mrs. Lucy Case Harwood in memory of her husband, Bert C. Harwood, a painter, who came to Taos in 1917, and died here. Many of his paintings are in the gallery. Every summer the artists of Taos exhibit jointly in the large, well-lighted hall.

8. The TRUJILLO HOUSE (pronounced *Tru-heé-yo*) on Ranchitos Road facing the placita of Our Lady of Guadalupe Church, one block W. of the plaza, is an outstanding example of the original flat-roofed type of Spanish-Colonial house with a portal supported by posts. This house was built in 1856 and was used as a storehouse by Antonio José Valdez; it represents the type of structures which at one time surrounded the plaza.

9. The MONTAÑER HOUSE, on Padre Martínez St., three blocks W. of the plaza, was one of a group of buildings, including a

near-by chapel which belonged to Padre Antonio José Martínez, who lived in Taos from 1826 until his death in 1867. The house occupies the site of his school for boys and girls.

10. The MANBY HOUSE, on the E. side of Pueblo Road, opposite Governor Bent St., and adjoining the Martin Hotel, was the home of A. R. Manby, an English eccentric and adventurer who came to Taos in 1894-5. His decapitated body was found in his house on the evening of July 3, 1929. The incident stands today as one of Taos' unsolved murder mysteries.

11. The HOUSE OF GOVERNOR CHARLES BENT in Spanish-Colonial one-story type of architecture, is on Governor Bent St., where Governor Bent was scalped during the insurrection of 1847. His family escaped by digging through the adobe wall to the house next door.

## POINTS OF INTEREST IN ENVIRONS

Placitas, 0.7 *m.;* Ranchos de Taos, 4.4 *m.;* Arroyo Hondo, 12 *m.;* Kiowa Ranch, D. H. Lawrence Shrine, 17.5 *m.* (*see Tour 3a*).

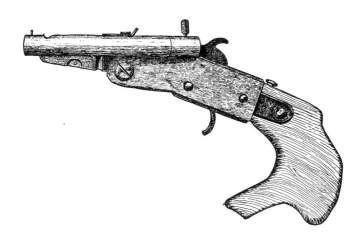

# PART III
## The Most Accessible Places

# *Tour* 1

(Trinidad, Colorado)—Ratón—Las Vegas—Santa Fe—Albuquerque—
Los Lunas—Socorro—Las Cruces—Anthony—(El Paso) ; US 85 and
US 80.
Colorado Line to Texas Line, 523.1 *m.*

Two-lane, bituminous-paved roadbed. Blizzards sometimes block Ratón Pass.
Atchison, Topeka & Santa Fe Railway roughly parallels entire route.
Accommodations in principal towns.

North and east of Santa Fe US 85 follows the old Santa Fe Trail
and south of Santa Fe approximates *El Camino Real* (the royal
road). Both have played important parts in the history of the State.
Over the Santa Fe Trail came the first white men to enter New Mexico
from the East (French fur traders and trappers) followed by pack
trains and wagon trains. General Kearny marched his Army of the
West in 1846 through the valleys and passes between Las Vegas and
Santa Fe where later the Union armies defeated the Confederates and
thwarted their plan to block the flow of gold from California to the
Union government.

South of Santa Fe is the country traversed by explorers, colonizers,
and those engaged in trade between Santa Fe and Chihuahua, Mexico;
in the lower Rio Grande Valley the famished Spaniards first came
upon the Indian fields of corn, beans, and pumpkin. *El Camino Real*
was the name given the route taken from Chihuahua by Augustín
Rodríguez in 1581.

*Section a.* *COLORADO LINE TO SANTA FE, 194.7 m.*

The northern part of US 85 goes through Ratón Pass and crosses
alternating mountains and plains, connecting occasional villages of adobe
houses. The magnificent views with their vast expanses of sky and
level, grassy lands that sweep clear to the mountains are characteristic
of the entire route.

US 85 crosses the NEW MEXICO LINE, 0 *m.,* which is 15
miles south of Trinidad, Colorado, over Ratón Pass, so named for the
many pack rats on the mountainside.

The WOOTTON RANCH HOUSE, immediately north of the New
Mexico-Colorado Line, was rebuilt by Colonel Owensy on the exact
spot where Uncle Dick Wootton obstructed the highway with heavy
chains to insure payment of toll for the twenty-seven miles of road he
had constructed in 1866 over Ratón Pass, until that time the most difficult section of the Santa Fe Trail.

The usual charge for wagons was $1.50 and old-timers relate how
Uncle Dick would hitch his mules outside the combination general store

and bank in the nearest town while he carried in a whisky keg full of silver dollars.

Through his gate passed freighters, soldiers, homeseekers, outlaws, and Indians. Only the latter were not asked for payment. Wootton believed they would not understand the toll system and wanted to avoid angering or delaying them. But those Spanish-speaking travelers who also found his barrier objectionable had their protests settled with diplomacy or a club. Cattle thieves were a source of trouble to Uncle Dick. Often they would seek employment at his ranch house in order to steal the animals of travelers who were spending the night there.

Dick (Richens Lacy) Wootton had many ventures beside his toll road. He was born in Virginia in 1816, given a "fair business education," and at the age of seventeen worked on a tobacco plantation; a year later he was employed on a Mississippi cotton field where he heard stories of adventures in the West that led him to Independence, Missouri, starting point for caravans leading over the Santa Fe Trail. The money being made in furs appealed to young Dick who became a trapper with headquarters at Fort Bent (now Colorado).

From this point in 1838 Dick Wootton and a dozen kindred spirits set forth on a trapping adventure that took them into the far northwest, then into California. When several days distant from the fort the discovery was made that no one had an almanac, so a Frenchman named Charlefou was elected to keep track of time by cutting a notch on a stick for each day. Charlefou had cut thirty-one notches when his horse failed in a leap across a chasm and both crashed down a hundred feet. When Dick Wootton and others arrived at the place several hours later they found the Frenchman with both legs broken lying on top of a dead horse. The plainsmen got Charlefou out of the chasm by nightfall and yanked the bones of his legs together then completed the job by using branches from saplings as splints. They carried Charlefou in a litter for two months, or what they estimated to be two months, for the board on which the notches had been cut was lost. Soon it came to be a joke that no track could be kept of the days and they agreed to give up the attempt. When they arrived in California they thought the seasons had been advanced two months, only to reach another conclusion when on the way east they were caught in a snow storm. They were absent from Fort Bent a year and a half and upon arrival learned that their "dead reckoning" was six weeks too fast.

For a time Dick Wootton served as hunter for the fort. He described the herds of buffalo as extending to the horizon and the plains at times appeared to be undulating fields of black. He rescued an Indian woman who was embedded in a snowdrift and dying and thus won the friendship of the Arapahoe.

Wootton, now known as Uncle Dick, turned his attention to a buffalo farm where the young were nourished by milch cows. Once when caught in a snow storm he became so hungry that he swam the South Platte to retrieve a goose he had shot the afternoon before. He learned while in a Ute village that the chief was dying and that custom required the killing of a stranger when a chief died—so he made a hurried departure. Once while trapping with several others he was cornered by Indians who rolled rocks down on the white men and injured several. He won a fight against wolves and another time had difficulty in balancing his 240 pounds in a tree where he was imprisoned for several hours by a grizzly bear.

Following the murder of Governor Charles Bent and other Americans, Wootton led a party of volunteers that assisted regulars in crushing the Taos revolution. Again he led volunteers who sought the Indians that perpetrated the massacre of stagecoach passengers on the Santa Fe Trail and abducted Mrs. White, her child, and a Negro nurse. By watching the flight of ravens Wootton directed the soldiers to the Indians' camp and during the fight that followed his life was saved by a suspender buckle over his heart. Learning that sheep were selling in California at ten times the cost price in New Mexico, Uncle Dick with four assistants, eight goats, and a shepherd dog drove nine thousand head to Sacramento; the trained goats led the way across rivers. Attacked by Utes, Wootton grabbed Chief Uncotash around the waist, wrestled with him, then sat on the chief's stomach, a knife in hand, until peace was promised.

In 1852 Uncle Dick was invited to visit at the home of Brigham Young in Salt Lake City. He was worried about his attire because he expected to meet several Mrs. Youngs. His buckskin trousers had stretched every time he crossed a stream and he had cut off the bottoms little by little. In the dry air of Utah they shrank until they came up to his knees. He made the visit but did not meet any feminine Youngs.

After his return to Fort Bent, Uncle Dick carried $14,000 in gold in his saddle bags to St. Louis. Once more in New Mexico he joined Tom Tobin in hunting the bandit Espinosa and a companion. Both resisted and were shot down. Tobin cut off their heads which he carried in a bag to Santa Fe and thus made sure of the rewards.

Uncle Dick Wootton's next enterprise was equipping a freight train to travel the Santa Fe Trail, a freight train nearly a mile long, comprising thirty-six prairie schooners with five pairs of oxen to each, and an ambulance that carried anyone who was sick, also passengers. Forty drivers and herders were on the train which averaged 16 miles a day and each round trip netted Uncle Dick $10,000. He also organized a rapid transit stagecoach line; fourteen days, Santa Fe to Independence, Missouri, one-way fare $250; passengers were fed, usually pork and beans, by the company; no stops were made at night and travelers were compelled to sleep sitting up.

Between Wootton and Ratón the highway skirts sheer cliffs and cutaways as it winds over the Pass. The terrain is heavily wooded with pine, piñon, and juniper; the wild pink locust so fragrant in spring is abundant. The mountain crossed at RATÓN PASS (7,800 alt.) is protected from erosion by a thick cap of lava. There are views of

Bartlett Mesa to the east, of the vast plains to the south, and coal-bearing, lava-capped rocks to the west; behind them loom the lofty peaks of the Culebra (snake) Mountains. South of the REGISTRATION STATION, 6 *m.*, the highway circles in gradual descent. To the right the plains reach far into the distance, the view extending more than a hundred miles. Johnson MesaL., a stark, lava-capped, table-topped mountain, is conspicuous in the east.

Halfway down the grade a road and several footpaths lead to a clearing on GOAT HILL (R), 8.5 *m.*, where cars can be parked.

RATÓN, 9.9 *m.* (6,400 alt., 7,594 pop.), the seat of Colfax County, is a stock-raising, railroading, and coal-mining town. A government forage station was established here in the 1860's at the Willow Springs Ranch on Ratón (formerly Willow) Creek. Accessibility to a limited water supply soon made this point the logical watering place between the Wootton Ranch on the Pass and the Canadian River to the south. In May 1871 Charles B. Thacker moved his family from Colorado into a small vacant *jacal* (Mex., plaited wood and mud hut) here and, after sinking a well to supplement the meager water supply, began raising cattle. In 1879 the railroad was built to Otero, five miles south of Willow Springs Station, and the latter developed so rapidly as a railroad junction that the population of Otero moved here. Ratón, renamed for the Pass, has prospered with the development of near-by coal mines. Its population is mostly of Spanish and Mexican descent, though there are many Anglo-Americans and a few Greeks, Italians, Central Europeans, and Negroes.

The NEW MEXICO MINERS' HOSPITAL AND HOME FOR OLD MINERS here, accommodating 50 persons, is maintained by the State.

In Ratón is the junction with US 64 (*see Tour 2*) which unites with US 85 between this point and Hoxie. Occasional traces of the old Santa Fe Trail are visible along US 85 south of Ratón. MESA NEGRA (black tableland) of *malpais* (bad lands or lava) formation, volcanic in origin, is on the left. A series of flat mesas and conical hills of lava are near Ratón and extend southward three miles. Sandstone foothills of the Sangre de Cristo Mountains are cn the right.

Grama grass plains gradually open up, become more expansive and sandy, and stretch to the horizon. Grama grass is the name given to the many species of the genus *Bouteloua,* but in New Mexico it refers to those perennial grasses on the cattle ranges, especially the side-oats grama so valuable for feed. Sagebrush, yucca, and cactus are sparsely scattered over the plains. A towering windmill and ranch house break the monotony of the tawny grazing lands, domains of great cattle kings of the past century.

A short distance from the highway at 16.1 *m.*, just south of the Canadian River are the ruins of the CLIFTON HOUSE (R), a hostelry and stage station for the Barlow and Sanderson Stage Line which traversed the plains of Kansas and continued to New Mexico during the 1860's. Built in 1867 by Tom Stockton, a rancher, as headquarters for the cattle roundups in that section, it attracted attention of stage officials who subsequently leased it, added a blacksmith shop and stables, and made it an overnight stop for travelers. The Clifton House was one of the West's best known stop-overs.

In HOXIE, 24.6 *m.,* a settlement of few dwellings, is the southern junction with US 64 (*see Tour 2b*) which branches R.

The valley of the Canadian (locally known as the Red) River and its several tributaries fed from the snowy summits of the Sangre de Cristo Mountains to the west was cow country until the turn of the century, its lush grazing land having been dominated by the Maxwell Land Grant Company and several other large ranch interests. The impounding of water and subsequent development of beet, fruit, alfalfa, and grain crops since 1900 have brought wealth to the heirs of the original owners. The old cow lands have been fenced and subdivided; near the highway, but not in sight, are nine reservoirs that impound nineteen thousand acre-feet of water and feed all lands adjacent to US 85 (L) as far south as Maxwell. Other similar irrigation projects extend almost to Las Vegas.

MAXWELL, 36.8 *m.* (5,555 alt., 439 pop.), named for Lucien Maxwell, is a shipping center for cattle, sheep, and farm produce. In the late eighties the Maxwell Land and Irrigation Company, an organization of Hollanders, began making surveys of the district for irrigation purposes. A general store, still operating, together with a saloon, hotel, and livery stable marked the beginning of the town. The original land company sold out, and with the change of management many Hollanders left for other States.

The vicinity of Maxwell is well adapted to the growing of sugar beets and for a decade this was a flourishing industry. A refinery built just outside the city limits was abandoned later when grain and legume crops supplanted beet raising. Recently extensive acreage is again being planted with beets, and the factory may be reopened.

From Maxwell are good views of TINAJA (Sp., bowl) and EAGLE TAIL PEAKS, slightly to the northeast (L); the former is 6,965 feet high and the latter 7,000.

FRENCH, 42 *m.* (5,804 alt., 398 pop.), named for Captain William French who owned practically all the land in this locality, is a frame town that suddenly sprang into prominence when this point on the Santa Fe Railway became a junction with the Southern Pacific, which runs northwest to Dawson and its mines (*see Tour 2b*). Irrigated lands around the junction have been developed to produce beets, grain, and fruits, and French has become a trading and shipping point. From this point is an exceptionally fine view (R) of the snow-clad Sangre de Cristo Mountains in Colorado.

Left from French on a dirt road to CHICO, 22.3 *m.,* and the INGERSOLL RANCH, until 1892 the home of Colonel Robert R. Ingersoll (1833-99). The ranch and grazing lands formerly belonged to ex-Senator Dorsey and came into possession of Ingersoll as a fee for successfully defending Dorsey (1883) in a "Star routes" mail case. The place now has several owners, and the two ranch houses are unoccupied.

SPRINGER, 51.9 *m.* (5,832 alt., 1,312 pop.), a thriving crossroads town, was named for Springer Brothers, owners of stock ranches.  In 1882 it was made the seat of Colfax County, but in 1897, after a protracted and bitter political fight, the seat was moved to Ratón and the Supreme Court denied Springer's appeal.  At that time the population was more than fifteen hundred but approximately five hundred residents left during the following year.  Then, as now, it was the trading center for a wide cattle- and sheep-raising area.

The New Mexico Industrial School for Boys and the district headquarters of the State Highway Department are in Springer.

Left from Springer on NM 58, a paved and graded road, to a junction with NM 39, a paved road, 20 *m.*; R. to ROY, 46 *m.*; L. from Roy on NM 120, a graded road, to BUEYEROS, 91 *m.*, heart of the extensive DRY ICE FIELDS of Harding County.  Discovery of carbon dioxide gas seeping from crevices in an extensive anticline leads many to believe that dry ice may become an important item of commerce from this region.

Besides its uses for refrigeration and air conditioning, dry ice has been employed by physicians for many purposes and by moving-picture directors to create fog.

The rock formation of the CORNUDOS (horned) HILLS, 60 *m.* (6,250 alt.), is popularly known as Wagon Mound because it resembles a covered wagon.  This pile of rock was one of the notable landmarks on the Cimarrón branch of the old Santa Fe Trail.

Between Springer and Las Vegas are several railroad sidings, stations, and abandoned villages, now containing not more than one or two families each.  They testify to the optimism of early settlers who came when the railroad pushed its way along the valley.  In many instances buildings in these mushroom settlements were loaded on flat cars and transported several miles to communities that had grown in size and importance.

COLMOR, 62.6 *m.* (5,800 alt., 274 pop.), a shipping point, consists of a hotel, feed store, a district school, and several small dwellings.

WAGON MOUND, 71.9 *m.* (6,250 alt., 852 pop.), was founded in 1850 by stockmen who were attracted by pasturage possibilities. They first named their settlement Santa Clara for their patron saint. It is now a flourishing trading center and a wool- and stock-shipping point for Ocaté Valley (R) and Mora Valley (L).  Wagon Mound has an exciting history.  Plains or mountain Indian tribes, out foraging or passing by on buffalo hunts, met here, and raiding Indians attacked overland traffic many times at this point.

Dr. H. White, a popular resident of Santa Fe, returning with his wife and child from a visit to the East, had reached a point near Wagon Mound on May 10, 1850, when he was attacked by Indians.  White and eleven of his party were murdered and scalped, and his wife, child, and nurse were kidnapped.  When news of the outrage reached Santa Fe ten days later, Congress appropriated $1,500 for recovery of the prisoners, and a large body of volunteers joined the regulars and started in pursuit of the marauders.  William Kroenig, in later years a resident of the Mora Valley below Wagon Mound, was at Santa Fe at the time and he thus described efforts made by the punitive force:

"The Apaches and Utes were very bad. I joined the company at Santa Fe. We went by way of Las Vegas to get the Indians who had killed Dr. White and captured his wife. After a long march toward Taos we arrived at a place where the Indians had camped the day before. It was about two hours before sunset when we struck the Indians' trail. Our captain, José María Valdez, sent me to the major commanding the regulars for two shift horses to locate the camp before night; our request was refused at first but later, about sunset, he gave us the horses, but it was now too dark and the Mexicans lost the trail and returned to camp. At daylight, the pursuit was renewed and after a chase of more than twenty miles the Indians were overtaken and charged by the regulars. In this charge the commanding officer was struck in the chest by a stray bullet, but owing to the fact that he had a pair of heavy gauntlets in his blouse the bullet was deflected. The regulars now dismounted, waiting for the volunteers, the latter securing a position between the Indians and their horses. A skirmish was kept up for some time, the Indians having made the temporary stand in order to permit the escape if possible of their families.

"The Indians finally made their escape and during the pursuit I saw the body of Mrs. White lying against a willow tree, pierced with arrows. The color, however, had not entirely left her face, showing that she was murdered during the skirmish. Some Indian children were taken prisoners. The nurse and child of Dr. White were never recovered. . . ."

The volcanic rock that covers the plains (R) for several miles beginning at 84 *m.* has interested geologists because it is different from outcroppings in the surrounding terrain.

Between Wagon Mound and Watrous the TURKEY MOUNTAINS (R), a series of sandstone foothills, are visible about five miles from the highway. US 85 passes through plains country where the grazing lands (R) are given over to cattle and a small herd of buffalo owned by a cattle company.

At 94 *m.* behind a filling station (L) is the old TRADING STATION (*now a private residence*) erected in 1830 by Samuel B. Watrous, pioneer trader. His old store, built in sections, was a rendezvous for Fort Union soldiers on leave and here they mingled with Spaniards, Mexicans, Indians, and cowboys.

At 94.2 *m.* is the junction with a dirt road.

Left on this to VALMORA SANATORIUM, 4 *m.*, in the Traverse Valley of the Mora River, protected on three sides by green hills. Consisting of a central hospital and numerous cottages, it accommodates 60 patients. Valmora is financed by several large wholesale houses in Chicago and St. Louis for the benefit of their employees.

WATROUS, 94.8 *m.* (8,398 alt., 406 pop.), at the junction of the Sapello and Mora rivers, is a trading and shipping center serving a farming and ranching community and the Valmora Sanatorium.

Large lumber shipments from Mora or Shoemaker Canyon to the east are loaded here.

Right from Watrous on a dirt road to the RUINS OF FORT UNION, 9 *m.*, in a broad valley at the base of the Turkey Mountains. Started in 1851 it became headquarters of the Ninth Military Department which was transferred from Santa Fe by Colonel Sumner and remained here until the fort was abandoned February 27, 1891. Fort Union was built with Army labor on a reservation eight miles square. The principal buildings were erected around the parade ground, in the center of which was a bandstand. Close to the fort were the quarters of traders, freighters, and storekeepers, and a group of Masonic buildings was within its boundaries. During the 1860's the headquarters store did a business of $3,000 daily; and more than a thousand carpenters, wagon builders, smiths, harnessmakers, and laborers were constantly employed.

A half mile north of the fort was the arsenal from which ran an underground tunnel connecting the main buildings. The badly eroded walls of the arsenal, hospital, and barracks still stand, although the supporting timbers have been removed. Stark chimneys contribute to the desolate appearance. In the jail cells, still standing, Gerónimo and Billy the Kid were once imprisoned.

The fort strategically placed to protect traffic along the Santa Fe Trail was the most important post in this section, both as a supply center for minor forts and as a base for troop movements. It was the heart of a military region comprising an area of more than five hundred square miles. During the Civil War Fort Union became the principal objective of the Confederate troops under General Sibley. But the Confederates were defeated at Pigeons' Ranch, Glorieta, and Apache Canyon (*see below*) by troops from the fort and the Colorado Volunteers, and Sibley was forced to abandon his campaign in New Mexico. Fort Union in the 1860's had all the conveniences of a small town and was a lively social center. Kit Carson served during this period as lieutenant-colonel of the New Mexican Volunteers. In the neighborhood of Fort Union are still visible, stretching across the prairies, the deep ruts and wagon marks of the old Santa Fe Trail; and in many places are the hoofprints of horses, oxen, and mules.

At 113.8 *m.* is the junction with NM 3, an improved road (*see Tour 11*).

LAS VEGAS (Sp., the meadows), 114.6 *m.* (6,391 alt., 12,318 pop.), was originally known as Nuestra Señora de los Dolores de Las Vegas (Our Lady of Sorrows of the Meadows) after the patron saint of the town. In 1821 Luis María C. de Baca petitioned the Mexican government for a grant of land here bordering the Rio Gallinas—then called the Vegas Grandes—for himself and his 17 sons. Though the grant was made in 1823, it was never completely occupied because of encroachment from Indians.

In his *Commerce of the Prairies,* Dr. Josiah Gregg, describing the places along the Santa Fe Trail in 1831, related that after leaving the Mora River he reached "the Gallinas, the first of the Rio del Norte waters—here the road stretches over an elevated plain unobstructed by any mountain ridges. At Gallinas Creek we found a large flock of sheep grazing upon the adjacent plain; while a little hovel at the foot of the cliff showed it to be a rancho." This was the rancho of the De Bacas and the beginning of the present town.

The first settlement of any size was established in 1833 when a group of men from San Miguel del Bado on the Pecos River petitioned for a grant. The tract was given under the conditions that a plaza be erected for protection against Indians and as a meeting and market place. This settlement seems to have been the beginning of Old Town or West Las Vegas, on the west side of the Gallinas River which divides the present city. Dr. Wislizenus in his *Memoir of a Tour Through Northern Mexico in 1846-47* found the settlement about a mile from the Gallinas and described it as a place of "100 odd houses and poor dirty-looking inhabitants." It was in this latter year that General Kearny arrived with his Army of the West and from a house-top on the plaza issued a proclamation taking possession of the territory for the United States. A military post was established, and Las Vegas was a seat of military operations until the erection of Fort Union in 1851.

Until the coming of the railroad Las Vegas was a typical adobe town, a stopover on the Santa Fe Trail, and a trading center. About 1879 New Town (now East Las Vegas) harbored one of the worst gangs of rascals and cut-throats that ever infested the West. A list of their aliases includes Caribou Brown, Dirty-face Mike, Hoodoo Brown, Scar-face Charlie, Pawnee Bill, Kickapoo George, Jack-knife Jack, Flyspeck Sam, Mysterious Dave, Hatchet-face Kit, Durango Kid, Pancake Billy, Cockeyed Frank, Rattlesnake Sam, Split-nose Mike, Web-fingered Billy, Wink the Barber, Doubleout Sam, Jimmie the Duck, Flapjack Bill, Buckskin Joe, Cold-deck George, Pegleg Dick, Red River Tom, Hog Jones, Long Lon, Soapy Smith, Stuttering Tom, and Tommy the Poet. After the respectable citizens were aroused, a windmill in the plaza center became the favorite gibbet used by the Vigilantes. March 24, 1882 a placard announced:

"Notice to thieves, thugs, fakirs and bunko-steerers among whom are J. J. Harlin, alias 'Off Wheeler,' Saw Dust Charlie, Wm. Hedges, Billy the Kid, Billy Mullin, Little Jack the Cutter, Pock-marked Kid and about twenty others: if found within the limits of this city after ten o'clock p.m. this night you will be invited to attend a grand neck-tie party, the expense of which will be borne by 100 substantial citizens." Hangings became so numerous that the owner of the windmill had it dismantled.

In the early years of the town, wealthy dons were accustomed to take advantage of impoverished citizens, seize huge tracts of land, and run the tenants off. According to the original grant, lands not allotted to persons were to be used as public grazing areas. The Herrera family after their lands had been confiscated organized an order, *Los Caballeros de Labor* (gentlemen of labor), whose purpose was to destroy all fences so that livestock of poor men could find forage. They worked secretly at night wearing white robes and pointed caps and so became known as *Gorras Blancas* (white caps). The order became so powerful that the lands again came into possession of the community.

Today Las Vegas is a shipping point and supply depot for 140,000 acres of irrigated land and the large ranches in the counties of Mora and San Miguel that graze hundreds of thousands of sheep and cattle on more than a million acres. The town is also noted for the number and quality of its schools and for its climate which is beneficial to sufferers from pulmonary diseases.

On the OLD PLAZA, freighters on the Santa Fe Trail unloaded their goods. Back of the plaza is the first courthouse and jail, oldest building in the town, where Billy the Kid spent a few anxious hours. OUR LADY OF SORROWS CHURCH on Church St., erected in 1836, is now occupied by a grocery store. CHURCH STREET in Old Town was formerly known as *Sodomía* and *La Calle de la Amargura* (the road of suffering and bitterness). Its walks were flanked by bawdy houses, dance halls, and saloons; many were robbed and murdered along this street. In the KING STADIUM, just outside the town, is held the Las Vegas 111th Cavalry Horse Show (Aug.) that attracts persons from all over the West. From 1906 to 1911, the old race track was in Gallinas Park near the Montezuma Hotel (*see below*).

Right from Las Vegas on NM 65, a graveled road, to MONTEZUMA HOT SPRINGS, 5.5 *m.*, and the MONTEZUMA HOTEL, now used by the Roman Catholic Archdiocese of Santa Fe as a seminary for the training of priests. For many years, commencing in 1880, several hotels occupying this site in succession served as playgrounds for millionaires from the East, as well as for famous and infamous westerners. The original castle-like Montezuma Hotel, one of the first million dollar resort hotels of the West, was built in 1880 by the Santa Fe Railway to accommodate the many visitors attracted by the springs. The first unit incorporated a bathhouse that surrounded 23 springs and had a capacity of 1,000 baths daily. The springs, ranging in temperature from 50° to 144° Fahrenheit, contain lithia, sulphur, and sodium compounds.

After this hotel burned in 1881 and another erected on the site proved too small, the management built still another structure which covered three acres and contained 300 rooms set on six elevations. Vast wine cellars, card rooms, a dining room seating 500, and a casino for 1,000 were included in the new undertaking. Walls were covered with oak paneling, fireplaces were of marble, and the furnishings were valued at $1,000,000. In 1885 a third fire was followed by another rebuilding. The erection of El Tovar in Grand Canyon drew heavily from the Montezuma's clientele, and the Santa Fe found it impossible to maintain two such establishments, so closed the Montezuma on October 13, 1903.

Since that time it has changed hands several times. First it was sold to the Young Men's Christian Association for a dollar; next it was given to the Bible Film Company for use as a location. In 1921 it became a Baptist college and was so used for a decade.

At 118 *m.* US 85 crosses a series of foothills over a winding course. Scattered over the hillsides are many squatters' shacks and adobe houses, mainly inhabited by workmen employed at Las Vegas.

A few miles south the highway cuts through the rugged granite of Kearny's Gap, opening on fertile valleys in the foothills south of the Gallinas River. This aperture was named for General Stephen W. Kearny, commander of the Army of the West, who passed through here August 17, 1846, on his journey to Santa Fe. Here he prepared to meet a large force of Mexicans reported to be marching against him, but they never were encountered.

In ROMEROVILLE, 120.3 *m.* (6,287 alt., 130 pop.), a cross-roads trading center, are the ruins of the old ROMERO RANCH HOUSE (R), built by Don Trinidad Romero in 1880. It is a two-story adobe structure with a dozen high-ceilinged rooms paneled in walnut and costing $100,000. Here Don Trinidad, a member of the United States Congress, entertained President and Mrs. Hayes and General Sherman. After the house was sold by the Romero family, it became a sanitarium, then a dude ranch, and finally burned in 1932. Only the walls remain.

West of Romeroville is the ROMEROVILLE CANYON, a gorge cut eight hundred feet deep in the mesa south of Las Vegas.

TECOLOTE (Aztec, ground owl), 125.8 *m.* (6,010 alt., 192 pop.), is a trading center settled in 1824 by Salvador Montoya. During the U.S. Army campaigns against the Indians in the last century, Tecolote was one in a chain of posts established to furnish forage and corn to Army units. The ruins of the headquarters buildings and the large stables still remain.

Crossing the bridge over Tecolote Creek at the edge of the village, US 85 traverses the old Tecolote Grant and rises gradually to the long slopes of hard sandstone characteristic of this region.

BERNAL, 131.4 *m.* (6,068 alt., 284 pop.), first called Bernal Springs, was the first station on the Las Vegas-Santa Fe section of the old stage lines. Today it comprises only a store, gas station, and a church built around a plaza.

There is a view (L) of STARVATION PEAK (7,000 alt.) where, it is said, 120 colonists—men, women, and children—took refuge from pursuing Indians and starved to death. A Penitente cross surmounts the highest point.

Between Bernal and San José the highway passes three large ranches (R), private estates of wealthy eastern landowners. On the left is the eastern extremity of Glorieta Mesa.

At 138.9 *m.* is a junction with a dirt road.

Left on this road to SAN MIGUEL DEL BADO (St. Michael of the Ford), 2.8 *m.* (6,000 alt., 500 pop.), one of the oldest towns in New Mexico. Originally settled by a group of Indians who had been cast out of their tribes because of their conversion to Catholicism, it soon became an active and well-settled community augmented by the influx of Mexican herders and farmers. During the era of Mexico's sovereignty, San Miguel was the seat of the third division of the Central District. The present county was named for the town. Padre José Francisco Leyba, the first resident priest, is buried on the gospel side of the altar of the CHURCH OF SAN MIGUEL DEL BADO. He served the settlements of the Pecos Valley, traveling the entire territory on horseback through hostile Indian country for 32 years. His ministry was a saga of service. The CHURCH OF SAN MIGUEL DEL BADO, built in 1806, is of rock. It was constructed by the Indians of the parish under direction of the priests. Its walls were three feet in thickness and twenty feet high. Gold and silver donated by the faithful were cast into two bells which today are in the care of the parish priest. The first floor of the church covers the coffins of wealthier inhabitants of the village. The pews are all hand-hewn and decorated. Many old statues, the work of the parishioners, are incorporated in the church appointments. The records, intact for many decades, give the religious and civil history of this section. San Miguel was an important way-stop on the

Santa Fe Trail. Here many Texans were imprisoned when they invaded New Mexico in 1847.

Residents of SAN JOSÉ, 148.3 *m.* (6,387 alt., 556 pop.), a typical New Mexico village on the banks of the Pecos River, depend on farming for a livelihood. Many of the houses are of native architecture but have peaked corrugated iron roofs that detract from their charm, but prevent melted snow from dripping in. The *corrida del gallo* (chicken pull) is an annual event (June 24) still popular in New Mexico among Indians and whites. From surrounding villages come men with their best trained, fleetest horses and, after a series of eliminations, a representative of each community is chosen. The final test is to ride a horse from a starting point to a fat live rooster partly buried in the sand, snatch it while still mounted and successfully defending possession of the fowl, gallop back to the starting point. The winner is guest of honor at a feast and dances with the prettiest señorita in the village.

San José was a camping site for General Kearny on his march to Santa Fe.

West of San José the highway winds over gently undulating country; small ranches, usually perched on the higher spots, break the monotony of the terrain. The land is channeled by the inevitable arroyo, carved out of the brown and gray shales that make up the surface to the north. To the south (L) is the main part of Glorieta Mesa, a tableland of gray sandstone that extends to the Sangre de Cristo Range. This mesa presents a continuous line of cliffs with a level lava-capped crest which descends to the valley of the Pecos.

KOSLOSKIE'S RANCH, 165.2 *m.,* was founded by Andrew Kosloskie, later owner of the first store in Rowe, as a main-stop for the Barlow and Sanderson Stages on the Santa Fe Trail. A large spring in a dense copse, 300 yards from the ranch house and corral, provided water for horses and passengers. To this place the Union forces retreated after the first day's battle with the Confederates in Apache Canyon and were joined by 300 reserves, regulars of the Union Army, who, with the full complement of Colonel Slough's Colorado Volunteers, had come in from Bernal during the night. Throughout the battles in Apache Canyon, Kosloskie's was used as Union headquarters.

At 167.2 *m.* is a junction with a dirt road.

Left on this road within the Pecos State Monument to the RUINS OF THE PECOS PUEBLO, 0.7 *m.,* the strongest pueblo in the fourteenth century and the most eastern inhabited Indian village in the days of the Spanish Conquest. Always a trading point between the Plains Indians and the Pueblos, its situation was good economically; the land was productive, the water supply ample, and the proximity to the buffalo country a great advantage.

The pueblo, a quadrangular structure built on a sandstone formation about 1348 (according to the tree-ring date of a beam), consisted of two great communal dwellings of four stories each; they contained respectively 585 and 517 rooms. From the balconies of these rooms the entire circuit of the village could be made without setting foot on the ground. The Pecos people once numbering about two thousand were rich, proud, independent, and war-like;

# *History*

SAN ILDEFONSO PUEBLO,
WITH HISTORIC TUNYO (BLACK MESA) IN BACKGROUND

HOUSE IN UPPER LAS VEGAS (c. 1850)

*Ina Sizer Cassidy*

SETTLERS (c. 1890)

DUG-OUT SCHOOL (c. 1903), NEAR CLOVIS

LISTENING TO THE GRAMOPHONE IN BALDY, A MINING TOWN (c. 1891)

CORNER OF LAGUNA PUEBLO

*Ernest Knee*

OLD COURT HOUSE, LINCOLN

"INDIAN RATION DAY," FLOUR MILL, CIMARRÓN (c. 1865)

EL TORREON, TOWER USED AS A FORT BY EARLY SETTLERS, LINCOLN

SANTA FE AND VICINITY FROM THE EAST
Drawing from Lieutenant Simpson's Report of the Arkansas Route

ST. FRANCIS CATHEDRAL, SANTA FE

*Paul Odor*

PLAZA, LAS VEGAS (c. 1880)

SAN FELIPE DE NERI CHURCH AND PLAZA, OLD ALBUQUERQUE

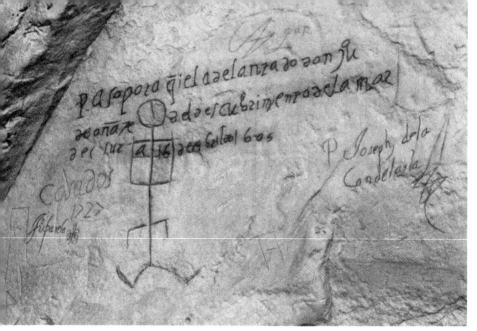

INSCRIPTION BY OÑATE ON INSCRIPTION ROCK (1605)

SALLYPORT, FORT BAYARD (c. 1874)

but the situation of their city was not as good defensively as it was economically. In 1540 it was conquered by Coronado and in 1541 Fray Luis de Escalona voluntarily remained as a missionary at Pecos. The belief is that he was killed soon afterward, becoming the first Christian martyr in New Mexico. Pecos then remained unvisited until 1583, when Antonio de Espejo stopped at the pueblo for a brief time. In 1590 Castaño de Sosa and his handful of soldiers (plus two brass cannon) attacked the well-fortified pueblo, which surrendered. After Oñate's settlement in 1598, it became the seat of a mission. The massive adobe walls of NUESTRA SEÑORA DE LOS ÁNGELES (Our Lady of the Angels) CHURCH, which was built in 1617, are visible from the highway. In 1680 the priest at Pecos, Fray Fernando de Velasco, was killed within sight of the Galisteo pueblo where he had hurried to warn his superior of the Pueblo Revolt. Pecos participated in this uprising, and the tree-ring dating shows that the church was either restored or rebuilt after the revolt.

Although harshly treated by Coronado, who referred to the village by its Tewa name Cicuyé, Pecos suffered less from the Spaniards than did some of the other pueblos and offered no resistance to the reconquest by De Vargas (1693). Until 1720 the town prospered, but attacks by marauding plains tribes—chiefly Apache and Comanche—had considerably reduced the population by 1750 when Pecos sent its entire man power to carry war into the enemy country. This force was ambushed and cut to pieces by the Comanche, only one man escaping. In 1768 an epidemic of smallpox left only 180 survivors; and in 1805 attacks of mountain fever, a form of typhoid (or dysentry), prevalent throughout the mountain region at that time (from impure water), further reduced it to 104; and it was finally abandoned in 1838, when 17 survivors joined their kindred at Jémez (*see Tour 9*). There are believed to be about two hundred descendants of the Pecos refugees now living at Jémez; until recently a few of them were said to make a ceremonial visit twice each year to their sacred cave in the upper Pecos Valley. After the exodus Pecos fell rapidly into decay, a process aided by those living near who robbed it of beams and timber for firewood. The north building kept its form for a few years, and its plaza served as a prison to hold Texans captured by Armijo in 1841. In 1869 the beams of the church were removed and used as corral posts, and its unprotected walls gradually disintegrated. The pueblo proper went to pieces even more rapidly; its upper walls fell, the timbers below rotted away or were pulled out, and not until a sheltering mound had formed itself over the lower stories was the process of ruin arrested.

In 1915 Mr. Barry Kelley, owner, deeded the ruins to the Museum of New Mexico. Since then extensive excavations sponsored by Phillips Academy of Andover have been made, and the great mission repaired. Among the most interesting objects found are pipes and figurines; the pipes included the plain tubular form of very early times and the large elaborately carved and incised types of the historic period. The figurines are small clay representations of human beings, birds, and animals. Although crude they are noteworthy because objects of this nature have so rarely been found in Southwestern ruins. Other excavations show that the population of Pecos kept moving about from one part of the mesa to another, building and rebuilding. Ruin is piled upon ruin, presenting a vivid history of a people that practiced arts and crafts, created a government, and participated in religious ceremonies resembling those in the pueblos of today.

The Indians have a legendary explanation of Pecos' decline. Like most of the pueblos, Pecos regarded the snake as a beneficent deity. A huge one was kept in the *kiva,* regular offerings being made to it, including, according to Spanish tradition, human sacrifice—supposedly young children. A sacred fire necessitating constant care was kept alive on the *kiva* altar. As the Indians drifted away from their paganism into Christianity, the sacred fire went out, and the sacrifices were almost abandoned. The climax was reached when a particularly disastrous epidemic carried off most of the small children of the pueblo. The *cacique* after ceremonial fasting, hoping to appease the wrath of the gods, called for a child to be sacrificed. Exercising his rights of office, he chose the son of his war captain. Having already given one of his children and having only one left (owing to the epidemic), the war captain gave his son to the priest to hide and substituted a kid for the sacrifice. The sacred snake, however, was not deceived. Deciding that his people were definitely abandoning their religion for that of the alien, the huge reptile crawled from the *kiva,* then on to the Rio Grande which he followed to its mouth and disappeared in the Gulf of Mexico. The Galisteo River (*see below*) is said by the Indians to be the path made by the snake on its way out. This marked the final fall of Pecos. The native inhabitants of the Pecos Valley today tell of the Indian boy, the son of the war chief, who was brought up without knowledge of his origin under the care of the priest. He married among their people and had a family whose descendants still live in the vicinity, but the Pecos Indians have never learned of the deception.

PECOS, 169.8 *m.* (6,800 alt., 1,029 pop. including vicinity), named after the Pecos Indians, is a trading center for stock and dude ranches. It is also the starting point for many hunting and fishing expeditions into the Pecos River Valley. Outfits and guides can be procured.

Right from Pecos on graveled NM 63 which winds along the banks of the Pecos River, crossing and recrossing it, to VALLEY RANCH, 1.7 *m.* (*Accommodations for 85 guests; fishing, horseback riding, tennis courts, swimming pool, and golf course*).

The countryside is part of the SANTA FE NATIONAL FOREST. Heavy pine, aspen, and fir clothe the mountain sides. This region is a hunting and fishing ground; trout and other fish are abundant; turkey, grouse, bear, deer, and elk mingle with alpine marmot and pika. Efforts are being made by the State Game Department to replenish the area with beaver.

North, the highway enters the broad river canyon which after a short distance narrows considerably. Here are irrigated farms, with hardy willows and cottonwoods along the cultivated fields.

LISBOA SPRINGS FISH HATCHERY, 2.2 *m.,* is the principal unit of the State's fish propagation system established in 1921. This hatchery propagates rainbow, Loch Leven and steelhead trout, crappie, and Chinook salmon.

Beginning at 7.4 *m.,* the mountains crowd close to the highway, and the Pecos River tumbles over a rocky bed.

In FIELD'S PUBLIC CAMPGROUND 9.6 *m.* the Forest Service maintains ample parking space, picnic, and camping facilities. At various points tourist camps are available at reasonable rates.

Directly across the river is the BRUSH RANCH, 11.7 *m.* (*hunting and fishing: open all year; riding and pack trips*).

In Holy Ghost Canyon (L) are numerous private fishing and hunting lodges as well as a public campground maintained by the Forest Service on the shore of Spirit Lake at the head of the canyon. Rito Espíritu Santo (Holy Ghost Creek) enters the canyon from the left and tumbles into the Pecos. In a nook near by, not discernible from the highway, is a cave said to be the outlet of a series of subterranean passages that extend to the mountains east of Nambé Pueblo (*see Tour 3a*) and used for ceremonials by the Pecos Indians. Exploration has disclosed a passageway for about a mile but no extensive tunnels to the west.

West of Pecos US 85 winds through foothills covered with piñon and juniper and crosses a railroad spur that goes north (R) to the mill of the American Metals Company. The highway enters the mouth of APACHE CANYON, west of Glorieta Pass, scene of a battle during the Civil War.

Field headquarters for the Union forces was at PIDGIN'S RANCH (R), also called Pigeon's, 174.9 *m.*, owned and operated by Alex Valle, a Frenchman who cut fancy "pigeon's wings" at dances. The old adobe ranch house is still standing, and the adobe corral with its port holes is just east of a steep rocky bluff that projects out toward the highway. Topped with an American flag, the bluff is marked with a tablet commemorating the first encounter with Confederate forces in the canyon. The battlefield itself, west of the ranch house, centered around an arroyo that threads across the highway now crossed by a bridge. It was not far from this point that the Union cavalry was forced to leap its horses sixteen feet across the same arroyo after the Confederates had destroyed the log bridge.

In a small forest of piñon and jack pine is GLORIETA, 175.9 *m.* (7,432 alt., 381 pop.), a trading center and loading station for the Santa Fe railway near the highest point in the canyon at the beginning of GLORIETA PASS. In this gateway through the Sangre de Cristo Mountains to Santa Fe and the West a large uninscribed boulder (R) marks the site of another encounter between the North and South.

In March 1862 after the defeat of the Union forces at the Battle of Valverde (*see below*) Confederate General Sibley advanced on Santa Fe. The small Union detachments in the area fell back to Fort Union after having destroyed all government stores in the capital to prevent their falling into the Confederates' hands. These Union troops were later joined by Colorado units under Colonel Slough, who assumed command of the forces at Fort Union and advanced against the Confederates, who had by that time captured Santa Fe. From Bernal (*see above*) Slough sent Major Chivington forward with a small force to check the Confederates. On March 26, in Apache Canyon, about 15 miles from Santa Fe, Chivington's troops engaged the enemy. The Federal loss in this encounter was 5 killed, and 14 wounded; the Confederate loss was 32 killed, 43 wounded, and 71 prisoners. On the 28th when the main forces of both sides met in Apache Canyon, Colonel Slough held the main body of the Confederates in the canyon and sent Major Chivington on a wide sweep around the flank of the Southern Army. The major succeeded in destroying, without the loss of a man, the Confederate ammunition and supply train which was at Johnson's ranch. The main battle was indecisive, but the loss of all of his trains and supplies forced the Confederate commander to retreat to Santa Fe in a demoralized and destitute condition. Colonel Slough, having stopped the Confederate advance toward Fort Union, retired to that place, his aim accomplished.

US 85 leaves the canyon at CAÑONCITO, 181.3 *m.*, where the detachment of Major Chivington's Union forces captured the Confederate supply trains. During occupation by the Army of the West in 1846, General Kearny passed through the canyon at this point. It was here Governor Armijo drew up his forces to oppose the invaders, only to flee to Galisteo before the arrival of United States troops.

On the rise of the hill at Cañoncito is an old ranch house and

church (R).  The adobe house (L) was an old stage station, JOHN-
SON'S RANCH, important on the stage and freighter lines, and the last
stop on the old Trail before reaching Santa Fe.  It was the last station
closed before the abandonment of the stage lines from the East.

At 184.2 *m.* is the junction with US 285 (*see Tour 7b*) which
unites with US 85 between this point and Santa Fe.

US 85 winding over rolling country passes through heavy stands
of piñon and cedar, following the old Pecos Trail.  Just east of Santa
Fe three mountain ranges are seen: the Sandía and Manzano to the
south behind the cone-shaped Cerrillos Hills, the Jémez Range to the
west, and the Sangre de Cristo to the east.

SANTA FE, 194.7 *m.* (7,000 alt., (20,237 pop.) (*see Santa Fe*).

*Points of Interest:*  The Plaza, Palace of the Governors, Museum of New
Mexico and Art Gallery, State Capitol Building, and others.


### Section b.  SANTA FE to SOCORRO, 133.6 m.

This section of the route, like the first, contains mountains, plains,
farms, grazing land, here and there a stream, with the overspreading,
brilliant sky to hold it all together and make it sparkle; it also has
coal and turquoise mines and Indian pueblos whose residents are not
only farmers and craftsmen but excellent artists as well.  The highway
borders the Rio Grande—on whose banks the Pueblo Indians have
built some of their villages—which runs swiftly through the land it
rules, a headstrong, benevolent despot, bestowing largesse on the tilled
fields and giving hope when the sky withholds it.  At flood stage it is
unpredictable and earns the other name, *Bravo,* the Spaniards gave it,
meaning fearless, bullying, savage, wild, fierce, or untractable—all of
which it is.

Southwest of Santa Fe, 0 *m.,* US 85 crosses the SANTA FE
PLATEAU.  To the south (L) are the little Cerrillos Hills outlined
against the Ortiz Mountains, with the Sandía (watermelon) Mountains looming along the horizon.  Detached buttes stud the lava-capped
mesas which slope to the valley of the Rio Grande (R), from one-half
to five miles from the highway.  All farming in this area is subsistence
and is carried on along the banks of the Rio Grande.  Corn and beans
are the main crops; melons, peas, and other vegetables are also raised.

At 14 *m.* is a junction with a graded dirt road.

Left on this road into the Cerrillos region, an area noted for its minerals.
Turquoise was mined here by the Pueblo Indians long before the discovery of
the country by the Spaniards, while gold was mined here as early as 1722
at La Mina de la Tierra (the mine of the earth) on a Spanish grant of 1696.
There was an exciting gold discovery here thirty years before the 1849 strikes
on Cherry Creek in Colorado.  In addition to turquoise and gold the area
contains lead, zinc, silver, and a little copper; yet today the region is mined
only for coal in the shale upthrusts.

A dilapidated two-story house, 1.5 *m.,* is all that remains of BONANZA,
once a town with two thousand inhabitants.  The strike that boomed the town

occurred in 1879 though the site was staked out in 1800 after the discovery of sulphide ores, lead, zinc, and silver. The two-story structure, still standing, was a hotel and gaming house that lingered after the town had crumbled and was used as a rendezvous for thieves and outlaws.

At 3.2 *m.* is a junction with a dirt road.

Right on this road 3.4 *m.* past the ruins of Carbonateville, Chalchilhuitl, Cash Entry, and Mina de la Tierra Mines to the GEM TURQUOISE MINES (*25¢ to visit*) the most extensive of the mines near Santa Fe, formerly owned and worked by the Tiffany interests. An agent of the company lives on the property and guides visitors through the workings. The Indians probably found this mine by following a seam of turquoise exposed by volcanic action, and they worked downward, breaking the ledge with stone hammers. Three hundred or more of these hammers have been found here. The whole Cerrillos region is pitted with old Indian turquoise diggings some of which were mined later by the Spaniards.

The mines opened during the last half century, including the Sky Blue, Gem, Morning Star, Blue Bell, and Costello Claims, have produced turquoise of highest quality, being harder than most varieties of turquoise and truer in color with the copper matrix laced through in intricate patterns. Turquoise, representing the "Sky Powers," has always had deep significance for the Indians. Even today groups have been seen at several old workings performing ceremonies which end with the planting of prayer plumes. Gems from the Cerrillos Hills, identified by their peculiar color and hardness, have been found in southern Mexico where they were undoubtedly carried by traders. When Pedro de Tovar, one of Coronado's men, visited the Hopi in Arizona during the first *entrada* of 1540, they presented him with splendid gifts of turquoise which, it is claimed, came from the Cerrillos region.

There are other interesting mines in this area, but they are almost impossible to find without local guides.

The graded dirt road continues to a junction with NM 10 (*see Tour 15*) at 9 *m.*

US 85 gradually descends and declines sharply at LA BAJADA (the descent) HILL, 19.2 *m.,* a sheer bluff capped with black basalt at the end of LA BAJADA MESA.

At 22 *m.* is the junction with a graded dirt road.

Right on this road toward the Jémez Mountains and across a flat plain bordered (R) by La Bajada basaltic cliffs to a junction with a graded dirt road at 3.2 *m.* Right on this to BAJADA (descent), 5.2 *m.,* a small hamlet at the base of La Bajada Hill. In Spanish Colonial days Bajada was a *visita* of Peña Blanca and later a stage station and overnight stopping place on the road to Santa Fe. Continuing westward across the flat plain, the dirt road traverses the northern part of the Santo Domingo Pueblo Grant. On this flat the Indians graze herds of cattle, sheep, and horses (*drive carefully*). In springtime, especially following a winter of much snow, the entire flat is purple with locoweed (*Astragalus mollissimus*) which causes a nervous disorder in cattle that eat it.

Clumps of wild four o'clock (*Mirabilis*) provide shade for the horned toad and sand lizards. Few snakes are found here, but rabbits and field mice scurry to cover as a car glides by at night. Hawks, meadow larks, field sparrows, and mocking birds share the plain with a few road runners (chaparral cocks) and prairie foxes, whose pelts are included in ceremonial dance costumes. This country below La Bajada was known to the early Spanish colonists as Rio Abajo (down river), and on account of its sheltered position and proximity to the Rio Grande was seriously considered in the late seventeenth century as a site for the provincial capital.

At 9.3 *m.* the road crosses the fence boundary of the Cochití Pueblo Grant and 10.6 *m.* is a fine view of the expansive RIO GRANDE VALLEY, with cultivated fields in the foreground. The descent into the valley from Las Lomas de la Peña Blanca (the hills of white rock) begins here.

PEÑA BLANCA, 11 m. (5,042 alt., 1,006 pop), settled in the early seventeenth century, was a Spanish wedge driven between the two Keresan villages of Santo Domingo on the south and Cochití on the north, and was always a bone of contention; both pueblos claiming ownership of the land. One or two cases arising from the conflicting land claims were so complicated they had to be sent to Spain for adjudication by the King. In 1867 the parish of Peña Blanca was taken from the Franciscans and given to the Jesuits who maintained it till 1910, when it was returned to the Franciscans. Unlike members of their order in other parts of the State who were of French descent, the Franciscans here were German. Until 1876 Peña Blanca was the seat of Santa Ana County, one of the seven original counties into which the territory was first divided; and during the semiannual terms of the district court Peña Blanca was a busy place.

After a flood on July 24, 1930, had inundated almost the entire town, destroying 30 or 40 houses and adjoining fields and doing nearly $50,000 damage, dikes were built at the upper and lower ends of the village.

At 11.1 m. the side route follows a street between small adobe houses; corn and wheat fields beyond lie between the road and the Rio Grande (L). The road crosses the broad dry sandy stream bed of the Santa Fe Wash (*dangerous when water is flowing*) at 11.9 m.

COCHITÍ PUEBLO (*Governor of pueblo sells permits to photograph; cars must be left in open space*), 16.5 m. (5,600 alt., 590 pop.), is a pre-Columbian Keresan pueblo, with one-story adobe houses built around a plaza; near by are a government day school, a seventeenth-century Catholic mission, and two large half-sunken circular *kivas*. Just south of the village a tree-covered island in the river is used for pasturage and maize cultivation. Cochití's old Spanish land grant of 1689 was confirmed by the United States December 22, 1858, surveyed for more than twenty-four thousand acres in 1859, and patented in 1864. Though land has been bought and sold at various times, the present holdings of the pueblo are about the same as in 1864. In 1598 Oñate found the Indians living on this site and from their old Keresan word, Kot-fe-te (of obscure etymology) gave them the name Cochití. The first Spanish mission, San Buenaventura de Cochití, was established early in the seventeenth century, and Juan de Rosas was placed in charge, but little is known of its earliest history.

In 1650 when the Cochití conspired with Jémez Pueblo (*see Tour 9*) and with the Apache to drive the Spaniards from the country, Captain Baca discovered the plot and notified Governor Hernando de Ugarte y la Concha, who hanged some of the leaders and sold others into slavery. Although the Cochití took part in the Pueblo Revolt of 1680, no priest was killed there. According to a legend the Cochití priest was warned by the Indian sacristan of the church. In 1681 the people fled before the army of Governor Otermín—who was attempting reconquest of New Mexico—and with their kinsmen from San Felipe and Santo Domingo took refuge at Potrero Viejo, a massive rock that towers 700 feet above the canyon about twelve miles east of here. They remained there until 1683 or 1684, when they returned. At the approach of De Vargas in 1692, the people of Cochití joined by those from San Felipe, San Marcos, and some tribes from the north again fled to Potrero Viejo and on its summit built a stronghold named Cieneguilla (little marshy meadows) by the Spaniards. De Vargas visited them there and persuaded them to return to their homes. But after a brief time the Cochití again returned to the rock. On April 14, 1694, De Vargas marched to the Potrero with 70 soldiers, 20 colonists, and 100 Indian allies from San Felipe, Santa Ana, and Zía. He drove the Cochití from their stronghold, destroyed Potrero Viejo, and returned to Santa Fe with a large quantity of corn and over 150 captive women, who were liberated after the Cochití warriors had returned to their pueblo here. Fray Antonio Carbonel was given charge of the missionary work; and SAN BUENAVENTURA DE COCHITÍ MISSION, which had been destroyed between

1680 and 1682, was rebuilt in 1694 by De Vargas on the same site. This building, still standing, is 34 feet wide and more than 100 feet long, a fine example of early Spanish-Indian mission architecture. The exterior has been remodeled in recent years. The old flat roof and Franciscan belfrey have been replaced by corrugated iron and a pointed steeple. The outside balcony has been removed and the entrance enclosed by an adobe porch having three arches—the only attempt at decoration—but the interior is still typical of the early Indian mission. Old tin candlesticks brought from Chihuahua, Mexico long before New Mexico was part of the United States, still firmly hold lighted tapers. Above the altar a large painting of San Buenaventura adorns the center of the wall, while the Nativity, the Transfiguration, the Last Supper, and three scenes of the Crucifixion are on the reredos. The ceiling of the chancel is decorated with moons, horses, and other figures which the Cochití executed in yellow, black, and red. Thirty-eight great *vigas,* most of them with Indian carving, support the roof. The church possesses three wooden statues representing San Buenaventura, the patron saint of the pueblo. The largest of these statues is of French workmanship, the next in size was done by a Mexican Indian, and the smallest and most revered is an antique. In their pottery the Cochití confined themselves to black-on-white ware until the recent revival of pueblo arts, when they included some reds. The designs representing rain, planting, growing, and harvesting frequently appear all over the vessels.

Cochití's fiesta is July 14th, when the annual Festival of San Buenaventura, patron saint, is held in connection with the Rain Dance. During the early morning, Mass is said by a priest from Peña Blanca. Late in the seventeenth century the Cochití people were converted to Roman Catholicism, but they still retain their ancient Indian rites and traditions. The rather elaborate Mass is a prelude to their dance for rain, the Green Corn Dance as it is sometimes called. Outside the church are stationed an Indian with a rifle and another with a large drum. At the close of Mass the crack of the rifle and boom of the drum summon members of the *kiva* group who climb up the ladder through the hole in the roof of their *kiva.* Led by the bearer of the staff fetish, they march in single file to the plaza where a large booth hung with Navaho blankets has been built to shelter the statue of San Buenaventura carried from the church after Mass. Following the dance, the participants slowly march to the statue and each member kisses the robe of the patron saint before retiring to the *kiva.* Sometimes as many as fifty take part in the dance. The men dressed in white rain kilts with fox skins hanging behind have their legs and the upper part of their bodies painted. Hopi rain belts and strings of sleigh bells are around their waists. A gourd rattle is carried in one hand, a bundle of pine twigs and a branch waved rhythmically with the other. On their feet are moccasins topped with skunk pelts; and at the knees, woven bands and a turtle rattle. The women wear the black Hopi skirt with long red belts wound around their waists; on their heads are *tablitas* (headdresses carved from a board and painted in bright colors.) Small girls and boys similarly dressed follow at the end of the line. A man with a large drum leads a chorus of male singers dressed in velveteen and brilliant silk or rayon shirts, with printed calico or white cotton trousers and buckskin moccasins; some are adorned with handmade silver belts, and all wear long necklaces of turquoise, coral, shell, or silver. Some have buckskin "leggins," but all wear gay-colored head bands. *Koshares* (delight makers) wearing only a black breech clout and a headdress, their bodies painted white and black, dance at the side of the procession. The groups dance alternately until late afternoon, then sometimes join for the final dance.

The highway passes over the Santa Fe Railway at 22.2 *m.* and just beyond that crosses Galisteo Creek in its arroyo-like bed, a lazy rivulet in dry seasons, of practically no use for irrigation, but in flood times a torrent, dangerous along its entire length.

At 26.2 *m.* is the junction with a dirt road.

Right on this road, 4.5 *m.,* to the large PUEBLO OF SANTO DOMINGO (*obtain permission to photograph*). This village is inhabited by one of the most rigidly integrated of all tribes whose dances, similar to those of Cochití, are considered exceptionally fine. On August 4 is their fiesta and magnificent Corn Dance. These people are a sturdy, handsome tribe and, though reserved, are hospitable and welcome all visitors who behave with consideration.

The long concrete bridge over Arroyo Tunque, 33.2 *m.,* marks the junction with a dirt road.

Right on this past HAGAN JUNCTION, 2.2 *m.,* a loading point on the Atchison, Topeka & Santa Fe Railway, and across the bridge over the Rio Grande to SAN FELIPE PUEBLO (alt. 5,700; pop. 641) 2.8 *m.* These hospitable and friendly people (*obtain permit to photograph*) hold their most interesting dances on their May first fiesta and on Christmas Eve, when they dance in the SAN FELIPE CHURCH, an adobe building erected in the early part of the eighteenth century. The entrance portal is flanked by twin towers with open belfries and protected from the sun by a wooden gallery with lattice railing. A shed roof over the gallery is supported by a large, wooden beam resting on decorative brackets at either end. The severity of the exterior side walls is relieved only by the projecting ends of the ceiling *vigas.*

ALGODONES (cotton), 37.7 *m.* (5,088 alt., 867 pop. of township), a small trading center for ranchers, was named according to local tradition for cotton fields that existed here at one time.

The highway at 37.9 *m.* dips slightly over a wide arroyo, which in flood times is dangerous. (*Do not cross when water is high.*)

A farming settlement of Santa Ana Indians, locally known as EL RANCHITO (the little ranch), is (R) at 42.1 *m.* (*see Tour 9*). At 43.1 *m.* is the junction with NM 44 (*see Tour 9*).

BERNALILLO (little Bernal), 45.4 *m.* (5,033 alt., 2,213 pop. of township), seat of Sandoval County, is on the east bank of the Rio Grande. It was settled in 1698 by the descendants of Bernal Díaz del Castillo who was associated with Cortés in his conquest of Mexico. Bernalillo marks the approximate site of Coronado's headquarters, 1540-42, and of his departure for Quivira (Kansas) in 1541. This region, long before the Spanish conquest, was the province of the Tiguex Indians, one of whose pueblos Coronado occupied as his headquarters. Isolated Spanish ranches and haciendas existed in the neighborhood before the Pueblo Rebellion of 1680; six years after reconquest by De Vargas in 1692, a Spanish village called Bernalillo was founded by settlers and a garrison of soldiers. In this place De Vargas died in 1704 leaving a will that directed: "If His Divine Majesty shall be pleased to take me away from the present life, I desire and it is my will that a Mass be said while the corpse is present in the church of this town of Bernalillo . . ." Situated in a rich part of the Rio Grande Valley, the town is now a trading center for Indian and white farmers, a shipping point for cattle and lumber from the Jémez country, and retains some of the atmosphere of the old Spanish days.

South of Bernalillo the highway traverses the fertile farming lands of the Sandía Pueblo Grant.

At 48.9 *m.* is a junction with an unimproved road.

Left on this road, 0.4 *m.*, to SANDÍA PUEBLO (128 pop.), a village of Tewa speaking Indians, remnant of the once populous Tiguex province of Coronado's time. Nafait or Nafaid (Ind. dusty place), the native name of this village, was recorded as Napaye by Oñate in 1598. The pueblo on a grant of more than 24,000 acres has a government day school, a cluster of low one-story adobe houses enclosing a plaza, and an adobe mission dedicated to Neustra Señora de los Dolores (Our Lady of Sorrows), on whose day, June 13, is the annual fiesta and dance. The old mission and monastery, established by Father Estevan de Perea in the early seventeenth century, is now nothing but a heap of adobes. It was here that Governor Don Pedro de Peralta, having displeased the officers of the Inquisition in the Royal Villa, was imprisoned in 1710 for a year with Father Perea his jailer. Sandía's mission, dedicated to St. Francis, continued in importance until the Pueblo Revolt of 1680 when the Indians, according to the old chronicles, burned and destroyed the church and convent, "committing many outrages" and "desecrating the holy altars in the most indecent manner." Following the reconquest (1692) by De Vargas, the Sandía Indians scattered rather than submit again to the Spaniards, some fleeing to the Hopi pueblos in Arizona, where they stayed for 62 years. In 1742 they were persuaded by the Franciscan missionaries to return to the ruins of their old home. According to report, 3,000 or more left and only 441 returned. In 1748 by petition of Father Juan Manchero, Governor Don Joachín Codallas y Rabal set aside lands and renewed the old grant for the pueblo. This was confirmed by Congress in 1858.

ALAMEDA (poplar grove), 55 *m.* (5,000 alt., 1,350 pop. of township), lines both sides of the highway. So thickly populated is the highway between Alameda and Albuquerque that it is difficult to determine the village boundaries. Farms here are irrigated by a series of modern canals recently constructed by the Middle Rio Grande Conservancy District. Alfalfa, chili peppers, fruits, grains, and sorghums are the principal crops. On the mesa east of the village, discernible from the highway (L), is the newly constructed NAZARETH SANITARIUM, a large modern hospital supervised by the Third Order of Dominican Sisters.

West of the village (R) at the river's edge are the Alameda Pueblo Ruins, a pre-Columbian Indian village, one of the original Tiguex pueblos.

US 85 winds through the typical cluster of small homes set in garden patches, through lanes of gas stations, stores, roadside stands, and restaurants on the outskirts of Albuquerque.

ALBUQUERQUE, 62 *m.* (4,943 alt., 26,570 pop.), (*see Albuquerque*).

*Points of Interest:* State University of New Mexico, Old Town Plaza, Church of San Felipe de Nerí and Convento of San Felipe de Nerí Church, Harvey Indian Museum, Casa de Armijo, U. S. Veterans' Hospital, and Huning Castle.

In Albuquerque is the junction with US 66 (*see Tour 6*).

US 85 crosses Barelas Bridge over the Rio Grande and traverses the level river-bottom plains composed of fertile alluvial deposits. This region is given to small farms and orchards, irrigated and intensely cultivated under an agricultural program conducted by county agents.

Coronado and many of the conquistadores passed up and down this valley, and in the historical records mention is made of many Indian communities whose ruins border the highway.

ARMIJO, 65.3 *m.* (4,950 alt., 100 pop.), a suburban community of Albuquerque, is a group of *ranchitos* closely packed along the west bank of the Rio Grande. These little farms in the rich bottom lands are watered by a new system of irrigation ditches planned by the State's soil conservancy program. The highway is lined with filling stations, roadstands, and small stores. The two PUEBLO RUINS (R) together with a score of others dotting the river valley as far north as Bernalillo antedate the Spanish Conquest. The larger of the two was the site of a Tewa pueblo, called *Los Guajolotes* (turkeys) by Espejo in 1582. All *estancias* and *haciendas* in this vicinity were destroyed in the Indian uprising of 1680.

PAJARITO (Sp., small bird), 69.5 *m.* (4,900 alt., 435 pop.) is surrounded by ranchitos on both sides of the river and on the table-lands between the Manzano Mountains and the Rio Grande.

The highway leaves the river bottom south of Pajarito and traverses a higher country along the Mesa de Los Padillas (R), where are the RUINS OF PURETUAY PUEBLO, a 60-room settlement of the Tiguez Province.

LOS PADILLAS, in early times known as SAN ANDRES DE LOS PADILLAS (Andrew of the Padillas), 72.5 *m.* (1,165 pop.), was settled by the Padillas family in 1705. Small ranches surround it.

Southward a tableland mesa rises directly out of the plain, a part of the Isleta Pueblo Indian Reservation which stretches to the right and left. Two adobe trading posts are at 74.3 *m.*

LOS LUNAS, 82.1 *m.* (4,800 alt., 596 pop.), seat of Valencia County, named for the Luna family, was founded early in Spanish colonial days. Some of the New Mexico dishes popular today are from this section. Two of these are *enchiladas* served with beans (*frijoles*) and *posole,* which is hominy cooked with pork.

Los Lunas is on the San Clemente Grant, granted to Don Felix Candelaria in 1716, two years after his mother petitioned for the land; subsequently it was owned by the Luna family and granted to their heirs in 1899 by the United States.

Among the old Spanish Archives (No. 462) are the papers of Antonio de Luna, "dying intestate at the hands of the enemy Apaches on June 9, 1779." The following inventory of his possession was made so his children's share in his estate could be determined: "one tract of land in said place of Los Lunas; 13 cornfields, small ones and large ones; three rooms of an adobe house; two small houses and one house lot; five pictures of 3 handbreadths painted in oil colors with their frames and one Infant Jesus in sculpture of 3 fingerbreadths; one hoe of medium weight; one plow with equipment; one medium sized kettle and one iron griddle, both very old; one mortar; one spit;

two benches; one pair of trousers of scarlet cloth and one jacket of black cholula cloth; one old cloak of *Queratano* cloth; one pair of useless blunderbusses; one branding iron; one horse and one mule; one cart; four oxen; two cows with calves; four bulls two years old; eight calves one year old; 600 breeding ewes and 412 lambs born in that year." All this was appraised at 3,607 pèsos. In accounting for the property, the widow reported that the hoe had worn out; she had paid the trousers for four masses, receipt for which she had lost; she had given the jacket for twelve masses and the horse for twenty masses; the cloak was worn out in service; she sold the mule for one yoke of oxen; the cart was entirely useless; 300 sheep died because of carelessness and the plague of lice; she had given 40 ewes as a burial fee for her deceased husband; 118 were lost by the *major-domo* of the herd, "which he still owes"; 2 oxen were killed by the enemy (Indians); one ox she gave for the shroud.

Los Lunas was made the county seat in 1875, but it was not until 1914 that modern county buildings were constructed. In a region given to raising alfalfa, grains, and sheep, Los Lunas is a trading and exchange center.

South of Los Lunas the highway runs along the Rio Grande's fertile bottom lands. Along the river bank and irrigation ditches are farms with the usual adobe ranch homes.

LOS CHÁVEZ, 87.8 *m.* (523 pop.), a trading center, is another small cluster of adobe houses and corrals.

BELÉN, 93.2 *m.* (4,600 alt., 3,035 pop.), first named BELÉM (Bethlehem), was a settlement provided by the Spanish authorities for *Genizaros* (Sp., begotten by parents of different nations), captives ransomed by the Spaniards from the Apache and Comanche Indians and subsequently released from slavery. The *Genizaros* also included the Spaniards' prisoners, whose status was that of slaves, but who eventually were redeemed or released. Though the pueblo here was destroyed in the revolt of 1680 some settlement continued, for when land here was granted to 24 petitioners by the "Mayor of Alburquerque," about 1740 the *Genizaros* of the pueblo protested that the land was already occupied. An archive (No. 1,226) reveals that the settlement of *Genizaros* at Belén had risen to the dignity of a *partido* (district) in the late eighteenth century and that the natives were aiding the Spaniards in their campaign against the hostile Indians.

In the heart of the most fertile section of the Rio Grande Valley modern Belén is a shipping and trading center for the near-by agricultural and more remote grazing lands and also a railroad center, with large railroad yards, roundhouse, repair shops, loading pens, coal chutes, ice plant, and the largest flour mill in the State. The main east and west line of the Santa Fe crosses the main north and south line here, a division point which holds the record in New Mexico for tonnage and number of cars handled on the Santa Fe Railway. In this rich sandy loam four or five cuttings of alfalfa a year are the rule, cereals do exceptionally well, and wheat grown here has taken first prize repeatedly at many fairs. Corn, oats, and fruit are also important crops. The large Church of Our Lady of Belén houses ecclesiastical records begun in 1793. Little remains of the ruins of the original church near by. The DON CHÁVEZ MANSION (*private*) within the city limits on US 85, has long been a landmark. The barn is surmounted by a high cupola, used as a lookout in the days when the Apache made repeated raids.

South along US 85 are irrigated sections of the Rio Grande Valley. To the east, miles in the distance, the Manzano Mountains (L) loom against the horizon; toward the west are high mesa lands covered with luxuriant grasses that feed sheep and cattle.

In JARALES, 97.2 *m.* (4,000 alt., 890 pop.), a trading center with a population almost entirely of Spanish and Mexican descent, old customs are still faithfully observed.

BOSQUE (woods), 99.2 *m.* (4,770 alt., 269 pop.), a small farming community, was started in the eighteenth century as a small *Genizaro* settlement (*see above*). The Federal government has established a resettlement project here to rehabilitate farmers from drought-stricken areas. Twenty-four hundred acres have been cleared and irrigated and homes built for 300 families, each with a well-watered five-acre tract of farm land suitable for intensive cultivation. A modern school and community hall serve the new project.

US 85 south of Bosque traverses the old Apache country. For a century this nomadic tribe harassed the colonists, stole their flocks, and raided their homes.

SABINAL (Sp., place of cedar thickets), 99.7 *m.* (282 pop.), is a small hamlet formerly the home of a large band of Apache who settled here in 1791, after signing a peace treaty with the Spanish authorities. But the "Apaches de Sabinal," notwithstanding the so-called peace treaty of 1791, again became hostile and continued their depredations and guerilla warfare until the Apache were finally subdued by the campaigns of Generals George Crook and Nelson A. Miles in the 1880's.

LADRÓN (robber) PEAK, visible from the highway (R) south of Sabinal, was a rendezvous for the Navaho and Apache horse thieves long before the advent of American rustlers. It is the highest summit in the Ladrones Mountains, a lateral range whose slopes on the north wall in the Rio Salado (salty), one of the main tributaries of the Rio Grande from the west. South of the Rio Salado are the Bear Mountains, a short range, backed farther west by the Gallinas (chickens) and Dátil (date) Mountains, two great uplifts that redden the high country which stretches far to the west. These three ranges, all in the Cíbola National Forest, are contiguous to the southern banks of the Rio Salado, and abound in game, fish, and fowl.

In BERNARDO is the junction with US 60 (*see Tour 8a*) which unites with US 85 between this point and Socorro. Across the Rio Grande, (L) which continues its course to the south, gently rolling country gives way to the bulk of the Manzano and Pinos Ranges.

Through the southern and northern extremities of these two ranges, the Belén cutoff of the Santa Fe Railway makes its trail to the east.

This colorful arid country has lazily rolling hills and an occasional mesa that rises abruptly. Mesquite, yucca, desert willow, and wild verbena abound; and south of here is creosote.

At 119.3 *m.* is the junction with a side road.

Left on this road to SAN ACACIO, 2 *m.* (100 pop.) a Spanish-Mexican hamlet on the banks of the Rio Grande. The SAN ACACIO DAM, constructed here by the Middle Rio Grande Conservancy in 1934, differs from most dams in that it is a floating one, erected on a soft alluvial bottom and tied to a concrete blanket by a series of cables strung along both banks of the river. In case of a washout of the dirt bottom, the main part of the dam would be held securely by the cables.

The highway passes through a fertile valley lined with groves of tamarisks whose fluffy pink blossoms in springtime add a vivid touch to the predominant beige of the land.

POLVADERA (dusty place), 123 *m.* (6,000 alt., 347 pop.), another hamlet where Spanish customs still prevail, takes on color only in late summer and fall when strings of crimson chili hang in the sun from the beams of the adobes, and in early summer when the prickly pear and cactus abound with flame-colored blooms. The ruins of the SEVILLETA PUEBLO, the most northerly settlement of the Piro Indians, are just west of the present village. Oñate visited this place in 1598 and called the village *Nueva Sevilla.* The pueblo was evidently destroyed by the Apache before 1629, for Benavides describes rebuilding the pueblo in that year and founding the mission of San Luis Obispo. In 1681 when Otermín passed through he found the pueblo as deserted as it is today. Also on the Rio Grande at this point are the ruins of Fort Connelly, one of the early United States Army forts, established in territorial days.

LEMITAR, 126.6 *m.* (5,000 alt., 243 pop.), is on the Rio Grande opposite the almost leveled ruins of the Piro Indian village of TEY-PANA, where in 1541 Coronado with 30 of his men camped and in May, 1598, Oñate was hospitably received and given a supply of much-needed corn. In recognition of this friendly reception and welcome aid the Spanish Conquistador named this settlement Socorro (succor) in honor of Nuestra Señora del Socorro (Our Lady of Succor).

SOCORRO, 133.6 *m.* (4,616 alt., 3,701 pop.), seat of Socorro County, is built on the site of the Piro Pueblo, Pilabo (or Piloque, as the Oñate documents record it). The name Socorro was applied to the present city by Friar Alonso de Benavides under whose direction the Franciscan mission was erected here in 1628 (*see below*).

Socorro is in the nearly level secondary bottom of the Rio Grande Valley, at the foot of a projecting range of hills (R). The Socorro Mountains, about 3 miles west of town, are in the foreground (R) and farther west loom the Magdalena, Dátil, and Black Ranges, with the San Mateo Range to the southwest. These magnificent mountain masses do not run in parallel ridges but consist of apparently independent groups thrown up in haphazard fashion. Rich in everything that mountain, mesa, and valley can yield, this region is best known as a producer of minerals, shipping out gold, silver, copper, lead, galena, and zinc. Cattle, sheep, goats, and horses are raised on the grassy plateaus. Orchards, truck, and grain farms fill the valley drained by streams that are fed from the mountains, where much big game abounds. The streams, stocked with fish, are visited by numerous waterfowl.

Socorro was a focal point in the events of the Spanish occupation, the Pueblo rebellion, and the re-conquest by De Vargas. For protection against the Apache it was the policy of the friars to segregate the inhabitants of the Piro Pueblos into concentrated areas, one of which was Socorro, and from the time of its founding more or less peaceful terms were maintained between the Spaniards and the Piro in the Rio Grande Valley; although it is recorded that in 1665 warriors of these opposing tribes banded together on two occasions to drive out the Spaniards. But the Piro living at Socorro took no part in the Pueblo Revolt in 1680. They feared retribution from the northern Pueblo Indians and joined Otermín in his retreat to El Paso, where Socorro del Sur (Succor of the South) was established for them on the north side of the Rio Grande. During their absence, the northern Indians of the rebellion attacked the deserted pueblo. Otermín and his men, returning the following year (1681), found the pueblo partly ruined and ordered the remaining buildings demolished to prevent the enemy from occupying them.

It was not until 1817 that the ancestors of the present families settled in Socorro. In a grant from the Spanish Crown, 21 families including the Montoyas, Bacas, Abeytas, Garcías, Padillas, Gallegos, Lunas, Vigiles, and others now prominent in New Mexico's affairs were given holdings to encourage the permanent colonization of the land. Dependent upon agriculture, cattle, and sheep raising exclusively, they settled on the hillside and valley floor, irrigating their crops from mountain springs and the Rio Grande, and lived a leisurely life until 1861 and 1862 when the officers of the Union garrison at Fort Craig made Socorro their rendezvous. The freighting and storing of supplies here for the Civil War campaign created a bustling activity that completely transformed the town.

After silver was discovered near by in 1867, Socorro began to grow so steadily that during the 1880's it was the largest city in New Mexico. As the center of one of the richest mining areas in the country, it had 44 saloons lining its thoroughfares and was a supply and shipping point for the 200 wagon trains that served the mines. This mining activity continued until the middle of the 1890's when the price of silver declined. Since then the mines have been worked only at intervals and, with the exception of the hydrocarbons and zinc ores, with discouraging results.

The CHURCH OF SAN MIGUEL, situated in the exact center of Socorro, is one of the oldest churches on the North American Continent. It is a fine example of early Spanish-Indian mission architecture, having been remodeled twice; one of its present walls being the wall of the first Franciscan mission built in 1598. It has massive five-foot walls, hand-hewn rafters, old paintings, and sacred ornaments.

In May 1598 when Oñate stopped at Teypana, he had in his expedition Fray Salazar and Fray Martínez of the Franciscan Order who remained behind when the main expedition resumed its march to the north. A small edifice was erected at Pilabo (present site of Socorro), the nearest large Piro Indian settlement south of Teypana, and from here the Indian communities were served. When this was burned or destroyed at the turn of the century, the present mission at Socorro was founded by Friar García de San Francisco Zuñiga early in the seventeenth century. In 1628 Friar Alonso de Benavides, the first *custodio* of an organized mission field north of Mexico, visited Pilabo, found this Franciscan mission established, and dedicated it to Nuestra Señora del Socorro de Pilabo, to commemorate the aid given Oñate by the Piro Indians in May 1598. This building was badly damaged in 1680 by the northern Indians, and in 1692 De Vargas describes sleeping in a cell of the tumble-down convent. It was almost a century later that settlers rebuilt the mission.

The old PARK HOTEL (1836) just west of the plaza has housed many prominent men including General Lew Wallace, sent to New Mexico to check the Lincoln County War. During 1861-62 this was headquaters for the Union forces.

The NEW MEXICO SCHOOL OF MINES, founded here by the Territorial Legislature of 1889, has a campus of 32 acres on the western outskirts of the city.

In Socorro is the southern junction with US 60 (*see Tour 8b*).

### Section c. SOCORRO to TEXAS LINE, 194.8 m.

Footprints of men and women who made New Mexico history, ruts of their wooden-wheeled carts, and tracks of the blooded horses of *caballeros* determined this route. Much of *El Camino Real,* of which US 85 approximates portions, was the main artery of New Mexico. Early Spanish and Mexican colonists built their homes in the valley through which this route lies. Few strayed from it, few wanted to. This was enemy territory, and safety demanded they keep together. To the east across the Rio Grande was the dreaded Jornada del Muerto (journey of death) across 90 miles of desert and lava beds, with little or no water—a grueling, heart-breaking experience that required more than courage and demanded the utmost in strength. The Santa Fe Railway now dashes through this area, and on the west side of the Rio Grande automobiles rush by over a modern road; irrigation systems enrich the region; and the Royal Road, no longer imprinted in the sand or bottom lands, has been lifted to the low tablelands by engineers and paved.

South of Socorro, 0 *m.,* US 85 runs through areas of creosote and cactus with mountains on both sides.

SAN ANTONIO, 10.8 *m.* (4,500 alt., 432 pop.), is a trading point for ranchers on the site of the Piro settlement, Senecu, a corruption of the aboriginal Tzenocue. The Spanish San Antonio is a survival of the name applied to the mission here in 1629 by Fray Antonio de Arteaga and Fray García de Francisco de Zuñiga, its founders. Bandelier records that the remains of the latter are buried at Senecu.

The banks of the Rio Grande are level on both sides here and water is available by gravity flow and by pumping. Alfalfa is the most important crop raised in the approximately 5,000 acres under cultivation in this area. West of the town is the beautiful boxlike Nogal Canyon with walls ranging perpendicularly from 300 to 1,000 feet high.

San Antonio is at the junction with US 380 (*see Tour 12b*).

At 27.8 *m.* is the junction with a dirt road.

Left on this road past SAN MARCIAL, 2.1 *m.* (70 pop.), a trading center for ranchers and a loading station on the Santa Fe Railway, to the VALVERDE BATTLEFIELD, 6 *m.* Subsequent to the American occupation of New Mexico, a number of army posts were built along the Rio Grande by the several commanders of the United States Army and nearly all of the forts were garrisoned until the final subjugation of the Apache in 1886 by General Nelson A. Miles. Two of these were Fort Conrad, a few miles north of here on the Rio Grande, and Fort Craig about five miles south of here on the west bank of the river. At Fort Craig occurred the first encounter between the Union and Confederate forces in New Mexico, beginning February 16, 1862, when General H. H. Sibley and his Texans appeared before the fort and were engaged by Union cavalry from the garrison. The Confederates then withdrew and on the 19th crossed the river; the following day a force of Federal troops crossed and made a feint of attack on the Confederates. This attempt was beaten off without much loss to either side. Some troopers in one of Kit Carson's companies of New Mexico volunteers even lassoed a Confederate cannon cowboy style and dragged it into the Union camp. On the night of the 20th Captain Paddy Graydon who commanded an independent company of scouts was permitted to make a night attack on Sibley's camp. He equipped two old mules with packs containing explosives attached to short fuses. Then with several of his men he approached the Confederate camp, lit the fuses, and started for home after impelling the mules toward the sleeping bivouac. The mules, instead of continuing toward the camp, followed their masters, who fled the faster. The perambulating bombshells finally blew up and awakened the Confederates, thus making a surprise attack out of the question.

The same Paddy Graydon had an ingenious method of filling his ranks. Whenever one of his men was killed, wounded, or just went over the hill, he would find some inoffensive peon, accost him under the name of the missing man, and put him into the service as the other man, paying no attention to the impressed victim's howls of protest. In consequence Captain Graydon at the time his troop was mustered out had not only a full complement of men but, judging from their recorded names, the same men the troop had originally contained.

On the morning of the 21st, Sibley moved his camp up the river to a point about a mile east of this site. While Sibley's men held the fords at the foot of the Mesa de la Contadera, the Union troops appeared in force on the western bank.

The Federals crossed the Rio Grande here and drove the Confederates back from their positions on the river bank. Toward noon, when the battle had been fiercely contested for two hours, the main force of the Texans came on the field. Two charges were made, one against the left flank of the Federals being successful while the charge against the right flank was thrown back. This latter was met with a countercharge which scattered the Confederate troops. Meanwhile the Union left flank was stormed and the bulk of the army's artillery was captured. The whole battlefield resembled nothing so much as a swinging door with the left flanks of each retreating and the right advancing. By good management and considerable luck, the Federals who had their backs to the river managed to withdraw to Fort Craig, while Sibley went on to take Albuquerque and Santa Fe.

US 85 south of the junction with the road to San Marcial leaves the route of El Camino Real which until 1919 turned east from San Marcial, crossed the Rio Grande, and traversed the dreaded Jornada del Muerto, a trackless desert valley that had been the bed of the Rio Grande until lava in Quaternary times diverted the river to the west.

The width of the Jornada is approximately 35 miles and its length exceeds 90 miles. Only two places were known in the old days where water could be found: one at the Ojo del Muerto (spring of death) in a steep canyon of the Fray Cristóbal Mountains and the other at Laguna del Muerto (lake of death), a mere sinkhole occasionally filled during the rainy season. For the journey over the Jornada, full water kegs were necessary. Records left by several of the *conquistadores,* early Spanish colonists, and Indian fighters reveal the hardships of the trip. The "old road," as it is now known, is used only by local residents. Between the junction of the side road to San Marcial and Hot Springs (*see below*), US 85 parallels the ELEPHANT BUTTE RESERVOIR (L), a lake 45 miles long made by the waters of the Rio Grande impounded by the Elephant Butte Dam (officially named Wilson Dam) five miles north of Hot Springs. From this lake thousands of acres of land in this area are irrigated.

Visible ahead are the Magdalena Mountains and the San Mateos (R); left of the highway the Fray Cristóbal and Caballo ranges push their rugged, colored peaks and escarpments into white clouds and misty halos. The first mine registered in New Mexico (1685) is believed to be the Nuestra Señora del Pilar de Zaragonza (Our Lady of Pilar of Zaragonza), supposed to be a gold claim in the Fray Cristóbal range. It was discovered and registered by Pedro de Abalos, who accompanied Cruzate in 1683 for the reconquest of the Province. Southward, US 85 dips and crosses numerous gulches, canyons, and arroyos, up and down over the plateau-like terrain. This topography is so cut up by small streams and arroyos that it is readily apparent why the *conquistadores* and Spanish colonists used the Jornada on the east rather than the west bank of the Rio Grande. An Indian trail had long existed on the west bank but was seldom used until American occupation when General Kearny took his column down this side and over the mountains to the west.

The western bank was also followed by the first wagon road across the continent, established in 1846-47 by the Mormon Battalion of infantry, 400 strong, commanded by Lieutenant Colonel Philip St. George Cooke. Early in that year, when war with Mexico seemed inevitable, the Church of Latter-day Saints had become involved in difficulties in Illinois, Missouri, and Arkansas, and Brigham Young decided to move his flock west. The battalion was organized to blaze the way, and when Brigham Young offered its services to the War Department, Cooke was put in command with instructions to join Kearny's main body at the Gila River near where that stream crosses from New Mexico into Arizona. In Cooke's journal which covers day by day this memorable march to the Pacific, it is stated that the battalion was completely formed at Santa Fe on October 13, 1846 and a few days later a march south was begun. When 200 miles had been covered word came from Kearny, now breveted a major general, that he had abandoned his wagons, acting upon advice given by Kit Carson, and was proceeding westward with supplies on pack mules.

Cooke, having in mind instructions that he establish a wagon road, consulted his guides and decided not to attempt a meeting with Kearny; he continued another 200 miles in a southward direction before turning due west.

Though the Mormon Battalion left Santa Fe with no knowledge of military tactics, it was drilled on the way and marched into San Diego Mission on January 29, 1847 a well-organized unit of the United States Army. That evening Lieutenant Colonel Cooke reported to General Kearny at San Diego six miles from the mission. Next morning, in "Order No. 1" issued to the battalion, Cooke commended his men thus: "The lieutenant-colonel commanding congratulates the battalion on their safe arrival on the shore of the Pacific ocean, and the conclusion of the march of over two thousand miles. History may be searched in vain for an equal march of infantry. Nine-tenths of it has been through a wilderness where nothing but savages and wild beasts are found, or deserts where, for want of water, there is no living creature. There, with almost hopeless labor, we have dug deep wells which the future traveler will enjoy. Without a guide who had traversed them, we have ventured into trackless prairies where water was not found for several marches. With crowbar and pick and ax in hand we have worked our way over mountains which seemed to defy aught save the wild goat, and hewed a passage through a chasm of living rock more narrow than our wagons. To bring these first wagons to the Pacific we have preserved the strength of our mules by herding them ever over large tracts, which you have laboriously guarded without loss. The garrisons of four *presidios* of Sonora, concentrated within the walls of Tucson, gave us no pause. We drove them out with their artillery, but our intercourse with the citizens was unmarked by a single act of injustice. Thus, marching half naked and half fed, and living upon wild animals, we have discovered and made a road of great value to our country." Though Cooke failed to mention it, several members of the battalion wrote stirring descriptions of their one battle which took place in the San Pedro Valley when the battalion was attacked by wild bulls. Sixty or seventy bulls had been killed, one or two pack mules gored to death, and several of the battalion injured before, as the battalion poet expressed it:

Whatever cause, we did not know
But something prompted them to go;
When all at once in frantic fright
The bulls ran bellowing out of sight.

With the opening of the silver mines around Deming, the western bank of the Rio Grande was used more frequently and about the middle of the nineteenth century became definitely a roadway.

West of the highway is the BLACK RANGE (R), an unbroken chain of mountains 120 miles in length which extends laterally north and south, a treasure house of minerals. Its prominent peaks attain an altitude of 8,000 to 10,000 feet. The slopes and valleys are covered with thick growths of pine and other valuable timber, the dark appearance of which has given rise to its name. Bear, deer, and other wild game abound. Mining has been carried on in this region since 1880. The lands that stretch west of the highway to and into the Black Mountains are fine for grazing; this being one of the best stock regions in the State. There is a good underground water supply and sheep and goats do well, especially Angoras. Does and bucks from several of the goat ranches have won many prizes.

At 68 m. is the junction with NM 52.

Right on this road to CUCHILLO (knife), 6.4 m. (145 pop.), a small community composed of several stores and dwellings. CHLORIDE, 25.7 m. (158 pop.), was started in 1879 as a mining camp by Harry Pye, who hauled freight to military posts in the West. Pye knew something about minerals and while traversing this terrain with a pack train, espied a quantity of ore where Chloride now stands. He took a sample, had it assayed, and found he had made a silver strike. When his contract with the government was completed, he and a party of friends returned to this site and began working. The name Chloride was given to the mining camp because of the character of the ore. Pye did not live to enjoy his wealth as roaming Apache killed him and several settlers shortly thereafter. Today there is little activity in this area but it has been steadily productive.

HOT SPRINGS, 81.6 m. (4,200 alt., 2,740 pop.), the largest town in Sierra County and a trading center for the surrounding mining, stock raising, and farming areas, has good stores, cafes, hotels, modern camp grounds, sanitary bathhouses, and up-to-date motion picture theaters. It is a health resort and its population is increasing rapidly. The town is underlaid with hot rocks; at a depth of 120 feet a temperature of 120° is encountered. The Springs of Palomas, now called Hot Springs, furnish an uninterrupted supply of hot mineral water highly alkaline and nonlaxative. Hot mineralized mud and water baths, with competent attendants in charge, are available at all times. THE CARRIE TINGLEY HOSPITAL for crippled children, a Work Projects Administration project, was erected (1937) at a cost of $1,000,000 for the treatment of infantile paralysis cases. This is a modern, fireproof hospital with a capacity of one hundred beds. The grounds which comprise 118 acres are owned by the State. President Franklin D. Roosevelt took an active interest in its construction.

The Elephant Butte Regatta is held in Hot Springs annually (1st Sat. and Sun. in June.)

Near Hot Springs in the Black Range is excellent hunting and fishing. Many of the ranches have accommodations for visitors; there are guides and pack trips into the mountains. The Black Range (R) is heavily timbered and abounds with deer, bear, turkey, and numerous small game.

At 90.5 *m.* is the junction with a dirt road.

Left on this road to LAS PALOMAS (Sp., the doves), 0.8 *m.* (286 pop.), a primitive hamlet near the ruins of a pueblo. Almost deserted today, it was until recent years a bustling health resort. Indians, Spanish colonists, cowboys, and miners stopped here before there were any accommodations at Hot Springs. The name refers to the thousands of doves that lived in the cottonwoods along the river and around the springs.

In CABALLO, 98.9 *m.,* is the junction with NM 180 (*see Tour 1A*).

To the west at 112 *m.* are the MIMBRES MOUNTAINS, extending from the terminus of the Black Range to the northernmost point of Cooks Range, a continuation of this immense north-to-south uplift.

SALEM, 127.2 *m.* (128 pop.), a small trading center, was an early Spanish village named Plaza, but in 1908 a group of New Englanders, mainly from Salem, Massachusetts, settled here and renamed it.

US 85 crosses the Rio Grande to the west bank at 129.3 *m.*

The approximate SITE OF FORT THORN is at 137 *m.* At this military post, established in 1853 and abandoned in 1859, General Sibley in 1862 joined his several columns of Confederates and marched north. The Rio Grande Valley now broadens; and the Mesilla Valley, a fertile plain dotted with numerous farms yielding fine crops, stretches far to the west.

The highway recrosses the Rio Grande at 138.6 *m.* and at 140 *m.* are the ruins of FORT SELDON (L) with massive unroofed adobe walls, all that is left of a very important post established in 1865 as a means of protection against raids by Gila Apaches.

South of Fort Seldon is MOUNT ROBLEDO (R), named for Pedro Robledo, a member of Oñate's 1598 expedition who was buried near it. This mountain was used by the United States Army as a heliograph station during the campaigns against the Apache and other Indians, the messages being flashed from Fort Bliss to Fort Seldon. Later it was used as an astronomical observation point (1882) to study the transit of Venus.

The land on both sides of the highway is planted with cotton, which yields an exceptionally good crop.

At 162.5 *m.* is the junction with a dirt road.

Left on this road to DOÑA ANA, 1.3 *m.* (348 pop.), a Spanish-Mexican settlement untouched by time and modernity. The old church was erected with the founding of the town in 1843 by Don José María Costales, who with 116 settlers received from the governor of Chihuahua, Mexico, a grant on the east bank of the Rio Grande, known as El Ancón de Doña Ana (Doña Ana bend). After an influx of Texans many of the old settlers decided to seek homes under Mexican jurisdiction. In March, 1850, they moved across the river ·to the west bank and colonized the Mesilla Grant, several miles south. Within two decades the Americans moved out, and Doña Ana became again the Spanish-Mexican village that it is today. Colonel Doniphan and Lieutenant Colonel Gilpin in December, 1846, stopped at Doña Ana after a hard march through the Jornada del Muerto. They and their armies rested here for two days, purchased supplies, and then continued their journey southward.

LAS CRUCES (the crosses), 171.2 *m.* (3,895 alt., 8,355 pop.), is the seat of Doña Ana County. A caravan of oxcarts, en route from Chihuahua, was attacked by Indians at the point where the city now stands and was entirely destroyed. A few days later another freight party from Doña Ana found the bodies, buried them, and erected crosses over the graves. From that time the site has been known as Las Cruces.

Settled in 1848 it has become a prosperous city in the center of a rich agricultural district with fine schools and churches, two banks, a State Farm Bureau, many civic and social clubs, a country club, and a golf course. Several trails lead from Las Cruces to the mountains east and west and to the Mesilla Valley, a land of beauty and of vast resources, agricultural and mineral. The AMADOR (lover) HOTEL on Amador Street was built by Don Martín Amador, a Santa Fe Trail stage driver in 1853, and was furnished with massive walnut pieces of the 1850's brought by oxcarts from the East. In addition to the fine old furniture, girls' names over the doors—La Luz, María, Esperanza, Natalia, Dorotea, Muñeca and others, 23 in all—recall the days when the *casa* was the rendezvous of officers and men from Fort Seldon to the north and Fort Fillmore to the south. There was a variety theater, dance hall, and games of chance—a frontier stopping place typical of the time. Court was held in the dining room and the kitchen was converted into the jail—the jury debating over a murder verdict to the rhythm of the *vals* or the *Varsoviana* in the great hall adjoining. The displays in the great hall include old paintings, lace *mantillas,* fans under glass, pre-historic pottery, and other relics.

One of the oldest branches of the Loretto Academy for Girls, founded in 1852, is in Las Cruces. In 1870 five members of the Sisters of Loretto Order and the Reverend Father Bernal started the school in a private home with six pupils.

The THOMAS BRANNIGAN MEMORIAL LIBRARY houses a noted collection of books and manuscripts.

Las Cruces has enjoyed a marked growth in recent years. There has been a population increase of over 2,500 in the decade following 1930. Cotton, alfalfa, corn, sugar beets for seed, cantaloupes, onions, chili, sweet potatoes, asparagus, pecans, and various fruits are grown in the surrounding irrigated lands. Fine dairy herds are also found in this area.

Left from the center of Las Cruces on Mesa Road 2.6 *m.* to the NEW MEXICO STATE COLLEGE (coeducational), founded with seventeen pupils about

1890 through the efforts of Hiram Hadley. The College now has 1,400 students and offers courses in agriculture, engineering, and the general sciences as well as in business administration, home economics, music, and the other arts. It was accredited by the North Central Association and Engineering Council for Professional Development. The buildings have some interesting murals by Olive Rush, Howard Schleeter, and Edna Pierce, including two by Olive Rush in the entrance to the Biology Building that are true fresco.

At 172.2 *m.* is the junction with a paved road, NM 28.

Right on this road, 2.8 *m.*, to OLD MESILLA (3,857 alt., 606 pop.), whose old plaza and surrounding flat-topped adobe houses sleep in the sun, dreaming of the days when this was the capital of a vast new state that combined the lower part of New Mexico with all of Arizona; of the days of Emperor Maximilian who, according to local tradition, sought sanctuary here; and of the days of Billy the Kid and the Lincoln County War. After the close of the Mexican War a group of New Mexicans who preferred to remain under Mexican protection settled at this site, then a part of Chihuahua, Mexico, and in 1853 they received the land under the Mesilla (little tableland) Colony Grant. The settlement, nevertheless, became a part of the United States when, by terms of a treaty signed here, Mexico received $10,000,000 and the United States an additional strip of land known as the Gadsden Purchase, that included the entire Mesilla Valley. On July 4, 1854, there was a flag-raising ceremony in the plaza at La Mesilla in confirmation of the treaty. Governor Merriwether from Santa Fe was present, as were troops from Fort Fillmore and a large crowd of citizens. In 1857 Mesilla became a central point on the Overland Mail route established by John Butterfield to run between Missouri and California, and a wager was laid as to which coach would reach Mesilla first—the one from the East or the one from the West. The latter won. A newspaper, *The Mesilla Times,* was started in 1860. In July, 1861, Lieutenant Colonel Baylor of the Confederate Army, after capturing Fort Fillmore with little resistance, made his headquarters at Mesilla, proclaiming himself military governor and Mesilla the capital of the new territory of Arizona, which included all of New Mexico south of the 34th parallel, a part of Texas, and all of Arizona, Nevada, and California. After August, 1862, when the Confederates fled before the California Column under General James H. Carleton, La Mesilla was made headquarters of the Military District of Arizona under the United States.
La Mesilla was on the west side of the Rio Grande until 1865 when the river changed its course. The walls of the tumble-down adobe house, which held the courtroom in which Billy the Kid once stood trial, still stand on the corner of the plaza. The main interest of the town, aside from its special charm and mellowed quality, is the privately owned BILLY THE KID MUSEUM (*open 9 to 12 and 1 to 5, 25¢*) that contains authentic relics of Billy the Kid. Other items include relics said to be of Maximiliano and Carlotta of Mexico, a Breeches Bible, rare maps, old branding irons, swords, guns, and blankets.

In Mesilla is the junction with US 70 (*see Tour 10b*).
At 174.2 *m.* is the junction with a dirt road.

Left on this road to the TORTUGAS INDIAN VILLAGE, 0.5 *m.,* built around a small nondescript plaza, with a handsome stone church in modernized Gothic style. They speak no native Indian language, but still cling to their tribal myths and legends. Little is known about them, but E. W. Gifford, curator of the Museum of Anthropology and associate professor of the University of Southern California, says they are descendants of Indians who were expelled from Isleta del Sur, south of El Paso, several generations ago. According to local tradition, their ancestors were Isleta Indians, who at the time of the Pueblo Revolt (1680) were taken from their home near Albuquerque

by Governor Otermín retreating to El Paso. Though most of them were settled by him at the present Indian village of Isleta del Sur about 18 miles
southeast of El Paso, a few who were too old or too ill to continue the journey
settled here and were the founders of Tortugas.

BRAZITO SCHOOL HOUSE (L), 179.9 *m.,* marks the site of the only
Mexican War battle that occurred on New Mexico soil. After United
States troops under Colonel Doniphan had defeated a force here under
General Ponce de León on Christmas Day, 1845, Colonel Doniphan's
march into Mexico was without opposition.

In Conklings Cave near MESQUITE, 182 *m.* (2,430 alt., 195
pop.), at the southern end of the ORGAN MOUNTAINS, bones of
ancient sloths, camels, and cave bears have been found.

At the REGISTRATION STATION (*all trucks must stop*), 193.5 *m.,* out-
of-state trucks pay a road tax and tourists whose cars are not properly
licensed must buy license plates.

In ANTHONY, 194.8 *m.,* US 85 crosses the Texas Line, 20 miles
north of El Paso, Texas.

# *Tour 1A*

Caballo—Hillsboro—Santa Rita—Junction with US 260; NM 180.
68.5 *m.*

Two-lane, graveled roadbed.
Route crosses a spur of the Atchison, Topeka & Santa Fe Railway at Santa Rita.
Accommodations in principal towns; tourist camps, gas stations frequent.

This route is up from the Rio Grande Valley and across the Black
Range with its exceptionally fine panoramas, hunting, and fishing, past
the very large open-pit copper mines at Santa Rita that are visible from
the road, and on to Silver City, largest town in this area. Parts of the
road are through Gila National Forest, which, like the rest of the route,
was the camping and hunting ground of the Gila Apache and is rich
in Indian, mining, and historical lore of the frontier. The Mogollón
Range, beyond Silver City, has many pueblo and cliff dwelling sites of
pre-Columbian days, as well as habitations of a more recent period, and
is an exciting region for the archeologist; and no less interesting to the
hunter and fisherman who must pack in to reach the best spots. There
are many places where pack trips into the areas inaccessible by automobile can be arranged, especially in the Gila Wilderness, which is
being kept primitive.

From CABALLO, 0 *m.* (76 pop.), at a junction with US 85, 15
miles south of Hot Springs (*see Tour 1c*), NM 180 runs west over a

barren stretch to the foothills of the Black Range, away from the Sierra Caballos (ridge of the horses) across the Rio Grande, a wide, blue reservoir at this point. A series of curves precede a long stretch over a wide plain covered with creosote bushes that hide the chaparral cock, sand lizards, and various reptiles, while the sparse grass provides food for the grazing flocks.

HILLSBORO, 17.9 *m.* (5,238 alt., 320 pop.), is the seat of Sierra County, once the center of a rich mining district. Millions in gold, silver, and other ores have been taken from the surrounding hills. Large flocks of goats and sheep and herds of cattle graze on the slopes and plains. Hillsboro's history began in 1877 when two prospectors discovered gold near by. They were joined later by other prospectors working in the near-by Mimbres Mountains. Each miner had a name for the new site, so each wrote his choice on a slip of paper, placing it in a hat. One member drew from the lot and the name Hillsborough was chosen, contracted in later years to Hillsboro. The main thoroughfare of the town is lined with cottonwood, and the old stores, all landmarks of the earlier camp, are still the hangouts of citizens who lived and knew the boom days of the town. The Gold Pan Restaurant, a miners' rendezvous, is still feeding chuck to bearded prospectors who were in the rush, and according to the proprietor "much mining is still done on the plank bench in front of the store." This bench has been studded with large nails to protect it from assault by whittlers.

The LAKE VALLEY REGION, south of Hillsboro, was one of the best ore producers in the Southwest and is still potentially valuable. The history of all the finds in this district is full of action; joy, heartbreak, and battles with the Indians being a part of it. This section was the part-time home of Victorio, the Apache chief, and his lieutenants, Loco and Nane. The silver ore is of high grade, and a strike in the district furnished an illustration of the romance connected with mining in New Mexico. Two miners in the early 1880's struck an ore vein near the settlement of Lake Valley and sold out for $100,000. Two days after the sale, the lead ran into what is known as the Bridal Chamber, a subterranean room and the working of which produced upwards of $3,000,000 in horn (free) silver. A spur track from the railroad was run into the room and the silver loaded directly into cars. The expense of working this room was so small that one man offered the owners a large sum for the privilege of entering the mine and taking down all the silver he could pick single-handed in one day.

In the mining boom days, stagecoaches were the means of transport and the one from Hillsboro to Lake Valley was the busiest. Sadie Orchard, still living in Hillsboro (1939), was owner and one of the drivers. She came to the territory in 1886 from London when Hillsboro was teeming and Kingston a wild town of 5,000 people; the silver boom was at its height and dance halls and saloons in full swing. It was in this setting that she and her husband, with two Concord coaches and an express wagon, started their stage and freight line to the outlying mining camps. Sadie took her full turn at the lines, driving every day from Kingston to Hillsboro to Lake Valley. She proudly boasts that her stage was never in a holdup. One of her coaches is now on display in the Museum of New Mexico at Santa Fe.

Between Hillsboro and Kingston, the highway traverses PERCHA CANYON, a rugged, niche-like channel cut through mountains that tower on both sides. This stretch in the early days, as Sadie Orchard relates, was "always troublesome for us stage drivers; Indians lurked along the way and the road was surely trying."

The GILA NATIONAL FOREST is entered at 25.8 m.

KINGSTON, 26.7 m. (6,353 alt., 76 pop.), with only one store, the old hotel, and several frame buildings, was a beehive of activity in the 1880's, the contiguous country having produced approximately $10,000,000 in silver and related ores. The highway passes the store, but the old town (R) is hidden from view by the trees. The first mineral discovered near Kingston was in 1880; the news of the find started a boom, and within five years the town had a population of 7,000. Several landmarks stand, one the fire bell, used in those days to summon the volunteers, today calling the few settlers for their mail. The Victorio Hotel (see below), built in 1882, still stands; the register, in use since 1887, still serving. A story is told of an old Washington Hand Press that was used during the gold rush days. It had been brought hundreds of miles overland to Old Mesilla on the Rio Grande, where a small newspaper was published (see Tour 1c). During the Civil War, after the capture of Mesilla by the Confederates, the press was thrown into the Rio Grande where it lay in the sand for many years. With the activity at Kingston it was retrieved, and itinerant printers got out crude newspapers and hand-bills on it, first at Kingston and then at other boom towns in the area. It is still in operation (1939), publishing a small newspaper in the town of Hatch (see Tour 1c). Sheba Hurst, Mark Twain's humorous character in Roughing It, was the wit of Kingston; a plain pine slab bearing the name "Sheba" marks his last resting place in the old graveyard outside the town. Victorio, the Apache raider, and his cohorts paid several surprise visits to Kingston, but the tough miners were too much for them. Their victories made them generous, and they named the three-story hotel Victorio. In its prime, Kingston had 22 saloons, several dance halls, a theater at which Lillian Russell and her troupe once played; many stores, three hotels, and three newspapers. It was suggested that the town needed a church, so hats were passed in saloons. Dance hall girls tossed diamond rings into them; gamblers dropped money and stickpins, and miners weighted the kitty with gold nuggets. The collection totaled $1,500, which built the church. The walls of stone are still standing, and behind the altar the appropriate sign, The Golden Gate, still blazons.

West of Kingston, NM 180 gradually ascends the east slope of the BLACK RANGE, through extensive forests of pine, spruce, and juniper, passing from Sierra into Grant County. The highway trails over the mountain slopes with expanded views of mountain and plain.

Wooded canyons thick with mountain flowers and quiet meadows crossed by mountain streams add to the beauty of the Black Range Highway. A number of United States game refuges have been established in the Black Range, but special permits for hunting and fishing outside these areas may be obtained from any forest officer. The highway leaves the Gila National Forest at 45.1 *m.*, drops down in the Mimbres Valley, and crosses the Mimbres River. San Lorenzo, a small trading center, is reached at 52.9 *m.* Here is the junction with a side road.

Left on this road is MIMBRES HOT SPRINGS, 10 *m.*, a quiet, isolated health resort in a ranch country of great natural beauty. Modern buildings are clustered about 20 springs of hot water ranging in temperature from 120° to 144° F. Near by is a group of Indian pueblo ruins.

The VALLEY VIEW STORE AND CAMPGROUNDS are passed at 54.1 *m.*, with a fine view of the Mimbres Valley Plains.

The KNEELING NUN, a pinnacle rock formation rising abruptly from a mesa some distance (L) is a landmark visible at 61.2 *m.*

Pavement begins at 62.2 *m.*

SANTA RITA, 62.3 *m.* (6,311 alt., 2,565 pop.), site of the large open-pit copper mines, is a small city practically surrounded by its own excavations. Two immense bowls, worked at different benches (shelf-like levels) have produced many thousand tons of copper yearly since 1800. These bowls, created by continuous digging, lie in a well-defined widening of the Santa Rita Valley, the rim of the basin being highest at the Santa Rita Mountain (7,365 alt.). The remainder of the basin rim was originally formed by a series of hills rising 100 to 450 feet above the basin floor. Some of the hills have been removed, wholly or in part, by steam shovels.

The Santa Rita mine was discovered in 1800 by Lieutenant Colonel Manuel Carrisco, a Spanish commandant in charge of military posts in this section of New Mexico. The Spaniards had made Santa Rita a penal colony, and it is said that convict labor was employed in developing the property under the ownership of Don Francisco Manuel Elguea, of Chihuahua, who bought the mine from Carrisco. The copper was of so fine a quality that the Royal Mint contracted for the output to be used in coinage. The metal was transported to the City of Mexico on pack mules, 300 pounds loaded on each animal, and it is recorded that 100 mules were constantly employed in this work. In 1807, Zebulon Pike, American explorer, told of a copper mine in this part of the Territory (undoubtedly Santa Rita), "producing 20,000 mule teams of copper annually."

Don Francisco died in 1809, and the mine was worked until 1822 under various leases made with his widow. Robert McKnight held it from 1826 to 1834. Because of the Apache, the mine was abandoned for a few years, but from 1840 to 1860 it was worked by Siqueiros. In 1862, when all the mines in the Territory were closed down, Sweet and LaCosta were proprietors. At various periods from

1862-70, it was worked by Messrs. Sweet, LaCosta, Brand, and Fresh, using for their labor Mexicans from Chihuahua and as a smelter a small Mexican blast furnace with a capacity of about 2,000 pounds of refined copper per month.

The mass development of the Santa Rita Copper Camp really dates back to 1873, when it came under American management. Work continued steadily until the early 1880's when a decline in price caused the mines to close down until the late 1890's. Then the Hearst estate secured an option which in 1899 was sold to the Amalgamated Copper Company for $1,400,000. Now (1939) the mines are owned by the Nevada Consolidated Copper Company, and the ore is treated at Hurley, 10 miles south of Santa Rita. The concentrate is shipped to the American Smelting and Refining Company at El Paso, Texas.

Evidence of old Spanish and Mexican workings have been found in the mines, even skeletons and old fills together with many old timbers. Since the beginning of steam shovel operations, there have been further developments. In stripping the Romero section the skeleton of a very tall man of the Indian type was unearthed, the skull and teeth practically replaced by carbonate of copper. Two copper bars three feet in length were also found. They had been punched with a hole at the end and showed that they had been hammered into shape. Several vessels of hammered copper have been unearthed, also mining tools and bullets. On the northern extremity of what is known as the Hearst pit, while stripping, 50 skeletons were taken out from a depth of 6 feet above the natural slope and about 15 feet under an old dump. Legend has it that at one time 50 convict miners were imprisoned in this mine by a cave-in and their bodies never recovered.

Encircling the pits of the mine the highway leads westward, passing the flag station stop of Cobre, 65.6 *m.,* branch railroad from Hurley to the mines, and Bayard Station, 67.5 *m.,* an unloading point for the Fort Bayard Hospital, joining US 260 at 68.2 *m.*

At 68.5 *m.* is the junction with US 260 (*see Tour 18*).

US 260 and NM 180 are united to Silver City (*see Tour 18*).

# *Tour 2*

(Kenton, Oklahoma) — Valley — Folsom — Ratón — Hoxie — Colfax—Cimarrón—Taos; US 64, NM 72, US 64.
Oklahoma Line to Taos, 197.3 *m.*

Bituminous-paved roadbed between Ratón and Colfax; elsewhere two-lane graded graveled.

Spur of the Atchison, Topeka & Santa Fe Railway parallels route between Hoxie and a point near Ute Park.
Hotels at Ratón and Taos; accommodations at Folsom and Capulín; gas stations at short intervals.

This route traverses mountainous terrain and rolling prairie with farms and typical New Mexico villages of adobe houses and passes a volcanic cone incredibly perfect. Warriors, trappers, traders, thieves, spendthrifts, and exploiters have all left their mark on this country. The route between Colfax and Taos should be driven carefully. Sometimes it is very slippery; sometimes rocks fall; and snowdrifts make it dangerous in Cimarrón Canyon.

*Section a.  OKLAHOMA LINE to RATÓN, 98.6 m.*

On the Carrizozo Creek Bridge US 64 crosses the NEW MEX-ICO LINE, 0 *m.*, 2.3 miles west of Kenton, Oklahoma, and winds through high, rolling prairie cut by many canyons. The road gains altitude across the northern part of Union County, paralleling the Cimarrón (wild) River between hills and mountains as far as Folsom. This river, fed by small creeks and innumerable springs, is often referred to locally as the Dry Cimarrón because it flows underground for most of its course. Mesas, evenly formed buttes, and rugged cliffs present an ever-changing picture of enchanting beauty with black rimrock and reddish earth and rocks sharpening the contrasts.

VALLEY, 23.6 *m.*, is a placita with a population of 71 persons. DEVOY'S PEAK (R), 48.5 *m.*, a formation covered with piñon and juniper trees, rises from the center of a high mesa named for one of the earliest settlers of the Dry Cimarrón region. Michael Devoy, known as the Father of the Cimarrón, came to Madison—near the present Folsom—about 1870 and founded the first post office in what was to become Union County. He bought a ranch eight miles northeast of Madison where he lived till his death in 1914. He operated a small store for cowboys and raised prize short-horn cattle, the first in northeast New Mexico. Near Devoy's Peak are a few Indian graves, and many believe that treasure was buried on the mesa by outlaws in the days of the Wild West. Between the peak and Folsom there is good fishing in the Cimarrón.

At 52.2 *m.* is a junction with a dirt road.

Right on this road 3.2 *m.* are the Sierra Negra Ice Caves which have supplied the neighboring residents with ice since their discovery about 1921.

At 54 *m.* is a fine view (L) of EMERY'S PEAK (9,000 alt.), which like the gap west of it and the vanished town of Madison at its foot, was named for Madison Emery (*see below*). The rocky, timbered slopes of the peak and the adjacent hills were often used by the settlers as retreats when they heard rumors of Indian attacks.

Through TOLL GATE CANYON (R), 55.3 *m.*, which is a four-mile branch of the Dry Cimarrón Canyon, Bill Metcalf, a frontiersman, built a toll road in the early 1870's. The ruins of his combination toll house, grocery store, and saloon are still visible in the canyon. This, one of the few good wagon roads between Colorado and northeastern New Mexico, is said to have brought Metcalf so much wealth that he handled his money with a shovel.

At 56.3 *m.,* a few hundred yards from the highway, are The Falls. They are located about 3 miles from Folsom and afford excellent trout fishing and swimming.

FOLSOM, 59.2 *m.* (6,500 alt., 392 pop.), named for President Cleveland's wife Frances Folsom, and surrounded by unusually beautiful mountains, is a typical western cattle- and sheep-shipping town. Half the population speaks Spanish and the other half English. Near by is the site of the former village of Madison, settled in 1865 by Madison Emery, who came here first in 1862 when the grass in the Cimarrón valley grew so high that it nearly hid a man on horseback, and the hills were covered with pine, piñon, and juniper trees, and wild game and fish were abundant. As various families continued to settle here, Madison acquired a store, saloon, blacksmith shop, flour mill, and post office.

Though trouble with Indians was frequent, the villagers sometimes barricaded themselves in their houses only to learn that rumors were the cause of their anxiety, or that the Indians on the warpath were on the trail of an enemy tribe. If an Indian even camped near the town there was alarm. On one occasion Bud Sumpter, Emery's stepson, found an Indian lying apparently asleep, behind the store. Rolling him over he discovered that the man had died of too much "fire-water!" Emery hearing of the tragedy and fearing trouble called the chief to his house for a conference. Just as the chief stepped inside Emery's door, a shell accidentally thrown into the stove exploded. It took a great deal of explaining to convince the chief he was not going to be assassinated. Finally the tribe was given the fattest cow Emery possessed, and the death of the Indian was soon forgotten.

Coe and his notorious outlaws whose headquarters were at "Robbers Roost," north of Kenton, Oklahoma, frequently visited Madison, then the settlement nearest their hide-out. Upon arrival at the town the bandits would turn their horses loose and force some one to unsaddle and feed them. They demanded food at Mrs. Emery's and lodged as a rule at a bunkhouse belonging to the Emerys.

United States cavalry companies from Fort Union, New Mexico and Fort Lyons, Colorado, also were frequent visitors while seeking the bandits. Coe was finally captured and jailed at Fort Lyons but escaped and made his way to Madison on a pony stolen from an Indian. He came to Mrs. Emery, demanding food and lodging. As soon as he was asleep, Mrs. Emery sent her eldest son Bud on his pony to the encampment of the Fort Union troops, who were seeking Coe. Bud brought them back to town, and Coe surrendered peacefully. As he was being led away, he noticed Bud's pony, and said: "That pony has had a hard ride." Believing that Coe, should he escape again, would return to Madison and murder Mrs. Emery, her son, and possibly others in town, vigilantes took him from the jail at Pueblo, Colorado, where he had been locked up, and lynched him. Years later a skeleton was found with a ball and chain on its feet and handcuffs on its wrists.

The advent of the Colorado & Southern Railroad—which reached Folsom in 1887-88 and was the only railroad in the northeastern part of the State until 1901—marked Madison's end and Folsom's beginning. From a railroad construction camp called Ragtown because the saloons, restaurants, and houses were all tents, Folsom soon developed into a bustling town and for a time had the largest stockyards north of Fort Worth. By 1895 Folsom had two mercantile stores, three saloons, and other business establishments and was contributing to the outlaw history of New Mexico's early Anglo-American settlements.

W. A. Thompson, proprietor of the Gem Saloon and deputy sheriff, left Missouri with a price on his head, charged with murder of a man in his home town. Insanely jealous and hot-tempered he piled up as bloody a record as any man in the West. On one occasion he shot a man because he "had the nerve" to become intoxicated in a rival saloon. John King, owner of a grocery store and a saloon, loved to taunt Thompson by setting men up to drink at his bar. One morning after King had treated a native boy to a drink Thompson started after the lad who dashed around the corner of a house belonging to Mrs. George Thompson and started to cross the yard. Thompson fired and the bullet entered Mrs. Thompson's kitchen, barely missing her. She ran out just as the gunman shot again, and saw the boy fall to his knees. While she was berating Thompson, the lad, uninjured, took to his heels. Thompson returned to his store, got a shotgun and came out again. Seeing Billy Thatcher, a fellow-officer and bitter enemy, he began to fire at him. As Jeff Kehl came out of King's store to see what was going on, a bullet pierced his abdomen, and he died that night.

A gun fight followed, with Thatcher using a revolver, and the rifle was shot from Thompson's hands. He ran to his saloon, barricaded himself in the basement, and began drinking. The entire town was out to lynch him but could not get him out without burning his saloon and with it the entire block of buildings. That evening, however, Thompson, dead drunk, surrendered and was taken into custody. He was placed in the Clayton jail for safe keeping, then removed to the Springer jail. Released on bond, he returned to Folsom and disposed of his business. When tried, he was acquitted, went to Trinidad, and married the girl because of whom he had committed his first murder. They went to Oklahoma where Thompson killed another person, was again acquitted, and there spent the remainder of his life.

The decline of Folsom as a shipping center began in 1908 when a flood swept away most of the buildings and drowned seventeen persons. Near the north end of the town is the foundation of an old telephone exchange, marking the SITE OF THE HOME OF SARAH J. ROOKE of whose heroism the townspeople still speak. On a night in August, 1908, Sarah, a telephone operator, heard the buzz on her switchboard and answering it, was told: "The river has broken loose! Run for your

# Along the Highway

*Ernest Knee*

IN NORTHERN NEW MEXICO

US 66, EAST OF GRANTS

LUMBERJACKS IN LINCOLN NATIONAL FOREST

VIEW OF RATON FROM RATON PASS

CLIFF RUINS IN FRIJOLES CANYON

NAVAHO RODEO AUDIENCE, GALLUP          *Milton Snow*

CARNIVAL

PACK TRIP, SAWMILL PARK TRAIL

RED RIVER VALLEY, LOOKING TOWARD SANGRE DE CRISTO MOUNTAINS

*Milton Snow*

WINTER, SANTA FE NATIONAL FOREST

VALLE GRANDE, THE LARGEST MEASURED EXTINCT VOLCANIC CRATER

WOOD HAULER WITH BURROS

CHRISTMAS PREPARATIONS, MADRID

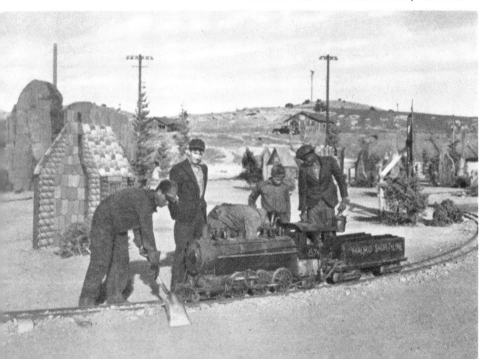

life!" She did not run. Realizing that many persons were unaware of the impending disaster she called them, one by one, till the flood swept her cottage away; her body was found in the wreckage eight miles below the town. In the Folsom cemetery a granite monument to Sarah Rooke was paid for by over 4,000 contributors.

Folsom is the junction with NM 72. The tour continues straight ahead over NM 72 while US 64 (L) turns south.

Left on US 64, 7 *m.*, is a junction with a graded dirt road. Left on dirt road to the CAPULÍN NATIONAL MONUMENT, 10 *m.* (8,268 alt.). This area, supervised by the National Park Service, contains MOUNT CAPULÍN (8,368 alt.) and nine smaller extinct volcanic craters. Mount Capulín, a huge cinder cone of geologically recent formation, is described as the most nearly symmetrical volcanic cone in North America. It is about a mile in diameter at the base and 1,450 feet in diameter at the top. The road completely encircles the mountain to the rim, 6 *m.*, where a trail leads into the crater, which is 700 feet deep and overgrown with grasses and brush. Capulín is the name of a Mexican cherry. Some believe the mountain was named for fruit trees that formerly grew in its crater. The Indian explanation of the name is a legend about Capulín, the son of a chief whose tribe lived on the slopes of the mountain. Capulín was sent on a mission of peace by his father and during his absence, Oogah, his brother, shot and killed the powerful Thunderbird, guardian of the mountain. On Capulín's return, he found the entire tribe wiped out by volcanic eruptions which he interpreted as a punishment from God. He made his way to the top of the crater, gazed into the molten depths and cried: "O Great Spirit! If my life will atone, it is thine!" Then he threw himself into the seething mass. Many years later when other Indians ventured up to the crater's rim, they saw a pine tree growing from the heart of the crater, and as the wind moaned through its branches, the Great Spirit whispered: "Capulín, Capulín!"

US 64 continues to junction with US 87 in Capulín 10.6 *m.* (*see Tour 4*).

Right from Folsom, NM 72 traverses JOHNSON MESA, a lava-capped tableland that extends most of the distance between Folsom and Ratón which was named for Lige Johnson, a pioneer cattleman who owned a ranch on its southern slopes. The mesa was seldom scaled by other cowboys before 1887, when a settler, Marion Bell, attracted by the cowboys' reports of the rich, crumbling soil, the springs of pure mountain water, the perpetual sunshine, and the magnificent scenery built a house on its top.

At 68.7 *m.* is a junction with an unimproved dirt road.

Left on this road is the CROWFOOT RANCH of J. L. Johnson and Sons 1.3 *m.* where the Folsom point finds in 1926 gave evidence that man was living here more than 10,000 years ago (*see Archeology*).

BELL, 82.5 *m.* (8,460 alt., 32 pop.), on the Mesa, was settled in 1887 by a group of dissatisfied miners from Bossburg, New Mexico who wanted to farm and followed Bell up the steep canyon leading to the mesa and settled on this island above the clouds. Here in a strange new world nearly 20 miles long and 4 to 6 miles wide, they built their homes, school, and church. Most of the houses are constructed of stones and earth, for protection against snows and blizzards, as temperatures of 30° to 40° below zero are not infrequent. The soil is remarkably rich, and regular rains and the spring flows keep it well watered. Potatoes and oats are the principal crops. Not far from here, under the north rim of the Johnson Mesa, are the ICE CAVES discovered in 1934, when Eli and Fred Gutierrez of Ratón entered them by descending from the top of the mesa by a rope. Later with two other adventurers, they found a second entrance. In the caves are rooms with solid ice floors and walls. Strata of dust alternate with ice, and through these it may be possible to date the formation of the caves. In one cave there is no ice, but it is extremely difficult to enter since it is necessary to crawl over jutting ledges and across fissures, and there is a drop of about 200 feet. In April 1936, Dr. S. B. Talmadge of the New Mexico School of Mines discovered in the caverns the miniature TALMADGE GLACIER, which is slowly flowing through breaks in the lava rock that forms the top of the mesa. The glacier is about 200 feet long, over 30 feet thick in places, and from 2 to 25 feet in width. Seepage of melting snow, augmenting the ice of the glacier, serves to keep it moving.

YANKEE, 94.3 *m.* (6,710 alt., 148 pop.), was started as a coal town by A. D. Ensign, representing eastern investors who promoted the Santa Fe, Ratón & Eastern Railroad from Ratón to Yankee. The venture failed and the town was abandoned, but since then a few families have moved into some of the abandoned houses and now dig their own coal.

RATÓN, 98.6 *m.* (7,594 pop.), is at a junction with US 85 (*see Tour 1a*) which unites with US 64 between Ratón and Hoxie.

### Section b. RATÓN to TAOS, 98.7 m.

Between RATÓN, 0 *m.*, and Colfax the road is two-lane bituminous; the remainder is graded gravel. This is one of the most attractive routes in the State. US 64 continues southwest through level plains country, following a route of the old Santa Fe Trail. To the north and west the foothills of the Sangre de Cristo Mountains are visible. Because of numerous dips in the road and straying cattle and horses, it is well to drive carefully.

At 28.2 *m.* is the junction with a dirt road.

Right on this road is DAWSON, 5.4 *m.* (7,500 alt., 2,698 pop.), a busy coal mining camp, now owned by Phelps-Dodge interests. J. B. and L. S. Dawson, brothers, who came to New Mexico between 1867 and 1870, had a ranch here till coal was discovered on the property about 1895; some of J. B. Dawson's ranch houses are still standing. It is estimated that there are enough undeveloped veins at Dawson to last for more than 50 years. Besides Americans, the population consists of Slavs and Italians.

Northwest of Dawson the road is unimproved and at times almost impassable. It follows the Vermejo River to its source near the Colorado State Line. VERMEJO (vermilion) PARK, 26 *m.*, is a magnificent private club and game preserve extending eastward 40 miles from the eastern slopes of the Sangre de Cristo Mountains. W. H. Bartlett, millionaire grain operator of Chicago, bought the ranch in 1900 after his physician had warned him concerning his health, and lived here for 18 years. Bartlett built a home for himself and for each of his sons, with guest houses, an electric plant, an ice plant, a fish hatchery and made other improvements. The streams were stocked with bass and trout and, operating under a park license, Bartlett drew up his own game and fish laws. After Bartlett and his sons had died in 1918 the property was in the care of trustees until 1927, when a group of Los Angeles capitalists, headed by Harry Chandler, president of the *Los Angeles Times-Mirror,* purchased the ranch and incorporated it into a private club, using Bartlett's home as clubhouse. The original 75 members included Will Rogers, Cecil B. De Mille, Douglas Fairbanks, Max C. Fleischman, Will Hays, and Andrew Mellon. The property totals nearly a half million acres. Today the ranch includes a large game preserve, where 5,000 elk, 15,000 mule-deer, 20,000 wild turkeys, pheasants, bears, wildcats, and other animals roam freely.

COLFAX, 28.5 *m.* (6,550 alt., 100 pop.), comprises a gas station, general store, railroad station, an abandoned school house, and a few dwellings. The nearest post office is at Dawson.

Southwest of Colfax the highway continues almost in a straight line through sagebrush, where fine herds of cattle and sheep graze and occasional ranch houses are seen.

CIMARRÓN, 39.5 *m.* (6,427 alt., 700 pop.), divided into New Town and Old Town by the Cimarrón River, is on the narrow shelf of land that divides the Rayado and Cimarrón Valleys from the Sangre de Cristo Range and is well protected from mountain gales. To the north and west rise lofty mountains, and to the south and east are two of the most fertile valleys in the State. In addition to the Cimarrón River, the water of the Ponil and the Cimarroncito (little wild) Canyons supply adequate water for the town and the irrigation of crops. Near-by mountains provide ample fuel, timber, and game and there is good trout fishing in the surrounding streams. Cimarrón has had several gold-mining booms but no "strike" of importance. Large stock ranches near here produce excellent cattle, particularly purebred Herefords. Since 1933 a polo field and race-horse stable have been established, and eight large ranches are devoted to the breeding of thoroughbreds.

The filing of a petition for the Beaubien and Miranda Grant, one of the largest in all New Mexico (in 1841), marked the beginning of settlement here. In that year Carlos Beaubien, a French trapper, and Guadalupe Miranda of Taos requested the land from Governor Armijo, but it was not until 41 years later that the litigation concerning the grant finally ended. About 1849 Lucien B. Maxwell, originally of Kaskaskia, Illinois, a hunter and trapper who had accompanied General Frémont on his first and third expeditions and had married Beaubien's daughter, settled on the grant and, after Beaubien's death at Taos in 1864, bought out the remaining heirs. By 1865 Maxwell and his wife were the sole owners of 1,714,765 acres, a territory three times the size of Rhode Island. The Maxwell Grant, as it was called, included the site of Springer, French, Maxwell, Otero, Ratón, Vermejo Park, Ute Park (*see below*), Elizabethtown; and in Colorado, Vigil, Stonewall, Torres, Cuarto, Tercio, Primero, and Segundo. Maxwell was a powerful man, an expert horseman; he loved gambling, drinking, and almost any extravagance. Buying costly furniture was a hobby. In the days of his greatest prosperity he had 500 peons working on the grant, with several thousand acres of land under cultivation. Thousands of cattle and sheep grazed on the fertile plains. Travelers held up by storms were entertained lavishly. For many years he did a thriving business with the government, selling livestock to near-by army posts.

He started many a small rancher in the stock business, giving him a herd of cattle, sheep, or horses and a small ranch to be run on shares. The agreement was always a verbal one, and sometimes two or three years would pass without a division. Then when Maxwell needed more stock, hay, or grain to fill his government contracts, he would call in his shareholders, ask for an accounting, always verbal, and direct them to bring in the surplus to him, which was done without question. In 1860-62 Maxwell was associated with "Buffalo Bill" Cody in a goat and sheep ranch near Cimarrón. The finding of gold on the grant in 1867 was disastrous for Maxwell who invested a fortune in the venture, which failed. In 1870 the grant was sold to three financiers for a sum believed to have been between $650,000 and $750,000. Three months later it was purchased by an English syndicate for a reported price of $1,350,000.

Maxwell's next venture was banking. He founded the First National Bank of Santa Fe, today the only one in the capital. In December 1870, when the charter was granted, stock certificates bore a vignette of Maxwell with a cigar in his mouth. But his lack of banking experience (on the Maxwell Grant he had always kept his money in a cowhide trunk in his bed room) caused him to sell out in 1871 and invest $250,000 in bonds of a corporation formed for the construction of the Texas Pacific Railroad. This proved to be a complete loss, and Maxwell died in comparative poverty on July 25, 1875. He was buried in the old military cemetery at Fort Sumner, where his son Peter and Billy the Kid were also interred (*see Tour 8a*).

The MAXWELL HOUSE, now in ruins, was built about 1864 by the former trapper. As large as a city block, it housed a gambling room, billiard room, and dance hall, as well as a rear section which the women were not allowed to leave. Every evening sums of money changed hands as the gambling gunmen and ranchers gathered to play faro, roulette, monte, cunquién, poker, and dice. Maxwell's soon became the principal stopping place for travelers on the Santa Fe Trail and the starting point for prospectors, hunters, and trappers, as well as the "cowboy capital" of northern New Mexico. Its guests are said to have included Kit Carson, Ceran St. Vrain, Jesús Abreu, Charles Bent, Davy Crockett, Clay Allison, "Buffalo Bill" Cody, Tom Boggs (grandson of Daniel Boone), and many others. In the same year in which the mansion was built, there was erected a stone GRIST MILL in which was ground the wheat grown on the ranch. It is now used by the Polo Club for storing grain and hay. After Maxwell had been appointed a U. S. Government Indian agent, he used it to house provisions for the Ute. Across from the Maxwell House, the St. James Hotel, now operated as the Don Diego Tavern, was built in 1870-80 and run by Henry Lambert, who before coming to New Mexico had been chef for General Grant and Abraham Lincoln. This inn was frequented by outlaws and was the scene of 26 killings. Whenever a man was shot in the hotel, townspeople would say, "Lambert had a man for breakfast." The *Las Vegas Gazette* once reported: "Everything is quiet in Cimarrón. Nobody has been killed for three days." As the gunmen of the Southwest continued to come to Cimarrón, 15 saloons, 4 hotels, a post office, and a newspaper, the *Cimarrón News and Press,* were established. The paper, housed in a warehouse used as the Indian Agency Headquarters, was said to have been printed on the press brought to New Mexico by Padre Antonio José Martínez and first used by him in 1835 to print school books, religious propaganda, and a Taos paper, *El Crepúsculo* (the dawn). It is related that one evening Clay Allison and some of his cohorts, angered by an item in the newspaper, battered in the door of the building, smashed the press with a sledge hammer, and finally dumped the type cases and office equipment into the Cimarrón River. Not satisfied, Allison and one of his men went back to the plant next morning, found a stack of the previous day's papers, and went from bar to bar selling the papers at 25¢ a copy. As if Cimarrón did not have enough of its own gangsters, "Black Jack" Ketchum of western Oklahoma frequently dropped into town between train robberies. He was finally hanged at Clayton (*see Tour 4*).

It was in Cimarrón that Buffalo Bill organized his famous Wild West show, rounding up almost all of the Indians and pinto ponies in the region. Whenever possible, he would spend Christmas here giving a party for children at the St. James Hotel. On one occasion each child received a plush-seated tricycle, and some of the recipients still keep these gifts as cherished mementoes.

Cimarrón was the home of Frank Springer, one of the founders of the State Museum of Art at Santa Fe. Coming from Iowa in 1873, he settled here and became one of the leading lawyers of the Southwest. He was also the author of numerous works on paleontology, a member of the Archeological Institute of America, and the outstanding patron of the School of American Archeology at Santa Fe. He contributed generously to the expense of building the Art Museum in the capital and donated some of the finest collections in both Santa Fe museums. His brother, Charlie Springer, was for many years one of the State's most prominent citizens.

Cimarrón was the seat of Colfax County from 1872 to 1882 but declined with the transfer of the county seat to Springer. A new wave of prosperity came in 1905-06, when a branch line was built by the St. Louis, Rocky Mt. & Pacific Railroad (later sold to the Atchison, Topeka & Santa Fe Railway) to Cimarrón and Ute Park (*see below*). The Cimarrón Townsite Company bought a tract of land on the north side of the river called New Town and sold residence lots to the homeseekers who came in with the railroad. In addition to the two hotels

Cimarrón's interesting buildings include: the AGENCY WAREHOUSE, built 1848, still in good condition and now occupied as a residence; the old COUNTY JAIL AND COURTHOUSE, both built in 1854. The NATIONAL HOTEL built in 1858, the first hotel in town, is behind the Don Diego; adjoining the Canyon Lunch in Old Town, is SWINK'S GAMBLING HALL, built in 1854, now a garage. Swink's Hall rivaled Maxwell's home as the best place in Cimarrón for one to become rich —or poor—overnight. In the CIMARRÓN CEMETERY graves of many pioneers of Colfax County are marked by wooden headpieces, many of them illegible. The remains of Davy Crockett, the desperado, killed in September 1876, when he refused to surrender to Deputy Sheriff Joe Holbrook, are in a grave whose marker was stolen by a stranger claiming to be his relative.

The CIMARRÓN POLO FIELD AND RACE TRACK is at the west end of New Town.

Left from Cimarrón on NM 21 to the PHILMONT RANCH, 1.8 m., owned by Waite Phillips of Oklahoma, a private game preserve where buffalo, elk, antelope, and other animals are protected by a 12-foot fence. It had formerly been Kit Carson's Rayado Ranch, established in 1849 when the noted scout hoped to settle down. His services were too valuable to the government, however, and he spent only a short time here. CARSON'S HOME, a two-room adobe, was recently restored and put in good condition. Beyond the Philmont Ranch is a junction with a dirt road, 3.1 m. Right on this road is a rock called the TOOTH OF TIME, 4.2 m., an eroded formation resembling an immense incisor, a landmark for miles around. For several years a glass jar has been left there, in which visitors deposit slips of paper with the name and date of their visit.

At 40.3 m. is junction with dirt road.

Left on this road is CHASE RANCH, 3.1 m., a large estate occupied by Lew Wallace (one time governor of New Mexico) when he was working on *Ben Hur.*

CIMARRÓN CANYON, 44.8 m., is a narrow, twisting gorge whose stone walls seem to hang over the highway. Scrub pine, juniper, and aspen cover the sides coming down to the very edge of the road. Fine camping spots privately owned are along the highway (*50¢ charge for camping*).

The north walls of Cimarrón Canyon are chiefly of cretaceous sandstone, while those of the south side are broken with diorite, making alternate ridges and gulches that slope to the river.

CIMARRONCITA CAMP (L), 53.1 m., a camp for girls established in 1931, is near the site of a fierce battle between the Ute and Comanche.

UTE PARK, 56.6 m. (7,706 alt., 100 pop.), was named for the Ute Indians, who lived on the east slope of near-by Mount Baldy. The rebellious Ute resisted their white oppressors, and an Indian Agency and military force were maintained at Cimarrón to keep them subdued, until they were finally moved to a reservation in southern Colorado and Utah. The village of Ute Park, opposite the mouth of Ute Creek, is the terminus of an Atchison, Topeka & Santa Fe Railway branch that parallels US 64 and is a distributing point for freight for Moreno Valley, Red River, and Taos.

West of Ute Park, US 64 follows the twisting Cimarrón River through a region that abounds in thick pine and aspen forests. The CIMARRÓN PALISADES (R), a formation of red sandstone that rises eight hundred feet above the highway, extend for about two miles along the railroad. In certain lights the Palisades are a mass of color, and even on cloudy days their strength and beauty of form are striking.

After two hairpin turns, the highway climbs over the hills into MORENO VALLEY, and at 64.6 *m.* (L) EAGLE NEST LAKE (*boats and tackle for rent*) is visible. Considered by some the best trout lake in the State, this body of water is annually visited by hundreds of fishermen. The State Game Department stocks the lake with fish and the public is permitted to fish from the banks without charge.

At 68.1 *m.* is the junction with a dirt road.

Left on this road past EAGLE NEST LODGE to EAGLE NEST DAM, 0.5 *m.*, built by the Springer Brothers in 1912. The dam is 140 feet high and impounds 100,000 acre-feet of water, which is used to irrigate 70,000 acres of land and to provide electric power for Springer, Maxwell, French, and other points. Here is the EAGLE NEST FISH HATCHERY, a Federal hatchery that is in operation only during the spawning season for trout.

EAGLE NEST, 68.4 *m.* (8,500 alt., 400 pop.), was formerly called Therma (Gr. hot). For several years both names were used, but in 1935 the name of the post office was officially changed to Eagle Nest. About the first of May an annual Free Fish Fry here is attended by about 5,000 persons. There are three restaurants, two of which offer night-club entertainment. The population, including some German and Irish as well as Spanish-Americans, is largely engaged in cattle raising and mining.

Right from Eagle Nest on NM 38, a graded gravel road, to ELIZABETH-TOWN, 4.8 *m.*, (142 pop.), a ghost mining town. NM 38 continues through the RED RIVER CANYON, one of the most beautiful in the State, to a junction with NM 3 in QUESTA, 30.2 *m.* (1,029 pop.) (*see Tour 3a*).

South of Eagle Nest US 64 follows a winding course through the Moreno (dark or brunette) Valley. In autumn this area of farming and grazing land is beautifully colored with the yellow of aspen trees, the red of the oak on the surrounding hills, and vivid purple wildflowers dotting the carpet of brown grass.

AGUA FRÍA (cold water), 77.5 *m.* (9,800 alt., 372 pop.), is on the CIENEGUILLA (little marsh) CREEK which empties into Eagle Nest Lake. One of the surrounding peaks, bearing the same name as the village, is nearly 11,000 feet high.

West of Agua Fría US 64 makes a series of switchbacks over the Sangre de Cristo Range, climbing PALO FLECHADO (tree shot with arrows) HILL. The unusual name comes from an old Taos Indian custom of shooting the remaining arrows into a large tree after buffalo hunts. At the summit of the mountain near PALO FLECHADO

PASS (9,038 alt.) is the tree containing the arrows. The highway enters Taos County and continues down into TAOS CANYON in another series of hairpin turns, passing through the settlement of GUS-DORF, 84.6 *m.,* a village of 50 inhabitants.

The highway crosses a section of the CARSON NATIONAL FOREST. Here along Taos Creek four public campgrounds (L) are maintained by the Forest Service, providing water, wood, and sanitary facilities for free camping.

CAÑÓN, 96.6 *m.* (7,100 alt., 546 pop.), at the head of Taos Valley, is one of the oldest Spanish-American settlements in the valley, settled between 1700 and 1725. The site was chosen because of the abundance of water and because it was outside the boundaries of the Taos Pueblo Indian Land. TAOS PEAK (12,282 alt.) visible (R.) is referred to as the Sacred Mountain by the Taos Pueblo Indians, whose pueblo is at its base. The road leads across the valley through well-cultivated ranches.

TAOS, 98.7 *m.* (7,050 alt., 1,847 pop.), (*see Taos*).

# *Tour 2A*

Pojoaque—San Ildefonso—Ótowi—Frijoles Canyon (Bandelier National Monument)—Valle Grande—Cuba; 79.3 *m.,* NM 4 and NM 126.

Graveled road with steep grades and sharp curves; arroyos dangerous in flood time.
Accommodations at Ótowi and Frijoles Canyon.
Route intersects Denver & Rio Grande Western Railroad at Ótowi.

Along this route is a visual record of the ages written in the land itself; multiformed stone, volcanic thrusts, mesa lands, wind- and water-gouged canyons, and the rugged mountains are vestiges of the time, eons ago, when the violent earth outlined its contour. Another chapter of a later day when this area was peopled is found in the ruins of dwellings atop high plateaus, in caves, and in carvings on cliffs.

In the Indian pueblos, of early origin but still occupied, is preserved the mode of living found by the conquering Spaniard 400 years ago. Along the arroyo banks are *ranchitos* with adobe houses, juniper-post corrals, and barns similar to those of the Spanish colonists who first established them. These, together with larger *haciendas* of later Americans, make the contemporary scene. Tuff cliffs and mesa table-lands; monumental natural carvings resembling cathedrals, or cubistic statuary; sequestered valleys interlaced by irrigation ditches, dotted with apricot and peach orchards, wild plum thickets, and chili patches; inhabited pueblos and ruins—these and much more are passed in turn.

NM 4 branches west from US 64 (*see Tour 3a*) in POJOAQUE, 0 *m.* and winds along the south bank of the Nambé River through small ranches; land once owned by Indians, now by others. Generally nondescript, these farms become colorful in the fall when the scarlet strings of drying chili, golden leaves of cottonwoods, and the russet basket willows make vivid the countryside. To the right across the river and paralleling the highway almost to the Rio Grande rises a long, high, eroded range of pinkish hills, the Santa Fe marl.

The TESUQUE RIVER, 0.2 *m.,* a sandy bed except during floodtime (*dangerous to ford if more than 3 inches deep*), is crossed near its confluence (R) with the Nambé River, called the Pojoaque River west to its junction with the Rio Grande.

JACONA (Ha-kó-nah), 1.9 *m.,* a small settlement, is on the site of Jacona Pueblo, abandoned in 1696 when the inhabitants joined other Tewa Pueblos. At the time of the 1680 rebellion this was a *visita* of the Nambé Mission. In 1709 the Jacona grant became the property of Ignacio de Roybal.

At intervals along this portion of the road are the adobe homes of Fred Glidden, John Glidden, and Edith Warner, writers; Allan Clark, sculptor; and Cady Wells, painter. These houses, though finely furnished, are inconspicuous among the externally similar homes of the native inhabitants.

West of Jacona, the highway crosses a sand flat caused by the overflow of the Pojoaque River; the many sandy arroyos here are hazardous immediately after a hard downpour.

A good view of TUNYO (Ind., very spotted), also called Black Mesa or Orphan Mesa (R), a stark, isolated volcanic butte, is at 3.5 *m.* This is the traditional home of Savayo or Tsabiyo, a giant who ate the children of the San Ildefonso Pueblo. After long suffering the *cacique* made medicine for protection, and in answer to his prayers the Twin War Gods killed the giant by allowing him to eat them and then cutting open his stomach. At the instant of his death, smoke and flame burst from the mountains in the four corners of the earth and his blood flowed out in the form of steaming lava.

At 4.5 *m.* is the junction with a dirt road.

Right on this road to the PUEBLO OF SAN ILDEFONSO (*obtain permission to photograph*), 1.2 *m.,* a Tewa-speaking village on the east bank of the Rio Grande below the mouth of the Pojoaque River. Don Juan de Oñate in 1598 gave the name Boye to the old village that was about a mile from the present pueblo. The Tewa name Ci-po-que means place where the water cuts through. San Ildefonso people say their ancestors once lived in the cliffs across the Rio Grande, in the ruins of Ótowi and Tsánkawi on the Pajarito Plateau (*see below*). According to tradition, when water grew scarce they moved to the place in the valley now marked by large village ruins. The present settlement on the east bank consists of many one-story and several two-story adobe houses built around two large plazas. The mission and monastery were founded in 1617 under Friar Cristóbal de Salazar. In 1628 Benavides wrote that the church at San Ildefonso "upon which the Religious have put much care" was very beautiful.   While General Juan Francisco Treviño was governor and captain-general of the Province in 1675, Indians of the Tewa nation were accused of having bewitched Friar Anares (Andrés) Durán, superior of the convent at San Ildefonso, his brother, sister-in-law, and an Indian interpreter.   More than 40 persons were arrested and all pleaded guilty. Forty-three were sentenced to be whipped and sold into slavery and four to be executed.   Of the four, one was hanged in Nambé, another in the pueblo of San Felipe, a third in Jémez, and the fourth hanged himself. At the time of the Pueblo Revolt in 1680 the village had about 800 inhabitants and two resident missionaries, with Santa Clara and San Juan as *visitas*.   During the revolt of that year Fray Luis de Morales and his assistant, Antonio Sánchez de Pío, were murdered.

When De Vargas reconquered New Mexico in 1692, San Ildefonso acknowledged its allegiance without protest; but later in 1694, when De Vargas marched against the northern tribes, the San Ildefonsons entrenched themselves on Black Mesa.   Although the Spaniards fought valiantly for a time the Tewa repelled all their attacks but were eventually conquered.

After the declaration of peace in 1694 the missions were reestablished, but in 1696 several of the Pueblo tribes again rebelled and during the night of June 4 the San Ildefonso Indians closed all the openings and set fire to both church and convent.   Fray Francisco Corvera as well as Fray Antonio Moreño of Nambé, who was visiting him, were burned alive.   Immediately after, the Indians fled to Black Mesa where Spanish forces again forced them to surrender.

Spanish archives record that between 1717 and 1722 a new chapel was erected at San Ildefonso.   However, a part of the 1696 monastery remained until late in the nineteenth century.   Nothing is left of the beautiful old church and monastery, which were torn down before 1900 to make way for the present church west of the north plaza, a simple white-washed adobe structure.   Several paintings, some on elk and buffalo hide, materials used in early times because of the scarcity of canvas, formerly decorated the interior.

The San Ildefonso Pueblo Grant first made by Spain was confirmed by the United States in 1858 for 17,292 acres.   The GOVERNMENT DAY SCHOOL that children of the pueblo attend is slightly north of the North Plaza.

San Ildefonso has long been known for the skill of its craftsmen and through the encouragement of the School of American Research, the Indian Arts Fund, and particularly the endeavors of Mr. Kenneth Chapman, expert on Indian ceramics and design, today it is a leader in art and pottery. It was here that Crescencio Martínez developed the old technique in Indian watercolor painting under the patronage of Dr. Edgar L. Hewett, director of the Museum of New Mexico.   Awa Tsireh, Louis Gonzales, Abel Sánchez, and other well known painters live at San Ildefonso, which is the home of Julian Martínez and his wife Marie, said to be the best known designers and makers of the famous black and red pottery.   Here may be seen bowls, vases, plates, and jars in all the processes of molding, firing, decorating, and polishing.   Because of the ready market for its handicrafts, the village has a high pro rata income.

The site of this pueblo is especially attractive with the Jémez Range on the west, the Truchas on the east, and the Black Mesa directly north.   The construction of homes and the daily life of the inhabitants, who are a friendly and courteous people, seem to be much the same as many years ago.   On January 23, which is their fiesta, the Buffalo and Comanche dances are performed on alternate years.

Near the pueblo are four sacred springs and hill-top shrines, which are not visited by the general public.   The volcanic butte Tunyo is also venerated as the home of the giant.   Though the Twin War Gods killed him long ago, even today Tsabiyo is occasionally used by Tewa mothers as the bogeyman to frighten their children into obedience.   Every autumn in some of the Tewa villages an impersonator of Tsabiyo, dressed in traditional costume, comes to the village with whip in hand to punish men, women, and children who have transgressed during the year.

NM 4 at 6.3 *m.* approaches the bottom farm lands (R) of the Rio Grande, the majority of which belong to the San Ildefonsons. In the spring before the Indians start work on irrigation ditches, cleaning them of debris and preparing for the spring flow, they usually hold dances asking the boon of plentiful water. In autumn they thresh their grain on primitive earthen threshing floors, using goats or horses to tramp it out.

Beyond rolling hills with a mesa (L), NM 4 crosses a suspension bridge over the Rio Grande. ÓTOWI, 7.8 *m.,* contains EDITH WARNER'S TEA ROOM (*overnight accommodations for a limited number arranged in advance*), the only place along this part of the route where lunches, teas, and dinners are served.

Between Ótowi and the Cochití Pueblo approximately 20 miles to the south (L), the White Rock Canyon walls in the Rio Grande. This canyon marks the eastern extremity of the PAJARITO (little bird) PLATEAU, a part of the more extensive Jémez Plateau over which the highway continues to Frijoles Canyon. This crescent-shaped plateau, bordered on the east by the Rio Grande, on the north by the Rio Chama, and on the south by Cañada de Cochití, is about 50 miles long and 12 miles wide. Much of it is covered by a sheet of volcanic tuff, varying in thickness from 100 to 1,000 feet, and it is cut by many canyons, mostly east–west gorges, all made by streams tributary to the Rio Grande, which are intermittent in dry seasons. The only permanent stream in this region is the Rito de los Frijoles (*see below*). In this area are 27 large ruins, including the pueblos on the mesas and cliff dwellings, or combinations of both, as well as many small house pueblos and cliff dwellings that have not been touched by the archeologist.

Although the territory was not especially accessible to the nomadic tribes, the fertility of the soil in the canyons and the natural protection of the cliffs and the tuff deposits, that provided an easily worked building material, attracted a considerable population. Just when the "Pajaritans" left the plateau has not been determined, but it is believed the struggle with drought caused the exodus to the Rio Grande pueblos during the fourteenth, fifteenth, and sixteenth centuries.

At 8.1 *m.* is a junction with a gravel road R. that leads north to junction with road to Puyé (*see Tour 7A*).

West of Ótowi the highway ascends a roadway cut in the side (R) of Los Alamos Canyon, which it traverses for five miles. Cliff-like sides of igneous rock rise sheer and rugged, and formations stand out from the bluffs and ridges in groups of illusive images that seem to increase enormously as they apparently rush toward the observer.

At 12.2 *m.* is the junction with a dirt road alternative NM 4.

Right on this road 0.8 *m.* to a side road R. This road, usually passable for cars, leads to the ÓTOWI RUINS (Ind., a gap where water sinks), 1.5 *m.,* on a high square ridge on the valley floor. These were the nucleus of the Ótowi settlement, a large pueblo ruin surrounded by clusters of excavated dwellings in the near-by cliff. The ruins of another pueblo of considerable dimensions, comprising seven small houses, are on a parallel ridge to the south of the main dwelling. The main pueblo ruin at Ótowi differs in plan from others of this region. With the exception of one detached house it consists of a cluster of five houses, situated on sloping ground and connected at one end by a wall. Investigators believe that these houses were a counterpart of the present terraced houses at Taos, though somewhat smaller. Altogether the five houses contained about 450 rooms on the ground floor. The number of superimposed rooms is estimated at 250. The circular *kivas,* all subterranean and outside the walls of the buildings with two exceptions, are incorporated in the Ótowi ruins. Two types of excavated cliff dwellings are found. The crude fireplaces were generally placed beside the doorway but seldom provided with smoke vents. The rooms, rectangular in shape, vary in size; the well-plastered walls are three to four feet high, and the floors levelled and packed.

On the valley floor about 0.7 *m.* north of the main ruins is a cluster of separated conical formations of white tuff, 30 feet high, popularly called "tent rocks." They are honeycombed with caves, both natural and artificial; some have been utilized as human habitations.

Returning to the highway at 0.8 *m.* one may continue up the hill R. Here the road winds over a high plateau until LOS ALAMOS RANCH SCHOOL for boys is reached at 5.9 *m.* This lies in a fertile valley surrounded with rolling fields. From here retrace to the southern NM 4 leading to Frijoles Canyon or proceed over a winding mountain road through forests to another junction with NM 4 beyond the Frijoles turn-off at 11.1 *m.*

At 13.0 *m.* is a junction with an unimproved dirt road, impassable for cars and hardly recognizable.

Left on this road to an Indian trail, 0.2 *m.* L. or R. on this up the mesa to TSÁNKAWI CLIFF DWELLINGS AND RUINS, 0.3 *m.,* a smaller eminence perched upon a larger. The name Tsánkawi, given by the Pueblo Indians, is the Tewa equivalent for "the place of round cactus." This ruin is between Los Alamos and Sandía canyons of the Pajarito Plateau on a long, irregularly shaped mesa, the sides of which are strewn with sharp-edged volcanic rocks common to this region. The sides of the lower mesa contain numerous caves, some formed by erosion and others by human labor. At the summit of the first mesa a path in the rock is well defined, worn fully a foot deep in places by the constant tread of feet in bygone ages. This trail leads to the abrupt walls of the superimposed mesa whose rock sides are indented with a large and forbidding group of petroglyphs evidently devised to frighten enemies away.

A narrow passage, a few feet from the rock etchings, leads to the summit of this mesa. The defile, easily defended, proves the near-impregnable character of the summit. The opening, about ten feet high and two feet wide, extends snakelike in the rock wall; it is a climb of approximately 20 feet to the upper mesa with its magnificent view of the Pajarito Plateau, mountains, valleys, and canyons. Westward (R) is the Jémez Range and far to the east the Sangre de Cristo Range. The main ruin is about 1,000 feet from the citadel, a three-story pile of stone outlining approximately 200 rooms in each story. No excavating has been done, and the hewn stones still lie in heaps. It has been estimated that the inhabitants lived here until the fifteenth century.

South from Tsánkawi 2.5 *m.,* on an ancient trail in the rock, definable for most of the distance, lived Tsánkawi's nearest neighbor of the same period, the combined cliff dwelling and pueblo RUIN OF NÁVAWI. Doubtless the ancient inhabitants were constantly passing back and forth between the four towns of the Pajarito Plateau—Návawi, Tsánkawi, Tshírege, and Ótowi. These communities engaged in common occupations, mainly agriculture; that they watered their crops by irrigation is evident from remains of ditches and reservoirs. No excavation has been done on this ruin, but the main handmade caves and entwining steps are plainly visible. At the top of the mesa, reached by four well-worn stone paths, is the game trap for which the community is named, a pit cut down in solid rock for the purpose of capturing deer, bear, and other game. About six feet long and three feet wide at the top, it widens out as it reaches a depth of fifteen feet.

NM 4 at 14 *m.* runs through yellow pines and in many places are wild flowers indigenous to mountain regions. All this section, now part of the Bandelier National Monument (*see below*), was part of the Ramón Vigil Land Grant.

In PAJARITO CANYON, 18.1 *m.,* cliff caves honeycomb the entire canyon wall beginning at the highway 18.1 *m.*

At 19.1 *m.* is the junction with a dirt road at a sign reading "Guard Station—3 *m.*"

Right on this road 0.2 *m.* (park the car beside the road and walk over one of the trails to the Right) to TSHÍREGE (Ind. bird) RUINS, 0.3 *m.*

Tshírege, with the extensive cliff dwellings clustered about it, was the largest aboriginal settlement in the Pueblo region with the exception of Zuñi. The main dwelling contained approximately 600 rooms with 10 *kivas* of the circular subterranean type. A defensive wall extended from the southwest corner of the main building to the rim of the cliff 150 feet away. Below this wall, cut on the face of the cliff, is one of the best petroglyphs in the Southwest, a representation of a plumed serpent seven feet long. The cliff dwellings along the mesa side, extending for three quarters of a mile, contain the largest number of caves in one group.

Tshírege is said to have been the last of the Pajarito Plateau villages to be abandoned, undoubtedly because the water supply here was greater than at any other Pajaritan settlement. From a spring in the arroyo a quarter-mile away water flows during all seasons; Pajarito Creek in wet seasons also carries water, and reservoir ruins on the mesa top show that river water must have been impounded. W. S. Stallings, Jr., on the staff of the Laboratory of Anthropology, Santa Fe, has determined the date of Tshírege as approximately 1480 to 1581.

Traversing the highlands, NM 4 winds through extensive stands of yellow pine and juniper where the floor of the forest is covered with rabbit brush and a shrub called Apache plume.

A winding descent begins at 22.7 *m.* through Water Canyon (*drive carefully*) and interlacing gorges.·

At 23.9 *m.* is the junction with a graveled road.

Left on this road 3.2 *m.* into BANDELIER NATIONAL MONUMENT, a 26,000-acre reserve in Frijoles Canyon named for Adolph F. Bandelier, American of Swiss parentage who gained world renown as ethnologist, archeologist, and writer. He was the first scientist to make an extensive survey in this region; also the first to study the ethnology and mythology of the Indian groups living around Santa Fe as well as in Mexico and Peru. He worked in this region between the years 1880 and 1886, living in one of the *kivas* of Frijoles Canyon ruins. At the end of his stay he wrote *The Delight Makers,* an ethno-historical novel depicting life of the early Tewa, with Frijoles Canyon and the Tyuonyi Ruins as its setting. El Rito de los Frijoles (the little river of the beans), fed by several springs and the snows of the Jémez Range, threads its way through the canyon, passing between cliffs that contain prehistoric dwellings of a Pajaritan tribe whose cliff caves and community structure have become noted throughout the world. As the highway approaches the ruins, deep clefts in the earth (L) and sheer stony sides capped with basalt form a natural barrier to this prehistoric home of the Indian.

At 3.2 m. the road ends in a small plaza which affords ample parking space. Around this plaza are the FRIJOLES CANYON LODGE (*guides and horses available*), the only available accommodations in the canyon, the WAYSIDE MUSEUM, and the ADMINISTRATION BUILDING (*free guides for foot tours through the ruins*), both operated by the National Park Service. This canyon, a deep gash 17 miles long and varying from 300 to 600 feet in depth, runs from the east slope of the Jémez Mountains to the Rio Grande, entering White Rock Canyon and cutting through a great crescent-shaped volcanic plain that spreads out like a huge fan south and east of the mountains. This plain, formed by ash thrown by once active volcanoes of the Jémez Range, is overlaid in many places with later flows of basalt. The canyon floor is a sedimentary soil, tillable and easily worked. Yellow pine and spruce, interspersed with cottonwood, box elder, and willow, line the creek banks. It is thought that Frijoles Canyon was first occupied about 1250 A.D. During 300 years the inhabitants built 13 groups of houses, which in their heyday might have held a population of between 1,500 to 2,000. These village ruins extend for 2.5 miles in the lower part of the canyon. Each village, built of lava blocks, contained 20 to 25 rooms and stood one to four stories high. Above them were cave rooms varying in dimensions from a few feet to as large as 10 feet square. The rooms, both on the canyon floor and in the cliff caves, were usually coated with a plaster of rotted gypsum, which remains intact. The *kiva* (Ind., ceremonial room), circular in form and either sunken below ground level or cut back into the cliff, was an important part of each village. The circular form and sunken position is said to symbolize the original earth passage through which the early Indians came in their transition from the original "down below" world to this world of light. These *kivas* served as council chambers for the men and were the center of the religious activities of the clan.

Of the three other villages on the canyon floor, the great community house of TYUONYI and its isolated *kivas* are the major remains and are adjudged by archeologists the central point of population. Although a fair composite picture of the ruins may be obtained from the Administration Building, the individual village, the *kivas,* and caves become much more interesting upon closer inspection.

Left (*on horseback*) from Frijoles Canyon Lodge on a trail winding up the south side of the canyon wall and across the south mesa to the SHRINES OF YAPASHI (a name given to fetishes representing human forms), part of the prehistoric Yapashi Ruins Pueblo on the plateau between Capulín and Álamo Canyons southwest of the west rim of Frijoles Canyon. This pueblo, similar to other major ruins, consists of a single great community house or group of houses with some outlying cliff dwellings. It has been estimated that several hundred inhabitants lived here. Forming a triangle with the pueblo ruins are two shrines, 9 m., one commonly known as the STONE LIONS and the other designated as the SHRINE OF THE STONE ALTAR. The Stone Lions lie west of the pueblo ruins in a circular enclosure, 23 feet high. Two parallel walls of similar height, forming a passageway five feet in width, extend from one side for a distance of 20 feet. Within this enclosure are life-sized effigies of crouching mountain lions or pumas carved from lava. While crude, these figures are of graceful proportions and are readily identified. They are 16 inches high and each is two feet wide at the base and six feet long. The Tewa and other Pueblo Indians still visit this shrine and sprinkle the figures with sacred meal. The trail continues to the SHRINE OF LA CUEVA PINTADA (the painted cave), 12 m., a large cavity in the northeast wall of Capulín Canyon. Stairs for hand- and foot-holds, cut in the vertical face of the tuff wall, afford a perilous ascent to the cave, 50 feet from the base of the cliff, where two communicating rooms facing southwest are carved high in the cliff. A crude stairway of 16 hand- and foot-holds leads up to the door of the room on the left and a similar stairway passes down from the door of the room on the right. Between the stairways at the cliff's base rises a column of stone three feet high and two feet thick, in the top of which is carved a basin more than a foot in diameter and half of that in depth. The larger room has a banquette extending around the sides and back, above which are etched many pictographs, easily distinguishable in the smoke-stained walls and ceiling.

On the circular wall at the back of the cave conventional symbols, such as clouds, lightning, masked dancers, and the sun are painted with carbon, calcite, and red ocher. Occupying a conspicuous position in the center of the frieze is a great plumed serpent, the *Awanyu,* keeper of the waters, or rain god of the Tewa.

Continuing from the junction NM 4 before crossing the JÉMEZ MOUNTAINS with magnificent views of ranges on the north, east, and south, arrives at junction with alternative NM 4 (*see above*) at 32.3 *m.*

VALLE GRANDE, 35.2 *m.,* long thought to be a valley, has been identified as an extinct crater (8,500 alt. of floor; 9,000 alt. of rim), 176 square miles in area, said to be the largest measured crater on earth. Mountains rise up from its sides, and down in the crater cattle, horses, and sheep graze. Its grassy, smooth immensity with trees on the slopes above and a vast expanse of sky, makes it one of the most attractive places in the vicinity of Santa Fe. (*During bad weather make inquiry concerning road.*)

In Valle Grande is the junction with NM 126 which the route follows over the NACIMIENTO RANGE through grassy mountain meadows with vistas of great beauty at several points along the road. As the road ascends the eastern slope of the range, there is a fine view of REDONDO MOUNTAIN (11,250 alt.) to the east toward Valle Grande. On through forests of aspen, fir, and pine, past many attractive camping spots, to the top of the pass (9,000 alt.), then continuing over a dirt road rich red against the dark green of the forests down into Señorita Canyon, with magnificent vistas ahead to the west as the road twists and turns in its descent. On past and over mountain streams and more red road to the plain on which Cuba is situated. This last part of the trip is easy when the road is dry. (*Inquire about road conditions after a rain.*)

In CUBA, 79.3 *m.,* is the junction with US 84 (*see Tour 9*).

# *Tour 3*

(San Luis, Colo.)—Costilla—Questa—Taos—Velarde—Santa Fe—Galisteo—Moriarty—Willard—Corona; NM 3, US 64, US 85, NM 41, US 60, NM 42.
Colorado Line to Junction US 54 with NM 42, 239.7 *m.*

NM 3 is a two-lane, bituminous-paved road to Questa; graded gravel to Taos. US 64 is graded gravel between Taos and Velarde, bituminous-paved to Santa Fe.
US 285 is graded gravel; US 60 bituminous-paved; NM 41 graded gravel; NM 42 gravel and dirt.
A.T. & S.F. Ry. roughly parallels Section b. between Galisteo and Willard.
Hotels in Taos and Santa Fe; limited accommodations elsewhere.

The first section of this route is through mountainous country, with superb vistas and panoramas. Care should be exercised because of curves, steep hills, and occasional rock slides. There are forests, mountain streams, small irrigated farms, mining, dude ranches, some cattle and sheep, Indians, scenery, and history. The second section is one of vast expanses of level farm and grazing land, with mountains along distant horizons. Herds and flocks are seen, more numerous than in the first section, with large ranches in the Estancia Valley.

### Section a. COLORADO LINE to SANTA FE, 117.1 m.

NM 3 crosses the broad Taos Valley and winds through the Sangre de Cristo range, seldom dipping below altitudes of 7,000 feet.

In the tiny hamlet of GARCÍA, NM 3 crosses the State Line, 0 m.

COSTILLA, 1.4 m. (7,500 alt., 805 pop.), a trading point for ranchers, named for the Rio Costilla (Rib River) which curves through the town, is in the southern end of the SAN LUIS VALLEY, whose northern extremity reaches far into Colorado.

In the surrounding area known as Sunshine Valley sheep raising and crops of beans, corn, and chili are the main sources of revenue; a large reservoir on the Rio Costilla north of town provides water for irrigation. UTE PEAK (R), named for the Indians who owned this land, raises its pine-topped head abruptly from the valley floor and has always been used by Indian, hunter, and trail makers as a landmark. Far away COSTILLA PEAK (12,634 alt.), is visible (L), the highest of a series of five hogback formations along the Colorado-New Mexico Line.

Instead of one plaza Costilla had four. In 1852 an expedition of settlers from Taos and Arroyo Hondo, under the leadership of Juan de Jesús Bernal, journeyed to the site of Costilla and laid out the four plazas on land acquired by Carlos Beaubien, who also filed the Maxwell Grant (see Tour 2b). Two of the plazas, LA PLAZA DEL MEDIO (middle), the first constructed, and LA PLAZA DE ABAJO (lower), part of which lies in Colorado, are along the highway.

Though Costilla remains an unhurried community that observes the feast days it has had many flurries of excitement. Rumors of gold strikes on several occasions have attracted floating populations, and the formation of a million-dollar Dutch company to irrigate and exploit the fertile valley for a time focused attention on this area.

LA PLAZA DE ARRIBA (upper) was built at the southeastern end of the original settlement. A torreón (tower) here, now partly in ruins, was a part of the PLAZA DEL PELEE. It was four stories high, and through its portholes guards kept long vigils for marauding Ute and Apache who made repeated attempts to steal sheep and horses.

Left from the post office in Costilla on a dirt road the highway threads the level floor of Sunshine Valley. The SANGRE DE CRISTO MOUNTAINS (13,306 alt.), rugged and snow-capped, barricade the blue horizon (L). Enveloped at times by violet haze, encircled at others with lazily rolling, fleecy clouds, they afford an ever-changing picture of grandeur, strength, and beauty. The soil is loose and rocky; lack of water makes it suitable only for sheep raising. The Rio Grande flows south through the valley, and some farming is done on its banks. Small close-huddled communities dot the river bottom at intervals, the economic life of the residents being dependent chiefly on the raising of sheep. The valley, approximately 20 miles in width, is a vast stretch of sage and rabbit brush. The species of sagebrush common in northern New Mexico plateau regions is *Artemisia tridentata,* a woody, erect bush, with pungently aromatic foliage, which usually grows from two to three feet high.

The rocky sides of beautiful RED RIVER CANYON (L), 21.5 *m.,* are outlined with varicolored jagged peaks, their green sides covered most of the year with snow.

QUESTA (sloping land where runs a road), 22.2 *m.* (7,469 alt., 1,029 pop.), originally named San Antonio del Rio Colorado, the third largest town in Taos County, is on a ridge of gravel on the north side of Red River and west of Cabestro Creek. There is an attractive free camping ground at the mouth of the canyon. Unadorned by anything modern and with a large majority of its residents of Spanish and Mexican stock, Questa is still an authentic picture of life as it was during the Mexican regime. Agriculture is the main pursuit. Sheep are raised in considerable numbers, crops are watered from the Red and Cabestro (rope) streams, and some placer mining is carried on in near-by mountains.

Questa had several beginnings and sudden endings because the Ute and Apache discouraged adventurous settlers who wished to work the fertile river bottoms.

In 1829 Don Francisco Laforet built a home on the river bottom but was forced to move to the ridge the better to watch for marauders. These settlers held out and in 1872 obtained a grant containing 115,000 acres. Old documents show that in 1849 one hundred families were living in Rio Colorado and eagerly greeted the mountain men and traders who came in covered wagons on the old Taos Trail. Indians attacked again in 1854 and during this campaign a six-foot wall with only one entrance was built around the town. The church, erected in 1873, is Questa's oldest building. In 1884 when the town acquired a post office, the name was changed to Questa.

NM 3 dips into a wide fertile valley and passes the tiny settlement of EMBARGO, then climbs through an evergreen area for several miles. Beyond the woods is the San Cristóbal Valley, checked with small farms, well-irrigated and well-kept.

SAN CRISTÓBAL, 34.3 m. (7,450 alt., 291 pop.), is a half-hidden farming community settled in 1860, and inhabited almost entirely by descendants of Spaniards and Mexicans. Until 1930 there was no post office, and prior to 1912 all trading was done at Arroyo Hondo, 4 miles south.

At 35.2 m. at the top of a hill is a junction with a dirt road.

Left on this road along LOBO MOUNTAIN (12,104 alt.) to the log HOME OF MISS DOROTHY BRETT, 2.1 m., English painter and writer (see Literature). KIOWA RANCH, 5 m., home of Frieda Lawrence, widow of D. H. Lawrence (1885-1930), the English author (see Literature), stands below a knoll on which is a mausoleum containing Lawrence's ashes. The road to Kiowa Ranch is dangerous when wet and is sometimes impassable in winter.

ARROYO HONDO (deep brook), 40.5 m. (6,998 alt., 519 pop.), settled in 1823, has three plazas. It is in the Hondo Valley among the fertile fields along the river bottom. In addition to crops, sheep and cattle are raised. At the turn of the century, a mining boom caused an influx of prospectors and gold seekers, but as the output was limited the boom soon collapsed and the community settled back to its former way of life. Two chapters of the Penitente order are active in Arroyo Hondo, and their WEST MORADA (no visitors) in the central plaza is recognized by its large wooden cross.

The REAL HOME (L) on NM 3, an old, two-storied, balconied house, is owned by the Real family, prominent in the early affairs of the community. Beyond the Real home, the highway makes a right-angle turn, crosses a bridge over the Hondo River, and continues up a steep grade. Near the top of the grade (R) is MARTÍNEZ STORE (1826), which once was the granary and trading center of the village. Adjacent to the store and residence are the ruins of the private chapel of the Martínez family.

1. Right from Arroyo Hondo on a dirt road to a charred mass of ruins, 2 m., all that remains of TURLEY'S MILL AND DISTILLERY. Simeon Turley, an American, came to the canyon in 1830 and in a few years had the most flourishing ranch in the Taos district, with herds of cattle and sheep and acres of corn and wheat. With characteristic Yankee enterprise, he built a dam, impounded the waters of the Hondo, and erected a grist mill which for many years served a large section. He added looms and spinning wheels, and on his ranch were the town's industries. All things necessary to a comfortable, civilized life were made here. Many natives and Pueblo Indians worked for him and were well paid and well fed. He is mentioned as jolly, good-natured, kind, and generous. Then came the uprising of 1847.

During the insurrection Turley at first took no precautions, believing he had no enemies, but when warned that natives and Indians had risen in revolt, that Governor Bent had been killed (see Taos), and that a party of raiders was approaching his establishment, he barricaded the ranch and prepared for its defense. The besiegers offered him his life if he would turn over the ranch and nine Americans with him, but this he contemptuously refused to do, and for two days a pitched battle raged. On the second day the attackers set fire to the mill. Enveloped by smoke Turley and another made their escape. On the way north, Turley met a neighbor whom he had befriended and confided in him. This man told Turley to hide in a deserted ranch near by, and he promised to return the following night with food and a mule. Then he rode straight to the mill and informed the raiders of Turley's whereabouts. At night 30 of them returned to the deserted ranch, called Turley, and when he came out he was riddled with bullets.

2. Left at the Real House in Arroyo Hondo to UPPER PLAZA, 1 *m.,* and the CHURCH OF NUESTRA SEÑORA DE LOS DOLORES. The EAST MORADA (*no visitors*) of the Penitentes, with large wooden crosses at the east of the entrance, stands on a hill south of the church plaza.

South of Arroyo Hondo, NM 3 climbs a series of switchbacks.

The 300-acre ranch (R) at 49.6 *m.* was purchased in 1935 by Baron and Baroness Von Maltzahn. WHEELER PEAK (13,123 alt.), second highest peak in the State, is plainly visible (L). All the mountains of the Sangre de Cristo Range at this point have an altitude in excess of 10,000 feet.

The EL PRADO TRADING POST (L) and ranch owned by Gerson Gusdorf, an early pioneer of Taos, is passed at 50.3 *m.* The settlement here is known as PRADO, south of which the route crosses the Rio Lucero (river of the morning star), which, fed from the north slopes of Taos Mountain (L) and the Rio Pueblo, is the source of irrigation for Taos Valley.

In the small hamlet of PLACITA, 50.8 *m.,* is an adobe church belonging to the Church of Jesus Christ of Latter-day Saints (Mormon).

In TAOS, 51.7 *m.* (7,050 alt., 1,847 pop.), (*see Taos*), is a junction with US 64, which the route now follows.

RANCHOS DE TAOS, 55.4 *m.* (6,900 alt., 1,035 pop.), an old village of adobe, is a quiet community and the home of many members of the Penitente Order. Near the foothills of the Sangre de Cristo Mountains, Ranchos commands a splendid view of the whole valley and specially of Taos and its protective background of rugged peaks. There is little activity at any time except during festive periods, such as St. Francis Day, October 4, and the annual play, *Los Comanches,* which is held on January 25 in co-operation with the adjoining village of Llano Quemado. This play in Spanish, enacted on horseback, has as its plot the rescue of two children captured by Comanche. The play ends with a grand entrance into the church.

According to Indian tradition, Ranchos de Taos was founded by members of Taos Pueblo who sought better fields for their crops. With the coming of the Spaniards, the settlement became known as Las Trampas (the traps). As with other frontier towns of New Mexico, it was raided by Apache and Comanche. In the center of the village is the SAINT FRANCIS OF ASSISI MISSION (*Guide service within the church, 25¢ usual gift; disregard small boys outside*) built by the Franciscans. It fell into disuse and was rebuilt about 1772, but there is a dispute as to the date of its founding. This fortress-like adobe building, famous for its exceptionally thick walls supported by great abutments and its white stucco exterior, is 120 feet long and is surrounded by a six-foot wall. The bells are in two front towers, one slightly higher than the other. Two of the abutments on the front facade are the full width of the towers and form two great pylons flanking an unusual arched entrance portal having surface tracery and double, paneled doors. Buttresses are also placed at the corners of the transepts, and at the end wall of the apse. At the crossing are four diagonal bracings aiding two heavy beams supporting the nave and transept *vigas,* spaced unusually close together and springing from double-scrolled brackets. The only modern note in the interior is the altar of French design. The large reredos, 25 feet high, with its carved pillars and wooden partitions, contains seven paintings so old that it is impossible to tell which saints most of them represent. There are also several old paintings done on wood by native artists.

In Ranchos is a junction (L) with NM 3 (*see Tour 11*).

US 64 parallels the Rio Grande, running beside the river for 14 miles. (*Drive carefully through the canyon because of occasional rock slides.*) Along here are many places where it is safe to park; also vantage points for fishing.

PILAR, 62.2 *m.* (6,550 alt., 130 pop.), a primitive farming community on a cone-shaped delta surrounded by rugged hills and canyon walls, is an area cultivated by the Jicarilla Apache in pre-Spanish times. In 1694 their village was burned by De Vargas. Finally in 1795 twenty families were given a grant here, one of the provisions being that all pastures and watering places must be communal. That settlement is now known as Cieneguilla (little marsh).

In 1822 Governor Melgares ordered that the Jicarilla Apache be allowed to live and farm in Cieneguilla, but the Spanish-Mexicans protested so vigorously that the order was never enforced. Forgotten by the American government, the Indians were in dire straits, starving close to the land that really belonged to them. In 1854, when the territory had become American, they revolted and were engaged in battle near the village by the U. S. dragoons. An unknown number of them were killed, as well as 22 soldiers. The dragoons retreated to Fort Burgwin where Kit Carson and his niece, Teresina Bent, helped bury the dead. Meanwhile, a larger body of soldiers pursued the Indians, but they escaped. Later that year they were compelled to sign a treaty. The old bridge at Pilar, erected in the early 1880's, is the newest of a series of bridges that have been built at this spot, the earliest believed to be in 1598. A large cross tops a conical hill near by, while ahead is a great copper-colored cliff. This has been one of the chief gold-mining sections of New Mexico for many years.

GLEN-WOODY BRIDGE, 65.2 *m.,* is a suspension bridge that crosses the Rio Grande and leads to the RUINS OF GLEN-WOODY MINING CAMP on the west bank. A town was laid out here in 1902, and a large flume, in which was installed a 160-horsepower turbine, was built just north of the bridge on the east bank to supply power for mining machinery. A hotel and other buildings were erected and hopes were high. But the venture was a failure, and the town literally rotted away. Mining activities in this region, embracing the area east of US 64 about as far as Picurís, have been widespread. Copper mining, very active about 1900-02, has been practically abandoned owing to the low prices of this metal. The only mine open is the Lilac, producing lepidolite used in the manufacture of shatter-proof glass and glass cooking utensils.

Near RINCONADA (Sp. place in the corner), 69.4 *m.*, the river valley widens between towering cliffs on both sides of the river.

At 72.6 *m.* is the junction with NM 75, a graded dirt road.

Right on NM 75, 15.2 *m.* to the junction with a dirt road.

Right on this road 5.4 *m.* to LAS TRAMPAS (Sp. the traps) (106 pop.) known as the "Place of the Early Settlers." This adobe-walled town with flat-roofed mud houses is a part of seventeenth century Spain and Mexico set down in the heart of New Mexico. Customs go back to Spanish colonial days and farming is carried on in the manner of the past, crops being harvested by hand, goats or horses stamping out the grain in the primitive manner. Wooden plows are still used on some of the *ranchitos.* On the plaza here is the *Santo Tomás del Rio de Las Trampas Church,* first known as The Church of the Twelve Apostles and later as La Iglesia de San José. It is built of adobe, with walls four feet thick and 34 feet high relieved of their severity only by small towers on the front façade. Between these two bell towers is an outside choir balcony from which in the old days the choir sang while the procession moved outside the church. All took part in this, the men on the left and the women on the right; at its head marched four men carrying the canopy to cover the Holy Spirit of the Estandartes. Behind these came two more who chanted the *Ave Maria* and sang hymns. Tradition says 350 years is its age, but *Historic Building Survey* gives its date as 1760. There were two bells—both containing gold and silver—which were rung by striking them with a rock. One because of its gentle tone was named Gracia (Grace) and was rung for Mass and for the deaths of infants, while the other with a heavier tone, called Refugio (Refuge), was rung for masses for the dead or for the death of an adult. Since Refugio was stolen a few years ago, Gracia is used on all occasions. The reredos is a fine example of early painting, said to have been brought from Spain through Mexico. Within the entrance of the church a door (R) leads to a small room in which is kept the death cart of the Penitente Order. A black draped, carved skeleton is mounted on a crude two-wheeled cart; its wheels, three feet in diameter, hewn from solid logs. Doña Sebastiana (as the figure is called) holds a bow and arrow in her bony fingers. She is trundled by two men in the Holy Week processions of the Order, and tradition has it that the image has been known to discharge the arrow at an unrepentant sinner.

Trampas has long been a center of the Penitentes, their rites being performed during Holy Week of each year, with a procession of cross bearers and the Death Cart to the *Calvario* (Sp. Calvary), a quarter of a mile from the church.

East on NM 75, to a junction (L) with a dirt road, 16 *m.* Left on this road 0.9 *m.* to PICURÍS PUEBLO, (8,400 alt., 98 pop.), formerly a prosperous village. The name is from Keresan *Pikuria* meaning "those who paint." The walls are of puddled adobe, laid without forms, one of the few inhabited pueblos so constructed. At present the Picurís make culinary pottery, do some weaving, and embroider black *mantas.* However, farming and goat raising are the principal means of livelihood. Picurís celebrates San Lorenzo's Day, August 10th, with Mass in the morning followed by traditional dances. After the pueblo had been visited by the Coronado Expedition in 1540 there was no further record of Europeans being here until 1598, when Oñate commenced organized mission work, establishing San Lorenzo (St. Lawrence) de Picurís Mission with Fray Francisco de Zamora in charge. The church was built soon after 1620 with Fray Martín de Arvide, later murdered on his way to the Zuñi country in 1632, as the missionary. By 1629 San Lorenzo was an important mission, and the priest was in charge of a number of smaller neighboring villages. Father Alonzo de Benavides, the priest-historian, wrote in 1630 that there were about 2,000 Indian converts at Picurís; he said these Indians were the most savage in the province and were often "miraculously restrained" from killing the Franciscans. Under increasing Spanish domination during the seventeenth century, the Picurís grew more and more discontented, and Luis Tu-pa-tu, governor of the pueblo, with Jaca of Taos and Catiti of Santo Domingo, ably assisted Po-pé in organizing the Pueblo Revolt of 1680. After the Spaniards left New Mexico in 1680 it was Tu-pa-tu of Picurís who succeeded Po-pé, the main leader of the revolt. There were then about 3,000 Indians at Picurís and Tu-pa-tu was the most powerful and influential chieftain in the entire province.

Following the Reconquest by De Vargas in 1692, Tu-pa-tu, mounted on a fine horse, appeared in full Spanish costume at the governor's palace in Santa Fe and offered not only his allegiance but his assistance in subduing the still hostile tribes. The Picurís had abandoned their pueblo in 1680, but soon after 1692 the pueblo was rebuilt on or near the old site, and SAN LORENZO DE PICURÍS CHURCH, cruciform with a walled forecourt, was erected. It is one of the most interesting of the old missions in New Mexico. The only decorative element on the exterior is the false, stepped gable end, placed in the center and pierced with a rectangular opening for a bell. Inside is a gridiron representing the instrument of torture upon which San Lorenzo was slowly burned to death; and hanging on the wall near the door is a human skull covered with a white cloth whose history is no longer known. The altar screen has some very old paintings.

Between 1695 and 1696, Picurís joined with other tribes in asking for wide distribution of resident Franciscans in the various pueblos, the concealed reason for the request being the desire to scatter the Spanish forces. In 1696 they joined in the revolt in which five Franciscans and 21 Spaniards were killed. In the autumn of 1696 the Picurís feigned a desire for peace in order to save their crops, but De Vargas fearing treachery marched against them, captured 84, many of them women and children whom he distributed as servants among the soldiers and citizens who had accompanied him on the expedition. The Picurís realized by December 1696 that there was nothing to do but submit to the Spanish authority. In 1704 because of some superstition, the remaining Picurís again abandoned their pueblo and fled to Cuartelejo, a Jicarilla Apache settlement about 350 miles northeast of Santa Fe. In 1706 the captive Picurís, through their chief Lorenzo, sent a messenger to Governor Cuervo y Valdez, praying for forgiveness and asking aid to return to their old home. The petition was approved in a council of war in Santa Fe, and Juan de Ulibarri was selected as commander of the expedition to go to Cuartelejo and bring back the repentant and homesick Indians.

The Picurís tribe has intermarried with both whites and Apaches. Less than a score of the inhabitants are said to be of pure Pueblo blood.

NM 75 continues to PEÑASCO (Sp. rocky) 16.6 *m.* (8,000 alt., 699 pop.), given its name because of the rocky outcroppings near by. The town is a survival of several tiny settlements of the eighteenth century.

In the year 1796 three Spanish-Americans from San José petitioned Governor Fernando Chacón for permission to build two towns in this vicinity. According to Private Land Claim 114, the governor acquiesced with the proviso that "at least 50 individuals must *repopulate* the place and hold the land against sale for ten years." Thus it is construed that the valley had been settled prior to this date although no record of this is found. Seventy-seven took advantage of the grant and three settlements were started, Llano (Sp. plain) ; Llano Largo (Sp. large plain) and Santa Barbara. The present Peñasco was probably the lower portion of Santa Barbara and the present village of Rodarte the center of the old Santa Barbara.

The village church, an adobe structure, its front faced with tin sheeting, is interesting because of the white marble statue group in the churchyard.

The residents of Peñasco depend mostly upon farming and sheep raising but some weaving is also done.

Passing for a mile through clustered tiny villages, the highway makes an abrupt left turn 19.1 *m.* at the ranger station.

VADITO, a small farming village is passed at 21.2 *m.*

At the settlement of RIO PUEBLO in the valley (R) the highway joins NM 3, 22.7 *m.* (*see Tour 11*).

US 64 follows the Rio Grande past the rural post office (L) of EMBUDO (funnel), 73.1 *m.* (6,500 alt., 6 pop.), a former Indian pueblo now little more than a few ranches, and across the river a station on the Denver & Rio Grande Western Railroad, a narrow-gauge railroad line (*see Tour 17*) that parallels US 64 between Embudo and Puyé City (*see below*). In the Spanish archives are bills of sale, dated March 21, 1707, and February 17, 1732, for land in and adjacent to Embudo.

At 80.5 *m.* US 64 leaves the canyon and enters the RIO GRANDE VALLEY.

VELARDE, 81.5 *m.* (5,600 alt., 624 pop.), center of a farming community with fine peach orchards, was formerly called La Joya but was later named for a prominent family.

LOS LUCEROS (Sp. the morning stars), 87.4 *m.,* was once the capital of the *departamento* of Rio Arriba and from 1855 to 1860 was the seat of Rio Arriba County. In 1860 the county seat was transferred to Alcalde (*see below*), then called Plaza del Alcalde, and in 1880 to Tierra Amarilla where it is now.

ALCALDE (Sp. magistrate, judge), 88.8 *m.* (484 pop.), is a trading point consisting of flat-roofed adobe houses, a small chapel, and a Penitente morada.

US 64 continues along the base of Mesa Prieta (dark mesa) or Mesa Canoa (canoe) as it is sometimes called.

At 96.2 *m.* is the junction with Truchas Road (*see Tour 3A*).

PUYE CITY, 96.6 *m.* (5,590 alt., 100 pop.), formerly called Riverside, is the junction with US 285 which is united with US 64 to Santa Fe.

As the highway crosses the Santa Cruz River and mounts a hill, there is a glimpse (L) of the village of SANTA CRUZ (*see Tour 3A*). Descending the hill, US 64 continues across two extremely wide sandy arroyos and traverses a rolling desert country. This section, known as the POJOAQUE (pronounced po-wháh-ke) BADLANDS or SANTA FE MARL, is said to be one of the most nearly perfect exposed sea beds in existence. Here, in a region of miniature canyons, mesas, and cliffs, smooth pebbles, grasses, and multi-colored rock strata, the bones of many prehistoric animals have been found. Remains of mammoths and other Pleiocene animals have been shipped to eastern museums, notably the Museum of Natural History, New York City.

POJOAQUE, 104.2 *m.* (539 pop.), the site of an early Tewa-speaking Pueblo, whose survivors died only two score years ago, marks the junction with NM 4 (*see Tour 2A*).

Left from Pojoaque on a dirt road to RANCHO DE BOUQUET, 0.1 *m.* (*privately owned*), once a noted stopping place for stage coaches. Nambe Pueblo is 3.07 *m.*

US 64 passes through the little village of CUYAMUNGUÉ (Tewa Ind., the place where they threw stones), 107.6 *m.* This is a settlement of adobe houses whose walls are hung with clustered strings of red chili in the fall and surrounded in summer by small orchards and wide green fields of alfalfa. The ruins of the old pueblo of Cuyamungué are one mile below the village on the west bank of the Tesuque River (R). South of the settlement are excellent views of the Jémez Range (R) and the Sangre de Cristo Range (L). Roundabout are countless eroded formations in the sandstone-capped hills, the most distinctive of which is the CAMEL ROCK (R).

At 111.3 *m.* is the junction (R) with a dirt road.

Right on this road to TESUQUE PUEBLO, 1 *m.* (135 pop.) on the west bank of the Tesuque River, the southernmost village of the Tewa-speaking branch of the Rio Grande Pueblo Indians. The present form of the name is from the Tewa *Tat'unge'onwi*, meaning "pueblo down at the dry spotted place." This pueblo, first discovered by Coronado's expedition in 1540, is the Indian pueblo nearest Santa Fe. The seat of a mission, San Lorenzo de Tesuque, in the early seventeenth century, destroyed in the Pueblo Rebellion (1680), it was reconquered in 1692 by De Vargas and established under the name of San Diego de Tesuque. It became a *visita* of Santa Fe in 1760, and of Pojoaque in 1782. In the latter part of the nineteenth century the Mission and its *convento* (monastery) gave way because of age and lack of care. The original sacristy became the present Tesuque Mission. The walls of the chapel probably date from the early seventeenth century.

The United States Government Day School for the pueblo was built several years ago and in addition to the regular curriculum, interesting work is done in native Indian arts and crafts. In spite of its proximity to Santa Fe, Tesuque is tenacious of its Indian customs and life. The annual feast day on November 12th in honor of its patron saint, San Diego, is celebrated by Indian dances directly following a morning Mass. Ceremonies and dances that occur during the year include the Corn dance, the Eagle dance, the Bow and Arrow dance and others. The pottery is distinctive; the water color paintings are purely Indian in theme and design.

*Piki* or *bunjabe,* a paper thin wafer bread, is still prepared by the older women of the pueblo, especially for ceremonial purposes. These thin sheets of corn meal are also useful on journeys.

Tesuque owns its land by virtue of an original grant from the Spanish crown, ratified by the Republic of Mexico 1821, and confirmed by the United States in 1848.

SANTA FE, 117.1 *m.* (7,000 alt., 20,237 pop.), (*see Santa Fe*). In Santa Fe is the junction with US 85 (*see Tour 1*) and US 285 (*see Tour 7*).

### Section b.  SANTA FE to CORONA, 122.6 m.

From SANTA FE, 0 *m.,* over US 85-285 (*see Tour 7b*) to their junction with NM 41 (R), 17.9 *m.,* following NM 41 through the richly productive Estancia Valley.

GALISTEO, 23.7 *m.* (6,400 alt., 300 pop.), is a typical New Mexico farming village in the center of a stock-raising area. Within the Galisteo Valley are nine pueblo ruins, two on the north side and seven on the south side, in the Galisteo Basin. Five of these were occupied when the Spaniards came, the best known being Galisteo pueblo, 1½ miles above the present village. First called San Lucas by Castaño de Sosa (1591), it was renamed Santa Ana by Oñate (1598). During the Pueblo Rebellion (1680), the missionaries here and in neighboring pueblos were killed, and these Indians established themselves in Santa Fe until De Vargas drove them out in 1692. In 1706 Governor Cuervo y Valdez re-established the pueblo, which was renamed Santa María and later called Nuestra Señora de los Remedios, with 90 Tano Indians, whose number by 1749 had increased to 350; but smallpox and Comanche raids reduced them so greatly that in 1794 the few survivors moved to Santo Domingo (*see Tour 1b*) where a few Tanos now live.

One of the ten churches in the Province of New Mexico in 1617 was at Santa Cruz de Galisteo. Coronado came here in 1541 on his way to Pecos (*see Tour 1a*), and the pueblo was visited by Espejo in 1583.

Southward, past Stanley and Otto, NM 41 continues through the Estancia Valley to the Junction with US 66, 51.6 *m.* From the junction the route proceeds south on NM 41. MORIARTY, 52.7 *m.* (6,200 alt., 396 pop.), is the center of a farming and stock raising area.

ESTANCIA, 68.7 *m.* (6,117 alt., 634 pop.), is the seat of Torrance County. It raises cattle, but beans and wool are its principal products. There is no irrigation. Estancia (small farm) was first a cluster of ranch houses around Ojo del Berrendo (Antelope Springs), the property of the Otero family. It was here that Don Manuel Otero, scion of the prominent New Mexico family of that name, was killed (1883) as the result of a dispute over the title of his land. There are different versions of the encounter, but according to Frank M. King, who wrote an account of it in the *Western Livestock Journal* for April 28, 1936, Whitney and his men came up and took charge of the Otero property while Don Manuel was away. When he returned he asked Whitney by what authority he was there. Whitney was seated beside a table in the room and near him was his pistol. He took it up, saying, "By this authority," and fired. The narrator of the story said he didn't remember who fired first but that "there was plenty shootin'." Otero was killed and Whitney had his right jaw shot away. In addition, he had two slugs in his body. Another man was killed and two were slightly wounded. According to one version, Whitney was placed in a light wagon drawn by two ponies, driven to Chilili where a spring wagon and a team of mules were secured, then driven as rapidly as possible to Santa Fe, where he was kept in hiding in a house now owned by Judge Holloman. There he was apprehended and taken to Los Lunas by special train. At the trial that resulted he was acquitted. The property was sold by the Otero estate to the New Mexico Central Railroad, which needed the location for a water tank.

At 77 *m.* is a junction with US 60, and the roads are united for 2.2 miles (*see Tour 8a*).

WILLARD, 79.2 *m.* (6,091 alt., 461 pop.), is in the center of a large stock raising region. Here the route follows NM 42 (R).

At 84 *m.* (L) is a chain of natural salt lakes from which, according to a Spanish document dated 1668, burros laden with salt were driven more than 700 miles to the silver mines in southern Chihuahua, Mexico. The Spaniards were operating these mines with the aid of Indian slaves and needed salt for smelting the ores. The salt traffic, however, had gone on for centuries before it was resumed by the Spaniards. It had been a staple of trade among the Indians of the Southwest, and was known to the Mexican Indians, although it was not then carried by burro.

NM 42 continues to CEDARVALE, 110.2 *m.* (6,400 alt., 245 pop.), center of another dry-farming region.

NM 42 continues across the northeast corner of the Lincoln National Forest, with views of North Peak and Cougar Mountain (R).

CORONA, 122.6 *m.* (6,666 alt., 717 pop.), is situated in an agricultural district in Lincoln County. Mining, wool, and cattle raising are the principal industries.

In Corona is a junction with US 54 (*see Tour 13*).

# *Tour 3A*

Junction with US 64—Santa Cruz—Chimayó—Truchas—29.8 *m.* Truchas Road.

Two-lane, graded dirt roadbed between US 64 and Truchas; rough dirt elsewhere throughout.
Accommodations limited.

This route runs through farming communities and mountain villages of the Chimayó Valley which is the center of the Chimayó type of weaving and has some of the most spectacular scenery in the State. Old customs are observed in this section and the Penitente Brotherhood flourishes here; El Santuario, a noted sanctuary, is on the route. The winding road and sharp turns necessitate careful driving.

The Truchas Road runs east from its junction with US 64, 0 *m.* (*see Tour 3a*) and passes EL SANTO NIÑO (Holy Child), 0.5 *m.,* an old section of Santa Cruz.

SANTA CRUZ, 2.5 *m.* (4,582 alt., 592 pop.), of importance during the early Spanish period, is a Spanish-speaking village of adobe houses around a sleepy plaza with a large modern concrete cross in the center. It was first settled by colonists who came with Oñate in 1598 and, attracted by the fertile lands along the Santa Cruz River (R), established *haciendas*.

For over 300 years Santa Cruz was on the main road between Santa Fe and Taos, but a few years ago the village was by-passed about a mile to the west by the new highway.

Abandoned by the Spanish in 1680 at the time of the Pueblo Rebellion, Santa Cruz was occupied by Indians from the Tano pueblos of San Cristóbal and San Lázaro who established new pueblos here and remained in possession until the reconquest in April 1692, when De Vargas ordered them to vacate. Some went to live at Chimayó, some to San Juan de los Caballeros, and one group to the Hopi country in Arizona where they established the pueblo of Hano on the First Mesa. The first settlement of Santa Cruz had been on the south side of the Santa Cruz River, but the new village was established on the north bank, the second Royal Villa (Santa Fe being the first) in New Mexico, under the name of *La Villa Nueva de Santa Cruz de los Españoles Mexicanos del Rey Nuestro Señor Don Carlos Segundo* (The New Town of the Holy Cross of the Spanish Mexicans of the King our Master Carlos II) and made the military headquarters of the district.

Sixty families of colonists from Zacatecas, Mexico were given grants in 1695, and 19 families from Zacatecas in 1696. De Vargas assisted the colonists in every way. In his official proclamation, he says that he will "take the colonists on his saddle-horses, furnishing pack-mules for any clothing and house-furnishings they may have, and muleteers to help them load." Houses, together with adjoining fields and seed-corn for planting, were to be provided. Antonio Moreño, a Franciscan friar, accompanied the settlers and under his direction a church was erected.

Later the village was temporarily deserted, with crops left standing in the fields, owing to lack of sufficient military protection, but was resettled and a Mission with resident priests was established in 1706. About 1710 more settlers were brought by Juan Jaez Hurtado.

When Major Z. M. Pike passed through the village in 1807, he reported a population of more than 2,000. Under Mexican rule from 1821 to 1846, Santa Cruz was of great political importance and known as one of the "wildest" towns of the southwest.

In the so-called Chimayó Rebellion of 1837 (*see History*), Santa Cruz was the scene of a significant battle between the Mexican Federal troops and the Insurrectionists. Juan José Esquival, *alcalde* (magistrate or judge) of the town, was one of the leaders in the revolt. In August 1837 Governor Pérez marched with 200 troops (the majority of whom were Indians) from Santa Fe against Santa Cruz. Upon meeting the rebel army on the outskirts of the village, many of his own men deserted at the first fire from the enemy. Only a few remained loyal, but in the first charge by the insurgents even those were routed, seven killed and many wounded. The governor with 23 others managed to escape to Santa Fe but on the next day, while attempting to flee the country, he was met by a group of rebellious Santo Domingo

Indians a short distance outside of Santa Fe, and was assassinated. His head was cut off and carried back in triumph to the rebel camp at Santa Cruz.

During the Taos Revolt of 1847, following American occupation, on January 24 when the American army under Colonel Sterling Price was advancing to Taos to avenge the death of Governor Bent, another noteworthy battle was fought here, the Americans defeating a large force of Indians and Mexicans under Chávez, Montoya, and Tafoya. Two Americans were killed during the engagement and several wounded; Colonel Price then proceeded to Taos, where the revolt was summarily suppressed.

During Territorial days, Santa Cruz's reputation for disorder increased. Thomas A. Janvier in *Santa Fe's Partner* says:

"Santa Cruz de la Canada . . . was said to have took the cake for toughness before railroad times. It was a holy terror Santa Cruz was! The only decent folks in it was the French Padre—who outclassed most saints—and hadn't a fly on him—and a German named Becker. He had the government forage station, Becker had; and he used to say he'd had a fresh surprise every morning of the five years he'd been forage agent—when he woke up and found nobody'd knifed him in the night and he was keeping on being alive."

Dominating the plaza is the SPANISH MISSION, a massive cruciform church erected in 1733, one of the largest in New Mexico. It has simple exterior lines, a steep gabled front, and square, buttressed corner towers. The arched belfries surmounting the towers have pyramidal roofs, and the severity of the facade is unrelieved by the usual decorations for a church of this late period. The interior is a treasury of Spanish-Mexican art. The walls of the nave are adorned with Mexican pictures of Our Lady of Sorrows, St. Joseph, St. Stephen, and Our Lady of Guadalupe. On the north wall is a long niche containing figures which represent Christ in the Tomb. Near it is a remarkable seventeenth century Spanish wood carving, a figure of St. Francis. The high altar is similarly adorned with religious paintings. At the south side of the altar, richly painted and paneled doors lead into the Chapel of St. Francis. On the north side, the chapel of Our Lady of Carmel contains a modern Virgin and two paintings on metal—one of St. Anthony of Padua and the other of St. Joseph. Adjoining this chapel is the sacristy, containing religious ornaments from Mexico and several Spanish paintings that originally hung in the nave and suggest the work of Murillo. Here also are stored richly embroidered sacerdotal vestments, altar furnishings of gold and silver, and several very old books.

This church was the central seat of the Confraternity of Our Lady of Carmel and contains a register of all its members, "made by the authority of the Pope and the Bishop of Durango" in 1760.

The church has priests in residence, who minister to a large parish including several pueblos, and many Tewa-speaking Indians are christened and married by them. The babies of the parish are still baptized in the old Chapel of Saint Francis.

The bell, according to Nina Otero in her *Old Spain in the Southwest,* was brought from Spain in the early eighteenth century and its lovely tone is the result of gold and silver jewelry given for its casting by Spanish ladies of the period.

The church in the beginning was flat dirt-roofed, but after several disastrous rains, the resident priest constructed the present hip roof in order, as he said, "to save the church itself!" Changes in the interior include the remodeling of the northern chapel about 1920. Preserved in the church are historical and ecclesiastical records beginning in 1695 and described as the most perfect and complete in the Southwest.

A Catholic Mission School has been built next to the Church in modern times. The *casa de cura* (house of the resident priest) directly back of the church, is an old adobe building with a large barn and corrals that recall the days, not so far distant, when all the priest's journeys to Chimayó, Córdova, Truchas, and other parishes were made by a two-horse team and buggy over roads often almost impassable.

On Santa Cruz Day (*May 3*)—the feast of the finding of the Holy Cross—the cross in the Plaza is always draped in white, and every second year *Los Moros* is presented. This play representing the Conquest of the Moors by the Christians and the recapture of the Cross is enacted on horseback, as it was by the soldiers of Don Juan de Oñate in 1598 at San Juan de los Caballeros, shortly after their arrival in this new province of Spain.

This performance is given at a number of villages by players descended from the families of those who first took part in 1598. The original manuscript in verse was, no doubt, brought from Spain but long ago was lost and the dialogue is now preserved orally.

East of the Plaza is the PENITENTE MORADA, a secret chapel of the Penitente Brotherhood of New Mexico, a survival of the Third Order of Saint Francis.

East of Santa Cruz this is an improved dirt road following the narrow Santa Cruz Valley that is planted with fields of corn, chili, *frijoles* (Mexican or pinto beans), apple and peach orchards, and walled in by grotesquely eroded sandstone cliffs. A gravelly rock-strewn stream curves across the valley floor changing its course from day to day, never man-controlled. Adobe houses nestle against tawny cliffs or perch defiantly on lookout hilltops; and in May, lilac-draped mud walls rise from barren grounds; young children in joyous mood and dress play in the roadway beside wayside crosses that mark the resting places of their ancestors. A chapel here, a *morada* there, or a stark Penitente cross on a hilltop bear testimony to the people's piety.

CHIMAYÓ, 9 *m.* (6,872 alt., 573 pop.), is on the site of a pueblo inhabited by a group of Tewa Indians who were called the Tsimajó (Ind., flaking stone of superior quality) and were fine weavers. It is supposed the few Spaniards living here before the Tewa abandoned their pueblo learned the craft from them. Chimayó was the eastern boundary of the Province of New Mexico from 1598 to 1695, the frontier place of banishment for offenders, which in those days meant punishment greater than prison. After the Reconquest in 1692, it was known as *San Buenaventura de Chimayó* (Chimayó of the Good Venture). Today, because of its sheltered position, it is the center of farming, fruit culture, and weaving. The road, winding through the village, is lined with lilac hedges and with adobe houses and patio walls that are covered in June with the yellow rose of Castile. In the fall when the shimmering gold of the cottonwoods contrasts with strings of scarlet chili that drape the houses, the harvesting of the crops is carried on, and grain is threshed on primitive threshing floors with goats and horses tramping it out. During Lent processions of Penitentes, creeping up to the hilltop cross, scourge bare backs with yucca whips. Sometimes, in the spring of a dry year, can be seen a procession of men and women, the leader carrying an image of the Virgin or the Santo Niño (holy child) and all chanting prayers for rain as they walk across the dry fields. Here are the homes of generations of weavers whose gaily colored Chimayó blankets have been called the link between the Navaho blankets of New Mexico and the Saltillo of Mexico. Every other house contains a hand loom with father, mother, and sometimes children operating it. Weaving in New Mexico had so deteriorated by the beginning of the nineteenth century that the Spanish authorities sent to Mexico for expert craftsmen to teach the colonists; in the spring of 1805 the brothers Bazán, Don Ignacio and Don Juan, certified master weavers, came to Santa Fe under a six-year contract to teach the youth. At the capital they found conditions not to their liking so moved to Chimayó, which was established as a weaving center, a position it holds today though there have been periods of inactivity followed by revivals.

For a time the craftsmen used wool bought from manufacturers instead of that prepared from neighbors' sheep as formerly, but are now restoring their blankets' popularity by turning again to native wool, hand spinning, and local vegetable dyes.

At Chimayó is the junction with a secondary dirt road.

Right on this road over a small stream to a cluster of adobes surrounding EL SANTUARIO DE CHIMAYÓ 1.3 *m.,* a Christian sanctuary, believed to be on the site of the old Tsimajó Pueblo.

The low-flat-roofed adobe church with its tapering front towers and twin belfries is entered through a wall-enclosed garden with towering cottonwoods. It was built as a thanks offering by Don Bernardo Abeyta in 1816, and is very well preserved. The wide main portal is in the center of a thick retaining wall which supports a terrace immediately in front on the church structure. Between the front towers at the gallery level is a narrow porch with timber posts and roof. Here a smaller doorway opens into the choir loft within. The interior is notable for its characteristic Spanish-Pueblo decorations—a heavy timber ceiling of closely spaced *vigas,* supported at the ends on carved brackets and crude plaster walls lined with a low painted dado and hung with numerous religious paintings. There are also pierced tin candelabra and a small *bulto* of Santo Niño. In front of the high altar is an interesting chancel rail with perforated wooden balusters. Behind the draped altar is a high reredos, naively decorated with painted conventional designs and religious symbols, and over it a cross found in the pine tree that grew on this site. It is an exact replica of the cross at Esquipulas, Mexico in the Iglesia de Santo Niño.

A privately-owned square chapel about 50 feet from the Santuario also contains a small statue of Santo Niño Perdido, the lost Child. The custodian here will respond to the ringing of a bell, which hangs in the campanile, and sell layettes of value, blessed by Santo Niño, to expectant mothers. It is said that these images of Santo Niño go out during the night on errands of mercy to the poor, in consequence of which new shoes must be bought for them every six months, although many thank offerings consist of doll-size shoes for their wear. The Santuario was in possession of the Abeyta family until the fall of 1929, when Mary Austin (*see Literature*) obtained from an anonymous donor $6,000 with which the Society for the Preservation and Restoration of New Mexico Churches purchased the property and transferred it to the Roman Catholic Church.

Continue (R) on this road to the SANTA CRUZ RESERVOIR (*park cars at dam base and climb on foot to water's edge*), 0.8 *m.*, built in 1929. The water here irrigates about 6,000 acres and provides lake trout fishing (*boats 50¢ an hour*).

The road continues to climb along the crest of a hogback dividing two small valleys, with TRUCHAS PEAK (13,306 alt.), highest in New Mexico, and TAOS MOUNTAINS ahead, and with the JÉMEZ RANGE (L).

At 13 *m.* is the junction with a dirt road.

Right on this road, which crosses a small stream and winds up the steep foothills, to CUNDIYÓ, 2.1 *m.* (5,621 alt., 100 pop.), another hill town where a native craft center has recently been established. The specialty is hand-tanned goat skins from local goats, each family owning a small flock kept for this purpose as well as for milk and meat. About 100 feet above Cundiyó, at the foot of a small round hill, called by the Nambé Indians the "round hill of the little bells," are the ruins of a large adobe pueblo, said to be one of the ancient villages of their people.

At 19.2 *m.,* is the junction with a dirt road.

Right down this narrow road, which tortuously winds across low spurs of hills, to CÓRDOVA, 0.5 *m.* (5,742 alt., 573 pop.), said to have first been an Indian pueblo, now entirely Spanish-American. Its one street leads along the lower edge of a hill. On the left native type adobe houses with portals of pink, mauve, blue, and yellow are set in diminutive yards; on the right are chicken houses, stables, and corrals that slope steeply to the mountain stream. Between the stream and the towering foothills the yellow-green of spring wheat and the vivid green of alfalfa fields are outlined with wild plum. There is an adobe church dedicated to San Antonio de Padua where the bier, still used at funerals, is near the door; for there is no room here for the modern hearse. Córdova was the home until his death in May 1937 of the wood carver, José María López, who fashioned with his penknife from juniper and piñon firewood, birds, squirrels, and beavers, as well as the figures of Adam and Eve, in dejection, leaving the Garden. On a point at the upper end of the village is a large cross and MORADA OF THE PENITENTES.

The route continues (L) to the crest of a steep hill where there is a group of wooden crosses (R) set among the rocks, many ornamented with framed photographs of the departed ones.

At 22.9 *m.* is a sharp turn. Here the road winds through several dry river beds to TRUCHAS (Sp. trout), 29.8 *m.* (7,622 alt., 722 pop.), mentioned in a Spanish Archive of 1752 as Nuestra Señora del Rosario de las Truchas, a name longer than its main street. An archive dated 1762 tells of the transfer of its people, together with those of Las

Trampas, to the Parish of Picurís. In March 1772 another archive records the requests of the villagers for 12 muskets and powder and protection from the Comanche. "Denied" is written in answer to both requests. The walls of the adobe houses here are unusually thick (Truchas is a very cold place in winter) ; and handsome, hand-carved doors are numerous. There is a small Roman Catholic mission of early days and a Presbyterian Church and mission training school. Behind the village rise the TRUCHAS PEAKS. From Truchas on a clear day are visible the La Plata Mountains 150 miles away in southern Colorado; the JÉMEZ RANGE and the PEDERNAL (9,857 alt.) to the west; SANDÍAS, 75 miles to the southwest; and MT. TAYLOR, 150 miles south of west. Spread below is the entire Tewa world and a magnificent panorama of the Rio Grande Valley.

Numerous trails lead out from Truchas into the CARSON NATIONAL FOREST (*good hunting and fishing*). East of Truchas, a rougher and more erratic road leads into and through the Forest, and another, north, runs over mountain trails and across canyons to Trampas (*see Tour 3a*)—a very difficult and dangerous road, not to be undertaken except under the best conditions and then only by those experienced in mountain driving. It is safer as a pack trip.

# Tour 4

(Texline, Texas) Clayton—Des Moines—Capulín—Ratón US 87. Texas Line to Ratón, 92.6 m.

Two-lane, bituminous-paved roadbed throughout.
Atchison, Topeka & Santa Fe Railway roughly parallels the route between Clayton and Mt. Dora, and the Colorado & Southern Railroad between Clayton and Des Moines.
Hotels in Clayton and Ratón; tourist camps and gas stations at short intervals.

This route cutting across the northeast corner of New Mexico traverses a region strewn with masses of black lava rock. In the old days this was a cattle country and great herds roamed here until the spring roundups.

US 87 crosses the TEXAS LINE, 0 *m.*, at a point 36 miles northwest of Dalhart, Texas.

CLAYTON, 9.3 *m.* (5,200 alt., 3,171 pop.), the county seat and the largest town in Union County, is on a high plateau and its lights are visible for miles around. The town is on two railroads and serves as trading and shipping point for ranchers and farmers of the entire eastern part of the country, which usually has enough snow in winter to provide moisture in the spring for crops. Clayton's population is chiefly Anglo-American, although there is a large Spanish-American group.

Clayton began as a camping ground for cattle drovers in 1888, when the railroad was built and accepted cattle for shipment. Its first store was a tent from which supplies were sold to the cattlemen. In the 1880's such large herds were being driven from points in Texas to Springer, New Mexico, and Granada, Colorado that a railroad through the northeastern part of New Mexico was planned.

Senator Dorsey's foreman, John C. Hill, suggested the establishment of a trading post here and persuaded General Granville Dodge, construction manager for the Denver & Fort Worth Railroad Company, to make the proposed new town a division point on the Colorado & Southern, a part of the Denver and Forth Worth system.

The first building was a shack put up by C. M. Perrin in October 1887 a month before the town site was surveyed. The first post office was housed in a small frame structure with a canvas roof, and soon the Clayton House (hotel) was built. A store was opened on January 13, 1888 in Perrin's cabin. Another building was used as schoolhouse, courtroom, and public meeting place. In the early 1890's the first minister came to Clayton.

In March 1888 the first passenger train was run from the Texas Line to Trinidad, Colorado. From then on the town had a rapid growth; in 1900 the population was 750. One setback for the determined settlers was a severe snowstorm during October and November 1889, when Clayton was cut off from the outside world for several weeks and train service from the north was held up for 13 days. The snow averaged 25 inches in depth and piled up in drifts as high as 7 feet. Frozen horses, sheep, and cattle, as well as human bodies, were found when the snow melted. Five cowboys and two sheepherders died in the blizzard. Two passenger trains were snowbound at Texline for several days. Stock shipments from Clayton were practically discontinued for the winter.

Another hazard that made life interesting for the Clayton settlers was the wild career of Black Jack Ketchum and his several gangs of train robbers. When he was tried and hanged at Clayton on April 26, 1901, a stockade was built around the gallows to frustrate any possible attempt at rescue by members of his gang.

This two-gun bandit came into Arizona from Texas in the middle 1890's. He was large in stature, swarthy as a Mexican, and dangerous as a rattler. Following one of their train robberies, in which the loot totaled many thousands of dollars, Ketchum and his gang made for their hideout on the Diamond "A" ranch south of Separ. It was a November morning, 1896, when the desperadoes rode down the mountain slope into the withering fire of a posse in ambush. A number were killed, but Black Jack escaped. Then for several years he operated in southeastern Arizona, a part of New Mexico, and northern Sonora. Single handed, he held up a train at Twin-Mountain Curve, but this proved to be the climax of his career. He was wounded in making his escape and was found next morning by a sheriff's posse, wandering on the desert in a crazed condition. When a nervous hangman fumbled with the noose at his hanging, Black Jack called out, "Hurry it up; I'm due in hell for dinner." He asked to be buried face down. One of his last requests was for music at the end, and a violin and guitar were played in accordance with his wishes.

When Union County was created in 1893, Folsom and Clayton contested the honor of being made county seat. After a bitter struggle, Clayton won and a courthouse was built in 1895 that served until 1908 when a gale unroofed the building and killed several persons. Soon afterward the present courthouse was erected. When district court was held in the earlier building, in April and October, Clayton put on a festive air.

A story is told about Judge Mills, who was attending a formal evening party when he was summoned to the courthouse to receive a verdict. He rushed to the building, still in evening clothes, opened court, heard the verdict, then adjourned. The next day a stranger who had attended the session asked a local attorney if it was the custom for the judge to preside in full dress. "It is," the lawyer assured him; "in Clayton no man would think of going out in the evening in anything but a full dress suit."

When Phlem Humphrey, one of three county commissioners, was taken to the new courthouse to be tried for murder, he saw the marker on the building with the names of the commissioners, including his own, and said: "Don't that beat hell! I'm the first one tried for murder in my own courthouse." He was acquitted a year later.

The CROSS SALES PAVILION, owned by W. A. Cross, was built in 1933 of adobe in typical New Mexico style. It is a two-story sales ring with an arena that seats 500. At the rear is a stockyard accommodating 1,500 head of cattle and connected by an alley with the Santa Fe Stockyards.

Clayton's Old Western Dance held each winter during the holiday season, usually for three nights, is attended by visitors from many other States. Guns are checked at the door and prizes are offered for the best costumes, the best waltzers, the most recently married couple, the longest whiskers, and many other "bests" or "mosts."

The Union County Fair, held for three days in the early autumn, is sponsored by the 4-H Clubs, the Junior Chamber of Commerce, farm-women's clubs, Clayton businessmen, and other groups.

A familiar figure in Clayton is Ernest Thompson Seton, whose *Lobo, King of the Currumpaw* deals with a giant wolf that terrorized the ranchers northwest of Clayton for more than five years before he was trapped in 1894. So great was the dread of this animal that the price on its head finally reached $1,000.

In this area fossils of sea shells, fresh water snails, and fish have been found. In 1935 two distinct species of dinosauria were excavated north of Clayton, one carnivorous and one herbivorous. Indian petroglyphs, arrowheads, stone implements, and other artifacts have been uncovered.

RABBIT EAR MOUNTAIN (R), 19 *m.,* is named for a Cheyenne chief, called Rabbit Ears (*Orejas de Conejo*) because his ears had been frozen, who was killed in battle and buried on this mountain. Here in 1717 a volunteer army of 500 Spaniards, eager to put an end to Comanche raids, killed several hundred of them and took 700 prisoners. A long truce followed. The Star Mail Route from Kenton, Oklahoma to Clayton, carried at first by team and wagon, skirted Rabbit Ear Mesa near here. In 1910 it was decided to take a short cut across the mesa; but, owing to a legal technicality, the road could not be changed unless it was proved that the mail was already using a part of the proposed route. So W. G. Howard, the mail carrier, persuaded a group of interested men to "hold up the coach" atop the mesa and carry it down the steep sides. The problem was not yet settled, however, for at the foot of the mesa lived "Shotgun Mary" Goodin, who had definite ideas about roads crossing her ranch. The 24 men were effectively held at bay by her, and it seemed the new route was doomed until John Spring, a member of the Clayton police whom Mary held in great respect, persuaded her to allow the road to go through.

North of Rabbit Ear Mountain in an unnamed box canyon (inaccessible by car) is a green pool covered with an oily scum that conceals its depth. No water flows from it except after heavy rains. The canyon walls have areas charred by fires and an unexplored opening three feet in diameter. It is believed that the region formerly contained oil that has been burned out.

Senator Dorsey, who served from Arkansas 1873-79, is responsible for several place names in this area. Clayton and Clayton Peak were named for his son; Mt. Dora for his sister-in-law, and Mt. Margarite and other hills for other members of his family.

MT. DORA, 27.2 *m.* (5,280 alt., 250 pop.), at the foot of the mountain that bears the same name, has had a post office since 1912. It is a shipping point for cattle and sheep as well as for grains and produce, but since 1929 it has had only a fraction of its former business.

GRENVILLE, 36.4 *m.* (5,300 alt., 231 pop.), conspicuous for its grain elevator, is another shipping point for ranch and farm products. It developed as a station on the Colorado & Southern Railroad and experienced a boom in 1919 when the Snorty Gobbler oil well, five miles north, was brought in; its growth stopped in 1925 when the oil company failed. There is a good fishing resort at Wetherly Dam, 10 miles west of town.

At 44.5 *m.* is the junction with an unimproved dirt road.

Right on this road 4.1 *m.* is COW MOUNTAIN, in the west side of which is the GRENVILLE CAVES. The second cave is about a half-mile long and branches into two tunnels that connect in the back of the cave. The last room contains an aperture about one and one-half feet wide, through which a strong, warm wind is said to blow at five minute intervals. The cause of this has not been discovered. The floors, covered with boulders of various sizes, resemble a creek bed. Since a compass will not register accurately within the caves owing to the magnetic iron content of the surrounding rock it has never been determined in what direction the caves extend. The walls contain many small holes believed to be the homes of rattlesnakes, hence the alternative name, Rattlesnake Caves. The geologist thinks the caves were caused by air bubbles in the hot lava poured by the surrounding volcanoes over this land.

US 87 crosses a wide plateau through a sparsely settled ranch country where lava rock is frequently visible and limestone is also found.

DES MOINES, 54.5 *m.* (6,620 alt., 362 pop.), named for Des Moines, Iowa, is a trading and shipping point for an extensive dry farming and ranching area. When the Colorado & Southern Railroad extended its lines through New Mexico in 1887-88 a station was set at the foot of the Sierra Grande and named Des Moines. For 19 years there was no town at this site; but in 1907 two sites were surveyed and settled, one founded by R. M. Saavedra, the other by J. F. Branson. The former was named for its founder; the latter was called Des Moines. Saavedra erected the first building on his property and opened a store; within a year Branson's site had a lumber yard, several saloons, restaurants, stores, and a post office. In 1915-16, Saavedra took the lead in population and several business houses of Des Moines moved there. Then the Townsite Company, assisted by railroad interests, bought 17 acres lying between Saavedra and Des Moines and this tract drew the two groups together. When this land had been acquired, the name Des Moines was adopted for the consolidated areas. For a time the population increased so rapidly much of it was housed in hastily built shacks. An early settler named Rogers became known as the Shack Builder after constructing 75 of these shelters in 90 days.

By 1920 the town reached its peak with a population of 800, but with drought and the 1929 economic depression it declined to one-half that figure. In 1936 a rich deposit of carbon dioxide started a dry ice industry like that of Bueyeros (*see Tour 1a*).

Twin Mountains, 4 miles northwest of Des Moines, is largely composed of red cinders, and has supplied the Colorado & Southern Railroad with material for its roadbed and furnished settlers with material for construction.

CAPULÍN, 63.6 *m.* (6,868 alt., 285 pop.), formerly called Dedman, was later renamed for Mt. Capulín. Near by is the beautiful Sierra Grande (Big Ridge), 40 miles in circumference at the base and having an altitude of 11,500 feet. In Capulín is the junction with US 64 (*see Tour 2a*) which is united with US 87 between Capulín and Ratón (*see Tour 1a*).

In the Capulín-Folsom region, archeological discoveries indicate the existence of a human race here some 15,000 years ago. Spear heads of stone, called the Folsom points, have been found in close proximity to bones of mammoths and an extinct species of bison, indicating that they were the tips of weapons used by these primitive people in hunting game. In spite of the Folsom finds, northeastern New Mexico has not been very extensively explored by archeologists. That future explorations may greatly enhance knowledge of prehistoric man is indicated in a report by Edward T. Hall, Jr., archeologist, who has made a study of this area and says: "Small rock shelters in the sides of canyons have produced evidence of occupation by a people who are thought to have been linked with the ancient Basket Makers. Pictographs that were undoubtedly made by the ancient inhabitants have been located in various parts of this area. Indications on the ground surface lead the archeologist to believe that a nomadic hunting people roamed this plain in search of buffalo, and the early Spaniards report meeting various groups of Plains Indians camped in this district. We have evidence of occupation here from about thirteen thousand years ago, and it is easy to see why the Buffalo Nomads would pick northeastern New Mexico as a place to live, since there must always have been an abundance of large game that provided not only food but shelter and clothing. . . . Since they did not build large permanent houses of masonry, evidence of their presence in this region is more difficult to find and can be easily overlooked, but it is here nevertheless."

CUNNINGHAM, 81.6 *m.,* directly south of Johnson Mesa (*see Tour 2a*), is a small agricultural and stock-raising settlement.

In RATÓN, 92.6 *m.* (6,400 alt., 7,594 pop.), is the junction with US 85 (*see Tour 1a*).

≪≪≪≪≪≪≪≪≪≪≪≪≪≪≪≪≪≪≪≪≪≪≪≪≪≪≪≪≪≪≪≪≪≫≫≫≫≫≫≫≫≫≫≫≫≫≫≫≫≫≫≫≫≫≫≫≫≫

# *Tour 5*

(Antonito, Colorado)—Palmilla—Taos Junction—Ojo Caliente—Española; NM 74. Colorado Line to Española, 85.7 *m.*

Two-lane graveled and dirt road.
Denver & Rio Grande Western Railroad roughly parallels the route between the Colorado Line and Taos Junction.
Accommodations in Ojo Caliente.

This is approximately the route followed in 1778-79 by the Spanish Governor, Lieutenant Colonel Juan Bautista de Anza, in his campaign against the Comanche chief, Cuerno Verde (Green Horn), for whom the Greenhorn Mountains in southern Colorado were named. When the discoverer of Pike's Peak was made a captive he was led along here en route to Chihuahua, Mexico. Though the region has beautiful scenery it is known chiefly for mineral springs at Ojo Caliente.

From the COLORADO LINE, 0 *m.,* six miles south of Antonito, Colorado, NM 74 crosses a flat, grassy plateau lying between distant mountains.

VOLCANO HILL, 12 *m.,* is an extinct crater. West of here are vast open cattle ranges (R). (*Drive carefully to avoid animals that stray across the highway.*) SKARDA, 17.2 *m.,* is only a railroad station.

NO AGUA (Sp. no water), 19.5 *m.,* another railroad station, has a store, small church, and two or three houses. No Agua Mountain (R), on a division of the Carson National Forest, looms against the horizon.

TRES PIEDRAS (three stones), 25.7 *m.* (317 pop.), is a REGISTRATION STATION. This small settlement, with railway station, store, and a half-dozen homes, was named for sandstone outcroppings that surround it. The majority of the population live in the vicinity where there are large ranches devoted to stock raising. Many potato and grain fields also border the highway. Scattered piñon and juniper border the route; in the spring the blue of the lupine and later the red of the Indian paintbrush color the countryside.

SERVILLETA, 38.3 *m.,* is another railroad station and small settlement.

TAOS JUNCTION, 49.2 *m.* (6,900 alt., 65 pop.), was for many years the railway station nearest to Taos.

Left from Taos Junction on graded NM 96 to JOHN DUNN BRIDGE, 10 *m.,* over the Rio Grande in Rio Grande Canyon (*see Tour 3a*).

A flat-topped, wind-eroded mesa (R) at 52 *m.* hems in a narrow valley with a dry arroyo that leads into the bed of Comanche Creek which is dangerous in floodtime.

OJO CALIENTE (6,283 alt., 107 pop.), 61.2 *m.,* has a store and gas station and adobe houses that have changed little in a hundred years, although there are more peaked roofs. There are fields of corn and beans as in earlier times, and in the low hills near by are a number of pueblo ruins and several mineral springs for which the town is named.

Though the Spanish outpost that existed here in 1766 had a fortress for protection against the Ute and Comanche and assessed a fine of 200 pesos and imprisonment in chains against any settler who deserted, the place was abandoned in 1790 as indefensible and was not reoccupied for 20 years.

When Governor Juan Bautista de Anza, who had explored California and founded a colony of 200 at San Francisco in 1776, reached Santa Fe in 1778, he saw the necessity for a show of force against warring tribes to the north, especially the Comanche, Ute, and Apache. Cuerno Verde, chief of the Comanche, was an implacable foe who hated the Spaniards for the death of his father and Anza was determined to break his power.

He set out from Santa Fe August 15, 1779 with 400 Spanish soldiers and 200 Indian allies, marched north and crossed the Rio Grande, following closely the present route of the Denver & Rio Grande Western Railroad.

Ojo Caliente, which had already been abandoned, was one of his stops. From this point he marched directly north into Colorado where his columns met the full force of the Comanche war party at Fountain Creek on August 31. During the battle Anza succeeded in luring Cuerno Verde into a trap along with some of his lieutenants and his best warriors. Anza records his admiration for their courage, saying, "There, without other recourse, they sprang to the ground and intrenched behind their horses made in this manner a defense as brave as it was glorious. Notwithstanding the aforesaid Cuerno Verde perished with his first-born son, the heir to his command, four of his most famous captains, a medicine man who preached that he was immortal and others who fell into the trap. A larger number might have been killed, but I preferred the death of this chief even to more of those who escaped, because of his being constantly in this region the cruel scourge of this kingdom." The power of the Comanche was broken, but the terror and hazard of those days was long remembered.

In 1790 eighteen families living in Bernalillo received permission from Governor Fernando de la Concha to settle at Ojo Caliente providing they formed "a well ordered and regular settlement on the outskirts of the Cañada de los Comanches." It was to be heavily fortified "since experience has proven that nobody can last there on account of its fatal position."

After Major Zebulon M. Pike, seeking the headwaters of the Colorado River in 1807, had been arrested by Spaniards near Taos, he was brought through this village, which he describes thus: "The difference of climate was astonishing, after we left the hills and deep snows, we found ourselves on plains where there was no snow, and where vegetation was sprouting. The village of the Warm Springs or Ojo Caliente (in their language) is situated on the eastern branch of a creek of that name and at a distance, presents to the eye a square enclosure of mud walls, the houses forming the wall. They are flat on top, or extremely little ascent on one side, where there are spouts to carry off the water of the melting snow and rain when it falls, which we were informed, had been but once in two years, previous to our entering the country . . .

"Inside of the enclosure were the different streets of houses of the same fashion, all of one story; the doors were narrow, the window small, and in one or two houses there were talc lights (window panes of mica). This village had a mill near it, situated on the little creek, which made very good flour.

"The population consisted of civilized Indians, but much mixed blood. Here we had a dance which is called the *Fandango*, but there was one which was copied from the Mexicans, and is now danced in the first societies of New Spain, and has even been introduced at the court of Madrid. This village may contain 500 souls. The greatest natural curiosity is the warm springs, which are two in number (there are actually five), about 10 yards apart, and each affords sufficient water for a mill seat. They appeared to be impregnated with copper, and were more than 33° above blood heat."

Right from Ojo Caliente on a dirt road across the Rio del Ojo Caliente to the OJO CALIENTE HOT SPRINGS (*bathhouses, pools, hotel, cottages*) at the foot of Ojo Caliente Mountain. The five springs containing arsenic, iron, sodium sulphate, lithia, and soda, and varying in temperature from 98° to 113° Fahrenheit, were valued by the Indians as medicinal springs before the Spanish conquest. The Tewa called the place P'soi (spring of mossy greenness) for its green-stained rocks, and regarded it as a dwelling place of tribal gods. The springs themselves were the openings between this world and the "down below world," whence their people first came. The grandmother of Poseyemo, a Tewa hero, is said still to live in one of the springs.

The Spaniards had a settlement here that might have existed before the Pueblo Rebellion of 1680. On one of the hand-hewn beams of the old CHURCH appears the date: 1689, probably the year the church was finished. In 1747 the settlers petitioned the governor to permit their removal to a safer place, but it is recorded that they returned here in 1768.

On the mesa above are the HOMAYO RUINS and HOUIRI RUINS as well as POSE-UINGGE (or Posege) RUINS, where after considerable excavation archeologists have concluded that the Indian towns of the Chama, to which these ruins belong, are a link between the archaic Pajaritan culture and that of the living towns. Posege was occupied at the time of the Spanish Conquest. It is said by the Tewa to have been the birthplace of Poseyemo, their legendary hero, who was born of a virgin, comes here annually to visit his grandmother, and will some day return from the East with the rising sun to rejoin his people.

South of Ojo Caliente the road winds near the eroded slopes of Dark Mesa or Mesa Canoa (L), following the general course of Rio del Ojo Caliente and passing small ranches with flat-roofed adobe houses. A mound (R), 62.7 *m.*, near a group of cottonwoods, is all that remains of a Tewa ruin.

Beside a small mesa (L) which the Indians appropriately named Stove Ashes Mesa, is GAILAN, 64.6 *m.*, a group of scattered houses. Here according to legend Poseyemo battled with Josi, god of the Christians, but the tale does not name the victor.

Weather-beaten wooden crosses are visible at intervals along the roadside, standing among white ones more recently erected. These mark hallowed spots where coffins in rural funeral processions were lowered from the shoulders of the pallbearers and prayers for the dead were said. A little farther Mesa Canoa comes into full and impressive view.

The valley widens at 72 *m.* and the road winds among masses of antler cactus, with a great volcanic dyke ahead. At 77 *m.* the highway enters the Chama River Valley near the mouth of the Rio del Ojo Caliente. Along here the road is only a few feet above the muddy red waters of the river. The Jémez Mountains are visible (R) and the Sangre de Cristo Mountains (L) across the Rio Grande. On great black boulders along this stretch of the road are many old pictographs.

NM 74 crosses the Chama Valley, passing cultivated fields and typical New Mexican settlements, and at 85.7 *m.* joins US 285 (*see Tour 7*) in ESPAÑOLA (*see Tour 7*).

━━━━━━━━━━━━━━━━━━━━━━━━━━━━━━━━━━━━━━━━━━━━━━━━━━━━━━━━━━━━━━

# Tour 6

(Amarillo, Texas)—Tucumcari—Santa Rosa—Moriarty—Albuquerque
—Grants—Gallup—(Holbrook, Arizona) ; US 66.
Texas Line to Arizona Line, 376.3 *m.*

Bituminous-paved, two-lane road throughout.
Chicago, Rock Island & Pacific Railway parallels route between Glenrio and
Tucumcari; Southern Pacific Railroad between Tucumcari and Santa Rosa;
Atchison, Topeka, & Santa Fe Railway between junction with NM 14 and the
Arizona Line.
Hotels chiefly in cities; tourist camps and gas stations at short intervals.

Over US 66, one of the main transcontinental highways, went many
of the farmers who fled from the dust bowl and became migratory
workers in the fruit valleys of California. It is the route described
in John Steinbeck's *The Grapes of Wrath.* Because US 66 crosses
the section of Oklahoma in which Will Rogers was born, some of his
admirers met in Albuquerque in 1939 and gave this road his name,
though all US highways are officially designated by numbers.

The two sections of this route are as different as the opposite ends
of a cow. At the eastern end, the land is as flat as a cowboy's purse
the morning after pay day and so level that in the old days the pioneers
had to drive stakes across it to find their way. It is a continuation of
the Texas Panhandle terrain and the western terminus of the Llano
Estacado (staked plains). There is a gradual rise to the western
section, where the hills and mountains predominate. Agricultural
areas are passed at different points, mostly irrigated, although there is
some dry farming in the eastern and central sections. Cattle are
numerous in the eastern part, but there are more sheep in the western
part. Because of migrations from Texas and Oklahoma into the eastern half, the linguistic stock is largely English, and this is especially
true in the larger towns; but farther west, and in the remote villages
throughout, both customs and language are Spanish.

*Section a. TEXAS LINE to ALBUQUERQUE, 217.3 m.*

Between the Texas Line and the Pecos River lies the western section
of the staked plains; home of the buffalo, hunting ground of the
Comanche, then the Spaniard, and later the Americans; repository for
the bleached bones of those who were either killed in battle or who
failed to find the water holes. Among the many accounts of the name
is the Indian legend that stakes were driven in the plains to guide the
Great Chief who was to come from the east and deliver the Indians

from their enemies.   Chambers' Encyclopedia and Encyclopedia Americana credit the name as coming from the yucca, which viewed from a distance is thought by some to resemble poles.   The International Encyclopedia gives its literal translation, "Palisaded Plain," as the meaning.   One plausible explanation, however, is that because there were no trees to blaze, the trails to the water holes were staked out, till this vast stretch of grim and forbidding country became marked with stakes pointing the way to water.   Llano Estacado is a plateau flanking the Pecos River and running north to south for 400 miles, from a point 40 miles north of Fort Sumner down to the dry canyons which form the headwaters of the Colorado east of Pecos, Texas, then sloping eastward about 150 miles to the caprock of Texas, an area of some 60,000 square miles.   Its maximum altitude of 5,500 feet is on the western border, its minimum is 2,000 feet along its southern and eastern terminus.   The plain remains much the same as it was in the days of the buffalo, the bull-whacking buffalo hunter, and the terrifying Comanche, except for the windmills that mark the white man's successive triumphs in his search for water.

Captain R. B. Marcy, in a report written in 1849, describes the Plains as a view ". . . boundless as the ocean.   Not a tree, shrub, or any other object, either animate or inanimate, relieved the dreary monotony of the prospect; it was a vast illimitable expanse of desert prairie—the dread 'Llano Estacado' of New Mexico; or, in other words, the great Sahara of North America . . . even the savages dare not venture to pass it except at two or three places, where they know water can be found."   In his *Commerce of the Prairies,* Gregg says, "I have been assured by Mexican hunters and Indians that there is but one route upon which this plain can be safely traversed during the dry season; and even some of the watering places on this are at intervals of fifty to eighty miles and hard to find."   Coronado's expedition to the Jumano Indians undoubtedly traversed the northern part before turning north to Quivira, and Guadalajara and Castillo are credited with crossing it a century later; but subsequent trail makers from the east skirted the plateau, and in their journals gave as their reason, "The Plains country we avoided because it is so vast and is barren of anything to eat . . . and of water."   On his survey for a wagon road between Fort Smith and the Colorado River in 1858 Edward F. Beale reached the Llano Estacado on December 20 and reported: ". . . we ascended the mesa of Llano Estacado, and encamped on its summit without wood or water, but with abundant grass. . . . Before reaching our camp a fresh Indian trail was passed, apparently not twenty minutes old; this makes us doubly watchful to-night, as well as anxious, lest possibly we may lose a mule or two, to say nothing of the train.

"December 21 . . . traveling over the dead level plain, we camped for an hour to graze our animals on the prairie.   The grass . . . is everywhere abundant, but of water there is none, unless at times the rains may leave a pool or two standing in the old buffalo wallows. We saw not a living thing but a prairie dog and antelope or two, and a crow, in crossing this extensive plain. Evidences enough exist that years ago buffalo have grazed on its fine grasses, but now there is not one to be seen, or the sign of one less than ten years old."

Edward Fitzgerald Beale (1822-93) was well acquainted with the West. He was a junior officer on the U. S. frigate *Congress* when it reached Monterey in 1846 and took part under Robert F. Stockton in the annexation of California. Beale was with a detachment that reached General Kearny just before Kearny's forces were surrounded by the Mexicans in the battle of San Pasqual, and with Kit Carson, Beale made his way through the enemy lines to summon Stockton's aid. Later he and Carson were sent overland to Washington with dispatches and while crossing the desert Beale conceived the idea of using camels for transportation. He persuaded Jefferson Davis, then Secretary of War, to import camels, which Beale used in 1857 on his survey of a wagon road from Fort Defiance to the Colorado River. His report of this trip contains interesting glimpses of New Mexico as well as praise for the camels and condemnation of their drivers.

"July 16, (1857) . . . The camels arrived nearly as soon as we did. It is a subject of constant surprise and remark to all of us, how their feet can possibly stand the character of the road we have been traveling over for the last ten days. It is certainly the hardest road on the feet of bare-footed animals, I have ever known. As for food, they live on anything, and thrive. Yesterday they drank water for the first time in twenty-six hours, and although the day had been excessively hot they seemed to care but little for it. Mark the difference between them and mules; the same time, in such weather, without water, would set the latter wild, and render them nearly useless, if not entirely break them down.

"August 12. Started my train on, it being necessary for me to remain until the arrival of the express from Santa Fe. I was anxious, moreover, to get the men out of town as soon as possible, as the fandangos and other pleasures had rendered them rather troublesome. This morning I was obliged to administer a copious supply of the oil of boot to several, especially to my Turks and Greeks, with the camels. The former had not found, even in the positive prohibitions of the prophet, a sufficient reason for temperance, but was as drunk as any Christian in the train, and would have remained behind, but for a style of reason much resorted to by the head of his church, as well as others, in making converts, *i.e.,* a broken hand. Billy Considine says he has seen a cut glass decanter do good service, when aimed low, but to move a stubborn half-drunken Turk give me a good tough piece of wagon spoke, aimed tolerably high.

"August 17 . . . We find this valley, cultivated by the Indians, in far better condition, as far as crops and prospects are concerned than any part of New Mexico we have yet seen. They seem to have plenty of corn and wheat, and are, altogether, quite as well off as their Mexican neighbors."

During the Civil War the camels were neglected. Eventually they were sold to mining companies and circuses or were turned loose.   For many years they wandered about the Southwest and even found their way into Indian legends.   Beale kept a few camels on his California ranch and before he left his retirement to serve as minister to Austria-Hungary, frequently created a stir in Stockton by arriving in a carriage drawn by camels.

The Comanche were finally driven out of this territory in 1874, when Colonel Nelson A. Miles descended upon them from Fort Dodge, Kansas; Colonel R. S. Mackenzie advanced from Fort Sill, Oklahoma, attacking on the east; and troops from Fort Union, New Mexico, threatened from the west.   The former "scourge of the plains" were taken to an Oklahoma reservation under the guns of Fort Sill, and the American Army completed what Indians, Spaniards, Mexicans, and the Republic of Texas had attempted.

In the 1870's when buffalo hunting was a lucrative commercial enterprise several "floating outfits" (consisting of a cook and several "hands" who lived on the plains for a year at a time) killed buffalo by the thousands for their hides.   Their greed made short work of the enormous herds and in 15 years the buffalo had gone from this region.   By watching the movements of the animals the hunters had discovered not only water holes but undersurface water as well.   After the buffalo disappeared, western cattle were brought to graze on the luxuriant grasses.   Prairie schooners brought homesteaders whose settlements grew into towns, and the Staked Plains became staked-out areas where men struggled to establish homes and provide food for their families.

US 66 crosses the Texas Line at GLENRIO, 0 *m.* (4,286 alt., 80 pop.), at a point 73 miles west of Amarillo, Texas.   Glenrio is a cluster of stores and gas stations among small frame houses.

ENDEE, 4.7 *m.* (350 pop.), a blowoff town for the cowpunchers in the early years of its existence, is now a sunbaked ruin of dilapidated shacks and frame buildings.   In its heyday, the town had regular Sunday morning burials for those who had been too slow on the draw.   It is said that in preparation for their reception, a trench was dug each Saturday on the edge of town.

BARD, 12.9 *m.* (4,290 alt., 30 pop.), a trading point for ranchers, consists of a few shacks and houses about a store and filling station.

SAN JON, 18 *m.,* an eastern REGISTRATION STATION (4,192 alt., 541 pop.), is a busy trading center of ranchers but has no overnight accommodations.

TUCUMCARI, 42.2 *m.* (4,135 alt., 6,163 pop.), has increased its population 50 per cent since the official census was taken in 1930. It is a division point on the main line of the Rock Island Railroad, which here meets the Southern Pacific.   The town is named for the near-by mountain but the origin of the mountain's name is obscure.

Tucumcari was only a small trading point for cattlemen, until the Rock Island arrived in 1901; in 1903, when Quay County was organized, this was made the county seat.   About 40 per cent of the present (1940) population is of Spanish and Mexican descent but each year more people from Central Texas and Oklahoma move here attracted by the dry-farming area where wheat and sorghums are raised. The town also ships cattle, but the tourist business is its chief source of income. This is the border between the Central Standard Time zone and the Mountain Standard Time zone (west bound tourists set their watches back one hour).

Tucumcari is at the junction with US 54 (*see Tour 13*).

The Tucumcari Metropolitan Park Area, with Tucumcari State Park is (L) at 46.7 *m.* alongside US 66, within sight of the highway.

Westward US 66 parallels the railroad through tawny-yellow formations and cultivated fields with farm houses and windmills in the distance. Yucca and bunch grass clothe the plain, and the landscape is vivid with red, purple, and green. Fenced pastures enclose beef cattle, farm houses, windmills, and corrals.

There is an especially fine view from 54 *m.,* and at 60 *m.* are high mesas and rock upheavals, conspicuous in this generally level land. Before the military campaigns drove off the Comanche and confined them, the BLUFFS OF THE LLANO ESTACADO (L) were the rendezvous for renegade Mexicans and white Americans who acted as "fences" for Comanche cattle thieves. This was known as the "Comanchero trade." The Indians would drive off cattlemen's stock and sell them to the renegades who, in turn, marketed them after altering the brands. Charles Goodnight (*Charles Goodnight* by J. Evetts Haley) tells of three well-defined trails used exclusively by the Indians and those who bought their loot, and all three crossed the Llano Estacado. The illicit trade flourished for 20 years, during which time thousands of cattle were stolen. The Indians usually got the worst of the bargain. On this point, Goodnight writes, "One cow went for a loaf of bread or a cheap trinket, whereas a quart of whiskey called for the transfer of a large herd." Military forces who put a stop to this were aided by cowmen, trail drivers, and law officers who took a substantial toll with their own guns.

A typical BOOT HILL CEMETERY (L) marks the eastern edge of the hamlet of MONTOYA, 62.6 *m.* (152 pop.), a loading point for the Southern Pacific Railroad. "Boot hill" cemeteries are to be distinguished from others in that decent folk, who died in their beds as a result of so-called natural causes, were laid away in "hallowed ground," while those whose trigger-fingers were a trifle sluggish, or who felt the ire and the bullets of an enraged citizenry, were grudgingly flung with their boots on into a pit beside others who had suffered violent deaths.

West of Montoya the route traverses plains broken here and there by sandstone, rock ridges, and small hills with stunted juniper, mesquite, and cactus.

NEWKIRK, 73.3 *m.* (4,330 alt., 239 pop.), an unloading station for construction supplies, is increasing in population since work on the Conchas Dam was started.

Right from Newkirk on graded dirt NM 129, to CONCHAS DAM, 25.2 *m.*, a PWA project, approved in 1933. The quarters of the engineers are at the dam's site, and the workers live at Gate City, which is a collection of huts, 6.8 miles south. The project consists of a concrete main dam in the canyon of the South Canadian River and earth wing dams contiguous. The main dam is 235 feet above the roadway, with a crest length of 1,250 feet. When the water is level with the top of the emergency spillway, this reservoir has a storage capacity of about 600,000 acre-feet and covers about 26 square miles extending up the South Canadian Valley about 14 miles and up the Conchas Valley about 11 miles. It is estimated that this reservoir will reduce flood damage in Texas and Oklahoma, providing water for 100,000 people and for irrigating 45,000 acres of neighboring land.

West of Newkirk more red mesas are visible, with cattle grazing on the wide plains.

CUERVO (crow), 81.9 *m.* (4,300 alt., 287 pop.), is a group of frame buildings, a store, and several gas stations.

As the road climbs over the bluffs of the Llano Estacado, there is a panorama of the Pecos Valley with rolling grasslands reaching to distant mountains, and at the top of a rise, Corazón (heart or core) Hill (6,220 alt.) comes into view (R).

The Pecos River rises in the Sangre de Cristo Mountains and flows south into Texas draining the eastern part of New Mexico; after the buffalo had been killed off, this section became cattle country and the tall tales of the buffalo hunters were dwarfed by the taller tales of the cowboys. A favorite among them was the legend of Pecos Bill who originated in Texas, but eventually covered the entire Southwest, for wherever cowpunchers gathered, the spirit of Pecos Bill was invoked in song and story. Many of the legends, including the story of the Perpetual Motion Ranch, were based on actual incidents. In the finished version the ranch was on a conical mountain so that the cattle grazed low on its sides in winter but climbed higher in summer and so required little herding by the cowboys. It was offered for sale to an Englishman who, when he arrived with his sedate wife and ebullient daughter, Sluefoot Sue, insisted upon a count, and sat down to check off the number as the cattle were driven past. The enraged cowboys made up for the great discrepancy between the actual number in the herd and that listed in the contract of sale by driving the small herd around and around the mountain while the buyer counted. After one bald-faced steer had hobbled past a dozen times, the Englishman asked how many of that breed there were, and when told there were twelve of that highly valuable strain, he signed the deed and paid the money. Pecos Bill, hearing what had occurred when he returned to the Perpetual Motion Ranch, slipped away on his horse, Widow Maker, and drove thousands of cattle from the plain onto the ranch—more than enough to make the count an honest one.

Another Pecos Bill story accounts for the appearance and name of the Llano Estacado. When Pecos Bill lassoed a tornado that threatened his vast herds the tornado bucked, sunfished, and sunned its sides in its efforts to escape; it ranted and tore around until everything was so bare that people had to drive stakes across the country to find their way about.

In the late 1860's, Charles Goodnight and his partner drove cattle along the Pecos from Texas to Fort Sumner (*see Tour 8a*), and from there, under a contract with Santa Fe supply men, drove a hundred head a month to that capital.

After the coming of the railroad early in the twentieth century, each succeeding year brought changes and deepened the gulf between the old and new ways of living. Tiny settlements that originated as trading points for ranchers became agricultural and shipping centers, and from populations of ten, twenty, or a hundred, towns grew amazingly. Settlers migrated from Oklahoma and central Texas to the cities, steadily raising the percentage of resident Americans, but the small villages were little affected and still retain their charm, simplicity, and Spanish language and customs.

SANTA ROSA, 100 *m.* (4,616 alt., 1,127 pop.), on the banks of the Pecos River, is the seat of Guadalupe County (*small hotels, tourist camps*). It is a trading place for ranchers and a shipping point for livestock and wool, with about 85 per cent of its population of Spanish and Mexican descent. The first settlement here was called Agua Negra Chiquita (little black water). It developed here after 1865 when Don Celso Baca came from Mexico and became lord of the region under the old custom of range domain. In Santa Rosa is the western junction with US 54 (*see Tour 13*).

Left from Santa Rosa on NM 11, a dirt road, to PUERTO DE LUNA (doorway of the moon), 10.4 *m.*, where Coronado is said to have built a bridge in 1541. The town, founded in 1862, was the seat of Guadalupe County until the railroad so increased Santa Rosa's importance that the county seat was moved there. In the winter of 1862 a committee of thirteen men was appointed to examine this site to determine its advantages for settlement. At their favorable report, six families moved in. A dike thrown across the Pecos River the following spring provided water for irrigation, and land cultivation began. Then the Navaho came, raiding the herds of the village and killing the herder. Later, they returned, killed a boy, and drove off more of the stock.

In the spring of 1864 the Indians attacked in greater force, but the settlers were better armed, and succeeded in driving them off, killing three. As late as 1866 a band of twenty-five Indians drove off a large flock of sheep belonging to a man from Antón Chico known as Cuate Real (colloq. Royal Pal). Twelve men set out on horseback from the settlement, followed later by thirteen men on foot. The Indians were overtaken about 25 miles from the village, but the dust raised by the sheep afforded them a screen, and under cover of this they surprised their pursuers, who barely managed to drive them off. The sheep were recovered, however, as well as a herder whom the marauders had captured and who had been compelled to carry water while goaded ahead by repeated jabbing with Indians' lances.

West of the Pecos River at 100.3 *m.* is the southern junction with US 54 (*see Tour 13*).

In a filling station at 101.8 *m.* is a BILLY THE KID MUSEUM. Most of its relics are from Maxwell's house (*see Tour 8a*). There is also an old account book from Lucien Maxwell's days in Cimarrón (*see Tour 2b*), showing purchases in 1851 by Christopher (Kit) Carson, the guide and scout.

At 117.8 *m.* is the junction with US 84, part graded gravel and part graded dirt.

Right on US 84, which runs through open range country dotted occasionally with cane cactus and revealing vistas of seemingly endless rolling country.

At DILIA, 24 *m.*, is the junction with a dirt road; L. on this 6 *m.* to ANTÓN CHICO (5,270 alt., 500 pop.), near Tecolote (owl) Creek which joins Cañón Blanco about 5 miles south of here. Antón Chico (nickname for Sangre de Cristo) is a shopping place for ranchers and during the season for sportsmen attracted by the excellent deer and turkey hunting in the country immediately to the west. Stock raising is the principal occupation.

US 84 continues to a junction with US 85 at ROMEROVILLE, 56 *m.* (*see Tour 1a*).

US 66 crosses flat plains with sparse growths of scrub juniper and piñon and occasional flocks of sheep guarded by lone herders.

PALMA, 148.3 *m.,* is a crossroads hamlet.

Right from Palma on NM 3 a graded gravel road, across Cañón Blanco, to VILLANUEVA, 24 *m.*, center of a game-hunting area.

At 150 *m.* CERRO PEDERNAL (flint peak) is visible (L). Although not high, it is an outstanding landmark in this level country. Stories of buried treasure on its summit have caused it to be pitted with excavations by hopeful fortune hunters. There is a large spring at its base, which makes the place a natural camping ground. Many fights over possession of this spring took place in the heyday of the cattlemen. The name refers to the many arrowheads found around its base.

On the plains is CLINES CORNERS, 156.8 *m.* Westward the terrain becomes undulating, with more heavily wooded areas of piñon and juniper. (*Avoid straying cattle on the highway.*)

In BUFORD, 178 *m.*, another crossroad, is the junction with NM 41, a bituminous-paved, two-lane road (*see Tour 3b*).

West of BARTON, 190.9 *m.,* which consists of a tourist camp, a store, and a gas station, the road winds through hilly country into Tijeras Canyon, passing trading posts and wayside gas stations.

At 200.4 *m.* is the junction with NM 10 (*see Tour 15*).

TIJERAS (Scissors), 201.4 *m.* (467 pop.), is within the boundaries of CÍBOLA NATIONAL FOREST; west of the village where US 66 emerges from the canyon there is a fine view of the Rio Grande Valley and of Albuquerque in the distance.

ALBUQUERQUE, 217.3 *m.* (4,943 alt., 26,570 pop.) (*see Albuquerque*). In Albuquerque is the junction of US 85 (*see Tour 1b*).

*Section b. ALBUQUERQUE to ARIZONA LINE, 159 m.*

US 66 passes the fertile farms and orchards of the Rio Grande valley. Beyond these are arid, grass-covered plains and plateaus that sweep toward mountains. The gray-green clumps of sage, desert grasses, and low bushes, yellow with flowers in summer and autumn, meet the blue-green trees that dot the sides of hills and mountains. The road cuts through occasional stretches of earth whose vivid reds and yellows sharpen the contrast with the soft deep blue of the mountains and the brilliant turquoise of the spreading sky. It is a landscape of changing colors. Brilliantly colored geologic formations appear, some with smooth contours and others with the sharp outlines of a violent upthrust. Near the road are a few tiny villages of Indians or Spanish-speaking Americans or the solitary dwelling of a Navaho family. This is a sparsely peopled region whose lifeblood is water—where it flows is nurture.

For more than 400 years, over parts of this route or on roads branching from it, have moved soldiers of fortune, prospectors, priests and missionaries, colonists and caravans, traders and trappers, thieves and murderers, sheepherders and cowboys with their herds and flocks. Where the dwellers of the plains once roamed and hunted, docile sheep now set the mood, supply food and covering, and signify capital resources. Near the Arizona Line, where the highway approaches the southern boundary of the Navaho reservation (*see Tour 6C*), there is an occasional glimpse of a *hogan* (Navaho dwelling) with an Indian tending his flock of sheep near by. Approaching Gallup, the sandstone cliffs on the right stand higher, looking down with changeless calm upon those who now hurry by, safeguarded inheritors of adventurers who paved the way.

West of Albuquerque, 0 *m.,* are vistas of richly colored mesas and desert, stretching to the Arizona Line. The color and the forms are even more fantastic farther north (R), and the artist who attempts to paint this country must wrestle with the problem of light that shifts so rapidly he has scarcely time to outline a scene before it has changed entirely. This is especially true at sunset, when there is usually such a riot of color that if it could be accurately presented it would seem a gross exaggeration to those unfamiliar with the country. Here is such vastness of sky, such piling up of cumulus clouds on the horizon, that at times the whole universe seems to be made of sky and cloud. Though many come to New Mexico for the benefits of its sunny, dry climate, even more are attracted by the beauty of the landscape. The San José River (R) parallels US 66 as it crosses the eastern boundary of the LAGUNA INDIAN RESERVATION, 32.6 *m.,* a grazing area of 125,225 acres set aside for the Indians of the Laguna Pueblo. The Rio Colorado (Red) empties into the San José river at 32.6 *m.*

At 40.6 *m.* is a junction with a dirt road.

Right on this road to MESITA, 0.6 *m.,* a small settlement of Pueblo Indians from the Laguna grant. The cluster of adobe houses, at the foot of a red- and buff-colored mesa, rests on a lava bed.

US 66 dips into the San José river bottom through a broken, colorful country. Along the river bank is a great lava dike; dark mesas are tapped with sand dunes and black lava beds protrude on both sides. From the top of the rise is a glimpse of the Laguna Indian Pueblo.

Across the San José River is the settlement of Old Laguna (L), 45 m., and the junction with a graded dirt road, good in dry weather (difficult when wet).

Right on this road to PAGUATE, 7.2 m., a Laguna village of about 500 Pueblo Indians who raise sheep.

SEBOYETA (from Cebolleta, tender onion), 13.8 m. on the dirt road, is one of the oldest settlements (7,500 alt., 400 pop.) in this region and was long an outpost in enemy territory. A temporary settlement was made in 1746, and in 1749 the Franciscans established a mission for the Navaho who promised to live in the walled town; but after a year of sedentary life these strolling herders deserted and resumed their old ways. When colonists were sent up from Mexico, the Navaho regarded them as invaders and waged war. There is a long record of strife in the old Spanish archives. The colonists were aided from time to time by friendly Laguna Indians, who hated the Navaho, and by a detachment of soldiers who were sent to garrison the fort; but time and again, their cherished crops were stolen. In later years when the villagers grew stronger, the young men of the town would go out on raids and steal Navaho boys and girls for slaves. It was the custom when a marriage was arranged in the town to give the *Cebolleteños* an order for one or two Navaho boys or girls as a wedding present. The town now has a day school, whose curriculum includes two years of high school, and a vocational school established in 1936 for those over 16, who are taught tanning and woodworking. As in many remote New Mexico communities, Seboyeta men belong to the Penitente brotherhood. In the little adobe church, built in 1823, are two objects used in their processions—a cart in which the effigy of death (*la muerte*) is carried and El Santo Entierro (The Holy Sepulchre), constructed on a wooden frame with two handles at both ends. Within, plainly visible, is the Cristo dressed in long garments of white with the crown of thorns pressed down tightly on the head and drops of blood painted on the face. In the choir loft (L) is a sacred painting in oil, and one of a patriarchal figure (R) with the words "Elias Francis and Son" in the lower left corner. Elias Francis was a Syrian peddler who visited Seboyeta about 1880, settled there, and for 50 years was its most influential citizen.

Left (inquire directions in village) 1 m. from the church on a dirt road to a SHRINE OF OUR LADY OF LOURDES (L) in a natural recess under overhanging rock. The altar is carved out of the rock wall. At the base of the rock near the altar flows a spring of clear water, which runs off into the Paguate River. The story is that in the early days, after the Navaho had reduced the settlement's male population to 15, the colonists walked to Chihuahua, Mexico with their families, begging to be sent back to Spain; but the Viceroy insisted they return to Cebolleta and perform their contract to colonize. So they walked once again the thousand and more miles back to Cebolleta and erected a shrine to Our Lady of Mercy, vowing that so long as Cebolleta stood, they would hold feasts each year in Her honor. Cebolletta stands. And there is the shrine, though the present image of Our Lady is not as old as the shrine itself.

LAGUNA PUEBLO, 47.3 m. (5,795 alt., 2,451 pop.), was named for a near-by lake that has since disappeared. There was a small settlement of Indians at this place in 1697, but the pueblo was not established until 1699 when the Spanish governor, Pedro Rodríguez Cubero, ordered it done, while he was on an expedition to Zuñi. This is the only pueblo establishment subsequent to the Spanish invasion and is the largest east of the Continental Divide. Its people are a mixture of four Pueblo linguistic stocks: Tano, Keres, Shoshone, and Zuñi.

It is the "mother pueblo" of seven summer or farming villages scattered within a radius of a few miles at points where there is irrigation. The houses are mainly of stone plastered with adobe.

There are Government schools at all the little Laguna settlements roundabout so nearly all the people can speak English though the language they use mostly is Keresan. This pueblo is one of the most progressive, perhaps owing to the influence of three young American surveyors who came here in 1870 and married Laguna girls. Many of these Indians, in addition to attending the Government schools, have worked on the railroad, and this has made them more willing to accept white men's customs, though they have managed to retain much of their native culture and blend it with their Roman Catholic religion. Like other Pueblos, they are farmers.

Because of its accessibility this pueblo is often visited and is well known. It is a trading center for the Navaho, especially on the feast day, September 19, when a harvest dance is given. Other dances, such as Buffalo, Tablita, and Deer, are given at intervals during the year.

SAN JOSÉ DE LAGUNA CHURCH (1699), unlike many of the New Mexico mission churches, is of stone with plain, massive walls having only four openings of any size—the doorway, a window in the middle of the front facade, and two small belfry openings in the false gable front, with a glistening cross above. The rooms adjoining the church, which once were a convent, add to its massive appearance as does the churchyard enclosed by an adobe wall. The plaster on all the buildings is of native earth and the walls have been smoothed down to their present lines by time and weather. The decorations of the interior are the works of Indian craftsmen. All around the side walls are designs in red, yellow, and green bordered with heavy black lines with birds at intervals. On the ceiling of the chancel are painted Indian symbols of the sun, moon, stars, rain, and a rainbow; on the walls hang paintings of two saints, Santa Barbara on the north and San Juan Nepumoceno on the south. A large painting of St. Joseph done on elk's skin hangs on the reredos, and above are the figures of the Trinity, their halos triangular instead of circular. The altar is covered with animal skin, tightly drawn and painted with Christian symbols. The ceiling of the nave is of the usual carved and ornamented *vigas*.

PARAJE (place) 50.5 *m.,* is a small settlement of Laguna Indian farmers, a trading post, and also the junction with NM 23 (*see Tour 6A*).

At 55.7 *m.* is the junction with a dirt road.

Right on this road 1.4 *m.,* to CUBERO (6,210 alt., 1,340 pop.), a village of old adobe houses, that was named for the Spanish governor. It was formerly occupied by Indians from San Felipe and other pueblos. There is a pueblo ruin near by, but it is difficult to find without a guide.

From Cubero the dirt road continues 7 *m.* to a fork; L. from the fork 22 *m.* to a second fork and L. 8.6 *m.* to SAN MATEO (383 pop.) in the Cibola National Forest. This small village is a trading center for sheep ranchers. North of it are the remains of PUEBLO ALTO, which was approximately 100 feet wide and 200 feet long. Enough of the walls remains to show that it was a two-story structure.    In the western part is a tower, square on the outside and round within.    The pottery found is of the Chaco Canyon type (*see Archeology*).    Ruins of a stone pueblo are also within the town limits, and small house ruins are east and west of the village.

From 56 *m.* MT. TAYLOR (11,369 feet) is visible (R), the highest peak in this section.

US 66 continues through stretches of desert with multi-colored formations and with but little cultivated ground, except in the settlements off the road.    These native villages are as unchanging as the woman in one of their stories.    When she was called before a local justice he asked her age.    "I have 45 years."    "But," said the justice, "you were forty-five when you appeared before me two years ago."    "Señor Judge," she replied proudly, drawing herself to her full height, "I am not of those who are one thing today and another tomorrow!"

SAN FIDEL, 59.6 *m.,* is a small trading center for the ranchers of the district.

SANTA MARÍA DE ÁCOMA, formerly known as McCarty's, 66 *m.,* just off the road (L) is a farming community of Ácoma Indians. A number of adobe houses clustered against the rocky hillside, the new stone church, and the people themselves, present a picture of yesterday. Along the road in summer are Ácoma women and children in traditional Pueblo costumes seated under brush shelters with baskets of Ácoma pottery to sell.

There is an underpass of the Santa Fe Railway at 66.1 *m.,* and at 68 *m.* are LAVA BEDS.    Black basalt masses cooled and hardened in waves from 50 feet to 200 feet wide, winding and curving about the flat valley for 20 miles; where blisters had formed and broken are large caverns in the lava's rough surface.    A Navaho legend says that this lava is the blood of the great giant who was slain by the Twin War Gods in the Zuñi mountains (*see Folklore*).

GRANTS, 78.3 *m.* (6,464 alt., 1,541 pop.), is a railroad town and trading center for a large agricultural and ranching territory.    Its history begins in 1872 when Don Jesús Blea settled here and called his home under the cottonwoods Alamitos (little cottonwoods).    In 1873 came Don Ramón Baca with his family.    When the Santa Fe Railway reached this point in 1881, Alamitos became a coaling station and was renamed for the Grant brothers who constructed the railroad.

At 79.2 *m.* are the junctions with NM 53 and NM 174 (*difficult when wet*).    The former unites with US 66 west for 4 miles.

1. Left on NM 174 through SAN RAFAEL, 3.3 *m.* (1,059 pop.), a farming community, to the PERPETUAL ICE CAVES, 27.2 *m.*    In a volcanic sinkhole, its crevices are perpetually packed with solid ice, aquamarine in color and banded with dark horizontal stripes.    The ice bed is approximately 50 feet wide and 14 feet high.    Its depth underground is unknown.    E. R. Harrington, a scientist, thus explains the phenomenon: "The basaltic formation offers perfect drainage for melting snow, and my investigations show that the greatest amount of ice forms during the spring when the snow is melting on the surface.    Conditions such as the slant of the sun, temperature, formation of the cave, etc., result in free circulation of air in winter, freezing ice and drawing the cave full of

very cold air. In summer changes in conditions result in practically no circulation of air. Cold air in the cave has a tendency to remain there, and what few eddy currents of warm air enter are chilled to the freezing point. Thus the perpetual ice." Ranchers from the vicinity used to come here for ice during the summer. Farther south in the lava flow are several other ice caves that are less well known. A myriad of recent folk legends surround the lava flow and its various features. (*Tourists should wear stout shoes for walking over the lava bed.*)

2. Left on NM 53 to PAXTON or PAXTON SPRINGS, 20 *m.*, a logging camp (7,500 alt.), and the terminus of the Breece Company Railroad which carries logs and lumber to the main line of the Santa Fe at Grants. The spring, a stream of cool clear water, was named for the Paxton family, early settlers. NM 53 crosses the CONTINENTAL DIVIDE at Oso (Bear) Ridge just before its junction at 22.2 *m.* with NM 174. From here to the ice caves (alternate route) it is 1.7 *m.* farther.

Through groves of pine standing on a rocky terrain, the united roads pass several ranches. Red sandstone bluffs begin to mark the landscape at the approach to El Morro (headland) which is visible at 33 *m.* The settlement of EL MORRO is at 38.5 *m.* and at 40.6 *m.* is EL MORRO NATIONAL MONUMENT comprising a tract of 240 acres, established in 1906 to preserve INSCRIPTION ROCK, a camping place on the old Ácoma-Zuñi trail.

The rock, with a base roughly triangular and narrowing to a rounded and comparatively thin edge at the eastern end, covers about 12 acres. The stratification is slightly tilted. The top stratum is much harder than the bottom and has served as a shield to protect the softer layer below and preserve the outlines of the rock. Here, in centuries past, with what instruments it is difficult to say, perhaps sword points, the Spaniards and others carved historical "entries." The earliest now legible (1605) is that of Governor Oñate, the first colonizer of New Mexico. It is thought Coronado passed this point 65 years earlier, but there is no record in the rock which contains more than 500 deciphered inscriptions and names. Numerous Spanish governors following Oñate left their names. General Don Diego de Vargas, who reconquered the Pueblos after the rebellion of 1680, carved a brief record of his conquest, as did many explorers and members of expeditions into the Pueblo country. One of the names is that of Lieutenant Edward Fitzgerald Beale (*see above*). Members of freight and immigrant trains likewise recorded their passage. Soldiers, scouts, traders—all sorts and conditions of men—left their mark, the only claim to immortality some of them have. On top are ruins of two pueblos, which eventually will be excavated and restored. They are said to be the remains of an early Zuñi habitation. The cleavage, a blind canyon, runs deep into the heart of the rock, and in this an old spring has been uncovered. It had been reported by members of earlier expeditions, but was lost in later years and was rediscovered recently by an old Navaho who had served under the Apache, Gerónimo.

Drainage from the rock accumulates in a deep basin on its south side, forming a natural reservoir which for the past hundred years has been used as a public watering place.

NM 53 continues to a junction with NM 32 (*see below*) at 42.7 *m.* NM 32 continues through RAMAH, 53.6 *m.*, which is 3 miles east of the Zuñi reservation (*see below*).

US 66 passes over the Santa Fe Railway, 81 *m.*, and at 82 *m.* is the western junction with NM 53, a rough dirt road which also leads to SAN MATEO (*see above*).

BLUEWATER, 90.9 *m.*, is a railroad loading station.

Red sandstone cliffs (R) are at 92 *m.* and the volcanic cone (R) El Tintero (inkwell) from which lava is said to have flowed as far east as Grants. From this point are good views of the western slope of Mt. Taylor showing the high, lava-capped plateau from which it rises.

In SOUTH CHÁVEZ (R), 106.2 *m.*, a railroad siding, is a junction with a dirt road.

Left on this road (*almost impassable in wet weather*) to BLUEWATER RESERVOIR (*cabins, fishing, boating, swimming*), 3.6 *m.*, which contains the impounded waters from the Zuñi Mountain watershed and fills three great depressions in the high tablelands. A dam constructed in 1926-27 by the Toltec-Bluewater Irrigation District across two lofty natural walls of solid rock creates a deep lake one mile wide and seven and one-half miles long.

At 109.8 *m.* is the junction with a secondary road (alternate NM 164) to Chaco Canyon (*see Tour 6B*).

US 66 crosses the CONTINENTAL DIVIDE at 114 *m.*

At 131 *m.* is the junction with a graded dirt road.

Left on this road to FORT WINGATE, 3.3 *m.* (461 pop.), the integral part of the FORT WINGATE MILITARY RESERVATION comprising 64,000 acres. The fort is named for Captain Benjamin Wingate who was killed in 1862 at the Battle of Valverde (*see Tour 1c*). In 1850 a post named for Wingate was established at Cebolleta (Seboyeta) by the United States War Department and maintained as such until 1862, when it was moved to El Gallo near the present settlement of San Rafael, five miles south of Grants. This latter was the second Fort Wingate as established by Brigadier General James H. Carleton in the fall of 1862. Quarters were furnished for six companies of men, but the first garrison actually consisted of two companies. In 1863 this was increased to three companies, including one of California volunteers and two of New Mexico volunteers. It was headquarters of Kit Carson when he rounded up the Navaho but after the Navaho were brought back from their exile at Bosque Redondo (*see Tour 8a*), old Fort Wingate was abandoned, and in 1868 the new fort was established here. This place was called Ojo del Oso or Big Bear Springs and was the site of a fort called Fort Fauntleroy (established in 1860) after General Thomas Turner (Little Lord) Fauntleroy, an army officer who later resigned his commission in order to join the Confederates. Because of this desertion Fort Fauntleroy was renamed Fort Lyon, but in 1866 when the post at El Gallo was moved here, the name was changed to Fort Wingate.

From 1882 on the fort was often used as headquarters and outfitting post for ethnological and archeological expeditions. Fort Wingate was retained by the government as a military depot until about 1910. In 1914 the old buildings were used for housing 4,000 Mexican troops and their families who had been forced from Mexico into Texas at Eagle Pass during the Villa uprising. Some time after 1925 Congress appropriated $500,000 for a school for the Navaho on the Fort Wingate Military Reservation. The barracks have been made into dormitories, and the square where soldiers drilled is now a ball field. Included in the equipment is a golf course, three reservoirs, and irrigated gardens and fields.

The Magazine Area, where explosives are stored by the army, comprised in 1936 about 5,000 acres with 114 storage buildings. Large quantities of explosives were kept there immediately after the World War, when this area was taken over by the Ordnance Department. These storage plants are visible from US 66. In 1929 all land north of the Santa Fe tracks, approximately 1,500 acres, was turned over to the Bureau of Indian Affairs to be used as Indian grazing land.

From the top of the hill south of Fort Wingate is one of the finest views in McKinley County. Stretching for miles is a broad expanse of red sandstone cliffs colored like the Painted Desert of Arizona. Before the coming of the Americans, the Navaho under Chief Mariano used this section as an agricultural and watering place, called Shash'titgo (Navaho, bear springs). Lake Mariano to the north was named for this chief whose descendants still live in this vicinity.

The road continues through forests of pine, spruce, and juniper and groves of white aspen to McGAFFEY (8,300 alt.), 10 *m.*, which was a sawmill town before the lumber company cut out the timber and moved away. There is a transient camp here, a spring near the site of the old McGaffey sawmill, and a small lake (*fishing*). McGaffey is in the Zuñi District of the Cibola National Forest over which the Forest Service has jurisdiction, and the entire military reserve is a Federal game refuge (*no hunting*).

West of Pyramid Rock (R), 135 *m.*, US 66 continues along a red shale valley near the foot of great red cliffs. At 135.4 *m.* is an unobstructed view of a rock formation called NAVAHO CHURCH, an object of veneration by the Navaho. In these formations are several large caves, and it is said Kit Carson, in his roundup of the Navaho, used one of them to shelter his small party during a storm.

In REHOBOTH, 137.7 *m.* (6,461 alt., 378 pop.), is REHOBOTH MISSION, a school and hospital for the Navaho maintained by the Christian Reformed Board of Missions with headquarters at Grand Rapids, Michigan. Approximately 120 students are enrolled each year. The school opened in 1903 with six Indian pupils under the supervision of the Reverend L. P. Brink.

Near Gallup, the sandstone cliffs (R) seem to push themselves out of the ground. A gigantic upheaval which tilted the cliffs from horizontal into a semi-vertical position, known as the Zuñi Uplift (*see Geology*), marks the southern terminus of these beautiful formations. Beyond this, on a lower level, is another sandstone formation extending almost to the Arizona line and inclosing the coal beds for which Gallup is noted. Near Gallup the road passes through breaks in several intrusive dikes.

GALLUP, 142.2 *m.* (6,503 alt., 7,031 pop.), is a railway division point and a thriving industrial and trading center. Its principal industry is coal mining, most of the mines being in the immediate vicinity. Half of the population is Spanish and Mexican; Americans, Slavs, Italians, and other small groups complete the total. Its history is recent, dating back to 1879, when the Atchison, Topeka & Santa Fe Railway sent two mining engineers to prospect for coal, which was found here in large deposits. The railroad pushed through the section in 1881. Before this, sheep and cattle men occupied the territory, but when the government granted to the railroad alternate sections of land on both sides of the tracks in a forty-mile strip, ranchers were forced to graze their stock farther inland. Before the railroad was built there was only a saloon and general store here—it was built about 1880, was called the Blue Goose, and is still standing—that served as a stop on the Westward Overland Stage. After this point was made a railroad station and the mines were opened, settlers came in increased numbers, and the town grew steadily. Incorporated in 1891, it organized a local government and in 1901 was made the county seat of newly-formed McKinley County.

The coal mines have been operated continuously. Two in the immediate vicinity have offices in the town, and three others are within a radius of ten miles. Two large brick kilns have been built here because of the coal. Gallup is the main shipping point and buying center for the Navaho wool clip, thousands of pounds being shipped annually; it is also a buying center for the growing piñon nut industry. Wool combing and packing and the shipping of sheep and cattle from the grazing lands of the Zuñi mountains are important activities here, and the town serves as a trading point for the Zuñi and Navaho from the near-by reservations.

Gallup is most crowded during the four days of the Intertribal Indian Ceremonial, which until 1939 was held the last Wednesday, Thursday, and Friday of August, now advanced a week because the Hopi rain makers to the north have "batted a thousand" in their annual Snake Dances and the Gallup Indian Ceremonial virtually coincides with it. By getting a jump on the Hopi rain priests it was hoped that the Gallup show would not be dampened.

The Ceremonial originated in 1922, when a small group of Gallup businessmen organized a modest exhibit and invited a few Indians to dance at the McKinley County Fair in order to encourage the Indian to preserve his ceremonials and to improve his arts and crafts, also to inform people generally of the artistic excellence of the Indian artist and craftsman. Now it includes more tribal dances of various kinds than could be seen in years of going to Indian dances, more beautiful costumes, more color, more fascinating choregraphy than any ballet or tribal dances elsewhere produces. Here Navaho, Apache, and Pueblo Indians, hundreds of them, take part in the dances and contribute to the arts and crafts display. Navaho men make sand paintings and Navaho women weave blankets, while on the concourse men and boys race bareback, and undemonstrative Indians from a score of tribes look on without showing the intense excitement they feel. Here Indians from all tribes trade, many attending the ceremonial as much for this reason as for the dances, races, and general excitement. Groups of three or four Indians will squat on the ground, the men in a huddle, the women near by pretending a lack of interest in the proceedings which their sharp, keen glances belie. Perhaps none of the traders speak the same language, so that signs are used, fingers are pointed and heads nodded in agreement or an averted glance indicates that the signaled propositions are not agreeable. If goods are being traded, fingers point to the article held by the one offering it and then point to the article or articles desired in exchange. If money is offered, one extended finger means one dollar, another finger laid across it means one and a half, and so on. No outward sign or behavior indicates the battle for advantage, no flicker of eyelash or facial expression conveys any inkling of the real status of the transaction or how near to agreement the parties are. And when the deal is made or no deal results, they separate and move off without the slightest outward evidence of elation or satisfaction.

Gallup is the junction with US 666 (*see Tour 6C*).

Left from Gallup on NM 32-36, a graded dirt road, to ZUÑI PUEBLO, 41.7 *m*. (2,180 pop.), on the north side of Zuñi River, whose waters are used for irrigation. Approaching the large village of red sandstone houses, the ruined mission is visible in the center of it and corrals are interspersed among the houses. Vegetable gardens are visible across the Zuñi River. At the entrance to the pueblo are some trading posts, with others farther on at the southern and western bounds of the settlement. The Zuñi are farmers and sheepherders, noted for their dances and their arts and crafts—particularly the making of turquoise jewelry.

The ZUÑI MISSION CHURCH (1705) is a crumbling ruin. Its massive front towers flank remains of a once deep and shadowed entrance loggia. The timber floor of the loggia balcony is still intact as is its supporting, bracketed post.

Zuñi is most interesting to visitors during the Shalako, a festival in which the gods enter the village, late in November or early in December, to bless the new houses. The Zuñi houses are built of red sandstone, with high-ceiled and spacious rooms. The six Shalako who come to bless them present a most imposing appearance; they are about ten feet high and have glossy black hair five feet long hanging down their backs. Each great mask, executed with superb artistry, is supported by a man who works, by hidden controls, the huge, beak-like mouth of the god and at intervals utters his bird-like cries. The masks are the largest of any group of American Indians.

The name Zuñi is a Spanish adaptation of the Keresan *Sunyi'tsi* or *Su'nyitsa,* the meaning unknown. The name of the tribal range is *Shi'wona,* corrupted to Cíbola (see-bo-la). In 1539 Fray Marcos de Niza, seeking the seven cities of Cíbola, set out from Mexico with Estevan, a Barbary Moor or Negro (there is conflict of opinion) who had accompanied Nuñez Cabeza de Vaca on his journey from Florida to Mexico. Great excitement attended the departure of this expedition, for it was believed that gold, silver, and jewels were to be found in greater abundance in Cíbola than the Mexican conquerors had ever known. When word reached Fray Marcos that the Zuñi had killed Estevan, who had been sent ahead with the Indian guides, Fray Marcos hurried forward. From an adjacent eminence he viewed Háwikuh (Ahacus), the principal of the seven villages, and it is thought that in the golden rays of the setting sun Fray Marcos believed this mass to have walls of gold, which made all the fabulous stories seem credible. Without entering any of the villages, he hastened back to Mexico, where his glowing accounts hastened the later Coronado expedition which marched upon Cíbola (1540). In this meeting with the Spaniards the Indians were on guard and suspicious. Friction developed, and after the engagement that followed, the Indians retreated.

The Spaniards continued their advance to Háwikuh, which Coronado called Granada. He carried the place by storm, but found nothing of value. The "Kingdom of Cíbola" consisted of just seven ordinary pueblos, and Coronado reported that Fray Marcos "had said the truth in nothing that he reported." Háwikuh became the base of operations for a time, and from here expeditions were sent to Tusayan (the Hopi country), the Grand Canyon of the Colorado, and to the Rio Grande and beyond, where, after the arrival of the main force, the Spaniards entered winter quarters.

Cíbola was visited by Chamuscado in 1580. He reported but six villages. In 1583 came Espejo, who was the first to call the village, known as Halona, Zuñi—adding that its other name was Cíbola. He found some Mexican Indians who had been left there by Coronado. Espejo also reported six villages, one of them Háwikuh, indicating that one of the villages had been abandoned between 1540 and 1583. The ruins of Háwikuh are on the Zuñi River about 18 miles south of Zuñi. Part of these have been excavated, and much valuable information uncovered. In 1598 Oñate, first colonizer of New Mexico, visited Zuñi and the six villages, now in ruins.

The first mission was established at Háwikuh in the summer of 1629 by the Franciscan order, which sent three missionaries. Between this date and 1632, Fray Francisco Letrado was sent to Zuñi, where he was murdered by the Indians on February 22, 1632. Five days later Fray Martín de Arvide, who was en route to Zuñi, was overtaken by a band and killed. Fearing reprisals by the Spaniards, the Indians again fled to their stronghold, Taaiyalone (Corn Mountain), as in Coronado's time, and remained there until 1635. From then until 1670, their history is almost a blank. On August 7 of that year the Apache (some say the Navaho) raided Háwikuh, killed its missionary, Fray Pedro de Avila y Ayala, and burned the church. Háwikuh was never re-established as a mission. At the time of the Pueblo Rebellion, 1680, there were but three villages beside Háwikuh. The Zuñi took part in the rebellion, slaying their missionary and again fleeing to Taaiyalone, where they remained until New Mexico was reconquered by De Vargas in 1692. They built a new pueblo on the north side of the Zuñi river, the present Zuñi pueblo. A church was erected about 1699, but in 1703 the village was again without a resident priest, owing to the killing of a few Spanish soldiers who had mistreated the Indians. After this act of violence, they again fled to Taaiyalone, where they remained until 1705, when they settled in the plain, and the missionary returned to them. A garrison was kept at the pueblo for several years. There were times when they were at enmity with the Hopi, but peace was restored in 1713. There was a mission throughout the eighteenth century and well into the nineteenth, but the church gradually fell into ruins and was only occasionally visited by priests. For some time after the territory became part of the United States, Zuñi was entirely abandoned by white people.

In 1857 when Edward Fitzgerald Beale (*see above*), was surveying for a wagon road he wrote the following account of this place:

"August 29.—Arrived at Zuni, an old Indian pueblo of curious aspect; it is built on a gentle eminence in the middle of a valley about five miles wide, through which the dry bed of the Zuni lay (sic). As we approached, cornfields of very considerable extent spread out on all sides, and apparently surrounded the town. This place contains a population of about two thousand souls. The houses, although nearly all have doors on the ground floor, are ascended by ladders, and the roof is more used than any other part. Here all the cooking is done, the idle hours spent, and is (sic) the place used for sleeping in summer. Each house or family has a little garden, rarely over thirty feet square, which is surrounded by a wall of mud. Inside of these, and completely encircling the town, are the corrals for sheep, asses, horses, which are always driven up at night. We saw here many Albinos, with very fair skins, white hair, and blue eyes. The Indians raise a great deal of wheat, of a very fine quality, double-headed. The squaws are more expert at carrying things upon their heads than our Southern Negroes. I saw one ascend to the second story of a house by a ladder, with an earthen jar containing a full bucket of water without touching it with her hands. It was quite amusing to see the men knitting stockings. Imagine Hiawatha at such undignified work. The old Jesuit church is in ruins; but a picture over the altar attracted our attention from the beauty of four small medallion paintings in each corner, which are very beautifully done. . . . White intercourse (traders) with these Indians seems to have destroyed with them all the respect they had for the Catholic religion, without giving them any in return. Like all Indians who have a fixed abode, they are quiet and inoffensive. . . . We found here a few indifferent peaches, the only effect of which was to carry us back, in fancy, to home at this season. The melons also are quite poor, almost unfit to eat."

Two years later another survey again brought Beale through this country and he records: "March 16. . . . I . . . found it hard to realize that we had reached by so excellent a trail, & without a single hard pull, the dividing ridge of the dreaded Rocky Mountains. The country here, even at this forbidding season, is beautiful, & the forests of pine and abundant grass render it particularly favorable for settlement. . . . Tomorrow I shall despatch two wagons to the Indians at Zuni, in hope to find corn there, and the Indians in a selling humor. In this respect all Indians are singular. They either sell readily and for little or nothing, or not at all, & are as capricious in their dispositions as possible." "March 27.—We entered Zuni today. . . . The day was very disagreeable, with a high wind blowing the dust in every direction, reminding us of Washington City in a winter gale. . . . The old governor met me in the town with many compliments and congratulations. . . . He had a long list of grievances. The United States had persuaded him into an alliance with the troops as auxiliaries in the late war with the Navahoes; his people had fought with our troops side by side like brothers; the United States had found it convenient to make peace with their enemies, & had left their auxiliaries the prey of their powerful & numerous foes. I told him I thought it served him right for meddling in things which did not concern him, and warned him for the future to avoid all 'entangling alliances.' "

In recent years the government has built extensive irrigation works here and established a large Indian school; the younger generation is being educated and is learning the English language. In character and customs, the Zuñi resemble Pueblo groups generally. They are quiet, good tempered, industrious, and friendly toward Americans, but distrustful of the Navaho and hate the Mexicans. There are several trading posts at the pueblo, where the various arts and crafts may be seen and bought.

US 66 leaves Gallup and the REGISTRATION STATION is passed.

From Gallup the countryside is desert-like plains with occasional sandstone outcrops in fantastic shapes.

The road veers to the southwest at 151 *m.,* passing Defiance trading post and Rocky Point trading post which serve the Navaho. Half a mile farther the Santa Fe Railway again crosses the route on an underpass. MANUELITO, 158.5 *m.* (8,260 alt., 75 pop.), is also a trading center for the Navaho, and a wayside museum is maintained. A number of Navaho *hogans*—roughly octagonal or round structures of timbers or masonry walls with timber and dirt roofs and side walls chinked with mud—are seen here along the route. The settlement was named for Manuelito, a prominent Navaho chief, elected in 1855 when a treaty, not ratified by Congress, was arranged with the Navaho to end their depredations. Lawlessness on their part continued for another eight years, however, until they were all finally subjugated. Manuelito was made head of the police force and proved loyal to his trust.

At 159 *m.* US 66 crosses the ARIZONA LINE, 54 *m.* east of Holbrook, Arizona (*see Arizona Guide*).

# Tour 6A

Junction with US 66—Ácoma Pueblo; 13.7 *m.*   NM 23.

Unmarked dirt road.
No accommodations.

This route to Ácoma Pueblo, the Sky City, crosses the tilled fields of the Ácoma Indians and a sandy plain sparsely covered with rabbit brush and dotted here and there with juniper trees.   NM 23 branches south from its junction with US 66, 0 *m.* (*see Tour 6*) at a point 4.6 miles west of New Laguna and winds through the settlement of CASA BLANCA (white house) at 0.7 *m.*   The characteristic caprock formations of the Ácoma area appear along the mesa tops at 4 *m.,* closing in the plain to a valley confine.   NM 23 crosses the northern boundary of Ácoma Reservation at 10.3 *m.*

The ENCHANTED MESA (L) 10.6 *m.* called by the Ácoma, *katzimo* (Ind., enchanted), is a sandstone butte 430 feet high, golden brown, outlined by precipitous walls and sharply turreted pinnacles, with heaps of sharp detritus at its base (*only experienced climbers should attempt the ascent*).   The Ácoma have a tradition that their ancestors once lived on its top, but the path was closed by a storm.   The people tending their fields on the plain below were not able to regain their homes, and those who were caught on the summit died of starvation.

On ÁCOMA ROCK, 13.7 *m.,* which is of fairly level topped sandstone covering 70 acres and rising abruptly 357 feet from the windswept plain is ÁCOMA PUEBLO (7,000 alt., 1,168 pop.).   (*Admission $1; permission to photograph must be obtained from the governor. Usual fee: $1 for small cameras and $5 for movies.*)   This pre-Columbian Keresan-speaking pueblo is said to be the oldest continuously occupied village in the United States.   From a distance the pueblo appears to be part of the natural cliff and not readily distinguishable as a habitation.   Approaching the high fortress-like city are well-defined foot trails, which are still used, but some of the Indians prefer to ascend by the ancient toe- and finger-hole trail.   The only trail accepted as existing before 1629 is the ladder trail on the northwestern side, formed by a combination of ladder and toe- and finger-holes cut in the solid rock and tortuous passages worn deep by years of age.   This came to be known as "Camino del Padre" after Father Ramírez made his famous ascent.   The Burro Trail, built under the direction of the same priest, so that a more comfortable and less hazardous route might be possible, has at its top a large wooden cross, which is still decorated with flowers on "Cross Day" in May.   The trail principally used by visitors today is the one to the right of the Ladder Trail, leading over a wind-deposited sand rampart to a short ascent by stone steps. If taken leisurely it is not tiring to those able to do a moderate amount of uphill walking.

The dwellings, 1,000 feet long and 40 feet high, are built in three parallel lines of stone and adobe running east and west. Each structure consists of three stories terraced and built in the usual Pueblo style. The first story, between 12 and 15 feet high, originally had no openings except a trap door on top, being used exclusively for the storage of supplies. Ladders led from the ground to the second story, but the third story and roof are reached by steep narrow outside steps against the division wall. In appearance these long rows are community houses, but there is no communal or socialistic mode of life. Each family is completely separated from the others by substantial division walls. Many of the oldest houses still have windows of selenite, mined in the vicinity. The house groups are separated by streets of medium width, the one between the south and middle row being wider than the others and providing a plaza for ceremonials and festivities. The rooms of these groups have low ceilings, and at one end stand three lava-rock *metates* enclosed in a low wooden bin, sloping somewhat like a washboard in a tub, and used for grinding corn. The women use a small beveled stone or lava slab called a *mano* to crush the grain. This falls over the edge between the slabs, each *metate* grinding finer meal. There is also a fireplace for warmth and cooking. Outside are beehive-shaped ovens where all baking is done, save that of the *guayave* or paper-thin bread (called *piki* in Hopi and *hewe* in Zuñi). This bread, which is given great care, is baked on highly polished stones and placed upon a special firebox directly over the blaze. Usually made from blue cornmeal, the bread tastes something like popped corn and is sustaining on long journeys.

Men do all the heavy part of house construction including the carpenter work, but the women often build the adobe walls and do the plastering. Once a year, before the Saint's festival, the inside walls of the houses are freshly whitewashed. Against them are hung garments of skins, blankets, guns, trinkets of all kinds, and silver jewelry made by Ácoma artisans. Adding color to this array are twisted strings of red chili and dried muskmelon, bags of dried peaches, jerked mutton from the family's flock of sheep, and jerked venison from the pueblo hunt, all hung from the beams as winter food supply. At night wool *colchones* (mattresses) are laid on the floor; during the day they are rolled and placed against the walls where, covered with gay blankets, they make comfortable seats.

Ácoma pottery is thin and slightly less durable than that of Zuñi, but its designs have more variety. Flowers, birds, trees, and leaves are introduced with geometric patterns. Reds and grays, applied before firing, approach an accidental glaze afterward.

Instead of the inhabitants of the Great Rock going to the farming villages just for the planting and harvesting seasons as was their custom, more of them live in the summer towns the year round, returning to the mesa top only for ceremonies or festivities at stated intervals. The annual festival at Ácoma (*Sept. 2*) honors Saint Stephen, their patron saint, and is unlike that of any other pueblo, being the dramatic representation of Saint Stephen's arrival in New Mexico. Early in the morning a long procession appears several miles away on the plains below the citadel and slowly approaches. At the foot of the mesa it is met by the governor and war captain of the pueblo, who, after a conference, escort the "strangers" up the steep trail to the top and welcome them to the villages. After more ceremonies, both parties enter the church. A feature of this ceremony is a small hobbyhorse which is conducted into the church and up to the very altar itself, where more ceremonies take place; afterwards games and dances continue outside.

Ácoma is much the same as it was in 1540, when Captain Hernando de Alvarado of Coronado's army discovered it and called it Acuco. The native name, *Ako,* is of obscure etymology. The Ácoma call their own people Akomi (the "mi" meaning people); it has been translated as "people of the white rock." Charles F. Lummis called it "the sky city." Just when the pueblo was built on this natural stronghold no one can say. The Indian tradition gives the time as following the destruction of the Enchanted Mesa, ages ago. It was here when Fray Marcos de Niza sought the Seven Cities of Cíbola in 1533; and Antonio de Espejo in 1563 remarked upon the precipitous trail cut in the solid cliff leading to the top. The first Spanish foothold in Ácoma was in 1598 when the pueblo voluntarily submitted to the authority of the Spanish crown as represented by Don Juan de Oñate, but only that they might trick him later. Oñate refused to be lured into a room by Chief Zutucopan, however, and escaped the fate of Don Juan de Zaldivar who, with his detachment, was attacked without warning, and all but four soldiers were killed. Those leaped off the rock. The following months (December 1598), as soon as Oñate could marshal the weakened Spanish force, a band of 70 under the leadership of Vicente de Zaldivar, who insisted on the right to avenge his brother's death, were sent to punish Ácoma. They engaged in the assault on the 22, 23, and 24 of January 1599, and the forcing of that fortress was an epic struggle.

The mission here was assigned to Fray Andrés Corchado in 1598 and later to Fray Gerónimo de Zarate-Salmerón; but because of the hostility of the inhabitants, a church was not established here until 1629, when Fray Juan Ramírez, the first permanent missionary, was escorted to Ácoma by Governor Francisco Manuel de Silva Nieto on his expedition to Zuñi during July and August, 1629. Legend says that Father Ramírez walked alone from Santa Fe to Ácoma, having no defense save his cross and breviary, and that as soon as he was seen by the Ácoma attempting the ascent of their stronghold, he was pelted by rocks and arrows sufficient to kill a dozen men, but not one pierced his habit. It happened too, in the tumult on the top caused by his appearance, that a little girl was inadvertently pushed off and fell upon the pointed rock 60 feet below. The good Franciscan reached her, knelt and prayed beside her, then carried her unharmed up to her astounded relatives and neighbors. It was then the Ácoma received him as one more than human, and soon after became his followers.

After the Pueblo Revolt in 1680, the Ácoma people remained hostile for 16 years. In November of 1692, De Vargas and his small army reached a watering place called El Pozo (the well), a place from which the rock of Ácoma could be seen. In his journal, De Vargas wrote: "We descried the smoke made by those traitors, enemies, treacherous rebels and apostates of Zueres (Keresan) tribe." Within musket-shot of the Penol, the greeting of "Hail" was exchanged between the Spaniards and the Indians, but it required all the patience De Vargas could muster to finally persuade this most difficult of all pueblos to submit.

The Spanish Grant of 1659 was confirmed by the United States, December 22, 1858, but the Ácoma Indians formally applied for their land in 1863, when seven Pueblo governors went to Washington to confer with President Lincoln and settle boundaries. After the conference, Lincoln presented each governor with a silver-headed cane upon which was engraved (varying only as to the name of the particular pueblo):

> "A. Lincoln
> Prst. U.S.A.
> Acoma
> 1863"

This cane is passed to each succeeding governor when he is elected in January, and constitutes his badge of office. When the governor is away his representative keeps the cane. In 1877 the Ácoma had more than 95,000 acres; 17,400 acres have been added since by executive order making the present area more than 113,000 acres, 900 acres of which are irrigable, with 600 acres cultivated at Acomita and Pueblito.

SAN ESTEBAN REY (Saint Stephen the King) MISSION is claimed by some historians to be the church built here through the efforts of Fray Ramírez in 1629, with additions made after the Pueblo Revolt of 1680; others say the original edifice was destroyed in 1680, when Fray Lucas Maldonado, the Ácoma missionary at the time, was murdered. However, the present church, undoubtedly remodeled in 1699 and repaired in 1923 by the Museum of New Mexico, is one of the finest of all the old pueblo missions. It is 150 feet long and 40 feet wide, with walls 60 feet high and 10 feet thick, a marvel of adobe construction. Every ounce of material used in the mission, as well as the soil for the *campo santo* (burial ground), was carried up the steep passage on the backs of zealous Indian women. The heavy roof beams, each 40 feet long by 14 inches square, were cut in the Cebollata (tender onion) Mountains, 30 miles distant, and carried on men's backs to the top. The front walls of the church, devoid of architectural ornament, are so sloped that they form great buttresses, topped with square towers and open belfries. On the end wall of the chancel, contrasting with the bare, white walls of the nave, is a richly carved and painted reredos. It is divided into panels by twisted, serpentine columns, each panel having a painting of a saint placed above scroll and shell motifs. The huge carved *vigas* are supported by elaborately carved scroll brackets. Adjoining are the priest's residence, patio, and a lookout, the latter a vantage point from which an enemy might be seen. This affords a magnificent view of the countryside. The burying ground is perhaps a greater marvel than the church, and probably the only one of its kind in the world. The Ácoma converts wanted their dead in consecrated ground near by, so they built a stone retaining wall almost 10 feet high at the outer edge, enclosing an area 200 feet square; then from the plain below they carried up enough earth, a sackful at a time, to make their sacred graveyard. That the name of the mission was changed at one time to San Pedro is evidenced by the inscription on the old bell in the northeast tower of the church, which notes "San Pedro, 1710." Subsequently, Saint Stephen resumed his sway.

One of the most unusual law suits in the United States, in which the Pueblo of Ácoma was plaintiff and the Pueblo of Laguna defendant, was fought through the courts from 1852 to 1857 for possession of the painting of Saint Joseph, now at Ácoma. The picture was said to have been presented to Father Juan Ramírez by King Charles II of Spain, and taken by him to Ácoma in 1629, when he founded the mission here. The natives of Ácoma believed (and still do) that Saint Joseph endowed the painting with miraculous powers, and it is still held in great veneration. During all the Ácoma prosperity, the neighboring Pueblo of Laguna, which had suffered from drought, epidemics, floods, and other calamities, grew envious and asked to borrow the picture. The Ácoma consented. From this time, so the story goes, Laguna fortunes changed; those ill became well, the crops were good, the women bore children. Months passed, and the Ácoma, weary of waiting for the return of their beloved picture, sent messengers to inquire the reason for the delay. They received no satisfaction. A council was held. After a solemn Mass it was agreed that lots should be drawn. Twelve slips were prepared, eleven of them blank; on the twelfth was a rude sketch of the prized picture of San José. All twelve were shaken up in a jar, and two little girls, one from Ácoma and one from Laguna, were chosen for the drawing. On the fifth drawing, the Ácoma child drew the sketch of San José. "So," said the priest, "God has decided in favor of Ácoma," and the sacred painting was taken triumphantly to its former home.

One morning while Ácoma was still rejoicing its people went to pray before their beloved saint, only to find the picture gone! A war would have followed had not Father López counselled that the matter be taken to the United States District Court at Santa Fe. His advice was followed. The decision was in Ácoma's favor, but Laguna appealed the case to the Supreme Court. However, in 1857, the final decision also went to Ácoma. Rejoicing over their victory, a committee was appointed by the Ácoma to bring back the sacred painting, absent more than half a century. They had gone but half the distance to Laguna when, "miracle of miracles," they found the painting of San José under a tree! The Ácoma believe that San José had already heard of the decision and started to return, but being weary, tarried under the tree where he was met by his jubilant people.

# *Tour 6B*

Junction US 66—Crownpoint—Chaco Canyon National Monument—64.3 *m.* NM 164.

Graded dirt road entire distance; sharp declines over dry arroyos and washes, bad to impassable during rainy season; dusty when dry
Limited accommodations.

This route, through one of New Mexico's most important pueblo ruins, courses a high flat country bordered with sandstone upthrusts and cut by arroyos and hills that are sparsely covered with grama grass, piñon and juniper. The region is vast and open, with far horizons.

NM 164 branches right from US 66, 0 *m.* (*see Tour 6b*) at a point 17.8 miles west of Bluewater and parallels the Atchison, Topeka & Santa Fe Railway for a short distance. In the first few miles great sandstone ridges, magnificently sculptured, border the road on the left. For the most part the land is flat with occasional hills and rugged gullies, and everywhere the color is alluring, especially at sunset. Despite the general aridity, numerous springs of clear, pure water are present, seepages from formations in the substrata.

The ANTOME INDIAN MISSION, 5.3 *m.,* is operated under the auspices of the Christian Reformed Church. Winding northward, the highway courses over valley country, flanked again by hilly countryside.

Towerlike KINYAI RUIN (Navaho, tall house), 23.5 *m.,* is the ruin (R) of a pueblo believed to have been constructed by peoples affiliated with those of Chaco Canyon. Surrounding the ruins are remains of a well-defined Navaho irrigation system, two reservoirs, and a main canal 25 to 30 feet wide and in several sections 3 feet deep.

CROWN POINT, 26.3 *m.* (523 pop.), is at the edge of a plain, surrounded by low-lying hills opening at the north end of Devil's Canyon, three miles from the crown-shaped butte for which it was named. Before all the Navaho subagencies were consolidated at Window Rock, Arizona, this was the seat of the Eastern Navaho Agency; it still has a United States Indian School.

Although NM 164 runs a few miles east of the Navaho reservation, it traverses typical Navaho country, on which the Navaho have lived and grazed their flocks for centuries. From the highway are glimpses of *hogans* (Navaho dwellings) blending into the brown soil, solitary Navaho riding their ponies, rude wagons containing the entire Navaho family and their inevitable dog, and flocks of sheep tended by child herders. Grass is plentiful, and in summertime wild flowers abound after the periodic rains. The high altitude gives clarity to the atmosphere, and distant views are brought into sharp relief.

SEVEN LAKES, 42.8 *m.,* is a one-family settlement but has a gasoline pump. An unused country school for white children, a water hole for cattle, and the family home comprise the settlement. Formerly there were seven lakes in this vicinity, but at present three lake beds are dry. Oil was first discovered in 1923, but the wells were shallow and the output so limited that pumping operations have been abandoned. Fifteen miles to the east a small field is still in operation.

CHACO CANYON NATIONAL MONUMENT at Pueblo Bonito (*admission 25¢*), 64.3 *m.,* containing some of the greatest surface ruins in the United States, consists of 32 sections of land owned by the United States Government, the School of American Research, the University of New Mexico, and a private individual. It is in and about Chaco Canyon, a valley roughly ten miles long and a mile wide, eroded through a sandstone cap, in whose bottom during the rainy season flows the Chaco River.

The Monument is administered by the National Park Service. A permanent custodian is stationed near the ruins of Pueblo Bonito (Beautiful Village) to give information and assistance. A campground and trading post afford limited accommodations. Among the 18 major ruins and countless smaller ones, archeologists have identified house sites of the Basket Makers (*see Archeology*). Here also are the unit-type houses of the first Pueblo Indians. This culture period developed through Pueblo II and flowered in the Pueblo III or classic period.

In the monument a branch road leads (R) just over the bridge, passing most of the large ruins that are not on the main road.

Beginning with Pueblo Bonito and Chetro Ketl the most noted ruins are Taba Kin (Pueblo del Arroyo), Casa Rinconada (corner house), Kin Kletso (Navaho, yellow house), Pueblo Alto (high village), Casa Chiquita (little house), Peñasco Blanco (white rock), Hungo Payi, Una Vida (a life), Tzin Kletzin (Navaho, black house), Kin Biniola (Navaho, house of the winds), Wijiji, and Pueblo Pintado (painted village). In addition are innumerable sites which may be classed as accessories of the Pueblo culture—single-house ruins, sanctuaries, reservoirs, stairways, trails, and ditches. All these evidence a civilization that utilized its economic resources and had a religious, social, and aesthetic development. And since, in the main, the Pueblo III ruins of the Chaco have characteristics in common, Pueblo Bonito and Chetro Ketl can be taken as examples.

PUEBLO BONITO, close to the perpendicular north wall of the canyon, is the largest, the best-known, and most completely excavated of the main ruins in the Chaco region. The Hyde Expedition (1896-99) ·centered their research work on it and subsequent excavation was undertaken by the National Geographic Society (1922-26) under the direction of Neill M. Judd, curator of Archeology, United States National Museum. Through tree-ring dating, experts conclude that Pueblo Bonito was under construction in 919 A.D. Additions were made in the years 1017, 1033, and 1102 and the village was undoubtedly occupied in 1127. Pueblo Bonito differs from the majority of the ruins, being D-shaped rather than rectangular, or E-shaped. The building, surrounding three sides of a court, is terraced back from an initial height of one story at the court to three or more stories at the rear. The straight, fourth side of the court was enclosed by a tier of one-story rooms. Pueblo Bonito contained over 800 rooms and could easily have sheltered 1,500 people at one time. The masonry of its walls is of particular interest. They are composed of medium-sized stones hewn with stone implements, and so reinforced with small spalls that they present an almost mosaic-like pattern. Some of the rooms still have their ancient timbered ceilings; it was from these timbers and an occasional log found in the walls that the dating was accomplished. Within the court were 32 *kivas,* where clan and fraternal religious rites were observed. That Bonito was an exceptionally wealthy community, is in accord with the Navaho myths of No-qoil-pi, the Great Gambler, who not only won the possessions of the people of the region, but enslaved them as well. Among the rich artifacts found here are thousands of dish-shaped, perforated turquoise beads, turquoise and shell pendants, exceptionally fine turquoise and shell mosaics, carved birds and insects, and a frog of jet with eyes of inlaid turquoise. The most spectacular find was an extraordinary turquoise necklace recovered by Mr. Judd in 1924.

Pottery here was elevated to the plane of a fine art. The potter's wheel was unknown, but a crude substitute in the form of a shallow basket or the bottom of a broken *olla* (jar), was sometimes used as a movable work table upon which a new vessel was fashioned. The Chaco Canyon ruins contained beautiful pitchers, ladles, and bowls. The tracing of thin black lines over their highly polished (not glazed), gray surfaces, to form unusual and exquisite patterns, was the art of Bonito women. Tall, cylindrical jars, unlike those from other regions with design rarely if ever duplicated, show that their pottery stands close to the apex of ceramic achievment among pre-Columbian people of our country.

It is the regret of the archeological world that the main burial grounds of these large ruins have never been found. Only a scant number of burials have been unearthed.

CHETRO KETL, a large partly-excavated major ruin of a community home, which if set down in a modern American city would occupy an average city block, is a quarter of a mile east of Pueblo Bonito. Dr.

Edgar L. Hewett, director of the School of American Research in Santa Fe and in charge of the excavation, says, ". . . as a community dwelling, built by people for their own domestic purposes, I know of nothing to compare with it—ancient or modern." Chetro Ketl consists of a large main house and a succession of talus villages built against the cliff for a thousand feet. Basically, Chetro Ketl followed the "E" plan of architecture, but it varied from the type in that one of the wings of the "E" was completely extended and the other only partly. The great curved front which tied in the two ends of the "E" was not merely a wall but also a rampart of one-story rooms. Beneath this rampart was a walled trench about eight feet deep (probably covered) which prior to the construction of the rampart served as a protected passage-way from one wing of the town to the other, and was an instrument of defense. It had the usual terraced rooms, three to five stories high along the back wall, which was over 470 feet long. These rooms, as at Pueblo Bonito, surrounded three sides of a court containing the *kivas*. The *kivas* of Chetro Ketl are of three types—the great *kivas*, the small *kivas*, and the tower *kivas*. *Kiva* "G" the upper of a vertical series of *kivas* was constructed 1103 A.D., according to the tree-ring dating. The great *kivas* are always very large, and the one at Chetro Ketl measures 60 feet in diameter. In this sanctuary were three successive levels built one upon the other, each a replica of the pattern. The lower part of each of two main walls is encircled by a bench of masonry; near the middle of the floor is a raised fireplace, and on both sides of it a rectangular, vault-like structure of rock. Whether the great *kiva* was roofed has not been determined. A series of small rooms partly surrounds the *kiva* on the south side. Interesting are the crypts of the lower levels, safe-like sealed caches which yielded many strings of beads and turquoise pendants and ritualistic talismans.

The small *kivas* at Chetro Ketl, seldom more than 25 feet in diameter, have, like the larger ones, a low bench about the base of their walls. On each bench are several small blocks of masonry, 12 or so inches high, set an equal distance apart; each block usually encloses a short, heavy beam which runs back into the main wall of the *kiva*. Near the center of the floor is a firepit, and under the south wall runs the air duct or ventilator, opening through the floor near the firepit. West of the firepit is a single rectangular, masonry-lined vault. The tower *kivas*, built within the walls of the community houses, were completely surrounded by living rooms. Circular in shape, they were enclosed by walls in a square to separate them from the living quarters and obviously to fit into the general square layouts of the main entrance. The caverns were filled with earth. Pottery and bead work, tools, and artifacts are of the same general type as found at Pueblo Bonito, and archeologists have agreed that the inhabitants of Chetro Ketl were contemporaries of the Bonitians.

The Chaco group of ruins has been recognized as one of the most important archeological districts north of the Mexico Plateau, and its excavations an important archeological project in the Southwest. The permanent research station here, erected by the University of New Mexico and the School of American Research, consists of a headquarters building, a shop, bathhouse, and photographic laboratory, eleven dormitories (modeled after Navaho *hogans*), dining hall and kitchen, and storerooms. Two large *hogans* serve as a field museum laboratory and as a seminar room. A water system has been completed and camping quarters to accommodate classes of visiting students are planned. (*No camping is permitted on this property.*)

Field sessions in Anthropology of the University of New Mexico are conducted here each summer, and provisions are made for full-time work throughout the year for special students.

Pueblo Bonito is the southern terminus of NM 56 and the northern terminus of NM 164. NM 56, an unimproved dirt road, continues through OTIS, 26 *m.,* to a junction with US 84, 29 *m.* (*see Tour 9*).

# *Tour 6C*

Gallup—Shiprock; 94.3 *m.,* US 666.

Bituminous-paved two-lane road for 11 *m.;* remainder graveled.
During July and August high water makes arroyos dangerous to cross.
Do not attempt to ford if water is more than a few inches deep. Assistance can be obtained at trading posts. Watch out for sheep crossing to pastures. These flocks, usually tended by children, will be frightened and scatter if motorists approach too closely or suddenly.
Limited accommodations.

Most of this route is through the Navaho Indian Reservation with stretches of grass-grown desert and red soil and rocks eroded into formations of great beauty.

US 666 branches north from US 66 in GALLUP, 0 *m.* (*see Tour 6b*), passing the Santa Fe Railway shops. In the low-lying hills (R) are outcroppings of coal in the sandstone and shale composing this area.

GAMERCO, 2.1 *m.* (6,750 alt., 1,221 pop.), is a large modern coal camp, built by the Gallup American Coal Company since 1921. It includes homes for mine officials and employees, an executive office building, and a company store.

Sub-bituminous coal is mined here through shafts 400 feet deep. Underground are 30 miles of track, the longest haul being 2.5 miles. The mines and the power house supply electricity to near-by towns, including Gallup; are open for inspection by application to company headquarters.

Nationalities represented in Gamerco are Spanish, Mexican, American, Italian, Greek, Negro, Indian, Japanese, Welsh, and English.

Ruins of pueblo homes and *kivas* on the knolls around Gamerco are of recent discovery. In 1932 a miner on his way to work stepped on a skull a few feet from the mine tipple. On brushing aside the sand he uncovered the skeleton of a man in the position of a flexed burial, knees under chin. Less than half a mile north of town miners have unearthed nine rooms and the rounded walls of a *kiva* believed to be very old. Deposits of pottery and beads have also been discovered.

From a ridge at 4.5 *m.* is a splendid panorama; close at hand and also far in the distance loom mountain ranges, mesas, peaks, and buttes. Near these points have occurred encounters between Indian tribes fighting among themselves, between Spanish *conquistadores* and aborigines, and still later between the United States Army and the Navaho.

The road gradually ascends to the Tohatchi Flats, and at 10.5 *m.* the southern boundary of the NAVAHO INDIAN RESERVATION (22,010 pop. in New Mexico) is crossed. An Indian School is visible (L) at 15.7 *m.,* and at 16 *m.* there is a bridge over the Navaho River.

At 18.4 *m.* is the junction with a graveled road.

Left on this road to MEXICAN SPRINGS, 3.6 *m.,* called by the Navaho *Nakai Bito* (Mexican springs). The Department of Agriculture's Soil Conservation Service has an Experimental Station here. Fenced areas on both sides of the road have abundant grass, grown to retard both wind and water erosion.

On the Navaho's sacred CHUSKA PEAK (L), 23 *m.* (8,000 alt.), ceremonies to the Rain Makers are performed by medicine men. When rain is needed a medicine man goes to each family and collects beads or pieces of turquoise beads, offering them to the gods while he prays for rain. The turquoise is left on the peak where no Indian except the medicine man ever ventures. The name Chuska is a corruption of Shashgai (Navaho, white spruce).

TOHATCHI (Navaho, scratch for water), 24.6 *m.* (6,425 alt., 90 pop.), is an Indian village built around a United States Indian Service School and Hospital. The school, established in 1895, has been steadily enlarged to accommodate 265 pupils. Though a few of the children live in the dormitories, most of them are day pupils transported by three Government busses, each traveling 60 miles a day. Clothes and hot lunches are furnished.

Tohatchi, so named because water is obtained simply by scratching below the top soil in the arroyos, was called Little Water by the first white settlers. After the Reverend L. P. Brink came here in 1900 as a missionary of the Christian Reformed Board of Missions, he succeeded in putting a part of the Navaho language into writing. Tohatchi has a Roman Catholic mission also, and across the line in Arizona the Franciscan Fathers compiled a Navaho grammar and dictionary in addition to translating hymns and psalms into Navaho. The trading post here has been operated by Albert Arnold since 1909. (*Limited accommodations are available at a club maintained for government employees.*) The Navaho Chapter (similar to the Eastern grange) in this village is one of four which signed an agreement to co-operate with the Experimental Station of Soil Conservation Service at Mexican Springs in the reduction of stock and grazing.

A Navaho family living in Coyote Canyon near by tells of the days when their grandfather, a Mexican, had been captured and enslaved by the Zuñi. In a battle with this tribe, the Navaho captured the Mexican and took him to live with them. This incident is related to an even earlier era, when the capture and enslavement of Indians was introduced by the Spaniards, who used them for work in their *haciendas*. The Indians retaliated by enslaving Spaniards and later Mexicans. For years this practice was continued on both sides.

On the summit of Tohatchi Peak (L) is the Forest Ranger lookout. Bears still inhabit this region, which abounds in lakes and pine trees; and since the Navaho do not kill them because they are held sacred and hunting on the reservation is forbidden, the bears have greatly increased. At 25.6 *m.* is a wide panorama.

The eastern flank of Chuska Mountains (L) as seen from the highway is an imperfectly graded slope of 16 to 20 miles, rising from the valley at a rate of 200 to 300 feet per mile up to the 8,000 foot contour above which steep and frequently precipitous cliffs extend to the edge of the plateau-like summit. Stream channels gash the surface from one to three miles apart, in places cutting into bedrock. The streams, lakes, and numerous springs are frequently surrounded by small meadows near the base of the upper cliffs. Flowers remarkable for their abundance and variety grow at moderate altitudes. White spruce, piñon, juniper, alder, and aspen cover the slopes. Oaks and a few magnificent yellow pines grow along the higher benches above 7,000 feet. In these mountains are remains of breastworks marking a fight that occurred before 1850, according to Navaho legend, between their warriors and Mexican troops.

DROLET'S, 42.9 *m.* (5,850 alt., 40 pop.), is a trading post and Government Day School whose Navaho name is *Narshitty* (badger) ; J. M. Drolet now owns the trading post, the oldest on US 666. Both a Christian Reformed mission and a Roman Catholic chapel are here.

At 49 *m.* is the junction with a graded dirt road.

Left on this road, 14.2 *m.,* to WASHINGTON PASS, named in honor of Lieutenant Colonel John M. Washington, civil and military governor of New Mexico, 1848-49, and commander of the expedition against the Navaho in 1848. Locally this is called Cottonwood Pass, though the Navaho name is *Breath-kil-chee-begez* (stream running from two peaks). The pass leads left over Chuska Mountains to CRYSTAL, 18 *m.,* a trading post, and across the Arizona State Line to the upper end of Canyon de Chelly where Kit Carson rounded up the Navaho (*see Tour 8a*). On the summit of the mountains near Washington Pass are numerous mountain meadows with rain-filled ponds where Navaho often camp during the summer months to plant fields of corn and squash and to graze their flocks.

From 47 *m.* are views of Arnold's Rock, Bennett's Rock, and Mitten Rock, straight ahead and left (north and northeast). Along the road is a pipe line running from the Rattlesnake Oil Fields to Gallup with booster stations at intervals and storage tanks.

NEWCOMB'S, 58.8 *m.* (5,440 alt., 25 pop.), is a Navaho trading post, day school, and community center. The trading post established here in the 1800's was called Nava till the post was bought in 1914 by its present owner, Arthur J. Newcomb. Mrs. Arthur J. Newcomb (Franc J.) is the recorder and co-author with Gladys A. Reichard of *Sand Paintings of the Navajo Shooting Chant* (1937), a valuable record of the sacred sand picture of this Navaho ceremonial, recorded under the supervision of Klah, an outstanding medicine man, who died in 1937.

During the early years of the present century, when this post consisted of one small building and a dugout in the hillside, two young freighters, Roy and Clinton Burnham, cousins, drove up with a dead man. They had left Farmington for Gallup the day before with freight and one passenger, an old prospector named Saunderson. The party camped by the roadside that night. The two younger men, up at dawn, called to Saunderson, but there was no answer. Laying a hand on the older man's shoulder, they found him cold and unresponsive. After recovering from their shock, the cousins debated what disposition to make of the body. The law required that the deceased remain untouched until arrival of an officer. As this obviously was impossible, they decided to move the body to the trading post and from there dispatch an Indian runner back to the justice of the peace in Farmington. Wrapping the corpse in canvas, they strapped it to the wagon top, throwing a wagon sheet over it in deliberately careless fashion. On arriving at the post, the white men told their story to the trader. His business would have been ruined if the Navaho had learned of the corpse, for they immediately leave the vicinity of a dead body. However, the trader allowed the body to be locked in a dugout after dark. The runner was started back, and the cousins went on without arousing the Indians' suspicions. On their return with a load of Christmas turkeys for Farmington, they stopped again at the post, only to learn that the justice had instructed *them* "to bury the body there!" After dark they chopped a hole in the frozen ground with axes, then Saunderson was laid on his own pillow and bedding, and the earth was slowly and reverently shoveled in and leveled. The cousins immediately departed. Neither cross nor handboard marked the newly-made grave, but the story lives on in reminiscences of early traders.

The Indian Day School, with three residences for employees, was established with the addition of a community house, blacksmith shop, and bathhouse.

For many years the Navaho have raised fields of corn along the banks of Tunsta Wash which runs through Newcomb's; a retention dam, recently built at the head of the wash by the Soil Conservation Service, has greatly increased the water supply for irrigation.

Numerous pre-Columbian ruins near Newcomb's have yielded beautiful Pueblo pottery specimens—corrugated, white-and-black, and red-and-black of a pre-Mesa Verde type. In near-by clay cliffs bordering the Chaco Wash east of Newcomb's, fossil remains have been discovered, including bones of extinct mammals, and forms of invertebrate and plant life. This whole northwest corner of New Mexico is rich in fossil remains.

The CHUSKA MOUNTAINS (L) are of porous, friable gray Chuska sandstone (*see Geology*) with caps resulting from volcanic flows of the Tertiary age. Although the range is essentially uniform in geologic structure and topography, the Navaho call the northern section LUKACHUKAI (beautiful mountain), the central part TUNITCHA (Tgo Teo, large or much water), and the southern section, CHUSKA.

Forming junctions with US 666 are numerous dirt roads, graded and graveled, leading to small trading posts, Indian settlements, and schools.

In the wide amphitheater south of Beautiful Mountain (8,340 alt.) short streams with permanent or intermittent flows emerge from the network of deep canyons that gash the east face of distant Tunitcha Mountain, farther south (R). Closer to the highway Bennett Peak (L) and Ford Peak (R), igneous necks, rise abruptly from the floor of the valley. Both peaks have long served as landmarks in exploring and mapping the surrounding terrain. Along this road are many canvas-covered, horse-drawn wagons transporting entire Navaho families to trading posts or ceremonials; also horsemen riding to the post to trade blankets for groceries or to pawn their "hard goods" (silver, shell, and turquoise necklaces and bracelets). On the hills are occasional *hogans,* doors facing east, the homes of the Navaho whose flocks of sheep and goats, tended by their children and followed by sheep dogs, graze in the valley.

From 56 *m.* SHIPROCK (L), an igneous cliff formation, resembles a giant ship, full sail on a calm sea. The Navaho call it *tae-bidahi* (the winged rock).

This rock that towers 1,400 feet above the surrounding country has served both Indian and white man as a landmark. There are many legends connected with it, and the Navaho explain its origin thus: Long ago when they were besieged by Utes, and almost overcome by them, the medicine men held a ceremony, making medicine all day and night. As the second night came on, and all the besieged people were praying and chanting, the rocky ground on which they stood rose in the air, its crags formed wings, and it sailed away, leaving the enemy behind. All night it sailed and until sundown of the next day, when it settled in the midst of this great open plain, where it has since remained, a sentinel and a sacred mountain.

The valley floor along which US 666 winds is marked by a labyrinth of broken mesas, flat-topped ridges, and low hogbacks eroded into fantastic knobs and pinnacles. The red sandstone mesas are of various sizes and forms and in the slanting light of sunset or dawn are indescribably beautiful.

In SHIPROCK, 94.3 *m.* (4,903 alt., 2,131 pop.), is a junction with US 84 (*see Tour 9*).

<<<<<<<<<<<<<<<<<<<<<<<<<<<<<<<<<<<<<<<<<<<<<<<<<<<<<<<<<<<<<<>>>>>>>>>>>>>>>>>>>>>>>>>>>>>>>>>>>>>>>>>>>>>>>>>>>>>>

# *Tour* 7

(Alamosa, Colorado) — Chama — Tierra Amarilla — Ábiquiu — Española — Santa Fe — Vaughn — Roswell — Carlsbad — (Pecos, Texas) ; US 285.
Colorado Line to Texas Line, 403.8 *m.*

Graded gravel and bituminous-paved road throughout.
Denver & Rio Grande Western Railroad roughly parallels route between Colorado Line and Chama; Atchison, Topeka & Santa Fe Railway parallels route between Roswell and the Texas Line.
Accommodations in the larger towns.

This route winds through mountainous country and high plateaus, through quiet farming villages and places important in New Mexico history. Part of the way is through two national forests and near fishing, hunting, and recreational areas. In midwinter parts of US 285 in northern New Mexico are blocked by snow (*inquire locally*). South of Santa Fe, the route lies through grazing lands and farm areas, having a much warmer climate; the altitude of the highway varies from 10,000 feet in the north to 3,000 feet in the south.

*Section a. COLORADO LINE to ESPAÑOLA, 96.2 m.*

Through Cumbres Pass (10,003 alt.) US 285 crosses the COLORADO LINE, 0 *m.,* at a point 70 miles southwest of Alamosa, Colorado.

In 1848 Cumbres Pass was the scene of an attack by United States troops on a large band of Utes and Apaches. The hero of the battle, Old Bill Williams, was praised by the commanding officer for gallantry but condemned by his admirers for ingratitude.

William Sherley Williams (1787-1849) was one of the most eccentric characters in New Mexico. He was born in North Carolina but raised in Missouri. For a time he was an itinerant preacher, then made his home with the Osage Indian Nation in Missouri. Preacher Bill's attempts to convert the Indians ended in his accepting their belief and being adopted by the tribe; he married an Indian and became the father of two girls. After his wife died, he left the Osage to become a trapper, hunter, and guide.

Old Bill Williams, as he now was called, preferred to trap alone and would start on a trip with six traps on his back, each weighing five pounds, also a blanket, a rifle, and a knife always whetted to a razor-like edge. He would return after a few weeks bent nearly double under a burden of pelts. These sold, and cash in pocket, he would carouse in Taos until his money was gone then start forth again. Once he traded a stack of pelts for a barrel of whisky at Fort Bent, knocked the top off the barrel, invited all hands to join him and did not leave the spot until the barrel was empty.

Williams, six-feet-one in height, was thin and bony but tougher than most plainsmen; when he walked he always zig-zagged from side to side; when he rode it was with a short stirrup-leather that made him crouch in the saddle till he resembled a hunchback. His voice was high-pitched and his words had a peculiar emphasis that suggested the various Indian tongues with which he was familiar. His blue eyes had the furtive expression of one always on the alert; he wore buckskin shirt and trousers, which he never changed until they were worn out. In such clothing and with his tawny hair reaching his shoulders he visited his daughter Mary, who was living near St. Louis. By this time Mary had a daughter, who screamed when she saw her grandfather and hid under the bed.

Soon after this visit Williams decided to settle down and opened a store in Taos. But haggling with Mexican women over prices got on his nerves and he quit business by moving his stock into the street, throwing bolt after bolt of printed calico as far as he could, and yelling, "Take the damn stuff since I can't sell it to you." For a time he enjoyed the scramble for calico which was priced a dollar a yard, then he started out with his traps again and apparently gave no further thought to his store.

Old Bill shot with a double wabble but was reputed one of the best shots of his time and was always eager to wager a hundred dollars on his marksmanship; he tagged his pelts "Bill Williams, Master Trapper."

He lived with Indians more often than with persons of his own race, was adopted by the Ute as well as by the Osage, and accepted their belief in transmigration. He prophesied his reincarnation would take form as a buck elk, and it is related that several plainsmen refrained from killing buck elks for several years following Old Bill's death.

His friendship with Indians served him a good turn and made him useful as an interpreter. But the old scout's fondness for liquor finally caused him to break a life-long record for square dealing. Early in 1848 the Ute entrusted him with a quantity of furs to be sold in Taos. The deal concluded, Old Bill hied himself to a saloon where he continued a spree until all the Indians' money was gone. Afterward he couldn't return to them and a few months later was hired as a guide by Major W. W. Reynolds who was about to lead a punitive expedition against a band of Apaches. The troops followed the Apaches into these mountains where they were joined by some Utes and together made a stand at Cumbres Pass. Thirty-six Indians and two white soldiers were killed during the engagement that followed. In his report to the War Department Major Reynolds wrote, "Williams, a celebrated mountaineer, who behaved himself gallantly, was wounded badly."

A shattered arm kept Old Bill at Fort Bent for several weeks. He probably was glad for the respite. Not only had he defrauded his friends the Utes but he had led soldiers against them and he knew that for some time the life of a trapper would not be safe for him. Such was his condition when he was asked to join Frémont's fourth expedition, financed by private capital, and organized to survey a cross country railroad route.

John C. Frémont, who within five years had risen from lieutenant to lieutenant colonel in the topographical division of the army, had been appointed governor of California by Stockton and court-martialed for refusing to take orders from Kearny, left Fort Bent at the head of a well-equipped force late in 1848. Asked why he undertook the journey at such a season Frémont said that he wished to experience the most unfavorable conditions that a railroad would encounter. In that he was successful.

Dick Wootton started out as Frémont's guide but soon said, "There is too much snow ahead for me." Efforts to engage Kit Carson, who was at Taos, proved unsuccessful and Frémont finally selected Old Bill Williams to lead this, his most important enterprise. The truth of what happened in the Sawatch Mountains and the Sangre de Cristo did not become known for several years, not until reports made by several survivors had been published and analyzed. Meanwhile Old Bill Williams was charged with having lost his way, was held responsible for the death by freezing of eleven men, and was even accused of cannibalism.

Facts subsequently brought to light proved that Williams advised that what now is known as La Veta Pass be used to cross the Sangre de Cristo, but Frémont insisted upon using Cochetopa Pass over the Sawatch and sent Old Bill to the rear, selecting another guide. In January squads from the ill-fated expedition commenced arriving at Taos. It took three men ten days to make forty miles; feet and hands frozen they "crawled on ice or through snow." Old Bill Williams was saved from starvation by the capture of a deer. His first act was to cut out the liver and eat it raw. Then he "took the meat in his bony hands and began tearing off great mouthfuls of raw flesh like a savage animal."

Two months later Williams and another scout set out for the mountains to recover the goods and money cached by Frémont. It happened that a fortnight prior to this a junior lieutenant of dragoons, sent against a party of Utes, had obeyed orders too literally and had killed a score who had been ambushed. The Utes, seeking revenge, came upon Williams and his companion who were smoking as they sat beside a campfire. Both were fatally shot by the Indians. It is said that notwithstanding Old Bill Williams' misuse of money and his part in the battle at Cumbres Pass, the Utes mourned the death of their adopted son and gave him a chief's burial.

CHAMA, 8.6 *m.* (7,850 alt., 743 pop.), is a lumbering and trading center at the confluence of Archuleta and Willow Creeks. Lumber yards, a saw mill, general stores, and small industries engage the townspeople. It is a shipping point for the new oil fields opened up in 1937 in Chromo Valley, just over the Colorado Line. At a REGISTRATION STATION (*all trucks must stop*) on the south edge of town, trucks must pay a road fee and out-of-state cars not properly licensed buy additional tags.

The route crosses the Rio Brazos, 20.3 *m.,* and runs through an open valley.

At 21.9 *m.* is the junction with NM 112, a graded gravel and dirt road.

Right on this road to EL VADO DAM AND RESERVOIR (*trout fishing;*

*hotels, tourist camps, campgrounds*) 14.9 *m.,* a storage reservoir on the Chama River. El Vado (ford) Dam is part of the Middle Rio Grande Conservancy Project for flood control and irrigation.

TIERRA AMARILLA, 24 *m.* (6,800 alt., 1,097 pop.), named for the yellow earth in this vicinity, is the seat of Rio Arriba County, one of the old Mexican districts settled by Spaniards and Mexicans, and also one of the original counties set up in 1852 under the United States. Tierra Amarilla was the ration headquarters for the Ute and Jicarilla Apache in 1871-72, before the Ute were moved to a reservation in San Juan County and the Apache to the western part of this county.

CANJILÓN, 43.2 *m.* (7,800 alt., 644 pop.), a trading point for farmers and sheep ranchers, is reputedly the town where lived the descendants of De Vargas, *conquistador.*

US 285 crosses the CHAMA RIVER at 58.8 *m.*

ÁBIQUIU, 72.9 *m.* (5,930 alt., 530 pop.), in the center of a farming and stock raising area, is on the site of pueblo ruins. In the middle of the eighteenth century it became a settlement of *Genizaros* (*see Tour 1b*) and in 1778 was one of the stops on the Spanish Trail to the new village of Los Angeles, California.

CHAMITA, 90.7 *m.* (5,800 alt., 275 pop.), with a general store, church, chapel, and a cluster of small houses, is the trading center for Indians of San Juan Pueblo across the road (L).

As US 285 traverses the Chama Valley the Rio Grande is in the distance (L).

ESPAÑOLA, 96.2 *m.* (5,600 alt., 625 pop.), a shipping point for fruit, stock, and other farm products, is on the west bank of the Rio Grande. On the east bank is a junction with US 64, with which this route is united to SANTA FE, 121.4 *m.* (*see Tour 3a*).

*Section b.* SANTA FE to TEXAS LINE, 307.6 m.

Between SANTA FE, 0 *m.,* and a junction at 9.8 *m.,* US 285 is united with US 85 (*see Tour 1a*), then branches R. over hilly pasture land with vistas of the Sangre de Cristo Mountains (L) and the Cerrillos Hills, Manzano, Sandía, and Jémez Mountains (R). The road curves frequently as it descends into a ravine of Apache Creek Canyon.

LAMY, 15.5 *m.* (6,457 alt., 329 pop.), a junction point on the Atchison, Topeka & Santa Fe Railway for passengers to Santa Fe, was named for Archbishop Lamy (*see Religion*).

South of the junction with NM 41, US 285 is flanked by Pankey's Pasture (R), named for Benjamin Pankey who early in the twentieth century accumulated more than half a million acres of grass land in New Mexico stocked with thousands of cattle; but he failed, and his property passed into other hands. The route is through miles of grassy plains with hills on both sides and cattle or sheep grazing near the road. A filling station, store, and cafe called CLINES CORNERS, 49.9 *m.,* mark the junction with US 66 (*see Tour 6a*). Southward, the highway traverses more plains and rolling country peopled only by scattered ranchers.

In ENCINO, 82.4 *m.* (610 pop.), is a junction with US 60 (*see Tour 8a*) with which this route is united to EAST VAUGHN, 98.3 *m.* (*see Tour 8a*).

South of East Vaughn, US 285, paved, proceeds over a graded and graveled roadbed across a high rolling prairie. For nearly 100 miles plains country is suitable for grazing and stock raising, and there are few settlements.

Underlying this area is the ARTESIAN BASIN, where hundreds of artesian wells bring cold, pure water from the limestone depths (*see Geology*). Water from heavy rains and melting snows of the mountains, together with the drainage from the basins of streams tributary to the Pecos, is caught in the honeycomb channels of porous limestone strata that underlie the top soil and "valley fill." This porous deposit outcrops on the east flank of the Sacramento Mountains (*see Tour 13*) and extends underground to the bluffs east of the Pecos River, serving as a natural channel to convey the water downward to the valley floor. The natural hydrostatic pressure is sufficient to force water from the basin surface when tapped and in many cases is sufficient to "push out" the springs, many of which are in this area. Water from these wells, which have been drilled to depths of 700 feet though the average depth is 250 feet, transforms 60,000 acres of arid lands into good farm lands.

Irrigation farming has been practiced in the Basin since 1880, the water at first being obtained from the large springs near Roswell or diverted from tributaries of the Pecos. It was not until 1905 that irrigation from artesian wells began to assume importance.

At 190.1 *m.* is the junction with US 70 (*see Tour 10*).

ROSWELL, 193.9 *m.* (3,600 alt., 13,443 pop.), in less than seventy years has grown from a barren plains trading post to one of the most modern and attractive cities in the State with miles of wide, paved streets shaded by fine old cottonwoods and willows, and attractive homes, gardens, and public buildings. Its many industries include a flour mill, cotton gins, creameries, and meat-packing plants. It has an airport, a railroad, bus lines, a radio station (KGFL), the fully accredited New Mexico Military Institute (*see below*), tennis courts, and a golf course (*fees 25¢ and 50¢*). Its population, which is 90 per cent Anglo-American, 9 per cent Spanish and Mexican stock, and 1 per cent foreign born, observes several festivals including San Juan's Day, June 24; Eastern New Mexico Old Timers' Reunion and Dinner, September 15; Mexican Independence Day, September 16; and the Eastern New Mexico State Fair and Roswell Rodeo which runs for a week, beginning about October 7. The State Fair is the most popular with the townspeople and usually attracts 50,000 visitors. Many wear costumes common when Roswell was a lone store on a cattle trail in the wilderness, and all gather around the chuck wagon; but instead of "sow belly and beans," eat barbecue meat, buns, pickles, and drink black coffee.

Roswell's modern history begins with 1865 when a group of settlers, known as the Missourians, attempted to establish the Missouri Plaza, 15 miles to the southwest, but were forced to abandon the site because of insufficient water. In 1869 a professional gambler named Van C. Smith, who came from Omaha by way of Santa Fe with his partner, Aaron O. Wilburn, constructed two adobe buildings here that served as general store, post office, and attic sleeping quarters for paying guests.

March 4, 1871, Van Smith filed the first claim; three years later he was appointed postmaster, and the place was named Roswell for his father. Captain Joseph C. Lea came in 1877 and bought Smith's holdings, and a year later his father-in-law Major W. W. Wildy bought out Wilburn and two other settlers, presenting this property to his daughter, Sally Wildy Lea. This gave the Lea family entire ownership, and their influence kept peace and order during the Lincoln County War of 1877-79 (*see Tour 12b*). Mrs. Lea's struggles in behalf of education and civic improvements attracted other settlers to Roswell in the early 1880's, and the village became an important trading center.

When the accidental discovery of an artesian water source (1891)' on the Nathan Jaffa place near Roswell revealed an unlimited supply of water, ditches were cut through the plains and irrigation begun that now results in annual crops in this region of staple cotton, alfalfa, apples, corn, small grain, and garden truck worth more than $2,000,000.

After the railroad (1894) had replaced carts drawn by burros and oxen, there were two land booms and an oil boom, bringing many more persons. Since then growth has been steady.

The NEW MEXICO MILITARY INSTITUTE is 1 mile north of the center of town. The central campus consists of 75 acres of level mesa land situated on a hill overlooking the main part of Roswell and shaded by numerous trees. The total value of buildings, furniture, and fixtures approximates $1,500,000. Hagerman Barracks, Lea Hall, Willson Hall, Luna Memorial Natatorium, the Hospital, Headquarters, Cahoon Armory, Mess Hall, Thomas Memorial, and the houses of the Superintendent and the Executive Officer are all handsome buff brick structures.

The Institute Library occupies the south wing of Willson Hall to the right of N. Main St. entrance. There are 15,000 volumes including encyclopedias, dictionaries, atlases, and similar works, and the fields of English and American literature, science, history, biography, and the best fiction are well represented in the collection, providing supplementary reading for the academic courses and recreational reading for the cadets. In addition to the books the library has a number of daily newspapers and nearly 100 of the best weekly and monthly periodicals.

In the J. Ross Thomas Memorial Building, are large murals by Peter Hurd, depicting incidents and scenes in the early history of Roswell. These can be seen by visitors at any time during the day. In the classroom of Captain Starr are five paintings by the same artist, illustrating *The Last of the Mohicans*.

In Roswell is the junction with US 380 (*see Tour 12*).

South of Roswell, US 285 parallels the PECOS RIVER famed as the boundary line of western justice. The "law west of the Pecos" is a western idiom signifying justice summarily dealt. The cattle kings whose empires flourished in the Pecos valley in the nineteenth century have moved to the north and east; irrigation has turned the valley into a luxuriant garden spot, and the big ranches have been divided.

CHISUM RANCH (R), 198.3 *m.,* is now owned and operated by Cornell University, under direction of Dr. A. D. Crile, as an experiment station on range control and diversification of crops. John Chisum came from Tennessee to Paris, Texas, where he served as county clerk. Soon after the Civil War he drove three small herds of cattle to Little Rock and sold them to a packing house owned partly by himself. This enterprise failed and he filed papers in bankruptcy. As his only assets were wild Texas cattle, inaccessible for attachment and inconvertible into cash, Chisum started life again while judgments against him became waste paper.

Charles Goodnight and Oliver Loving had already blazed the trail up the Pecos River, and Chisum started his new drive over the same route with a motley gang, establishing headquarters in the Bosque Grande 30 miles south of Fort Sumner in the Pecos Valley, on a ranch site previously established by Goodnight. His first herd of 600 beeves he sold at Fort Sumner and obtained a contract to deliver 10,000 more. Realizing the riches of the Pecos Valley, he determined to make it his home and on his second drive he made his permanent headquarters at this ranch, though he maintained two other cow camps. Between 1870 and 1881 Chisum was credited with having the largest holdings of cattle in the world. His ranch then extended from Fort Sumner on the Pecos for 200 miles southward to the Texas Line. Though his petition to President Grant for a patent to the whole area was denied, for some time no one dared dispute his rule; he enforced his edict, "settlers are unwelcome," and the cattle with the "long rail" brand and "jingle bob" earmark (vertical split in both ears) multiplied. His ranch had more than 100,000 head of cattle at its zenith about 1878 before Indian raids, rustlers, and competition from other owners diminished his power and his wealth.

After his death in 1884 litigation made further inroads. In 1893 a Colorado business man, J. J. Hagerman, and a group bought the Chisum ranch. Hagerman was an empire builder of another sort and with Charles B. Eddy and other citizens of Roswell developed the transportation facilities of the valley. The Chisum Ranch in 1894 was the scene of an elaborate party celebrating arrival of the first railroad train to Roswell. In 1904 Hagerman remodeled the ranch house, but the main structure was left intact and made the central part of the new abode. At a later date the Hagerman estate sold it to Cornell University.

DEXTER, 211.2 *m.* (3,560 alt., 734 pop.), a town of gardens and a trading center for farmers, is surrounded by fertile cotton fields. It has a cotton gin and alfalfa mill. In the latter the alfalfa is dehydrated and ground into a fine powder, sacked, and shipped to manufacturers of prepared stock feeds.

Southward the highway is flanked on both sides by broad alfalfa fields that yield heavily.

HAGERMAN, 217.3 *m.* (3,520 alt., 855 pop.), named for J. J. Hagerman (*see above*), is a thriving farming community and the site of the MINERAL WELLS SANATORIUM.

ARTESIA, 236.8 *m.* (3,350 alt., 3,991 pop.), was settled in 1903 and owes its rapid growth to oil discoveries. When Artesia was incorporated in 1905 it had a population of 1,003, largely Yankees, but today there are approximately 500 of Spanish and Mexican stock, mostly recent arrivals from Mexico.

Oil was discovered here in the spring of 1923 and now (1940) there are oil refineries, huge gasoline storage tanks, and pipe lines, although farming and stock raising still hold high rank as industries. Thousands of sheep of the Rambouillet and other breeds are raised on the surrounding plains, while Angora goats are bred in the mountainous country to the west.

The homestead on which the town was built was a part of the Chisum holding, known as South Chisum Ranch. It was on the old stagecoach road between Eddy (now Carlsbad) and Roswell. Billy the Kid spent the winter of 1880 here.

In Artesia is the junction with NM 83 (*see Tour 14*).

DAYTON, 248.4 *m.* (3,300 alt., 567 pop.), now a small settlement, was expanded by an oil boom to a town of 2,000 inhabitants in

1927. MARABLE RANCH (R), formerly the Gilbert Ranch, is the oldest ranch in Pecos Valley.

Active artesian wells are not found south of Dayton, and irrigation of the lands is by a system of dams, canals, ditches, flumes, and siphons, known collectively as the CARLSBAD RECLAMATION PROJ-ECT. This project spreads the waters of the Pecos (which have been impounded in Lake McMillan and Lake Avalon) over the land up and down the valley. Farmers in the valley frequently receive some $27,000,000 for their crops, chief of which is long staple cotton.

Alfalfa is extensively raised but its acreage is decreasing in favor of cotton. Many crops, ranging from canaigre (a native plant from which a type of tannic acid is extracted) through varieties of sorghums and maizes to sugar beets, have been tried and all have had a fair measure of success. Grapevines and fruit trees were also introduced and likewise did well, but distance from markets and problems of distribution made such crops less profitable.

At 255.6 *m.* is the junction with an improved road.

Left on this road 2.1 *m.* is LAKEWOOD, (3,200 alt., 348 pop.), a trading center for farmers. Stretching to the eastward, the village overtakes Old Seven Rivers, settled in 1870 by "Pa" and "Ma" Jones who came from Virginia by ox wagon. As a stopping point on the cattle trail from Texas and trading post for the ranchers of the valley, Seven Rivers soon became a typical "wild and woolly" community. One saloon boasted a "door with easy hinges" that was readily removed and served as a stretcher for customers who had been too slow on the draw. Remnants of the old adobe walls and the old cemetery, where it is said most of the men were buried with their boots on, are all that is left of the community.

Rocky Arroyo, formerly called Indian Creek, is crossed at 266.2 *m.* The Carlsbad Flume is visible 100 yards (L) of the highway at 273.3 *m.* CARLSBAD MINERAL SPRING (L), in the center of a desert, contains solutions of soda, so that it is possible to take a "salt bath" here in so-called fresh water.

CARLSBAD, 276.3 *m.* (3,110 alt., 7,048 pop.), known as the potash capital of America, was settled in 1888, and in 1889 was organized as the town of Eddy. The old stockmen rode through knee-deep grass, but irrigation transformed the area into cultivated land. After a flood of the Pecos River in 1904 had nearly destroyed the private irrigation system, the United States Government bought it (1906) and developed the Carlsbad Reclamation Project which insures adequate irrigation for the valley with no danger from floods. The soil is especially adapted to alfalfa and cotton. Carlsbad boomed when operations in the near-by potash mines began in 1931 (*see Tour 16*).

LOVING, 286.5 *m.* (3,100 alt., 1,464 pop.), was first named Vough for Swiss settlers, then renamed Florence. It was later named for John Loving, who was one of the first to drive cattle up the Pecos from Texas. It is in the midst of a cotton and alfalfa section, though many residents work at the potash plants. A cotton-seed oil mill and two gins also provide employment.

MALAGA, 291.5 *m.* (3,045 alt., 1,472 pop.), also a trading point for farmers, is so named for the abundance of sweet wine grapes grown near by. There is also a cotton gin here.

At 307.6 *m.* US 285 crosses the TEXAS LINE 52 miles north of Pecos, Texas.

# *Tour 7A*

Española—Santa Clara Pueblo—Puyé Cliff Ruins.  NM 5.
Española to Puyé Ruins, 11.5 *m.*

Graded gravel road.
Route parallels Denver, Rio Grande & Western Railroad for five miles.
Accommodations at Española:

This route to the Santa Clara Pueblo and Puyé Cliff Ruins goes through the quiet low country and past the *ranchitos* of descendants of Spanish colonials who in the sixteenth century wrested the land from the Indian.

NM 5 branches south from its junction with US 285 in the western end of ESPAÑOLA, 0 *m.* (5,600 alt., 625 pop.) (*see Tour 7a*), and crosses a bridge over the bed of the Santa Clara River, 0.8 *m.*, dry the greater part of the year, but flowing in spring and during the rainy season in July and August.

NM 5 passes the *placita* of Güachepangue 0.9 *m.*, once an Indian village with a small adobe chapel.

At 1.9 *m.* is a junction with a dirt road.

Left on this road to SANTA CLARA PUEBLO (*obtain permission to photograph from the pueblo governor*), 0.3 *m.*, on a low mesa above the west bank of the Rio Grande. K'hapoo (Ind., where the water grows under) is the native name of this Tewa-speaking settlement, which covers 17,369 acres of land granted by the Spanish King and patented by the United States in 1864.

Their all-black pottery originated in Santa Clara is exceptionally good, the traditional shapes are maintained, and little innovation has been introduced in exterior decoration, the forms themselves constituting the intrinsic beauty of bowls, *ollas,* and *tinajas.* When an automobile appears in the plaza the women bring out their pottery and stand behind it while the visitor examines and makes his choice. They are about the same size as most New Mexican Indians, speak English, and are very courteous.

Archeologists verify the Santa Clara belief that their ancestors came from the clusters of artificial grottoes of Puyé and Shufinne (*see below*). It is not known when the pueblo was settled. A Franciscan missionary was assigned to Santa Clara in September 1598, and the first mission was built between 1626 and 1629 by Fray Alonso de Benavides, who is credited with conversions among the "Apaches de Navahu," whose range was on the west. Santa Clara joined in the Pueblo Revolt of 1680 and destroyed the church, the site of which is now marked by a mound of earth. After the Reconquest by De Vargas (1692) a new church and monastery—now also in ruins—were built, and at intervals during the next 100 years Santa Clara was changed from a *visita* to a mission and back again, until 1782 when it became a permanent mission with San Ildefonso as a *visita*. Bandelier says the church, built in 1760, was already in decay in 1893. It was built of adobe, 135 feet long, cruciform in plan, and with an entrance eight feet wide and ten feet high. The massive, deeply paneled doors were adorned with engraved escutcheons. These large doors were opened only on special occasion. Cut in one door was a smaller entrance, "the eye of the needle," three feet by six feet, for daily use. This church had a bell marked 1710 and two wooden side altars bearing the date 1782. The priest's quarters contained rude native carvings of animals; and stored away in old wooden chests and closets were ancient ecclesiastical vestments, as well as very old Spanish documents. The last mentioned are what remain of the Archives of the Franciscan Order in New Mexico, the *Custodia de la Conversión de San Pablo de la Nuevo México* (Custody of the Conversion of St. Paul of New Mexico). These have been in Santa Clara since the old military chapel of Santa Fe, Castruenza or Castrense, was condemned as unsafe in 1844. Concerning his efforts to examine these archives, Bandelier said that they remained in an old cupboard of the ruined convent until an illiterate Indian, who venerated old things, proposed they be given to some individual who would care for them. For a long time the *Principales* of the pueblo refused, protesting that the higher powers would be offended; but when these were finally consulted, the answer was in the affirmative, and the archives were removed from the ruins and placed in charge of a blind Indian who kept them in a back room of his house out of sight and guarded closely. It was only after arming himself with letters from the Archbishop at Santa Fe and the resident priest at Santa Cruz, that Bandelier finally was allowed to see them and make copies of those that had some bearing on New Mexico history. The originals are still at Santa Clara, guarded with superstitious care by an Indian who is as zealous of their safety as was the original tribesman-guardian.

In 1909 the massive church from which these documents were taken was being remodeled. After the roof with its supporting timber had been removed, a storm occurred, causing the walls to fall (as they did at Nambé) and the building was destroyed. The present church is designed in a modified version of Spanish-Pueblo style.

Records indicate that Santa Clara's decline was owing to numerous intertribal killings for the practice of witchcraft and to the ravages of disease. In less than two months during 1782 over 500 deaths occurred here and in one other pueblo. The Indians themselves blame their decline on internal disagreements. Though the Navaho were said to have cultivated fields in this vicinity, raids by other Navaho as well as inroads by the whites seriously depreciated the Santa Clara lands.

On the hills surrounding the pueblo are many shrines formed by arrangements of stones. Sacred meal and prayer sticks are still deposited at some of these places during certain rituals. August 12 the Feast Day of Santa Clara de Assisi, is usually celebrated with Mass followed by Indian dances and horse races.

NM 5 well graded here and paralleled (L) by the Denver & Rio Grande Western Railroad and the bottomlands of the Rio Grande, runs between the Black or Orphan Mesa (L) and the foothills of the Pajarito Plateau (R).

At 3.8 *m.* is junction with Puyé road. The route goes R. between gravelly, piñon-dotted hills and terraced, eroded cliffs and ascends a steep grade at 7 *m.* to the top of the level Pajarito Plateau, covered sparsely with rabbit brush and desert grass. The Jémez Mountains rise ahead on the horizon.

As the highway gives way to a dirt road through tall pines, tawny colored tuff cliffs are visible at 9.9 m., also the caves of Puyé Ruins.

After a turn (R) at 10.9 m., the road leads to the rock Guest House and Museum of the PUYÉ RUINS (Tewa, where cottontail rabbits assemble) (*adults 50¢; children 25¢*), 11.5 m. An Indian attendant is in charge.

Puyé's accessibility, serenity, and magnificent situation make it a popular point of interest. The ruins, remains of a prehistoric Tewa pueblo, occupy a commanding position on the Pajarito Plateau. It is one of the most extensive and interesting of the cliff villages. Though this was the first ruin in the Rio Grande Valley to be systematically excavated, and the second in the United States to be scientifically treated in order to preserve it, Puyé was never made a National Monument, but is supervised by the United States Indian Service and the Santa Clara Indians to whom the land belongs. The School of American Research, which conducted the excavation, still acts in an advisory capacity concerning the maintenance and preservation of the ruins.

Puyé is a splendid example of everything characteristic of Pajaritan culture (*see Archeology*). Here are all the Pajaritan forms of house ruins, typical in construction and placement with symbolical decorations following a well-defined order, *kivas,* pictographs, implements, utensils, and red pottery. None of the excavations have yielded evidence of any European influence. The glazing of pottery, an art practised long before the coming of the Spaniards, reached a high state of development here. On the excavated pottery the most prevalent design is the *Awanyu* (plumed serpent), guardian of springs and streams and thus the preserver of life, for without water, the Indians realized crops and life itself must fail. The great band across the concavity of water jars and food bowls represented the sky path of *Awanyu* or the circuit in which his power habitually moved. *Awanyu* "threw himself across the sky" and left his trail in the Milky Way, according to Tewa legend.

The tree-ring calendar shows that Puyé was built between 1450 and 1475 and was at its height in 1540. It was the center of a population that occupied a number of villages in the northern section of the Pajarito Plateau (*see Tour 2A*). All were closely related, connected by trails worn deep in the rock.

The settlement of Puyé was made up of two aggregations of dwellings—the pueblo and the cliff houses. The Santa Clara Indians say their ancestors lived in the winter in the caves excavated in these pumice cliffs and in the pueblo on the mesa above in the summer.

The CLIFF VILLAGES are a succession of houses built not only against but also within the cliff walls, usually at a level where the slope met the vertical escarpment. They extend along the cliff for more than a mile. There were three kinds of dwellings in these villages: excavated, cave-like rooms serving as domiciles with no construction in front; others with open rooms or porches built on in front; and stone houses, one to three stories high with the same number of terraces built upon the rocky slope against the cliff. Two sections of the cliff are broken by a ledge about halfway up its height, which goes back a few yards and then meets another straight wall. On this ledge, against and within this vertical wall, are the remains of another succession of dwellings which are continuous for about 700 yards. These and the dwellings on the lower level show what remains of the houses that covered a distance of a mile and a half. Stairways cut in the rock ascend to the great community houses on the mesa above; this house stands near the edge of the cliff and its southwest corner reaches to within 20 feet of the very brink.

One subterranean *kiva* is found against the outer wall of the East House and another, slightly larger, is about 35 feet in diameter, with one *kiva* on the ledge halfway to the top. All these sanctuaries were dug into the rock. Others are found on the ledge of the cliffs below, and still others in rocks at the cliff's base.

The PUEBLO, a great quadrangle on the mesa top, was an arrangement of four huge terraced community houses surrounding a court and forming an effective fortification. The outside rooms in each group are noticeably small and they are believed to have been used for the storage of grain and other supplies. All the rooms were connected by small doorways, the sills of which were always about 18 inches above the ground. Small round ventilation holes, five to ten inches in diameter, were cut in the sills. Stone plugs were used when ventilation was not needed. The main entrance to this great community house is at the southeast corner and is about 17 feet wide at the eastern end, enlarging to double that width before it opens into the court. A narrow passageway about 13 feet wide at the southwest corner of the court separates the South House of the quadrangle from the other sides.

# *Tour 8*

(Amarillo, Texas) — Texico — Clovis — Fort Sumner — Willard — Bernardo — Dátil — Quemado — (Springerville, Arizona) ; US 60. Texas Line to Arizona Line, 363.9 *m.*

Two-lane, bituminous-paved road most of the route; graveled the remainder. Atchison, Topeka & Santa Fe Railway roughly parallels the route between the Texas Line and Magdalena.
Accommodations in principal towns.

US 60 which links Norfolk, Virginia and Los Angeles, California runs across the center of New Mexico, east to west, from the wide reaches of the level Staked Plains (*see Tour 6a*), across extensive farming areas, over mountain ranges, and through cattle and mining country.

### Section a. TEXAS LINE to BERNARDO, 220.7 m.

In the eastern part of the State the route crosses a grassy plateau utilized for stock raising and the growing of grains, legumes, broomcorn, and various crops. It is a region of color, stillness, and mirages—those pranks of nature that added to the suffering of thirst-crazed travelers in the early days.

US 60 crosses the Texas Line, 82 miles southwest of Amarillo, Texas, at TEXICO, 0 *m.* (569 pop.), a continuation of Farwell, Texas, and a trading center for ranchers.

Texico began after the Pecos Valley Railroad built a siding here in 1902 and its early boom subsided when the division point was established at Clovis, eight miles west. Texico has a REGISTRATION STATION (*all trucks are required to stop*) and is on the boundary between Central and Mountain Standard time zones (*west-bound travelers set watches back one hour*).

In CLOVIS, 9.7 *m.* (9,931 pop.) (*see Tour 10a*), is the junction with US 70 (*see Tour 10a*).

PORTAIR, 13 *m.,* is the airport for Clovis and a loading point for grain, cattle, and produce.

GRIER, 20.9 *m.* (4,270 alt., 291 pop.), was named for a fur trader who established a trading post here for pelts of antelope, great herds of which overran this district.

MELROSE, 33.5 *m.* (4,100 alt., 1,226 pop.), is a typical plains community and a shipping point and feeding stop for cattle. Broomcorn is grown around here more extensively than elsewhere in the State; wheat and maize are also important crops. A WPA Art Center has been established here.

At 54.9 *m.* is the junction with a graded dirt road.

Left on this road to the crumbled mud walls of OLD FORT SUMNER, 2.5 *m.,* in the BOSQUE REDONDO (round grove of trees) on the east bank of the Pecos River. This shaded spot, said to have been on the trail followed by Coronado in 1541 and Espejo in 1583, was a campground of the Comanche before the Spaniards came. In 1851 a licensed trading post was established here, and in 1862 a fort named for General E. V. Sumner, Commander of the Ninth Military Department in New Mexico, was erected. John Cremony, on the staff of Captain Updegraff who selected the site in accordance with the plan of General James H. Carleton, reports that the structure was built by the soldiers of the California Column and was "beyond comparison the handsomest and most picturesque in the Union."

Carson, to force the Navaho into submission, gave orders that their crops should be destroyed and if they still refused to surrender, the women and children should be taken as prisoners to Bosque Redondo and all armed braves shot. Kit Carson was given command of the regiment assigned to bring in the Navaho. During his eight years service as Indian agent, Carson had continuously worked for the Indians' welfare. In a report dated August 31, 1858 he wrote ". . . as Indians generally learn the vices and not the virtues of civilized men, they will become a degraded tribe, instead of being, as they are now, the most noble and virtuous tribe within our Territory. Prostitution, drunkenness, and the vices generally are unknown among them. Humanity, as well as our desire to benefit the Indian race, demands that they be removed as far as practicable from the settlements. Have farmers, mechanics, etc., placed among them, to give instructions in the manner of cultivating the soil to gain their subsistance, and teach them to make the necessary implements to carry on said labor." Yet as colonel he pursued them relentlessly, even succeeding in dislodging those who took refuge in Canyon de Chelly, Arizona, and in marching more than 7,000 of them across New Mexico to the Bosque Redondo—the Navaho "long walk."

It was believed that the Navaho would quickly adjust themselves to the new way of life, but the results were disappointing. In spite of efforts to farm this land, insects, drought, floods, insufficient supplies, and unseasonable extremes of cold worked such hardships on these captives that the experiment failed. To make matters worse, the Comanche and Kiowa from the east and south made several raids on the flocks and herds. In the spring of 1868, discouraged and bitterly resentful, the Navaho planted no crops; and on promise of good behavior, their plea to be allowed to return to their homeland was granted.

They kept their word and are now a vigorous tribe increasing in strength, numbering nearly 50,000. After they left, Fort Sumner was demilitarized and put up for auction. Lucien B. Maxwell (*see Tour 2b*) bought the improvements from the War Department and remodeled the officers' quarters into a house of 20 large rooms. He lived here on a lavish scale until his death in 1875 when his son Peter inherited the property. In 1881 Billy the Kid (*see Tour 12b*) was killed by Sheriff Pat Garrett in Peter Maxwell's bedroom.

In 1884 a group of Colorado cattlemen bought the property, but drought and the economic depression of 1894 caused failure of the venture and they abandoned it, razing the house for the lumber. Near the ruins of the fort is the Fort Sumner cemetery containing the GRAVE OF BILLY THE KID as well as that of Peter Maxwell and others.

FORT SUMNER, 57.9 *m.* (4,050 alt., 1,666 pop.), seat of De Baca County, has made marked gains in population and importance in recent years. Near the Alamogordo Dam, which serves as supplemental storage for the lands of the Carlsbad Irrigation District (*see Tour 7b*), Fort Sumner's chief industries are cattle, sheep raising, and farming. It is a natural business center as well as an important shipping point. The principal crops are alfalfa, sweet potatoes, apples, grapes, and melons.

Right from Fort Sumner on US 84—a two-lane, graded gravel road for 7 miles, then graded dirt. It follows the concrete underpass of the Santa Fe Railway, 0.4 *m.*, then over a bridge across Alamogordo Creek, 1.2 *m.*, to a rise at 1.9 *m.* where is a view of open range, coarse grasses, soapweed, and grazing cattle and horses. To the east (R) are the Bluffs of the Llano Estacado (*see Tour 6a*).

At 3 *m.* is a graded dirt road; (L) 14 *m.* on this to ALAMOGORDO DAM which impounds the waters of Alamogordo Creek for irrigation. At 13.6 *m.* on US 84 the dam is visible to the west (L) and there is a fine vista of blue water, red bluffs, and silvery grasses with a few white-faced red cattle grazing.

There is another fine view from a rise at 16.8 *m.* To the north are trees along the banks of Alamogordo Creek. The road descends and crosses a bridge over this creek, then rises after it crosses the Guadalupe County line and gains another rise at 24.1 *m.* This is especially attractive in summer. There is a view ahead of the brown road winding across and up the side of the valley; the grass is green and rich, masses of purple wild verbena and yellow wild flowers stretch for miles alongside the road.

At 26.9 *m.* is a clump of handsome cottonwoods beside a bridge over an arroyo. These quick-growing shade trees that thrive where other trees can't grow are a blessing to this land. Cane cactus appears farther on with occasional growths of low piñon and juniper.

At 38.9 *m.* is an adobe hut with a corral, the first sign of human habitation in 25 miles. The red-brown road becomes redder and by contrast the grasses appear greener.

At 41.2 *m.* is the junction with a dirt road. US 84 turns sharply (L) past thicker growths of piñon and juniper. The odor of burning piñon, that unmistakable incense of New Mexico, comes up on the breeze as Santa Rosa is approached. The road dips past a reservoir to a cluster of cottonwoods and houses, which is SANTA ROSA, 42.4 *m.* (*see Tour 6a*).

YESO, 79.9 *m.* (4,600 alt., 239 pop.), a trading point for ranchers, was established in 1906 when the railroad came. When it was discovered that the land was suitable only for grazing and sheep herding, many settlers who had filed claims moved on.

EAST VAUGHN, 115.5 *m.* (5,950 alt., 501 pop.), called "the oasis" for its shade trees, is a division point on the Santa Fe. Its roundhouse is the town's chief source of employment.

Here are junctions with US 54 (*see Tour 13*) and US 285 (*see Tour 7b*) with which US 60 is united between East Vaughn and Encino. This is good sheep raising country.

The ruins at 127.9 *m.* are an old fort (L) used in the Indian campaign of the 1860's, when the countryside was harassed by the Apache and Comanche.

ENCINO, 131.4 *m.* (6,200 alt., 610 pop.), is a trading center for ranchers and headquarters for an annual coyote roundup by automobile. Here is the western junction with US 285 (*see Tour 7b*).

PEDERNAL MOUNTAIN (7,580 alt.) 146.2 *m.,* an important landmark, is visible (R).

WILLARD, 167.3 *m.* (6,091 alt., 461 pop.), is a trading point for a large stock raising area.

Left from Willard on NM 42, 4.8 *m.* to a chain of NATURAL SALT LAKES now leased to the New Mexico Salt Company. According to a Spanish document dated 1668, burros laden with salt here were driven more than 700 miles to southern Chihuahua, Mexico, where the Spaniards with the aid of Indian slaves were operating silver mines and used the salt in smelting the ores. Salt had been a staple in trade among the Indians of the Southwest for centuries before the Spaniards arrived.

At 168.5 *m.* is a junction with NM 41 (*see Tour 3b*).

West of Willard are raised most of the pinto beans grown in the United States. New Mexicans eat large quantities of pinto beans and chili, which are very nourishing. The United States Bureau of Home Economics reports that chili is rich in vitamin A and the beans in vitamin B. Beans, a concentrated food containing protein and carbohydrate, also contain calcium and phosphorous as well as iron and copper. A pound of pinto beans furnishes as much energy as 2.3 pounds of lean beef, or 20 eggs, or 1.3 pounds of bread. The New Mexico Experiment Station has found that pinto bean straw and pinto bean culls are satisfactory feed for farm animals. Straw that contains large

amounts of the beans needs little additional grain to make feed sufficient to carry cattle in good condition through the winter.

MOUNTAINAIR, 181.1 *m.* (6,550 alt., 1,483 pop.), in the heart
of the fertile Estancia Valley, is a shipping center. for the pinto bean
industry. In this region are several pueblo ruins (*see Tour 15*).

Westward the Manzano (apple) Mountains (R) are visible, and
the route continues through fine vistas, including the northern escarpment (L) of the Chupadera Mesa, which stretches far to the south.
This mesa, home of deer, wild turkey, and wild horses, is a favorite
hunting ground. To the south (L) are the wooded boundaries of the
Cíbola National Forest.

ABO, 188.2 *m.* (318 pop.), is a flag stop on the Santa Fe Railway
named for the Piro Indian Pueblo ruin.

At 191.2 *m.* is the junction with an unimproved road.

Right on this road 0.8 *m.* to the ABO PUEBLO RUINS, the remains of an important pueblo built on beautiful red sandstone with a *kiva* of unusual design
and structure. The church of the ABO MISSION, which was built in 1646, has
been excavated by the Museum of New Mexico and repaired and preserved.
This church is the only building with walls standing above the surface, the
village and *convento* walls being level with the ground.

Past SCHOLLE, a small roadside stop at 194.2 *m.,* US 60 continues over Abo Pass in Los Pinos Mountains to DRIPPING
SPRINGS, 197.5 *m.,* a tourist camp near a spring (R), which is unusual in this arid region, and crosses the Rio Grande Valley.

In BERNARDO, 220.7 *m.,* is the junction with US 85 (*see Tour
1b*) with which US 60 is united to SOCORRO, 247.7 *m.,* (*see Tour
1b*).

*Section b.   SOCORRO to ARIZONA LINE, 143.2 m.*

West of SOCORRO, 0 *m.,* the road winds through a region of
great natural beauty where the Apache roamed and hunted; the road
twists uphill and down, through canyons and arroyos, near big game
territory and mining country. On both sides of the road are sections of
the Cíbola National Forest. Here among millions of board feet of
sawtimber lies a sportsman's paradise, for the area abounds in wildlife.
The mule and whitetail deer are abundant and may be hunted in season
(*see General Information*), furnishing sport and recreation for more
than 700 hunters annually. Beaver, bear, turkey and antelope may also
be found. Camping is free throughout the forest. Many natural camp-
sites among the tall pines can be found short distances from the highway and visitors are encouraged to use the many recreational areas established for their pleasure by the National Park Service. Windmills
mark infrequent habitations and old prospectors still whittle away on
tavern benches as they swap stories of lost mines or load burros and
head toward the canyons to search again.

US 60 skirts the southern end of the Socorro Mountains (R),
passing small adobe houses. The rugged Polvadera Mountain and the

Bear Mountains are also visible (R). The road lies through a narrow valley with dark outcroppings of volcanic rock (R) and the dark reds of other igneous rock (L). Where the road inclines cane cactus appears, and juniper on both sides begins the march of evergreens up the mountain.

MAGDALENA, 27 *m.* (6,548 alt., 1,371 pop.), the second largest town in Socorro County, was named for Mary Magdalene. It is a trading and shipping point for cattle ranchers as there is no other railroad station between Magdalena and Arizona. In the spring large herds of cattle are driven here, and in June the season's clip arrives in long wagon trains packed with sacks of wool. Though Magdalena is the last stronghold in New Mexico of the old cattle barons and the gateway to vast grazing plains, settlers are moving in along the arroyos and mountain streams and before long irrigated farms probably will occupy the area. Meanwhile the annual rodeo (Sept.), barred to professional performers, brings together the cowpunchers, their friends and backers, and many visitors.

The town was founded in 1884 by miners who worked small claims. The railroad came very soon, and the town began to flourish. Money was free and easy, liquor was abundant, and the old frontier lived lustily here. When mining declined Magdalena declined too; then it turned to livestock and flourished again.

AUGUSTINE, 52.3 *m.* (7,200 alt., 10 pop.), was named for the Plains of St. Augustine (L) to the south and was reputedly trod by the Spanish missionaries and after them the traders.

DÁTIL, 63.9 *m.* (7,855 alt., 174 pop.), was named by the early Spaniards for a fruit resembling dates found in the mountains. It is a trading center for ranchers and a supply point for hunters. The United States Army built a fort here in 1888 to protect settlers from raids by the Apache.

Left from Dátil on NM 12, an improved dirt road, past mountains, ranches, springs, and forests where the Apache roamed before their subjugation. HORSE SPRINGS, 25.9 *m.* (6,980 alt., 310 pop.), and the springs (R) near by, named for the wild horses that roamed this section, are now owned by a syndicate of cattlemen. At 39.6 *m.* the road enters the APACHE NATIONAL FOREST, which is two-thirds western yellow pine, the remainder being Douglas fir, white fir, and spruce. Large herds of cattle, horses, and sheep graze here under government permit. West of the CONTINENTAL DIVIDE (7,500 alt.), the roads go through TULAROSA CANYON, 45 *m.*, a winding gorge cut by the Tularosa River, which is dry most of the year but swift and dangerous in rainy weather. This region is the heart of the old Apache country where these ferocious fighters for many years carried on guerrilla warfare led by Mangas Coloradas, Victorio, Gerónimo, Chato, and Cochise. Tradition has it that these Indians were peaceful and hospitable to the first trappers, colonists, and explorers but when later pioneers settled in the country and took their land and water, it was thought that the first friendly "pale-faces" had been annihilated by the later, and more aggressive, tribe. This opened a half century of warfare that was not curbed until the final surrender of Gerónimo to General Nelson A. Miles in 1886.

ARAGÓN, 49.1 *m.* (7,135 alt., 370 pop.), is a trading center in the narrow Tularosa Valley. Small irrigated farms, with cattle and sheep raising, comprise the interests of the villagers, mostly of Spanish and Mexican stock. Fort

Tularosa was built here in 1870 and maintained for four years, and here is the burial ground for soldiers from the neighboring territory. There are several pueblo ruins in this vicinity, locale for the story about Mangas Coloradas and a captive Mexican girl. He added her to his household with the same status as that of his two wives, contrary to tribal law which decreed that she should serve them as a slave. They exercised their right of appeal to their relatives, and a brother of each wife challenged Mangas to defend his right to keep her. Mangas, a tall, exceptionally powerful man, fought the two before the assembled tribe. They were clad only in breech clouts and were armed with long knives. After Mangas had killed them both no one questioned his right to wench or wife as he pleased.

RESERVE, 69.2 *m.* (5,769 alt., 226 pop.), is seat of Catron County, the only county in New Mexico without a railroad. On the banks of the San Francisco River, in the heart of the cattle country, it is surrounded by forests and mountains. Farming and lumbering are also carried on in the neighborhood. It is a starting point for pack trips and hunting parties. In Reserve in 1882, Elfego Baca, deputy sheriff, had an exciting adventure when he attempted the arrest of a drunken cow hand. At the time of his arrival the cowboy, named McCarthy, having filled up on Mr. Milligan's bad whiskey, was riding up and down the main street looking for trouble.

Elfego Baca, a deputy sheriff, saw that the wild McCarthy was endangering people's lives and that the local authorities would take no action, so he proceeded to disarm the cowboy and place him under arrest. Word soon went to his friends at the nearby ranches, and a mob rode into town determined to rescue McCarthy and teach Baca a lesson.

In this engagement, Baca killed one of the mob, wounded another, kept his prisoner, and drove the entire mob down the street with well-directed shots kicking up the dust behind them. The local Justice of the Peace, afraid of the Texans, refused to hold court. It was the wish of Baca to try McCarthy on the spot, and thus avoid having to take him to Socorro, the county seat. Eventually he brought his prisoner from the middle plaza where he had taken him for safe keeping, a Justice of the Peace was found, and court opened. All the cow-punchers and saloon loafers had followed Baca and his prisoner, and the court room was so crowded that not more than half the people could enter. The verdict rendered was "drunk and disorderly and a five dollar fine."

Baca was disgusted. He left, went down the street and entered a cabin, presumably to rest. On the scene appeared four men who stated they had an order from the presiding justice to arrest Baca for shooting a man at the time of McCarthy's arrest. These men proceeded to the door of the cabin, which Baca had entered. Hern, who was in the lead, knocked on the door and asked if anyone was inside. Getting no reply, he kicked the door and demanded admittance. In reply a bullet fired through the door got Hern in the stomach. He cursed, and falling backward was dragged around the corner of the house. Two of the four men were so badly frightened they fled. The one who dragged Hern out of danger laid him on the ground. A man known as Old Charley, leading a saddled horse belonging to an English ranchman named French, heard the shots and came galloping down the street, pulling up in front of the cabin door. He was shot at twice, both bullets passing through his peaked hat. Old Charley had business away from there, and at once, but the lead horse balked. French seeing the trouble ran and grabbed the reins of his horse, but in the excitement lost his hat, it falling off just in front of the cabin door. French determined to retrieve his hat and made a dash for it. While he was picking it up Baca fired three shots through the brim.

Dan, the deputy, now agreed with the mob that Baca should be arrested, but he couldn't do it as he had to have some sleep. He had been up the entire night before, he said.

The mob got behind adobe walls and poured bullets into the shelter, but whenever any of them showed a head or an arm he was greeted by a bullet from Baca. The attackers thought that perhaps the best way would be to take the cabin by assault; but this idea was abandoned.

The little house was not of stone, logs, or adobe, but what is called a *choza*. It was a light structure consisting of upright poles supporting a mud roof, with a little gable roof over one room and a small window in the end. Why Baca was not killed no one could imagine, for up to this time, it is said, 3,000 shots had been fired into the house, but that he was very much alive was shown whenever anyone showed himself.

After a particularly fierce fusillade by the storming party, Baca's fire ceased, and all thought him dead.

Night coming on, sentries were posted to prevent his escape. During the night Hern died. Several of the sentries fell asleep on duty, and had Baca so desired, there was nothing to have prevented his walking out of the door and going where he pleased though he also was probably asleep.

Early the next morning French, curious to know if Baca were still in the cabin, ran as fast as he could past the cabin and received a salute from his guns. French was satisfied that Baca was still alive.

While all this excitement was going on, several Spanish-Americans made a hurried trip to Socorro to get help from the officers. While they were gone, all kinds of inducements, couched in flowery Spanish, were offered to Baca to surrender, the mob not realizing that Baca spoke better English than most of them.

Presently an attempt was made to set the house on fire. Blazing branches were thrown on the roof, but because it was covered with a foot or so of dirt it wouldn't burn.

The sun was going down on the second day when a buggy containing three men drove up rapidly from the direction of Socorro. From the buggy stepped a deputy sheriff named Rose. He said he had come in response to a message from Elfego Baca, brought by the Spanish-Americans who accompanied him. As Socorro was over 125 miles from the plaza where the shooting had occurred, both the messengers and the returning sheriff had made fast time.

Dan the local deputy, who had been drunk and asleep all this while, now was much in evidence, telling what he had done to enforce the law. Rose did not pay any attention to him, but asked questions from others regarding the affair, which offended Dan who returned to Mr. Milligan's for liquid consolation.

Mr. Rose now endeavored through a friend of Baca to communicate with him. When Baca recognized his friend's voice, he agreed to come out on the following condition: Everyone except his friend and Rose was to retire from in front of the house; he would then surrender to them. When these terms were accepted, Elfego came out, not through the door as expected but through the little gable window in the end of the house. He was stripped to his pants and had a gun in each hand, glancing on each side as if afraid of some treachery. He then walked up to Rose who disarmed him.

Dan, still pretty drunk, now appeared and formally turned "his prisoner" over to Rose, thereby compensating for the slight to his dignity.

When questioned, Baca explained he had escaped by lying on the floor, which like typical New Mexico dwellings was a foot or more below the level of the ground.

This fight in which one man had stood off a mob of over 80, holding out for over 33 hours, as testified in court during Baca's trial, won for Elfego Baca a secure place among the colorful characters of New Mexico.

Southwest of Stark Weather Canyon, NM 12 goes through an open rolling valley studded with tall pines and stands of juniper. Ahead are the beautiful San Francisco Mountains. At 76.4 *m.* is the junction with US 260 (*see Tour 18*).

US 60 runs through a narrowing valley and crosses at 65.3 *m.* the boundary of CÍBOLA NATIONAL FOREST, which it traverses for 20 miles.

A Ranger Station (R) and cabins for tourists (L) are at 66.7 *m.*

An upthrust of rock towers above the road (R) as it rises past tall pines on wooded slopes. The valley opens again, the way descends.

US 60 crosses the CONTINENTAL DIVIDE, 84.1 *m.*, and continues through a section of magnificent vistas. Outcroppings of colored sandstone border the road.

PIE TOWN, 86.1 *m.* (6,810 alt., 50 pop.), started with a filling station whose owner had taken up a mining claim on this site. His third occupation was baking pies, hence the name. This is a marketing point for piñon nuts gathered in this area by Indians who sell to traders or to wholesalers.

OMEGA, 101.0 *m.* (6,900 alt., 30 pop.), formerly called Sweazeaville, was the original site of Quemado, established in 1870 by Felipe Padilla.

QUEMADO (Sp. burnt), 108.7 *m.* (7,000 alt., 284 pop.), the largest town in Catron County, is named for an Apache chief whose hand, legend says, was burned in a campfire. Coronado's route in 1540 was through this region.

US 60 continues through rugged country to the ARIZONA LINE, 143.2 *m.,* 17 miles east of Springerville, Arizona.

# *Tour 9*

(Cortez, Col.)—Shiprock—Farmington—Aztec—Cuba—Bernalillo.
US 84 and NM 44.
Colorado Line to Bernalillo, 233.7 *m.*

Two-lane, graveled road to Shiprock, bituminous-paved to Aztec, gravel and dirt to Cuba, bituminous-paved to Bernalillo.
Denver & Rio Grande Western Railroad roughly parallels route between Farmington and Aztec; Santa Fe Northwestern Railway between San Ysidro and Bernalillo.
Accommodations in larger towns.

This route offers fine vistas and panoramas as it runs through the fertile orchards and farms of the San Juan Valley, crosses the Navaho and Apache reservations and passes oil fields, fossil beds, grazing lands, and pueblo ruins.

US 84 crosses the COLORADO LINE, 0 *m.,* 27 miles south of Cortez, Colorado. Between the Colorado Line and Farmington the route is within the NAVAHO INDIAN RESERVATION (22,010 pop.), a desert-like country covered with coarse grasses grazed by Navaho sheep. Geologic formations rich in color appear at intervals as the route descends to the San Juan River.

SHIPROCK, 15.4 *m*. (4,903 alt., 2,131 pop.), named for an imposing rock mass (R), was the headquarters for the Northern Navaho
Indian Agency from 1903 till the subagencies were all consolidated at
Window Rock, Arizona, in 1938. It is now a Navaho district office.
The Rattlesnake Oil Fields (R) near Shiprock contain some of the
highest grade oil in the United States but the flow is limited and the
lack of marketing facilities further reduces their value. From these
and two other fields on their reservation the Navaho receive annually
a total of about $50,000 in royalties. There is an annual Navaho Fair
held here early in October with sports and exhibits of arts and crafts
(*see Indians*). In Shiprock are junctions with US 666 (*see Tour 6C*)
and with US 550, which the route follows through the fertile San Juan
Valley, the most prosperous section of the Navaho Indian Reservation.

FRUITLAND, 33.3 *m*. (5,200 alt., 455 pop.), is a farming village
settled in the winter of 1877-78 by Mormons under Luther E. Burnham, who changed the name from Olio to Fruitland. On the south side
of the San Juan River there is an irrigation project supplying water to
more than 3,000 acres. This has been divided into ten-acre tracts on
which the Navaho expected to raise corn, beans, and other subsistence
crops, but so far, because of their distrust of the situation, these Indians
have not availed themselves of this land.

In the heart of this agricultural region is FARMINGTON, 45.1 *m*.
(5,305 alt., 2,151 pop.), at the confluence of the San Juan, Las Ánimas,
and La Plata rivers. First settled by whites in 1876, Farmington was
incorporated in 1901 and now is the largest town in San Juan County
and a flourishing commercial center; but it grew despite many pioneer
hardships. This region was occupied by the Navaho, claimed by the
Apache, and plagued with unruly cowboys.

In the spring of 1883 after a drunken cowboy had shot and wounded
an Indian on the street of Farmington, the Indians threatened to go on
the warpath, and several hundred of them surrounded the town.
Gregorio, a friendly Indian, warned the white settlers and told them
that if the plowmen and ranchers stayed in their homes they would not
be hurt, for the Indians were after the *tejanos* (Texans or cowboys).
After many hours of suspense the war chief arrived and quieted his
followers. In 1885 when Largo Pete, a sub-chief, turned his horses
loose in W. P. Hendrick's grain field, serious trouble threatened until
troops arrived from Fort Lewis and the Indians subsided. The following year after Largo Pete rode into a wire fence strung by the Virden
Brothers, traders, and died of the injury, the Indians were so aroused
by the accident that the militia was again called out, but after a conference the Indians were bought off with a small amount of provisions.

The Reverend Griffin, Farmington's first resident preacher, arrived
in 1885 and remained for many years despite trouble with the cowboys.
When he refused to drink with them, they shot holes in the floor around
his feet, but he stood his ground until they ceased. A professional show-
man was not so brave; he attempted to hold a stereopticon show in the

schoolhouse, but when cowboys shot the canvas screen to bits, the show-man jumped out the window.

The cattle business, which preceded land cultivation here, had its ups and downs. "Uncle" Washington Cox, who once refused $100,000 for his branded stock, died a pauper. In co-operation with McGalliard the Virden Brothers built the first irrigation ditch. It carried water two-and-one-half miles on the north side of the river irrigating about four acres.

Development of the fruit industry began in 1879, when William Locke came here from Florence, Colorado. On his second trip, he brought peach, walnut, and other seeds and later small fruit trees including plum, apple, pear, and nectarine, as well as blackberry and raspberry bushes. In a few years there were many fine orchards, notably that owned by C. H. McHenry. A brick kiln and a flour mill followed, and Farmington became a center of varied activity.

AZTEC, 59.1 *m.* (5,590 alt., 740 pop.), is the seat of San Juan County and one of its principal trading centers. Before 1826 when the beaver were exterminated trapping was a profitable industry here. Though the townsite was laid out in 1890 it showed little growth for the next 15 years. Its location in a prosperous fruit growing center has been responsible for a steady, continuous growth since 1905.

At 59.4 *m.* is the junction with a dirt road.

Left on this road 0.7 *m.* to AZTEC RUINS NATIONAL MONUMENT (*adm. 25¢; ranger guides*). This large E-shaped pueblo contained approximately 500 rooms. The ceilings, where standing, are supported by beams that were cut and dressed with stone tools between 1110 and 1121 A.D. according to tree-ring dates. The sandstone walls are fine examples of pueblo masonry. The American Museum of Natural History, which gave the land to the United States for a National Monument, has excavated the ruins and established a small museum here.

BLOOMFIELD, 68.2 *m.* (5,400 alt., 1,407 pop.), settled in 1881 by William B. Haines, an Englishman, was the home of the notorious Stockton Gang. Its early history is one of cattle rustling, terrorism, and violent death. Port Stockton was made a peace officer because of his expert marksmanship, but when divested of authority because he could not be trusted with a gun, he became an outlaw again. He is said to have shot and wounded a barber who had cut him slightly while shaving him; to have jumped a ranch below Aztec while the owner, a widow, was visiting relatives 50 miles away; to have forced his way into a dance where he knew he was not wanted, and danced all night with a six-gun strapped to his waist; to have rustled cattle and held up stage-coaches. He was aided by Bloomfield's lack of peace officers and courts and by local ranchers' preoccupation with raids on their herds by the Eskridge gang from Durango, Colorado. In Stockton's gang were Ike Stockton, Harg and Dice Etheridge, Bert Wilkerson, and a giant of a man named Lacey. Cattle stolen by them were sold to army posts or to markets, and the gang even operated a butcher shop in Durango. At one time two score ranchers of the San Juan Basin were in their saddles day and night trying to safeguard their property.

Port Stockton, who is said to have had 15 notches on his gun when he blew into Bloomfield from the Lincoln County War (*see Tour 12b*), was killed in 1881 while hiding a man named Truitt who had shot a man at a dance. When the posse went after Truitt, Stockton refused to surrender him. Shooting began, and after the smoke had cleared Stockton was dead. His wife rushed from the house with a rifle, which she rested on a wagon wheel for a better sight. One of the posse, in trying to shoot the gun out of her hand, hit the gun barrel and mangled her hand; but she recovered and soon was married again.

Shortly after Stockton's death a man named Blancett arrived at Bloomfield and opened a saloon. Although he was so lame that he was compelled to use a crutch, Blancett was ready for anything when armed and soon his bar became headquarters for gunmen. Many of them had drifted in from the upper San Juan Valley, after having been run out, and they found Blancett to their liking.

Several violent deaths were instigated by him and he was finally killed in Utah, where he was shot in the back. Nothing was ever done about his death; it was considered a providential disposition.

Bloomfield finally settled down and became a prosperous little town; now it is an agricultural center and surrounding farms produce large crops of grain, beans, and other produce. In 1906 land owners here organized the Citizens' Ditch and Irrigating Company to reclaim 6,000 acres. This company was organized on May 19, 1906 and was absorbed in March, 1911 by the Bloomfield Irrigation District, which took over all rights and properties and has been functioning since. The system is fed from the San Juan River by a canal 30 miles long and irrigates 4,000 acres. It is said to have the best heading, that is, the best constructed intake facilities, of any similar system in this country.

South of the San Juan River, US 84 crosses Kutz Canyon Wash and follows a hilly winding route that is bordered with juniper and gives a superb view of KUTZ CANYON (L), a ravine broken by gray mounds.

ANGEL'S PEAK (L), a desolate mountain of blue and gray shale that resembles a group of winged angels, is visible from 82.5 *m*. This is the chief landmark of the GARDEN OF THE ANGELS, which covers 80 square miles and is almost completely devoid of vegetation, but has been eroded into a great confusion of mesas, buttes, and boulder-strewn canyons. These badlands are arid, completely uninhabited except by the Navaho, and most uninviting. But to the artist they present a challenge.

From 89.3 *m*. is a view (L) of EL HUÉRFANO PEAK (7,000 alt.) with sides rising sheer for 500 feet. The solitary position of the peak gives it the name, The Orphan. On the summit, according to Navaho legend, is a sacred spring. Only Indians have been allowed to climb it.

EL HUÉRFANO TRADING POST is at 93.4 *m.* near the foot of the peak.

At 133.8 *m.,* is the junction with a dirt road.

Left on this to HAYNES, 5 *m.,* a small trading post on the edge of CANYON LARGO, an eroded gorge about 40 miles long, and one of the most desolate spots in the State. The road continues through this canyon whose sides are brown sandstone cliffs from 100 to 300 feet high. The effect at night is weird and fantastic.

The CONTINENTAL DIVIDE (7,680 alt.) is crossed at 154.4 *m.* and the western boundary of the SANTA FE NATIONAL FOREST at 161.3 *m.*

At 164.7 *m.* is the junction with NM 44 which the route follows R. US 84 branches north.

CUBA, 166.8 *m.* (7,000 alt., 841 pop.), originally named Naci-miento (nativity), is the center of a ranching country where cattle and sheep are abundant. It is situated in a valley between the Sierra Naci-miento and the Cejita Blanca (little white peaks) Ranges. In Cuba is a junction with NM 126 (*see Tour 2A*).

LA VENTANA, 181.7 *m.* (6,400 alt., 263 pop.), formerly a coal mining town, is no longer active, production having ceased.

Less than a mile south of La Ventana, NM 44 traverses what was once one of the largest land grants in New Mexico—the OJO DEL ESPÍRITU SANTO (spring of the Holy Ghost). According to tradition the name of the grant came from the experience of a peon who stood guard one night after dinner. Suddenly he rushed toward the camp, crying out: "El Espíritu Santo! El Espíritu Santo!" and the others, leaving camp, saw two wraith-like spirals rising from the ground in a near-by canyon. For them it was a manifestation of the Holy Ghost. This led to the discovery of the springs from whence the "miracle" came.

The De Bacas, members of the family of Cabeza de Vaca, the ex-plorer, were given this area of more than 113,000 acres by the Spanish Crown. The grant extending westward almost to the Rio Puerco (dirty river) and Cabezón (big head) Peak and eastward as far as the Naci-miento Mountains, contains mountains, foothills, and valleys and in-cludes much valuable pasture land and a deposit of gypsum. The estate was sold later in 1934 to the United States Government for the use of the Pueblo Indians.

CABEZÓN PEAK (R) is visible from 194.8 *m.*

NM 44 parallels the Rio Salado (saline river) as far as San Ysidro, where the stream joins Jémez Creek (*see below*). The Rio Salado flows southward from its source in the Salado Canyon in the heart of the Ojo Espíritu Santo grant, leaving the grant at its southeast corner. The river, containing calcite, has warm currents of water caused by springs along its course.

The highly colored mountainous terrain gives way to relatively level land at 199 *m.*

Improved highways have developed SAN YSIDRO, 209 *m.* (5,450 alt., 414 pop.), from a post office, store, and filling station patronized by tourists and ranchers into a small village.

Left from San Ysidro on NM 4 over the Jémez River and across the railroad tracks. JÉMEZ PUEBLO (*Pueblo governor for a fee grants permission to photograph*), 4.7 *m.* (5,800 alt., 675 pop.), was established sometime between 1696 and 1700. On August 2, Pecos Day is celebrated in memory of the survivors from Pecos Pueblo who came here a hundred years ago (*see Tour 1a*), and the patron saint of the village is honored on November 12. The Jémez people make little pottery but specialize in elaborately embroidered ceremonial shirts and are noted for their weaving; they make a distinctive type of flat basket with yucca leaves. On the western edge of the village stands the modern Chapel of San Diego, built in 1937 at a cost of $4,000. Grouped round it are the post office, the parochial day school, and the ruins of the old church that burned.

Jémez took a prominent part in the Pueblo Revolt of 1680. In June 1696 a small detachment of Spaniards from Bernalillo, with allies from Zía, attacked the Jémez and defeated them. The Jémez retreated to the Navaho country, remaining several years, then returned to establish the present village. Because of its proximity to Navaho country and the friendly relations between the two peoples, there were many intermarriages. Some anthropologists say that Jémez is "more than half Navaho" and that one of their outstanding leaders, Nazle, was Navaho born. Navaho come here in numbers at fiesta time for the purpose of trade. The population of Jémez was given as 3,000 in 1630 and as 5,000 in 1680, but from the middle of the eighteenth century to the beginning of the twentieth remained between 250 and 500. JÉMEZ SPRINGS, 17.7 *m.* (677 pop.), is a hamlet with a post office, a dispensary, a cafe, and a trading post with lunch room and gas station. A string of houses along both sides of the road make up the village.

The JÉMEZ STATE MONUMENT (R), 19.6 *m.* contains the ruins of the MISSION OF SAN JOSÉ DE JÉMEZ, with walls in some places, six to eight feet thick and thirty feet high. Across the road from the entrance to the monument is a large stone hotel (*open in summer*). This was the site of ancient Giusewa (Ge-oó-see-wah), one of the many pueblos occupied when the early Spaniards came. It is supposed there were about 800 inhabitants. In 1617 when the mission was built this was an important village of the Jémez Valley but was abandoned in 1622 owing to the aggressions of the Navaho. The story of the Jémez pueblos and missions is a stormy one, full of revolt, abandonments, and re-establishments at various sites.

The site of Giusewa, covering about six acres, was acquired by the Museum of New Mexico in 1921 and created a State Monument in 1935. In 1921-22 excavations were continued by the School of American Research after earlier collaboration with the Bureau of American Ethnology and the Royal Ontario Museum, and in 1935 they were resumed in co-operation with the Universtiy of New Mexico.

SODA DAM (R), 19.8 *m.*, is a natural dam extending like a huge misshapen mushroom from the canyon floor. Numerous conical rocks and sulphur springs are above the dam. A private residence with white stucco buildings and extensive grounds is at 20.4 *m.*

Between San Ysidro and Santa Ana, NM 44 follows Jémez Creek. At 215.6 *m.* is the junction with a dirt road.

Left 1 *m.* on this road across a wooden bridge to ZÍA PUEBLO (*Pueblo governor for a fee grants permission to photograph*). These people, like those at other pueblos, are farmers but have difficulty growing anything on this poor soil. They manage to raise corn, wheat, and alfalfa and in their gardens work hard to produce watermelons, chili, beans, and cabbage. The tribe participated in the Pueblo Revolt of 1680, and in 1687 when the Spaniards were attempting to reconquer the pueblos a bloody battle was fought here. General De Posada, acting under orders of Governor Cruzate, marched from El Paso as far as this pueblo. Historians say that 600 Indians were killed and 70 taken prisoners. The latter were condemned to slavery for ten years with the exception of a few old men who were executed. The mission was reestablished by De Vargas, and from the ruins of the old church the present adobe MISSION OF NUESTRA SEÑORA DE LA ASUNCIÓN was built October 24, 1692. It is a simple structure with massive buttresses on the front facade. The second-floor gallery porch over the entrance has a solid railing with a pattern of crude, circular openings cut out along the bottom. In the center above the gallery's wooden roof is a bell hung in a stepped adobe gable.

Zia has always made fine pottery which is distinctive in color and design. Their annual fiesta (August 15) honors Our Lady of the Ascension, their patron saint.

At 224.5 *m.* is the junction with a dirt road.

Left on this road .2 *m.* then across a ford in the Jémez River. This crossing is difficult, often dangerous, and unless others are near by to render aid or to advise about conditions, it is better not to attempt it, for even when the river bed is dry the sand is deep and treacherous.

SANTA ANA PUEBLO (*obtain permission to photograph*), 0.8 *m.* (5,500 alt., 258 pop.), is usually in charge of caretakers while most of its people are at the farming settlement, El Ranchito (*see Tour 1b*). The CHURCH OF SANTA ANA DE ALAMILLO was rebuilt by De Vargas in 1692 on the site of the mission church erected about 1600 and burned in 1687. It is an adobe structure with a walled forecourt and low, one-story buildings on both sides. Over the entrance to the church proper is a crude wooden gallery supported at each end by an extension of the church's side walls and protected from the weather by a flat canopy above. In the center of the entrance facade, a stepped gable with a bell opening rises above the square mass of the church.

At 230.1 *m.* on NM 44 is the junction with a dirt road.

Left on this road 1.5 *m.* to the junction with a dirt road. Left on this in the CORONADO STATE MONUMENT are two pre-Columbian Tiguex pueblo ruins: KUAUA (R), 2 *m.,* and PUARAY (L), 3 *m.,* two of the several pueblos of the pre-Columbian "province of Tiguex" where Coronado had his headquarters in 1540-42. It is not known definitely in which one of the dozen or more Tiguex pueblos in this region Coronado quartered his soldiers, and there is even disagreement over the identification of Kuaua and Puaray. In 1581 the Rodríguez-Chamuscado expedition entered the Tiguex province, and the three Franciscan leaders chose a town called Puaray as the site of their missionary labors; all three were killed by the Indians. By 1680 when the pueblos revolted only four of the Tiguex villages were inhabited but these took an active part in the rebellion.

Archeological research has been done here by the University of New Mexico and the School of American Research at Santa Fe with financial aid from the Federal Emergency Relief Administration and Work Projects Administration. The most interesting find was a series of murals along three sides of a square subterranean *kiva.* The walls had been covered with 29 washes of adobe plaster, and from 7 to 12 of these layers contained mural decorations. The walls were removed intact, after being covered inside and out with reinforcements of plaster of Paris, glue, and burlap, and all the successive layers have been removed at the State University where copies were made of the drawings on each layer.

NM 44 joins US 85 at BERNALILLO, 233.7 *m.* (*see Tour 1b*).

*Tour 10*

Clovis—Portales—Roswell—Hondo—Tularosa—Alamogordo—Las
Cruces—Deming—Lordsburg—(Duncan, Arizona); US 70.
Clovis to Arizona Line, 445.8 *m.*

Two-lane bituminous-paved road except through Mescalero Apache Reserva-
tion.
Atchison, Topeka & Santa Fe Railway roughly parallels route between Clovis
and Roswell; Southern Pacific Railroad between Tularosa and the Arizona
Line.
Accommodations in principal towns.

This route which connects modern Roswell with historic Las Cruces
crosses level plains extending west of Roswell, traverses Lincoln County,
scene of Billy the Kid's daring exploits in the Lincoln County War, and
winds between beautiful mountains in the Mescalero Apache reservation. It cuts through the White Sands National Monument and west
of the Rio Grande gains altitude, crossing the Victoria and Pyramid
Mountains near the Arizona Line.

*Section a.* CLOVIS *to* ALAMOGORDO, *228.8 m.*

In the eastern part of the State US 70 runs through plains made
productive by irrigation and crosses the Mescalero Ridge and the Pecos
Valley, in pioneer days a famous cattle run and a region where Billy
the Kid operated.

US 70 branches south from US 60 (*see Tour 8a*) in CLOVIS,
0 *m.* (4,218 alt., 9,931 pop.), which was named by the daughter of a
Santa Fe Railway official for the first Christian King of France. The
town began in 1907 as Riley's Switch, a siding on the Santa Fe, but
grew rapidly after the railroad brought its shops and warehouses here
from Melrose (*see Tour 8a*). It is now a four-way division point of
the Santa Fe, a junction of US 60 and 70, two important east-west
highways, and NM 18, a north-south artery which taps the rich oil
centers of southeastern New Mexico. Clovis is also a jobbing center
with many warehouses, a storage point with four large elevators for
wheat and other grain grown in this area, and a feeding point for livestock being shipped east. Cattle from the western grazing lands are
often sent on a "stop in transit" billing that permits a stop-over at the
Clovis feeding pens for fattening. Several Federal and State agencies
for agriculturists and ranchers maintain offices here.

Adjoining the southern city limits is HILLCREST, a 140-acre
municipal park with an 18-hole golf course, a $20,000 swimming pool,

sunken garden, wading pool, tennis courts, zoo, a lake stocked for fisher-men, and a baseball park.

EASTERN NEW MEXICO STATE PARK (L), 10 *m.,* in the Blackwater Draw, covers 380 acres. Work on this was under super-vision of the National Park Service and all labor was performed by the Civilian Conservation Corps.

The Blackwater Draw, a series of shallow dry basins and lakes tributary to the Portales Valley, was made by a prehistoric river that headed somewhere in the vicinity of present Taiban and Krider (*see Tour 8a*) near the western escarpment of the Staked Plains and ex-tended southeast through the site of Portales (*see below*) to the Double Mountain Fork of the Brazos River in west Texas. An upheaval—probably the one that raised Llano Estacado—formed a dike that turned the river into the course of the present Pecos. Its abandoned bed in the Portales Valley developed numerous sinks now almost obliterated by sand dunes built by wind erosion. Lake La Tule, Tierra Blanca, and Great Salt Lake are among the salt and alkali lakes that mark the old river bed.

PORTALES (Sp. entrance) 19.3 *m.* (4,002 alt., 5,091 pop.), the seat of Roosevelt County, is in the well-irrigated Portales Valley. In 1890 when shallow underground water was discovered, cattlemen and farmers moved into this region. Although the Portales Irrigation Company organized in 1910 failed financially in 1918, several farmers continued to raise irrigated crops here. Today 385 private wells are furnishing water for 14,000 acres that produce tomatoes, peanuts, and sweet potatoes that are shipped to all parts of the country; also melons, strawberries, cucumbers, and grapes. Dairying has become a consider-able industry in outlying farms.

Southwest of Portales the highway crosses typical grazing lands and more farming areas chiefly planted with sorghums, which are converted into syrup.

The Brazos River, which flows principally through Texas, is crossed at 21.3 *m.*

ELIDA, 44 *m.* (4,280 alt., 325 pop.), was settled in 1880 by George Littlefield whose son now owns 16,000 acres in the vicinity, and has always been a trading point for ranchers.

From KENNA, 54.1 *m.* (4,200 alt., 133 pop.), established in 1906 as a cattle-shipping point, Kenna Mesa is visible (R).

ACME, 85.2 *m.* (3,750 alt., 30 pop.), was named for the Acme Cement Company which in 1905 constructed a cement mill near by. Plaster and cement blocks were manufactured until 1931, when high freight rates caused the plant to close down, though a small plant here still operates.

A long bridge crosses the PECOS RIVER, 94.2 *m.,* which is usually a small, sluggish stream but in flood times mounts close to the bridge floor. West of the Pecos, the highway traverses an irrigated farming district.

In ROSWELL, 110.5 *m.* (3,600 alt., 13,443 pop.) (*see Tour 7b*), are junctions with US 285 (*see Tour 7b*) and US 380 which is united with US 70 between Roswell and Hondo. West of Roswell, the route begins a gradual ascent of the WHITE and CAPITÁN MOUN-TAINS (R). On the hillsides the rich green of the junipers accents the soft brown and gray of the countryside.

PICACHO (Sp., peak) HILL, 142.9 *m.,* so steep in stagecoach days it was a hazard for inexperienced drivers, has been graded. Prickly pear, cactus, and ocotillo eight to ten feet high and in spring tipped with scarlet blooms, grow on the hilltop. The highway winds around the summit, presenting far vistas of great beauty. In the canyon at the base of the hill wild walnut, hackberry, and mesquite grow in profusion.

The highway winds beside the cottonwood and mesquite-lined banks of the Hondo River, a main tributary of the Pecos, from which many small farms are irrigated. This valley divides the White Mountains and the El Capitán country (R).

PICACHO, 148.9 *m.* (4,964 alt., 410 pop.), named for the peak (R) which dominates the little adobe village, is a trading center for farmers from the surrounding goat and sheep ranches, fruit orchards, and truck farms. The first ranchers came from the Rio Grande settlements about 1865, braving attacks from the marauding Apache. The cattlemen moved in about 1875.

TINNIE, 153.8 *m.,* originally named Analla for one of its earliest settlers, but renamed for the daughter of the first postmaster, is also a trading point. In the broad expanse of the Hondo Valley apples are the principal crop.

HONDO, 157.8 *m.* (5,280 alt., 854 pop.), at the confluence of the Bonito (Sp., pretty) and Ruidoso (Sp., noisy), mountain streams which unite to form the Rio Hondo, is a typical New Mexican settlement built around the original homestead claim of L. W. Coe, a cousin of Frank and George Coe, who were involved in the Lincoln County War (*see Tour 12b*).

In Hondo is the western junction with US 380 which branches (R) (*see Tour 12b*).

US 70 traverses the scenic Ruidoso Canyon, noted for its forests of tall conifers, trout stream, and recreation areas for campers in summer and skiers in winter, and from a hilltop is a vast panorama.

SAN PATRICIO, 161.3 *m.* (5,550 alt., 300 pop.), on the Rio Ruidoso, is in a crop-growing and grazing area. This village was settled about 1875 by farmers and cattlemen from neighboring hamlets and by migrants from the Rio Grande. The church built here by the first settlers 60 years ago was for many years the only one in an area infested by cattle rustlers and outlaws. San Patricio was a favorite resort for Billy the Kid and his band (*see Tour 12b*).

US 70 crosses the eastern boundary of the LINCOLN NA-TIONAL FOREST at 164.2 *m.,* an area of 1,500,000 acres covered with large pines and crossed with canyons and ravines. The mountain-sides are stocked with game.

Southwest of GLENCOE, 168.6 *m.* (6,000 alt., 575 pop.), another

trading center, US 70 crosses the northern boundary of the MES-
CALERO INDIAN RESERVATION (752 pop.), 182.7 m., which
is 35 miles long and 25 miles wide.

In MESCALERO, 197.9 m. (6,475 alt., 771 pop.), is the agency
headquarters. Before 1872 the Mescalero Apache were quartered at
Fort Stanton with the Navaho. In 1866 the related Athapascan groups
quarreled, and the Mescalero resumed their former nomadic life, murdering, pillaging, and stealing through eastern and southern New Mexico. After the Army had succeeded in returning 800 of them to the
Fort Stanton Agency, a reservation there was set apart for them. A
series of executive orders had been issued, each giving the Mescalero a
new home, before the present boundaries were established March 24,
1883. Of their 427,320 acres, 2,000 acres are suitable for cultivation
and the remainder for grazing.

. In 1868, on the sides of ROUND MOUNTAIN (R), a conical-
shaped hill visible from 206 m., United States soldiers and the Apache
fought one of the fiercest engagements of the Indian campaign. The
Indians captured many guns and much ammunition but were not able
to use them; and the troops stampeded many Indian horses, so that the
engagement became a succession of individual forays. Though neither
side won a decisive victory the battle saved the settlement of Tularosa,
the objective of the Indian marauders.

The name of TULAROSA, 215.5 m. (4,515 alt., 1,445 pop.), is
derived from *tule* (Sp., reed or rush) and *rosa* (Sp., rose). Founded
in 1860 by Spanish and Mexican immigrants from the Mesilla Valley
after the Rio Grande at flood stage had wiped out their small farms, it
prospered for one year, but the Apache raided the settlement so frequently that it was abandoned. The second attempt to colonize was
in 1862 when the present townsite was surveyed and platted into 157
*hortalizas* (Sp., garden or orchard tracts). Tularosa is a thriving
community, with a large lumber mill and cotton gin. It is also a loading point for cattle.

In Tularosa is the junction with US 54 (*see Tour 13*), which is
united with US 70 to a point 2 miles south of Alamogordo.

Right from Tularosa on NM 52, a graded dirt road, which runs through a
valley of gypsum and lava beds and crosses Rhodes Pass in the San Andrés
Mountains, to a barbed wire fence (R) at 46.7 m. Right (*on foot*) under this
fence; then R. 100 *yds.*, and L. (west) 35 *yards*, to the GRAVE OF EUGENE
MANLOVE RHODES (1869-1934) beloved New Mexican author. Plain wooden
boards are set in the ground about 10 feet wide and 15 feet long. A tall
piñon, with a small juniper rooted at its feet, leans over to shade the spot.

South and west of Tularosa US 70 crosses the TULAROSA VAL-
LEY, a 125-mile long desert basin, bounded by block plateaus or gently
tilted stratified formations. It extends south into Texas and north to
the Chupadera Mesa in the Cíbola National Forest and lies between
the east-facing scarp of the San Andrés Mountains (R) and the west-
facing scarp of the Sierra Blanca and Sacramento Mountains (L).

Between Tularosa and Alamogordo are deltas of rich soil formed by the La Luz (the light) and Alamogordo Rivers; underground water is abundant and farming is the chief occupation.

ALAMOGORDO (big cottonwood tree), 228.8 *m.* (4,300 alt., 3,947 pop.), was settled in 1898 when the railroad selected this site for its proximity to water from Alamo Canyon, three miles southeast of the present city. During its first year, Alamogordo was made a division point and its population grew to 1,200. Although the railroad removed part of its shops in 1903, the natural advantages of Alamogordo's position had already made it a trading and recreational center; and as the terminus of the Southern Pacific branch line that taps the lumber regions of the Sacramento Mountains, it continued to serve the lumber industry. There are large mills, a railroad tie plant, repair shops, and a marble works, utilizing the pink marble found at Marble Canyon two-and-a-half miles east of the city.

The NEW MEXICO SCHOOL FOR THE BLIND, a State institution, is situated here. It is a part of the public school system for the education of children unable to attend the regular school because of partial or total blindness. It has a nine-month session, and room, board, tuition, and medical care are furnished free. Kindergarten and twelve full grades are taught with the texts transcribed into Braille, and the high school is on the State's accredited list.

*Section b.  ALAMOGORDO to ARIZONA LINE, 217 m.*

South of ALAMOGORDO, 0 *m.,* US 70 traverses the far-reaching wind-swept plains of the Tularosa Valley. The few ranches are away from the highway, near the water holes in the valley.

At 2 *m.* is the southern junction with US 54 (*see Tour 13*) which branches L. from US 70.

At 16.1 *m.* is the junction with a dirt road.

Right on this road to the WHITE SANDS NATIONAL MONUMENT (*adm. 25¢*) 0.2 *m.,* an area supervised by the National Park Service and including only a third of the 176,000 acres that are covered with gleaming white sands.

One explanation of the origin of the sands is that gypsum in solution was washed down from the surrounding hills and carried sometimes on top of the ground and sometimes beneath, finally settling in the old lake bed to the south. Hot sunlight and a dry atmosphere caused evaporation, leaving exposed the grains of gypsum which the prevailing southwest winds piled in dunes and drifts. A second theory is that there are underground beds of pure gypsum here and water pushing upward (the water level is only 225 feet below the surface) dissolves the gypsum, bringing it to the surface. Within the Monument area is a poisonous boggy old lake bed 10 miles wide and 20 miles long. Settlers say toads and frogs washed down in the summer freshets soon die and that no life can exist on the lake bed. Topographically the area is diversified with dunes and banks, in many forms and sizes—some reaching 100 feet in height. Plant life is confined generally to the outer zones and differs from similar species elsewhere. Mice, insects and beetles, numerous here, are white or a near-white shade. Of special interest to scientists is the presence of plant life in an area free of nitrogen. It is believed that these plants create their own supply.   If subjected to intense heat (dehydrated) the white sands become plaster of Paris.

The Park Service road continues past interesting formations to a place, 8 m., where the sands are rippled and glistening white (*picnic grounds*).

Land adjacent to this area is being developed into a wild game preserve. Two-hundred-acre Lake Lucero, created from a mineral well, will serve as a breeding and resting ground for duck and other fowl that come in from the San Andrés and Sacramento Mountains.

US 70 proceeds across the valley, skirting the southern part of the sands.   Colonel A. J. Fountain, a former army officer, took this road to his home in Las Cruces from a court session at Lincoln, where he had been prosecuting cases against some of the notorious cattle thieves caught during the Rustlers' War which followed the close of the Lincoln County War (*see Tour 12b*).   He was driving in a democrat wagon accompanied by his twelve-year-old son, and was seen last at Apache Wells.   When he failed to reach Las Cruces a posse was sent out. Somewhere between White Sands and SAN AUGUSTÍN PASS (alt. 5,654), 47.1 m., marks indicated that his team had been forced off the road at a gallop; the posse found the wrecked wagon, Fountain's rifled traveling bags, his legal papers scattered about; but no trace of him or his son.   Though large rewards were offered for information leading to the recovery of the bodies, they were never found.   It is supposed that some of the thieves being prosecuted ambushed the father and son and disposed of the bodies in one of the many deep arroyos in the vicinity.   Rumors that Fountain and his son had been seen in Mexico were traced to his supposed abductors but still persist.

The Organ Mountains (9,108 alt.) which the highway crosses through San Augustín Pass, are spectacular from both sides of the range.   They contain valuable ores.

On FUNERAL BUTTE (L), 50 m., the Mescalero Apache and other earlier tribes buried their dead.   Row after row of remains with accouterments of all descriptions have been found.

In LAS CRUCES, 68.1 m. (8,355 pop.), is the junction with US 85 (*see Tour 1c*).

West of Las Cruces, US 70 passes through fields of cotton, corn, and alfalfa surrounding numerous dairy farms.   A little north of US 70 between Las Cruces and Deming is the route followed by the Overland Mail between 1851 and 1861.   John Butterfield's stages ran from St. Louis, Missouri to San Francisco, California, by way of El Paso and Yuma to avoid the snows of the Rocky Mountain region.   The trip usually took a little more than three weeks; the record was 21 days. About every 20 miles along this 2,800-mile route were stations established primarily as points to change horses or mules.   In New Mexico the stations were of adobe, and like those elsewhere, designed to afford only temporary shelter and protection to travelers.   Mowry Station near Deming, now a ruin on a private ranch, was an ideal site for its purpose, having water and pasturage for stock.   It was named Mimbres, but later called Mowry for Major Mowry who was in command of Fort Webster near by.   Mowry resigned his commission, went over to the Confederate Army, and was captured by the California Column. After 1861 the Overland Mail moved to a route farther north.

From FAIR ACRES, 72.1 *m.*, a cotton gin, a service station, and a store, Robledo Mountain is visible to the north (R).

The highway traverses a rolling desert between foothills and a region where continuous fields of yucca grow masses of creamy blossoms in spring.

CAMBRAY, 101.3 m. (20 pop.), has a post office, gas station, and several tourist cabins.

The FLORIDA MOUNTAINS (pron. Flo-ryé-da locally), 113 *m.*, to the south (L) are noted for their purple evening hues and their rugged, sharp outlines against the background of flaming sunsets.

At DEMING AIRPORT AND RODEO STADIUM (L), 123.9 *m.*, a rodeo is held every year (Nov. 9-11).

DEMING, 127.4 m. (4,342 alt., 3,591 pop.), the seat of Luna County, is more like the rapidly growing towns in the eastern section of the State with their Texas flavor than a typical New Mexico town. It is in the Mimbres Valley, which contains many thousand acres of fine farm land. The Mimbres River has its source in Grant County to the northwest of Deming. Until it reaches a point approximately 20 miles north of Deming its course is above ground. It then passes underground for the entire remainder of its length emptying into a drainless lake in Chihuahua, Mexico. Water from this underground supply, shown by U. S. Government test to be 99.9 per cent pure, is tapped to irrigate valley lands which are most suitable for tomatoes. Many varieties of fruit also are produced and cattle, horses, hogs, and goats graze on the uncultivated areas. To the north and south the valleys are dotted with mines. Lead and zinc are found in the Cook's Peak district, 20 miles north; gold, silver, copper, and onyx in the Tres Hermanas Mountains, 20 miles to the south; manganese in the Florida Mountains, 10 miles to the southwest, and fluorspar is mined a few miles northeast of Deming and milled at the city limits.

In Deming is the junction with US 260 (*see Tour 18*).

The vast fields of yucca, west of Deming, produce a quality fibre used in the manufacture of cordage, binder twine, upholstery, bagging, mattress materials, and auto seat pads.

GAGE, 147.1 *m.* (102 pop.), is a railroad settlement and a small trading point.

The CONTINENTAL DIVIDE (5,000 alt.) is crossed at 159 *m.*

From SEPAR, 167.9 *m.* (220 pop.), a cattle loading station and trading point for ranchers, the Pyramid Mountains are visible (L).

LORDSBURG, 187.5 *m.* (4,249 alt., 3,091 pop.), formerly named Lordsborough for a construction engineer for the Southern Pacific Railroad, is the seat of Hidalgo County. Radio and meteorological stations are maintained here, and Army personnel is on duty. Next to catering to tourists, mining is the chief occupation. Large mining operations are now being carried on five miles south of Lordsburg in the Pyramid

Mountains. The surrounding mountains are rich in copper and a gold strike is occasionally reported.

Directly south of the town (L) is the Lordsburg Airport, dedicated by Colonel Charles A. Lindbergh in 1927.

US 70 crosses the ARIZONA LINE, 217 *m.*, 3 miles east of Duncan, Arizona.

---

# *Tour 11*

Ranchos de Taos—Mora—Junction US 85. NM 3.
Ranchos de Taos to Junction, 74.7 *m.*

Two-lane, graded gravel roadbed throughout.
Accommodations in Mora; places to camp out.

This route is noted for its magnificent vistas and panoramas, especially in the autumn, when the color is richer than at any other time and there is snow on the mountains. It lies through forests and tiny settlements, over mountain passes on an all-weather road, and past farms and cattle ranches. The highest elevation of the road itself is 9,041 feet.

South of RANCHOS DE TAOS, 0 *m.*, NM 3 traverses the Talpa Valley, passing the home (R) of Dr. Gertrude Light, physician, well known in Taos and the vicinity, 0.4 *m.* The village of LLANO QUEMADO (burnt plain) is a settlement (R) named for the ruins to the south excavated in 1920 by direction of the Smithsonian Institute. Some anthropologists believe the Taos Indians lived here first. The reredos from the church at Llano Quemado is now in the Palace of the Governors at Santa Fe.

TALPA, 1.9 *m.* (458 pop.), is on the old Spanish land grant of Don Cristóbal de la Sena. NM 3 crosses the Rio Chiquito (little river) for which the settlement was formerly named and passes the private chapel of the Durán family, a small adobe structure built about 1820.

On a side road (L) near the highway lives Juan Pedro Cruz (born about 1855), a village weaver whose handmade loom and spinning wheel are still in use. Before machine-made blankets and carpets were sold, he supplied the Taos Indians with most of their *sarapes* and the surrounding villagers with the black, brown, and white checked *jergas* (small rugs) with which they carpeted their dirt floors. He also wove the white *sabanillas* used as foundations for the elaborately embroidered *colchas* (bed spreads) now sought and prized by collectors of Spanish handicrafts.

Close to the village are the PONCE DE LEÓN HOT SPRINGS, where the Indians of ancient times and the early Spanish settlers bathed. Before Taos had plumbing, the springs were known as the Taos Bathtub, since many of the town's citizens would journey here for baths.

New buildings have recently been added—a tea room, where home-cooked meals are prepared while the guest swims, and two excellent swimming pools, one indoor and one outdoor.

South of Talpa the highway begins a long climb through forests over U. S. Hill in the Sangre de Cristo Mountains. It is so called because United States soldiers camped in this region in 1847. At sunset the coloring of the distant mountain ranges is exceptionally beautiful. From the summit of U. S. Hill (8,500 alt.), 12.3 *m.*, parts of the old wagon road can still be seen (L) just below the edge of the present highway. Over this, a section of the old Santa Fe Trail used as late as 1933, Colonel Price brought his troops from Las Trampas to Taos to quell the uprising of 1847. They marched for three days in January through deep snow and over the rough mountain trails.

At 13.1 *m.* is junction with dirt road.

Right on this road 5.4 *m.* is Picurís Pueblo (*see Tour 3a*).

The highway crosses a boundary of the CARSON NATIONAL FOREST at 14.4 *m.*, then dips sharply downward into a small high valley. It then follows the Rio Pueblo de Picurís, a tiny stream of sparkling mountain water. For several miles the creek seems to be flowing upward. A Forest Service public camp (R) is at 17.6 *m.*, and the Agua Piedra (stony creek) Recreational Area is at 23.6 *m.* In a pocket of the Sangre de Cristo Range near TRES RITOS (three creeks), 25 *m.* (7,500 alt., 15 pop.), is the confluence of the Rio La Junta (junction river), the Agua Sarca (blue water), and the Rio Pueblo de Picurís. Another Forest Service Sub-station and the La Junta Recreational Area are in the village (L). At the latter place is a campground with stone fireplaces, tables, and sanitary facilities. Good water and wood are provided, and there is no charge for camping.

The Rio Pueblo de Picurís drains a valley on the western slope of the Sangre de Cristo Range about 10 miles long and 6 to 8 miles wide above the crossing of the highway. It affords good trout fishing. Tres Ritos was used as a camping ground for freighters on the old Taos-Las Vegas Trail. The Angostura Camp Fish Hatchery (R) is passed on the climb toward the summit of Holman Hill. At 29 *m.* is the Angostura Public Camp Ground (R), maintained by the Forest Service of Carson National Forest. The crest of Holman Hill (9,041 alt.) is at 30.2 *m.*

South of Holman, NM 3 requires great care in driving. It twists and turns through hilly country and an additional hazard is provided by the many horses, cows, and chickens that wander onto the highway.

HOLMAN, 37.4 *m.* (7,500 alt., 30 pop.), is in Mora Valley, approximately 15 miles long and from one-half to two miles wide. In pre-Spanish times this valley was the home of the "wild tribes" of

Indians, the Ute, Comanche, and at times the Jicarilla Apache, which greatly retarded its early settlement. According to Spanish archives, the upper part of the valley was called Valle de San Antonio, while the lower in which the town of Mora is, was called Valle de Santa Gertrudes, the name first given to the town. The valley was first visited in 1696 by De Vargas in pursuit of the Picurís and other Pueblo Indians, leaders of the second Pueblo revolt, but no permanent settlement was attempted until the nineteenth century. De Vargas on this campaign was the first Spanish officer to cross the main range of the Sangre de Cristo Mountains in winter. In his journal he describes in detail the immense snowdrifts. Some Frenchmen and at least one American, about 1804, had come on this route with bands of Plains Indians to trade with the Indians and whites of Taos. This afterward became a part of the Dry Cimarrón route of the old Santa Fe Trail, and detachments of troops from Santa Fe were kept along this section of the trail to prevent smuggling and to collect revenues from the freight caravans going to Taos.

CLEVELAND, 40.7 m. (7,400 alt., 626 pop.), was formerly called San Antonio and later named for President Cleveland. The establishment here of a store, still operating, by Dan Cassidy and other Irishmen said to be from County Donegal, Ireland in the latter part of the nineteenth century, was the beginning of this settlement. Another store and a post office have been added to the adobe houses that are the town. (*Good fishing at a small lake 1 mile west of the post office.*)

Left from Cleveland on a graded dirt road to ROCIADA (dewy), 17 m. (6,989 alt., 164 pop.), settled in 1846 by Spanish-Americans and so named for the frequently heavy dews. At one time this was the home of José Baca, Lieutenant Governor in 1924, whose widow Marguerite P. Baca was secretary of state of New Mexico from 1930-34. On the hills above Rociada is the elaborately equipped dude ranch, the JAY-C BAR RANCH comprising 2,000 acres of land.

Entering Mora, the COUNTY COURTHOUSE (R), with the jail behind it, is the meeting place for residents of the many small rural communities in the vicinity. The great square yard about the stone building is usually filled with horses and wagons of all descriptions.

MORA, 43.5 m. (6,528 alt., 1,049 pop.), was settled in 1835. The original name, Lo de Santa Gertrudes de Mora, is thought to be a contraction of el ojo (the spring), and of mora, meaning mulberry; but the French called it L'eau des Morts (water of the dead), after a French beaver-trapping party had discovered human bones in the stream now called the Mora River. The citizens are mostly of Spanish and Mexican stock, though some are Irish, German, and Syrian, and there are two descendants of early French settlers. When the original Mexican grant was made by Governor Albino Pérez in 1835 to 76 men and women, in a ceremony symbolizing possession of the land the grantees "pulled up weeds, threw stones, scattered handfuls of dirt and gave thanks to God and their nation."

But constant raids by Comanche Indians made it necessary for them to build their houses very close together, and there was much hardship in clearing the land. In 1843 a party of Texans, led by Colonel Charles A. Warfield, an ambitious adventurer, led an unsuccessful raid on the town. On the day following the massacre of Governor Bent in Taos, a party of traders returning to Missouri were captured here by the insurgents under command of Manuel Cortés, a Mexican outlaw. The entire party was taken out and shot, and their wagon train and goods confiscated. Among those killed was Lawrence L. Waldo of St. Louis, who had been engaged in the Santa Fe trade for many years and was well acquainted with this section. Six days before his death in a letter to his brother, who was a captain in Doniphan's regiment, Lawrence Waldo expressed the belief that "not one in one hundred native Mexicans" was content under the rule of the United States.

Ceran St. Vrain (1798-1890), who had come to Taos from St. Louis in 1830, settled here in the 1860's. He had been a partner of Governor Charles Bent, and had served as colonel of the First New Mexico Volunteer Infantry, but ill health caused him to resign, and his lieutenant colonel, Kit Carson, succeeded him. His *hacienda,* which contained many thousands of acres under a Spanish grant, followed the lavish traditions of French and Spanish hospitality. Scores of servants, peons, and Negroes from a Virginia plantation—said to be run-away slaves—as well as captured Indian children who had grown up in the household, served the St. Vrains. He died in 1890 and was buried on a low hill near the village.

In its early years Mora was seldom a peaceful town; the feuds, murders, lynchings, and terrorism of the scores of Las Vegas gangsters (*see Tour 1a*) extended throughout Mora County and sometimes centered in this village.

Near the SCHOOL OF THE SISTERS OF LORETTO, founded by Father Salpointe—later assistant to the Archbishop of Santa Fe—is a linden tree imported from France by Father Güerín. It is one of two found in northern New Mexico. Mora has a tanning school for boys and a WPA supervised school for girls that teaches carding, spinning, dyeing, and weaving. As at the boy's school, only native dyes and barks are used. There is also a woodwork school for boys.

In Mora is the junction with NM 38, a dirt road.

Left on this road to BLACK LAKE, 27.2 *m.,* a region popular with fishermen.

Southwest of Mora, along the Mora River, the highway crosses La Cueva Valley, a beautiful, well-irrigated section of 50,000 acres or more with fine orchards.

LA CUEVA (the cave), 49.2 *m.* (6,500 alt., 375 pop.), in the heart of the valley, is in an amphitheater of hills with lofty mountains behind them. Shortly after the building of Fort Union (*see Tour 1a*) in 1851, La Cueva was established as its chief supply ranch for forage and grains. The founder of the town, Vicente Romero, is remembered chiefly for his remarkable irrigation system at La Cueva, still functioning. La Cueva produces livestock, vegetables, flour, and fruits, particularly apples and apricots.

The highway passes DON TOMÁS, 57 *m.* (7,000 alt.), and SAPELLÓ, 61.9 *m.* (6,900 alt., 169 pop.), at the junction of the Manuelitos and Sapelló creeks. Don Tomás consists of a post office, two stores, and several frame buildings that serve the wheat and alfalfa farmers in the surrounding area and the hunters who come during deer and turkey season. Southwest of Sapelló the highway leaves Sapelló Creek and continues across the plain, gradually losing altitude. Along here is a fine view (L) of the TURKEY MOUNTAINS, a low range running north to south.

At 74.4 *m.* is the junction with US 85 at East Las Vegas (*see Tour 1a*).

# *Tour 12*

(Brownfield, Texas)—Tatum—Roswell—Hondo—Carrizozo—San Antonio. US 380.
Texas Line to San Antonio, 246 *m.*

Two-lane, bituminous-paved roadbed, except between Adobe and San Antonio. Hotels in Roswell, Carrizozo; tourist camps, gas stations at short intervals.

Near the Texas Line US 85 crosses flat plains country, where stock grazing and agriculture are the principal industries. West of Roswell it runs through mountainous country and the scene of the Lincoln County War.

### Section a. TEXAS LINE to HONDO, 139 m.

US 380 crosses the TEXAS LINE, 0 *m.,* at a point 33 miles west of Brownfield, Texas, crossing the lower end of the Staked Plains (*see Tour 6a*) and climbing almost imperceptibly to the caprock formation, whence it descends to a lower sandy plain of grasses and low bushes. This is primarily a cattle and sheep grazing plain, but oil wells are encroaching, and this area will probably be exploited for oil as vigorously as the region to the south.

At 14 *m.* is the REGISTRATION STATION where out-of-state trucks pay a mileage tax and licenses are sold to out-of-state cars not properly licensed.

TATUM, 15.3 *m.* (3,950 alt., 598 pop.), was founded in 1909 by James G. Tatum, who started a small general store. With funds realized from neighborhood dances and box socials, a school was built and the settlers had a permanent community. Though several oil leases have recently attracted attention to this locality, no development has yet (1940) been started. Dry farming of maize and corn produces abundant crops.

US 380 continues through a section of sheep and cattle ranches where Indian artifacts, camping sites, and flint mounds are evidence of an Indian use of these lands, though the absence of burial grounds indicates temporary, rather than permanent, occupation. The Spanish explorers recorded finding the Comanche, Kiowa, and Apache here. Piles of broken flint recently uncovered indicate the meeting place of Apache and Comanche, who visited and traded, meanwhile shaping and working points for spears and arrows. Traces of trails in the caprock between watering places usually course a direct route. The Indian's knowledge of the short-cut gave him an advantage when pursued over the plains. Several rock mounds along the Mescalero Ridge (*see below*) are believed to have been buffalo traps used in the days before the Indians had horses.

The most primitive and dangerous method of hunting buffalo was on foot. Wearing wolf skins, the Indian stalked his prey until he was within bow shot. This slow and tedious method was succeeded by trapping. Wearing a buffalo pelt, the Indian attracted the animals by his antics. As they moved nearer the edge of the cliff, the Indian darted behind a mound for protection, and other Indians who had crept up behind the buffalo frightened them, causing them to stampede over the edge to their destruction. A third method came in with the horse, when the Indian, covered with a buffalo robe, worked his way into the herd and killed several before there was a stampede. Later, some Indians used the rifle but the majority relied on the spear or bow and arrow.

Women also had a part in the hunt. Once the animal had been killed, regardless of the method employed, a man's work was done and the woman's begun. Squaws with sharp stone or bone knives fell to skinning and quartering. If the kill had been large, they were busy for days taking care of the meat and every part of the buffalo carcass. If the weather was cool, much of the meat, after a few days' cooling, was folded in leather blankets, to be carried away to their permanent home or stored in underground pits for future use. When the weather was warm, they sliced it almost paper thin, and smoked and dried it in the sun. This was called *charqui* or "jerked" meat. Dried meat was often pounded with fat and seasoned with herbs and berries to make pemmican, the forerunner of sausages. Many of the hides were tanned with the hair on to be used for robes and covers, but others were made into leather for tepees, moccasins, clothing, and other coverings. The tanning was a laborious process of soaking, scraping, oiling, and rubbing, but the finished product was an exceptionally fine, light, and almost pliable leather, so soft that rain would not harden it. Sinews were saved and split for thread. Bones were made into various tools and teeth into ornaments. It is an old Indian saying that the buffalo supplied the bowstring to kill himself, the tools with which to carve himself, the fuel with which to roast himself, and the thread and needle with which to sew himself into garments as well as to make articles for trade. With the buffalo available, the Indian felt that he could easily sustain himself, and it was for possession of the buffalo that the Comanche fought so desperately to keep the white man from these plains.

Between Tatum and CAPROCK, 40.3 m. (165 pop.), a tiny hamlet, the highway traverses the Simonola Valley, a depression in the plains having several well known ranches where water is easily obtained.

A definite break in the caprock of the Staked Plains occurs at about 45 m. MESCALERO RIDGE, named for an Apache tribe of mescal eaters who came there to hunt, is a north to south uplift, marking the western boundary of the higher plains, the lower being, geologically, the valley floor of the Pecos River.

At 74.1 m. is a junction with a graded dirt road.

Left on this road to BOTTOMLESS LAKES STATE PARK, 9 m., an area of great natural beauty in this arid region. Crystal-clear and mirroring the tinted bluffs that encircle them, the lakes are from 45 feet to 600 feet deep and vary in size from a few hundred square feet to 2,500 acres. The cowboys who discovered these lakes thought them bottomless because numerous weighted lariats tied together never came to rest on the bottom. This was later accounted for when it was discovered that a flow below caused the lines to be moved along. Geologists say that the lakes were formed when pressure of underground water on soluble rock caused a weakening of the substrata and a consequent caving in from the surface.

In ROSWELL, 91.7 m. (3,600 alt., 13,443 pop.) (see Tour 7b), are junctions with US 285 (see Tour 7b) and with US 70 with which US 380 is united between this point and HONDO, 139 m. (see Tour 10a) where US 380 branches R.

### Section b.   HONDO to SAN ANTONIO 107 m.

West of HONDO, 0 m., are vistas of green hills, the Bonito Valley, and mountains in the distance. This is Lincoln County, scene of a bloody quarrel between cattlemen called the Lincoln County War (1877-78). John H. Chisum, the reputed cattle king of New Mexico, declared that small owners were running off his stock, and those with fewer herds accused the Chisum forces of similar practices. Allied with Chisum were Alexander McSween, a lawyer, and John H. Tunstall, a wealthy Englishman who furnished capital for the partnership. McSween and Tunstall were dealers in livestock and real estate in Lincoln, the county seat. Opposed to this combination was the firm Murphy-Dolan whose supply store was patronized by the opposition.

Neither Chisum, Tunstall, nor McSween was accused of lawlessness during this period, but many of their ranch hands were, and evidently the principals made no effort to restrain them. Such a situation caused Lincoln County to become a magnet, attracting desperadoes from other sections of New Mexico, from Colorado, Texas, and even from regions south of the Rio Grande.

In and out of this turbulent scene rode Billy the Kid, who killed to amuse himself, to avenge a fancied insult, to aid a friend, or to plunder and obtain funds that he promptly lost at a gambling table. The Kid (William H. Bonney), who was born in New York City (1859), moved with his family to Kansas where the elder Bonney died and the widow married a man named Antrim. They soon moved to New Mexico and finally settled in Silver City where it is reported that at the age of twelve the boy committed his first murder by stabbing a man who had insulted his mother. That started him on his career of killing and Billy the Kid never saw any member of his family again. He was next heard from in Arizona where he killed three peaceful Indians for their ponies and blankets. Turning these into cash he enjoyed the hospitality of soldiers at Fort Bowie until he killed an enlisted man who worked as a blacksmith. The Kid fled to Mexico where he killed at least three men, stole horses, and dealt monte. At the age of 17 he started north and somewhere in Texas killed eight Indians, picking them off one by one with his Winchester and thus saved an emigrant train. Arriving in New Mexico again he joined forces with Joe Evans who had belonged to a gang once led by the Kid in Silver City. The Kid and Evans crossed and re-crossed the Rio Grande several times; they stole horses on one side and sold them on the other, and during this period three murders were committed. In avoiding punishment for his crimes, the Kid depended as much on his expert riding as on his shooting. Sheriff Pat Garrett describes the dismay of the Kid's enemies who "gazed at the sight of a gray horse, saddled and bridled, dashing across the valley with no semblance of a rider save a leg thrown across the saddle and a head and arm protruding from beneath the horse's neck, while at the end of this arm the barrel of a pistol glistened in the sunlight. . . ."

"The Kid had a lurking devil in him," Garrett continues. "It was a good-humored, jovial imp, or a cruel and blood-thirsty fiend, as circumstances prompted. He always laughed when killing, but fire seemed to dart from his eyes." Because Joe Evans joined the Murphy-Dolan forces in the cattle rustling war the Kid did likewise, but later—influenced by his deep admiration for Tunstall—withdrew from the war and for several months quietly 'tended range cattle for the Englishman. When the latter was murdered by members of a deputy sheriff's posse after he had surrendered and handed over his gun, the infuriated Kid resumed his former life, killing Sheriff Brady and others.

From then until the war ended with the bloody battle in the county seat (*see below*), Joe Evans fought for one faction and the Kid for the other.

After the war the Kid continued his savage career. He was finally captured by Sheriff Garrett and at the age of 22 was sentenced to be hanged. Because he had small hands and large wrists he was able, after starving himself for several days, to shake off his handcuffs; he killed his guard and also the jailer and then took time to do a triumphant jig on the balcony of the jail, singing his defiance, before he mounted a horse and, with one leg iron still dangling, escaped. A year later Sheriff Garrett trailed the Kid to Pete Maxwell's house in Fort Sumner (*see Tour 8a*) where well directed revolver shots put an end to Billy the Kid.

Americans of Spanish and Mexican stock founded the first settlement in the present county in 1855, and other settlements followed, but it was a region of large ranches, and except for Lincoln, the county seat, sparsely populated.

For most of the distance between Hondo and Carrizozo US 380 traverses the LINCOLN NATIONAL FOREST.

This area comprises five mountainous divisions that provide timber and water that are so essential to the general development of this section of the State. Along the upper reaches of the Rio Bonito, Rio Ruidoso, Rio Hondo, Rio Felix, and Rio Peñasco, which feed the Pecos River, there are several prosperous farms. There are great expanses of high, wooded slopes. It was named, as were the county and town of Lincoln, for the Civil War President. Settlement of the Sacramento division of this forest began as early as 1851 on the west side in the La Luz and Tularosa valleys. The stockmen from west Texas began to settle the east side in 1870.

Timber for some of the early Spanish missions was carried from the forest a hundred miles or more. It is said that the *vigas* (beams) for the old church at Juárez, Mexico came from the Sacramento area, but lumbering on a large scale did not begin until the completion of the railroad to Cloudcroft, about 1910.

Notorious in the late 1870's as the scene of part of the Lincoln County War, it is now famous as a stock grazing region and a popular recreation area. There are numerous public campgrounds with conveniences, as well as many attractive camping sites. There are many summer homes, and campers and visitors are encouraged to make use of the area. Game is plentiful and the region attracts scores of hunters and fishermen.

LINCOLN, 10.2 *m.* (5,600 alt., 438 pop.), is near the first settlement in this county on the Rio Bonito. Later settlements were a village on the Hondo called the Missouri Plaza (*see Tour 7b*), and, in the Ruidoso Valley, settlements at Hondo and San Patricio (*see Tour 10a*). Irrigation systems were laid out so that this fertile land could be farmed. Because of the rich grass, stock raising was also important. When Lincoln was settled in 1859 it was named Las Placitas (small settlements), but after the county was named for President Lincoln the name of the town was changed. It was the county seat until 1913, when the seat was transferred to Carrizozo.

LINCOLN COUNTY COURT HOUSE STATE MONUMENT (*open 9 to 5*) has (L) been restored and is administered by the Lincoln County Society of Art, History, and Archeology as a branch of the Museum of New Mexico. It once held the Murphy-Dolan store, downstairs, while the second floor contained the courtroom, jail, and bedrooms. The courtroom upstairs is now the auditorium and one of the bedrooms is an art gallery, in which exhibits of local artists as well as traveling exhibits from the Museum of New Mexico are shown. The two rooms on the first floor house historical and archeological material. The History Room includes economic exhibits, such as mining and cattle raising as well as mementoes of the Lincoln County War. The Archeology Room represents the Mescalero Apache, pueblo ruins, cave ruins, and cave dwellings. Cases of exhibits are installed in both rooms, and above the cases are dioramas explaining the use of the items.

In the final battle of the Lincoln County War, Evans and his men occupied the Murphy-Dolan store in this building and the Kid and 19 followers were entrenched in the spacious McSween home diagonally opposite, where Watson's drug store was later erected. For two days rifle fire was exchanged and there were several casualties. General Lew Wallace, who later wrote *Ben Hur,* ordered a detachment into Lincoln to put an end to the conflict. No attention was given the militia, however; the McSween House was set on fire and finally Billy the Kid escaped with several of his gang, leaving dead or wounded behind. Thus ended the Lincoln County War.

Near the site of the McSween house, on the same side of the street, is the TORREÓN (*caretaker next door west; 10¢ customary*), built by early settlers in 1852 for protection against Indian raids. It is of red-brown adobe brick, three stories in height, with loopholes in each floor level and gun embrasures on the roof. Ascent is by a ladder inside. It was restored by the Chaves County Historical Society of Roswell in 1935.

At 17.2 *m.* is the junction with a graded dirt road.

Left on this road 3 *m.* to FORT STANTON, now a United States Marine Hospital Reservation. It was established on the Bonito 2 miles south of this site in 1855 to restrain the Mescalero and White Mountain Apache, but was more of a stockade than a fort, with few buildings and little equipment. In 1861 the crude fortifications were destroyed by Confederate troops from Texas. Reoccupied by Union forces in 1863, it was rebuilt in 1868. Still later, when the site was moved here, substantial buildings were erected, most of which still stand, and are occupied by officers, attendants, and patients. The last of the soldiers left in 1896, and three years later it was turned over to the Public Health Service, and now is operated as a sanitorium. In the old days when the railroad was more than a hundred miles away, the fort depended to a large extent on food raised in the neighborhood, and all prices were high. Prairie hay sold at $50 per ton, corn at $2.50 per bushel, and other commodities in proportion.

CAPITÁN, 22.3 *m.* (6,500 alt., 926 pop.), was named for the Capitán Mountains (R) to the northeast. When the old El Paso and Northeastern Railway ran its line up from El Paso in 1897 to the coal deposits here, the village, named Gray for a homesteader in the cattle business (1887), was established, and while it was on the main line it flourished. Later the route was changed, and is now a branch line of the Southern Pacific, successor to the El Paso and Northeastern.

Capitán is in the center of mining, stock raising, and farming areas, has excellent hunting and fishing and a reputation as a health resort.

West of CARRIZOZO, 42.8 *m.* (1,432 pop.), the junction with US 54 (*see Tour 13*), the route is over lava beds and many miles of open country, with the beautiful Oscura (dark) Mountains on both sides. There are few settlements and little traffic along the route in this vast, silent, barren country.

BINGHAM, 75.5 *m.* (6,000 alt., 15 pop.), is a post office near the old Carthage coal mines that were developed in the 1880's when a spur of the Santa Fe Railway was laid from San Antonio (*see below*). When the mines were no longer productive, they were abandoned, and the town declined.

US 380 passes the little settlement of San Pedro and crosses the Rio Grande just east of SAN ANTONIO, 107 *m.,* in which is the junction with US 85 (*see Tour 1c*).

<<<<<<<<<<<<<<<<<<<<<<<<<<<<<<<<<<<<<<<<<<<<<<<>>>>>>>>>>>>>>>>>>>>>>>>>>>>>>>>>>>>>

# *Tour 13*

(Dalhart, Texas)—Santa Rosa—Carrizozo—Alamogordo—Newman; US 54.
Santa Rosa to Texas Line, 347.2 *m.*

Two-lane, graded graveled roadbed; bituminous-paved between Alamogordo and Texas line.
Southern Pacific Railroad parallels entire route.
Hotels in principal towns; tourist camps, gas stations frequent.

This route running alternately through level plains and mountains gives access to forests, fishing, and hunting grounds as well as mines, pueblo ruins, and grazing lands.

US 54 crosses the TEXAS LINE, 0 *m.,* at a point 41 miles west of Dalhart, Texas and runs through a section of the Dust Bowl. Near the Texas Line a soil erosion demonstration project is sowing Johnson and grama grass on areas made barren by drought and overgrazing in order to restore forage and prevent further erosion.

West of the demonstration project is a semiarid countryside of sheep and cattle ranches. Except for a few cultivated rows near the widely separated ranch houses, no crops are grown here.

In NARA VISA, 4.5 *m.* a trading point for ranchers, is a REGIS-TRATION STATION for all trucks (*see General Information*).

The Llano Estacado (*see Tour 6a*) here is broken by ravines, arroyos, sharp cliffs, and red sandstone outcrops that create a magnificent picture in the slanting light of the setting sun.

LOGAN, 28.6 *m.* (675 pop.), another trading point for ranchers and a station on the Rock Island Railway, was named for Captain H. Logan, a Texas ranger who had filed a claim on this site.

US 54 crosses a grassy plain and at 43.2 *m.* is a view of the DON CARLOS HILLS (R).

Near the AGRICULTURAL EXPERIMENT STATION, 49.5 *m.,* is a large depression (L) that when full of water becomes a red lake.

In TUCUMCARI, 51.9 *m.,* is the junction with US 66 with which this route is united to SANTA ROSA, 113.2 *m.* (*see Tour 6a*). Here US 54 branches southwest over high plains, level and rich in pasturage, a cowman's and sheepman's paradise. During the 1880's and 1890's, the territory was used exclusively for cattle grazing, but at the turn of the century with the development of the ranches on the Staked Plains (*see Tour 6a*), the cattlemen moved eastward and left this section to the sheep. As a result, Guadalupe County became and has continued to be a wool-raising region, the annual clip exceeding three million pounds.

PASTURA, 131.9 *m.,* is merely a small trading center in the midst of pasture land which stretches away on all sides.

US 54 joins US 60 at EAST VAUGHN, 152.5 *m.* (501 pop.) (*see Tour 8a*), passes through VAUGHN, 153.3 *m.* (*see Tour 8a*), and branches (L) from US 60 at 155.8 *m.* winding over high plains country.

DURÁN, 168.2 *m.* (6,000 alt., 452 pop.), a shipping point for the wool industry, preceded Tucumcari as a division point on the Southern Pacific Railroad.

TORRANCE, 179.6 *m.* (5,860 alt., 25 pop.), now only a flag stop and a small cluster of adobe houses, was formerly a terminus of the New Mexico Central Railroad with a population of 1,500.

South of Torrance, US 54 rises gradually through high plateau country covered with juniper and piñon trees. Piñon nuts provide revenue for the inhabitants, and the timber is used for ties and fence posts.

CORONA, 187.7 *m.* (6,666 alt., 717 pop.), at the foot of the GALLO (rooster) MESA just north and east of the GALLINAS (chickens) MOUNTAINS (R), is a thriving trading and shipping center, serving a wide territory. Founded in 1899 upon land homesteaded by Captain Frank A. DuBois of Shelby, Ohio, it has steadily grown in importance. Cattle, sheep, and goat ranching are the leading industries, though considerable dry farming is carried on and beans are a major crop.

West of Corona lies a part of the Lincoln National Forest, its eastern boundary extending along the highway 15 miles north and south.

The huge Gallo Mesa known as the Gallinas Mining Area was for a time the scene of feverish mining activities. Five mines, Old Hickory, Hoosier, Corona Queen, Red Cloud, and Deadwood, produced mostly copper and zinc. Except for the holdings of the Corona Lead and Zinc Company, operations are now suspended here. On this mesa was a mine called the Millionaire, which for a time produced considerable copper but at a depth of 150 feet was underlain by rock so hard that it could not be drilled. As the walls of the shaft showed rich copper, the owner who called himself "Lord Lincoln" had no trouble in managing a sale at a good price, but in the contract he always inserted a clause that the purchaser must sink the shaft 50 feet during the ensuing year or the holdings would revert to "Lord Lincoln." The baffled lessee always lost, and the mine was repossessed each year. "Lord Lincoln" lived in luxury for a decade until his location rights ran out, and another jumped his claim.

ANCHO (wide), 213.7 m. (6,160 alt., 269 pop.), in wide Ancho Valley (L), is the trading center for miners who work the gullies and streams of the Jicarilla Mountains (see below) for gold and for the ranchers who graze their cattle and sheep on the mountainsides. Ruins of 16 brick kilns are all that remain of a $250,000 investment to use clay deposits found near by. The plant was never operated, the venture suffering a financial collapse before operations were started.

South of Ancho the highway winds through the foothills of the Jicarilla Mountains (L), named for the Jicarilla Apache. The mining district is rich with placer gold, but the absence of water has impeded development except in the White Oaks district (see below).

At 234.5 m. is the junction with a dirt road.

Left on this road is WHITE OAKS, 7.8 m. (6,400 alt., 109 pop.), which at one time boasted a population of 2,000.

John Wilson, who had a price on his head, discovered gold on the site of Baxter Mountain in 1880 but did not profit from the find because he preferred the life of a desperado. Wilson, escaping from a Texas jail, cut across the mountains to visit two friends, Jack Winters and Harry Baxter, who were placer miners. The day after his arrival, Wilson started for the top of Baxter Mountain to obtain a view of the country through which he expected to travel. He took a pick with him and jokingly said that he was going to find a gold mine. Halfway to the summit he sat down to rest and began to chip pieces from the rock. Examining the chips, he found them speckled with yellow. When he returned to the cabin Winters asked Wilson if he had found his mine and Wilson passed over the chips. One glance at the rock sent Winters into the air with a yell, and Harry Baxter, awakened from a nap, became equally excited. It was now pitch dark, but the three made a climb for the spot by lantern light. The two miners set out stakes, and when Wilson was asked for his full name, so they could locate the claim for the three, he answered, "I have no use for gold." Thus the North Homestake and South Homestake claims came into being and were later sold for $300,000 apiece. Wilson left next day with nine silver dollars and a good pistol, a present from the two prospectors. The Old Abe Mine, the original strike, has produced $3,000,000 and is still being worked.

The stark buildings still standing in this great ghost town include the Exchange Bank, whose second story housed the young lawyers W. C. McDonald, later the first governor of New Mexico under statehood, H. B. Fergusson, delegate to Congress, and John I. Hewitt, a powerful *politico* of territorial days. In the Little Casino, Madam Varnish, so called for her slick ways, dealt faro, roulette, and poker during the two decades when White Oaks boomed and was noted for its bawdy gaiety. East of White Oaks are iron ore deposits and soft coal. The latter is burned in the power plant that supplies electricity to Carrizozo and other near-by communities.

Emerson Hough, a reporter on the *Golden Era,* a weekly newspaper published during the 1880's, wrote *Heart's Desire* with White Oaks for its locale.

CARRIZOZO, 237.7 *m.* (5,425 alt., 1,432 pop.), the thriving seat of Lincoln County, has a name derived from the Spanish word *carrizo,* a reed grass that grows abundantly in surrounding regions. The town is on the eastern side of the wide elevated valley between the Carrizo and Sierra Blanca Mountains (L), and bounded on the west by the low Oscuras (R). This valley is approximately 30 miles wide and is generally known as the CARRIZOZO PLAIN.

Carrizozo had its beginning with the coming of the El Paso & Northeastern Railroad (*see Transportation*) in 1899. The town was laid out by a subsidiary of the railroad company and soon after was made a division point with the erection of a roundhouse and shop employing many workmen. In a short time it became a supply center and shipping point.

Carrizozo is at the junction with US 380 (*see Tour 12b*).

US 54 south of Carrizozo crosses the Tularosa Valley (*see Tour 10a*) with the White and Sacramento Mountains forming a protective wall on the east. The basin extends to the Texas Line, walled in on both sides by uplifts that protect the valley from high winds and give it an equable temperature. Water from the mountains fills deltas on the east side of the valley, where cattle find abundant grasses.

THREE RIVERS, 253.3 *m.* (4,562 alt., 362 pop.), trading center and railroad loading point, has gained world-wide attention because it is the station for the famous TRES RITOS (three rivers) RANCH, formerly owned by Albert B. Fall, Secretary of the Interior in the Harding cabinet. The settlement of Three Rivers began when Patrick Coghlan came to this section in 1874 and devoted his energies to building a cattle empire. His holdings eventually were purchased by Fall, as were those of Mrs. Susan Barber, widow of Alexander McSween (*see Tour 12b*), who had a large ranch here late in the 1890's. Many stories are told of the Cattle Queen of New Mexico who rode as hard and shot as straight as any man, and never asked for quarter. In 1917 she also sold out to Fall and retired to White Oaks.

The holdings of the Hatchett Land and Cattle Company, another large ranch, together with the Fall Ranch and grazing lands, are now owned by the Palomas Cattle and Land Company, which at the present time (1939) is actively engaged on all properties.

1. Left from the railroad station on a dirt road through the 90,000 acre Fall estate to the FALL RESIDENCE, 2.7 *m.,* an old adobe converted into a two-story Spanish-Colonial house with grey cement stucco finish. There is a portal extending the full length of the house on the south side with large square pillars that run to the top of the first floor. The grounds are landscaped with trees and shrubs and near by are the buildings for the household servants and several huge barns. Near here is the ROCK HOUSE built by Mrs. Barber.

2. Left from Three Rivers on a dirt road to some exceptionally fine examples of pictographs (L) and petroglyphs, 4 *m*. Black rocks, covering several acres and ranging in size from one foot to ten feet across, are covered with representations of animal life and geometric figures. Early artists used the contours of the rocks to aid their design, the corner of a rock representing the human face, with an eye and an ear on each side of a pointed corner representing the nose.

In TULAROSA, 271.9 *m*. (4,436 alt., 1,445 pop.), is the junction with US 70, with which US 54 is united at 287.3 *m*. (*see Tour 10a*) where US 70 branches R.

As US 54 traverses the Tularosa Valley the road is bordered by the Sacramento Mountains (L) and the Jicarilla Mountains (R) while the southern terminus of the San Andrés Range (R) slants into the western sky. Still farther south are the Organ Mountains (R) and the Hueco (hollow) Range (L), a low uplift near the Texas Line.

The valley between these ranges is a windy, semiarid region fairly suitable for grazing and permitting some dry farming.

The name of VALMONT, 294.5 *m*. (4,024 alt., 127 pop.), a hamlet on a level plain bordered by the Sacramento Mountains, is derived from vale and mountain. When it was founded in 1900 as a farming community it was called Dog Canyon for a near-by canyon of the same name. Later it became Camp City, then Shamrock, and finally Valmont. Drought caused so many farmers to leave in the 1920's and 1930's that it has shrunk to a small trading point.

ORO GRANDE (much gold), 318.4 *m*. (4,170 alt., 268 pop.), on the plains southeast of the JARILLA MOUNTAINS and first called Jarilla Junction, grew from a camp to a town, then a little city when a gold rush occurred in 1905-6. It was a lively community for two years with a peak population of 2,000. Two smelters were built here and the railroad constructed a spur to the Silver Hill mining district where the ore was found. Occasional mining is done now. This area has long been noted for its turquoise, which was mined by the Apache, and later by white men under both the Spanish and Mexican regimes. The Tiffany interests purchased the properties, but no work is now carried on. Valuable specimens of pottery, *metates, manos,* and broken fragments of various stone utensils have been taken from the hills in this area which was occupied by the Apache.

In Oro Grande is a REGISTRATION STATION where all trucks must stop (*see General Information*).

NEWMAN, 347.2 *m.,* a border hamlet, was named for a real estate man from El Paso who sold building sites to home seekers. Archeologists say Newman is an old Indian pueblo site and many relics of pueblo habitation have been uncovered here. At Newman US 54 crosses the Texas Line 17 miles northeast of El Paso.

≪≪≪≪≪≪≪≪≪≪≪≪≪≪≪≪≪≪≪≪≪≪≪≫≫≫≫≫≫≫≫≫≫≫≫≫≫≫≫≫≫≫≫≫

# *Tour 14*

(Seminole, Texas) — Lovington — Artesia — La Luz — Junction US 54; NM 34, 83.
Texas Line to Junction with US 54, 198.7 *m.*

Two-lane, graded and graveled road, except for 60 miles bituminous-paved. Terminus of Texas & New Mexico Railroad at Lovington; route crosses Atchison, Topeka & Santa Fe Railway at Artesia and parallels a spur of the Southern Pacific between Cloudcroft and La Luz.
Accommodations in Lovington and Artesia; few tourist camps, gas stations.

This route connects the oil-producing plains around Lovington with the mountain and recreation region in Lincoln County. Between the Texas Line and Artesia in the Pecos Valley no houses are seen for several miles. Across this area thousands of cattle were driven to the plains of eastern New Mexico in the latter part of the nineteenth century. West of Artesia the road rises and enters Lincoln National Forest, scene of many encounters with the Apache in territorial days; now it is a resort for Texans anxious to escape summer heat.

NM 34 crosses the TEXAS LINE, 0 *m.,* at a point 50 miles northwest of Seminole, Texas, and traverses a level plains country.

LOVINGTON, 18.7 *m.* (3,944 alt., 1,904 pop.), seat of Lea County and the northern terminus of the Texas & Pacific Railroad, is in the center of an area where the ground water level is near the surface. Its principal industries are truck farming, oil, and cattle raising. When the town was founded in 1908 on the homestead of R. R. Love who became its first postmaster, mail had to be brought from Knowles, 20 miles southeast. As the white man drove out the Indian from this region, cows supplanted buffalo and cattlemen from Texas established small ranches here. A one-room schoolhouse was built and free residence lots given to school patrons. The first teachers homesteaded. In 1909 Lovington had its first bank, its first newspaper, and its first church. For a time Lovington prospered with farms and gardens, but a drought not only destroyed crops but caused cattle prices to slump, and the town suffered. Oil development in the late 1920's saved many ranchers from ruin, and brought an extension of the railroad to this point in 1930.

In Lovington is the junction with NM 83, now the route.

Around Lovington are ranch houses three to five miles apart, some with irrigated gardens, some raising their garden truck by dry farming. As underground water is near the surface, windmills make irrigation possible and grain, sorghums, alfalfa, and other feeds are raised. Fruit growing is uncertain because of frosts, but dairying and poultry farming are successful. There are sand storms but no winds severe enough to destroy property. When asked why there were no cyclones an old-timer answered: 'Humph! there couldn't be. Our straight winds would blow the hell out of a cyclone." Lea County, containing nearly 3,000,-000 acres, is fortunate in having an underground water supply for there is not a stream of any kind within its boundaries. Nevertheless several grasses clothe the plain: buffalo and grama on the harder soil, sedge and shinnery (a low-growing shin oak) on the sandy areas. There are mesquite and some varieties of yucca and cactus. The wildlife is limited to coyotes, skunks, badgers, prairie dogs, jack rabbits, eagles, hawks, prairie chickens, blue quail, and doves.

This recently developed region is known as Little Texas. There are no New Mexican missions here; Methodists and Baptists had the field to themselves till a Catholic Church was built in 1930. Seldom is Spanish heard, and feasts and holidays celebrated in other parts of New Mexico are unknown. There are no natural swimming or fishing holes, and because there is little shade picnics are never held before sunset; but there is shooting in season, and toward the end of the summer, usually the last week in August, Lovington has a three-day rodeo and county fair.

Between Lovington and Artesia the route crosses the lower end of the Staked Plains and the Mescalero Ridge (see *Tour 12a*), a region of ranches and vast grazing lands where mirages are seen but seldom last more than an hour. When the buffalo disappeared and cattle came the grass was so thick and high that many herdsmen were not aware of outcropping rock until a few years of close grazing cut the grass down near the sod. More of the rock appeared when they began fencing. Such land grows the best grazing feed, the most nutritive grasses; and because the State designated such land as unfit for farming—a fact for which the stockmen never ceased being grateful—it was saved for cattle. The farmer may have some livestock, but the sheep or cowman rarely farms, and many, especially those who have witnessed the dust storms and the horrors of uncontrolled soil erosion, refuse to allow the sod to be broken by a plow. So dependable and so persistent are native grasses that Will Rogers once said the Texas Panhandle's wind erosion problem was "good enough for the fools who had plowed up such a wonderful turf and ruined the grandest cow country in the world."

The climate here, though in many ways delightful, is variable. Ground freezing is rare. It seldom rains, but when it does it is usually in the form of a downpour. The altitude is sufficient to insure pleasant nights on the warmest days, and cold spells in winter are never sustained.

Around the roadside stop of MALJAMAR, 43.6 *m.*, is a large game refuge principally for blue quail and dove. A few protected antelope are in outlying districts. The natural breeding grounds of the prairie chicken to the north and east and over into West Texas are said to be the most extensive in the Southwest, but the season on them has been closed both in New Mexico and Texas until their number has increased.

West of Maljamar the route traverses the plains to the Pecos Valley (*see Tour 6a*), crossing the Pecos River at 78 *m.*

In ARTESIA, 82.9 *m.* (3,350 alt., 3,991 pop.), is the junction with US 285 (*see Tour 7b*).

West of Artesia, NM 83 goes through open range country covered with short, coarse grass and with occasional cane cactus and a clump of soapweed and Spanish dagger. From the Artesia Golf Club, 85.5 *m.*, is a view of silvery grasses reaching to the horizon in a smooth line broken only by the sharp spikes of Spanish dagger. Occasional flocks of sheep graze near the yucca and greasewood. Lombardy poplars appear at 100 *m.* with orchards and cottonwoods; the road rises gently.

HOPE, 106.3 *m.* (3,450 alt., 275 pop.), was called Badgerville when it was settled in 1885 because the homes were dug out of the ground and the roofs alone were of timber. The name was changed to Hope when a post office was opened in the same building as Jim Jerald's store and saloon; the saloon had to be moved to the rear because of a law prohibiting a post office and saloon being under the same roof. The Rio Peñasco supplied sufficient water for irrigation until 1922 when the supply failed owing to drainage of marshes on the Peñasco and the deforestation of near-by mountain slopes. The complete failure of crops discouraged many, and the town dwindled to 175. Another adversity befell in 1912 when construction was begun on a railroad between El Paso and Artesia. While a station was being built here, Lord Pierson, head of the syndicate that was to buy the rails, lost his life in the *Titanic* disaster. The road was never finished, and the frontier opportunists left the stricken community for greener pastures.

The Resettlement Administration in 1937 provided markets by trucking and resettled some of the farmers in other parts of the State—around Fort Sumner, Taos, and Los Lunas.

West of Hope the Sacramento Mountains form an effective background for the thick clumps of cactus growing beside the road. Bands of light encircle the Guadalupe Mountains to the south (L), where the ribbon-like line of its crest runs across the sky. Cattle graze on the foothills of the Pajarito (little bird) Mountains (R).

Cane cactus becomes profuse as a succession of hills piles up one after the other; and in the foreground are groves of trees by the Peñasco. Dark hills run high across the upper end of the valley.

LOWER PEÑASCO, 140.8 *m.* (208 pop.), is a small farming community.

Near PEÑASCO, 141.0 *m.,* the road looks down on a narrow gorge, with the valley beyond.

Winding across the floor of the valley, it passes a graveyard (L) surrounded by poplars. At Culbertson's Saw Mill, 143.2 *m.,* conifers appear (R), giving notice of the approach of Lincoln National Forest.

ELK, 148.8 *m.* (5,350 alt., 65 pop.), named for near-by Elk Canyon, is a farming and stock raising community settled in 1885 and 1887. Archaeologists have removed artifacts from several sites in this vicinity; in one an unbroken bowl containing burnt beans indicated a hasty flight. This region had its Indian troubles too. The first settler was killed in 1871; and near here Captain Stanton was slain (*see below*). Large herds of elk roamed this section in early times.

In the James Valley, NM 83 crosses the eastern boundary of the LINCOLN NATIONAL FOREST at 148.1 *m.*

MAYHILL, 161.2 *m.* (6,500 alt., 309 pop.), settled in 1876 as Upper Peñasco by migrants from Texas, is interested in lumbering, sheep ranching, farming, fruit, and truck gardening. An Apache stronghold was formerly in the hills west of the village; and in 1854, Captain Stanton raided the settlement and destroyed 200 Apache dwellings. Stanton was later killed on Mayhill Mesa. The doctor attending him froze his body and took it to Old Mesilla for burial, but later the Rio Grande's channel changed its course and the graveyard crumbled off into the river and disappeared (*see Tour 1c*).

The pines are taller and the road climbs higher west of Mayhill.

CLOUDCROFT, 180 *m.* (8,640 alt., 265 pop.), is a shipping point for timber and a recreation center, with a summer population increase of several thousand. It was settled when J. A. and B. C. Eddy built a branch of the Southern Pacific east and up from Alamogordo (*see below*) to the timber here. The Eddys abandoned the project, but the son of a surveying engineer took a transit and surveyed a switchback, and the railroad became a reality. Later the legislature dedicated 2,300 acres for a summer resort, and the railroad gave up its land. Camps were laid out for summer visitors as well as those who wished to remain the year round.

There are many of Spanish and Mexican stock here, some of the latter recently from Mexico, being unskilled workers who are either naturalized or have applied for papers.

West of Cloudcroft the route lies along Fresnal Canyon, descending to MOUNTAIN PARK, 186.9 *m.*, a farming community which was once a resort for tuberculous patients. The road twists and turns on the descent, offering many fine panoramas of the Sacramento Mountains and passing HIGH ROLLS, 188.2 *m.*, whose hotel and cabins are deserted. Both Mountain Park and High Rolls (named for the character of the country) are trading centers. There are large orchards and truck farms in this area.

Past more magnificent vistas of mountains covered with greasewood, soapweed, and bunch grass on their lower slopes, the road emerges from the forest over rich red land with groves of cottonwoods at the bottom of the canyon. Tall Spanish dagger is conspicuous as the road crosses to the other side of the canyon and looks down upon the railroad. The road levels off and the Sacramentos are left behind. Ahead are the tilted San Andrés Mountains.

# Arts and Crafts

Laura Gilpin

NAVAHO SILVERSMITH

NAVAHO WOMEN ON HORSEBACK
Painting by Gerald Nailor, Navaho Artist

*"Frashers"*

NAVAHO SANDPAINTING

MARÍA, POTTER OF SAN ILDEFONSO PUEBLO

THE PLASTERER
Painting by Ernest L. Blumenschein

Wyatt Davis

FAMILY PORTRAIT
Painting by Paul Lantz

OCTOBER IN NEW MEXICO—Painting by Sheldon Parsons

RIO TESUQUE—Color Woodcut by Gustave Baumann

*Ernest Knee*

BOY FROM THE PLAINS
Painting by Peter Hurd

*Laura Gilpin*

ÁCOMA PUEBLO WOMAN, WEARING TYPICAL DRESS AND SILVER AND
TURQUOISE BRACELETS AND BEADS OF INDIAN CRAFTSMANSHIP

LA LUZ, 196.3 *m.* (4,850 alt., 146 pop.), is a farming community best known for the beauty of its setting, its public cactus garden, and the La Luz pottery made near by. The name is an abridgement of Nuestra Señora de la Luz (Our Lady of Light), the mission founded in 1719 by the Franciscan padres. The first settlers here were immigrants from Mexico, but its beautiful setting and delightful winter climate have attracted a more cosmopolitan population. Its courteous citizens, when asked by visitors to point out the burial place of Anthony Adverse, indicate different places—under the chapel, under a clump of cactus, or in any other spot that impulse leads them to designate.

Mountain ranges border the road and directly west are the San Andrés Mountains, with the White Sands (*see Tour 10b*) a ribbon of silver in the distance.

At 198.7 *m.,* is the junction with US 54 (*see Tour 13*), 5.4 miles north of Alamogordo and 7 miles south of Tularosa.

# *Tour 15*

Junction with US 85—Madrid—Quarai—Mountainair—Gran Quivira—Junction with US 54; 180.5 *m.* NM 10 and NM 15.

Two-lane, graded graveled road except for 11 miles of bituminous pavement south of US 66.
Limited accommodations.

Although this route is through a region of exceptionally fine vistas and of coal, gold, and turquoise mines, it is known particularly as the route to Gran Quivira National Monument.

NM 10 branches south from its junction with US 85, 0 *m.,* at a point 9.1 miles south of Santa Fe, and traverses the Santa Fe Plateau, skirts the Cerrillos Hills (R), and cuts through pastures and grazing land. Ahead are the Ortiz Mountains, where gold was first discovered in New Mexico, and the Sandía Mountains (R).

At 7.2 *m.* is the junction with a dirt road.

Right on this road to the TURQUOISE MINES, 3.4 *m.* (*see Tour 1b*).

Southward from 11 *m.* is a fine view of the Galisteo Valley. Winding downward, NM 10 crosses several washes that are dangerous when the water is running.

CERRILLOS (hills), 14.3 *m.* (5,688 alt., 765 pop.), is the center of a mining district and a railroad loading point. After the larger mines were abandoned at the turn of the century, Cerrillos lost most of its population and became a trading center.

South of Cerrillos, NM 10 crosses the Galisteo River, usually dry but in flood times rampant; then enters the foothills of the Ortiz Mountains whose sides bear piñon and scrub juniper and are marked with mine drifts and abandoned workings. Tree cactus and yucca, blooming in June, are abundant.

MADRID, 17.3 *m.* (6,000 alt., 1,116 pop.), is owned and operated by the Albuquerque & Cerrillos Coal Company. Of all the mines on the Santa Fe Plateau and contiguous country, the coal mines of Madrid alone have a record of comparatively steady production. Veins of both anthracite and bituminous yield approximately 100,000 tons annually. Coal was discovered here in 1835, but not until 1869, when the operation of the old placer mines near by created a steady market, was any appreciable amount produced. Madrid's Christmas celebration has become well known. Thousands come from afar to see the illumination.

Southward, NM 10 traverses the region of mines operated by lone prospectors or long ago abandoned. Ahead are views of the Jémez Range (R) and of the Sandías.

GOLDEN, 28.9 *m.* (112 pop.), now a small village, was active during development of the new placer mining district in the San Pedro Mountains (R) and has a history of placer mining dating back to the sixteenth century, when the Spaniards worked deposits with Indians as slaves. In 1933 power shovels of idle contractors started operations, but without success, although local residents found free gold in gulches after rains and cloudbursts. There is little placer mining now.

In the San Pedro valley (R) on the old San Pedro Grant, south of the mining camp of San Pedro are the RUINS OF PAAKO (Paw-aw-ko; San Pedro de la Cuchilla), a former Indian pueblo known also as San Pedro Ruins. There is doubt whether this was a Keres or a Tewa speaking pueblo. It possibly marks the southernmost limit of the Tano Pueblos, and is separated from the Tewa villages to the south and west by the densely wooded Sierra de Carnue. Oñate in 1598 called it Tano, and the Keres of Santo Domingo say it belonged to their people. Many of the early Spanish documents refer to it as a Tewa speaking settlement, and add "San Pedro," its patron saint, to its name. Its houses, according to Hodge, were apparently constructed of rubble and generally consisted of two stories. The village had three *kivas*. Bandelier records that it was inhabited as late as 1626 but abandoned before 1670. Shea, in his *Catholic Missions,* says that a mission was founded in 1661 at "San Pedro de la Cuchilla," which is supposed to be the same site. This ruin enclosed by a barbed wire fence is owned and has been in part excavated (1936) by the University of New Mexico.

The small settlement of SAN ANTONITO (7,000 alt., 250 pop.), 36.6 *m.,* is a typical New Mexican mountain village whose residents support themselves mainly by dry farming and grazing sheep. Considerable wood is hauled to Albuquerque from the near-by Sandía Mountains and foothills.

At 37.4 *m.* is the junction with the graded Sandía Rim Drive (*see Albuquerque*).

Traversing TIJERAS CANYON, main pass between the Sandía and Manzano Mountains, the highway passes CEDAR CREST, 40.9 *m.,* a mountain resort where many residents of Albuquerque have summer homes.

In TIJERAS (scissors), 42.8 *m.* (6,318 alt., 467 pop.), two canyons intersect in such a way as to form an outline similar to open scissors; hence the name.

NM 10 reaches a high point at 56 *m.* that offers broad views, and at 63 *m.* is a magnificent panorama of the wide, luxuriant ESTANCIA VALLEY (L) with its bean farms.

CHILILÍ, 63.7 *m.* (6,000 alt., 473 pop.), on the Arroyo de Chililí, one of the Saline pueblos, was first visited by Chamuscado in 1581 and by Oñate, seventeen years later. At that time the site of the pueblo was south of the present town, but practically no ruins of the once flourishing village are now visible. Benavides in 1630 also mentioned the pueblo as a mission dedicated to *Nuestra Señora de Navidad* (Our Lady of Nativity). Here were interred the remains of Fray Alonzo Peinado who came to New Mexico in 1608 and to whom was accredited the conversion of the Pueblo Indians and the erection of the old church which stood on the bluff south of town, across Chililí Creek. The pueblo was abandoned between 1669 and 1676 on account of the hostility and continued raids of the Apache, the inhabitants joining the Tewa along the Rio Grande. It was again populated in 1680, so Vetancurt records, and was the home of 500 Piro-speaking Indians at that time; although Bandelier claims they were Tewa. This pueblo, one of the seven "cities that died of fear" was abandoned by its inhabitants to avoid the marauding Apache. From this region came exciting tales of buried gold and treasure uncovered beneath the altar of the church.

TAJIQUE (pron. Ta-*hee*-ke), 77.6 m. (325 pop.), is a village of farming mountaineers at the foot of the eastern slope of the Manzano Range. Tajique is probably phonetic Spanish for the Tewa *Taskike,* name of the pueblo that once was here and of which nothing now remains but a mound. Old records concerning Taskike show that Fray Gerónimo de la Llana, who built the mission at Quarai (*see below*), died here. His body was removed to Santa Fe 100 years later. This pueblo was a refuge from the Apache for the people of Quarai in 1674. Vetancurt, in his *Crónica,* records the escape of a priest and two Spaniards in one of the early raids. Taskike was credited with 500 inhabitants in its heyday and possibly was inhabited prior to the seventeenth century.

TORREÓN (tower) (6,991 alt., 540 pop.), 80 *m.,* is a mountain village of small ranches and farms. Here too are ruins of a Saline pueblo, so called because of proximity to the salt lakes eastward.

MANZANO (apple), 87.3 *m.* (6,960 alt., 708 pop.), a cluster of red adobes surrounded by verdant fields, was settled about 1829 and is still a primitive settlement. Tewa Indians now living near El Paso claim to have come from this place. Tradition claims the trees in an old apple orchard that gives the town its name were planted during the mission period before 1676, but Professor Florence M. Hawley, University of New Mexico, dates them from ring growth as being planted no earlier than 1800. MANZANO PEAK (10,608 alt.) towers (R) above the town and at its base is EL OJO DEL GIGANTE (giant spring), a flow of cold water that forms a lake around which cluster adobe houses. At the southern extremity of the lake is a torreón (tower) built as a defensive work and watch tower.

PUNTA DE AGUA (point of water), 92.3 m., commonly known as QUARAI (393 pop.) because of its proximity to Quarai Ruins, is a village of farmers and woodcutters.

Here is the junction with a dirt road.

Right on this road to QUARAI RUINS, 1.1 m., the southernmost pueblo of the Saline region. It was the seat of a Spanish mission (1629) founded by Fray Francisco de Acevedo and contains the ruins of the IMMACULATE CONCEPTION MONASTERY AND CHURCH built of red and brown sandstone. Some church walls standing 20 feet high extend to the former roof height, but the thinner monastery walls have been half razed to furnish building stone. It is in a meadow near a cottonwood grove, in which is a spring now walled and covered. In the grove are camping accommodations with outdoor grills, tables, seats, and other conveniences.

These mission ruins are surrounded by those of the ancient pueblo, now showing only as grass-grown mounds. Vetancurt says that Quarai had 600 inhabitants immediately prior to its abandonment. During a period of friendliness with the Apache, sometime between 1664-69, the people of Quarai conspired with the Apache to drive out the Spaniards but the plot was discovered and the leaders executed. The Apache compelled the abandonment of the pueblo about 1674, when the inhabitants fled to Tajique, where they remained perhaps a year longer. When Tajique was abandoned, the Tewa fled to El Paso and settled in the village of Ysleta del Sur, farther south on the Rio Grande, where their descendants live today. Twenty-two skeletons have been found, also pottery and a number of artifacts pointing to a long pre-Spanish occupation. Quarai, spelled variously in the old documents Cuara, Cuaray, Coarae, and Cuarae, figures prominently in the Spanish annals as an important outpost. Conversion to Christianity is credited to Fray Esteban de Perea between 1617 and 1630, probably about 1628. Among the missionaries perhaps the best known was Fray Gerónimo de Llana, 1659.

Besides the scourge of the Apache, there were other contributing causes to abandonment, such as epidemics and drought. Quarai was at one time a walled city, as was Pecos and even Santa Fe. Along the road to the ruins at times are seen small processions of devout women carrying the image of the Virgin in their arms and chanting prayers.

In MOUNTAINAIR, 100 m. (7,550 alt., 1,483 pop.), is the junction with US 60 (see Tour 8). A view of GRAN QUIVIRA at 117 m., reveals a pile of blue-gray limestone austere and aloof against the sky. At the small settlement of GRAN QUIVIRA, 125.7 m., is the junction with the Gran Quivira Road.

Left on this road to GRAN QUIVIRA NATIONAL MONUMENT, 1.4 m (7,000 alt.). These ruins, at the southern apex of the Mesa de los Jumanos, were known to the early chroniclers as TA-BI-RÁ, a former pueblo of the Tompiro, a division of the Piro Indians. In the early part of the seventeenth century the Piro, one of the principal Pueblo groups, comprised two divisions, one inhabiting the Rio Grande Valley from San Marcial northward to within 50 miles of Albuquerque where the Tewa settlement reputedly began (*see Tour 1c*). The other of the two divisions, called Tompiro and Salinero, occupied an area east of the Rio Grande in the vicinity of the salt lagoons extending for a distance of perhaps 25 miles southeast. This vicinity was first visited in 1581 by Chamuscado accompanied by three Franciscans. The first Franciscan missions among the Saline pueblos were established at Tabirá and Abo by Francisco de Acevedo in 1629. Chamuscado mentioned the existence of eleven pueblos in the region of the salt lagoons, but only six of these have been identified: Chililí, Abo, Tinabo, Tabirá, Cuarai, and Tajique. Governor Oñate visited these pueblos in 1598 and reported that "all rendered obedience to his Majesty." The ruins are commonly known as Gran Quivira, a name erroneously applied in the latter half of the nineteenth century because of their supposed identification with the Quivira of Coronado and Oñate.

In 1628 or 1629 Fray Alonso de Benavides visited the Saline groups and reported that within the 15 leagues there were 14 or 15 pueblos with more than 10,000 souls, 6 monasteries, and very good churches. He also reported that all the Indians were converted and most of them baptized; the others "are being catechised and taught, with their schools of all trades." He reported the land as "little fruitful, by reason of the many cold spells and the few waters." Tabirá was one of the larger of the New Mexico pueblos of that time with a population of 1,500. It comprised a group of three- and four-story terraced houses in parallel blocks facing each other across narrow streets. There were monasteries and two churches; one commenced between 1629 and 1644; the other probably between 1660 and 1670, the ruins of which remain. The larger church and perhaps the later one, at the western end of the village, is now a ruin with walls 30 feet high and 6 feet thick. Its front measures 202 feet and its depth 131 feet. The northern part of the ruin shows a cruciform room 30 feet long, with an eastern gateway 15 feet wide and 11 feet high and a mighty timber upholding another 15 feet of masonry. South of this room are many chambers of ordinary size divided by long halls with walls still standing to a height of 20 feet. Over many of the vacant doorways were found carved lintels.

Tabirá was involved in the Pueblo Rebellion (*see History*). An unbased tradition records that there were 70 priests and monks residing here and but two escaped. Prior to the massacre the priests were warned of the coming danger and buried the two bells, the sacred vessels, and other treasures of the church in a great pit dug outside the walls, with a map of its position carved on stone. This stone was buried near the altar, the two fleeing priests taking with them a map of its hiding place traced on paper. The bells were supposed to have been buried in the cemetery. Because of this legend (and the appearance of an amazing number of "secret maps") the churchyard and surrounding hillsides have been honeycombed with shafts and holes made by treasure seekers. The story has grown through the years until it now includes the gold and silver treasure of the Aztecs. No treasure is known to have been found by searchers during 350 years, and while no gold has come from any New Mexico mission this does not lessen interest in these ancient ruins, whose walls were laid, stone upon stone, by hands of patient Indian women under the direction of zealous Franciscan friars.

Gran Quivira, comprising 160 acres, was dedicated as a National Monument November 1, 1909. The area was increased to 423.7 acres on November 25, 1919 in order to protect the many ruins adjacent to the church. A resident custodian lives near, and plans are under way (1940) to provide adequate and comfortable camp sites for those who wish to spend time inspecting the ruins.

NM 15 continues south and southeast through the village of CLAUNCH (6,700 alt., 50 pop.), 139.7 *m.,* in an area of bean farms.

Claunch, named for the Claunch Cattle Company that grazed cattle and sheep here, has had a post office since 1931.

South of Claunch is rolling terrain; small thistle poppies blow white in late spring and early summer, and purple wild verbena mingles with them. That rare bird, the snowy-white heron, has been seen along this road. The trees are few and desert flora take their place; the Jicarilla Mountains appear to the east and southeast.

At 180.5 *m.,* is the junction with US 54, seven miles north of Carrizozo (*see Tour 13*).

# *Tour 16*

(Seminole, Texas) — Hobbs — Carlsbad — (Van Horn, Texas) ; NM 83, US 62.
Texas Line to Texas Line, 111.6 *m.*

Two-lane, bituminous-paved road, except for 30 miles graveled road between Hobbs and Carlsbad.
Texas & New Mexico Railroad touches the route at Hobbs; the Atchison, Topeka & Santa Fe Railway at Carlsbad.
Hotels at Hobbs and Carlsbad; tourist camps, gas stations along the road.

This southeastern corner of New Mexico gushes oil, the gross value of which in 1938 was nearly $36,000,000, nine-tenths of the State total. Culturally, topographically, linguistically, and in background Lea County is so typically Texan that it is called Little Texas. The eastern half, flat as a map, gleams with aluminum-painted tanks. Flares from wells wave flaming tongues as waste gas is carried upward through tall stacks or pipes, in order to safeguard public health.

When some of the first cattlemen settled in Lea County, more than 50 years ago, they found water near the present Monument (*see below*) at a depth of only six feet. They had no windmill, so horses were used for pumping. All of the ranchers who followed those pioneers knew that shallow water was to be found in many spots in the country, but it was 48 years—in 1932—before the United States Government made a survey of shallow waters suitable for irrigation. Before the Bureau of Chemistry and Soils made its soil and water survey, a number of ranch people had made use of the plentiful shallow water for irrigation of gardens and learned they could raise whatever they knew how to plant and tend.

NM 83 crosses the Texas Line, 0 *m.,* at a point 25 miles west of Seminole, Texas.

HOBBS, 5 *m.* (3,600 alt., 10,641 pop.), market center for a shallow water area of approximately a million acres, was founded in 1907 by James Hobbs, a Texan, and was a small settlement until the discovery of oil in 1927. Since then many wells have been brought in at Eunice and Monument to the south (*see below*), also in West Texas counties, and Hobbs, now the headquarters for oil well supplies, has grown so rapidly that the census of 1940 shows an increase in population of over 9,500. In Lea County alone there were 2,137 producing wells in April, 1939, with a pressure so great that only 4 per cent of them required pumps.

The town, having many new public buildings, is proud of its program of self-improvement and sure of its future since oil is not its only source of income. Lea County is an important ranching area, with large herds of cattle, flocks of sheep, and 800 farms. Of the 42,000 acres of farmed land, only 6,500 acres are regularly irrigated. Chief products of the irrigated areas are potatoes (both kinds), onions, corn, melons and cantaloupes, tomatoes, and many others, including grapes and berries. Irrigation has been recently established, and because the district is under-lain by shallow water, it is expected that truck crops and other produce will pay. There is also dairying and hog and poultry raising. Hobbs has a modern sewer system with disposal plant facilities, a community asset more rare in New Mexico than it should be.

There was no train service in Hobbs until April 19, 1930 when the Texas & New Mexico Railway came in. In addition to a large freight tonnage, there is good passenger service to various Texas centers.

In Hobbs are junctions with US 62, now the route, and with NM 18.

1. Left on NM 18, 20.7 *m.* to EUNICE (3,440 alt., 1,225 pop.), proclaimed a city by the Governor on April 26, 1937. The population given was in excess of 2,188 and the assessed valuation within the boundaries, $141,191. Eunice, named for the eldest daughter of J. N. Carson, was founded in 1909. Carson homesteaded the site which is at the southern end of the Staked Plains (*Llano Estacado*) on the Texas & New Mexico Railroad. After the homestead was filed, Carson opened a store and supplies were hauled from Midland, Texas. Mail was brought once a week from Shafter Lake, Texas and later twice a week from Monument, New Mexico (*see below*). A one-teacher subscription school was started by the homesteaders; a physician was advertised for and free living quarters provided, but there was not enough illness to support him.

The settlement remained fairly constant in appearance and population until 1927, when oil was discovered near Jal (*see below*), and the town was platted. Leases were made and they increased in value, but the greatest development did not begin until 1934 when the discovery well in this field was drilled. Production wells are now within three miles of the town. There are 125 of them, and the activity so overshadows everything else that other industries, including ranching, which was the principal interest before oil came, are scarcely noticed. Many homesteaders who held onto their claims through drought and hard times are now enjoying a reward they never anticipated in the form of lease and royalty money. Some have used oil incomes to pay off mortgages that had piled up on both ranch and stock during bad years. Oil derricks are scattered in the fields south and west of town and thousands of barrels of oil flow daily into pipe lines. Where cattle grazed, truckloads of workers and machinery rush by. Where buffalo fed, arrow and spear points were found in the early days, but no one bothers about artifacts now. The old 84 Ranch, two miles northeast, was one of the first in Lea County. Barney and Jim Whalen, former buffalo hunters, occupied this region by right of discovery in 1885, digging a well and putting a windmill over it. They controlled some 300,000 acres of Government grazing land that took care of 10,000 head of cattle. The encroachment of settlers reduced the open range until only a thousand acres now go with the old homestead that still stands.

2. JAL, 43.3 m. (3,000 alt., 1,155 pop.), was named for the old J A L Ranch in Monument Draw, six miles east of the present site. The post office that was opened on the ranch was moved here in 1916, but the town had no perceptible growth until 1927 when the Texas Production Company brought in its No. 1 Rhoads well. In 1910 in order to acquire the ranch post office, mail was carried free for three months by the sons of Charles W. Justice, the first postmaster. They rode horseback through 25 miles of deep sand from Kermit, Texas. The homesteads filed on at that time proved too dry for general farming and too small for stock raising, so that many people left for other sections. Supplies were hauled from Midland or Pecos, Texas; ten days for the round trip to Midland and five for Pecos. For a time Jal was just a country store 19 miles from the Texas Line. Now owing to oil discoveries there are several stores, lumber yards, an oil field supply house, machine shops, boiler works, and other enterprises, including hot-dog stands, beauty parlors, beer parlors, domino parlors, and pool halls. Most of these are housed in sheet iron and plaster board shacks hastily thrown together when Jal was expanding under its first oil boom. It has a Rotary Club and several oil companies have camps near by.

Hackberry trees, a ground tank, and parts of a rock wall at the edge of town mark the site of a well dug by hand in the old days. The oil is at a depth of 4,000 feet and drillers have brought up segments of mastodon bones. Although several wells are still active, the height of Jal's first boom has passed leaving a sprinkling of for-rent and for-sale signs, but there are indications of a new boom.

At 12.7 m., is the junction with a dirt road.

Left on this road, 5 m. to MONUMENT (4,200 alt., 88 pop.), named for an old monument erected to mark the location of water. In the spring of 1870, two buffalo hunters, Falkner and Hill, trailed a band of Indians traveling eastward, hoping they would lead them to water. On the fourth day the hunters came in sight of a hill surrounded by a pile of rock about 30 feet square and 18 or 20 feet high. This was the marker for the spring, which lay about a mile east.

No train comes to this section of the oil fields, but there is a daily mail car that carries passengers. The HAT Ranch house was built here in the early 1880's with thick walls and portholes.

There is plenty of shallow water around Monument, but not enough rainfall for successful farming, so stock raising became the chief occupation. Guy Falkner sold the Monument Springs for $400 in 1885 to an Englishman named Kennedy, who sold it four years later to General McKenzy, who later sold it to Winfield Scott and Sug Robinson in 1893. They named it the H A T for their old Texas ranch. Subsequently it was sold to Billy Weir. The Chisum Trail (*see Tour 7b*) passed through the ranch, and many persons, famous and otherwise, have visited or worked here at different times. Many large oil wells recently brought in are responsible for the present (1940) boom. A refinery has been built, also several pipe lines.

A few miles southwest of Monument is an Indian battlefield where hundreds of points of various sizes have been found. The people of Monument who have time to think of something besides oil like to imagine that the sculptured Indian that stands in the town facing toward the Monument is listening for the war cry of his people and the crack of the cowboys' forty-five.

## At 29.7 *m.* is the junction with a dirt road.

Left on this road to PEARL, 7 *m.,* at one time a post office in a residence —both gone. One autumn when most of the ranchers here had only grain-fed horses about their camps, the Indians succeeded in stealing so many horses that the owners started in pursuit. Four mounted men, Jim Ramer, Joe Nash, Boston Witt, and Tom Fennessy, with a pack horse took up the trail at John Aiken's camp and followed it north for more than 70 miles, then climbed the caprock. There they sighted three Indians with 20 or more stolen horses.

The Indians saw the ranchers just as quickly, and moved on with the stock. The ranchers fired a few shots and the Indians rode away, leaving the animals behind. The ranchers rounded up the horses, turned them back, then gave chase to the Indians, who had gained a lead of a mile, and soon disappeared over a rise. The pursuers kept on for two miles, then stopped to reconnoiter. In the distance were the Indians who had circled and recovered the horses. The thieves were too far away to warrant pursuit, and bobbing along with them was the ranchers' pack horse carrying food and blankets. To add to their discomfort the ranchers were out of water, and upon arriving at Monument Spring they had to strain the water through soiled handkerchiefs to keep out the insects and hoped that the dead buffalo in the pool wouldn't prove to be the death of them. This story wasn't told for some time. "We didn't talk about it because we were ashamed," said the narrator.

## At 56.6 *m.* is the junction with a dirt road.

Left on this road 3.1 *m.* to the UNITED STATES POTASH COMPANY MINE, producing since 1931.

According to a story in the Carlsbad *Daily Current-Argus,* potash was discovered 1,000 feet deep in this area by Dr. V. H. McNutt, geologist, who found a high percentage of polyhalite at several horizons in the Snowden-McSweeney oil test. It was McNutt's interest in this discovery and his appraisal of its value that led to the first core testing in the area. What once was the bed of an inland sea now is the Permian basin, extending over southeastern New Mexico into Texas and northward into Oklahoma and Kansas. In this basin, Carlsbad's two potash companies mine hundreds of thousands of tons each year. The lowest part of the Permian basin is in the Carlsbad area. Here were concentrated the intensely saline brines, concentrated by evaporation, in the closing stages of the basin's history. There is enough stored potash salts to supply the entire needs of the United States for many years.

Although potash has been manufactured in the United States since 1608, when Polish colonists skilled in making the salts from wood ashes plied their trade in the early colonies, it was not until 1916 that it was produced on an extensive scale at Searles Lake, in California; and it was not until 1931 that potash salts were mined.

Potash is of prime importance in agriculture as a plant food and is widely used in the chemical industry. Its name was derived from the manner in which it first was manufactured, by evaporating a solution leached from ashes of plants.

When natural potash salts were discovered in Germany in 1861, the subsequent educational programs devised to stimulate use of potash as a fertilizer made it in great demand. During the World War Germany's monopoly of the potash industry was keenly felt in the United States, and more extensive production of the salts was started in California. But it was not until 1931, with the United States Potash Company operations in the Carlsbad field, that the United States was freed from German monopoly. Although a recurrence of the war-time shortage with its ruinous high prices need never be feared again, the Carlsbad potash mines still face strong competition from Germany and other countries. Deposits are being worked in Germany, France, Spain, Russia, and Poland.

United States Potash Company started sinking its shaft in December 1929 and completed it in January 1931. The Potash Company of America (*see below*) started and completed its first shaft in 1933. Both mines follow the old room and pillar method in removing the ore from the bed of halosylvite, averaging about eight feet thick and about 1,000 feet below the surface.

Mechanical treatment of the crude salts is similar in both plants, except that the Potash Company of America does primary crushing underground. United States Potash Company refines potash salts by a process of solution and fractional crystallization. The final product is more than 99 per cent pure. Potash Company of America employs a newer method by which the crude salts are concentrated by flotation. Both are members of the Potash Institute, active in disseminating information regarding the uses of potash.

Potash from this area is marketed both in the crude form, called manure salts, and in the refined form. However, only a relatively small amount of manure salts is now shipped.

The Indians used wood ashes and fish to fertilize their crops, but since the discovery of potash, its use has increased steadily in the United States. During the World War of 1914-18, potash sold as high as $987 a ton, but in 1934 it was reported moving freely on the Atlantic seaboard at $27 a ton, although the lowest published price was $40.

At 58.9 *m.* is the junction with a dirt road.

Right on this road to the POTASH COMPANY OF AMERICA MINE, 6.1 *m.*, formed in 1933 and still active.

In CARLSBAD, 75.4 *m.* (3,102 alt., 7,048 pop.), is the junction with US 285 (*see Tour 7b*) with which US 62 is united for 2.7 miles.

WHITE'S CITY, 95.8 *m.*, is the junction with the road to Carlsbad Caverns (*see Tour 16A*).

US 62 continues through a rolling terrain, with the Guadalupe Mountains (R) to the west. Many tales of secret gold mines are told of these mountains. One of them concerns a man named Sublette, a water witch for the railroad, who with a hazel wand located wells along the right of way. It is said that his wand served him to even a better purpose and that one day he returned from a trip into the Guadalupe Mountains with a sack of gold bullion, but refused to tell where and how he had made the find. Repeated efforts to discover his secret were unsuccessful, for Sublette was a good shot and left no tracks. Some time after Sublette's death, a native sheepherder told two men who were looking for the mine that it had already been found by a man named Long, and express office records revealed that an Ed Long had consigned $30,000 in gold to himself in California.

The Guadalupes are also a rich field for archeologists. Dr. H. P. Mera of the Laboratory of Anthropology in Santa Fe spent two seasons excavating several Basket Maker II (*see Archeology*) cave sites in the limestone cliffs. Dr. E. B. Howard of the Museum of the University of Pennsylvania worked in the area and found Folsom points (*see Tour 4*) in association with the bones of extinct species of mammals. Dr. Deric Nusbaum of Gila Pueblo, Globe, Arizona, who has also studied these sites, says, "The known stages of the culture sequence in the area cover a period of ten or twelve millennia.  Folsom hunters occasionally penetrated the mountains from the Pecos drainage to the east and Crow Flat to the west.  Basket Maker II people occupied the dry, corridor-shaped caves as hunters and seed collectors; later they acquired maize and agricultural techniques.  Remains of two horizons of the later Pueblo-Mogollón phase are of common occurrence on shoulders of the foothills and around springs of water holes in the canyons. 'Mescal Pits,' hollow rings of burnt limestone, often contain habitation debris manifested by a surface sprinkling of potsherd and flint chips; most sand dune areas were used as camp sites; hearths, broken pottery, worked flint, and grinding stone speak of seasonal occupation by a semisedentary group of Indians who were subject to culture influence from the Plains tribes to the east.  A few halfbreeds are all that remain today of the aggressive Mescalero Apache, best known through the activities of their powerful chief, Gerónimo."

The Butterfield Trail, a main route to California during the gold rush days (*see Tour 10b*), rounds the southern point of these mountains. The limestone caves, partly hidden and easily defended, were favorite haunts of bandits who preyed upon wagon-train shipments of gold and merchandise; later the same caves served as hideouts for cattle rustlers and outlaws, including Billy the Kid (*see Tour 12b*), whose name appears on the wall of one of the canyons.

At 111.6 *m.* is the REGISTRATION STATION (*see General Information*) on the Texas Line, at a point 85 miles northeast of Van Horn, Texas.

# *Tour 16A*

Carlsbad—Carlsbad Caverns National Park, 27.5 *m.* US 62-285, Caverns Road.

Two-lane, bituminous-paved road throughout.
Accommodations: hotels in Carlsbad, tourist camps along route.

US 62-285 goes south from Carlsbad to a point, 2.7 *m.*, where US 285 turns (L); then straight ahead on US 62 to the junction with the Caverns Road (R) at White City.  The Caverns Road goes up Walnut Canyon through rocky mesas covered with Spanish-dagger (yucca), pricklypear, soapweed, and other species of desert flora, including chiefly cholla, cane cactus, ocotillo, and mesquite.  In the spring the snowy-clustered blossoms of the Spanish-dagger and the clear magenta of cactus bloom are points of color against the gray and green of the grasses.

## CARLSBAD CAVERNS NATIONAL PARK, 27.5 m.

*Three daily conducted tours with guide service, $1.50 per person for those over 16; elevator fee 25¢; elevator trip 12:30 to Big Room for those unable to walk; chief daily tour is 10:30 a.m.; lunch on tour, 50¢; comfortable walking shoes and light sweater recommended; temperature in Caverns, 56° summer and winter.*

The Caverns are openings made by water in a massive rock known as the Carlsbad limestone. This limestone was formed in a shallow inland extension of the ocean some 200 million years ago. After this, the area was dry land, although possibly resubmerged and covered by sediments at a later period. When the Rocky Mountains were formed, these uplifting and enfolding movements raised this area above sea level. This was about 60 million years ago. Since that time the Caverns have been hollowed in the limestone, and at a later time the amazing decorative deposits were formed. Repeated movements caused cracks and openings in the limestone, and along these cracks rain water made its way. This was the beginning of the Caverns, for once water enters, continued action slowly removes the limestone by solution. As openings become larger, channels are made, rocks cave in, and even larger holes result. Small seepages from above continue to find their way into the dry caverns, are evaporated, and instead of removal and solution, a deposit is left. These make stalactites, which hang from above. Where the water enters an opening too rapidly for evaporation, part of it falls to the floor, where it is evaporated, gradually forming stalagmites, which build up into various shapes and sizes. Sometimes a stalactite and a stalagmite meet, forming a column. A small amount of iron or other mineral matter in the limestone produces a delicate tinting. The brilliant and translucent formations result from saturation with water. They are said to be "growing." Those that are dry and dull in appearance (which results when the seepage of water is stopped) are called "dead."

Jim White, a cowboy, accompanied by a lad, discovered the Caverns in 1901. Attracted by a swarm of bats they found an opening leading far down into the earth. Entering, they made smudges to define their trail and reeled out lengths of string by which to find their way back. Marveling at the wonders he had seen, White talked about this to everyone who would listen, then took many in to see for themselves. News of the discovery resulted in an investigation by Mr. Robert Holley of the United States General Land Office and Dr. Willis T. Lee of the United States Geological Survey, who visited here in 1923 and 1924. Subsequently the National Geographic Society sponsored an expedition led by Dr. Lee and his reports were published in the *National Geographic* in January 1924 and September 1925. This was subsequent to the President's proclamation, October 25, 1923, which established the area as a national monument; in 1930, by act of Congress, it became Carlsbad Caverns National Park.

There is evidence of ancient use of the caves. A sandal of Basket Maker craft was uncovered, and there were other evidences of human beings.

Bats still inhabit the caves, emerging each evening, except during their winter hibernation. There are five species, the most numerous being the Mexican free-tail bat. While no ranger has stood by and clicked off the total, as is done each day with the tourists, their number is estimated at between three and five million.

One of the strangest industries in the country was established at Carlsbad in 1933. This was the Carlsbad Bat Guano Company, the only manufacturing plant of fertilizers in New Mexico and probably the only plant of this particular product in the United States. In recent years nearly 100,000 tons of guano have been taken out of the Caverns. Most of this fertilizer, which is mixed at the plant after being brought out of the caves, is shipped to California to be used on citrus fruit groves.

It is not yet determined how extensive the caverns really are. Thirty-two miles of them have been explored and three main levels discovered, the first 754 feet below the surface, the second, 900 feet, and the third, 1,320 feet. None of these has been completely explored. Well over a million and a quarter visitors have seen the caves, and statistics show a marked increase from year to year. The surface area within the Park has been increased from 700 to 9,960 acres.

Near the Pay Station is a cactus garden that contains all local varieties of cactus as well as some of the other plants of this area. There is also an old mescal pit that has been excavated.

## A TOUR OF THE CAVERNS

A siren is sounded at starting time and visitors assemble at the entrance where a large opening gives a view into the dim interior, from which rises the cool, slightly dank odor of undersurface regions. The dome-shaped entrance, rocky and discolored, gives a hint of what is to come, but is no preparation for it. After an introductory talk by one of the rangers, the line forms two abreast and moves slowly down toward the first objective, the Auditorium. Far below can be seen the place near which it is located, and the descending, expectant line can be seen below and above—those who have entered and those who are about to —moving like pilgrims toward a shrine. At a turn in the path a ranger clicks the attendance, while above at the Pay Station data is being compiled giving the States and foreign countries from which those registering have come, with the number from each section.

The descent suddenly steepens, still winding. At the lower recesses, blackened sides and top are seen for the first time. Where the exigencies of foot passage require it, the trail is cut through the solid rock, but where possible it is left as it was, except that the trail had to be made and dirt carried in to pack it and make it safe.

Inside, the artificial lights, ranging from 50 to 2000 watts, are carefully and skilfully concealed. There are 25 circuits, each illuminating

1000 feet of the caves. The vaulted heights close down as the trail descends; occasional areas of pale color are seen, and then the first stalactite.

At the BAT CAVE, which extends back half a mile from the trail, a turn (R) brings into view the entrance by which the long line has come. Here the ceiling is high again, and up above toward the front can be seen the diffused light of day pouring across the less powerful light below. Another turn, and the daylight is gone. From here until emergence at the end of the trip, the only light is artificial.

The group comes to rest in the AUDITORIUM, a spacious cave, where the guide gives an explanatory talk. Another hint of what will be seen is furnished by the formations here, modest in size and faintly colored.

The acoustics are excellent. Every word spoken in a moderate tone is heard, and the crowd is asked to speak in well-modulated voices for that reason.

A ranger is in the lead, with others along the double column, one for each 30 visitors, all charged with the responsibility of looking out for them and answering their questions. The long line proceeds to the next chamber along sentinel pillars, through low-ceiled passages flanked by stalactites, and past a lone column whose base rises from a clear, cool pool. Fine dust from the trail looks like a faint cloud of incense. There follows a fairly steep descent into a deep cavern. The lights at the side are adequate, but not too obvious. Formations grow in size and interest and are increasingly fantastic. Across this great space, high above, are formations suggesting ancient cliff ruins, this illusion being heightened by erosions which resemble those at Mesa Verde Cliff Dwellings.

The descent steepens sharply at a point where the ceiling is 125 feet above the trail. On past the *Whale's Mouth,* a formation cleverly lighted to show the ribbon-like stalactites which give the illusion; and then beyond loom depths of hundreds of feet. Where steps are needed, they are built of wood, with low rises, affording comfortable descent; and there are hand rails where the trail is at the outer edge of a parapet.

Lights issue from apertures at various points. At one the trail is 450 feet below the surface and the ceiling is 270 feet above. Then the trail winds through a low, rock-cut passage where gypsum crystals form sparkling bunches of "grapes" or "wasps' nests" on the ceiling. After a short climb up a flight of wooden steps there is another descent over the soft dirt trail. Here are weird formations: stalagmites, pillars rising near at hand, the *Baby Hippo* formation, and others resembling sea foam and waves. Walls rise smooth on one side, fantastically irregular on the other. Obelisks, monoliths, and pagoda-like forms come into view, some of them grotesquely aloof, stark and alone. Festoons of stalactites hang from the ceiling, which has dark clefts and fissures.

When a depth of 600 feet is reached, the guide invites those unequal to completing the trip to fall out and rest, taking a short cut to the lunch room. More stairs, and a continuing steep descent past huge solitary rocks; then over on the right side, past smooth, high walls, and again on the left, past the erosions and *The Iceberg,* largest "loose" rock in the caverns, which weighs about 200,000 tons. Here the ceiling, 358 feet, is cleft with a narrow opening in which shadows play; but the interior is not revealed because the light does not penetrate it.

The trail goes down into GREEN LAKE ROOM, rich in lacy, jagged stalactites, with ponderous pillars and varieties of cool and composed forms, chaste for all their irregularities. Above the trail a sentinel form stands motionless before what seems the votive light of a wayside shrine. Delicate traceries overhang Green Lake, an emerald pool whose clear waters disclose its depths; then on, past the *Frozen Water Falls,* named for its motionless cascade. In places huge rocks are heaped, appearing to have been tumbled there by turbulent waters.

The KING'S PALACE is 829 feet below the surface. Here the trail levels off under a profusion of hanging forms, some resembling Spanish moss, some having the quality of ecclesiastic architecture of the most ornate Gothic period, some rococo, some with arabesques and the delicate traceries of the best Moorish period. This room is circular and contains a riot of fantastic forms. Here is Mother Nature's laboratory, her plans revealed and her designs in process of execution. A niche high above holds a light; formations which hug the ground are brought into relief by lights, then the trail ascends to the QUEEN'S CHAMBER, winding through more of the same kind of shapes, except that they differ always in infinite variety.

More shallow pools, incredibly clear, and then on, past formations looking like sculptured scenes from The Arabian Nights, one in particular illustrating the adventure in which the genie rises from the fire in a waving column of smoke. Hydra-headed beasts thrust out from the sides; heads and bodies of marine monsters emerge from foaming waves. Delicate cavern flora appear just where they accent an especially graceful, flowing line. In the center of the room is a group resembling a Buddhist shrine. Subterranean debris is scattered along the sides of the trail, which is kept clear. The trail continues through a low, rockhewn passage to the PAPOOSE ROOM. Skirting the edge of this, it moves down, and after leveling off begins to climb in easy stages, a relief from the long descent.

A horizontal thrust above contrasts with the diagonal and perpendicular movements that flow in from the sides. Overhead, sprays seem to gush from the walls and freeze into identity with it. Fossils are seen, and walls tufted like quilted padding rise on the left. Tendrils of dark-colored stalactites are pressed against the damp ceiling. At the turns are pockets of light, and a cascade of pale forms falls to the left as the trail goes gently down again. At the right are wave-like forms stylized like the sea in a Hokusai print. On the left gigantic boulders seem pushed into place by mighty hands. Now dim, but never dark, the trail runs on, dimness succeeded farther on by comparative brightness, giving balance and quality to the illumination. Honeycombed fissures and crags are passed; high vaults alternate with low-ceiled grottoes, and the path enters a section of the BIG ROOM called the AMPHI-THEATRE, where a vast stage is set as for a cosmic play.

Away from this, through the GRAPE ARBOR, named for the clustered stalactites overhead, then under a vari-colored ceiling to the spacious, low-ceiled lunch room, reached at the end of two hours.

The lunch room was installed in 1927. While it accommodates 1,100 normally, as many as 2,500 have been served at one time. The efficient system enables the last one in line to have his lunch soon after he enters the room.

There is also an exhibit of the different kinds of formations, the "lily pads," aragonite (frost work), some branched and antlered helectites (unclassified), Iceland spar, dogtooth spar, and some fossils found in the Permian limestone.

After lunch the long line forms again, and at 1:15 moves toward the Big Room, the edge of which was skirted on the way to the lunch room. This is the largest chamber of them all, the culmination of the trip. The moving column traverses the Amphitheatre and passes the encrusted walls which rise to a multi-colored ceiling. Here is a glorified *malpais* (badlands), with forms suggestive of Tibet, Mongolia, China, Japan, Java, and Bali. Deep recesses withdraw behind interlaced draperies.

The way lies along the rocky transept of a churchlike interior, then through the "nave." Gigantic forms tower above vast, shadowy depths. Ornate sculptures stand out from huge masses. On the left the *Onyx Draperies* are flung from above. The ceiling arches high above forms which rise to points of accent. The way is past FAIRYLAND, a group of low, fantastically shaped stalagmites. As the van approaches a new section, the lights are switched on and a farther one stands out. Delicately tinted points depend from the ceiling. The trail is generally level throughout this part of the tour. The room is so large that it contains other caves. Distant forms stand out; fluted banners fly overhead. Fissures and lily-pads, flowers and laces, line the way to the TOTEM POLE, 40 feet high, standing apart where it is certain to be seen. The trail descends along a parapet that looks into shadowy depths on the left.

Another section of the room stands out as another light switch is turned. The trail here is through a narrow opening with a high-vaulted room on the left and past the entrance to a deeper cavern, 150 feet below this point. (This entrance has been abandoned). On past the JUMP-ING OFF PLACE, where this lower cave is seen and where the trail is just midway between its floor and ceiling, 150 feet in each perpendicular direction. Huge openings yawn above as the line moves past colored stretches along a parapet which overlooks a chasm on the left. There are vistas of dark halls leading off as the way curves past shallow pools, then pillars. More lily pads, then clusters of gigantic boulders flung in a towering heap. All sense of direction is lost and even forgotten, until a sign is encountered which points "North"—and the trail wanders past, going its own pace in its own direction.

Past MIRROR LAKE, another of the small, crystal-clear pools, looms the *Bottomless Pit,* 700 feet deep. Here the ceiling is 200 feet above the trail which now rises slightly, so that there is a view of the long serpentine line. Where the trail is moist from the dripping, a crunching sound of many feet is heard, but at other times—and for much the greater part—the trail is dry and the tread silent.

Ahead, on the right, is the *Shrine,* labeled and illumined, and beyond, another pool amid stalwart pillars. The largest growing stalagmite, *Crystal Spring Dome,* marks a point where the trail is damp again. From here the trail rises to a point at the *Rock of Ages,* an impressive stalagmite mass several millions of years old and second oldest in the Caverns, which stands to the left of the place where the group is now asked to be seated.

At the right can be seen those curious stalagmites, the *Giant Domes,* and other formations passed earlier in the tour. Away off in front, dim forms rise from below. Behind is a sheer drop of 150 feet to a cavern whose floor is 900 feet below the surface. This has not yet been opened to the public.

The mind plays with the dimensions of the Big Room: 4,000 feet by 625 feet and 300 feet high, the largest in the known world, requiring one and one-half hours to encircle. Of the 25 separate light circuits in the caverns only one is now turned on. When all are seated, the guide explains that the lights will be switched off for 30 seconds, making the room completely dark. This is done. After 30 seconds a dim light illumines a formation far off across the room and a quartet is heard in the hymn, "Rock of Ages." During the singing of two verses other sections in front are lighted in succession. At the end the voices fade to silence before the lights go up. The ranger gives the attendance figures and names the States and foreign countries represented, with the number from each.

At word from the guide, the group rises and follows along the farther trail past the *Polar Regions,* so named because of the resemblance to photographs of the Byrd Polar Expedition, then back to the lunch room, where the party divides, those returning by elevator passing to the left and those walking out going to the right.

At the surface again, until eyes are adjusted to the strong afternoon light, a rest of a few minutes is advised before regaining the parked car or bus.

# *Tour 17*

(Antonito, Colorado) — Taos Junction — Embudo — Española —
Santa Fe.
Colorado Line to Santa Fe, 119.6 *m.*

Denver & Rio Grande Western Railroad.
Narrow-gauge railroad with rough but adequate roadbed.
NM 74 roughly parallels route throughout.
Accommodations in Española and Santa Fe.

The trip on the old narrow-gauge railroad, the Denver & Rio
Grande Western, that runs between Santa Fe and Colorado points, connecting with the standard gauge line in Colorado, is such an interesting
trip and has such an old-world flavor, besides affording magnificent
views not possible from any of the highways in the State, that it is a tour
well worth-while taking. It is a funny sort of a road and New Mexicans poke fun at it, although they feel an affection for it, because it is
part of the New Mexico scene and gives such fine, surprising views of
the landscape. After all, there are few, if any, such railroads left in this
country, and it is a tie-up with that lush period of the railroads in the
1880's, since the engine and coaches are of that vintage. Although it
has charm and its own peculiar quality, it does furnish very fast freight
service into New Mexico from Denver, and this service will possibly be
the means eventually of pulling the road out of receivership. A ride
on this train is an amusing experience as well as a delightful one, and
the train serves a definite need in hauling freight.

This is the equivalent of a walking tour by train. The trip may be
made either from Antonito, Colorado near the New Mexico Line by
way of Denver or Alamosa, Colorado, or by round trip from Santa Fe.
There is service every day except Sunday. The trip from Santa Fe,
especially on upgrades, is leisurely enough to give the illusion of walking
through fields of grasses and wild flowers, and this is heightened by
growth right up to the tracks. There are panoramas not seen from any
highway in the State. The road, run into Santa Fe in 1881, has some
of the same rolling stock it had then, although the plush seats have been
replaced by imitation leather and the coaches improved. The fancy oil
lamps hanging from the ceiling still serve on this run, although there are
electric lights that can be used when the coach is hooked up with a train
that has electricity. The trip is made in daylight, but in winter it is
often dark by the time of arrival at either terminus. Small coal stoves
at each end of the coach furnish adequate heat. There is but one coach
in regular service, the rest of the train being made up of freight and

baggage or express cars. These are few, because when loaded the engine is taxed on the climbs. While it will pull as much as 400 tons on the level stretches, 187 tons are all it can drag out of Rio Grande Canyon, which offers a fairly steep climb as well as a magnificent view.

It takes about seven hours for the trip to Santa Fe from Antonito, Colorado, and about eight hours from Santa Fe to Antonito. There is water on the train, but lunch should be taken. Members of the train crew speak English but Spanish is used by a majority of the passengers. Mothers nurse their babies—there are usually babies—and older brothers and sisters help care for them, and so do other passengers. There are bundles and luggage and boxes and baskets, and from the latter chunks of cake are drawn and the children munch contentedly during the long ride.

When migratory workers from New Mexico go to the Colorado sugar-beet fields or the pea-packing plants, or return at the close of the season, the coach is crowded; at other times its capacity is not taxed. Because there is 24-hour service from Denver, the train carries freight on passenger-train schedules.

From the COLORADO LINE, 0 *m.,* 6 *m.* south of Antonito, Colorado, the Denver and Rio Grande Western Railroad runs across a high plateau flanked by mountains. The Sangre de Cristo Range (L) continues down into New Mexico, and beautiful San Antonio Peak (R) is a few miles south of the Colorado-New Mexico Line. (*See Tour 5 for a description of the towns along this route.*)

The track curves, skirting arroyos and hills. Yucca, cactus, locoweed, vetch, wild gourd vines, purple verbena, bee balm, aster, chamiso, and other wild flowers, including mallow and flowering grasses, give beauty to the foreground, while the hills and mountains in the distance make for greater loveliness, with sky and piling clouds over all. The train moves so slowly that instead of the confusing blur when close objects are passed at a rapid rate, form and color are defined and each object stands out for examination.

As the train approaches TAOS JUNCTION, the Taos Mountains are visible—more of them than from many points. This is the stop nearest Taos, and before the days of automobiles the stage from Taos here met passengers bound for that place.

The train descends into Rio Grande Canyon, looking down on the winding track below and over (L) at a panorama of the canyon—a world of mesas, peaked hills stepping back to the horizon, small cultivated fields in green patches on the canyon floor, occasional farm houses, and clumps of trees. Past aromatic sagebrush and black boulders strewn along the sides of the cut, the train clatters down into Embudo, which is on the Rio Grande. Here the canyon is narrow, and traffic is visible moving along the highway across the river. It is on this downgrade into Embudo that the accident described below occurred, according to the *New Mexico Daily Examiner,* which carried the following story:

## DENTAL MISHAP FAILS TO DELAY

Lost time and teeth seem to be of equal value to the D&RGW.

The Saturday afternoon train, right on time, was coming down the Embudo hill on its way to Santa Fe. Engineer Albee of Alamosa, Colo., felt an urge to cough, and inadvertently faced the cab window when he did so. As a result, his false teeth sailed out the window.

Engineer Albee immediately stopped the train, then backed it up to the hill to the place where the accident happened. The train crew and some of the passengers joined the search, and finally F. D. Casan of Chicago found the missing dental work.

Albee wiped off his teeth with his machine rag, replaced them, and raced the train into Santa Fe, arriving promptly on schedule.

On hearing yesterday of the dental mishap on the D&RGW, State Corporation Commissioner Bob Valdez announced that plans would be made to issue orders to all railroads, asking them to clear brush from the vicinity of the tracks in order that wigs, teeth, and other detachable objects might more easily be found.

Leaving Rio Grande Canyon, the train skirts the edge of Mesa Prieta (Dark Mesa) and follows the course of the Rio Grande past Alcalde and into Española, another stop. In the old days, visitors to Puyé ruins would take the train to Española and then by horse-drawn vehicle cover the remainder of the journey. One resident of those days, then new to the country, tells of waiting here for the train to Santa Fe. She asked when the train was due, and was told that it would be there soon, the station agent adding, "You'll know it's coming when you see the engineer's dog running down the track ahead of it."

*Placitas* and settlements tucked away down near the Rio Grande are visible; cultivated fields on both sides are seen in summer, but midsummer is not the most comfortable time for the trip, because of heat and flies.

As the train nears Ótowi, after passing Santa Clara Pueblo (L), the Black Mesa and San Ildefonso Pueblo (L) are visible across the river. A line of mesas (the Parajito Plateau) and the foothills of the Jémez Mountains (R) mark the limits of the sweeping view to the west. The train stops on signal at Ótowi, as at other places along the route, then crosses the bridge over the Rio Grande. On the face of cliffs (R) are some Indian petroglyphs. Along here, Paramount dammed the river and filmed water scenes for *The Light that Failed*. Here is Buckman, a shipping point for cattle in the old days, now abandoned. The views of the mesas around Buckman are extraordinary, giving a sense of this section of New Mexico that the tourist by motor never experiences.

Approaching SANTA FE, 119.6 *m.,* there is a view of the ancient city spread out below that is also different from the view from other points. Bundles are gathered up, along with babies and luggage and boxes. Near the little station, the train crosses a trestle in front of the Church of Our Lady of Guadalupe (R) with brave sound of bell and show of steam and at the station the engineer stands proudly by while passengers descend.

# Tour 18

Deming — Silver City — Glenwood — (Springerville, Ariz.) US 260.
Deming to Arizona State Line, 172.6 m.

Bituminous-paved road between Deming and point 16 m. beyond Cliff; else-
where two-lane graded graveled.
The Atchison, Topeka & Santa Fe Ry. parallels the highway (L) from
Deming to Silver City.
Good accommodations at major points along route.

US 260 north of DEMING, 0 m., courses through the Mimbres
Valley, a productive region adjacent to a highly mineralized area which
has always been the "promised land" for the inveterate prospector. As
the early home of the Mimbres tribe of Apache, it is also rich in history
and legend.

The mountains to the (R) of the highway are the COOK MOUN-
TAINS; the highest peak at the southern extremity is COOK'S PEAK,
an old landmark for early travelers and drivers of the stage on the Butterfield Trail.

At 24.1 m. is junction with dirt road.

Right on this road is FAYWOOD (also known as Faywood Springs) 2.1 m.,
primarily a health resort where numerous hot mineral springs give water
said to be very beneficial for the treatment of infantile paralysis.

Near the Springs, a few miles eastward (R) on the desert is the
so-called CITY OF ROCKS, a rock formation which creates the illusion of
a metropolitan skyline.

The tiny hamlet of APACHE TEJO (pronounced Teho) is passed
at 34 m. In the environs were the Apache *tejo* (quoit) pits and annually the champions of the several tribes would repair here to defend
their laurels. Fine springs are also located here.

HURLEY, 37.9 m., a company village owned by the Chino Mine
of the Nevada Consolidated Copper Company, is the site of the concentration mill for the Santa Rita Mine. It is directly connected by railroad with Santa Rita.

The village consists of 125 company houses, an ore mill, a steam
plant, and several stores and mercantile establishments. Until 1934
when the Santa Rita Mine closed down, it was completely occupied, a
behive of industrial activity. With the recent reopening of the mine,
work here has been resumed, and the 1940 census shows a population of
1,321.

At 42.5 m. is the junction with NM 180 (*see Tour 1A*).

CENTRAL, 43.8 m. (1,759 pop.), because of its proximity to
old Fort Bayard and the present United States Veterans' Hospital grew
from a small settlement to its present moderate size.

At 45.1 *m.* is a junction with a side road, NM 180 (*see Tour 1A*).

Right on this road is FORT BAYARD UNITED STATES VETERANS' HOSPITAL, 1 *m.* Originally an early fort and Army hospital, it was later transferred to the United States Public Health Service and now is under the guidance of the United States Veterans' Administration. Included in the physical equipment is the hospital with a capacity of 200 beds, several buildings for the hospitalization of tubercular patients, and quarters for the staff physicians, nurses, and employees. The government maintains its own dairy herd and considerable acreage is under cultivation.

CAMERON CREEK RUINS, 3 *m.*, south of Fort Bayard are the remains of a pueblo civilization, one of such units which thickly dot the Mimbres Valley. Inquire for directions at Fort Bayard.

Excavation work here has been carried on by private expeditions of the University of New Mexico and the University of Minnesota. The Cameron Ruins and the Swarts Ruins farther north are the main structures so far to receive the attention of the archeologists.

The Cameron Creek Ruins, located on a short ridge that projects into the Cameron Creek Valley, has yielded pottery, shell beads, necklaces, bracelets, skeletal material, and a structure of 135 pit rooms, a distinctive type of early pueblo architecture. The pit room type is so named because the first two to three feet of the structure was subterranean, the roof being about three feet from the ground level.

The burial grounds, also unusual, were oval pits under the ground floor of the rooms into which the bodies were placed in a flexed position. Personal belongings were buried with the deceased; notable are their personal jars. These mortuary jars were perfectly drilled through the bottom in most cases, said to be done to allow the spirit of the jar to escape with the soul of the departed. Interesting is the fact that no *kivas* have been found in the Mimbres ruins.

There is practically nothing left of these ruins except the walls of the rooms. Most of the "finds" have been taken to the Smithsonian Institute and to the Museum of New Mexico at Santa Fe.

At 48.5 *m.* is the junction with NM 187.

Right on this road is the GILA WILDERNESS AREA, 31.2 *m.*, supervised by the National Park Service. A gate at the entrance is kept locked and the key must be obtained from the ranger. Private automobiles are not permitted in the area, which is accessible only on foot or horseback. (*Write Silver City Chamber of Commerce for names of guides available for pack trips.*) From NM 180, junction with NM 187, the road is through broken, hilly country, with juniper, piñon, and oak on both sides. Abandoned mines and mine dumps are visible from time to time, with far vistas of mountain ranges on all sides; in the foreground are clumps of cholla, agave, and some mescal. Past peach orchards and cultivated fields, through the village of Pinos Altos, 5.9 *m.*, the road crosses the southern boundary of GILA NATIONAL FOREST, 7.6 *m.* Skirting the edge of Cherry Creek Canyon whose floor is 6,958 alt., past Forest Service Station, 13.1 *m.*, to M'MULLAN PUBLIC CAMP GROUNDS (R), 14.6 *m.* Through stands of Douglas fir, Ponderosa pine, spruce, piñon, and juniper, past fields of yellow genestra, blue lupin, and masses of ferns to the highest point on the road (7,431 alt.). Here there is a descent into the Gila drainage, then over Wild Horse Mesa to PINE FLATS PUBLIC CAMP GROUND, 20.2 *m.*, where stands of alligator-bark juniper are visible. At 25.2 *m.*, turn into Copperas Canyon Truck Trail (L), over a very rough, rocky road with fine panoramas, to the entrance of Gila Wilderness Area.

The GILA CLIFF DWELLINGS NATIONAL MONUMENT, an area of approximately 50 miles, is accessible only on foot or horseback. Wild turkey, wild deer, and birds seldom seen except in protected regions abound here. Up a canyon (L) off the west fork of the Gila River are the cliff dwellings. Too little research has been done on them as yet to obtain a complete picture of the life and work of these early people, but the ruins themselves, under a sheltering wall of rock, are sufficiently preserved to give some idea of the kind of community it was. Pueblo Indians lived in this area. Mr. Erik K. Reed, archeologist with the National Park Service, who has studied this section, states that the Pueblos living in the northern Southwest a thousand years ago spread down into southwestern New Mexico, changing and submerging the local people and culture. They cultivated maize, pumpkins, and beans, often employing irrigation. They hunted deer, jack rabbit, turkey, and many other animals; wore skins; had blankets and other articles of dress woven of cotton; made good pottery, also awls, needles, whistles, and other instruments from mammal and bird bones. They used various kinds of stones for axes and corn grinders, arrow-points, and knives. They made small ornaments from other kinds of stone, including turquoise, and had other ornaments made from sea shells from the Gulf of California, received by trade, and many of these cultural traits have persisted.

US 260 continues over a bituminous-paved roadbed to the outskirts of Silver City.

SILVER CITY, 50.5 *m.* (5,900 alt., 5,015 pop.), occupies a beautiful setting in the foothills of the Pinos Altos Range, an extension of the Mogollón Mountains. It is a shipping point for the near-by Chino mines and livestock ranches, business center of southeastern New Mexico, and home of the New Mexico State Teachers' College. It was founded in 1870 as a small Spanish settlement called San Vicente de la Cienega (St. Vincent of the Marsh), one of the camping sites of the Gila and Mimbres Apache Indians who claimed ownership of the entire district, contending that the United States should have negotiated with them, in 1847, instead of with the Spanish. In 1874 it became the seat of Grant County, formerly a part of Dona Ana County, which at first included the entire southern part of the territory acquired from Mexico by the United States under the treaty of Guadalupe Hidalgo (1848) and the Gadsden Purchase, 1854 (*see Tour 1c*). Silver City was the first town of its kind in New Mexico to be incorporated (1876).

Early in its history it was continually menaced by the Apache who, after several broken promises made by Spaniards, were irreconcilably hostile to all white men, and this animosity extended to those who came in following American Occupation. They drove off cattle grazing just outside the settlement and killed them, and roads were unsafe in all directions. They gave the highway to the army post at Fort Bayard special attention, for the whites depended upon this for protection. Tales of these raids are still told in Silver City. One that received Nation-wide attention was the capture on March 28, 1883, of little Johnnie McComas, son of Judge McComas, after his parents had been killed. It is not known for certain whether the boy was killed, for tales of his survival persist, the latest being the news story in May, 1938, of an archeological expedition into Mexico discovering a so-called lost tribe of Apache that had escaped from the United States at the time of

Gerónimo's capture. Their leader, red-haired and blue-eyed, was thought to be the lost Johnnie McComas.

Following an earlier raid upon Silver City on July 11, 1871, Captain John Bullard went into the hills and defeated an Apache war party. While bending over a supposedly dead Indian, the man grabbed his gun, and he was shot through the heart. This was on the slope of the peak that was named for him. One of the main streets in town also bears his name.

Like most western mining towns, Silver City had its share of notorious resorts. Soft-handed gamblers in wide-brimmed black hats, frock coats, and diamond-studded cravats presided at gaming tables. Cowboys strode up to the bar in high-heeled boots and demanded shots of red-eye, bug juice, or mescal for themselves and companions from Shady Lane. If their demands were not supplied immediately, they shot out the lights, the bar mirror, and any other attractive target, then turned over the roulette tables.

Before the railroad was built, prior to 1881, 12- and 14-horse teams hauled ore and bullion into Silver City from mining camps in the Mogollóns. Bricks of gold and silver were stacked on sidewalks outside shipping offices. Attempts at robbery were discouraged by numerous hangings. In the latter part of the last century, when the rich pockets of almost pure silver and gold placers were exhausted, the town declined, but the introduction of modern irrigation and farming into the Mimbres and the Gila River Valleys gave it new life. It became the shipping point for this region. About 1908 capital was again attracted when gold was found in the Mogollón Mountains and iron at Fierro, and the cattle industry was revived. It has continued to flourish, a thriving, modern city. The annual rodeo, July 2, 3, and 4, is known throughout the Southwest, and Silver City is the center for pack trips into the many hunting, fishing, and recreational areas in the surrounding mountains. It is headquarters for the Gila National Forest.

The COUNTY COURT HOUSE, with murals by Theodore Van Soelen, at 100 West Cooper Street, and the STATE TEACHERS' COLLEGE, 1008 West College Avenue, are points of interest. The very high curves and the deep depression running almost the entire length of the town, one block east of and paralleling Bullard Street, are the result of torrential rains, in 1895, which, falling on the denuded slopes of near-by hills, caused such flood conditions in the town that the main street was a river; stores and dwellings tumbled into the flood, and receding waters left a gaping, irregular gulch. In 1935 C.C.C. workers networked the hillsides with thousands of small dams to check the run-off and lined the Big Ditch with terraced masonry walls, transforming it into an attractive park.

At Silver City is the junction with NM 180.

Left on this road 12.7 m. is TYRONE (350 pop.), the de luxe model mining camp, called the most expensive in the world, which was designed by Goodhue and built by Phelps-Dodge interests at a cost of $1,000,000. The beauty and substantial character of the buildings and houses is incredible, unless actually seen. Tyrone, at the base of Little Burro Mountains, has a fine railroad station, large department store, and many modern dwellings, which rent for very little. All modern conveniences are available, and the setting and environs, in beautiful Tyrone Valley, are very attractive, with groves of cottonwood and lovely, quiet meadows. It is ideal for those whose health requires a salubrious climate, who desire quiet, or long for solitude, for scarcely anybody lives in Tyrone. It is a ghost town, dead since 1921, when the mines closed down. A few artists, writers, and others attracted to the place live here, but they must go to Silver City to do their marketing and buy supplies. Much ore has been mined and milled here, and there are turquoise mines too; but although they are said to be still rich in turquoise, they are not operating.

West from Silver City, US 260 skirts the edge of Gila National Forest (L), with mountains on both sides, crossing the Gila River at RIVERSIDE, 78.9 m. The Gila is important to irrigation in both New Mexico and Arizona. Rising in the Gila National Forest, its regular flow supplies water for the Coolidge Dam in Arizona. Several hot springs near its source and small tributary streams add to its flow.

At CLIFF, 81.4 m. (161 pop.), is the junction with a dirt road.

Right on this road 2.7 m. is GILA (769 pop.), one of the starting points and supply depots for pack trips into the Mogollón Mountains and the Gila Wilderness Area.

Several well-kept farms lie in the valley northwest of Cliff, and cottonwood and walnut trees line the banks of the Gila.

BUCKHORN, 88.9 m. (4,700 alt., 104 pop.), is a trading center. The MOGOLLÓNS, named for Don Juan Ignacio Flores Mogollón, Governor of the Province of New Mexico (1712-15), bound the valley (R). These mountains are one of the few places where the grizzly bear is found; black and brown bear are numerous; also white-tailed, fan-tailed, and mule deer. Mountain lion, bobcat, and coyote still prey upon the stock that grazes in this region under Government permit. Yellow pine, Douglas fir, white fir, and spruce are plentiful.

Past JACKSON, 97 m., a roadside stop, US 260 continues through mountainous areas covered with thick stands of timber.

PLEASANTON, 112.3 m. (4,637 alt., 15 pop.), is situated on the San Francisco River, surrounded by small farms, orchards, and cattle ranches.

GLENWOOD, 116.1 m. (4,746 alt., 135 pop.), is near the junction of several deep canyons, almost hidden in a grove of cottonwoods. In the midst of a hunting and fishing region, many trails into these areas lead from it.

At ALMA, 121 m., a small settlement, is the junction with NM 78.

Right on this road is MOGOLLÓN, 6.7 m. (200 pop.), a small settlement in the center of the Cooney mining district, named for Sergeant James Cooney who came to Fort Bayard in 1870. While on duty as a scout, he discovered gold quartz rock, but said nothing about it, and after his discharge came here with two buddies and worked the claim. The Apache, a continual menace, killed him, and he was buried in Cooney's Canyon in a sepulchre carved out of rock and sealed with gold-and-silver-bearing rock taken from the mine he discovered.

US 260 crosses Mineral Creek and the San Francisco River as it veers north to the junction with NM 12, 149.3 *m.,* at STEVENS SAW MILL (*see Tour 8b*).

LUNA, 164.3 *m.* (6,769 alt., 170 pop.), was first settled by Solomón Luna who grazed his sheep in the valleys and on mountainsides. Later this region was populated by Mormon families who journeyed from Salt Lake and who prospered here.

At 172.6 *m.,* US 260 crosses the ARIZONA LINE at a point 32 miles southeast of Springerville, Arizona (*see Arizona Guide*).

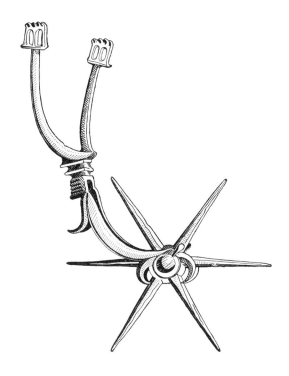

# PART IV
## Appendices

# Chronology

## INDIAN CHRONOLOGY

(The New World pre-history dates have been determined by tree-ring chronology)

?–300 A.D.  Basket Maker II: A semi-nomadic, pre-Pueblo people who inhabited the Southwest at the beginning of the Christian era. First agriculturists in New Mexico; excelling in basket weaving.

300–700  Basket Maker III: First truly sedentary people in New Mexico; built crude slab houses; cultivated corn, squash, beans, and tobacco; invented pottery in the Southwest.

700–900  Pueblo I: A roundheaded people, believed to have come from the Northwest, who conquered and absorbed the earlier Basket Maker people and their culture; introduced horizontal masonry, the bow and arrow, and developed pottery.

900–1150  Pueblo II: Sometimes called the developmental period; was a growth of the Pueblo I culture. The unit type house became the small village or group dwelling.

1150–1350  Pueblo III: The classic or great period of Pueblo culture.

1350–1700  Pueblo IV: The maximum expansion of Pueblo culture in New Mexico.

1700–  Pueblo V: Modern Pueblo.

## NEW MEXICO UNDER SPAIN
### 1540–1821

1528–1531  First rumors of inhabited cities in the north gained from an Indian in possession of Nuño de Guzmán, whose expedition fails to discover the cities, but explores country as far north as Culiacán, which he founded.

1536  Álvar Núñez Cabeza de Vaca, en route to New Spain from east Texas, passed through New Mexico. Indians farther south tell him of northern pueblos.

1539  In May, Fray Marcos de Niza, with the Negro Moor Estevan, discovers the "Seven Cities" of Cíbola (Zuñi); takes formal possession for Spain of region embracing present New Mexico.

1540  February 23, Coronado's expedition leaves Compostela to conquer Cíbola. He reaches region July 7, captures pueblo of Hawikúh; winters at Tiguex, near Bernalillo.

1541  April 23, leaving Tiguex, Coronado crosses buffalo plains to Quivira (Kansas-Nebraska border); returns to Tiguex for second winter.

1542  In spring, Coronado and army return to New Spain.

1543-4   The Franciscans Juan de Padilla and Luis de Escalona remain as first missionaries, and later martyrs, of New Mexico.

1546   Gastaldi map shows Cipola (Cíbola) and Nova Hispania, which appear north of Mexico, with "Le Sete Cita," north of Cipola.

1569   Mercato map shows Hispania Noua.

1581   June 6, missionary expedition of Fray Agustín Rodríguez and two other Franciscans with 12 soldiers under Capt. Francisco Sánchez Chamuscado follows new route up Rio Grande de Puaráy, one of the Tiguex pueblos, near Bernalillo.
Franciscans remaining after return of soldiers to New Spain are killed by Indians.

1582-1583   Relief expedition of Fray Bernadino Beltrán and Capt. Antonio Espejo to ascertain fate of the Franciscans. Casilda de Anaya, wife of a soldier, third of the white women in New Mexico. The name "New Mexico" appears for first time on title page of Luxán's Journal of expedition (1583).

1587   Hakluyt map on which appear Quivira, Tiguex, and Nuevo Mexico, north of Nova Hispania and Mexico.

1590-1591   First attempt (unauthorized) to colonize New Mexico: by Capt. Gaspar Castaño de Sosa, with 170 persons including women and children, and wagon train of supplies. After about a year Castaño arrested by Capt. Juan Morlete for having entered the country without a license and returned to Mexico.

1593-1594   Unauthorized exploring party under Capts. Humaña and Bonilla.

1595   September 21, Don Juan de Oñate given contract for colonization of New Mexico at his own expense.

1598   April 30. Oñate takes formal possession of New Mexico at point on Rio Grande below El Paso del Norte.
July 11, Oñate established first Spanish settlement and capital in New Mexico at San Juan pueblo.
August 11, Oñate begins work on first Spanish irrigation ditch.
September 8, first church built in New Mexico at new capital dedicated to San Juan Bautista. Franciscans assigned to missions in seven pueblos.

1599   January 22, 23, 24, battle of Ácoma; Spanish victory.

1600   Tattonus map shows Tiguex with church north of New Granada.
December 24, new capital of San Gabriel del Yunque established some time before this date at Yugeuingge on west bank of Rio Grande from San Juan.

1601   June 23, Oñate leaves San Gabriel for Quivira, probably reaching Wichita, Kansas; returns November 24.

1605   April 16, Oñate returning from Gulf of California leaves name on Inscription Rock, now El Morro National Monument.

1609   Death of Fray Cristóbal de Quiñones, first music teacher; installed organ and taught Indians to sing at San Felipe pueblo.
Plans made for new capital at Santa Fe.

1610 Santa Fe founded as new capital under the title La Villa Real de la Santa Fé de San Francisco de Assisi (The Royal City of the Holy Faith of St. Francis of Assisi), by Don Pedro de Peralta, third governor of New Mexico.

Regular mission supply service started between Mexico City and Santa Fe.

Villagrá's epic poem, *Historia de la Nueva México,* published at Alcalá de Henares, Spain; Villagrá first poet of present United States.

1613-1614 Fray Isidro Ordóñez, agent of the Inquisition, holds Gov. Peralta a prisoner at Sandía pueblo for nearly a year.

1617 Eleven mission churches in New Mexico.

White population 48 men.

1625 Fray Alonzo de Benavides arrives in Santa Fe as custodian of Franciscan mission province and agent of the Inquisition.

1627 Parish church built in Santa Fe.

1632 February 22, Fray Francisco de Letrado killed at Hawikúh.

December 28, Fray Pedro de Miranda, Taos priest, and guard of two soldiers killed by Indians.

1633 Fray Estevan de Perea, custodian and agent of Inquisition, investigates witchcraft, bigamy, and use of peyote.

1639 February 21, Cabildo (Town Council) of Santa Fe complains to viceroy in Mexico City against Franciscans, who declare Gov. Rosas persecutes them.

1644-1647 Religious persecution of Indians results in conspiracies and sporadic outbreaks against Spaniards. First outbreak caused by the whipping, imprisoning, and hanging of 40 Indians who refused to relinquish their native religion and become Catholics; uprising suppressed. Later, the Jémez and Apaches conspire, but are soon crushed, 29 being caught and punished.

1650 Pueblos of Jémez, Isleta, Alameda, San Felipe, and Cochití conspire with Apaches to expel Spaniards; plot discovered, nine ringleaders hanged, and others sold into slavery for 10 years.

At about this time Taos Indians plan general revolt, outlining their plans on deerskins; plot failed because the Moqui (Hopi) refused to join them. Many of the Taos fled to Cuartelajo in eastern Colorado, whence they were later induced to return.

1659 New Mexican Franciscans establish mission of Nuestra Señora de Guadalupe at El Paso del Norte on west bank of Rio Grande (now Juárez, Mexico).

1660 Conflict between civil and religious authorities so grave that Franciscans threaten to abandon New Mexico.

1661-1664 Gov. Don Diego de Peñalosa forbids exploitation of Indians by friars in "spinning and weaving cotton mantas." On return to Mexico City, Peñalosa tried by Inquisition for offenses against clergy; ruinous fine imposed. Later in Paris, Peñalosa's schemes stimulate expedition of La Salle (1684-1687) to limit expansion of Spanish possessions.

1675 Four Indians hanged, and 43 whipped and enslaved on conviction by a Spanish tribunal of bewitching the superior of the Franciscan Monastery at San Ildefonso.

1676 Apache destroy several pueblos and churches, killing Spaniards and converted Indians; those arrested are hanged or sold into slavery.

1680 August 10, Pueblo Revolt led by Indian, Po-pé; Spanish rule ended August 21; all Spaniards killed or driven from New Mexico, retreating to El Paso del Norte where capital was maintained for 13 years. The Coronelli map of about this year first notes that the Rio Grande empties into the Gulf of Mexico, not the Gulf of California.

1685 March 26, registration of mine, Nuestra Señora del Pilar de Zaragosa, in Fray Cristóbal Mountains.

1692 Reconquest by Gov. Don Diego de Vargas.
September 13, De Vargas enters Santa Fe; Indians yield peacefully.

1693 De Vargas recolonizes New Mexico with 70 families, 100 soldiers, and 17 Franciscans; reënters Santa Fe December 16.

1695 Franciscan missions reëstablished.
Villa of Santa Cruz de la Cañada refounded.

1696 In June, final Pueblo rebellion and defeat; Spaniards execute several Pueblo governors.

1706 Albuquerque founded by Gov. Don Francisco Cuervo y Valdés.

1710 San Miguel chapel restored by Gov. Peñuela.

1712 First fiesta season proclaimed in Santa Fe on September 16.

1716 Gov. Felix Martínez tries and fails to conquer Hopi pueblos.

1718 On the Delisle map appear Santa Fe, Cochití, Santo Domingo, and Albuquerque.

1720 Expedition under Capt. Pedro de Villasur (to investigate French activity on northeastern frontier) destroyed by Pawnee Indians, French allies.

1721 In August, public schools established by royal decree.

1725 Spanish Government forbids trade with French. Trade with Plains Indians limited to those coming to Taos and Pecos; beginning of Taos annual fairs.

1739 Mallet brothers and seven or eight other French Canadians visit New Mexico; two remain.

1743 A Bellin map shows Nouveau Mexique—Santa Fe.

1748 Sandía pueblo refounded.

1760 Bishop of Durango visits New Mexico; Cofradía (Confraternity) of Our Lady of Light organized in Santa Fe; Gov. Marín del Valle building the Military Chapel.

1767 Great flood in Santa Fe.

1776 In July, Fray Escalante and Fray Domínguez with eight companions leave Santa Fe to find trail to new missions at Monterey, California. Their route into central Utah became first stage in later famous Spanish Trail, Santa Fe to Los Angeles.

1779 Gov. De Anza's campaign against Comanches. Cuerno Verde and 38 principal Indians killed in battle 95 leagues northeast of Santa Fe.

De Anza passes in full view of peak later named for Zebulon M. Pike.

1780 Smallpox epidemic among Pueblos, Moquis, and Spanish following three year drought.

1787 Pedro Vial traces trail from San Antonio north to Red and Canadian Rivers on to Santa Fe.

1790 In November, total population in New Mexico including Indians, 30,953.

1792 May 21, Pedro Vial blazes trail from Santa Fe to St. Louis and returns following year; first complete journey across later famed Santa Fe Trail.

1800 Lt. Col. Carrisco discovers the Santa Rita copper mine near Silver City.

1804 First important mining development; Santa Rita mine worked by Don Francisco Manuel Elguea, of Chihuahua.
Baptiste Lalande, a Frenchman from Kaskaskia, reaches Santa Fe with a stock of merchandise, which he disposes of at a profit; forced to remain.

1805 First vaccination in New Mexico.
James Purcell (Pursley), a Kentuckian, having left St. Louis in 1802, after three years of wandering reaches Santa Fe.

1807 March 2, arrest of Maj. Zebulon M. Pike and party by Gov. Alencaster's order; brought to Santa Fe; later sent to Chihuahua, and finally released on Louisiana frontier.
Gov. Alencaster institutes measures to prevent American influences from entering New Mexico.

1810 August 11, Pedro Bautista Pino chosen first representative from New Mexico to the Cortes in Spain.

## NEW MEXICO UNDER THE REPUBLIC OF MEXICO
### 1821–1846

1821 September 27, independence of Mexico from Spain; New Mexico becomes a province of Mexico.

1822 In the spring, William Becknell, "Father of the Santa Fe Trail," brings first wagons from east across plains to Santa Fe.
April 27, first public school law in New Mexico; action of the provincial deputation: "Resolved, that the said *ayuntamientos* (town councils) be officially notified to complete the formation of primary public schools as soon as possible according to the circumstances of each community."
July 5, Francisco Xavier Chaves appointed political chief, relieving Facundo Melgares, the last governor of New Mexico under Spanish rule.

1824 July 6, New Mexico changed to a territory of the Republic of Mexico. Bartolomé Baca, political chief.

1825 United States survey maps route for Santa Fe Trail from Missouri to Taos.

1828   Republic of Mexico ratifies earlier treaty of 1819, regarding boundaries between Spanish possessions and the United States. Old placer gold mines discovered about 30 miles southwest of Santa Fe.

1829   June 3, first military escort furnished for Santa Fe Trail by U. S. Government; consisted of 170 men from Ft. Leavenworth, led by Capt. Bennett Riley.

1830   First oxen used on Santa Fe Trail.

1833   First gold lode or vein west of Mississippi River discovered and worked on famous Sierra de Oro (Mountain of Gold), now known as Ortiz Mine.

1834   In fall, first newspaper in New Mexico, *El Crepúsculo de la Libertad* (The Dawn of Liberty), published at Santa Fe by Antonio Barreiro on first press in New Mexico owned by Don Ramón Abreu, printer Jesús María Baca.

1835   In November, Padre Antonio José Martínez began printing pamphlets and school manuals on this press which had been moved to Taos, with Jesús María Baca as printer.

1837   August 3, dissatisfaction with revised Mexican constitution, centralizing power and imposing unaccustomed taxes, causes uprising; Gov. Albino Pérez assassinated. A counter movement, starting at Tomé and Albuquerque, is used by Gen. Manuel Armijo to seize control; his appointment as governor arrives from Mexico City in December.

1838   January 28, last rebel leaders captured and shot.

1841–1842   Armijo arrests members of Texas-Santa Fe expedition and sends them to Mexico City; released later due to pressure by U. S., British, and Texas Governments.

1843–1844   President Santa Ana closes the frontier custom house at Taos August 7, 1843, by decree, but repeals the act March 31, 1844.

1844   Printing press removed from Taos to Santa Fe for printing an official periodical called *La Verdad* (The Truth), edited by Donaciano Vigil; and after Kearny's occupation of the Territory in 1846, it was used for printing the laws of the Territory.

## AMERICAN OCCUPATION—NEW MEXICO A TERRITORY OF THE UNITED STATES
### 1846–1912

1846   May 13, proclamation of war with Mexico. United States plans to invade New Mexico.

August 18, Gen. Kearny occupies Santa Fe peacefully, declaring end of Mexican and beginning of American rule. Establishment of Kearny Code of law for New Mexico.

August 23, Missouri volunteers begin construction of Fort Marcy, Santa Fe.

September 22, proclamation of civil government; Charles Bent appointed civil governor.

November 22, Col. Doniphan makes first U. S. treaty with Navaho.
December 25, battle of Brazito, only battle of Mexican War on New Mexican soil; American victory.
Palace of the Governors said to be only building in New Mexico having window glass instead of gypsum panes.

1847 January 19, Taos Revolt; revolutionists and Taos Indians assassinate Gov. Bent and other officials; revolt spreads with preparations to march on Santa Fe.
February 3, Col. Price ends revolt by firing on insurgents in Taos pueblo church.
September 4, first English newspaper, *Santa Fe Republican*.
In December, first sawmill, erected on Santa Fe River.

1848 February 2, treaty of Guadalupe Hidalgo, providing that Mexico give up all claim to territory east of Rio Grande, and cede New Mexico and Upper California to United States.
August 28, first English school founded at Santa Fe.
October 14, people of New Mexico, in convention at Santa Fe, petition Congress for a territorial government, oppose the dismemberment of their Territory in favor of Texas, and ask protection of Congress against the introduction of slavery.

1849 Establishment of regular stage line between Santa Fe and Independence; round trip twice monthly, carrying mail by contract.
April 7, James S. Calhoun appointed first Indian Agent in New Mexico.

1850 U. S. Census reports population of New Mexico (including area of present State of Arizona and small portion of Colorado): 61,547.
In May, constitutional convention meets in Santa Fe, and frames constitution for State of New Mexico.
In June, F. X. Aubrey rode from Santa Fe to Independence, Missouri, 850 miles in five days and 16 hours on a wager, and won $10,000.
June 20, constitution for "State" of New Mexico, declaring against slavery, ratified by decisive vote and submitted to Congress. The State legislature under this constitution creates Socorro County.
September 9, Congress passed Organic Act creating Territory of New Mexico, and settling long controversy with Texas over region east of Rio Grande.
September 27, Congress authorizes monthly mail routes east and establishment of post offices.

1851 Santa Fe receives city charter.
March 3, James S. Calhoun inaugurated first governor under Organic Act.
July 14, first legislative assembly under Organic Act, makes Santa Fe territorial capital.
In summer, Rt. Rev. John B. Lamy, bishop of newly established Roman Catholic Diocese of Santa Fe, reaches capital; institutes important religious and educational reforms.

1853 Christopher (or Kit) Carson appointed an Indian Agent in New Mexico.

Beall & Whipple make railroad survey, 35th parallel route.

December 30, Gadsden Purchase adds to New Mexico southern half of Gila Valley, believed necessary for railroad to Pacific.

1854 Railroad survey made on 32nd parallel route.

January 15, first Protestant (Baptist) church in Territory dedicated at Santa Fe.

August 4, territory acquired from Mexico under the Gadsden purchase is incorporated within the Territory of New Mexico.

1856 Surveyor-general investigates Pueblo Indian land claims; recommends confirmation of grants to 18 pueblos.

1857 During summer, San Antonio, Texas, and San Diego, Cal., mail begins; service each way twice monthly. Contract to John Butterfield for carrying mail from St. Louis to San Francisco.

1858 July 24, first weekly mail from east.

Establishment of overland mail coach line to Pacific coast via Mesilla, making trip from San Francisco to southwest Missouri in 12 and 14 days.

1859 Mesilla Valley and settlers in Gadsden Purchase south of the Gila River apply to Congress for establishment of new Territory out of southern New Mexico to be known as Arizona; not granted.

December 26, Historical Society of New Mexico organized.

Territorial legislature passes act recognizing slavery as legally existing, and providing safeguards for its protection and security.

1860 U. S. Census reports population of New Mexico (including area of present State of Arizona and small portion of Colorado): 93,516.

Legislature passes first real public school law, providing for a school in each settlement.

1861 February 28, formation of Territory of Colorado reduces New Mexico in size; northern boundary fixed at 37th parallel.

July 1, Lt. Col. John R. Baylor of Confederate army occupies Mesilla; prepares to attack Fort Fillmore which Maj. Lynde evacuates. Baylor captures Lynde's entire force.

August 1, proclamation by Col. Baylor organizing all of New Mexico south of 34th parallel as Territory of Arizona; recognized by Confederate Congress.

1862 February 21, battle of Valverde between U. S. forces under Gen. Canby and Confederate forces under Gen Sibley; Confederate victory.

March 10, Confederate forces occupy Santa Fe without opposition; territorial government moved to Las Vegas.

March 27, 28, battle of Apache Cañon and Glorieta; Union victory; ends Confederate control in New Mexico.

April 8, Confederate forces evacuate Santa Fe.

April 11, Union forces reoccupy Santa Fe.

April 15, battle of Peralta; skirmish between Union and retreating Confederate forces.

1863 February 24, Territory of New Mexico again reduced by creation of Territory of Arizona

1864 Col. Kit Carson defeats Navaho in Canyon de Chelly stronghold, and transfers them to Bosque Redondo (circular grove of trees).

1867 Portion of New Mexico above 37° attached to Colorado.

March 2, Congress formally abolishes peonage, or debt servitude.

Gold discovered in Moreno district, Colfax County.

1868 U. S. Government returns Navaho to former area.

Daily mail from east.

1869 July 8, completion of military telegraph line from Fort Leavenworth to Santa Fe.

1870 U. S. Census reports population of New Mexico: 91,874.

Archives of New Mexico, partly destroyed in 1680, are further depleted under the rule of Gov. Pile, when reputedly sold for waste paper and only about one-quarter of them recovered.

1871 Legislature provides for common schools under a board of supervisors and directors elected by each county.

In November, total indebtedness of New Mexico, $74,000.

1875 February 12, archdiocese of Santa Fe created; Rt. Rev. John B. Lamy, archbishop.

U. S. military telegraph line completed from Santa Fe to Mesilla.

1876 Beginning of Lincoln County War between rival cattlemen and political factions; Billy the Kid takes leading part.

Legislature enacts a blue law.

1877 Extension of telegraph communication to San Diego, Cal. and El Paso.

In December, tri-weekly passenger coach line starts between Santa Fe and Garland City; time, 30 hours.

1878 During April—July, Ute Indians removed from New Mexico to the Colorado reservation.

October 1, President Hayes appoints Gen. Lew Wallace territorial governor for specific purpose of ending Lincoln County War.

October 7, presidential proclamation authorizes use of troops in Lincoln County to aid civil authority.

November 30, first railroad track laid inside Territory.

December 7, first locomotive crosses summit of Ratón Pass.

1879 February 13, first passenger train comes into New Mexico.

In March, mining camps established at Los Cerrillos.

In April, Chief Victorio and Apache, on warpath, leave Mescalero Reservation and terrorize southern New Mexico and Arizona.

July 1, railroad track laid into Las Vegas; railroad extended to Santa Fe, February 9, 1880; Albuquerque, April 22, 1880; crossed Rio Grande at Isleta, May 1, 1880; completed to Deming, March 10, 1881, forming first all rail route across New Mexico to San Francisco.

September 3, Apache begin massacres.

Gold discovered at White Oaks; mining camp established.

1880 U. S. Census reports population of New Mexico: 119,565.

January 12, first omnibus in Santa Fe.

February 10, Denver & Rio Grande Western Railroad enters Territory from north, having Rio Grande Valley and Santa Fe as objectives.

March 18, completion of Southern Pacific Railroad of Arizona and New Mexico to Tucson, connecting with San Francisco and Pacific system of railroads.

July 7–15, Gen. and Mrs. Ulysses S. Grant visit New Mexico.

December 5, gas lighting begun at Santa Fe.

1881 In July, completion of Atlantic & Pacific Railroad between Rio Grande Valley and Arizona boundary, via Laguna Indian Pueblo and Fort Wingate.

July 14, Billy the Kid shot by Pat. F. Garrett, sheriff of Lincoln County; buried following day in old military cemetery at Ft. Sumner.

October 3–8, first annual territorial fair held at Albuquerque.

October 9, Victorio killed in Chihuahua.

In November, telephone introduced in Santa Fe.

1883 Apache raids. Tertio-Millenial celebration at Santa Fe.

1885 Gerónimo flees San Carlos Reservation in Arizona, terrorizing southern New Mexico.

1886 New capitol building completed at Santa Fe.

September 4, Gerónimo surrenders to Gen. Nelson A. Miles.

In December, New Mexico Educational Association organized at Santa Fe.

Hemenway Expedition excavates ruins near Zuñi. First scientific excavation in New Mexico.

1889 Beginning of Pecos Valley Irrigation and Investment Company's great system.

February 28, Gov. Edmund G. Ross signs bill creating university at Albuquerque, agricultural college at Las Cruces, and school of mines at Socorro.

September 3–21, constitutional convention drafts a constitution for the proposed State of New Mexico.

1890 U. S. Census reports population of New Mexico: 160,282.

August 18, constitution amended; rejected by the people, October 7.

1891 Common school law enacted; first superintendent of public instruction appointed.

March 3, Congress approves act for establishment of Court of Private Land Claims, which finally settles Spanish and Mexican grant titles in Southwest.

1892 January 11, President creates Pecos Forest Reserve.

May 12, new capitol building burns at Santa Fe, destroying many public documents.

1893 New Mexico Normal University at Las Vegas and New Mexico Normal Training School at Silver City founded.

New Mexico School of Mines opens its first session September 5.

1894 January 18, prehistoric ruins near Santa Cruz opened and examined.

1895 June 25, Peralta land grant claimed by J. Addison Reavis for 12,-800,000 acres of New Mexico and Arizona declared fraudulent; Reavis sentenced to a term in prison.
July 23, Silver City suffers disastrous flood.

1898 April 23, President McKinley calls on New Mexico for 340 volunteer cavalrymen for Rough Riders in Cuba under Col. Leonard Wood and Lt. Col. Theodore Roosevelt in Spanish-American War. In eight days entire quota mustered into service at Santa Fe.

1900 U. S. Census reports population of New Mexico: 195,310.
June 4, dedication of completed new capitol building at Santa Fe.

1901 During March, Rock Island railroad enters Northeastern New Mexico.
August 19, unveiling of Kearny marble slab in the Plaza at Santa Fe by D. A. R.

1902 August 29, disastrous floods on Mimbres River, Grant County; hundreds homeless; governor asks public aid.

1904 During September and October, most disastrous floods in New Mexico's history; hundreds homeless; many lives lost; railroad traffic demoralized for two months.

1906 Electors of Arizona defeat proposed joint statehood.

1907 Palace of the Governors at Santa Fe becomes Museum of New Mexico and seat of the School of American Research.

1909 Spanish-American Normal School established at El Rito.
U. S. War Department classes New Mexico Military Institute as distinguished.
Oil discovered in encouraging amounts in well near Dayton, Eddy County.

1910 U. S. Census reports population of New Mexico: 327,301.
June 20, Congress passes Enabling Act providing for admission of New Mexico and Arizona into Union as separate States.

1911 January 21, voters adopt State constitution.
August 21, Congress passes and President Taft signs State Constitution.

## STATEHOOD
### 1912

1912 January 6, President Taft proclaims New Mexico 47th State of Union.
January 15, William C. McDonald inaugurated first State Governor.

1916 March 9, Francisco (Pancho) Villa raids Columbus, border town, killing American citizens.
March 15, Gen. John J. Pershing crosses Mexican border with expedition to capture Villa.
May 12, New Mexico National Guard mobolized at Columbus.
Elephant Butte Dam completed.

1917 In January, Gen. Pershing and entire force move back across border.
April 5, National Guard mustered out of service.

May 1, State Legislature in special session to provide for defense of State and assistance of government in World War, creates State Council of Defense to organize resources of State; appropriates $750,000 for war purposes.

In June 1,300 guardsmen mobilized at Camp Funston, Albuquerque. In September Battery A, machine gun unit of 146th Artillery, leaves for Camp Greene, North Carolina; before close of year, in France as first distinctively New Mexican unit, firing opening guns at Chateau-Thierry.

In October other New Mexican units to Camp Kearny, California; later to France. In all branches of service New Mexico contributed 17,157 men, larger number in proportion to population than average for whole country.

November 6, prohibition amendment to State constitution.

Art Museum dedicated at Santa Fe.

1920    U. S. Census reports population of New Mexico: 360,350.

1922    Discovery of Hogback and Rattlesnake oil fields on Navaho Indian Lands in San Juan County; assures importance of New Mexico as oil producing State.

Discovery of Artesia oil field, Eddy County.

1923    U. S. Geological Survey and Federal Land Office survey three miles of Carlsbad Caverns, later proclaimed National Monument by President Coolidge.

1924    In June, act of Congress creates Pueblo Indian Lands Board to settle non-Indian claims to land within or in conflict with Pueblo Land grants.

1930    U. S. Census reports population of New Mexico: 423,317.

In May, President Hoover creates Carlsbad Caverns National Park.

1933    U. S. and Mexico ratify treaty for regulating course of Rio Grande from El Paso to Fort Quitman, and building dam at Caballo just below Elephant Butte reservoir to assist control of lower Rio Grande flood waters.

September 19, voters of New Mexico repeal prohibition amendment of State constitution.

1935    State legislature establishes New Mexico Relief and Security Authority to assist unemployed to secure work on Federal Projects.

1936    Road mileage in State totals 31,950.6, of which 10,348.7 miles are State highways (all types), and 21,601.9 miles are rural roads.

Work begun for the Coronado Cuarto Centennial in 1940.

1937    May 15, New Mexico participates in a highway conference at Chihuahua City called by Gov. Talamantes with a view to reopening the sixteenth century highway from Mexico City to Santa Fe.

1938    Increasing number of oil wells brought in and developed in southeastern part of State.

1939    Conchas Dam completed.

Gross income from cattle and calf sales $29,079,880; gross income from all classes of livestock and livestock products more than $40,000,000.

Due to activity in oil fields around Hobbs, population increases make it fifth city in New Mexico.

Total road mileage in State increased to double that of 1936, approximately 62,000 miles.

1940 Coronado Cuarto (fourth) Centennial; celebration of Coronado *entrada* in 1540.

# Some Books about New Mexico

Amsden, Charles Avery. *Navajo Weaving*. Santa Ana, 1934.

Applegate, Frank G. *Indian Stories from the Pueblos*. Philadelphia, 1929.

—— *Native Tales of New Mexico*. Philadelphia, 1932.

Armer, Laura Adams. *Waterless Mountain*. New York, 1931.

Austin, Mary. *The Land of Little Rain*. New York, 1903.

—— *Land of Journey's Ending*. New York, 1924.

Bailey, Florence Miriam. *Birds of New Mexico*. Santa Fe, 1928.

Bailey, Vernon. *Life Zones and Crop Zones of New Mexico*. Washington, D. C., 1913.

—— *Mammals of New Mexico*. Washington, D. C., 1931.

Bancroft, Hubert Howe. *The History of Arizona and New Mexico, 1530–1888*. San Francisco, 1889.

Bandelier, Adolph F. A. *Final Report of Investigations Among the Indians of the Southwestern United States*. 2 vols. Cambridge, 1890–92.

—— *Hemenway Southwestern Archaeological Expedition*. Cambridge, 1890.

—— and Hewett, Edgar L. *Indians of the Rio Grande*. Albuquerque, 1937.

—— *The Journey of Álvar Núñez Cabeza de Vaca and His Companions from Florida to the Pacific, 1528–1536*. New York, 1905.

—— *The Delight-Makers*. New York, 1918.

Barker, Ruth Laughlin. *Caballeros*. New York, 1931.

Benavides, Alonso de. *The Memorial of Fray Alonso de Benavides, 1630*. Chicago, 1916.

Blake, Forrester. *Riding the Mustang Trail*. New York, 1935.

Bloom, Lansing B. and Donnelly, C. *New Mexico History and Civics*. Albuquerque, 1933.

Bolton, Herbert Eugene, ed. *Spanish Explorations in the Southwest*. New York, 1925.

Branch, E. Douglas. *The Hunting of the Buffalo*. New York, 1929.

*Bureau of American Ethnology Annual Reports and Bulletins,* Washington, 1879 to date.

Buttree, Julia M. *The Rhythm of the Red Man, in Song, Dance and Decoration*. New York, 1930.

Bynner, Witter. *Indian Earth*. New York, 1929.

Carson, Christopher. *Kit Carson's own story as dictated to Col. and Mrs. D. C. Peters About 1856–57*. Santa Fe, 1926.

Cather, Willa. *Death Comes for the Archbishop*. New York, 1936.

Chapman, Kenneth M., comp. *Decorative Art of the Indians of the Southwest*. Santa Fe, 1934.

—— , ed, and annot. *Pueblo Indian Pottery*. Nice, C. Szwedzicki, vol. 1, 1933 and vol. 2, 1936.

Church, Margaret Pond. *Familiar Journey*. Santa Fe, 1936.

Coe, George W. *Frontier Fighter*. Boston, 1934.

Cole, M. R. *Los Pastores; a Mexican Play of the Nativity*. Boston, 1907.

Conard, Howard Louis. *"Uncle Dick" Wootton*. Chicago, 1891.

Connelley, William Elsey. *The War with Mexico, 1846–1847*. Topeka, 1907.

Cook, James H. *Fifty Years On the Old Frontier*. New Haven, 1923.

Coolidge, Mary Roberts. *The Rainmakers*. Boston, 1929.

Corbin, Alice. *The Sun Turns West*. Santa Fe, 1933.

Cosgrove, H. S. and C. B. *The Swarts Ruin*. (Papers of Peabody Museum, Vol. XV., No. 1.) Cambridge, 1932.

Coues, Elliott, ed. *The Expedition of Zebulon Montgomery Pike to the Headwaters of the Mississippi River Through Louisiana Territory, and in New Spain During the Years 1805–1807*. New York, 1895.

Coze, Paul. *Rodeos de Cow-Boys et les Jeux du Lasso*. Paris, 1934.

Cremony, John C. *Life Among the Apaches*. San Francisco, 1868.

Crichton, Kyle S. *Law and Order, Ltd*. Santa Fe, 1928.

Cushing, Frank Hamilton, comp. and trans. *Zuñi Folk Tales*. New York, 1931.

Davis, William Watts Hart. *El Gringo*. Santa Fe, 1938.

De Huff, Elizabeth Willis. *Tay-Tay's Memories*. New York, 1924.

Dobie, J. Frank. *Coronado's Children*. Dallas, 1930.

Duffus, Robert L. *The Santa Fe Trail*. New York, 1930.

Dunton, Nellie. *The Spanish Colonial Ornament*. Philadelphia, 1935.

Espinosa, Aurelio Macedonio. *Los Comanches*. Albuquerque, 1907.

Fergusson, Erna. *Dancing Gods*. New York, 1931.

Fergusson, Harvey. *Rio Grande*. New York, 1933.

Fewkes, Jesse Walter. *Reconnaissance of Ruins in or Near the Zuni Reservation*. Cambridge, 1891.

Finger, Charles J. *The Distant Prize*. New York, 1935.

Fulton, Maurice Garland and Horgan, Paul. *New Mexico's Own Chronicle*. Dallas, 1937.

Fulton, Maurice Garland, ed. *Pat F. Garrett's Authentic Life of Billy the Kid*. New York, 1927.

Goddard, Pliny Earle. *Indians of the Southwest*. New York, 1931.

Gregg, Josiah. *Commerce of the Prairie*. Dallas, 1933.

Guthe, Carl. *Pueblo Pottery-Making*. New Haven, 1925.

Hafen, Le-Roy R. *The Overland Mail*. Cleveland, 1926.

Haley, J. Evetts. *Charles Goodnight, Cowman and Plainsman*. New York and Boston, 1936.

Hammond, George P. *Don Juan de Oñate and the Founding of New Mexico*. Santa Fe, 1927.

——— and Rey, Agapito, trans. and ed. *Expedition Into New Mexico by Antonio de Espejo, 1582–1583*. Los Angeles, 1929.

Haury, Emil W. *The Mogollón Culture of Southwestern New Mexico*. Globe, 1936.

Henderson, Alice Corbin. *Brothers of Light*. New York, 1937.

Hewett, Edgar Lee. *Ancient Life in the American Southwest*. Indianapolis, 1930.

Hewett, Edgar Lee. *The Chaco Canyon and Its Monuments.* Albuquerque, 1936.

Hodge, Frederick Webb. *History of Hawikuh, New Mexico.* Los Angeles, 1937.

—— *The Early Navajo and Apache.* Washington, D. C., 1895.

—— and Lewis, Theodore H., eds. *Spanish Explorers in the Southwestern United States, 1528–1543.* New York, 1925.

Hogner, Dorothy Childs. *Navajo Winter Nights.* New York, 1935.

Horgan, Paul. *From the Royal City of the Holy Faith of St. Francis.* Tesuque, N. Mex., 1936.

Hrdlicka, Aleš. *Physiological and Medical Observations Among the Indians of the Southwestern United States and Northern Mexico.* Washington, D. C., 1908.

Ickes, Anna Wilmarth. *Mesa Land.* New York, 1933.

Inman, Henry. *The Old Santa Fe Trail.* Topeka, 1916.

James, George W. *New Mexico, Land of the Delight-Makers.* Boston, 1920.

James, Thomas. *Three Years Among the Mexicans and Indians.* St. Louis, Mo., 1916.

Janvier, Thomas. *Santa Fe's Partner.* New York, 1907.

Jones, Fayette Alexander. *New Mexico Mines and Minerals.* Santa Fe, 1904.

Kidder, Alfred Vincent. *An Introduction to Southwestern Archaeology.* New Haven, 1924.

Larkin, Margaret. *The Singing Cowboy.* New York, 1931

Laut, Agnes C. *Romance of the Rails.* 2 vols. New York, 1929.

Lawrence, D. H. *Mornings in Mexico.* New York, 1928.

Leigh, William R. *The Western Pony.* New York, 1935.

Lockwood, Frank C. *The Apache Indians.* New York, 1938.

Lummis, Charles Fletcher. *Mesa, Canyon and Pueblo.* New York, 1925.

Mac Leish, Archibald. *Conquistador.* Boston, 1932.

Magoffin, Susan Shelby. *Down the Santa Fe Trail and Into Mexico.* New Haven, 1926.

Marcy, Randolph B. *The Prairie Traveller.* London, 1863.

Matthews, Washington. *Navajo Legends.* Boston, 1897.

Mera, Harry P. *Ceramic Clues to the Prehistory of North Central New Mexico.* Santa Fe, 1935.

Mills, Enos, A. *Romance of Geology.* Boston, 1932.

Morris, Ann Axtell. *Digging in the Southwest.* Garden City, 1933.

Nusbaum, Aileen. *Zuñi Indian Tales.* New York, 1926.

Otero, Miguel Antonio. *My Life on the Frontier, 1864–1882.* New York, 1935. Vol. II, Albuquerque, 1939.

Otero, Nina. *Old Spain in Our Southwest.* New York, 1935.

Parsons, Elsie Clews. *Tewa Tales.* New York, 1926.

Pearce, T. M. *Southwest Heritage, a Literary History and Bibliography.* Albuquerque, 1938.

Prince, L. Bradford. *Spanish Mission Churches of New Mexico.* Cedar Rapids, 1915.

Reichard, Gladys A. *Navajo Shepherd and Weaver*. New York, 1936.
Rhodes, Eugene Manlove. *Once in the Saddle* and *Paso por aquí*. New York, 1927.
Rollins, Philip Ashton. *The Cowboy*. New York, 1936.
Santee, Ross. *The Cowboy*. New York, 1928.
Saunders, Charles Francis. *Finding the Worthwhile in the Southwest*. New York, 1924.
Sears, Paul B. *Deserts on the March*. Norman, 1935.
Sedgwick, Mrs. William T. *Acoma, the Sky City*. Cambridge, 1935.
Segale, Sister Blandina. *At the End of the Santa Fe Trail*. Columbus, 1932.
Siguenza y Gongora, Don Carlos de. *The Mercurio Volante*. Los Angeles, 1932.
Siringo, Charles. *Riata and Spurs*. New York, 1921.
Sperry, Armstrong. *Wagons Westward*. New York, 1936.
Stacey, May Humphreys. *Uncle Sam's Camels*. Cambridge, 1929.
Stevens, Thomas Wood. *Westward Under Vega*. New York, 1938.
Thorp, N. Howard. *Tales of the Chuck Wagon*. Santa Fe, 1926.
Thwaites, Ruben Gold, ed. *Early Western Travels, 1748–1846*. 32 vols. Cleveland, 1904–1907.
Twitchell, Ralph Emerson. *Old Santa Fe*. Santa Fe, 1925.
——— *Leading Facts of New Mexico History*. 2 vols. Cedar Rapids, 1911-1912.
Vestal, Stanley. *The Mountain Men*. Boston, 1937.
Villagrá, Gaspar Pérez de. *History of New Mexico*. Los Angeles, 1933.
Walter, Paul A. F. *The Cities That Died of Fear*. Santa Fe, 1916.
Walton, Eda Lou, ed. *Dawn Boy*. New York, 1926.
Webb, Walter Prescott. *The Great Plains*. Boston, 1931.
Winship, George Parker, ed. *The Journey of Francisco Vásquez de Coronado, 1540–1542*. San Francisco, 1933.
Wissler, Clark. *The American Indian*. New York, 1932.

# Index